A Reference Publication in Literature

Joseph Katz, *Editor*

A BIBLIOGRAPHY OF JAMES JOYCE STUDIES

Second Edition, Revised and Enlarged

Robert H. Deming

G. K. HALL & CO., 70 LINCOLN STREET, BOSTON, MASS.

Library of Congress Cataloging in Publication Data

Deming, Robert H
    A bibliography of James Joyce studies.

    (Reference guides in literature)
    Includes index.
    1. Joyce, James, 1882-1941--Bibliography. I. Title.
Z8458.1.D4 1977   [PR6019.O9] 016.823'9'12 77-9545
ISBN 0-8161-7969-7

This publication is printed on permanent/durable acid-free paper
MANUFACTURED IN THE UNITED STATES OF AMERICA

Anne, Michael
Maura, Sean

Preface to the Second Edition

This second edition of <u>A Bibliography of James Joyce Studies</u> takes the 1964 first edition to December 1973, combining the old, first edition with materials from 1961 to 1973. Besides the accumulated materials of the twelve-year period, about 770 items from the pre-1961 period have been added, at least half of these through the efforts of Alan M. Cohn. Other items have been supplied during the past decade by Joyce scholars and friends who have written me of omissions, corrections, and additions. The total number of entries now reaches over 5,555 owing largely to the addition of three new sections to this second edition: I.E "Reviews of Joyce's Works"; I.F "Dissertations"; and I.G "Musical Settings, Theatrical Productions, Films, Radio Broadcasts, and Recordings." Most annotations of items, a worthwhile feature of the first edition, have been omitted; the sacrifice of this information should be compensated for by the greater completeness of this edition.

A few words on how this edition was compiled. For the first edition, almost everything was seen and inspected so as to provide annotations. For this edition very little was actually examined, except that checks were made to verify information, items were examined to determine their place in the various categories of the book, and correlative materials were investigated. But, for the most part, I have relied upon secondary sources of information. I have consulted the following secondary sources: Alan M. Cohn's annual <u>James Joyce Quarterly</u> supplements; the annual <u>MLA Bibliography</u>; the ten-year cumulative indices to <u>A Wake Newslitter</u> and <u>James Joyce Quarterly</u>; the <u>Bibliographie der fremdsprachigen Zeitschriftenliteratur (Internationale Bibliographie der Zeitschriftenliteratur)</u>; <u>Abstracts of English Studies</u>; <u>Dissertation Abstracts International</u>; Rosemarie Franke's dissertation, "James Joyce und der deutsche Sprachbereich: Übersetzung, Verbreitung und Kritik in der Zeit von 1919-1967"; <u>Index to Little Magazines</u>; <u>American Literature Abstracts</u>; <u>Index to Book Reviews in the Humanities</u>; <u>Yearbook of Comparative and General Literature</u>; <u>Bibliography of Comparative Literature</u>; <u>Annual Bibliography of English Language and Literature</u>; <u>Bibliographie der französischen Literaturwissenschaft</u>; <u>Seris Manual de bibliografía de la literatura española</u>; <u>Revista hispanica moderna</u>; <u>Handbook of Latin American Studies</u>; <u>Index analytique</u>; Jean Gilbert's unpublished 1952 SUNY at Buffalo M.A. Thesis, "A Card Index to the Press Clippings in the Joyce Collection of the Lockwood Memorial Library"; David Powell's "Annotated Bibliography of Myles na Gopaleen's 'Cruiskeen Lawn' Commentaries"; Carola Giedion-Welcker's <u>Schriften: 1926-1971</u>, edited by Reinhold Hohl; Rudolf Juchhoff's <u>Sammelkatalog der biographische und literarkritischen Werke zu englischen Schriftstellern des 19. und 20. Jahrhunderts</u>; D. G. Zhantieva's <u>Angliĭskiĭ roman XX veka</u>. I trust that there are other sources which I have forgotten to mention, and also other sources that I should have checked but didn't. For the latter omission I am apologetic.

A few words on the structure of this second edition. The large divisions in the first two sections of this edition follow the same arrangement as in the first edition, but the sub-divisions are more restricted and, I hope, more precise than before. To clarify this new arrangement of divisions and sub-divisions, a brief description of each follows.

Section I. I.A <u>Bibliography of Bibliographies, Checklists, Surveys of Joyceana, Exhibitions, Collections, Special Joyce Issues, and International James Joyce Symposia</u>. Separate categories are provided for each of these areas to facilitate easy location of specific items. The "Special Joyce Issues" area lists a main entry for the periodical concerned with a listing of its "contents"; these "contents" are then distributed in their appropriate places elsewhere in the book (with the exception of one item which was received too late for distribution of its "contents" throughout the book).

I.B.1 <u>General Critical and Biographical, Dictionary Entries, Encyclopedia Entries, Histories of the Novel, Etc</u>. Items which are only generally biographical-critical and very general comments on Joyce and the novel are included in this section rather than in the next section. I.B.2 <u>Biographical Background: Biographies, Relatives, Letters, Family, Friends, Ireland, Trieste, Pola, Paris, Zürich, Etc</u>. Items which are specifically biographical or are concerned with Joyce's background and life are included in this section. Other items which have a remote connection to Joyce's biography are listed in the block cross-references at the beginning of this section. Items which are not clearly "Reminiscences and Memoirs" are listed in this section and cross-references to these items are provided at the beginning of section I.B.4.

I.B.3 <u>Milieu Studies</u>. This section is now sub-divided into two parts--A. Milieu: Modernism, the 20s and 30s, Paris; and B. Joyce and Other Writers--Comparisons and Contrasts. The second sub-division ("B") is further divided with reference to the contemporary author with whom Joyce is compared or contrasted. Items are listed in this second sub-division only if a comparison or contrast is the <u>explicit</u> point of the book or article. Other comparisons and/or contrasts between a specific author and one of Joyce's actual works are listed under those works in Section II. A cross-reference to such an item is listed after the author's name in I.B.3. Other comparisons and/or contrasts between a specific author (not listed in I.B.3) and one of Joyce's works are listed in the block cross-references at the beginning of I.B.3. Authors who influenced Joyce are listed in I.C.1; authors influenced by Joyce are listed in I.C.3.

I.B.4 <u>Reminiscences and Memoirs</u>; I.B.5 <u>Interviews</u>; I.C.1 <u>Provenience: Influences Upon Joyce</u>. Cross-reference to other items concerned with influences upon specific works by Joyce are provided in the block cross-references at the beginning of each work in Section II. I.C.2 <u>Reputation Studies: General, Poems and Prose, Birthday and Anniversary Tributes, Obituaries</u>. Cross-references to other poems and prose works are provided in the block cross-reference at the beginning of this part. I.C.3 <u>Influence Studies</u>. Cross-reference to other items concerned with the influence of a specific work of Joyce's upon another writer are provided in the block cross-reference at the beginning of this part.

I.D <u>Comprehensive Studies of Joyce's Works</u>. This part lists items which deal, generally speaking, with all of Joyce's works but which do not give special attention to any one work. Cross-references to items in this part are found in the block cross-reference at the beginning of each separate work in Section II. Books which are collections or compilations of articles (e.g., Magalaner, editor. <u>A James Joyce Miscellany</u>, Third Series) are listed in this part with complete contents and a cross-reference number to the item's appropriate place in the book. A separate listing of each such item, with an abbreviated title, pages, and cross-reference number will be found throughout the text (e.g., O'Neill, Michael J. "The Joyces in the Holloway Diaries," in <u>A James Joyce Miscellany</u>, Second Series, pp. 103-110, No. 1613).

I.E <u>Reviews of Joyce's Works</u>. Reviews are listed chronologically for each work; each work is listed according to the date of its first publication.

I.F <u>Dissertations</u>. These are listed within the appropriate divisions of this work itself (i.e., a dissertation on <u>Ulysses</u> will be under II.H in this section). Cross-references are provided for publication of the dissertation in book form; but no effort has been made to determine from which dissertation specific periodical articles may have been derived.

I.G <u>Musical Settings, Theatrical Productions, Films, Radio Broadcasts, Recordings</u>. This section is divided into three sub-divisions: (1.) Musical Settings; (2.) Theatrical productions are listed first, followed by films, followed by radio broadcasts for each of Joyce's separate works; (3.) Recordings are listed for each of Joyce's separate works.

Section II. Every effort has been made in this section to list items under the appropriate heading for each of Joyce's works. Further distinctions have been made, for each of the works that require them, on the basis of the compiler's findings as to the most frequent areas of study and comment. The former distinction under II.H "<u>Ulysses</u>" between "General" and "As a Novel" has been eliminated, as has the distinction under II.I "<u>Finnegans Wake</u>" between "General" and "Work in Progress." Items in II.H.6 (<u>Ulysses</u>: Influence and Comparison) are often reviews in which Joyce's work is compared by the reviewer with the work being reviewed. Many of the items in this same section are closely related to those in I.C.1 and I.C.3; hence, cross-references from <u>Ulysses</u> to the earlier sections of the work are provided in the block cross-references at the beginnings of those sections in Section I. Controversies or items which have evoked numerous replies or letters to editors are all accumulated in one item. Internal cross-references are provided whenever one item has a reply or is a reply to another item.

Preface

Section III. This section contains two parts: (A.) Uncategorized items which have not been seen and/or could not be easily categorized within the book by title or by examination; and (B.) Unverified items which are "snags."

Index. An index of authors, editors, reviewers, translators, and unsigned articles and unsigned reviews is provided. Numbers in the Index refer to items, not to pages. Unsigned reviews of Joyce's works (from section I.E) are listed in the Index. All other unsigned reviews are listed under the particular reviewed work but not in the Index. Unsigned articles and editorials are listed in the Index under "Unsigned articles." Names beginning with "de" or "du" are listed in the Index under the main surname and a cross-reference is provided (e.g., "de Campos" is listed under "Campos").

NOTES ON THE TEXT

I have followed the University of Chicago Press's Manual of Style (12th edition) throughout. Exceptions to this style are that I provide a comma after the title of a periodical, I provide the month of issue for periodicals, where known, and I have adapted the Manual of Style's form for an article or chapter in a book (e.g., "McCarthy, Desmond. 'James Joyce,' in his Memories. New York: Oxford University Press, 1953, pp. 113-120"). I have made the latter adaptation in the interests of providing the most complete information possible. An asterisk (*) before an item indicates that it was not in the first edition and is a pre-1961 item. The form "n.t." is frequently used for items obtained from the extensive collection of reviews and periodical articles in the Poetry Collection at the State University of New York at Buffalo. Two lists are provided below: (1.) a list of titles and abbreviations of Joyce's works; and (2.) a list of journals which are given in abbreviated form under the "Contents" listing for items in the text.

LIST OF TITLES AND ABBREVIATIONS OF JOYCE'S WORKS

CM--Chamber Music

CW--Critical Writings of James Joyce

D--Dubliners

PAYM--A Portrait of the Artist as a Young Man

U--Ulysses

PP--Pomes Penyeach

ALP--Anna Livia Plurabelle

TTSS--Tales Told of Shem and Shaun

HCE--Haveth Childers Everywhere

Mime--Mime of Mick, Nick and the Maggies

CP--Collected Poems

FW--Finnegans Wake

SH--Stephen Hero

LIST OF ABBREVIATED JOURNAL TITLES

AL--American Literature

AUMLA--Journal of the Australasian Universities Language and Literature Association

BA--Books Abroad

BJA--British Journal of Aesthetics

CL--Comparative Literature

CLS--Comparative Literature Studies

DQR--Dutch Quarterly Review of Anglo-American Letters

EIC--Essays in Criticism

ELN--English Language Notes

ES--English Studies

JEGP--Journal of English and Germanic Philology

JJQ--James Joyce Quarterly

JJR--James Joyce Review

JML--Journal of Modern Literature

LJ--Library Journal

MFS--Modern Fiction Studies

MLJ--Modern Language Journal

MLQ--Modern Language Quarterly

MLR--Modern Language Review

MP--Modern Philology

N&Q--Notes and Queries

NMQ--New Mexico Quarterly

NYHTB--New York Herald Tribune Books

NYRB--New York Review of Books

NYTBR--New York Times Book Review

PBSA--Papers of the Bibliographical Society of America

RES--Review of English Studies

SAH--Svenska Akademiens Handlingar

SatR--Saturday Review of Literature

SoAtlQ--South Atlantic Quarterly

SoR--Southern Review

SSF--Studies in Short Fiction

TLS--Times Literary Supplement

VQR--Virginia Quarterly Review

WHR--Western Humanities Review

WN--A Wake Newslitter

ZAA--Zeitschrift für Anglistik und Amerikanistik

ACKNOWLEDGMENTS

I would like to again express my appreciation to those mentioned in the Preface to the first edition, especially to L. E. James Helyar, Editor of Library Publications and to John H. Langley, Director of the University Press of Kansas, who granted use of the copyright material of the first edition for this second, revised and enlarged edition.

For their assistance in the various stages of preparation of this edition, I would like to thank the following: K. C. Gay (Curator), Beverly Vander Kooy, Marti Gorman, and Kathy Abbey of the Poetry Collection at the State University of New York at Buffalo; Margaret Pabst and Dorothy Kokocinski of the Reed Library at State University College at Fredonia; Kanji Haitani; The State University of New York Research Foundation for two summer Research Fellowships which helped finance the research for this edition; Calvin Smith and Douglas Shepard of the Department of English, Fredonia; Diana George, Linda Cooper, and Rose Sebouhian who worked industriously as research assistants, the latter for many hours on annotations which were later annihilated; Dolores Bergstrand who for six months worked as research assistant and friend; Theresa Barber who typed most of the manuscript; Harrison T. Meserole, MLA Bibliographer, who provided early proof of the 1972 MLA Bibliography; George Sebouhian, Ruth and Jim Shokoff, Mort and Shirley Schagrin, Steve Warner, Mark Bradley, Becky Wilcox who assumed a fête and discovered index cards to be alphabetized; Willard Potts who supplied several missing items; many Joyce scholars who supplied items and answered my letters soliciting advice on the format of the second edition; and a very understanding and always sympathetic editor, Joseph Katz.

Anyone who has benefited from the bibliographical and general expertise of Alan M. Cohn will recognize my debt to him. He has not only provided me with items I would never otherwise have discovered but has also sustained and nourished this project through its second coming since 1964. He has also kept Joyce studies current since the first edition with his annual checklists in James Joyce Quarterly. Alan would wish to acknowledge his debt to Hensley C. Woodbridge and Fritz Senn. I also wish to thank all those previous James Joyce bibliographers listed in Section I.A.

A final but lasting debt of gratitude is only somewhat repaid by the dedication of this volume to my family.

Contents

Bibliographical, Biographical, and General Treatments

BIBLIOGRAPHICAL STUDIES

See also section II.H. "Ulysses": Herring. James Joyce's Ulysses Notesheets in the British Museum, No. 3595; Spoerri. "The Odyssey Press Edition of James Joyce's Ulysses," No. 4068; Dalton. "The Text of Ulysses," No. 3564; Silverstein. "Toward a Corrected Text of Ulysses," No. 4061; Thornton. "Joyce's Ulysses, 1922," No. 4091; Dodson. "Ulysses in America," No. 4363; II.F "Portrait": Adams. "Letters," No. 3287; Anderson. "The Text of James Joyce's A Portrait of the Artist as a Young Man," No. 3290; II.I "Finnegans Wake": Higginson. "The Text of Finnegans Wake," No. 4939; Brown. "Finnegans Wake," No. 5001; Hart. "Notes on the Text of Finnegans Wake," No. 5089; Higginson. "Notes on the Text of Finnegan's Wake," No. 5101; Dalton. "Advertisement for the Restoration," No. 4923; Fritz Senn. "James Joyce and Zürich," No. 1655.

BIBLIOGRAPHIES

1. CAHOON, HERBERT. "The Joyce Library of John J. Slocum." Antiquarian Bookman, 7 (23 June 1951): 2037-2038.

2. COHN, ALAN M. "Joyce's Bibliographies: A Survey." American Book Collector, 15, no. 10 (Summer 1965): 11-16

3. _____. "Corrigenda to the Joyce Bibliography (Slocum and Cahoon D 1-2), and a Possible Addendum." Papers of the Bibliographical Society of America, 65 (Third Quarter 1971): 304-307.

4. CONNOLLY, THOMAS E. The Personal Library of James Joyce: A Descriptive Bibliography. University of Buffalo Studies, vol. 22, no. 1. Buffalo: University of Buffalo Press, 1955.

5. EPSTEIN, EDMUND L., MARVIN MAGALANER, CLIVE HART, and THOMAS F. STALEY. "The Joyce Journals," American Book Collector, 15 (June 1965): 18-21.

*6. GILBERT, JEAN. "A Card Index to the Press Clippings in the Joyce Collection of the Lockwood Memorial Library." Unpublished M.A. Thesis, Buffalo, 1952. (Microfilm # 109, Wickser Collection: Lockwood Memorial Library, State University of New York at Buffalo.)

7. GILBERT, STUART. "The Wanderings of Ulysses." New Colophon, 2 (September 1949): 245-252.

8. HOFFMANN, FREDERICK, CHARLES ALLEN, and CAROLYN F. ULRICH. The Little Magazine: A History and a Bibliography. Princeton: Princeton University Press, 1946, pp. 59-60.

*9. JUCHHOFF, RUDOLF. "James Joyce," in Sammelkatalog der biographischen und literarkritischen Werke zu englischen Schriftstellern des 19. und 20. Jahrhunderts. Krefeld: Scherpe Vlg., 1959, pp. 136-140.

*10. LYNSKEY, WINIFRED. "Joyce." College English, 21 (December 1959): 188. [Surveys in-print editions of some of Joyce's works.]

11. MINKOFF, GEORGE ROBERT. Bibliography of Black Sun Press. Introduction by Caresse Crosby. Great Neck, N. Y.: G. R. Minkoff, 1970, pp. 21-22, 45.

12. MIZENER, ARTHUR. The Cornell Joyce Collection, Given to Cornell University by William G. Mennen. Ithaca: Cornell University Library, 1958.

13. O'HEGARTY, P. S. "A Bibliography of James Joyce." Dublin Magazine, 21, no. 1 (January-March 1946): 38-47. [Reprinted as A Bibliography of James Joyce. Dublin: A. Thom and Co., 1946.]

14. PARKER, ALAN. James Joyce: A Bibliography of His Writings, Critical Material and Miscellanea. Boston: F. W. Faxon and Co., 1948.

BIBLIOGRAPHICAL STUDIES

15. ROBERTS, R. F. "Bibliographical Notes on James Joyce's Ulysses." Colophon, n.s. 1 (Spring 1936): 565-579.

16. SCHOLES, ROBERT E. The Cornell Joyce Collection: A Catalogue. Ithaca: Cornell University Press, 1961.

17. SLOCUM, JOHN J., and HERBERT CAHOON. A Bibliography of James Joyce, 1882-1941. New Haven: Yale University Press, 1953; London: Rupert Hart-Davis, "Soho Bibliography." [Reprinted Westport, Conn.: Greenwood Press, 1971.]

18. _____. "A Note on Joyce Biography." Yale University Library Gazette, 28 (1953): 44-50.

*19. _____. "Periodical References about James Joyce and His Works." Unpublished microfilm. Compiled April 1955.

20. SPIELBERG, PETER. James Joyce's Manuscripts and Letters at the University of Buffalo: A Catalogue. Buffalo: University of Buffalo, 1962.

21. SPOERRI, JAMES F. "James Joyce: Books and Pamphlets Relating to the Author and His Works." Bibliographical Society of the University of Virginia: Secretary's News Sheet, no. 34 (October 1955): 2-12; supplements in no. 37 (September 1957): 2-3, no. 48 (June 1962): 5-6, and in no. 51 (February 1964): 5-6.

22. TANSELLE, G. T. "Samuel Roth's Love Secrets, 1927." Book Collector, 15 (Winter 1966): 486-487.

23. THORNTON, WELDON. "Books and Manuscripts by James Joyce." Library Chronicle of the University of Texas, 7, no. 1 (Fall 1961): 19-23.

24. VOSWINCKEL, BARBARA, and ERIKA JOERDEN. James Joyce, 1882-1941. Hamburg: Hamburger Öffentlichen Bücherhallen, 1965.

25. WALKER, BRENDA M. "James Joyce: A Bibliography." Manchester Review, 8 (Spring 1958): 151-160.

26. WHITE, WILLIAM. [n.t.]. Bulletin of Bibliography, 21 (January-April 1956): 199. [A note on Connolly, No. 4.]

27. _____. "James Augustine Aloysius Joyce, 1882-1941," in New Cambridge Bibliography of English Literature, vol. 4. Edited by I. R. Willison. Cambridge: Cambridge University Press, 1972, pp. 444-472.

28. WILEY, PAUL, compiler. "James Joyce (1882-1941)," in his The British Novel: Conrad to The Present. Northbrook, Ill.: AHM, 1973, pp. 65-71.

CHECKLISTS

29. BEEBE, MAURICE, and A. WALTON LITZ. "Criticism of James Joyce: A Selected Checklist with an Index to Studies of Separate Works." Modern Fiction Studies, 4 (Spring 1958): 71-99. [Also in Configuration critique de James Joyce, I, No. 1584; continued in Cohn and Herring, No. 45.]

30. _____, and PHILLIP HERRING. "Criticism of James Joyce: A Selected Checklist." Modern Fiction Studies, 15 (Spring 1969): 105-182.

31. BELL, INGLIS F., and DONALD BAIRD. "James Joyce," in their The English Novel, 1578-1956: A Checklist of Twentieth-Century Criticisms. Denver: Alan Swallow, 1958, pp. 71-86.

32. BONHEIM, HELMUT, and MANFRED PÜTZ, compilers. A Wake Newslitter, Ten-Year Index, 1962-1971. [1972] Available from Department of Literature, University of Essex, Wivenhoe Park, Colchester, Essex, England.

33. COHN, ALAN M. "Further Supplement to James Joyce Bibliography, 1950-1957." James Joyce Review, 2, nos. 1-2 (Spring-Summer 1958): 40-54.

34. _____. "Supplemental James Joyce Checklist, 1963." James Joyce Quarterly, 2 (Fall 1964): 50-60.

35. _____. "Supplemental James Joyce Checklist, 1964." James Joyce Quarterly, 3 (Fall 1965): 50-61.

36. _____. "Supplementary James Joyce Checklist, 1959." James Joyce Quarterly, 3 (Spring 1966): 196-204.

37. _____. "Supplemental James Joyce Checklist, 1960-1961." James Joyce Quarterly, 4 (Winter 1966): 141-153.

38. _____. "Supplemental James Joyce Checklist, 1965." James Joyce Quarterly, 4 (Winter 1967): 120-130.

39. _____. "Supplemental James Joyce Checklist, 1966." James Joyce Quarterly, 5 (Fall 1967): 53-67.

40. _____. "Supplemental James Joyce Checklist, 1967." James Joyce Quarterly, 6 (Spring 1969): 242-261.

41. _____. "Supplemental James Joyce Checklist, 1968." James Joyce Quarterly, 7 (Spring 1970):229-250.

42. _____ . "Supplemental James Joyce Checklist, 1969." James Joyce Quarterly, 8 (Spring 1971): 236-256.

43. _____ . "Supplemental James Joyce Checklist, 1970." James Joyce Quarterly, 10 (Winter 1973): 240-261.

44. COHN, ALAN M., and H. K. CROESSMANN. "Additional Supplement to James Joyce Bibliography, 1950-1959." James Joyce Review, 3, nos. 1-2 (February 1959): 16-39.

45. COHN, ALAN M., and PHILLIP F. HERRING. "Critique de James Joyce: Sélection bibliographique des études générales consacrées à Joyce, suivi d'un index pour l'étude des oeuvres particulières," in Configuration critique de James Joyce, II, pp. 223-244, No. 1584.

46. COHN, ALAN M., and RICHARD M. KAIN. "Supplemental James Joyce Checklist, 1962." James Joyce Quarterly, 1 (Winter 1964): 15-22.

47. DEMING, ROBERT H. A Bibliography of James Joyce Studies. University of Kansas Publications, Library Series, no. 18. Lawrence: University of Kansas Libraries, 1964; superseded by the present work.

48. KAIN, RICHARD M. "Portraits of James Joyce, A Preliminary Checklist," in A James Joyce Miscellany, Second Series, pp. 111-118, No. 1613. [See also Kain and Alan M. Cohn, "Portraits of James Joyce: A Revised List." James Joyce Quarterly, 3 (Spring 1966): 205-212.]

*49. _____ . "Supplement to Joyce Bibliography." James Joyce Review, 1 (December 1957): 38-40.

50. _____ . "Addenda to Deming Bibliography." James Joyce Quarterly, 3 (Winter 1966): 153-159.

51. PALMER, HELEN H., and ANNE JANE DYSON, compilers. "Joyce," in English Novel Explication: Criticisms to 1972. Hamden, Conn.: Shoe String Press, 1973, pp. 162-185.

52. SACKETT, S. J., compiler. "Masters' Theses in Literature Presented at American Colleges and Universities, July 1, 1964-June 30, 1965." Lit, 7 (Spring 1966): 89-165 (passim therein); "...July 1, 1965-August 31, 1966." ibid., 8 (November 1967): 45-174 (passim therein); with Herman A. Dreifke. "...September 1, 1967-August 31, 1970." ibid., 10, no. 2-11, no. 2 (1971-1973): passim.

53. SCHWARTZ, HARRY W. Checklists of Twentieth Century Authors. Milwaukee: Casanova, 1933, pp. 8-10.

54. SPOERRI, JAMES F. Finnegans Wake by James Joyce: A Check List, Including Publications under the Title Work in Progress. Evanston: Northwestern University Library, 1953.

55. STALEY, THOMAS F., compiler. James Joyce Quarterly, Five-Year Cumulative Bibliography [i.e., Index]. Fall 1963-Summer 1968. Available from University of Tulsa, Tulsa, Oklahoma.

56. VAN VOORHIS, JOHN, and JOHN METZNER, compilers. James Joyce Quarterly, Ten-Year Cumulative Index. Fall 1963-Summer 1972. Available from University of Tulsa, Tulsa, Oklahoma.

57. WHITE, WILLIAM. "James Joyce: Addenda to Alan Parker's Bibliography." Papers of the Bibliographical Society of America, 43 (First Quarter 1949): 93-96; 43 (Fourth Quarter 1949): 401-411.

58. _____ . "Addenda to James Joyce Bibliography, 1950-1953." James Joyce Review, 1, no. 2 (June 1957): 9-25.

59. _____ . "Addenda to James Joyce Bibliography, 1954-1957." James Joyce Review, 1, no. 3 (September 1957): 3-24.

60. WOOLMER, J. HOWARD. "James Joyce, Ulysses: Census of First Editions." Book Collector, 20 (Winter 1971): 533.

SURVEYS OF JOYCEANA

61. ADAMS, ROBERT M. "In Joyce's Wake." Hudson Review, 12 (Winter 1959-1960): 627-632.

62. _____ . "The Bent Knife Blade: Joyce in the 1960's." Partisan Review, 29 (Fall 1962): 507-518.

63. ALTICHIERI, GILBERTO. "Il fratello Stanislaus vuota il sacco." Corriere della Sera (Milan), 20 November 1966, p. 11. [Letter to the editor from Michele Risolo, husband of Amalia Popper and friend of Stanislaus; ibid., 13 December 1966, p. 11 and Altichieri's reply, ibid., 13 December 1966, p. 11.]

64. BARFOOT, C. C. [n.t.]. English Studies, 54 (August 1973): 368-369.

65. BEEBE, MAURICE. [n.t.]. Modern Fiction Studies, 5 (Summer 1959): 183-184, continuing in (Winter 1959-1960): 367-368; 6 (Summer 1960): 177-178; (Winter 1960-1961): 371-372; 7 (Summer 1961): 186; (Winter 1961-1962): 382; 9 (Summer 1963): 178-179, 191-192; 11 (Summer 1965): 201-202; 12 (Winter 1966-1967): 497-499; 13 (Winter 1967-1968): 528-529.

BIBLIOGRAPHICAL STUDIES

66. BENSTOCK, BERNARD. "The James Joyce Indus-
    try: An Assessment in the Sixties."
    Southern Review, n.s. 2 (January 1966):
    210-228.

67. BURGESS, ANTHONY. "The Joyce Industry in
    the United States." Atlas, 10 (July
    1965): 51-53.

68. CELATI, GIANNI. [n.t.]. Verri, no. 31
    (1969): 167-169.

69. CLARKE, AUSTIN. "All Hail, Great Master."
    Irish Times, 10 May 1958, p. 8.

70. COHN, ALAN M. "Haveth Critics Everywhere."
    Mad River Review, 2 (Summer 1966): 83-91.

71. DAICHES, DAVID. "Shifts in Emphasis," in
    English Literature. Englewood Cliffs,
    N.J.: Prentice-Hall, 1964, pp. 1-31.

*72. DEN HAAN, JACQUES. "Joyceana." Litterair
    Paspoort, 15 (October 1960): 170-172.

73. EPSTEIN, EDMUND L. [n.t.]. Modern Fiction
    Studies, 17 (Winter 1971-1972): 585-591.

74. FORD, JANE. [n.t.]. Modern Fiction Studies,
    19 (Winter 1973-1974): 638-642.

75. HALPER, NATHAN. "A Year of James Joyce."
    Nation, 184 (March 1957): 190-191.

*76. HELLER, A. "Megjegyzések egy Joyce-tanulmany
    hoz." Nagyvilag (Budapest), 4 (1959):
    1242-1244.

77. HOHOFF, CURT. "Neues über und von James
    Joyce." Merkur, 12 (October 1958):
    983-986.

78. HUTCHINS, PATRICIA. "James Joyce on View."
    Life and Letters, 54 (February 1950):
    123-130.

79. KANTERS, ROBERT. "Pour la majorité de
    James Joyce." Figaro littéraire, 14
    April 1962, p. 2.

80. KENNER, HUGH. "The Search for Joyce."
    Prairie Schooner, 36 (Spring 1962): 19-24.

81. KLEINSTÜCK, JOHANNES. "Dublin ist nicht die
    Insel Ogygia." Welt der Literatur, 27
    (March 1969): 18-19.

82. McLUHAN, HERBERT M. "A Survey of Joyce
    Criticism." Renascence, 4 (Fall 1951):
    12-18.

83. _____. "One Wheel, All Square." Renas-
    cence, 10 (Summer 1958): 196-200.

*84. MERCIER, VIVIAN. "In Joyce's Wake, A Boom-
    ing Industry." New York Times Book
    Review, 30 July 1961, pp. 5, 20-21.

85. _____. "More French Joyceana." James Joyce
    Quarterly, 4 (Winter 1967): 154-155.

86. MERTON, THOMAS. "News of the Joyce Industry."
    Sewanee Review, 77 (Summer 1969): 543-544.

87. MILLER, NOLAN. "Joyce and [Thomas] Wolfe."
    Antioch Review, 16 (Winter 1956-1957):
    511-517.

88. MORSE, J. MITCHELL. "The Book of Daublends
    Jined." Journal of General Education, 16
    (July 1964): 163-172.

89. _____. "By and About Joyce." Hudson Review,
    21 (Summer 1968): 381-390.

90. NAREMORE, JAMES. [n.t.] Modern Fiction
    Studies, 16 (Summer 1970): 235-240.

91. O'FLAHERTY, GERARD. [n.t.]. Dublin Magazine,
    6 (Spring 1967): 94-95; 8 (Spring-Summer
    1969): 89-90.

92. RODWAY, ALLEN. "Gnosers to the Grinsdown."
    Essays in Criticism, 10 (April 1960):
    181-194.

93. SENN, FRITZ. "In that Earopean End." James
    Joyce Quarterly, 6 (Fall 1968): 91-95;
    "In that Earopean End, II." ibid., 7
    (Winter 1970): 274-280.

94. STALEY, THOMAS F. "Joyce Scholarship in the
    1960's." Papers on English Language and
    Literature, 1 (1965): 279-286.

95. SWINDON, PATRICK. "Reviews and Comments."
    Critical Quarterly, 14 (Spring 1972):
    91-92.

96. THEALL, D. F. "Recent Contributions to the
    Joyce Perplex." University of Toronto
    Quarterly, 33 (April 1964): 329-337.

97. THORPE, MICHAEL. "Current Literature, 1968."
    English Studies, 51 (April 1970): 176,
    183-184.

98. VINGE, LOUISE. "Nyare Joyceforskning."
    Samlaren, n.F. 90 (1969): 201-203, 211.

99. Unsigned. "L'Homme Joyce." Roman, no. 1
    (January 1951): 75-78.

100. Unsigned. "Joyce in Deutschland." Die Zeit,
    4 February 1966.

101. Unsigned. "Joyceana." Choice, 5 (March
    1968): 30.

102. Unsigned. "A Fragment and Four Furrow."
    Times Literary Supplement, 23 May 1968,
    p. 526.

103. Unsigned. "Joyce in Exile." Times Literary
    Supplement, 24 April 1969, p. 430.

104. Unsigned. Foreløbigt katalog over Joyce-litteratur. Copenhagen: The James Joyce Society of Copenhagen, 1970. [A mimeo list of Joyceana available in Denmark.]

EXHIBITIONS

105. And Trieste, Ah Trieste. Introduction by Stelio Crise. Milan: All'Insegna del Pesce d'Oro, 1971. [Catalogue of exhibits in the Sala di Palazzo Costanzi and the Biblioteca del Popolo in Trieste for the Third International James Joyce Symposium.]

106. APPEL, ALFRED. James Joyce: An Appreciation Published upon the Occasion of an Exhibition. Stanford: Stanford University Libraries, 1964. [Reprinted Folcroft, Pa.: Folcroft Press, 1972.]

*107. BEACH, SYLVIA. "Les Années vingt: les écrivains américains à Paris et leurs amis, 1920-1930," in Catalogue of an Exhibition. 11 March-25 April 1959. Paris: Centre Culturel Americain, [1959].

108. BERCH, VICTOR A., EMILIA LANGE, and RICHARD A. PLOCH. James Joyce: An Odyssey. Checklist of an Exhibition held in Rapaporte Treasure Hall, 25 November 1969-16 January 1970. Waltham, Mass.: Brandeis University, [1969].

109. COHN, ALAN M. James Joyce: An Exhibition from the Collection of Dr. H. K. Croessmann. Carbondale, Ill.: Southern Illinois University Press, 1957.

110. DeLISIO, MICHAEL. Sculpture: Literary Figures. Catalogue of an Exhibition, Minnesota Institute of the Arts, 30 December 1970-3 February 1971. Minneapolis: [1970].

111. DEMPSEY, DAVID. "Pursuit of Joyce." New York Times Book Review, 21 January 1951, p. 8.

112. ELIOT, T. S. "Homage à Joyce." Arts (Paris), no. 233 (21 October 1949): 1.

113. GÊNET (JANET FLANNER). "Letter from Paris." The New Yorker, 25 (26 November 1949): 114-115. [Reprinted in her Paris Journal, 1944-1965. New York: Atheneum, 1965, pp. 111-112.]

114. GHEERBRANT, BERNARD. James Joyce: Sa Vie, Son Oeuvre, Son Rayonnement. Paris: La Hune, 1949.

115. MARRIOTT, R. B. "Bloom's Voyage." Art News and Review (London), 2, no. 11 (1 July 1950): 1. [Institute of Contemporary Arts Exhibition.]

116. MILLSTEIN, GILBERT. "A Valentine for Joyce: 'Tis an Exhibit out of the Wake." New York Times Magazine, 14 February 1954, p. 53. [Eight paintings and drawings by Else de Brun at Carstair Gallery exhibited on 13 February 1954.]

117. NYHOLM, J. "Joyce Exhibit at Northwestern." Library Journal, 78 (1 March 1953): 420-421.

*118. OLSON, RICHARD D. "The World of James Joyce: An Exhibit." Northwestern Library News, no. 21 (19 May 1967): 1-2.

*119. PIOVENE, GUIDO. "Joyce quasi vivi riappare a Parigi." Corriere della Sera (Milan), 30 October 1949.

120. PLUTZIK, ROBERTA. "You can feel at one with James Joyce." Rochester Democrat and Chronicle. Upstate Supplement, 19 March 1972, pp. 23-24, 26-29.

121. POWER, ARTHUR. "James Joyce Exhibition in Paris." Envoy, 2 (February 1950): 49-56.

122. [ROBERTS, WARREN]. "James Joyce," in A Creative Century: An Exhibition. Selections from the Twentieth Century Collections at the University of Texas. Austin: Humanities Research Center, University of Texas, 1964, pp. 33-35.

123. SENN, FRITZ. "James Joyce and Zürich," see no. 1655.

124. SIMMONDS, HARVEY. "John Quinn: An Exhibition to Mark the Gift of the John Quinn Memorial Collection." Bulletin of the New York Public Library, 72, no. 9 (November 1968).

125. SPOERRI, JAMES F. Catalog of a Collection of the Works of James Joyce. Exhibited at the Newberry Library, 1 March-26 March 1948. Chicago: 1948.

126. TAPLIN, WALTER. "James Joyce Exhibition." Spectator, 185 (7 July 1950): 14.

127. Unsigned. James Joyce: 1882-1941. London: Institute of Contemporary Arts, 1950.

128. Unsigned. "A James Joyce Exhibition." Times Literary Supplement, 23 June 1950, p. 396.

129. Unsigned. "James Joyce First Editions on View." Times (London), 29 May 1957, p. 7. [National Book League exhibit of Harriet Shaw Weaver collection.]

*130. Unsigned. "James Joyce-Archieve." Neue Zürcher Zeitung, no. 170 (23 June 1957).

131. Unsigned. "Ein Joyce-Museum." Neue Zürcher Zeitung, no. 189 (11 July 1964).

BIBLIOGRAPHICAL STUDIES

COLLECTIONS

132. BEACH, SYLVIA. Catalogue of a Collection Containing Manuscripts and Rare Editions of James Joyce, Etc. Paris: Shakespeare and Co., [1935].

133. BREADY, JAMES H. "Books and Authors." Baltimore Sun, 20 November 1966, p. 5D. [On George Leinwall's collection.]

134. COWIE, ALFRED T. "A Joyce Collection." PLA Quarterly (Private Libraries Association), 1 (January 1958): 58-62.

135. [DRIVER, CLIVE E.] "James Joyce," in Notable Acquisitions, 1966-1967. Philadelphia: Philip H. and A. S. W. Rosenbach Foundation, [n.d.], pp. 40-43.

136. GOTHAM BOOK MART. "James Joyce," We Moderns, 1920-1940. New York: Gotham Book Mart, 1940, pp. 38-41. [Bookseller's priced catalogue, listing 58 Joyce items.]

137. KAIN, RICHARD M. "On Collecting Joyce and Joyceana." American Book Collector, 15 (Summer 1965): 9.

138. M[ALKIN], S[OL] M. "Leinwall Joyce [Collection] to Dublin Museum." AB Bookman's Weekly, 43 (3 November 1969): 1441.

139. POTEGA, PATRICK H. "A James Joyce Collection." AB Bookman's Weekly, 42 (1-8 July 1968): 8, 10. [Winning entry for Loveman Award for college student book collectors.]

140. RICE, HOWARD C. "The Papers of Sylvia Beach." Princeton Alumni Weekly, 65, no. 17 (16 February 1965). [See also his "The Sylvia Beach Collection." Manuscripts, 18 (Summer 1966): 3-8, abridged from Princeton University Library Chronicle, 26 (Autumn 1964): 7-13.]

141. SILVERMAN, OSCAR A. "James Joyce: Paris-Buffalo, the Joyce Collections at the Lockwood Memorial Library." Grosvenor Society Occasional Papers, 1, no. 1 (February 1964).

142. SZLADITS, LOLA L. "The James Joyce Circle in France," in New in the Berg Collection, 1970-1972. New York: New York Public Library, 1973, pp. 36-39.

143. Unsigned. "School Gets Joyce Mss." New York Times, 4 August 1950, p. 19. [See also David Dempsey comment, New York Times Book Review, 20 August 1950, p. 8.]

144. Unsigned. "Cornell Receives James Joyce Items." New York Times, 26 May 1957, p. 51.

145. Unsigned. "Portrait of the Artist: Cornell's Rich New Joyce Collection." Times (London), 24 June 1958, p. 7.

146. Unsigned. St. Louis Post-Dispatch, 5 January 1959, p. 6A. [About Croessman collection at Southern Illinois.]

147. Unsigned. "The James Joyce Collection," in A Guide to the Collections. Lawrence, Kansas: Department of Special Collections, University of Kansas Libraries, 1964, pp. 9-10.

148. Unsigned. "Letters by Writers are Given to N.Y.U. by Frances Steloff." New York Times, 21 June 1965, p. 26.

SPECIAL JOYCE ISSUES

149. l'Arc, 36 (1968).
    Contents: Henri Ronse. "Retour à Joyce," 1-3; Michel Butor. "Joyce et le roman moderne," 4-5; Jacques Borel. "Joyce et la poésie," 6-12; Jean Michel Gardair. "Joyce et Svevo," 13-16; Italo Svevo. "Ulysses à Trieste," translated by Jean-Michel Gardair, 16-28 (French translation of Italian original first published in Il Convegno, 25 April 1937, reprinted in Svevo's Saggi e pagine sparse. Edited by U. Apollonio, 1954--No. 781 is the English translation of the first part of this essay); Umberto Eco. "Joyce et d'Annunzio: Les sources de la notion d'Epiphanie," translated by Elisabeth Hollier, 29-38; Ludovic Janvier. "Sames: Joyce et Beckett," 39-41; Denis Roche. "Joyce et Pound," 42-43; Ezra Pound. "Joyce et Pécuchet," 44-48, from No. 4511; Richard Ellmann. "Présentation de Giacomo Joyce," translated by Michel Perez, 51-54; James Joyce. "Giacomo Joyce," 54-58 (extracts in English); James Joyce. "Quartre lettres à Martha Fleischmann," 59-62, from Letters, vol. 2, No. 309; Roger Kempf. "Ma première impression de vous," 63-66; René Micha. "Le Dublin de Joyce," 69-72; Hélène Cixous. "Thoth et l'écriture," 73-79, from her l'Exil de James Joyce, No. 1543; Jean Schoonbroodt. "Sheminant avec Ulysse," 80-87; François van Laere. "Finnegans Wake, textuellement," 88-93; William Melvin Kelley. "Oswhole'-stalking," 94-95, from his A Wake In Progress; "Bibliography," 97.

150. Change, no. 11 (May 1972). A special James Joyce issue edited by Jean Paris.
    Contents: Jean Paris. "Pour changer d'ère," 9-10; François Rigolot. "l'Épreuve des langues," 12-25 (Joyce and Rabelais); Mitsou Ronat. "l'Hypotexticale," 26-33 (Joyce and Lewis Carroll); Robert J. DiPietro. "Sur quelques types de phrases joyciennes," translated by Marie-Jo Renard and Jean Paris, 34-46, original as No. 4290; S. M. Eistenstein. "Sur Joyce," compiled and translated by Léon Robel, 48-53; Gilles Deleuze, "Joyce indirect," compiled by Jean Paris, 54-59; from several books by Deleuze; Philippe Boyer. "Séries

noires," 60-69 (FW); Pierre Beaudry. "Une écriture 'attentative,'" 70-86; Pierre Gaudebout. "Divus Leopoldus: La Casartica de Joyce," 87-91; V. V. Ivanov. "Du Zaoum à Finnegans," translated by Yvan Mignot, 92-93 (Vygotski's "Transrational" and FW); James Joyce. "Scribbledehobble," 96-103; David Hayman. "Work in Progress," translated by Therese von Essen, 104-110 (from "Introduction" to No. 4936); Northrup Frye. "Quête et cycle dans Finnegans Wake," translated by Alain Delahaye, 111-119 (No. 5402); Jacques Aubert. "river-run," 120-130; Jean Paris. "l'Agonie du signe," 133-172; Danielle Collobert. "Ça des mots," 174-176, poem; André Hodeir. "Annamores Leep," 177-182 (musicality of U and FW); Giose Rimanelli. "Machine et montage," translated by Lucrezia Rotolo, 183-185 (the post-Joyce novel); and the following works showing Joyce influence: Giose Rimanelli. "Opera buffa," translated by Lucrezia Rotolo and Jean Paris, 186-194; Jean Paris. "Virgule," 195-210; Jean-Roger Carroy. "En chant (en) tier," 211-216; Michel Bulteau. "Hypodermique," 217-222.

151. CEA Critic (College English Association), 14, no. 2 (February 1952): 1-8.
    Contents: Elizabeth Drew. "The Difficulties of Joyce's Ulysses," 1, 6; Ellsworth Mason. "Ulysses, the Hair Shirt, and Humility," 6; Joseph Prescott. "A Semester's Course in James Joyce," 7; Denis Johnston. "God's Gift to English Departments," 4-5; Haskell Block. "Stanislaus and His Brother," 4; Kenneth Rothwell. "Who now Reads--?" 4.

152. Chesapeake Weekly Review, 12 June 1970. Bloomsday Issue.
    Contents: George Leinwall. "Bloomsday '70," 5; Richard Macksey. "The Ineluctable Modality of the Verbal," 6; Ed Gold. "Bloom Becoming," 7 (Levi-Straussian reading of U); Elliot Coleman. "Joyce's Grave," 7 (a poem); Paul G. Kreiner. "Joyce and Music," 9 (Diamond and Barber recordings).

153. Envoy, 5 (May 1951). See also No. 1644.
    Contents: Brian Nolan (Flann O'Brien, Myles na Gopaleen). "A Bash in the Tunnel," 5-11; Patrick Kavanagh. "Who Killed James Joyce?," 12 (a poem); Denis Johnston. "A Short View of the Progress of Joyceanity," 13-18; Andrew Cass (John Garvin). "Childe Horrid's Pilgrimace," 19-30; Niall Montgomery. "Joyeux Quicum Ulysse...Swissairis Dubellay Gadelice," 31-43; Joseph Hone. "A Recollection of James Joyce," 44-45; "Some Unpublished Letters of James Joyce," 46-61; W. B. Stanford. "The Mysticism that Pleased Him: A Note on the Primary Source of Joyce's Ulysses," 62-69; Patrick Kavanagh.

"Diary," 70-72; "Recollections of the Man," 73-78 (reprinted memoirs from the Irish Times, by C. P. Curran and Kenneth Reddin; reprints also from the Irish Press).

154. Levende Talen, no. 269 (June-July 1970).
    Contents: M. Buning. "Ten geleide," "Introduction," 413; "Ulysses in vertaling: De eerste bladzijde," 413-416; John Vandenbergh, Peter van Gestel, and anonymous announcer. "Voorrang: Ulysses van James Joyce," 416-425 (script of N.C.R.V., Amsterdam, radio broadcast of 27 October 1969); H. Vreeswijk. "Het James Joyce Symposium van Utrect," 425-427 (held 28 November 1969); A. O. H. Tellegen. "Ja, nee en geen van beide," 427-432; A. Vreeswijk. "Introduction to an Imperfect, Incomplete Ulysses-Commentary," 432-438 (from his book No. 4105); Rein Bloem. "Brief Encounters in Ulysses," 438-443 (in Dutch); Gerardine Franken. "Een portret van de Kunstenaar als jongeman," 443-447; Rudy Bremer. "The Poetry of James Joyce," 447-453; Izzy Abrahami. "The Joyce-Theatre Affair," 453-455 (theatrical adaptations of Joyce's works); Fritz Senn. "In het struikgewas van Finnegans Wake," translated by B. Wijffels-Smulders, 456-461 [second part of article originally in Zolliker Bote, 17 June 1966; first part translated in Utopia (June 1969)]; A. M. L. Knuth. "Joyce's Ouroboros: Kop en staart," 461-469; Fritz Senn. "A Reading Exercise in Finnegans Wake," 469-480; Clive Hart. "Select Bibliography," 481-483 (reprinted from his James Joyce's Ulysses, No. 3590).

155. Literatura na Świecie, no. 5 (25) May 1973.
    Contents: "Od redakcji," 3; Maciej Słomczyński. "Klucze otchłani," 4-41 (from his forthcoming book); Jerzy Strzetelski. "Finnegans Wake w oczach krytyki," 54-84 (survey of criticism); John Gross. "Nawiedzony kalamarz," translated by Hanna Zbierzchowska, 86-120 (chapter two of his James Joyce, no. 1580); Richard Ellmann. "James Joyce w latach 1921-1922," translated by Ewa Krasińska, 122-186 (chapter thirty of his James Joyce, No. 308); Alfred Döblin. "Ulisses J'a," translated by Barbara L. Surowska, 188-193 (revised from Deutsche Buch, 1928, No. 2093); Zbigniew Taranienko. "Poworty Ulissesa," 194-216 (motif of return in Ulysses); Zbigniew Lewicki. "Sceniczny Ulisses Słomczyńskiego," 218-240 (on Słomczyński's dramatization, with numerous photos of the Teatr Wybrzeze production); H[ieronim] M[ichalski?]. "Joyce in Zurych," 280-285; Z[bigniew] L[ewicki?]. "Ulisses na świecie," 286-289; English "Summary" of issue, 382.

156. Mercure de France, 349 (August-September 1963), edited by Jackson Mathews and Maurice Saillet: "Sylvia Beach (1887-1962)."

BIBLIOGRAPHICAL STUDIES

Contents: I. "Hommages": T. S. Eliot. "Miss Sylvia Beach," translated by Pierre Leyris, 9-12; Marianne Moore. "How do justice...," translated by Pierre Leyris, 13; Henri Hoppenot. "Pendant près d'un quart de siècle," 14-16; Bryher. "For Sylvia," 17-21; André Chamson. "Le secret de Sylvia," 22-24; Jackson Mathews. "My Sylvia Beach," translated by Yves Bonnefoy, 25-27; Yves Bonnefoy. "Le voyage de Grèce," 28-33; Archibald Macleish. "What one Remembers...," 34-47; Allen Tate. "Memories of Sylvia Beach," translated by Roger Giroux, 38-40; André Spire. "La rencontre avec Joyce," 41-45; Janet Flanner. "The Great American Publisher," translated by André Michel, 46-54; Pierre Leyris. "Sylvia remémorée," 55-56; Malcolm Cowley. "When a Young American...," translated by André Michel, 57-60; Marcelle Sibon. "Lettre du traducteur," 61-62; Justin O'Brien. "Sylvia Beach trait d'union," 63-65; Maria Jolas. "Le 16 Juin 1962," 66-69; John L. Brown. "12, rue de l'Odéon," 70-74; Maurice Saillet. "Mots et locutions de Sylvia," 75-81; Leslie Katz. "Meditations on Sylvia Beach," translated by Yves Bonnefoy, 82-89; II. "Petit Mémorial de Shakespeare and Company": Sylvia Beach. "Allocution prononcée le 24 mai 1927," 91-94; Gertrude Stein. "Rich and Poor in English," translated by Roger Giroux, 95-98; Valery Larbaud. "Sur 'Ulysses,'" translated by Marcelle Sibon, 99-101; James Joyce. "Who is Sylvia...," translated by George Adam, 102-103; Sherwood Anderson. "My friend Ernest Hemingway," translated by Roger Giroux, 104; Ernest Hemingway. "Dear Seelviah...," translated by Roger Giroux, 105-110; Adrienne Monnier. "Joyce rue de l'Odéon," 111-113; William Carlos Williams. "It was fine to hear from you...," translated by Roger Giroux, 114-118; Robert McAlmon. "Your check for the article...," translated by Roger Giroux, 119-122; S. M. Eisenstein. "Deux lettres de Moscou," translated by Roger Giroux, 122-126; Dorothy Richardson. "A few facts for you...," translated by Pierre Leyris, 127-129; André Gide. "Pour une aide effective...," 130; Jean Schlumberger. "Appel aux Amis de Shakespeare and Company," 131-132; Adrienne Monnier. "Lectures chez Sylvia," 133-135; Sylvia Beach. "Inturned," translated by Robert Soulat, 136-149; Paul Valéry. "Deux billets," 150-151; Pierre Reverdy. "Bonne chance," 152-153; Katherine Anne Porter. "Tell me about Adrienne...," translated by Marcelle Sibon, 154-157; Hilda Doolittle. "Will this reach you...," translated by Roger Giroux, 158-159; Cyril Connolly. "A rendezvous for writers," translated by André Michel, 160-166; Michel Mohrt. "Une Américaine à Paris," 167-170.

157. Modern Fiction Studies, 4 (Spring 1958).
Contents: A. Walton Litz. "Joyce's Notes for the Last Episodes of Ulysses," 3-20; Grant H. Redford. "The Role of Structure in Joyce's Portrait," 21-30; Julian B. Kaye. "The Wings of Daedalus: Two Stories in Dubliners," 31-41; D. J. F. Aitken. "Dramatic Archetypes in Joyce's Exiles," 42-52; H. K. Russell. "The Incarnation in Ulysses," 53-61; Robert Bierman. "'White and Pink Elephants': Finnegans Wake and the Tradition of 'Unintelligibility,'" 62-70; Maurice Beebe and A. Walton Litz. "Criticism of James Joyce: A Selected Checklist with an Index to Studies of Separate Works," 71-99.

158. Modern Fiction Studies, 15 (Spring 1969).
Contents: Bernard Benstock. "Every Telling has a Taling," 3-25; John White. "Ulysses," 27-34; Ralph Jenkins. "Theosophy in 'Scylla and Carybdis,'" 35-48; Phillip F. Herring. "The Bedsteadfastness of Molly Bloom," 49-61; William D. Jenkins. "It seems there were two Irishmen...," 63-71; Erwin R. Steinberg. "'Lestrygonians,' a Pale Proteus?" 73-86; George L. Greckle. "Stephen Dedalus and W. B. Yeats," 87-96; M. W. Murphy. "Darkness in Dubliners," 97-104; Maurice Beebe, Phillip F. Herring, and A. Walton Litz. "Checklist of James Joyce Criticism," 105-182.

159. Mosaic, 6 (Fall 1972). Special Issue: "Ulysses and The Waste Land: Fifty Years After."
Contents: William York Tindall. "Mosaic Bloom," 3-10; Michael Beausang. "Seeds for the Planting of Bloom," 11-22; Chester G. Anderson. "Leopold Bloom as Dr. Sigmund Freud," 23-44; Edward A. Kopper. "Ulysses and James Joyce's Use of Comedy," 45-56; Richard M. Kain. "Ulysses as a Classic: Some Anniversary Reconsiderations," 57-62; Marvin Magalaner. "The Humanization of Stephen Dedalus," 63-68; Thomas F. Staley. "Ulysses: Fifty Years in the Joycean Conundrum," 69-76; William T. Noon. "Song the Syrens Sang," 77-84; Mario Praz. "Notes on James Joyce," translated by Wallace Sillanpoa, extracted from Radiotelevisione Italiana lectures, 85-102; R. G. Collins. "Admiring a Bouquet of Blooms," 103-112; Julian Alberts. "A Bouquet for Bloom (woodcuts)," 113-126.

160. Studies in the Literary Imagination, 3 (October 1970). Special issue: "James Joyce in the 70's: The Expanding Dimensions of His Art."
Contents: Ted R. Spivey. "Editor's Comment," 1-2; Joseph Campbell. "Contransmagnificandjewbandtantiality," 3-18; Richard M. Kain, "James Joyce and the Game of Language," 19-26; William A. Evans. "Wordagglutinations in Joyce's Ulysses,"

27-36; Lodwick Hartley. "'Swiftly-Sterne-ward': The Question of Sterne's Influence on Joyce," 37-48; Ted R. Spivey. "The Re-integration of Modern Man: An Essay on James Joyce and Hermann Hesse," 49-64; Charles T. McMichael and Ted R. Spivey. "'Chaos-Hurray!--Is Come Again': Heroism in James Joyce and Conrad Aiken," 65-68; Potter Woodbery. "The Irrelevance of Stephen Dedalus...," 69-78; Joseph K. Davis. "The City as Radical Order: James Joyce's Dubliners," 79-96.

161. Umana, 20 (May-September 1971). Special issue for the Third International James Joyce Symposium.

    Contents: Aurelia Gruber Benco. "Commento a questo numero," 2; Niny Rocco-Bergera. "Benvenuto a Trieste il Terzo Simposio Joyciano Internazionale," 3-4; Bernard Benstock. "The First Two International James Joyce Symposia," 5; Silvio Benco. "Ricordi di Joyce," 6-12; Richard Ellmann. "James Joyce, Irish European," 13-15 [reprinted from Tri-Quarterly, 8 (Winter 1976)]; Augusto Guidi. "Gli anni trientini di Joyce," 16-20; Vera Rosa. "Gertrude Stein e James Joyce ovvero l'utopia nella letteratura del XX secolo," 20; Helmut Bonheim. "Umana in Finnegans Wake," 21-22; François van Laere. "Finnegans Wake, ou le triomphe des figures matricelles," 22-25; Stelio Crise. "James eats James," 26-27; Darcy O'Brien. "Cod be with You," 27-28; Maurice Beebe. "Joyce and the Limits of Modernism," 29-31 (article in full in Bates and Pollock, eds. Litters from Aloft, No. 1516 and in Journal of Modern Literature); Péter Egri. "The Place of James Joyce's Interior Mon-ologue in World Literature," 32-35 (trans-lated into English from his Alom, látomás válosóg, pp. 207-215, No. 1557); Vladimír Macura. "Polysemantization as a Construc-tional Principle of James Joyce's Novel," 36-37; Andrea Csillaghy. "La fortuna di Italo Svevo e James Joyce in Ungheria e l'evoluzione del concetto di'realismo borghese," 38-42; Tibor Szobotka. "James Joyce's Ulysses," 43-45 (in Hungarian with English abstract); Jan Parandowski. "Spotkanie z Joycem," 46-48 ("A Meeting with Joyce," with English abstract); Égon Naganowski. "Structura czásu przes-trzeni i postaci w Ulissesie Jamesa Joyce'a," 49-51 ("On Time, Space and Form in Ulysses," with English extract); Niny Rocco-Bergera. "La gelosia in James Joyce e in Italo Svevo," 52-56, reprinted in her Due saggi su James Joyce, pp. 53-71, No. 525; Thomas P. Staley. "Character and Structure in Italo Svevo's Una Vita," 57-59; Franco Carlini. "Italo Svevo per-sonaggio-attore," 60-63; Silvio Benco. "Italo Svevo," 64-68.

162. Utopia (Technische Hogeschool, Eindhoven), 8 (June 1969).
    Contents: J. M. H. Dassen and J. R. Durinck. "James Joyce: His Life as a Kind of Exejesus," 6-8 (in Dutch); "De Vertal-ing van Ulysses: Interview met J. Vanden-bergh," 9-12; J. M. H. Dassen. "Ulysses," 16-19; Fritz Senn. "James Joyce en zijn Ulysses," translated into Dutch by B. W[ijffels]-S[mulders], 23-26; J. R. Durinck. "Finnegans Wake is an Oral Book: It is Something to be Read Aloud," 27-28.

INTERNATIONAL JAMES JOYCE SYMPOSIA

163. First International James Joyce Symposium: Jacques Aubert, [n.t.]. Quinzaine littér-aire, 15-31 July 1967, pp. 10-11; Bernard Benstock. "The First Two International James Joyce Symposia." Umana, 20 (May-September 1971): 5; George Burrows. Daily Telegraph (London), 16 June 1967, p. 19; Julian Critchley. Sunday Times (London), 18 June 1967, p. 34; David Hayman. Books Abroad, 42 (Spring 1968): 214-217; John Kelly. Hibernia, no. 31 (June 1967): 8; Proinsias MacAonghusha. "Joycetown 1967." New Statesman, 73 (23 June 1967): 871-872; Proinsias MacAonghusha. "The First Blooms-day, June 16, 1904." Irish Times, 16 June 1967, p. 10; Quidnunc [Seamus Kelly]. Irish Times, 16 June 1967, p. 9; ibid., 17 June 1967, p. 9; Terry O'Sullivan. Evening Press (Dublin), 15 June 1967, p. 13; Harry Pollack. James Joyce Quarterly, 5 (Fall 1967): 3-8; W. L. Webb. Guardian, 17 June 1967, p. 7; Unsigned. Éire-Ireland, no. 762 (30 June 1967): 8-9; Unsigned. Irish Independent (Dublin), 17 June 1967, p. 8; Unsigned. Irish Press (Dublin), 16 June 1967, p. 3; ibid., 17 June 1967, p. 5; Unsigned. Irish Times, 16 June 1967, p. 8; Unsigned. New York Times, 17 June 1967, p. 33.

164. Second International James Joyce Symposium: Jacques Aubert. Quinzaine littéraire, 16-30 September 1969, pp. 9-10; Lionel Fleming. Irish Times, 13 June 1969, p. 5; Magnus Hedlund. Goteborgs Handels-och-Syrfarts-Tydning, 2, 9, 12 July 1969; Phillip F. Herring, James Joyce Quarterly, 7 (Fall 1969): 3-9; Patricia Hutchins. Irish Press, 16 June 1969; Hilda Kirkwood. Canadian Forum, 49 (December 1969): 218-219; Maciej Krasincki. Polityka (Warsaw), 12 July 1969; Juliusz Kydrynski, Zycie lierackie (Krakow), 903 (1969): 95; Mary MacGoris. Irish Independent, 11 June 1969, p. 13; Terry O'Sullivan. Evening Press (Dublin), 12 June 1969; "Quidnunc" [Seamus Kelly]. Irish Times, 7 June 1969, p. 9; ibid., 10 June 1969, p. 11; ibid., 11 June 1969, p. 11; ibid., 14 June 1969, p. 11; ibid., 17 June 1969, p. 11; Niny Rocco-

BIBLIOGRAPHICAL STUDIES

Bergera, Umana (Trieste), 18 (July-October 1969): 16-18; Eithne Strong. Irish Press, 16 June 1969; R. van der Pas. "Second International James Joyce Symposium, Dublin, June 10-16 1969." Levende Talen, no. 264 (1970): 27-34; Unsigned. Irish Independent, 12 June 1969, p. 7; Unsigned. Irish Times, 11 June 1969, p. 6; ibid., 12 June 1969, p. 10; ibid., 14 June 1969, p. 11; ibid., 16 June 1969, p. 10; ibid., 17 June 1969, p. 10.

165. Third International James Joyce Symposium: Leo Knuth. James Joyce Quarterly, 9 (Winter 1971): 266-269; William Peden, "Notes from Trieste: The Third International James Joyce Symposium." Contempora, 2, no. 1 (September-February 1972): 36-38; Nora Poliaghi. Gazzetta di Parma, 3 December 1970; Thomas F. Staley. Il piccolo (Trieste), 3 June 1971; Norman Silverstein. "The Third International James Joyce Symposium." James Joyce Quarterly, 9 (Spring 1972): 307-310; Florence L. Walzl. ACIS-Newsletter, 1 (December 1971): 4; TLS, 2 July 1971, p. 762.

166. Fourth International James Joyce Symposium: Frank Khan, Irish Independent, 9 June 1973, p. 12; Mary MacGoris. Irish Independent, 12 June 1973, p. 11; "Quidnunc" [Seamus Kelly]. Irish Times, 9 June 1973, p. 11; Desmond Rushe. Irish Independent, 13 June 1973, p. 16; Unsigned. Irish Times, 12 June 1973, pp. 5, 11; ibid., 13 June 1973, p. 11; Unsigned. ACIS-Newsletter, 2 (October 1973): 1.

BIOGRAPHICAL STUDIES

GENERAL CRITICAL AND BIOGRAPHICAL, DICTIONARY ENTRIES, ENCYCLOPEDIA ENTRIES, HISTORIES OF THE NOVEL, ETC.

Books

167. ABBAS, M. A. "Jems Jays," in Ulakappukalperra navalaciriyarkalum, navalkalum, vol. 1. Madras: Gemini, 1962, pp. 54-61. [In Tamil]

168. ALBÉRÈS, R. M. Histoire du roman moderne. Paris: Editions Albin Michel, 1962, passim; 4th edition, revised and enlarged, 1971.

169. ALLEN, WALTER E. The English Novel. London: Phoenix House, 1954, passim.

170. AMORÓS, ANDRES. Introducción a la novela contemporánea. Madrid: Ediciones Anaya, "Temas y estudios," 1971, passim.

*171. ANGIOLETTI, G. B. "Joyce, o i dinamitardi delle lettere," in I grandi ospiti. Florence: Vallecchi, 1960, pp. 185-189. [5th Edition, 1961.]

172. ARNOLD, I. V., and N. IA. DIAKONOVA. Analitischeskoe chtenie: Angliiskaia proza XVIII-XX vekov. 2nd Edition. Leningrad: Leningradskoe otd-nie, 1967, pp. 266-272. [In Russian]

173. BEREZA, HENRYK. "James Joyce," in Doswiadozenia: Z lektur prozy obcej. Warsaw: Panstwowy Instytut Wydawniczy, 1967, pp. 83-94.

174. BIHALJI-MERIN, OTO. "Dzems Dzojs," in Graditelji Moderne Misli u Literaturi i Umetnosti. Belgrade: Prosveta, 1965, pp. 73-113. [A Czech translation from the Serbo-Croatian by Irena Wenigova appears as "James Joyce." Svetova Literatura (Prague), no. 1 (1966): 175-199.]

175. BLOTNER, JOSEPH L. "James Joyce," in Masterplots Cyclopedia of World Authors, vol. 1. New York: Salem Press, 1958, pp. 586-589.

176. BROWN, MALCOLM. The Politics of Irish Literature from Thomas Davis to W. B. Yeats. Seattle: University of Washington Press, 1972, passim.

177. CAHILL, SUSAN, and TOM. "Portrait of James Joyce as a Young Man," "The Wandering of Ulysses," in A Literary Guide to Ireland. New York: Scribner's, 1973, pp. 231-257, 259-293, et passim.

178. CARPEAUX, OTTO MARIA. "Joyce," in As revoltas modernistas na literatura. Rio de Janeiro: Ediçoes de Ouro, 1968, pp. 213-220.

179. CHAPPLE, J. A. V. Documentary and Imaginative Literature, 1880-1920: History and Literature, vol. 4. London: Blandford; New York: Barnes and Noble, 1970, passim.

*180. CHATTOPADHYAYA (or CHATTERJEE), SISIR. "James Joyce and the Epiphany of Experience," in The Technique of the Modern English Novel. Calcutta: Firma K. L. Mukhopadhyay, 1959, pp. 110-167, et passim.

181. _____. The Novel as the Modern Epic. 2nd revised edition. Calcutta: K. L. Mukhopadhyay, 1965, passim.

182. CHURCHILL, R. C. "The Novel in Britain and America in the Age of Lawrence and Joyce," in The Concise Cambridge History of English Literature. Edited by George Sampson. 3rd edition, revised with additional chapters by R. C. Churchill. Cambridge: Cambridge University Press, 1970, pp. 866-899.

183. CONNELL, CHARLES. "James Joyce, 1882-1941," in World-Famous Exiles. Feltham, Middlesex: Odhams Books, 1969, pp. 182-187.

184. DAICHES, DAVID. "James Joyce," in The Norton Anthology of English Literature, vol. 2. Edited by M. H. Abrams et al. New York: W. W. Norton, 1962, pp. 1384-1462; revised edition, 1968, pp. 1611-1691.

185. DAVID, MICHEL. "Letteratura inglese," in Letteratura e psicanalisi. Civiltà letteraria del novecento, no. 10. Milan: U. Mursia, 1967, pp. 229-245, et passim.

186. DAY, MARTIN S. "The Novels and Short Stories of James Joyce," in History of English Literature. Garden City: Doubleday, 1964, pp. 382-389.

187. DURANT, WILL, and ARIEL. "James Joyce," in their Interpretations of Life: A Survey of Contemporary Literature. New York: Simon and Schuster, 1970, pp. 77-89.

188. EARNSHAW, H. G. "James Joyce," in Modern Writers. Edinburgh, London: W. and R. Chambers, 1968, pp. 134-139.

189. EASTMAN, RICHARD M. A Guide to the Novel. San Francisco: Chandler, 1965, passim.

190. EDEL, LEON. "James Joyce," in Atlantic Brief Lives: A Biographical Companion to the Arts. Edited by Louis Kronenberger and Emily Morison Beck. Boston, Toronto: Little, Brown, 1971, pp. 419-422.

191. EGRI, PÉTER. "James Joyce," in Az angol irodalom a huszadik században [English Literature in the Twentieth Century], vol. 1. Edited by László Báti and István Kristó-Nagy. Budapest: Gondolat, 1970, pp. 227-245.

192. ELLMANN, RICHARD. "James Joyce," in Masters of British Literature. Edited by Gordon N. Ray. Boston: Houghton, Mifflin, 1958, pp. 701-809.

193. EVANS, B. IFOR. "James Joyce," in his English Literature Between the Wars. London: Methuen, 1948, pp. 40-48.

194. EVERY, GEORGE. "James Joyce," in The New Spirit. Edited by E. W. Martin. London: Dennis Dobson, 1946, pp. 54-57. [Reprinted from The Student Movement.]

195. FORD, FORD MADOX. The March of Literature. New York: Dial Press, 1938, passim.

196. FRANULIC, LENKA, ed. Cien autores contemporaneos, vol. 1. Santiago de Chile: Ediciones Ercilla, 1940, pp. 429-439.

197. FRASER, G. S. The Modern Writer and His World. London: Derek Verschoyle; New York: Criterion, 1953, passim. [Revised edition, London: Andre Deutsch, 1964.]

198. FRASER, G. S. "The English Novel," in The Twentieth-Century Mind: History, Ideas and Literature in Britain, 1918-1945, vol. 2. Edited by C. B. Cox and A. E. Dyson. London, New York: Oxford University Press, 1972, pp. 373-416.

*199. FRICKER, ROBERT. "James Joyce," in Der moderne englische Roman. Gottingen: Vandenhoeck and Ruprecht, 1958, pp. 93-112; 2nd edition, revised and enlarged, 1966, pp. 103-123.

200. FRIEDMAN, ALAN. The Turn of the Novel. New York: Oxford University Press, 1966, passim.

201. FÜGER, WILHELM. "James Joyce (1882-1941)," in Das englische Prosagedicht: Grundlagen, Vorgeschichte, Hauptphasen, Anglistische Forschungen, Heft 102. Heidelberg: Carl Winter, 1973, pp. 320-335, et passim.

202. GILBERT, STUART. "James Augustine Joyce (1882-1941)," in Dictionary of National Biography, 1941-1950. London: Oxford, 1959, pp. 440-442.

203. GOLDMAN, ARNOLD. "James Joyce," in The Twentieth Century. History of Literature in the English Language, vol. 7. Edited by Bernard Bergonzi. London: Barrie and Jenkins and Sphere Books, 1970, pp. 75-105.

204. GUÉRARD, ALBERT. Preface to World Literature. New York: Holt, 1940, passim.

205. HALL, JAMES. The Lunatic Giant in the Drawing Room: The British and American Novel Since 1930. Bloomington, Ind., London: Indiana University Press, 1968, passim.

206. HEWITT, DOUGLAS. The Approach to Fiction: Good and Bad Readings of Novels. London: Longmans, 1972, passim.

207. HORTMANN, WILHELM. "James Joyce," in Englische Literatur im 20. Jahrhundert. Bern, Munich: Francke, 1965, pp. 48-52, et passim.

208. HUGHES, HELEN S., and ROBERT M. LOVETT. The History of the Novel in England. Boston: Houghton, 1932, passim.

209. IRASHEVA, V. V. "Dzheims Dzhois," Angliĭskaia literatura XX vek. Moscow: Izdatel'stvo "Prosreshchenie," 1967, pp. 38-66.

*210. KARL, FREDERICK R., and MARVIN MAGALANER. "James Joyce," in A Readers' Guide to

BIOGRAPHICAL STUDIES

Great Twentieth-Century English Novels. New York: Noonday Press, 1959, pp. 205-253; London reprint, Thames and Hudson, 1968, pp. 205-253; reprinted New York: Octagon, 1972.

*211. KATAOKA, JINTARO. "Solitude and Relief," "Liberation by Performance," in An Analytical Approach to World Literature. Tokyo: Shinozaki Shorin, 1959, pp. 119-123, 207-209.

212. KENNER, HUGH. "James Joyce," in Encyclopedia of World Literature in the Twentieth Century, vol. 2. New York: Frederick Ungar, 1969, pp. 187-191.

*213. KETTLE, ARNOLD. "The Consistency of James Joyce," in The Modern Age. Pelican Guide to English Literature, vol. 7. Edited by Boris Ford. Harmondsworth, Baltimore: Penguin Books, 1961, pp. 301-314. [Reprinted as A Guide to English Literature: The Modern Age, vol. 7. Edited by Boris Ford. London: Cassell, 1964, pp. 301-314.]

214. KNIGHT, GRANT C. The Novel in English. London: R. R. Smith, 1931, pp. 354-359.

215. KUNITZ, STANLEY J. "James Joyce," in his Living Authors: A Book of Biographies. New York: H. W. Wilson, 1931, pp. 201-204.

216. LALOU, RENÉ. Panorama de la littérature anglaise contemporaine. Paris: Simon Kra, 1926, pp. 196-205.

217. LARRETT, WILLIAM. "James Joyce," in The English Novel From Thomas Hardy to Graham Greene. Studien zur Sprache und Literatur Englands, no. 2. Frankfurt a. M.: Moritz Diesterweg Vlg., 1967, pp. 115-132.

218. LENNARTZ, FRANZ. "James Joyce," in his Ausländische Dichter und Schriftsteller unserer Zeit. Stuttgart: Kröner, 1955, pp. 335-338.

219. LODGE, DAVID. Language of Fiction. London: Routledge and Kegan Paul; New York: Columbia University Press, 1966, passim.

220. LONGAKER, MARK, and EDWIN C. BOLLES. "James (A. A.) Joyce," in their Contemporary English Literature. New York: Appleton-Century-Crofts, 1953, pp. 350-356.

*221. McGRORY, KATHLEEN. "Joyce," in McGraw-Hill Encyclopedia of World Biography, vol. 6. New York: McGraw-Hill, 1973, pp. 71-74.

222. MARTIN, GRAHAM. James Joyce. Arts: A Third Level Course. The Nineteenth-Century and its Legacy, unit 31. Milton Keynes, Eng.: Open University Press, 1973.

*223. MASARYK, THOMAS G. Die Weltrevolution: Erinnerungen und Betrachtungen, 1914-1918. Berlin: 1925, p. 110.

224. MASON, EUDO C. "James Joyce," in Englische Dichter der Moderne. Edited by Rudolf Sühnel and Dieter Riesner. Berlin: Erich Schmidt Vlg., 1971, pp. 285-298.

225. MERTNER, EDGAR. "James Joyce," in Englische Literaturgeschichte. Edited by Ewald Standop and Edgar Mertner. Heidelberg: Quelle and Meyer, 1967, pp. 630-635.

226. MEYLAND, JEAN-PIERRE. "James Joyce," in La Revue de Genève: Miroir des lettres européenes, 1920-1930. Geneva: Droz, 1969, pp. 390-395, et passim. [Paperback reprint of 1962 edition.]

227. MILLET, FRED B., ed. Contemporary British Literature. New York: Harcourt, 1935, pp. 38-39, 301-303.

228. MONOD, SYLVÈRE. "James Joyce," in Histoire de la littérature anglaise de Victoria à Elizabeth II. Paris: Armand Colin, 1970, pp. 305-312.

229. MOODY, WILLIAM V., and ROBERT M. LOVETT. A History of English Literature. New Edition by Fred B. Millet. New York: Scribner's, 1926, pp. 431-434, 479.

230. NAGAMATSU, SADAMU. "Life and Literature of Joyce," in A Study of Joyce, pp. 11-56, No. 1592.

231. NEILL, S. DIANA. A Short History of the English Novel. New York: Macmillan, 1952, pp. 312-320.

232. NOON, WILLIAM T., S.J. "James Augustine Joyce," in New Catholic Encyclopedia, vol. 7. New York: McGraw-Hill, 1967, pp. 1134-1136.

233. O'CONNOR, FRANK (Michael O'Donovan). "Antithesis-I," "Antithesis-II," in his A Short History of Irish Literature: A Backward Look. London: Macmillan; New York: Putnams' Sons, 1967, pp. 194-202, 203-211, et passim. [English edition entitled The Backward Look: A Survey of Irish Literature; the two chapters are reprinted as "James Joyce." American Scholar, 36 (Summer 1967): 466-490.]

234. O'CONNOR, ULICK. The Times I've Seen: Oliver St. John Gogarty. New York: Obolensky, 1963. [English edition, Oliver St. John

Gogarty: A Poet and His Times. London: Cape, 1964; "Joyce and Gogarty" reprinted in A Bash in the Tunnel, pp. 73-100, No. 1644.]

235. OPPEL, HORST. Englische-deutsche Literaturbeziehungen, II: Von der Romantik biz zur Gegenwart. Grundlagen der Anglistik und Amerikanistik, no. 2. Berlin: Erich Schmidt Vlg., 1971, passim.

236. PATERSON, JOHN. "James Joyce: It's All Won," in The Novel as Faith: The Gospel According to James, Hardy, Conrad, Joyce, Lawrence and Virginia Woolf. Boston: Gambit, 1973, pp. 107-142.

237. PIVANO, FERNANDA. "L'ingratitudine di Joyce," in America rossa e nera. Florence: Vallecchi, 1964, pp. 120-131. [Originally in Successo (January 1961).]

238. PRAZ, MARIO. "James Joyce," in La letteratura inglese dai romantici al novecento. New enlarged edition. Florence, Milan: Sansoni-Accademia, 1967, pp. 264-267. [Also in his Storia della letteratura inglese. 10th edition. Florence: Sansoni, 1968, pp. 693-697.]

*239. PRIESTLY, J. B. Literature and Western Man. New York: Harper, 1960, pp. 415-418, et passim.

240. PURNAL, ROLAND. "James Augustine Aloysius Joyce," in Dictionnaire biographique des auteurs, vol. 1. Edited by Robert Laffont and Valentino Bompiani. Paris: S. E. D. E., 1957, pp. 730-732. [First published in Italian. Milan: Bompiani, 1956-1957.]

241. RABINOVITZ, RUBIN. The Reaction Against Experiment in the English Novel, 1950-1960. New York, London: Columbia University Press, 1967, passim.

*242. RUSSE, ELLEN. "Englische Literatur," in Das geistige Europa, vol. 2. Edited by Friedrich Muckermann and H. van de Mark. Paderborn: F. Schöningh, 1926, pp. 201-205.

243. SARUKHANIAN, A. P. Sovremennaia irlandskaia literatura. Moscow: Izdatel'stvo "Nauka," 1973, passim.

244. SCHWARTZ, KESSEL. A New History of Spanish American Fiction, vol. 2. Coral Gables: University of Miami Press, 1971, passim.

245. SETH, RONALD. "James Joyce, 1882-1941," in 100 Great Modern Lives. Edited by John Canning. London: Odhams; New York: Hawthorne, 1965, pp. 482-488.

246. SHERMAN, STUART P. "James Joyce," in Men of Letters of the British Isles. Illustrated with portrait medallions by Theodore Spicer-Simson. New York: William E. Rudge, 1924, pp. 94-96.

247. SOUVAGE, JACQUES. An Introduction to the Study of the Novel with Special Reference to the English Novel. Ghent: E. Story-Scientia, 1965, passim.

248. STEIN, GABRIELE. "Joyce, James," in English Word-Formation over Two Centuries, Tübinger Beiträge zur Linguistik, no. 34. Tübingen: 1973, pp. 316-317.

249. STEVENSON, LIONEL. The History of the English Novel, vol. 11. New York: Barnes and Noble, 1967, pp. 208-230, et passim. [Continues E. A. Baker's history.]

250. TEMPLE, RUTH Z., and MARTIN TUCKER, eds. "James Joyce (1882-1941)," in their A Library of Literary Criticism: Modern British Literature, vol. 2. New York: Ungar, 1966, pp. 106-117.
    Contents: excerpts from Virginia Woolf. The Common Reader, No. 1840; Cyril Connolly. "The Position of Joyce," No. 1711; Jack Lindsay. "James Joyce," No. 939; Desmond MacCarthy. "James Joyce," No. 1050; L. A. G. Strong. "James Joyce," No. 1223; Richard Chase. "Finnegans Wake: An Anthropological Study," No. 5578; W. Y. Tindall. James Joyce, No. 1677; Marvin Magalaner. Joyce: The Man..., No. 1615; Richard Ellmann. James Joyce, No. 308; TLS, 20 November 1959, 5 February 1960; Donagh MacDonagh. London Magazine, (May 1960); Harry Levin. James Joyce, No. 1603.

251. TORRE, GUILLERMO de. Historia de las literaturas de vanguardia. Madrid: Guadarrama, 1965, passim.

252. URNOW, D. M. "Dzh. Dzhoĭs ĭ sovremennyĭ moderizm," in Sovremennye problemy realizma i modernizm. Edited by A. S. Miasnikov et al. Moscow: Izdatel'stvo "Nauka," 1965, pp. 309-345.

253. VAN DOREN, CARL, and MARK VAN DOREN. American and British Literature since 1890. New York: Century, 1925, pp. 303-304.

254. VON RECKLINGHAUSEN, DANIEL. James Joyce--Chronik von Leben und Werk. Frankfurt, a. M.: Suhrkamp Vlg., 1968.

255. WALCUTT, CHARLES CHILD. Man's Changing Mask: Modes and Methods of Characterization in Fiction. Minneapolis: University of Minnesota Press, 1966, passim.

256. WEST, PAUL. The Modern Novel. London: Hutchinson University Library, 1963, passim.

BIOGRAPHICAL STUDIES

257. ZHANTIEVA, D. G. "Dzheims Dzhois," in Angliski roman XX veka. Moscow: Izdatel'stvo "Nauka," 1965, pp. 14-67. [Translated by Anne White in Preserve and Create: Essays in Marxist Literary Criticism, AIMS Monograph Series, no. 4. Edited by Gaylord C. LeRoy and Ursula Beitz. New York: Humanities Press, 1973, pp. 138-172.]

258. _____. Dzheims Dzhois. Moscow: Izdatel'stvo "Vyshaia Shkola," 1967.

259. ZIOLKOWSKI, THEODORE. Dimensions of the Modern Novel: German Texts and European Contexts. Princeton: Princeton University Press, 1969, passim.

Periodical Articles

260. de ANTELIS, GUILIO. [n.t.]. Revista de letterature moderne, 1 (1950): 72-73.

261. ASCHAUER, JOSEF C., S.J. "James Joyce." Grosse Entschluss, 20 (February 1965): 221-224; (March 1965): 264-268.

262. ATKINSON, BROOKS. "Critic at Large." New York Times, 18 December 1962, p. 5 and 21 December 1962, p. 7. [Reprinted in his Brief Chronicles. New York: Coward-McCann, 1966, pp. 47-48.]

263. BEAUMONT, GERMAINE. "L'homme qui disait non." Nouvelles littéraires, 22 March 1962, pp. 1, 7.

264. BRAJNOVIC, LUKA. "Vida e obra literária de James Joyce." Rumo (Lisbon), 12 (August 1968): 139-150. [Translated as "Vida y obra literária de James Joyce." Istmo, 60 (January-February 1969): 42-57.]

265. BUTOR, MICHEL. "Joyce et le roman moderne." L'Arc, no. 36 (1968): 4-5.

266. CABANIS, JOSE. "Une vie de James Joyce." Preuves, no. 137 (July 1962): 77-79.

267. CINGRIA, CHARLES-ALBERT. "James Joyce." Aujourd'hui (Lausanne), 1 January 1931. [Appeared in his Oeuvres complètes, vol. 3. Lausanne: Éditions l'Age d'Homme, 1969, pp. 185-188.]

*268. CRASTRE, VICTOR. "Vue d'ensemble: James Joyce, 1882-1941," Critique, 6 (15 December 1950): 263-267.

269. EDGERTON, WILLIAM B. "Dzhoising with the Soviet Encyclopedias." James Joyce Quarterly, 5 (Winter 1968): 125-131 [Reprints English translations of three entries in different Russian encyclopedias in 1930, 1952, 1964.]

*270. FISCHER, ERNST. "Das Problem der Wirklichkeit in der modernen Kunst." Sinn und Form, 10 (1958): 461-483.

*271. FOGERTI, IU. "Dzhems Dzhois," translated by N. Belmin. Vestn. inostr. lit., no. 10 (1928): 119-128.

*272. FORD, WILLIAM J. "James Joyce, An Artist in Adversity." Quarterly Bulletin of Northwestern University Medical School, 23 (Winter 1949): 495-497.

273. FRANZERO, C. M. "Esuli di Joyce per la prima volta dopo oltre 50 sulle scene di Londra." Dramma, 46 (November-December 1970): 146-151. [General survey of life and works, not Exiles.]

*274. FRENK, MARIANA. "James Joyce." La palabra y el hombre, 4 (July-September 1960): 61-62.

275. GHEORGHIU, MIHNEA. "Note despre un om din Dublin." Romania literaria (Bucharest), no. 6 (February 1969): 21.

276. JACOBSON, DAN. "Muffled Majesty." Times Literary Supplement, no. 3246 (26 October 1967): 1007.

277. JAMESON, STORM. "The Writer in Contemporary Society." American Scholar, 35 (Winter 1965-1966): 67-77.

278. JANNATTONI, LIVIO. "Da Gogol a Joyce, fama europea del Belli." Letteratura, n.s. 11 (July-October 1963): 6-13.

279. JOHO, WOLFGANG. "Europaisches Streitgesprach über den Roman." Neue Deutsche Literatur, 11 (1963): 157.

280. _____. "Notwendiges Streitgesprach. Bemerkungen zu einem internationalen Kolloquium." Neue Deutsche Literatur, 13 (1965): 109.

281. KAIN, RICHARD M. "The Yeats Centenary in Ireland." James Joyce Quarterly, 4 (Winter 1966): 130-138.

282. KELLY, SEAMAS ("Quidnunc"). "An Irishman's Diary." Irish Times, 16 June 1962, p. 10. [History of Dublin Joyce Society.]

*283. LINATI, CARLO. "Joyce." Corriere della Sera, 20 August 1925.

284. NOON, WILLIAM T., S.J. "God and Man in Twentieth-Century Fiction." Thought, 37 (Spring 1962): 35-56.

285. PURDON, C. B. "James Joyce--The Irish Scholar." World Digest of Current Fact and Comment, 2, no. 9 (January 1940): 99-101.

*286. SCOTT, ROBERT IAN. "Modern Theories of Communication." James Joyce Review, 1, no. 4 (December 1957): 18-32.

*287. STARTSEV, A. "Dzhems Dzhoise." International Literature, no. 4 (1936): 66-68.

*288. ZORN, WALTHER. "Literaturberichte: Englisch." Monatsschrift für höhere Schulen, 31 (1932): 68-78.

*289. Unsigned. "Biografia de Jaime Joyce." Revista Paraguaya, 1 (April 1936): 34-35. [Headnote to translation of "A Little Cloud."]

BIOGRAPHICAL-BACKGROUND: BIOGRAPHIES, RELATIVES, FAMILY, LETTERS, IRELAND, TRIESTE, POLA, PARIS, ZURICH, ETC.

See also: Kain. Dublin in the Age of..., No. 332; Sheehy. "James Joyce," No. 335; Pearl. Dublin..., No. 3640; II.H "Ulysses": McCaffrey. "Joycean...," No. 4663; McCaffrey. "Barney Kiernan's," No. 3920; Ellmann. James Joyce's Tower, No. 4627; Friedman. "Three...," No. 3577; II.I "Finnegans Wake": Jolas, E. "My Friend James Joyce," No. 4944; Jolas, M. "Joyce's Friend Jolas," No. 4945.

Books

290. ADAMS, MICHAEL. Censorship: The Irish Experience. Dublin: Scepter; University, Ala.: University of Alabama Press, 1968, passim.

291. ALLT, PETER. Some Aspects of the Life and Works of James Augustine Joyce. Groningen: J. B. Walters, 1952. [Reprinted Folcroft, Pa.: Folcroft Press, 1971.]

292. ANDERSON, CHESTER G. James Joyce and His World. London: Thames and Hudson; New York: Viking-Studio, 1967.

293. BONHEIM, HELMUT. "James Joyce: Nation versus World," in Proceedings of the IVth Congress of the International Comparative Literature Association, vol. 1. Edited by François Jost. Fribourg: 1964; Hague: Mouton, 1966, pp. 462-466.

294. BUDGEN, FRANK. Further Recollections of James Joyce. London: Shenval Press, 1955. [Excerpts appeared in Partisan Review, 23 (Fall 1956): 530-544.]

295. BURGAUER, ARNOLD. James Joyce in Zürich. Zurich: Pro Helvetia, 1973.

296. BYRNE, J. F. Silent Years: An Autobiography with Memoirs of James Joyce and Our Ireland. New York: Farrar, Straus and Young, 1953. ["Diseases of the Ox" reprinted in A Bash in the Tunnel, pp. 221-233, No. 1644.]

297. COLUM, MARY. Life and the Dream. Garden City: Doubleday Doran, 1947, passim. [Revised and enlarged edition, Dublin: Dolmen Press, 1966, passim.]

298. COLUM, MARY, and PADRAIC COLUM. Our Friend James Joyce. New York: Doubleday, 1958; London: Gollancz, 1959. [Paperback reprint, Doubleday Dolphin, 1961; reprinted Gloucester, Mass.: P. Smith, 1968.]

299. COLUM, PADRAIC. The Road Round Ireland. New York: Macmillan, 1926, pp. 309-330.

300. CONNOLLY, CYRIL. "James Joyce: 1," "James Joyce: 2," "James Joyce: 3," in Previous Convictions. London: Hamish Hamilton, 1963; New York: Harper and Row, 1964, pp. 269-272 [a reprint of "A Note on James Joyce." New Statesman and Nation, 21 (18 January 1941): 59], pp. 273-276 [a reprint of a review of Letters, originally in Sunday Times (London), 2 June 19572, pp. 277-281 [a reprint of a review of Ellmann's James Joyce, originally in Sunday Times (London), 1 November 1959].

301. CORCORAN, A. T. The Clongowes Record 1814-1932. Dublin: Browne and Nolan, [n.d.].

302. COXHEAD, ELIZABETH. Lady Gregory: A Literary Portrait. London: Secker and Warburg, 1961, pp. 124-125. [2nd edition, revised and enlarged, 1966.]

303. CRISE, STELIO. Epiphanies and Phadographs: Joyce e Trieste. Milan: All'Insegna del Pesce d'Oro, 1967. [Brief extract translated by Gabriel A. Perez in JJQ, 9 (September 1972): 317.]

304. CURRAN, CONSTANTINE. James Joyce Remembered. New York: Oxford University Press, 1968.

305. _____. Under the Receding Wave. Dublin: Gill and Macmillan; London: Macmillan, 1970, passim.

306. DUFF, CHARLES. Ireland and the Irish. New York: Putnam, 1952, pp. 201, 203; London: T. V. Boardman and Co., pp. 168-171, et passim.

307. EGLINTON, JOHN. (W. K. Magee). "The Beginnings of Joyce," "A Glimpse of the Later Joyce," in his Irish Literary Portraits. London: Macmillan, 1935, pp. 131-150, 150-158. ["The Beginnings of Joyce" appeared in Life and Letters, 8 (December 1932): 400-414 and was reprinted in The Portable Irish Reader. New York: Viking Press, 1946; 1935 book reprinted Freeport, N.Y.: Books for Libraries Press, 1967, pp. 131-150, 150-158.]

308. ELLMANN, RICHARD. James Joyce. New York: Oxford University Press, 1959; paperback

reprint, Galaxy, 1965. [Translated by
Albert W. Hess, Karl H. Reichert, and
Fritz Senn. Zürich: Rhein Vlg., 1961
with "Zur deutschen Ausgabe" and "Bibliographie und Diskographie," pp. 9-10,
763-770 by Fritz Senn; translated by
André Couroy. Paris: Gallimard, 1962;
translated by Piero Bernardini. Milan:
Feltrinelli, 1964; chapter thirty translated by Ewa Krasińska. "James Joyce
w latach 1921-1922." Literatura na
Swiecie, no. 5 (May 1973): 122-186.]
  For the extensive reviews of this biography see: JJQ, 3 (Spring 1966): 198-
199; ibid., 3 (Winter 1966): 145-146;
ibid., 1 (Winter 1964): 17; ibid., 2
(Fall 1964): 53 (German translation);
ibid., 3 (Fall 1965): 53; see also William T. Noon. "A Delayed Review." JJQ,
2 (Fall 1964): 7-12; response by Robert
Scholes. JJQ, 2 (Summer 1965): 310-313;
and comment by Ruth Von Phul. "Noon and
Scholes." JJQ, 3 (Fall 1965): 69-72.
  Contains the following articles in
their previous appearance: "Ulysses the
Divine Nobody." Yale Review, 47 (Autumn
1957): 56-71; "The Grasshopper and the
Ant: Notes on James Joyce and His Brother,
Stanislaus." Reporter, 13 (December 1955):
35-38, No. 420; "A Portrait of the Artist
as Friend." Kenyon Review, 18 (Winter
1956): 53-67, No. 421; "Backgrounds of
'The Dead.'" Kenyon Review, 20 (Autumn
1958): 507-528, No. 3157; "Backgrounds of
Ulysses." Kenyon Review, 16 (Summer 1954):
337-386, No. 3794; "Limits of Joyce's
Naturalism." Sewanee Review, 63 (Autumn
1955): 567-575, No. 3795; Joyce in Love.
Ithaca: Cornell University Library, 1959.
  Portions appeared later as: "Edward
Garnett's 'Report by a Publisher's Reader'"
in Portraits of an Artist, pp. 19-21, No.
3260; Lettres nouvelles, no. 13 (April
1961): 54-64; "The Backgrounds of 'The
Dead'" in Joyce's The Dead, pp. 46-57, No.
3138; also in James Joyce's Dubliners, pp.
388-403, No. 2885; and in A Mirror for
Modern Scholars. Edited by Lester A.
Beaulire. New York: Odyssey, 1966, pp.
125-137; excerpts reprinted in A Library
of Literary Criticism, No. 250.

309. ELLMANN, RICHARD, ed. James Joyce, Letters.
  2 vols. (Three volume set; vol. 1 by
  Stuart Gilbert, revised.) New York:
  Viking Press; London: Faber and Faber,
  1966. [Ellmann's "Introduction" excerpted
  in Northwestern Review, 2 (Winter 1967):
  9-16; "Introduction" appeared as "Joyce:
  A Postal Inquiry." New York Review of
  Books, 7 (8 September 1966): 24-28, and
  reprinted in his Golden Codgers: Biographical Speculations. New York, London:
  Oxford University Press, 1973, pp. 113-
  131; letters to Ezra Pound of 17 March
  1915 and 22 October 1917 previously ap-

peared in Ezra Pound Perspectives. Edited
by Noel Stock. Chicago: Henry Regnery,
1965, pp. 112-113, 115-116; a group of
letters from vol. 2 are reprinted in Tri-
Quarterly, 8 (Winter 1967): 166-188; two
previously unpublished letters: (1) letter of 13 July 1913 in Letters to Macmillan. Edited by Simon Nowell-Smith. London: Macmillan; New York: St. Martin's,
1967, pp. 288-289; (2) letter to Kay
Boyle of 1 September 1937 with introduction by Ms. Boyle in Tri-Quarterly, 8
(Winter 1967): 195-197.]
  For the extensive reviews of the
Letters see: JJQ, 5 (Fall 1967): 54-55;
ibid., 6 (Spring 1969): 245.

310. ELLMANN, RICHARD, ed. Giacomo Joyce. New
  York: Viking Press, 1968; London: Faber
  and Faber. [Part appears, with illustra-
  tions by Joan Berg Victor and a brief introduction in Harper's Magazine, 236
  (January 1968): 27-30; extract in English
  in L'Arc, 36 (1968): 54-58; translated by
  Klaus Reichert, with additional notes by
  Fritz Senn. Frankfurt a. M.: Suhrkamp,
  1970; translated by Alfredo Matilla Rivas.
  Revista de belles artes, 19 (January-
  February 1968): 4-17; translated by Gerardine Franken, with Afterword by Fritz Senn
  translated by John Vandenbergh. Amsterdam:
  De Bezige Bij, 1969; translated by André
  du Bouchet. Ephémere, 10 (Summer 1969):
  265-283 from Gallimard edition; translated
  with Preface by Francesco Binni. Milan:
  A. Mondadori, 1968; Ellmann's "Introduction" translated by Michel Perez in L'Arc,
  36 (1968): 51-54; N. Kiashvili. Literatur-
  naya Gruziya (Tbilisi), nos. 9-10 (1969):
  79-86 (foreword to Russian translation).]
  Following items note coming publication: Marshalla Best. TLS, 11 July
  1968, p. 737; TLS, 23 October 1968,
  p. 526; Lewis Nichols. NYTBR, 8 Octo
  ber 1967, p. 66; Henry Raymont. New
  York Times, 28 September 1967, p. 1
  and Times (London), 28 September 1967,
  p. 1; Welt und Wort, 22 (October 1967):
  357; Richard Nickson. Explicator, 28
  (1969): item 38; Fritz Senn. JJQ, 5
  (Spring 1968): 233-236.

311. FABRICANT, NOAH D. "The Ocular History of
  James Joyce," in his Thirteen Famous Pa-
  tients. Philadelphia: Lippincott, 1960,
  pp. 128-139.

312. FRANCINI BRUNI, ALESSANDRO. Joyce intimo
  spogliato in piazza. Trieste: "La
  Editoriale Libraria," 1922.

313. FREUND, GISÈLE. and V. B. CARLETON. James
  Joyce in Paris: His Final Years. New
  York: Harcourt, Brace and World, 1965;
  London: Cassell, 1966. [Preface by
  Simone de Beauvior.]

314. FREUND, GISÈLE. La monde et ma caméra. Paris: Denoël/Gontheir, 1970, pp. 117-125, et passim. [Translated by June Guicharnaud as "James Joyce." The World in My Camera. New York: Dial Press, 1974, pp. 116-123, et passim.]

*315. GIEDION-WELCKER, CAROLA. "Nachtrag," in Herbert Gorman. James Joyce--Sein Leben und sein Werk. Hamburg: Claassen, 1957, pp. 345-375, No. 321. [Excerpted in Proben und Berichte (Hamburg), no. 8 (1957): 1-2.]

316. GILBERT, MARTIN. Sir Horace Rumbold: Portrait of a Diplomat, 1869-1941. London: Heinemann, 1973, pp. 178-179.

317. GILBERT, STUART, ed. The Letters of James Joyce, vol. 1. New York: Viking Press, 1957. ["Introduction," pp. 21-38; "Chronology of the Life of James Joyce" reprinted in Portraits of an Artist, pp. 4-11, No. 3260.]

318. GOGARTY, OLIVER ST. JOHN. "James Joyce as Tenor," in Intimations. New York: Abelard, 1950, pp. 58-69, et passim.

319. _____. It Isn't This Time of Year at All! New York: Doubleday, 1954, passim.

320. _____. Many Lines to Thee: Letters to G. K. A. Bell from the Martello Tower at Sandycove, Rutland Square and Trinity College Dublin, 1904-1907. Edited by James F. Carens. Dublin: Dolmen Press, 1971, passim.

321. GORMAN, HERBERT S. James Joyce. New York: Rinehart, 1939; revised edition, 1948. [Translated by Hans Hennecke and Hans Vogel as James Joyce: Sein Leben und Sein Werk, with an afterword by Carola Giedion-Welcker. Hamburg: Claassen, 1957.]

322. HARVEY, JOHN H. Dublin: A Study in Environment. London, New York: Batsford, 1949, pp. viii, x, 67, 74, 81.

323. HOLLOWAY, JOSEPH. Joseph Holloway's Abbey Theatre: A Selection from his Unpublished Journal. Edited by Robert Hogan and Michael J. O'Neill. Carbondale and Edwardsville: Southern Illinois University Press, 1967, passim.

324. HUTCHINS, PATRICIA. James Joyce's Dublin. London: Grey Wall Press, 1950. [A selection from this appeared in Irish Digest 38 (February 1951): 33-36.]

325. _____. "James Joyce on Holiday," in New World Writing: Eighth Mentor Selection, vol. 8. New York: New American Library, 1955, pp. 234-244.

326. _____. James Joyce's World. London: Methuen, 1957. [Translated by Roberto Sanesi and Cathy Berberian as Il Mondo di James Joyce. Milan: Levici, 1960.]

327. IRELAND, DENIS. From the Irish Shore: Notes on My Life and Times. London: Rich and Cowan, 1936, pp. 200-206.

328. JOYCE, STANISLAUS. An Open Letter to Dr. Oliver Gogarty. Paris: Editions Finisterre, 1953. [Appeared in Interim, 4 (1954): 49-56; see also Gogarty (No. 446) and Mary M. Colum (No. 389); correction of Gogarty's "They Think They Know Joyce" (No. 446).]

329. _____. My Brother's Keeper. Edited with an Introduction and Notes by Richard Ellmann. Preface by T. S. Eliot. New York: Viking Press, 1958. [Paperback reprint. New York: McGraw-Hill, 1964; translated by Arno Schmidt. Frankfurt a. M.: Suhrkamp, 1960; translated by Berta Sofovich. Buenos Aires: Fabril, 1961; translated by Anne Grieve. Paris: Gallimard, 1966; translated by Maciej Slomczyński. Warsaw: Państw, Instytut Wydawn, 1971; "The Bud" reprinted in A Bash in the Tunnel, pp. 101-133, No. 1644.]

330. _____. The Dublin Diary of Stanislaus Joyce. Edited by George Harris Healey. Ithaca: Cornell University Press; London: Faber and Faber, 1962. [Translated by Arno Schmidt as Das Dubliner Tagebuch. Frankfurt a. M.: Suhrkamp, 1964, paperback reprint, 1967; translated by Marie Tadie as Le Journal de Dublin. Paris: Gallimard, 1967.]

331. _____. The Complete Dublin Diary of Stanislaus Joyce. Edited by George Harris Healey. Ithaca: Cornell University Press, 1971.

332. KAIN, RICHARD M. Dublin in the Age of William Butler Yeats and James Joyce. Norman: University of Oklahoma Press, 1962.

333. KENNER, HUGH. "The Trivium in Dublin," in English Institute Essays, 1952. New York: Columbia University Press, 1954, pp. 202-228.

334. KIELY, BENEDICT. Modern Irish Fiction: A Critique. Dublin: Golden Eagle Books, 1950, passim.

335. LIDDERDALE, JANE, and MARY NICHOLSON. Dear Miss Weaver: Harriet Shaw Weaver, 1876-1961. London: Faber and Faber; New York: Viking Press, 1970, passim.

336. McALMON, ROBERT. Being Geniuses Together: An Autobiography. London: Secker and Warburg, 1938, passim. [Revised with

BIOGRAPHICAL STUDIES

supplementary chapters by Kay Boyle. New York: Doubleday, 1968.]

337. McCORMACK, LILY. I Hear You Calling Me. Milwaukee: Bruce Publishing Co., 1949, passim.

338. MEENAN, JAMES, ed. Centenary History of the Literary and Historical Society of University College Dublin, 1855-1955. Tralee: Kerryman Ltd. [1956], passim.

339. MORSE, J. MITCHEL. The Sympathetic Alien. New York: New York University Press, 1959.

340. NOËL, LUCIE. James Joyce and Paul Léon: The Story of a Friendship. New York: Gotham Book Mart, 1950.

341. NOON, WILLIAM T. "The Religious Position of Joyce," in James Joyce: His Place in World Literature, pp. 7-22, No. 1688.

342. O'CONNOR, FRANK. Leinster, Munster and Connaught. London: Robert Hale, 1950, pp. 29-32.

343. O'CONNOR, ULICK. "James Joyce in College," in Students' Handbook. Dublin: University College, 1965-1966, pp. 21-24.

344. O'NEILL, MICHAEL J. "The Joyces in the Holloway Diaries," in A James Joyce Miscellany, Second Series, pp. 103-110, No. 1613.

*345. ONO, YASUKO. "Joisu no Tegaini" ["Letters of James Joyce]," in Joisu Nyumon [An Introduction to James Joyce], pp. 197-206, No. 1511.

346. PICHETTE, HENRI. "Joyce au participe futur," in Rond-point, suivi de Joyce au participe futur et de pages pour Chaplain. Paris: Mercure de France, 1950, pp. 33-34.

347. POWELL, VIOLET. The Irish Cousins: The Books and Background of Somerville and Ross. London: Heineman, 1970, passim.

348. PRAZ, MARIO. "Joyce e l'ossessione di Dublino," in his Cronache letterarie anglosassoni. Letture di pensiero e d'arte, vol. 42. Rome: Edizioni di Storia e Letteratura, 1966, pp. 64-69.

349. ROCCO-BERGERA, NINY, with CARLINA REBECCHI-PIPERATA. Itinerary of Joyce and Svevo through Artistic Trieste. Trieste: Aziendo Autonoma Soggiorno e Turismo [1971]. [Also issued in Italian as Itinerario Joyciano e Sveviano a Trieste, published for the Third International James Joyce Symposium.]

350. ROGERS, W. G. Ladies Bountiful. New York: Harcourt, Brace and World, 1968, passim.

351. SENN, FRITZ. "Ergänzung der Anmerkungen zu Giacomo Joyce," in Giacomo Joyce. Translated by Klaus Reichert. Frankfurt a.M.: Suhrkamp, 1968, pp. 73-82.

352. _____. "Nawoord," translated by John Vandenbergh, in Giacomo Joyce. Translated by Gerardine Franken. Amsterdam: De Bezige Bij, 1969, pp. 85-98.

353. _____. "Vorwort," "Anmerkungen," in Briefe an Nora. Frankfurt a. M.: Suhrkamp, 1971, pp. 5-34, 147-172.

354. SETTANI, ETTORE. James Joyce. Venice: Cavallino, 1955.

355. SHARE, BERNARD. "James Joyce, 1882-1941," in his Irish Lives: Biographies of Fifty Famous Irish Men and Women. Dublin: Allen Figgis, 1971.

356. SHEEHY, EUGENE. "The Artist as a Young Man," "Francis Sheehy Skeffington, James Joyce, and Tom Kettle," in his May It Please the Court. Dublin: C. J. Fallon, 1951, pp. 21-29, 40-41.

357. SULLIVAN, KEVIN. Joyce Among the Jesuits. New York: Columbia University Press, 1958. ["Clongowes Wood and Belvedere" reprinted in Portraits of an Artist, pp. 120-142, No. 3260.]

*358. SVEVO, LIVIA VENEZIANI. Vita de mio marito. Trieste: Zibaldone, 1950. [2nd enlarged edition edited by Anita Pittoni. Trieste: Edizioni dello Zibaldone, 1958.]

359. TIERNEY, MICHAEL. Struggle with Fortune. Dublin: Browne and Nolan, 1954, pp. 49-50.

360. TINDALL, WILLIAM YORK. The Joyce Country. University Park, Pa.: Pennsylvania State University Press, 1960; paperback reprint, New York: Schocken, 1972.

361. de TUONI, DARIO. Ricordo di Joyce a Trieste. Milan: All'Insegna del Pesce d'Oro, 1966; also Milan: Vanni Scheiwiller, 1967. [Contains his "James Joyce nella vecchia Trieste." Fiera letteraria, no. 9 (1961): 5, and "James Joyce a Trieste." ibid., no. 22 (1961): 5.]

Periodical Articles

362. ANDERSON, CHESTER G. "Joyce's Letters and His Use of 'Place.'" James Joyce Quarterly, 4 (Winter 1967): 62-74.

363. ANDREASEN, N. J. C. "James Joyce: A Portrait of the Artist as a Schizoid." Journal of the American Medical Association, 224 (1973): 67-71. [See reply by J. B. Lyons, ibid., 225 (1973): 213-214.]

364. ANTONI, CLAUDIO. "A Note on Trieste in Joyce's Time." James Joyce Quarterly, 9 (Spring 1972): 318-319.

365. BENCO, SILVIO. "Un Illustre Scrittore Inglese a 'Trieste.'" Umana, 1, no. 4 (6 July 1918): 1-3. [Reprinted as "James Joyce in Trieste." Pègaso, no. 2 (August 1930): 150-165; appeared in Bookman (New York), 72 (December 1930): 375-380.]

*366. BERCE, LOJZE. "James Joyce v Trstu." Razgledi, 4, no. 8-9 (1949): 337-343.

367. BERGER, ALFRED PAUL. "James Joyce Advertising Man." Irish Times, 27 September 1965, p. 10.

368. _____. "James Joyce, Adman." James Joyce Quarterly, 3 (Fall 1965): 25-33.

369. BHANU, DHARMA. "James Joyce, An Appreciation." New Review (Calcutta), 29, no. 169 (January 1949): 40-47; no. 170 (February 1949): 134-137.

370. BIANCHINI, ANGELA. "Vita con James Joyce." L'Approdo letterario, 6, no. 10 (April-June 1960): 61-64.

371. BIANCHINI, ANGELA. "James Joyce e l'Italia." Tempo presente, 9 (March-April 1964): 51-56.

372. BLOCK, HASKELL M. "Stanislaus and his Brother." CEA Critic, 14, no. 2 (February 1952): 4.

373. BOLLETTIERI, ROSA M. B. "The Importance of Trieste in Joyce's Work, with Reference to His Knowledge of Psycho-Analysis." James Joyce Quarterly, 7 (Spring 1970): 177-185.

*374. [BONHEIM, HELMUT]. "Lettres de James Joyce à ses proches." Revue de Paris, 68 (December 1961): 34-49.

375. BORACH, GEORGES. "Gespräche mit James Joyce." Die Neue Zürcher Zeitung, no. 827 (3 May 1931). [Reprinted in Omnibus (1932): 141-142 and in Frankfurter Allgemeine Zeitung, 27 August 1955; translated by Joseph Prescott, College English, (15 March 1954): 325-327; also in Meanjin, 13 (Spring 1954): 393-396 and in London Magazine, 1 (November 1954): 75-78; original in James Joyce, Die Totem: Erzählungen. Zürich: Diogenes [1966], pp. 329-334.]

376. BOYD, ERNEST. "James Joyce: Memories." Decision, 1, no. 2 (February 1941): 58-59.

377. BRANCATI, VITALIANO. "Ricordo del Professore Joyce." Nuova stampa sera, 30-31 August 1948, p. 3.

*378. BROWN, T. J. "English Literary Autographs XL: James Joyce, 1882-1941." Book Collector, 10 (Winter 1961): 441.

379. BRUNO, FRANCESCO. "James Joyce in Italia." Idea (Rome), 17 February 1962, p. 6.

380. BURGER, HILDE. "Trieste: Europe's Window on the Adriatic." Journal of the Australasian Universities Language and Literature Association, no. 40 (November 1973): 219-239.

381. CAMPBELL, SANDY. "Mrs. Joyce of Zurich." Harper's Bazaar, 85 (October 1952): 170-171, 253-255.

382. CASS, ANDREW (pseud. of John Garvin). "Childe Horrid's Pilgrimace." Envoy, 5 (May 1951): 19-30. [Reprinted in A Bash in the Tunnel, pp. 169-179, No. 1644.]

383. CHALON, JEAN. "La femme d'Ulysse." Figaro littéraire, 26 February-3 March 1968, p. 18. [Amalia Popper.]

*384. CHISHOLM, FRANCIS P. [n.t.]. College English, 20 (February 1959): 249-250. [Report of Symposium on "The Biographical Element in Joyce" at 1958 NCTE Convention.]

*385. CHOCRON, ISAAC. "Dublan, Dublen, Dublin, Dublon, Dublun." Revista nacional de cultura, no. 144 (January-February 1961): 164-177.

386. CLARKE, AUSTIN. "Stephen Dedalus: The Author of Ulysses." New Statesman, 22 (23 February 1924): 571-572. [Reprinted in his Twice Round the Black Church. London: Routledge and Kegan Paul, 1962, pp. 26-28.]

387. COHN, ALAN M. "Joyce in the Movies." James Joyce Quarterly, 2 (Summer 1965): 317-319.

388. COLLINS, JOHN T. "The Family of James Joyce." Irish Times, 51 (September 1954): 20.

389. COLUM, MARY. "A Little Knowledge of Joyce." Saturday Review of Literature, 33 (29 April 1950): 10-12. [Condensed in Irish Digest, 37 (September 1950): 39-41; response to Gogarty, No. 446.]

*390. COLUM, PADRAIC. "With James Joyce in Ireland." New York Times Book Review, 11 June 1922, p. 10.

BIOGRAPHICAL STUDIES

391. _____ . "A Portrait of James Joyce."
New Republic, 66 (13 May 1931): 346-348.
[Reprinted in The Faces of Five Decades.
Edited by Robert B. Luce. New York:
Simon and Schuster, 1964, pp. 187-192.]

392. _____ . "Portrait of James Joyce." Dublin Magazine, n.s. 7, no. 2 (April-June
1932): 40-48. [Expanded from No. 391.]

393. _____ . "The Joyce I Knew." Saturday
Review of Literature, 23 (22 February
1941): 11. [See Gogarty, No. 446.]

*394. _____ . "Letter to the Editor." New
York Times, 4 December 1941. [Contra
Gogarty.]

395. _____ . "Working with Joyce." Irish
Times, 5 October 1956, p. 5; 6 October
1956, p. 7.

396. COMISSO, GIOVANNI. "Il buon Italiano di
James Joyce." Gazzetta del popolo
(Turin), 10 July 1965.

397. CONNELLY, STEVE. "Handball Prominent in
Literary Works of James Joyce: Irish
Renaissance Emphasized Values of Hand-
ball as Sport." Handball-U.S.H.A.,
(August 1972): 24-25.

398. CORKERY, TOM. "Joyce's Dublin." Ireland
of the Welcomes, 11 (July-August 1962):
23-26.

399. COYLE, KATHLEEN. "My Last Visit with James
Joyce." Tomorrow, 10, no. 2 (October
1950): 15-17.

*400. CRISE, STELIO. "Joyce e Trieste." Acca-
demie e biblioteche d'Italia, 29 (1961):
352-359.

401. _____ . "Ahab, Pizdrool, Quark," translated by Niny Rocco-Bergera. James Joyce
Quarterly, 7 (Fall 1969): 65-69.

402. _____ . "Humus triestino dell'opera di
James Joyce." Umana, 18 (November-
December 1969): 26-28.

403. _____ . "James eats Jams." Umana, 20
(May-September 1971): 26-27.

404. CRONIN, ANTHONY. "Joyce's Letters." Times
Literary Supplement, 31 May 1957, p. 335.

405. CRONIN, JOHN. "Gerald Griffin, Dedalus
Manqué." Studies, 58 (1969): 267-278.

406. CROWLEY, CHRISTINE. "When Joyce Ran a
Cinema." Irish Digest, 89 (May 1967):
46-48.

407. CURRAN, CONSTANTINE P. "When Joyce Lived in
Dublin." Vogue, 109 (1 May 1947): 144-149.

408. CURTAYNE, ALICE. "Ireland." Critic, 20
(April-May 1962): 66-68.

409. _____ . "Portrait of the Artist as Brother: An Interview with Joyce's Sister."
Critic, 21 (April-May 1963): 43-47.

410. DAICHES, DAVID. "James Joyce: The Artist as
Exile." College English, 2 (December
1940): 197-206. [Reprinted in Forms of
Modern Fiction. Edited by William Van
O'Connor. Minneapolis: University of
Minnesota Press, 1948, pp. 61-71.]

411. DALTON, JACK P. "Two New Fadographs of
James Joyce." James Joyce Quarterly,
5 (Winter 1968): 168-169.

412. _____ . "Joyce Could so Sing!" Spectrum,
18, no. 39 (8 March 1968): 4.

*413. DANEY, ERIC BURTON. "Det Forankira de Dub-
lin." Handelstidning (Goteborgs), 25
April 1932.

414. DASSEN, J. M. H., and J. R. DURINCK. "James
Joyce: His Life as a Kind of Exejesus."
Utopia, 8 (June 1969): 6-8.

*415. DEL BUONO, ORESTE. "Il suo capolavoro..."
Epoca, no. 529 (1960).

*416. DONOSO, JOSÉ. "Trieste. Encuentro con el
espectro de James Joyce." Ercilla (Santiago), no. 1339 (18 January 1961): 12-13.

417. DWYER, RICHARD A. "Being a Note on Joyce
and James Byrne (1820-97)." James Joyce
Quarterly, 5 (Winter 1968): 179.

418. EDEL, LEON. "James Joyce: The Last Journey."
Story, 32, no. 129 (Summer 1948): 139-147.
[Reprint of last chapter of his James
Joyce: The Last Journey. New York:
Gotham Book Mart, 1947.]

419. EGLINTON, JOHN (W. K. Magee). "Irish Letter."
Dial, 86 (May 1929): 417-420.

420. ELLMANN, RICHARD. "The Grasshopper and the
Ant: Notes on James Joyce and His Brother,
Stanislaus." Reporter, 13 (December 1955):
35-38. [Later appeared in his James Joyce,
No. 308.]

421. _____ . "A Portrait of the Artist as
Friend." Kenyon Review, 18 (Winter 1956):
53-67. [Later appeared in his James Joyce,
No. 308; also in Society and Self in the
Novel. Edited by Mark Schorer. New York:
Columbia University Press, 1956, pp. 60-77;
reprinted in Joyce's Portrait: Criticisms
and Critiques, pp. 88-101, No. 3223.]

*422. _____. "Joyce's Letters." Times Liter-
ary Supplement, 27 May 1960, p. 344; New
York Herald Tribune Books, 4 September
1960, p. 12.

423. _____. "Streiflichter auf James Joyce."
Akzente, 8 (April 1961): 145-155. [Ex-
tract from German translation of his
James Joyce, No. 308.]

424. _____. "James Joyce's Addresses."
American Book Collector, 15 (June 1965):
25, 27, 28, 29. [Appears in Letters,
vol. 2, pp. lv-lxii, No. 309.]

425. _____. "Uses of Adversity." American
Pen, 4 (Winter 1972): 15-17.

426. _____. "James Joyce, Irish European."
Tri-Quarterly, 8 (Winter 1967): 199-204.
[Reprinted in Umana, 20 (May-September
1971): 13-15.]

*427. FAIBANI, ENZO. "Il genio che sposo la fige-
ia del fornaio." Gente, 2 December 1960.

*428. FERRIERI, E. "Vita d'un vagabondo." Scena
illustrata (Florence), April 1941.

429. ffRENCH, YVONNE. "In the Steps of James
Joyce." Irish Illustrated, 1 (1956):
15-19.

430. FIFIELD, WILLIAM. "Joyce's Brother, Lawrence's Wife, Wolfe's Mother, Twain's
Daughter." Texas Quarterly, 10 (Summer
1967): 69-87.

431. FIRTH, JOHN. "Harriet Weaver's Letters to
James Joyce, 1915-1920." Studies in
Bibliography, 20 (1967): 151-188.

432. FIRTH, JOHN. "James Pinker to James Joyce,
1915-1920." Studies in Bibliography, 21
(1968): 205-224.

*433. FITZPATRICK, KATHLEEN. "James Joyce in
Paris." Irish Times, 22 March 1947.

434. FRANCINI BRUNI, ALESSANDRO. "Ricordi su
James Joyce." Nuova antologia, 441
(September-December 1947): 71-79.

435. FRANK, NINO. "Souvenirs sur James Joyce."
La Table Ronde (Paris), no. 23 (November
1949): 1671-1693. ["L'Ombra che aveva
perduto il suo uoma," translated by Paola
Angioletti. Il Mondo, 2 (3 June 1950):
11-12; (10 June 1950): 11-12.]

436. G., E. "Am Grade von James Joyce (At Joyce's
Grave)." Schweiz Suisse Svizzera Switzer-
land, 38 (November 1965): 18.

437. G., I. "James Joyce feiert seine silberne
Hochzeit." Querschnitt, 10 (May 1930).

438. GARVIN, JOHN. "James Joyce." Irish Press,
15 June 1967, p. 11; 16 June 1967, p. 11.

*439. GIEDION-WELCKER, CAROLA. "Der frühe James
Joyce." Neue Zürcher Zeitung, no. 1230
(5 July 1928): 1.

*440. _____. "James Joyce, Nachruf." Neue
Zürcher Zeitung, no. 76 (16 January 1941);
reprinted in In Memoriam, No. 1038.

441. _____. "James Joyce in Zürich." Die
Weltwoche (Zürich), no. 388 (18 April
1941): 5. [Translated in Horizon, 18,
no. 105 (September 1948): 207-212; reprinted in Zürcher Album. Edited by Ursula Isler-Hungerbühler, Wabern: 1970, pp.
12-15; reprinted in The Golden Horizon.
London: Weidenfeld and Nicholson, 1953,
reprinted in Turicum (Zürich), 2 (February 1971): 43-44; reprinted in Neue literarische Welt, 3 (1952): 4.]

442. _____. "Les derniers mois de la vie je
James Joyce." Figaro littéraire, 28 May
1949, p. 4. [In German as "Die letzte
Reise: 'Nachtrag,'" in the translation of
Gorman's biography. Hamburg: Claassen,
1957, pp. 367-375, No. 321.]

443. _____. "Ein beflügelter Dialog. Le Cor-
busier und James Joyce." Neue Zürcher
Zeitung, 19 September 1965, p. 5.

444. GILLET, LOUIS. "Recuerdos de James Joyce."
Sur, no. 87 (December 1941): 28-42; (January 1942): 53-65. [Appeared in Stèle
pour Joyce, No. 1568.]

445. GOGARTY, OLIVER ST. JOHN. "Joyce as a Friend
of Music." Tomorrow, 8 (December 1949):
42-45.

446. _____. "They Think They Know Joyce."
Saturday Review of Literature, 33 (18
March 1950): 8-9, 35-37; (8 April 1950):
24; (29 April 1950): 10-12, 24; (13 May
1950); 22; (27 May 1950): 23-24. [Arti-
cles condensed in Irish Digest, 37 (August
1950): 19-23; reprinted with "The Joyce I
Knew." Saturday Review of Literature, 23
(25 January 1941): 3-4, 15-16, in Saturday
Review Gallery. Edited by Jerome Beatty,
Jr. New York: Simon and Schuster, 1959,
pp. 251-260, 261-268; see also Stanislaus
Joyce (No. 330) and Mary Colum (No. 389).]

447. GOLDMAN, ARNOLD. "'Send Him Canorious':
James Joyce's 'Sullivanising.'" Listener,
88 (3 August 1972): 142-144. [See No.
535.]

*448. GOPALEEN, MYLES na (Flann O'Brien, Brien
Nolan). "Cruiskeen Lawn." Irish Times,
17 March 1943.

BIOGRAPHICAL STUDIES

*449. _____. "Cruiskeen Lawn." Irish Times, 18 December 1943.

*450. _____. "Cruiskeen Lawn." Irish Times, 18 June 1947.

*451. _____. "Cruiskeen Lawn." Irish Times, 15 August 1947.

*452. _____. "Cruiskeen Lawn." Irish Times, 21 January 1948.

*453. _____. "Cruiskeen Lawn." Irish Times, 21 November 1949.

*454. _____. "Cruiskeen Lawn." Irish Times, 6 October 1951.

*455. _____. "Cruiskeen Lawn." Irish Times, 7 July 1953.

*456. _____. "Cruiskeen Lawn." Irish Times, 9 June 1958.

*457. _____. "Cruiskeen Lawn." Irish Times, 18 January 1961.

*458. _____. "Cruiskeen Lawn." Irish Times, 3 August 1961.

459. _____. "Cruiskeen Lawn." Irish Times, 29 September 1965.

460. _____. "Cruiskeen Lawn." Irish Times, 6 December 1965.

461. GUIDI, AUGUSTO. "Gli anni triestini di Joyce." Umana, 20 (May-September 1971): 16-20.

*462. HABART, MICHEL. "Petit portrait de l'artiste en Irlandais." Lettres françaises, 16-22 February 1961, p. 3.

*463. HALL, DOUGLAS KENT. "James Joyce at 71, rue du Cardinal Lemoine." Brigham Young University Studies, 3 (Spring-Summer 1961): 43-49.

464. HALPER, NATHAN. "Joyce at Jammet's: A Meal Not Taken." James Joyce Quarterly, 9 (Winter 1971): 279. [On Ellmann's James Joyce, p. 40, No. 308.]

465. HARPHER, ALLANAH. "Some People in Paris." Partisan Review, 9, no. 4 (July-August 1942): 315-316.

466. HELWIG, WERNER. "Geheime Romanze in Zürich: Eine Erinnerung an James Joyce." St. Galler Tagblatt, 3 September 1971.

467. HENNING, JOHN. "A Footnote to James Joyce." The Bell, 11 (November 1945): 704-709.

468. HENSELER, DONNA. "The Psychic World of James Joyce." Psychic, 3, no. 4 (January-February 1972): 27-31.

*469. HULL, ROBERT R. "A Key to the Mystery of James Joyce." Fortnightly Review (St. Louis), 37 (1930): 223-225, 251-253, 274-276.

470. HUTCHINS, PATRICIA. "James Joyce's Tower." Life and Letters, 61 (April 1949): 10-15.

471. _____. "James Joyce and the Cinema." Sight and Sound, 21 (August-September 1951): 9-12. [Appeared in Irish Digest, (January 1952): 19-22.]

472. _____. "James Joyce's Correspondence." Encounter, 7 (August 1956): 49-54. [Translated by Adele Biagi in Tempo Presente, 1 (October 1956): 539-545.]

473. JOHN, AUGUSTUS. "Fragment of an Autobiography, XV." Horizon, 13, no. 73 (January 1946): 56-57. [Later appeared in his Chiaroscuro. London: J. Cape; New York: Pellegrini and Cudahy, 1952, pp. 216-218.]

474. JOLAS, MARIA. "Joyce en 1939-1940." Mercure de France, 309 (May 1950): 45-58.

*475. JOYCE, HELEN. "Joyce." New York Times Book Review, 8 November 1959, p. 56. [Letter to the Editor.]

476. JOYCE, STANISLAUS. "Ricordi di James Joyce." Letteratura, 5, no. 3 (July-September 1941): 25-35; no. 4 (October-December 1941): 23-35. [Recollections of James Joyce by His Brother. New York: James Joyce Society, 1950, is a translation by Ellsworth Mason from the Letteratura articles; same articles appeared in Hudson Review, 2, no. 4 (Winter 1950): 487-514, translated by Felix Giovanelli; translation reprinted as "Recollections of James Joyce," in Joyce's The Dead, pp. 58-59, No. 3138.]

477. _____. "Early Memories of James Joyce." Listener, 41 (May 1949): 896-897.

*478. _____. "Joyce's Dublin." Partisan Review, 19 (1952): 103-109.

479. KIM, CHONG-KEON. "Giacomo Joyce: Its Love Ethics." Yŏng-ŏ munhak: The English Language and Literature, no. 38 (Summer 1971): 3-24.

480. LaPORTE, NEURINE W. "A Word Index to Giacomo Joyce." Analyst, 26 (September 1971): 1-21.

*481. LAZARETT, PIERRE. "La célèbre écrivain anglais James Joyce, l'auteur d'Ulysse, même depuis 10 ans à Paris une vie studieuse et retirée." Paris-Midi, 9 April 1931, p. 2.

482. LENNON, MICHAEL J. "James Joyce." Catholic World, 132 (March 1931): 641-652.

*483. _____. "James Joyce and the Tenor Sullivan." Hibernia, 24 (16 October 1959): 11; (23 October 1959): 11.

484. LEVIN, HARRY. "Joyce's Sentimental Journey Through France and Italy." Yale Review, 38 (June 1949): 664-672. [Later appeared in his Contexts of Criticism, pp. 131-139, No. 938; translated in Configuration critique, I, pp. 261-271, No. 1636.]

485. LIDDERDALE, JANE, and MARY NICHOLSON. "Mr. Joyce's Dreadful Eye Attack." James Joyce Quarterly, 7 (Spring 1970): 186-190. [Also in No. 335.]

486. LIEPMAN, HEINZ. "James Joyce in Zürich: Begegnung des irischen Dichters mit einer Stadt." Die Welt, 12 January 1966.

*487. LOTRINGER, SYLVERE. "Une Dublincursion au pays de Joyce." Lettres françaises, 16-22 February 1961, p. 4.

488. LYONS, F. S. L. "James Joyce's Dublin." Twentieth Century Studies, no. 4 (November 1970): 6-25.

489. LYONS, J. B. "James Joyce's Miltonic Affliction." Irish Journal of Medical Science, 7 (April 1968): 157-165; (May 1968): 203-210. [Later appeared in his James Joyce and Medicine. Dublin: Dolmen, 1973, No. 1611; appeared as separate, Folcroft, Pa.: Folcroft Library Editions, 1973.]

490. _____. "James Joyce: Medical Student." Kilkenny Magazine, no. 18 (1970): 80-97. [Later appeared in his James Joyce and Medicine. Dublin: Dolmen, 1973, No. 1611.]

491. _____. "Joyce's Medical Dimension." Hibernia, 37 (13 July 1973): 12.

*492. McCAFFREY, JOHN. "James Joyce's Father." Irish Times, 2 January 1950, p. 5; 1 February 1960, p. 5. [Summarized as "John Stanislaus Joyce." Blarney Magazine, 18 (Summer 1960): 12-14; excerpted in Éire-Ireland, no. 470 (15 February 1960): 6-8.]

*493. MacCARVILL, EILEEN. "Joyce at the University." St. Stephens, Michaelmas Number (1960): 14-17; Trinity Number (1961): 19-24.

494. McHUGH, ROGER. "Hangman and Divine Assistance." James Joyce Quarterly, 2 (Summer 1965): 314-316.

495. _____. "A Setting for Stephen Dedalus." Arts in Ireland, 2, no. 1 (1973): 28-32.

496. MASON, ELLSWORTH. "Mr. Stanislaus Joyce and John Henry Raleigh." Modern Language Notes, 70 (March 1955): 187-191. [See No. 522.]

*497. MARTIN, KINGSLEY. "London Diary." New Statesman and Nation, 18 January 1941, p. 54. [Reprinted in his Critic's London Diary. London: Secker and Warburg, 1960, pp. 190-191; account of meeting with Joyce and the genesis of "From a Banned Writer to a Banned Singer."]

*498. MERCIER, VIVIAN. "The Old School Tie No. 3--Portora Royal School, Inniskillen." The Bell, 11, no. 6 (March 1946): 1081-1090.

499. MICHA RENÉ. "Le Dublin de Joyce." L'Arc, no. 36 (1968): 69-72.

500. M[ICHALSKI?], H[IERONIM]. "Joyce in Zurych." Literatura naświecie, no. 5 (May 1973): 280-285.

501. MORRISSEY, L. G. D. "Dedalus in Dublin." Westminster Magazine (Summer 1934): 89-112.

*502. MOSS, ARTHUR. "Over the River." New York Times (Paris), 4 September 1924.

503. MUCCI, RENATO. "Joyce a Roma: Cacciato di casa l'impiegato di banca." Fiera letteraria, 19 (21 June 1964): 1-2.

504. MURPHY, MAURICE. "James Joyce and Ireland." Nation, 129 (October 1929): 426.

*505. NOON, WILLIAM T., S.J. "Joyce and Catholicism." James Joyce Review, 1 (December 1957): 3-17. [Reprinted as "Joyce's Sense of Sin is Too Strong." Irish Digest, 63, no. 3 (September 1958): 102-109.]

506. NORDIO, MARIO. "Gli anni Triestini di James Joyce." Ateneo Veneto, 6 (January-June 1968): 77-86.

507. OAKES, E. "Joyce's Last Wish." Sydney Morning Herald, 4 May 1966, p. 12.

508. O'CONNOR, ULICK. "James Joyce at University College." Time and Tide, 37 (21 January 1956): 76.

509. O'CONLUAIN, PROINSIAS. "Portrait of the Artist as Ireland's First Cinema Manager." Irish Times, 25 September 1954, p. 8.

510. O'GRADY, DESMOND. "Joyce 'Trieste is Waking Rawly....'" New York Times, 12 December 1971, section 10, p. 7.

BIOGRAPHICAL STUDIES

511. O'MAHONY, EOIN. "Father Conmee and His Associates." James Joyce Quarterly, 4 (Summer 1967): 263-270. [Reprinted in A Bash
in the Tunnel, pp. 147-155, No. 1644.]

*512. OPASI, E. "Dzems Dzojs u Puli." Arena
(Zagreb), 12, no. 102 (1962): 6.

513. PARANDOWSKI, JAN. "Spotkanie z Joyce'em."
Odrodzenie, no. 32 (1948). [Translated
in Berliner Hefte, 4 (1949): 382-388; in
Weltwoche (Zürich), 17 (1949): 5; in
Dziela wybrane, vol. 3, Warsaw: 1956, pp.
468-477; translated by Leo Koszella.
"Begegnung mit Joyce." Deutsche Rund-
schau, 83 (1957): 279-284; in Umana, 20
(May-September 1971): 46-48.]

514. PAUL, ELLIOTT. "Farthest North: A Study of
Joyce." Bookman, 75 (May 1932): 156-163.

515. PHILLIPS, NANCY. "Jim Joyce--A Beautiful
Voice." Telegram (Toronto), 11 February
1964. [Interview with Mrs. May Joyce
Monaghan.]

516. PINGUENTINI, GIANNI. "James Joyce a Triesta
nella casa di Vie Bramante." Porta orientale, 6 (1970): 75-80.

517. POLLOCK, HARRY J. "The Girl Joyce Did not
Marry." James Joyce Quarterly, 4 (Summer 1967): 255-257. [Eileen Vance.]

518. PORTER, BERN. "Joyceana." Circle, no. 7-8
(1946): 14a.

519. PORTER, RAYMOND J. "Irish Messianic Tradition." Emory University Quarterly, 22
(Spring 1966): 29-35.

520. QUARANTOTTI-GAMBINI, P. A. "Vita italiana
di James Joyce." Il Tempo di Milano,
21 February 1950.

521. _____. "Un autore in vetrina." Giornale
di Trieste, 25 February 1950, p. 3.

522. RALEIGH, JOHN HENRY. "My Brother's Keeper--
Stanislaus Joyce and 'Finnegans Wake.'"
Modern Language Notes, 68 (February 1953):
107-110. [See No. 496.]

523. REYNOLDS, MARY T. "Joyce and Nora: The In-
dispensable Countersign." Sewanee Review,
72 (Winter 1964): 29-64. [35 of Joyce's
letters to Nora (Fall 1909) analyzed.]

524. RISOLO, MICHELE. "Mia Moglie e Joyce."
Corriere della sera, 27 February 1969,
p. 11. [Amalia Popper.]

525. ROCCO-BERGERA, NINY. "Triestinità di James
Joyce." Umana, 20 (January-April 1971):
22-31. [Reprinted in Due saggi su James
Joyce. Trieste: Edizioni "Umana," 1971,
pp. 7-49 as "I vincoli triestini di James
Joyce."]

526. _____. "James Joyce and Trieste." James
Joyce Quarterly, 9 (Spring 1972): 342-349.

527. ROCKWELL, KIFFIN. "A 'Bog-Latin' Letter to
James Joyce." Notes and Queries, 8
(March 1961): 108.

528. RODGERS, W. R. "Joyce's Wake." Explorations,
no. 5 (1956): 19-25. [Reprinted in Explorations in Communication. Edited by Edmund Carpenter and H. Marshall McLuhan.
Boston: Beacon Press, 1960, pp. 188-195.]

529. _____. "Joyce's Funeral." Irish Times,
20 June 1964.

530. ROONEY, PHILIP. "How Joyce Came to Kerry."
Irish Digest, 44 (February 1953): 37-38.
[Condensed from Sunday Express.]

531. RUFF, LILLIAN M. "James Joyce and Arnold
Dolmetsch." James Joyce Quarterly, 6
(Spring 1969): 224-230. [Reprinted from
Dolmetsch Foundation Bulletin, (October
1958): 3-5.]

532. RUSHMORE, ROBERT. "The Tenor of James Joyce."
Opera News, 32 (9 December 1967): 8-12.

533. RYAN, STEPHEN P. "James Joyce and Edward
Martyn." Xavier University Studies, 1
(Spring, 1961-1962): 200-205.

*534. S., I. "Triestinità de un grande scrittore
irlandese: James Joyce." Il popolo di
Trieste, 1 May 1926.

535. S., P. H. "Joyce Insult." Times (London),
27 May 1972, p. 14. [On Lucie Nöel Léon
and John Sullivan and Joyce. See No. 447.]

536. SCARRY, JOHN. "Joyce and Mario the Tenor."
Notes and Queries, 20 (Fall 1973): 32.

*537. SCHIFF, GERT. "Dublin and James Joyce."
Merian, 12 (1959): 33-36.

*538. SCHÜNEMANN-KILLIAN, PETER. "Irland: Notizen
aus einem Land, wo die Zeit stillsteht:
In Dublin auf den Spuren von James Joyce."
Christ und Welt, 17 December 1959.

539. SCOTTI, GIACOMO. "James Joyce a Pola."
Osservatore politico letterario, 18,
no. 1 (1972): 47-50.

540. SENN, FRITZ. "Hier wohnte Joyce." Du-Atlantis
(Zürich), 26 (September 1966): 735-736.
[Reprinted in his James Joyce: Aufsätze
von Fritz Senn. Zürich: 1972, pp. 16-21.]

541. _____. "Some Further Notes on Giacomo Joyce." James Joyce Quarterly, 5 (Spring 1968): 233-236.

542. _____. "It Teaches Me Better to Love." Neue Zürcher Zeitung, no. 541 (19 November 1972): 51.

543. SMIDT, KRISTIAN. "Joyce and Norway." English Studies, 41 (October 1960): 318-321.

544. _____. "Joyce's Norwegian Teachers." English Studies, 44 (April 1963): 121-217.

545. SINGH, V. D. "James Joyce: The Crucial Date in his Literary Career." Indian Journal of English Studies, 14 (1973): 40-43.

546. SMITH, HUGH. "Joyce's Boyhood Home near Dublin is up for Sale." New York Times, 4 March 1970, p. 38.

547. SOUPAULT, PHILIPPE. "Autour de James Joyce." Bravo (Paris), September 1930, pp. 16-17. [Later incorporated in his Souvenirs de James Joyce (1943, 1945), including a fragment from ALP, in French translation, pp. 71-91; a fragment of this book translated by Maria Jolas in her James Joyce Yearbook (No. 1596); another fragment appeared as "James Joyce" in his Profils perdus (1963), pp. 49-70.]

*548. _____. "Portrait de l'artiste à Paris." Lettres françaises, 16-22 February 1961, pp. 1, 3.

549. SPIELBERG, PETER. "Take a Shaggy Dog by the Tale." James Joyce Quarterly, 1 (Spring 1964): 42-44.

550. SPIRE, ANDRE. "La recontre avec Joyce." Mercure de France, 347 (August-September 1963): 44-45. [On Joyce's ingratitude to Ludmilla Savitsky.]

551. STALEY, HARRY C. "Joyce's Catechisms." James Joyce Quarterly, 6 (Winter 1968): 137-153.

552. STALEY, THOMAS F. "James Joyce in Trieste." Georgia Review, 16 (Winter 1962): 446-449.

553. STARK, HELMUTH. "Eine Begegnung aus dem Jahr 1915." Akzente, 8 (April 1961): 155-157.

554. STEPHENS, JAMES. "The Joyce I Knew." Listener, 24 October 1946, p. 565. [Reprinted in Irish Digest, 28 (July 1947): 38-41; reprinted in Harper's Bazaar, 96 (February 1963): 90-91, 163-164; reprinted in James, Seumas and Jacques. Edited by Lloyd Frankenberg. New York: Macmillan, 1964, pp. 147-155.]

555. STRAUMANN, HEINRICH. "Letzte Begegnung mit Joyce." Du (Zürich), 8, no. 12 (December 1948): 31-32. [Enlarged and translated by E[ugene] and M[aria] J[olas] as "Last meeting with Joyce" in James Joyce Yearbook, pp. 109-115, No. 1596; translated by Pierre Ajame as "Les derniers jours de James Joyce." Nouvelles littéraires, 28 July 1966, p. 3; reprinted in Contexts of Literature: An Anglo-Swiss Approach, Twelve Essays, Swiss Studies in English, vol. 75. Bern: A. Francke, 1973, pp. 65-68.]

556. _____. "Four Letters to Martha Fleischmann." Tri-Quarterly, no. 8 (Winter 1967): 177-188.

557. TAKADA, KUNIO. ["Dublin and Joyce--Usher's Island."] Caledonia, no. 7 (December 1971): 22-23. [In Japanese]

558. de TUONI, DARIO. "L'Ultima casa di Joyce a Trieste." Fiera letteraria, 16, no. 18 (30 April 1961): 1-2.

559. VACHON, JOHN. "The Dublin where James Joyce Lived." Look, 31 (18 April 1967): 34-40, 42.

560. VANDERPYL, FRITZ. "Pulchritudo tam antiqua et tam nova: Les Letterines de Lucia Joyce." transition, no. 22 (February 1933): 131.

561. VAN HOEK, KEES. "I Met James Joyce's Wife." Irish Digest, 35 (February 1950): 23-25. [Condensed from Irish Times]

562. VENEMA, ADRIAAN. "Dublin: Zwerftocht met Joyce door een vergrizende Stad." Studio (Amsterdam), 23-29 November 1969, pp. 6-11. [Photos by Ad van Denderen]

563. VIDAN, IDO. "Joyce and the South Slavs." Studia Romanica et Anglica Zagrabiensia, nos. 33-34-35-36 (1972-1973): 265-277.

564. VILAR, SERGIO. "Pèlerinage à Dublin," translated by Françoise-Marie Rosset. Lettres nouvelles, 15 (March-April 1966): 69-84.

*565. VILLASENOR TEJEDA, JOSÉ. "La evolucion del adolescente en Joyce." Revista de la Facultad de Humanidades (Universidad Autonoma de San Luis Potosi), 1 (January-March 1959): 55-59.

*566. VIRDIA, FERDINANDO. "Joyce in Italia." Fiera letteraria, no. 47 (22 November 1960): 1-2.

567. WEIR, LORRAINE. "Joyce, Myth and Memory: On His Blindness." Irish University Review, 2 (Autumn 1972): 172-188.

568. WILCOCK, J. RODOLFO. "Joyce a Roma." Il Mondo, 12 (7 June 1960): 8.

569. WILDER, THORNTON. "James Joyce, 1882-1941." Poetry, 57 (March 1941): 370-374. [Separately printed by Wells College Press,

BIOGRAPHICAL STUDIES

Aurora, New York in 1944; translated in
Merkur, 3, no. 2 (1949): 1086-1090; translated by Herberth E. Herlitschka as "James
Joyce: Leben und Werk." Universitas
(Stuttgart), 6 (May 1951): 531-535 and
reprinted as "Meine Bewunderung für James
Joyce." Freude am Büchern: Monatschefte
für Weltliteratur (Wien), 3 (1952): 36-37
and as "Dankan den Ulysses-Dichter James
Joyce." Die Zeit, 11 (12 January 1956):
4; Italian translation of Herlitschka
translation in Minerva, 71 (October 1951):
327-329; also reprinted as "James Joyce,
der Schöpfer des inneren Monologs: Zum 70.
Geburtstag des 1941 gestorbenen irischen
Dichters James Joyce am 2. Februar."
Frankfurter Allgemeine Zeitung, 2 February
1952; another translation as "Dualidad de
James Joyce." Revista de revistas, 38
(25 January 1948): 33.]

*570. WILDI, MAX. "James Joyce und die Stadt."
Neue Zürcher Zeitung, no. 85 (27 March
1954); no. 89 (31 March 1954).

*571. _____. "James Joyce in Zürich." Swiss
Review of World Affairs, 11 (May 1961):
19-24.

572. WOOD, TOM. "A Portrait of the Artist According to his Dwellings." James Joyce Quarterly, 10 (Fall 1972): 189-197. [Photo-
graphic essay]

573. YAMELLA, PHILIP R. "James Joyce to The
Little Review: Ten Letters." Journal of
Modern Literature, 1 (March 1971): 393-
398.

574. ZIMMER, DIETER E. "Dublin--und immer Joyce
im Kopf: Notizen von einer viell elcht
wahnhaften Reise." Die Zeit (Hamburg),
18 July 1969, p. 12.

575. Unsigned. "James Joyce's Sister, Nun, Dies
at 80 in New Zealand." New York Times,
16 March 1964, p. 45.

*576. Unsigned. "Joyce et Trieste." Il Piccolo
(Trieste), 26 April 1961.

*577. Unsigned. "Joyce in Porta Orientale." Il
Piccolo (Trieste), 9 September 1961.

578. Unsigned. "May Monaghon, A Sister of Joyce."
New York Times, 13 December 1966, p. 47.

579. Unsigned. "Two U.S. Joyceans to Tour
Writer's Paris Haunts." New York Times,
16 June 1965, p. 49. [Patric Farrell and
Else de Brun]

MILIEU STUDIES

See also Mason and Ellmann. "From a Banned
Writer to a Banned Singer," Nos. 2776, 2777;
Merchant. "From a Banned Writer to a Banned
Singer," No. 2778; II.C "Epiphanies": Beja.
Epiphany..., No. 2826; Beckson and Munro.
"Symons, Browning...," No. 2825; Friedman. "The
Cracked Vase," No. 2830; II.D "Dubliners": Blum.
"Shifting Point of View...," No. 3152; Pritchard.
"Related Exercise on Joyce and Faulkner," No.
2931; Male. "Story of a Sensitive Young Man,"
No. 2994; Ryan. "Dubliners and the Stories of
Katherine Anne Porter," No. 2934; Henning.
"Stephen Hero and Wilhelm Meister...," No. 3202;
II.F "Portrait": Altieri. "Organic and Humanist
Models...," No. 3288; Brandabur. "Stephen Dedalus
and Paul Morel," No. 3302; Egri. "Function of
Dreams and Visions in...," No. 3318; Fackler.
"Stephen Dedalus Rejects...," No. 3439; Geckle.
"Stephen Dedalus and W. B. Yeats," No. 3326;
Gillie. "Human Subject and Human Substance,"
No. 3238; Goldberg. "Joyce, Freud and the Inter-
nalization of Order," No. 3239; Heimer. "Betray-
er as Intellectual," No. 3337; Lind. "The Way of
All Flesh and...," No. 3419; Kurzweil. "Al schlo-
sha sippurei...," No. 3355; Pratt. "Women and
Nature," No. 3380; Mercer. "Stephen Dedalus's
Vision and Synge's," No. 3367; Warren. "Faulk-
ner's 'A Portrait of the Artist,'" No. 3409;
II.G "Ulysses": Buckley. "Leavis and his
'Line,'" No. 3739; Bulhof. Transpersonalismus...,
No. 3558; Carens. "Joyce and Gogarty," No. 3560;
Coleman. "A Note on Joyce and Jung," No. 4463;
Durzak. "Hermann Broch and James Joyce," No.
4469; Egri. "Parallelen zwischen...," No. 4218;
Egri. Avantgardism and Modernity, No. 4438;
Faas. "Formen...," No. 4220; Garnett. "Jacob's
Room," No. 3819; Gilikin. "Variations on a
Method," No. 4226; Guiguet. "Un-American Consid-
erations...," No. 4476; S. Kittredge. "Richard
Aldington's Challenge...," No. 3895; Kruse.
"Hemingway's 'Cat in the Rain'...," No. 4490;
Lorch. "Relationships between Ulysses and The
Waste Land," No. 4495; Marie. Le Forêt Symbol-
iste, No. 3625; O'Connor. Irish Statesman, No.
3975; Pritchard. "On Wyndham Lewis...," No. 4513;
Purdy. "On the Psychology...," No. 4514; Read.
"Ezra Pound...," No. 4511; Reck. "Julian Green
on...," No. 4009; Richardson. "A Few Facts for
You," No. 4013; Smoot. "Variations in Water
Imagery...," No. 4522; Wetzel. "Spuren des
Ulysses...," No. 4533; Woolf, L. Beginning Again,
No. 3676; Woolf, V. Writer's Diary, No. 3677;
Laney. Paris Herald, No. 3613; Russel. Living...,
No. 3648; Mitchell. "Joyce and Döblin...," No.
3958; Brick. "The Madman in his Cell," No. 3735;
Muir. "The Zeitgeist...," No. 4506; Stavrou.
"Love Songs...," No. 4526; Kenner. Flaubert,
Joyce and Beckett, No. 4443; White. "Labyrinths
of Modern Fiction," No. 4535; Friedman. "Three

Experiences of War...," No. 3577; Lillyman. "Interior Monologue in... and Otto Ludwig," No. 4234; Stanzel. "Ulysses," No. 4279; Isaacs. "Autoerotic Metaphor in...," No. 4304; II.I _Finnegans Wake_: Aldington. "A Critical Attitude...," No. 4972; Blish. "Long Nights of a Virginia Author," No. 4995; Behar. "McLuhan's _Finnegans Wake_," No. 4979; Glasheen. "Joyce and Yeats," No. 5062; Halper. "Joyce and Eliot," No. 5082; Harvey. _Ford Madox Ford_, No. 5525; Hassan. "Joyce-Beckett," No. 5093; Hayman. "Pound at the Wake," No. 5427; Korg. "Literary Esthetics of Dada," No. 5118; Staples. "Beckett in the Wake," No. 5497; Sullivan. "Tolstoy's _War and Peace_...," No. 5499; Miller. "Joyce and Wolfe," No. 87; "Dissertations," Nos. 2367-2389.

Milieu: Modernism, the 20s and 30s, Paris

Books

580. BELL, CLIVE. "Paris in the Twenties," in his _Old Friends: Personal Recollections_. New York: Harcourt, Brace, 1956, pp. 179-180.

581. EASTMAN, MAX. _The Literary Mind_. New York: Charles Scribner's Sons, 1931, pp. 97-102. [Contains "Poets Talking to Themselves." _Harper's Magazine_, no. 977 (October 1931): 563-574.]

582. FORD, HUGH, ed. _The Left Bank Revisited: Selections from the Paris Tribune, 1917-1934_. University Park, London: Pennsylvania State University Press, 1972, _passim_.

583. GAUNT, WILLIAM. _The March of the Moderns_. London: Jonathan Cape, 1949, pp. 199-208, 215-216, 219-220.

584. PUTNAM, SAMUEL. _Paris was our Mistress_. New York: Viking Press, 1947, _passim_.

585. RAY, MAN. _Self Portrait_. Boston: Little, Brown; London: Deutsch, 1963, pp. 186-188.

586. POWER, ARTHUR. _From the Old Waterford House_. Waterford: Carthage Press, 1940, pp. 148-155.

587. REID, B. L. _The Man from New York: John Quinn and his Friends_. New York: Oxford University Press, 1968, _passim_.

588. ROGERS, WILLIAM G. _Wise Men Fish Here: The Story of Frances Steloff and the Gotham Book Mart_. New York: Harcourt, Brace and World, 1965, _passim_.

589. SPECTOR, JACK J. _The Aesthetics of Freud: A Study in Psychoanalysis and Art_. New York, Washington: Praeger, 1973, _passim_.

*590. STARKIE, ENID. _From Gautier to Eliot_. London: Hutchinson; New York: Humanities Press, 1960, pp. 186-197. [Reprinted St. Clair Shores, Mich.: Scholarly Press, 1971, pp. 180-201.]

591. STERN, JAMES. "James Joyce: A First Impression," in A _James Joyce Miscellany_, Second Series, pp. 93-102, No. 1613. [Later appeared in _Listener_, 66 (28 September 1961): 461-463; reprinted in _Irish Digest_, 73 (December 1961): 113-116.]

*592. WEST, PAUL. "The Twentieth Century: The Poet's Novel," in _The Growth of the Novel_. Toronto: Canadian Broadcasting Corp., 1959, pp. 51-60.

593. WICKES, GEORGE. _Americans in Paris_. Garden City: Doubleday, 1969, _passim_.

594. ZERAFFA, MICHEL. _Personne et personnage: Le romanesque des années 1920 aux années 1950_. Paris: Klincksieck, 1969, _passim_.

Periodical Articles

595. ANDERSON, CHESTER G. "They Said 'Yes' to the Twenties." _Columbia Library Columns_, 17 (November 1967): 17-26. [Harry and Caresse Crosby]

596. BARNES, DJUNA. "James Joyce." _Vanity Fair_, 18 (April 1922): 65, 104.

597. BOYLE, KAY. "Paris in the Twenties." _Yale Reports_, no. 360 (25 April 1965): 7pp.

598. CALMER, EDGAR. "A New Issue of 'transition.'" _Chicago Sunday Tribune_ (Paris), 17 November 1929.

599. CODY, MERRILL. "James Joyce in the Twenties." _Connecticut Review_, 5 (April 1972): 11-15.

*600. GOPALEEN, MYLES na (Flann O'Brien, Brian Nolan). "Cruiskeen Lawn." _Irish Times_, 1 September 1944.

*601. _____. "Cruiskeen Lawn." _Irish Times_, 15 September 1950.

*602. _____. "Cruiskeen Lawn." _Irish Times_, 12 November 1955.

603. LOTTMAN, HERBERT R. "One of the Quiet Ones." _New York Times Book Review_, 22 March 1970, pp. 5, 28-29. [Maria Jolas; see also letter to the Editor by Robert N. Kastor, 10 May 1970, p. 22.]

604. POWER, ARTHUR. "Joyce Among the Poets: Memories of a Paris Evening's Talk." _Irish Times_, 17 December 1964, p. 10.

605. VALERY, PAUL. "L'Allocution de M. Paul Valery au banquet des PEN's Club." _Les nouvelles littéraires_, 4, no. 138 (6 June 1925): 1.

606. Unsigned. "The Forgotten Lawyer who found the Dollars (John Quinn)." _Times Literary Supplement_, 6 March 1969, p. 240.

BIOGRAPHICAL STUDIES

607. Unsigned. "Joyce i jego epoka ["Joyce in his Time"]." Dialog (Warsaw), 9 (December 1964): 126-135.

*608. Unsigned. "Lewis Portrays Dome 'Kultur': Gopher Prairie Discusses Paris Intellectuals." Chicago Tribune (Paris), 4 October 1925, p. 3.

Joyce and Other Writers--Comparisons and Contrasts

See also David Hayman. Joyce et Mallarmé, No. 932; Gilbert Highet. "Symbolist poets...," No. 933; Herbert Howarth. "Whitman and...," No. 936; W. H. Auden. "James Joyce and Richard Wagner," No. 956; J. R. Bambrough. "Joyce and Jonson," No. 957; Maurice Beebe. "James Joyce and Giordano Bruno," No. 959; Haskell M. Block. "James Joyce and Thomas Hardy," No. 962; Anthony Burgess. "Mark Twain and...," No. 966; Patrick Diskin. "Joyce and Charlotte Brontë," No. 971; Charles T. Dougherty. "Joyce and Ruskin," No. 974; Edmund L. Epstein. "James Joyce and The Way of All Flesh," No. 976; Donald Fanger. "Joyce and Meredith," No. 978; Rudd Fleming. "Dramatic Involution," No. 981; David Hayman. "James Joyce and Arthur Rimbaud," No. 988; Frank L. Kunkel. "Beauty in Aquinas," No. 996; Herbert M. McLuhan. "Joyce, Mallarmé, ...," No. 1000; William H. Marshall. "A Joyce-Santayana Parallel," No. 1003; Marion Montgomery. "Emotion Recollected...," No. 1005; J. Mitchell Morse. "Disobedient Artist...," No. 1006; J. Mitchell Morse. "Art and Fortitude...," No. 1007; J. Mitchell Morse. "Augustine's Theodicy...," No. 1008; J. Mitchell Morse. "Baudelaire...," No. 1009; Sister Marian Sharpless. "Hopkins...," No. 1016; M. T. Thomson. "James Joyce and Rimbaud's...," No. 1018; Simonne Verdin. "Mallarmé ...," No. 1021; David I. Grossvogel. "Joyce and Robbe-Grillet," No. 1372; Marshall McLuhan. "John Dos Passos...," No. 1383; Ben F. Stoltzfus. Alain Robbe Grillet..., No. 1409; Brom Weber. Letters of Hart Crane, No. 1414; Geoffrey Aggeler. "Comic Art of Anthony Burgess," No. 1418; Bernard Benstock. "On William Gaddis...," No. 1421; Pierre Boulez. "'Sonate...,'" No. 1423; G. Glauco Cambon. "La trilogia 'USA'...," No. 1429; Melvin J. Friedman. "Anthony Burgess...," No. 1442; Philip Henderson. "James Joyce and Lewis Carroll...," No. 1448; Roger B. Henkle. "Pynchon's...," No. 1450; Marianne Kesting. "Raymond Queneau...," No. 1462; Rob B. Male. "The Story of...," No. 2994; Marvin Magalaner. "Joyce, Nietzsche...," No. 3092; John Henning. "Stephen Hero and Wilhelm Meister ...," No. 3202; M. A. Goldberg. "Joyce, Freud...," No. 3239; Pedro A. Reyes. "A Difference...," No. 3383; Ilse Lind. "The Way of All Flesh...," No. 3419; Brian Dibble. "A Brunonian Reading...," No. 3313; Annis Pratt. "Women and...," No. 3380; Deena P. Metzger. "Variations...," No. 3524; Rima Drell Reck. "Julian Green...," No. 4009; W. J. Lillyman. "Interior Monologue...," No. 4234; Brion Mitchell. "Hans Henry Jahn...," No. 4239; Antonio R. Romera. "El monólogo...," No. 4243; Julian Palley. "The Periplus of Don Pedro...," No. 4428; Lila Aronne Amestoy. "Ulysses vs.

Rayuela...," No. 4435; Carlos Fuentes. "Rayuela ...," No. 4472; Augusto de Campos. "Um lance...," No. 5013; Charles T. McMichael and Ted R. Spivey. "Chaos-Hurray...," No. 5133.

General

*609. BAROIS, JEAN. "James Joyce parmi ses amis de Paris ou le retour d'Ulysse chez les civilises." Paris-Midi, 25 February 1934.

*610. BOYD, ERNEST. "Concerning James Joyce." The World (New York), 25 January 1925.

611. CRONIN, JOHN. "The Funnel and the Tundish: Irish Writers and the English Language." Wascana Review, 3, no. 1 (1968): 80-88.

612. HARUYAMA, YUKIO. "Joyce and his Contemporaries," in A Study of Joyce, pp. 169-188, No. 1592. [In Japanese]

613. HOANG-TRINH. "Tìm hiểu trở lai Macxen Pruxt, Jêm Joix, Uyliem Fôcnơ [Seeking to Understand the Future: Marcel Proust, James Joyce, William Faulkner]." Phu'o'ng tây văn hoc và con ngu'ờ'i [The West: Literature and Man]. Hanoi: Nhà Xuat Ban Khoa Hoc Xã Hôi, 1971, pp. 210-216.

614. JOLAS, MARIA. "Joyce et ses amis." Figaro littéraire, 20 January 1966, p. 13.

615. JORDAN, JOHN. "Joyce, One of the Boys." Hibernia, 24 (30 October 1959): 10, 12.

*616. LEWIS, SINCLAIR. "Self-Conscious America." American Mercury, 6, no. 22 (October 1929): 131-132. [On the Joyce cult in Paris]

617. SMYSER, WILLIAM LEON. "The Paris School of Irish Writers." Bulletin, 6, no. 7 (July 1927): 715-721.

618. SUZUKI, YUKIO. "Joyce as Seen by his Contemporaries," in A Study of Joyce, pp. 227-242, No. 1592. [In Japanese]

*619. WEISER, PETER. "Der Auseinandersetzungen müde: Wiener Premieren von Joyce, Sartre, Camus und Goetz." Frankfurter Allgemeine Zeitung, 21 January 1960.

AE (George Russell, "Y.O.")

[See also Richard M. Kain. "AE's Cooperative Watch...," No. 4484.]

*620. JACKSON, FRANCIS. "George Russell ('A.E.')." Bulletin (Sydney), 16 January 1929.

*621. O'CONNOR, FRANK. "A.E., A Portrait." The Bell, 1, no. 2 (November 1940): 49-57.

622. RUSSELL, GEORGE (AE). The Living Torch. Edited by Monk Gibbon. New York: Macmillan, 1938, pp. 139-140.

*623. _____ . "Letters from AE. Edited by Alan Denson. London: Abelard-Schuman, 1961, pp. 43, 50, 55-56.

Richard Aldington

[See also Selwyn Kittredge. "Richard Aldington's Challenge...," No. 3895.]

624. SENCOURT, ROBERT. "James Joyce and Richard Aldington," in T. S. Eliot: A Memoir. Edited by Donald Adamson. New York: Dodd, Mead, 1971, pp. 89-97; London: Garnstone Press.

625. THATCHER, DAVID S., ed. "Richard Aldington's Letters to Herbert Read." Malahat Review, no. 15 (July 1970): 5-44. [36 letters from Aldington to Read (1919-1960), mentioning Joyce, Dahlberg, Eliot, Wyndham Lewis, Pound.]

George Antheil

[See also Virgil Thomson. "Antheil...," No. 728.]

626. ANTHEIL, GEORGE. Bad Boy of Music. Garden City: Doubleday Doran, 1945, pp. 143-156 and passim.

Samuel Beckett

[See also Lionel Abel. "Samuel Beckett...," No. 1353; Ruby Cohn. "Joyce and Beckett...," No. 1362; Sighle Kennedy. Murphy's Bed, No. 1378; Lionel Abel. "Joyce the Father...," No. 1417; Melvin J. Friedman. "Novels of Samuel Beckett...," No. 1441; Vera Hickman. "Waiting...," No. 1451; Jan Hokenson. "A Stuttering Logos...," No. 1452; K. Stamirowska. "Conception of Character...," No. 1817; Allan Brick. "Madman in his Cell...," No. 3733; Hugh Kenner. Flaubert, Joyce and Beckett, No. 4443; Giorgio Cabibbe. "Francesco Flora...," No. 4460; Nathan Halper. "On an Anecdote of Beckett's," No. 5623.]

627. HASSAN, IHAB. The Literature of Silence: Henry Miller and Samuel Beckett. New York: Knopf, 1967, passim.

628. HAYMAN, DAVID. "A Prefatory Note" [Special Beckett Issue]. James Joyce Quarterly, 8 (Summer 1971): 275-277.

629. _____ . "A Meeting in the Park and a Meeting on the Bridge: Joyce and Beckett." James Joyce Quarterly, 8 (Summer 1971): 372-384.

630. JANVIER, LUDOVIC. "Sames: Joyce et Beckett." L'Arc, no. 36 (1968): 39-41.

631. JOLAS, MARIA. "A Bloomlein for Sam," in Beckett at 60: A Festschrift. London: Calder and Boyars, 1967, pp. 14-16.

632. 'Jude the Obscure.' "The H. U. Business Section." Honest Ulsterman, no. 30 (September-October 1971): 12-15. [See letter to Editor by Niall Cusack and Jude's response, no. 31 (November-December 1971): 24-27.]

Silvio Benco

633. BENCO, AURELIA GRUBER. "Between Joyce and Benco." James Joyce Quarterly, 9 (Spring 1972): 328-333.

André Biely

634. REAVEY, GEORGE. "Le mot et le monde d'André Biely et de James Joyce." Romàn, no. 2 (March 1951): 103-111.

Jorge Luis Borges

[See also L. A. Murillo. "James Joyce...," No. 4448.]

635. REVOL, E. L. "Elementos de Joyce," in La tradición imaginaria de Joyce a Borges. Cordoba, Argentina: TEUCO, 1971, pp. 10-29. [Previously published in his Al pie de las letras. Buenos Aires: 1949; reprinted in part in Escarabajo de oro, nos. 30-31 (1966?); part also appeared as "Joyce, la literatura y el lenguaje." Sur, no. 159 (January 1948): 75-86.]

Kay Boyle

636. BOYLE, KAY. "Letter from Joyce." Tri-Quarterly, 8 (Winter 1967): 195-197.

Hermann Broch

[See also Hermann Broch. Briefwechsel..., No. 1028; Manfred Durzak. "Die Ästhetik...," No. 1367; M. Irinoda. "Hermann Broch...," No. 1454; John McCormick. "James Joyce and...," No. 4444; Mandfred Durzak. "Hermann Broch...," No. 4469; G. C. Schoolfield. "Broch's Sleepwalker...," No. 4519.]

637. BIRĂESCU, TRAIAN LIVIU. "O paralelă literară: James Joyce-Hermann Broch." Analele Universităţii din Timişoara, Seria Ştiinţe filologice 7 (1969): 252-256.

William Burroughs

638. LODGE, DAVID. "Objections to William Burroughs," in The Novelist at the Crossroads and Other Essays on Fiction and Criticism. London: Routledge and Kegan Paul; Ithaca: Cornell University Press, 1971, pp. 161-171. [From an article originally in Critical Quarterly (1966).]

James Branch Cabell

[See also James Blish. "Long Night...," No. 4995; Nathan Halper. "Joyce and...," No. 5423.]

BIOGRAPHICAL STUDIES

639. HALPER, NATHAN. "Joyce/Cabell and Cabell/
Joyce." Kalki, 4 (1969): 9-24.

640. JENKINS, WILLIAM D. "Cabell/Horvendile and
Joyce/Stephen." Kalki, 5 (1972): 93-94.

*641. NEWMAN, FRANCES. "Review." Evening Post
(New York), 1 October 1927. [Joyce is
mentioned in a review of two of Cabell's
books.]

Paul Claudel

642. MOELLER, CHARLES. "James Joyce et Paul
Claudel: ou la transfiguration du monde."
Revue générale belge, no. 72 (1951): 898-
916.

Sidonie Gabrielle Colette

643. KRAHÉ, HILDEGARD. "Colette und Joyce:
Berühmte Namen in Kinderbuch." Die Welt
der Literatur, 3, no. 7 (1966): 37.

Joseph Conrad

644. WOLPERS, THEODOR. "Formen mythisierenden
Erzählens in der modernen Prosa: Joseph
Conrad im Vergleich mit Joyce, Lawrence,
und Faulkner," in Lebende Antike: Sympo-
sion für Rudolf Sühnel. Edited by Horst
Meller and Hans-Joachim Zimmerman.
Berlin: E. Schmidt, 1967, pp. 397-422.

Gabriel d'Annunzio

[See also C. P. Curran. "Joyce's d'Annunzian
Mask," No. 970; Corinna del Greco Lobner. "James
Joyce's 'Tilly'...," No. 2805; Umberto Eco.
"Joyce et d'Annunzio...," No. 2828; Barbara L.
Sloan. "The d'Annunzian Narrator...," No. 3096.]

645. ADAMS, ROBERT. "The Operatic Novel: Joyce
and D'Annunzio," in New Looks at Italian
Opera: Essays in Honor of Donald Grout.
Edited by William W. Austin. Ithaca:
Cornell University Press, 1968.

646. GRECO LOBNER, CORINNA del. "Speculations
Concerning an Altercation where Ippolita
and 'Gabriel of the Annunciation' Figure
Prominently." James Joyce Quarterly, 11
(Fall 1973): 57-60.

Donald Davidson

647. DESSOMMES, LARRY K. "The Antipodes of Mod-
ern Literature: A Discussion of Joyce and
Davidson." South Central Bulletin, 30
(Winter 1970): 179-181.

Édouard Dujardin

[See also Édouard Dujardin. Le monologue intérieure..., No. 928; Édouard Dujardin. "Der
roman...," No. 3784; Liisa Dahl. "A Comment on
Similarities...," No. 4214; Stuart Gilbert. "We'll
to the Woods...," No. 4225; Philip Handler. "The

Case for...," No. 4227; Rayner Heppenstall. "The
Bays are Sere," No. 4229; C. D. King. "Édouard
Dujardin...," No. 4233; Vivian Mercier. "Justice
for...," No. 4236; Unsigned. "Im Vorgeld...," No.
4253; Henry Edelheit. "Reflections on...," No.
5043.]

648. JOLAS, EUGENE. "The Spirit and the Troglo-
dytes." Living Age, 360 (May 1941): 255.

T. S. Eliot

[See also Joseph W. Alsop. "Some Aspects...,"
No. 1078; Unsigned. "Literature at the Cross-
Roads," No. 1246; Robert B. Kaplan. "Eliot's
'Gerontion,'" No. 1460; Anthony R. Kilgallin.
"Eliot, Joyce...," No. 1463; Selwyn Kittredge.
"Richard Aldington's Challenge...," No. 3895; A.
Walton Litz. "Pound and Eliot...," No. 3921; Eg-
bert Faas. "Formen der...," No. 4220; Robert A.
Day. "Joyce's Wasteland...," No. 4467; Claude
Edmonde Magny. "Note conjointe...," No. 4499;
Monique Nathan. "James Joyce et...," No. 4507;
Heinz Wetzel. "Spuren des Ulysses...," No. 4533;
Jack P. Dalton. "A Letter from T. S. Eliot," No.
5034; Nathan Halper. "Joyce and Eliot...," No.
5082.]

649. ANDREACH, ROBERT J. "James Joyce," in his
Studies in Structure: The Stages of the
Spiritual Life of Four Modern Authors.
New York: Fordham University Press, 1964,
pp. 40-71; London: Burns and Oates, 1965.
[Hopkins, Joyce, Eliot, Hart Crane]

650. BURNET, W. HODGSON. "Joint Affair: T. S.
Eliot and James Joyce Collaborate." Saturday Review, 159 (17 December 1932): 639.

651. DAY, ROBERT A. "Joyce's Waste Land and
Eliot's Unknown God." Literary Monographs, 4 (1971): 137-210.

652. HALPER, NATHAN. "Letter to the Editor."
James Joyce Quarterly, 9 (Winter 1971):
297-299. [Comment on Ruth von Phul, See
No. 656.]

*653. LÜDEKE, HENRY. "Die Auflockerung des
Reiches: Joyce und Eliot," in Die englische Literatur, Munich: 1954, pp. 120-
129.

654. POIRIER, RICHARD. "The Literature of Waste:
Eliot, Joyce, and Others," in his The Performing Self. New York: Oxford University
Press, 1971, pp. 45-61 and passim. [Much
changed version of article in New Republic,
156 (20 May 1967): 19-25.]

655. STOCK, NOEL. "Joyce and Eliot, 1915/1917,"
in The Life of Ezra Pound. London: Routledge and Kegan Paul; New York: Pantheon,
1970, pp. 176-200 and passim.

656. VON PHUL, RUTH. "Query about Joyce's Relationship with Eliot." James Joyce Quar-

terly, 8 (Winter 1970): 178-179. [See
reply by Nathan Halper, No. 652.]

James T. Farrell

657. WADE, MASON. "James T. Farrell and Dos
Passos." Colosseum (London), 4, No. 18
(July 1938): 114-129.

William Faulkner

[See also Peter Swiggart. Art of Faulkner's
Novels, No. 1412; Dudley Fitts. "Two Aspects of
...," No. 1440; M. Gidley. "Some Notes...," No.
1444; Morris Beja. Epiphany..., No. 2826; Ivo
Vidan. Romani Struje..., No. 4206; Robert M.
Slabey. "Faulkner's Mosquitoes...," No. 4521.]

*658. GAUNT, ROGER. "The Magic World within the
Mind: James Joyce-William Faulkner."
Debonair, 1 (February 1961): 56-63.

F. Scott Fitzgerald

[See Robert Sklar. F. Scott Fitzgerald, No.
1404; F. Scott Fitzgerald. "Fitzgerald on...,"
No. 4470; Unsigned. "F. Scott Fitzgerald's Copy
of Ulysses," No. 4537.]

Gustav Flaubert

[See also Haskell M. Block. "Theory of Language...," No. 925; Richard K. Cross. Flaubert
and Joyce, No. 1546; David Hayman. "Portrait and
L'Éducation...," No. 3334; Hugh Kenner. Flaubert, Joyce..., No. 4443; Ezra Pound. "James
Joyce et Pécuchet, No. 4274; Gabrijela Arneri.
"Les travestissements...," No. 4852.]

659. COLUM, MARY. "Literature of Today and Tomorrow." Scribner's Magazine, 100 (December 1936): 98-106.

Ford Madox Ford

660. FORD, FORD MADOX. It was the Nightingale.
Philadelphia: Lippincott, 1933, passim.

661. LUDWIG, RICHARD M., ed. Letters. Princeton:
Princeton University Press, 1965, pp. 161,
199, 320-323, et passim.

662. MIZENER, ARTHUR. The Saddest Story: A Biography of Ford Madox Ford. New York,
Cleveland: World, 1971, passim.

Waldo Frank

*663. FINGERIT, HULIO. "Waldo Frank." Criterio
(Buenos Aires), 6 (30 October 1929):
139-141.

André Gide

664. AMES, VAN METER. André Gide. Norfolk: New
Directions, 1947, pp. 183, 263.

665. MARKOW-TOTEVY, GEORGES. "André Gide et James
Joyce." Mercure de France, 339 (February
1960): 272-290.

Stuart Gilbert

[See also Patricia Hutchins. "In the Wake...,"
No. 1453; Montgomery Belgion. "Mr. Joyce and Mr.
Gilbert," No. 4458.]

Louis Gillet

[See also his Stèle pour James Joyce, No.
1568.]

666. EDEL, LEON. "James Joyce and the Academician,"
in A James Joyce Miscellany, 1957, pp. 44-
48, No. 1612. [Appeared also in Claybook
for James Joyce, pp. 7-11, No. 1568.]

667. MARKOW-TOTEVY, GEORGES. "James Joyce and
Louis Gillet," in A James Joyce Miscellany,
1957, pp. 49-61, No. 1612.]

J. W. von Goethe

668. HENNIG, JOHN. "Stephen Hero and Wilhelm
Meister: A Study of Parallels." German
Life and Letters, 5 (October 1951): 22-29.

Oliver St. John Gogarty

[See also Ulick O'Connor. The Times..., No.
234; Gogarty. It Isn't..., No. 319; Gogarty. Many
Lines..., No. 320; Gogarty. "They Think They Know
Joyce," No. 446.]

669. BREIT, HARVEY. "Avenger No. 1." New York
Times Book Review, 60 (21 February 1954):
8. [John J. Slocum on Gogarty]

670. O'CONNOR, ULICK. "James Joyce and Oliver St.
John Gogarty: A Famous Friendship." Texas
Quarterly, 3 (Summer 1960): 189-210.

Henrik Ibsen

[See Bjørn Tysdahl. Joyce and Ibsen, No. 952;
Vivienne MacLeod. "Influence of Ibsen...," No.
998; Kristian Smidt. "Joyce and Ibsen...," No.
1017; James T. Farrell. "Exiles and Ibsen...,"
No. 3487; Bernard Benstock. "Exiles, Ibsen...,"
No. 3500; Padraic Colum. "Ibsen...," No. 3503;
Amiya Dev. "The Artist in Ibsen...," No. 3505;
Fritz Engel. "Nach Ibsen," No. 3507; E. Iu.
Genieva. "Dzhois i Ibsen," No. 3511; Jacques Le-
marchand. "Un disciple...," No. 3520; Bjørn
Tysdahl. "Joyce's Exiles...," No. 3530; Marvin
Carlson. "Henrik Ibsen...," No. 5391.]

671. KENNER, HUGH. "Joyce and Ibsen's Naturalism."
Sewanee Review, 59 (January 1951): 75-96.

Henry James

672. SPENDER, STEPHEN. The Destructive Element.
Boston: Houghton Mifflin, 1936, passim.
[James' The Ambassadors and Joyce's U.]

BIOGRAPHICAL STUDIES

Eyvind Johnson

[See Örjan Lindberger. "Eyvind Johnsons...,"
No. 738.]

Carl G. Jung

673. COLEMAN, ELLIOT. "A Note on Joyce and Jung."
James Joyce Quarterly, 1 (Fall 1963): 11-
16.

Valery Larbaud

674. O'BRIEN, JUSTIN. "Valery Larbaud." The
Symposium, 3, no. 3 (July 1932): 315-334.

675. VIGNERON, ELISE. "Un ami de Larbaud."
Cahiers bourbonnais, no. 2 (1965): 289-
292.

D. H. Lawrence

[See also T. S. Eliot. After Strange Gods,
No. 696; William Deakin. "D. H. Lawrence's At-
tacks...," No. 733; Joseph W. Alsop. "Some As-
pects...," No. 1078; C. H. Sisson. "The Verse of
James Joyce," No. 2789; C. A. Enroth. Joyce and
Lawrence, No. 3130; Struther B. Purdy. "On the
Psychology...," No. 4514; G. Wilson Knight.
"Lawrence, Joyce...," No. 4565.]

*676. DAVIES, A. MERVYN. "Two Worlds in Revolt."
St. Louis Post-Dispatch, 6 December 1959,
p. 31. [On Southern Illinois University
symposia on Joyce and Lawrence.]

677. FRIEDMAN, ALAN. "The Other Lawrence." Partisan Review, 37 (Spring 1970): 239-253.

678. ROBSON, W. W. "Joyce and Lawrence," in Modern English Literature. London, New York:
Oxford University Press, 1970, pp. 73-92.

679. STOLL, JOHN E. "Common Womb Imagery in Joyce
and Lawrence." Ball State University
Forum, 11 (Spring 1970): 10-24.

Paul Léon

[See also Lucie Noël. James Joyce and Paul
Léon, No. 340.]

680. JOLAS, MARIA. "The Little Known Paul Léon,"
in A James Joyce Miscellany, Second Series,
pp. 225-233, No. 1613.

Wyndham Lewis

[See also Joseph W. Alsop. "Some Aspects...,"
No. 1078; Melvin J. Friedman. "Three Experiences
of the War...," No. 3577; William H. Pritchard.
"On Wyndham Lewis," No. 4513; Geoffrey Wagner.
"Wyndham Lewis...," No. 5228.]

*681. MORGAN, LOUISE. "Wyndham Lewis: The Great
Satirist of our Day." Everyman, 5, no.
112 (19 March 1931): 231-233. [Reprinted
in Writers at Work, (1931).]

682. ROSE, W. K., ed. The Letters of Wyndham
Lewis. Norfolk: New Directions, 1963,
passim.

*683. Unsigned. "Review." The Adelphi, 4, no. 10
(April 1927): 609. [Notes on Lewis' The
Enemy.]

*684. Unsigned. "Review." New Age, 2 June 1927,
p. 59. [Review of The Enemy, 1, no. 1
(January 1927) and much about Joyce.]

Hugh MacDiarmid (Christopher Murray Grieve)

685. LOW, DONALD A. "Joyce and Hugh MacDiarmid."
Joycenotes, 2 (September 1969): 3-9.

686. STEVENSON, RONALD. "MacDiarmid, Joyce, and
Busoni," in Hugh MacDiarmid: A Festschrift.
Edited by K. D. Duval and Sydney Goodsir
Smith. Edinburgh: K. D. Duval, 1962, pp.
141-154.

Marshall McLuhan

[See also Jack Behar. "McLuhan's Finnegans
Wake," No. 4979.]

687. HALPER, NATHAN. "Marshall McLuhan and Joyce,"
in McLuhan: Pro and Con. Edited by Raymond
Rosenthal. New York: Funk and Wagnalls,
1968, pp. 58-81

Thomas Mann

[See also Péter Egri. "Thomas Mann es...,"
No. 2908; Hannes Schiefele. "Freuds Bedeutung...,"
No. 4200; Péter Egri. "Parallelen zwischen...," No.
4218; Péter Egri. James Joyce es..., No. 4438;
Hans Robert Jauss. "Die Ausprägung...," No. 4442;
Otto Bihalji-Meria. "Faustus und Ulysses...," No.
4459.]

688. EGRI, PÉTER. "A Survey of Criticism on the
Relation of James Joyce and Thomas Mann."
Hungarian Studies in English, 2 (1965):
105-120.

689. _____. "James Joyce and Adrian Leverkühn:
Decadence and Modernity in the Joycean Parallels of Thomas Mann's Doktor Faustus."
Acta litteraria (academiae scientiarum
hungaricae), 8, no. 1-2 (1966): 195-238;
8, no. 3-4 (1966): 421-444.

690. FURST, LILIAN. "Thomas Mann's Interest in
James Joyce." Modern Language Review, 64
(July 1969): 605-613.

*691. HEILMAN, ROBERT B. "Variations on Picaresque
(Felix Krull)." Sewanee Review, 66 (Autumn
1958): 547-577.

*692. LENZ, SIEGFRIED. "Wie lebte der Mann, der
James Joyce haisess?" Die Welt, 14 December 1957.

693. MORSE, J. MITCHELL. "Joyce and the Early Thomas Mann." Revue de littérature comparée, 36 (July-September 1962): 377-385.

*694. SCHIROKAUER, ARNO. "Bedeutungswandel des Romans." Mass und Wert, 3 (September-November 1940): 575-590.

Katherine Mansfield

[See also Peter Hatter. "Die epiphanien...," No. 2865.]

695. BERKMAN, SYLVIA. Katherine Mansfield. New Haven: Yale University Press, 1951, pp. 159-177.

696. ELIOT, T. S. After Strange Gods. London: Faber, 1934, pp. 35-38. [Compares Joyce's 'The Dead,' Mansfield's 'Bliss,' and D. H. Lawrence's 'The Shadow in the Rose Garden.']

697. MORE, PAUL ELMER. "James Joyce." American Review, 5 (May 1935): 129-157. [Reply to Eliot, No. 696; reprinted in More's On Being Human. Princeton: Princeton University Press, 1936, pp. 69-96.]

H. L. Mencken

[See also Joseph Prescott. "Notes on Mencken," No. 1795.]

698. LEINWALL, GEORGE. [n.t.]. Menckeniana, no. 32 (Winter 1969): 11-12.

699. MENCKEN, H. L. Letters. Edited by Guy L. Forgue. New York: Knopf, pp. 64-65, 73-74.

Brian Moore

[See also Richard B. Sale. "An Interview...," No. 1491.]

700. GALLAGHER, MICHAEL P. "The Novels of Brian Moore." Studies, 60 (Summer 1971): 180-194.

George Moore

[See also Phillip Marcus. "George Moore's Dublin...," No. 2838; Karl Beckson. "Moore's The Untilled Field...," No. 2892; John R. Hart. "Moore on Joyce," No. 2918; Sister Eileen Kennedy. "Moore's Untilled Field...," No. 2922; Aristide Marie. Le Forêt Symboliste, No. 3625; Richard M. Kain. "AE's Cooperative...," No. 4484.]

701. HOARE, DOROTHY M. "Moore and Joyce--A Contrast," in Some Studies in the Modern Novel. London: Chatto and Windus, 1938, pp. 133-147. [Reprinted Philadelphia:

Dufour Editions, 1953; Port Washington, N.Y.: Kennikat, 1966; reprinted New York: Haskell House, 1972.]

Robert Musil

[See also Berhard Diebold. "Totentanz...," No. 735; Baruch Kurzweil. "Al shlosha sippurei...," No. 3355; Gerhard R. Kaiser. "Joyce, Ulysses," No. 3607.]

702. GARCIA PONCE, JUAN. "Musil y Joyce." Revista de bellas artes, no. 13 (January-February 1967): 13-31. [First part appeared in English translation in James Joyce Quarterly, 5 (Winter 1968): 75-86, translated by Boyd Carter and Eileen Carter.]

*703. PIKE, BURTON. Robert Musil: An Introduction to his Work. Ithaca: Cornell University Press, 1961, passim.

Vladimir Nabokov

[See also Karl Proffer. Keys to Lolita, No. 1398.]

704. NOËL, LUCIE LÉON. "Playback," in Nabokov: Criticism, Reminiscences, Translations, and Tributes. Edited by Alfred Appel and Charles Newman. Evanston: Northwestern University Press, 1970, pp. 209-219. [Also appears in Tri-Quarterly, no. 17 (Winter 1970).]

Brian Nolan

[See also Del Ivan Janik. "Flann O'Brien...," No. 3342; Howard Moss. "Tom Swift in Hell," No. 4504.]

705. BENSTOCK, BERNARD. "The Three Faces of Brian Nolan." Éire-Ireland, 3 (Autumn 1968): 51-65.

706. POWELL, DAVID. "An Annotated Bibliography of Myles na Gopaleen's (Flann O'Brien's) 'Cruiskeen Lawn' Commentaries on James Joyce." James Joyce Quarterly, 9 (Fall 1971): 50-62.

Sean O'Casey

[See also Atanas Slavov. "Ideyna nasochenost ...," No. 4328; Hugh B. Staples. "Mirror in his House," No. 5498.]

*707. KRAUSE, DAVID. Sean O'Casey. London: Mac-Gibbon and Kee; New York: Macmillan, 1960; New York: Collier Books, 1962, passim.

Frank O'Connor

708. EDWARDS, OWEN D. "O'Connor and Joyce." Scottish International, no. 8 (November 1969): 54-57.

BIOGRAPHICAL STUDIES

Sean O'Faolain

709. HARMON, MAURICE. *Sean O'Faolain: A Critical Introduction.* South Bend, London: University of Notre Dame Press, 1966, passim.

Boris Pasternak

*710. O'CASEY, SEAN. "Pasternak and Joyce." *Irish Times,* 19 July 1960. [See letters to the Editor: 'Quidnunc' [Seamus Kelly]. ibid., 20 July 1960; A. L. Wright. ibid., 22 July 1960; O'Casey. ibid., 26 July 1960; Monk Gibbon and A. L. Wright. ibid., 28 July 1960; James T. Farrell and F. R. O'Connor. ibid., 29 July 1960; Austin Clarke. ibid., 30 July 1960.]

Pablo Picasso

711. PACK, CLAUS. "Analogies: Joyce, Picasso, Klee," translated by Pierre Algaux. *Romàn,* no. 3 (June 1951): 264-268.

712. STEIN, GERTRUDE. *The Autobiography of Alice B. Toklas.* New York: Harcourt, Brace for the Literary Guild, 1933, p. 260.

Ezra Pound

[See also Noel Stock. "Joyce and Eliot...," No. 655; Enrico Falqui. "Marinetti...," No. 977; Jackson R. Bryer. "Pound to Joyce...," No. 3737; A. Walton Litz. "Pound and Eliot...," No. 3921; Egbert Faas. "Formen...," No. 4220; David Hayman. "Pound at the Wake...," No. 5427.]

713. ALVAREZ, A. "The Wretched Poet who Lived in the House of Bedlam." *Saturday Review,* 53 (19 July 1970): 27-29

714. GOODWIN, K. L. *The Influence of Ezra Pound.* London, New York: Oxford University Press, 1966, passim.

715. GUGLIELMI, JOSEPH. "Ezra Pound ou la saturation liveresque." *Cahiers du sud,* no. 389 (1966): 122-125.

716. HESSE, EVA, ed. *New Approaches to Ezra Pound.* Berkeley: University of California Press, 1969, passim.

717. KENNER, HUGH. *The Pound Era.* Berkeley: University of California Press, 1971, passim.

718. LEWIS, WYNDHAM. "Ezra: The Portrait of a Personality." *Quarterly Review of Literature,* 5, no. 2 (1949): 136-144.

719. MARÍN MORALES, JOSÉ A. "Radiografía epistolar: Joyce-Pound." *Arbor,* no. 318 (June 1972): 93-98.

*719a. NORMAN, CHARLES. *Ezra Pound.* New York: Macmillan, 1960, passim.

720. OLINTO, ANTÔNIO. "Renovaçao, Joyce e Pound," in *A verdade da ficçao.* Rio de Janeiro: Companhia Brasileira de Artes Gráficas, 1966, pp. 36-42.

*721. PAIGE, D. D., ed. *The Letters of Ezra Pound.* New York: Harcourt, Brace, 1950, pp. 51, 56, 109, 130, 133, 135, 153, 202, 221, et passim.

722. POUND, EZRA. "Past History." *English Journal,* 22 (May 1933): 349-358. [Reprinted in *College English,* 22 (November 1960): 81-86 and in Forrest Read's *Pound/Joyce,* No. 725.]

723. _____. "Tidings from Pound to Joyce." *Esquire,* 64 (December 1965): 152, 286-287. [Also in Read's *Pound/Joyce,* No. 725.]

724. READ, FORREST. "Ezra Pound et James Joyce: Les odysséens," translated by Pierre Alien. *L'Herne,* no. 7 (1966): 489-501. [Related to but different from his essay on Pound, Joyce and Flaubert in Hesse's *New Approaches to Pound,* No. 716.]

725. _____, ed. *Pound/Joyce: The Letters of Ezra Pound to James Joyce,* with Pound's Essays on Joyce. New York: New Directions, 1967; London: Faber and Faber, 1967. [Translated by Ruggero Bianchi. Milan: Rizzoli, 1968; translated by Mirko Lauer. Barcelona: Barral, 1971; translated by Philippe Lavergne. Paris: Mercure de France, 1970; translated by Hiltrud Marschall. Zürich: Verlag der Arche, 1972.]

726. _____. "Pound, Joyce and Flaubert: The Odysseans," in *New Approaches to Ezra Pound.* Edited by Eva Hesse, pp. 125-144, No. 716. [Also translated by Hiltrud Marschall in *Akzente,* 17 (June 1970): 266-286.]

726a. ROCHES, DENIS. "Joyce et Pound." *L'Arc,* no. 36 (1968): 42-43.

727. SCHNEIDAU, HERBERT N. "Pound and Joyce: The Universal in the Particular," in *Ezra Pound: The Image and the Real.* Baton Rouge: Louisiana State University Press, 1969, pp. 74-109.

728. THOMSON, VIRGIL. "Antheil, Joyce and Pound," in *Virgil Thomson.* New York: Knopf, 1966, pp. 73-83 and passim.

729. WAIN, JOHN. "The Prophet Ezra vs. 'The Egotistical Sublime.'" *Encounter,* 33 (August 1969): 53-70.

730. WIDMER, URS. "Ezra Pound: Abschied von James Joyce." *Woche,* 1 March 1967, pp. 6-7, 59.

Marcel Proust

[See also Wallace Fowlie. "Masques...," No. 982; H. D. Rankin. "Notes...," No. 1013; Floris Delattre. "L'influence de Marcel Proust...," No. 1366; Richard G. Stern. "Proust and Joyce...," No. 3209; Gerhard R. Kaiser, "Joyce, Ulysses," No. 3607; Hannes Schiefele. "Freuds Bedeutung...," No. 4200; Unsigned. "Proust, Joyce and...," No. 4255.]

*731. BROOKE, JOCELYN. "Proust and Joyce: The Case for the Prosecution." Adam, no. 297-298 (1961): 5-66. [With introductory notes by Miron Grindea, pp. 1-2, and Anthony Powell, pp. 3-4.]

732. BURGMÜLLER, HERBERT. "Zur Ästhetik des modernen Roman." Die Fähre, 1, no. 2 (1946): 111-120.

733. DEAKIN, WILLIAM. "D. H. Lawrence's Attacks on Proust and Joyce." Essays in Criticism, 7 (October 1957): 383-403.

734. DEBENEDETTI, GIACOMO. "Joyce e Proust," in Il romanzo del novecento. Milan: Garzanti, 1971, pp. 285-305.

*735. DIEBOLD, BERNHARD. "Totentanz: Von Proust und Joyce zu Musil." Neue Schweizer Rundschau, 12 (1944/45): 157-163, 210-219.

736. DREW, ELIZABETH A. The Enjoyment of Literature. New York: W. W. Norton, 1935, pp. 138-140.

737. KANTERS, ROBERT. "Rencontre entre deux univers." Figaro littéraire, 20 January 1966, p. 8.

738. LINDBERGER, ÖRJAN. "Eyvind Johnsons möte med Proust och Joyce." Bonniers litterära Magasin, 29 (1950): 554-563.

739. LINDSAY, JACK. "Time in Modern Literature," in Festschrift zum achtzigsten Geburtstag von Georg Lukács. Edited by Frank Benseler. Neuwied, Berlin: Luchterhand, 1965, pp. 491-501.

740. MONTGOMERY, NIALL. "Proust and Joyce." Dubliner, no. 4 (July-August 1962): 11-22.

741. MILLER, HENRY. "The Universe of Death." Phoenix, 1, no. 1 (Spring 1938): 33-64. [Reprinted in his The Cosmological Eye. Norfolk: New Directions Books, 1939, pp. 107-134.]

742. MIRSKII, DMITRII PETROVICH. "Dzheims Dzhois." Almanakh: God 16 (Moscow), no. 1 (1933): 428-450. [Translated by David Kinkead as "Joyce and Irish Literature." New Masses, 10-11 (3 April 1934): 31-34; translated by S. D. Kogan, International Literature, no. 1 (April 1934): 92-102.]

743. MURRAY, JOHN MIDDLETON. "Lemonade." The Adelphi, 4, no. 3 (September 1926): 193-149. [Extracted as "Proust, Joyce, Forster, and Lawrence," in Poets, Critics, Mystics. Edited by Richard Rees, Carbondale and Edwardsville: Southern Illinois University Press; London and Amsterdam: Feffer and Simons, 1970, pp. 55-58.]

744. PAINTER, GEORGE D. Proust: The Later Years. Boston: Little, Brown, 1965, pp. 340-342.

*745. TOMAS CABOT, JOSÉ. "En primera persona." Indice de artes y letras, 12 (March 1961): 3-4.

Arnold Schönberg

746. LAMBERT, CONSTANCE. Music Ho! A Study of Music in Decline. London: Faber, 1934, pp. 294-296; 3rd edition. London: Faber and Faber, 1966; New York: October House, pp. 249-252.

George Bernard Shaw

[See also William White. "GBS on Joyce's Exiles," No. 3531; Archibald Henderson. Table-Talk of GBS, No. 3593; William Hull. "Shaw...," No. 3874; George Bernard Shaw. "Letter," No. 4058; Shaw. "Literature and Science," No. 4060.]

747. BARR, ALAN P. "Shaw's Irish Contemporaries," in his Victorian Stage Pulpiteer: Bernard Shaw's Crusade. Athens: University of Georgia Press, 1973, pp. 41-54.

748. EGRI, PETER. "Ibsen, Joyce, and Shaw." Filológiai Közlöny, 13 (January-June 1966): 109-133. [In Hungarian]

May Sinclair

749. VINES, SHERARD. Movements in Modern English Poetry and Prose. Tokyo: Oxford University Press, 1927, pp. 264-271.

Gertrude Stein

[See also William Wasserstrom. "In Gertrude's Closet," No. 1022; Harry M. Beardsley. "James Joyce...," No. 4556.]

750. JOSEPHSON, MATTHEW. ["The Cult of James Joyce and Gertrude Stein"], in Fitzgerald and the Jazz Age. Edited by Malcolm and Robert Cowley. New York: Scribner's, 1966, pp. 105-107. [Reprinted from his Life Among the Surrealists, (1962).]

751. ROSA, VERA. "Gertrude Stein e James Joyce ovvero l'utopia nella letteratura del XX secolo." Umana, 20 (May-September 1971): 20.

BIOGRAPHICAL STUDIES

James Stephens

752. PYLE, HILARY. *James Stephens: His Work and an Account of his Life.* London: Routledge and Kegan Paul; New York: Barnes and Noble, 1965, *passim.*

Italo Svevo (Ettore Schmitz)

753. BENCO, SILVIO. "Italo Svevo." *Umana,* 20 (May-September 1971): 64-68.

754. CARLINI, FRANCO. "Italo Svevo personaggio-attore." *Umana,* 20 (May-September 1971): 60-63.

*755. de CASTRIS, A. LEONE. "Svevo e Joyce," in *Italo Svevo.* Saggi di varia unamità, no. 31. Pisa: Nistri-Lischi, 1959, pp. 323-340, *et passim.*

756. CSILLAGHY, ANDREA. "La fortuna di Italo Svevo e James Joyce in Ungheria e l'evoluzione del concetto di'realismo borghese." *Umana,* 20 (May-September 1971): 38-42.

757. DEBENEDETTI, GIACOMO. "Svevo e Joyce," in *Il romanzo del Novecento.* Milan: Garzanti, 1971, pp. 558-594.

758. DRAGHICI, SIMONA. "Joyce-Svevo-Professor şi Elev." *Secolul 20,* no. 6 (1968): 29-34.

759. ELLMAN, RICHARD. "Speaking of Books: Italo Svevo and Joyce." *New York Times Book Review,* 21 January 1968, pp. 2, 22.

760. FURBANK, P. N. "Svevo and James Joyce," in *Italo Svevo, the Man and the Writer.* London: Secker and Warburg; Berkeley and Los Angeles: University of California Press, 1966, pp. 78-91, *et passim.*

761. GALLI, LINA. "Livia Veneziani Svevo and James Joyce." *James Joyce Quarterly,* 9 (Spring 1972): 334-338.

762. GARDAIR, JEAN-MICHEL. "Joyce et Svevo." *L'Arc,* no. 36 (1968): 13-16.

763. JOYCE, STANISLAUS. "Joyce and Svevo." *The Stork,* 3, no. 12 (September 1932): 15-20.

*764. _____. "Introduction," to Svevo's *As a Man Grows Older.* Translated by Beryl De-Zoete. New York: New Directions, [c. 1950], pp. v-xii.

765. _____. *The Meeting of Svevo and Joyce.* Udine: Del Bianco Editore, 1965, 19pp. [First publication of lecture delivered at the University of Trieste, 27 May 1955, with a headnote by Sergio Perosa.]

766. KRATOCHWIL, GERMAN. "Svevo und Joyce in Trieste." *Süddeutsche Zeitung,* 11/12 September 1965.

767. LEVIN, HARRY. "Carteggio inedito Italo Svevo-James Joyce." *Inventario,* 2 (Spring 1949): 106-138. [Also in *Letters,* No. 317.]

768. MONTALE, EUGENIO. "Italo Svevo," translated by William Weaver. *Art and Literature,* no. 12 (Spring 1967): 9-31. [Appeared earlier in *Montale-Svevo: Lettere.* De Donato, Bari, 1966.]

769. PAIGE, D. D. "An Italian Joyce." *European,* no. 7 (September 1953): 36-45.

770. REDING, JOSEF. "Joyce's Sprachschuler: zu Italo Svevos Renaissance." *Welt und Wort,* 17 (February 1962): 39-40.

771. ROCCO-BERGERA, NINY. "La gelosia in James Joyce e Italo Svevo." *Umana,* 20 (May-September 1971): 52-66. [Reprinted in *Due saggi su James Joyce.* Trieste: Edizioni 'Umana,' 1971, pp. 53-71, no. 525.]

772. _____. "Joyce and Svevo: A Note." *Modern Fiction Studies,* 18 (Spring 1972): 116-117.

773. SELIG, KARL L. "Sveviana." *Modern Language Notes,* 71 (March 1956): 187-188.

774. SNOW, C. P. "Italo Svevo: Forerunner of Cooper and Amis." *Essays and Studies,* n.s. 14 (1961): 7-16.

775. SPAGNOLETTI, GIACINTO. "L'incontro con Joyce," in *Svevo: la vita, il pensiero, i testi esemplari.* Milan: Edizioni Accademia, 1972, pp. 69-74. [Reprints much of No. 781.]

776. SPAINI, ALBERTO. *Autoritratto triestino.* Milan: Giordani, 1963, *passim.*

777. STALEY, THOMAS F. "James Joyce and Italo Svevo." *Italica,* 40 (December 1963): 334-338. [Radio broadcast based on this article, James Joyce e Italo Svevo. Trieste: USIS and Associazione Italo-Americana di Trieste, 1965.]

778. _____. "The 'Italian Swabian': An English Assessment of Italo Svevo." *James Joyce Quarterly,* 3 (Summer 1966): 290-293. [Review of P. N. Furbank's *Italo Svevo,* No. 760.]

779. _____, ed. *Essays on Italo Svevo.* University of Tulsa, Department of English Monograph Series, no. 6. Tulsa: University of Tulsa, 1969, *passim.*

780. _____. "Character and Structure in Italo Svevo's *Una Vita.*" *Umana,* 20 (May-September 1971): 57-59.

781. SVEVO, ITALO. "Ulysses a Trieste." Il Convegno, 25 April 1937. ["James Joyce." Il Convegno, 18 (January 1938): 135-158 was originally a lecture delivered at Milan in 1927; brief portion of the latter appeared as "Trieste, 1907," translated by Herbert Alexander in Literary World, no. 1 (May 1934): 2; the lecture and later article were enlarged and were translated by Stanislaus Joyce as James Joyce. Norfolk: New Directions Books, 1950; entire thing reprinted in Svevo's "Scritti su Joyce," in Saggi e pagine sparse. Edited by Umbro Apollonio. Verona: Arnolda Mondadori, 1954, pp. 199-261; also translated by Jean-Michel Gardair. L'Arc, no. 36 (1968): 16-28; reprinted San Francisco: City Lights Books, 1969.]

782. SVEVO, LIVIA VENEZIANI (SCHMITZ). "Svevo et Joyce." Preuves, 5 (February 1955): 33-37. [See also No. 358.]

*783. TALARICO, E. "Svevo e Joyce." Fiera letteraria, no. 30 (1960): 1.

Jonathan Swift

[See also Thomas F. Staley. "The Poet Joyce ...," No. 2790; Robert Boyle. "Swiftian Allegory ...," No. 3113; Elaine M. Kauver. "Swift's Clothing Philosophy...," No. 3120; Lodwick Hartley. "'Swiftly Sterneward'...," No. 4480; L. A. G. Strong. "Three Ghosts...," No. 4290; Mackie L. Jarrell. "Joyce's Use of Swift's...," No. 4858; Mackie L. Jarrell. "Swiftiana...," No. 5435.]

784. STAVROU, C. N. "Gulliver's Voyage to the Land of Dubliners." South Atlantic Quarterly, 59 (Fall 1960): 490-499.

Arthur Symons

[See also Max Wildi. "James Joyce and...," No. 1025.]

785. BECKSON, KARL, and JOHN M. MUNRO. "Letters from Arthur Symons to James Joyce: 1904-1932." James Joyce Quarterly, 4 (Winter 1967): 91-101.

786. MUNRO, JOHN M. "Symons and the 'Moderns,'" in his Arthur Symons. Twayne's English Authors Series, no. 76. New York: Twayne, 1969, pp. 131-135.

John Millington Synge

787. PRITCHETT, V. S. "Current Literature: Books in General." New Statesman and Nation, 21 (19 April 1941): 413. [Reprinted as "The End of the Gael," in In My Good Books. London: Chatto and Windus, 1943, pp. 155-160.]

788. SULTAN, STANLEY. "A Joycean Look at The Playboy of the Western World," in The Celtic Master, pp. 45-55, No. 1583.

Dylan Thomas

[See also Walford Davies. "Imitations...," No. 1435; Horst Meller. "Zum literarischen...," No. 1471; Warren French. "Two Portraits...," No. 3324; Richard Kelly. "The Lost Vision...," No. 3349.]

789. BRUNS, GERALD L. "Daedalus, Orpheus, and Dylan Thomas's Portrait of the Artist." Renascence, 25 (Spring 1973): 147-156.

Joachim von Fiore

790. WEISS, WOLFGANG. "James Joyce und Joachim von Fiore." Anglia, 85, no. 1 (1967): 58-63.

Harriet Shaw Weaver

[See also Jane Lidderdale. Dear Miss Weaver, No. 335; Lidderdale. "Harriet Weaver...," No. 3916.]

791. PAINTER, GEORGE D. "The New Free Woman with Novel Inside: Harriet Weaver and James Joyce." Encounter, 36 (May 1971): 75-78.

792. PRITCHETT, V. S. "Passion of the Virgin." New Statesman, 80 (27 November 1970): 715-716.

Rebecca West

793. HALPER, NATHAN. "James Joyce and Rebecca West." Partisan Review, 16 (July 1949): 761-763.

Ludwig Wittgenstein

794. TORRE, GUILLERMO de. "Una crisis del lenguaje: Wittgenstein, Joyce, la 'Escritura de la Nada,'" in his Problematica de la literatura. Buenos Aires: Editorial Losada, 1951, pp. 85-89; second edition, 1958.

Thomas Wolfe

[See Elizabeth Nowell. Letters of Thomas Wolfe, No. 1393; Nathan L. Rothman. "Thomas Wolfe ...," No. 1400; Thomas Wolfe. Notebooks, No. 1416; Dudley Fitts. "Two Aspects...," No. 1440; Harry E. Netterville. "George Webber...," No. 1478.]

Virginia Woolf

[See also Morris Beja. Epiphany..., No. 2826; Melvin J. Friedman. "Three Experiences...," No. 3577; Leonard Woolf. Beginning Again, No. 3676; Virginia Woolf. Writer's Diary, No. 3677; David Garnett. "Jacob's Room," No. 3819; Karl Arns. "Die Bewusstseinskunst...," No. 4185; Liisa Dahl. Linguistic Patterns..., No. 4186; Liisa Dahl. "Attributive Sentence Structure...," No. 4212; Mihai Miroiu. "In the Stream...," No. 4238; Judith P. Moss. "Elijah Ben Bloom," No. 4573.]

BIOGRAPHICAL STUDIES

795. CHAMBERS, R. L. The Novels of Virginia Woolf. Edinburgh: Oliver and Boyd, 1947, pp. 25-28.

796. FRIED, ERICK. "James Joyce und Virginia Woolf." Die Brücke (Essen), no. 220 (1951).

797. GUIGUET, JEAN. Virginia Woolf and her Works. Translated by Jean Stewart. London: Hogarth Press; New York: Harcourt, Brace and World, 1965, pp. 241-245 and passim. [Translation of Virginia Woolf et son oeuvres. Études anglaises, no. 13. Paris: Didier, 1962.]

798. HATCHER, HARLAN. "A Scene of Confusion." College English, 4 (December 1942): 153-159.

*799. HENDERSON, PHILIP. "Virginia Woolf." Everyman, 2, no. 43 (21 November 1929): 453.

800. MIROIU, MIHAI. "Folosierea montajului în romanul englez Modern." Studii de literatura universala, 11 (1968): 173-181.

*801. MUIR, EDWIN. "Contemporary Writers: V--Virginia Woolf." Nation and Athenaeum, 17 April 1926, pp. 70-72.

802. O'FAOLAIN, SEAN. "Virginia Woolf and James Joyce, or Narcissa and Lucifer," in his The Vanishing Hero: Studies in Novelists of the Twenties. Boston: Little, Brown, 1956, pp. 170-204; London: Eyre and Spottiswoode, 1956, pp. 193-222. [Reprinted Freeport, New York: Books for Libraries Press, 1971, pp. 170-204.]

Thornton Wilder

[See also Joseph Campbell. "Skin of Whoose Teeth?...," No. 5012; John Modic. "Eclectic...," No. 5141; Henry M. Robinson. "Curious Case...," No. 5174.]

803. HABERMAN, DONALD. The Plays of Thornton Wilder. Middletown, Conn.: Wesleyan University Press, 1967, passim.

William Butler Yeats

[See also John A Lester. "Joyce, Yeats, and ...," No. 2924; Ben L. Collins. "Joyce's Use of ...," No. 3107; George L. Geckle. "Stephen Dedalus...," No. 3326; Herbert V. Fackler, "Stephen Dedalus...," No. 3438; Marion Witt. "A Note on Joyce and...," No. 4536.]

*804. ELIOT, T. S. "A Foreign Mind." Athenaeum, 4 July 1919, pp. 552-553.

805. ELLMANN, RICHARD. "Joyce and Yeats." Kenyon Review, 12 (Autumn 1950): 618-638. [Translated by Luigi Berti in Inventario, 4 (March-April 1952): 18-31; also in Ellmann's The Identity of Yeats. London: Macmillan,

1954 and in his Eminent Domain. New York: Oxford University Press, 1967, pp. 29-56 as "The Hawklike Man" which also appears in Yeats and Joyce. Yeats Centenary Papers, vol. 11. Dublin: Dolmen Press; London: Oxford University Press, 1967.]

*806. GOPALEEN, MYLES na (Flann O'Brien, Brian Nolan). "Cruiskeen Lawn." Irish Times, 11 April 1957.

807. _____ . "Cruiskeen Lawn." Irish Times, 15 January 1965.

808. MOORE, JOHN REES. "Artifices for Eternity: Joyce and Yeats." Éire-Ireland, 3 (Winter 1968): 66-73.

809. ROLLINS, RONALD G. "Portraits of Four Irishmen as Artists: Verisimilitude and Vision." Irish University Review, 1 (Spring 1971): 189-197. [Yeats, O'Casey, Synge, Joyce.]

810. SIDNELL, M. J. "A Daintical Pair of Accomplasses: Joyce and Yeats," in Litters from Aloft, pp. 50-73, No. 1516.

*811. TRENCH, W. F. "Correspondence: Dr. Yeats and Mr. Joyce." Irish Statesman, 2, no. 25 (30 August 1924): 790.

812. WOLFF-WINDEGG, PHILIPP. "Auf der Suche nach dem Symbol: James Joyce und W. B. Yeats." Symbolon, 5 (1966): 39-52.

813. YEATS, WILLIAM BUTLER. "A Poet on Writers." Daily Mail (London), 8 October 1932.

814. _____ . The Letters of W. B. Yeats. Edited by Allan Wade. New York: Macmillan, 1955, pp. 597, 598-599, 679, et passim.

815. _____ . Explorations. Selected by Mrs. W. B. Yeats. New York: Macmillan, 1962, p. 333.

816. _____ . The Senate Speeches of W. B. Yeats. Edited by Donald R. Pearce. Bloomington, Ind.: Indiana University Press, 1969, pp. 145-148.

Stefan Zweig

*817. ZWEIG, STEFAN. The World of Yesterday. New York: Viking Press, 1943, pp. 275-276.

REMINISCENCES AND MEMOIRS

See also Benco. "Un illustre scrittore...," No. 365; Borach. "Gespräche mit James Joyce, No. 375; Boyd. "James Joyce: Memories," No. 376; Bruno. "James Joyce in Italia," No. 379; Colum, P. "With James Joyce in Ireland," No. 390; Frank. "Souvenirs sur James Joyce," No. 435; Francini Bruni. "Ricordi su James Joyce," No. 434; Gillet. "Recuerdos de James Joyce," No. 444; Jolas, M. "Joyce en 1939-1940," No. 474; Joyce, S. "Ricordi di James Joyce," No. 476; Soupault. "Autour de

James Joyce," No. 547; Stephens. "The Joyce I
Knew," No. 554; Arthur Power. "Joyce among the
Poets," No. 604.

Books

*818. ACTON, HAROLD. Memoirs of an Aesthete.
London: Methuen, 1948, pp. 160, 161, 211.

*819. ADAMS, FRANKLIN P. The Diary of Our own
Samuel Pepys, vol. 1. New York: Simon
and Schuster, 1935, pp. 457, et passim.

820. ALDINGTON, RICHARD. Life for Life's Sake:
A Book of Reminiscences. New York:
Viking Press, 1941, pp. 143-144, 324-326.

821. BEDFORD, SYBILLE. Aldous Huxley: A Biography, vol. 1. London: Chatto and Windus,
1973, p. 216.

822. BLISS, ARTHUR. As I Remember. London: Faber
and Faber, 1970, pp. 100-101.

823. BUDGEN, FRANK. "Mr. Joyce," in his Myselves
When Young. London, New York: Oxford
University Press, 1970, pp. 181-204, et
passim.

824. BUTCHER, FANNY. Many Lives--One Love. New
York: Harper and Row, 1972, passim.

825. CALLAGHAN, MORLEY. That Summer in Paris:
Memories of Tangled Friendships with
Hemingway, Fitzgerald, and some Others.
New York: Coward-McCann, 1963, passim.

826. COWLEY, MALCOLM. Think Back on Us. Edited
by Henry Dan Piper. Carbondale, Ill.:
Southern Illinois University Press, 1967,
passim.

*827. CROSBY, CARESSE. The Passionate Years.
London: Redman, 1953, pp. 181-187.

*828. CUNARD, NANCY. "Visits with James Joyce,"
in Nancy Cunard: Brave Poet, Indomitable
Rebel, 1896-1965. Edited by Hugh Ford.
Philadelphia: Chilton, 1968, pp. 81-82.

829. _____ . These were the Hours: Memories
of My Hours Press, Reanville and Paris,
1928-1931. Edited by Hugh Ford. Carbondale and Edwardsville: Southern Illinois
University Press; London and Amsterdam:
Feffer and Simons, 1969, pp. 112-117.

830. DAHLBERG, EDWARD. The Confessions. New
York: George Braziller, 1971, passim.

831. ECO, UMBERTO. "Uno due tre: nessuno," "My
Exagmination," in his Diario Minimo. 3rd
Edition. Milan: Arnoldo Mondadori, 1966,
pp. 14-21, 109-125.

832. FLANNER, JANET (Genêt). Paris Was Yesterday,
1925-1939. Edited by Irving Drutman. New

York: Viking Press, 1972, passim. [See
also her "That was Paris." New Yorker,
11 March 1972, pp. 32-36.]

833. FRANK, NINO. "L'ombre qui avait perdue son
homme," in his Mémoire brisée, vol. 1.
Paris: Clamann-Lévy, 1967, pp. 27-64. [A
selection appeared as "La joyeuse partie
de campagne de James Joyce." Figaro littéraire, 8 May 1967, p. 27.]

834. GLASSCO, JOHN. Memoirs of Montparnasse.
Toronto, New York: Oxford University
Press, 1970, passim.

*835. GOGARTY, OLIVER ST. JOHN. As I Was Going
Down Sackville Street. New York: Reynal
and Hitchcock, 1937, pp. 83, 293-299;
London: Sphere, 1968, paperback reprint;
New York: Harvest, 1967, paperback reprint.

*836. _____ . Tumbling in the Hay. London:
Constable, 1939, pp. 188-194.

*837. _____ . Rolling Down the Lea. London:
Constable, 1950, pp. 116-117.

*838. _____ . "Joyce as a Joker," in his Start
from Somewhere Else. New York: Doubleday,
1955, pp. 82-85.

*839. GUGGENHEIM, PEGGY. Out of This Century. New
York: Dial, 1946, passim.

*840. HAMNETT, NINA. Laughing Torso. London:
Constable, 1932, passim.

*841. HOFFMEISTER, ADOLF. "James Joyce," "Osobnost
James Joyce," in Podoby. Prague: Čéskos-
lovenský Spisovatel, 1961, pp. 71-78, 118-
126. [Translated by Ela Ripellino. "Un
incontro con James Joyce." Europa letteraria, 2, nos. 13-14 (February-April 1962):
55-63; translated by François Kerel.
"James Joyce," "La personnalité de James
Joyce," in Visages écrits et dessinés.
Paris: Les Editeurs Français Réunis, 1964,
pp. 39-47, 48-60.]

842. _____ . Páríz & Okolí. Prague: Českoslov-
enský Spisovatel, 1967, passim.

*843. HUDDLESTON, SISLEY. Paris Salons, Cafés,
Studios. Philadelphia: Lippincott, 1928,
pp. 208-220.

*844. _____ . Back to Montparnasse. Philadel-
phia: Lippincott, 1931, pp. 192-203.

*845. IMBS, BRAVIG. Confessions of Another Young
Man. New York: Henkle-Yewdale, 1936,
passim.

846. JORDAN, JOHN. "Joyce without Fears: A Personal Journey," in A Bash in the Tunnel,
pp. 135-146, No. 1644.

BIOGRAPHICAL STUDIES

*847. KAHANE, JACK. Memoirs of a Booklegger.
London: Joseph, 1939, pp. 218, 238.

848. MacDIARMID, HUGH. The Company I've Kept:
Essays in Autobiography. Berkeley:
University of California Press, 1967,
passim.

*849. MAYOUX, JEAN-JACQUES. Vivants, piliers.
Paris: Juilliard, 1960, passim.

850. NICOLSON, HAROLD. The Desire to Please.
London: Constable, 1943, pp. 136-139.

851. _____ . Diaries and Letters, 1930-1939.
Edited by Nigel Nicolson. London, New
York: Atheneum, 1966, pp. 83-84, 164-
165, 401.

852. O'CONNOR, ULICK, ed. The Joyce We Knew.
Cork: Mercier Press, 1967.
Contents: Eugene Sheehy, from May it
Please the Court, pp. 13-35, No. 356;
William G. Fallon, 37-59; Padraic Colum,
from Our Friend James Joyce, 61-91, No.
298; Arthur Power, from From the Old
Waterford House, 93-123, No. 586.

853. POWER, ARTHUR. "James Joyce--The Internationalist," in A Bash in the Tunnel, pp.
181-188, No. 1644.

*854. QUENEAU, RAYMOND. Batons, chiffres et let-
tres. Paris: Gallimard, 1950. ["Une
traduction en joycien," pp. 171-173 is
the opening paragraphs of Gueule de
pierre, (1934), revised and enlarged as
Saint Glinglin, (1948).]

*855. RAIMONDI, GUISEPPE. "Qualcosa su James
Joyce," in his Lo scrittoio. Milan:
Edizioni "Il saggiatore," 1960, pp.
129-133.

*856. SLOCOMBE, GEORGE. The Tumult and the Shout-
ing. New York: Macmillan, 1936, pp. 220-
221.

Periodical Articles

857. BEASLAI, PIARAS. "Joyce among the Journalists." Irish Digest, 75 (September 1962):
71-74. [From the Irish Independent.]

858. BENCO, SILVIO. "Ricordi di Joyce." Umana,
20 (May-September 1971): 6-12.

859. BUDGEN, FRANK. "Joyce and Martha Fleischmann: A Witness's Recollection." Tri-
Quarterly, 8 (Winter 1967): 189-194.

860. COWLEY, MALCOLM. "When a young American...,"
Mercure de France, 347 (August-September
1963): 57-59.

*861. FRANCINI BRUNI, ALESSANDRO. "Ricordi person-
ali su James Joyce." Nuova antologia,
441 (September-December 1947): 71-79

*862. FRANK, NINO. "Visages a la minute: James
Joyce." Intransigeant (Paris), 6 February 1930.

*863. FREUND, GISÈLE. "En rouge et en noir." Fig-
aro littéraire, 20 January 1966, p. 8.

*864. GIEDION-WELCKER, CAROLA. "Eine Ausstellung
zum Gedächtnis von James Joyce." Basler
Nachrichten (Paris), no. 494 (18 November
1949): 1.

865. GILLET, GUILLAUME. "Un diner en ville."
Figaro littéraire, 20 January 1966, p. 9.

866. GOGARTY, OLIVER ST. JOHN. "James A. Joyce."
Times Herald (Dallas), 3 April 1949.

*867. HARMSWORTH, DESMOND. "James Joyce: A Sketch."
Harper's Bazaar, (April 1949): 128-129, 198.

868. HELWIG, WERNER. "Erinnerung an James Joyce."
Merkur, 24 (July 1970): 693-695.

869. "Hermes Rubrique." "Journal de Jacques Mercanton sur Joyce." Tel quel, 14 (Summer
1963): 42-43.

870. HONE, JOSEPH. "A Recollection of James
Joyce." Envoy, 5 (May 1951): 44-45. [Re-
printed in A Bash in the Tunnel, pp. 53-54,
No. 1644.]

871. JOLAS, EUGENE. "My Friend James Joyce."
Partisan Review, 8 (March-April 1941): 82-
93. [Reprinted in The Partisan Reader.
New York: Dial, 1946, pp. 457-468 and in
James Joyce: Two Decades of Criticism, pp.
3-18, No. 1570.]

872. KEMPF, ROGER. "Ma première impression de
vous." L'Arc, no. 36 (1968): 63-66.

873. KUEHL, JOHN. "A la Joyce: The Sister's Fitzgerald's Absolution." James Joyce Quarterly, 2, no. 1 (Fall 1964): 2-6.

874. LENNON, PETER. "James Joyce's 'Nurse' Remembers." Irish Digest, 74 (June 1962): 60-
64. [From the Guardian.]

*875. LÉON, PAUL. "In Memory of Joyce." Poésie,
no. 5 (1942): 35. [Also appeared in James
Joyce Yearbook, pp. 116-125, No. 1596.]

*876. LYND, SYLVIA. "Some Recollections of James
Joyce: In London." Time and Tide, 22, no.
4 (25 January 1941): 65-66.

877. McCARTHY, MARY. "Exiles, Expatriates and In-
ternal Emigres." Listener, no. 2226 (25
November 1971): 705-708. [Reprinted in
New York Review of Books, 18, no. 4 (9
March 1972): 4, 6-7, 8.]

878. MATTIONI, STELIO. "My Friend, James Joyce."
James Joyce Quarterly, 9 (Spring 1972):
339-341.

879. MEAGHER, JAMES A. "Stories of Joyce and Myself." Hibernia, 33 (6-26 June 1969): 19.

880. MERCANTON, JACQUES. "Les heures de James Joyce." Mercure de France, 348 (1963): 89-117, 284-315. [Translated by Lloyd C. Parks as "The Hours of James Joyce, Part I." Kenyon Review, 24 (Autumn 1962): 700-730; "The Hours of James Joyce, Part II." ibid., 25 (Winter 1963): 93-118; Les Heures de James Joyce. Lausanne: Éditions l'Age d'Homme, 1967.]

*881. MIRKOVIĆ, VLADIMIR. [n.t.]. Novine mladih (Zagreb), 13 (23 January 1954): 7; Nedeljne informativne novine (Beograd), 4 (28 February 1954): 65; Globus (Zagreb), no. 28 (1960): 43. [Memoirs of Amalija Globocnik.]

*882. MYERS, ROLLO H. "Some Recollections of James Joyce: In Paris." Time and Tide, 22, no. 4 (25 January 1941): 66.

883. _____. "Memories of Le Boeuf sur le toit." Listener, 25 February 1971, pp. 242-245.

*884. NICHOLS, LEWIS. "Joyce." New York Times Book Review, 7 February 1960, p. 8.

885. NORDIO, MARIO. "My First English Teacher." James Joyce Quarterly, 9 (Spring 1972): 323-325.

886. O'BRIEN, CONOR CRUISE. "Joyce's Ireland." Saturday Review, 50 (11 March 1967): 56-57, 88.

*887. PAŠTROVIĆ, STANKO. "Zagrepcanin--dak Jamesa Joycea." Vjesnik (Zagreb), 8, no. 3 (1966): 20.

888. POLIAGHI, NORA FRANCA. "James Joyce, An Occasion of Remembrance." James Joyce Quarterly, 9 (Spring 1972): 326-327.

889. PORTER, KATHERINE ANNE. "From the Notebooks of Katherine Anne Porter." Southern Review, 1 (July 1965): 570-573. [Reprinted in Collected Essays and Occasional Writings. New York: Delacorte, 1970, pp. 298-300.]

890. POWER, ARTHUR. "At a Party with Joyce." Irish Digest, 51 (September 1954): 27-29. [Condensed from Irish Tatler and Sketch; see also "Conversations with Joyce." James Joyce Quarterly, 3 (Fall 1965): 41-49.]

*891. QUENEAU, RAYMOND. "James Joyce, Auteur Classique." Volontés, no. 9 (1 September 1938): 20-23. [Reprinted in his Le voyage en Grèce. Paris: Gallimard, 1973, pp. 130-135.]

892. REES, LESLIE. "Clongowes, The Tower and a Meeting with James Joyce." Meanjin Quarterly, 27 (Spring 1968): 328-335.

893. SAVIO, ANTONIO FONDA, and LETIZIA FONDA SAVIO. "James Joyce, Two Reminiscences." James Joyce Quarterly, 9 (Spring 1972): 320-322.

*894. STARK, HELMUTH. "Eine Begegnung aus dem Jahr 1915." Akzente, 8 (April 1961): 155-157.

895. NO ENTRY.

*896. SUTER, AUGUST. "Some Reminiscences of James Joyce." James Joyce Quarterly, 7 (Summer 1970): 191-198.

*897. SVEVO, ITALO (Ettore Schmitz). "Ricordi zu James Joyce." Fiera letteraria, 27 March 1927.

898. WADSWORTH, P. BEAUMONT. "Visits with James Joyce." James Joyce Quarterly, 1 (Summer 1964): 14-18.

899. WESCOTT, GLENWAY. "Memories and Opinions." Prose, 5 (Fall 1972): 177-202.

*900. Unsigned. "Eine Erinnerung an James Joyce." Weltwoche, 17 January 1941.

901. Unsigned. "James Joyce w seietle biografii i wsoomnien." Dialog (Warsaw), 9 (December 1964): 124-126.

INTERVIEWS

See also Alice Curtayne. "Portrait of the Artist as Brother," No. 409; Phillips. "Jim Joyce...," No. 515; Staley. "James Joyce in Trieste," No. 552; Lansdell. "An Adventurer in Color," No. 908.

902. BINCHY, MAEVE. "Uncle Jimmy Remembered." Irish Times, 2 September 1971, p. 10. [Bozena Delimata, daughter of Eileen Joyce Schaurek.]

903. CHURCHILL, THOMAS. "An Interview with Anthony Burgess." Malahat Review, 17 (January 1971): 103-127.

*904. COWLEY, MALCOLM. Writers at Work. New York: Viking Press, 1958, pp. 40-275. [Interviews with: Mauriac, pp. 135-139; Faulkner, 173-179; Frank O'Connor, 198; Robert Penn Warren, 228; Alberto Moravia, 274-275.]

905. DALY, LEO. "James Joyce Interviewed by Leo Daly." Hibernia, 36 (3 November 1972): 17. [Imaginary]

906. FULFORD, ROBERT. "The Rising Cult of James Joyce." Toronto Daily Star, 21 August 1965, p. 22. [Interview with Harry Pollock.]

BIOGRAPHICAL STUDIES

907. LENNOX, MAUD. "My Father--By Giorgio Joyce." Sunday Press (Dublin), 18 June 1967, p. 17.

908. LANSDELL, SARAH. "An Adventurer in Color." Louisville Courier-Journal Magazine, 29 August 1965, pp. 33-39. [Henry Strater]

*909. LeFEVRE, FREDERIC. "une heure avec M. Valery Larbaud." Les nouvelles littéraires, 2, no. 51 (6 October 1923): 1-2.

*910. "Les Trieze." "Les Lettres." Intransigeant (Paris), 23 February 1933. [Hypothetic conversation between Joyce and Cesar Abin.]

911. M., I. "Seed Cake for Tea." Irish Independent, 12 February 1965, p. 13. [Interview with Mme. Paul Léon.]

912. O'DOHERTY, BRIAN. "A Sister Recalls Joyce in Dublin." New York Times, 3 February 1964, p. 25. [Mary (May) Joyce Monaghan.]

913. "Onlooker." "The Man Who Thinks There is too Much Literary Talent in Ireland." Irish Press, 29 July 1966, p. 10. [Fritz Senn]

*914. PEMBER, JOHN E. [n.t.]. Herald (Boston), 31 March 1929. [Interview with Thornton Wilder.]

915. TEGENBOSCH, LAMBERT. "Ontdekking von Eindhovense Huisvrouw." De Volkskrant (Amsterdam), 22 November 1969, p. 27. [Interview with Bernardine Wijffels-Smulders.]

*916. TERY, SIMONE. "Recontre avec James Joyce, Irlandais." Les nouvelles littéraires, 4, no. 126 (14 March 1925): 6.

*917. VINDING, OLE. "Et interview med Joyce." Forum: Tidsskrift for Teater, Musik, Literatur, Film, (1941): 21-22. [Shortened version in Perspektiv, 6, no. 8 (Summer 1959): 14-16; reprinted as "James Joyce i København," in his Vejen til den halve verden. Copenhagen: Gyldendalske Forlag, 1963, pp. 198-209.]

*918. W[EKKER], H[ERMAN]. "Cultus Wordt een Industrie." De Tijd (Amsterdam), 13 December 1969, p. 3. [Interview with Fritz Senn.]

*919. Unsigned. "Ecce Puer." New Yorker, 23 (5 April 1947): 26-27. [Interview with Stephen Joyce.]

920. Unsigned. "Interview with Mr. John Stanislaus Joyce," in James Joyce Yearbook, pp. 159-169, No. 1596. [Possibly Flann O'Brien, doubtless spurious.]

921. Unsigned. "Sister." New Yorker, 40 (14 March 1964): 34-36. [Interview with Mary (May) Joyce Monaghan.]

922. Unsigned. [n.t.]. Journal-Courier (Louisville), 24 February 1929. [Interview with Elizabeth Madox Roberts.]

*923. Unsigned. [n.t.]. Times-Start (Cincinnati), 3 November 1928. [Interview with Padraic Colum.]

GENERAL STUDIES

PROVENIENCE: INFLUENCES ON JOYCE

See II.B "Poetry": Staley. "Poet Joyce and the Shadow of Swift," No. 2790; del Greco Lobner. "James Joyce's 'Tilly' and Gabriel d'Annunzio's..," No. 2805; II.C. "Epiphanies": Marcus. "George Moore's Dublin 'Epiphanie' and Joyce," No. 2838; Wiehl. "Johannes V. Jenson's Myte and...," No. 2845; Walzl. "Liturgy of the Epiphany Season...," No. 2844; II.D "Dubliners": Carrier. "Dubliners: Joyce's Dantean Vision," No. 2897; Church. "Dante and Vico," No. 2899; Duffy. "Ernest Dowson...," No. 2906; Duffy. "Stories of Frederick Wedmore..," No. 2907; Kennedy. "Moore's Untilled Field...," No. 2922; Lyons. "James Joyce and Chaucer's Prioress," No. 2993; Taube. "Joyce and Shakespeare," No. 3018; Wilding. "James Joyce's 'Eveline' and...," No. 3020; Harmon. "Little Chandler and Byron's 'First Poem,'" No. 3039; Sider. "'Counterparts' and the Odyssey," No. 3054; Krandias. "Mr. Duffy and the Song of Songs," No. 3091; Reid. "The Beast of the Jungle and 'A Painful Case,'" No. 3094; Sloan. "The D'Annunzian Narrator...," No. 3096; Collins. "Joyce's Use of Yeats and...," No. 3107; Boyle. "Swiftian Allegory and Dantean Parody...," No. 3113; Kauver. "Swift's Clothing Philosophy...," No. 3120; Newman. "Land of Ooze...," No. 3123; Niemeyer. "Grace and Joyce's Method of Parody," No. 3124; Kelleher. "Irish History and Mythology...," No. 3167; Friedrich. "Bret Hart as a Source...," No. 3159; Moseley. "'Two Sights for Ever a Picture,'" No. 3177; Schmidt. "Hauptmann's Michael Kramer...," No. 3185; Ware. "Miltonic Allusion...," No. 3194; Verhaeghen. "Capriolen om Joyce...," No. 2938; II.F "Portrait": Eco. "Joyce et d'Annunzio," No. 2828; Walzl. "Liturgy...," No. 2844; Arnold. "Consideration of Joyce's Aesthetic Theory...," No. 3428; White. "Note on Joyce's Aesthetic," No. 3469; Fernando. "Language and Reality...," No. 3441; Gordon. "Dialogue of Life and Art...," No. 3332; Hayman. "Portrait of the Artist and L'Education Sentimentale," No. 3334; O'Connor. "James Joyce," No. 3460; Morin. "Joyce as Thomist," No. 3458; Reyes. "Difference of Grammar," No. 3383; Gillam. "Stephen Kouros," No. 3479; Feshbach. "Dramatic First Step...," No. 3442; Beebe. "Joyce and Aquinas," No. 3431; Bredin. "Joyce e l'Aquinate," No. 3435; II.G "Exiles": Benstock. "Exiles, Ibsen, and the Play's Function...," No. 3500; Dev. "Artist in Ibsen and Joyce," No. 3505; Lemarchand. "Un discipline egare d'Ibsen," No. 3520; Tysdahl. Joyce's Exiles and Ibsen," No. 3530; II.H "Ulysses": Hartley. "Swiftly Sterneward...," No. 4480; Jacobson. "Joyce and the Iliad," No. 4699;

Arneri. "Les travestissements...," No. 4852;
Kaplan. "Dickens' Flora Finching and Joyce's
Molly Bloom," No. 4598; Henke. "James Joyce and
Festus," No. 4481; Jarrell. "Joyce's Use of
Swift's 'Polite Conversation'...," No. 4858;
Lincecum. "Victorian Precursor...," No. 4235;
McMillan. "Influences of Gerhardt Hauptmann...,"
No. 4497; Mitchell. "Hans Henry John and James
Joyce," No. 4239; Moucheron. "Joyce and Shakes-
peare," No. 4505; Paley. "Blake in Nighttown,"
No. 4449; Reynolds. "Joyce's Planetary Music...,"
No. 4516; Ridgeway. "Two Authors...," No. 4517;
Starkie. "Miguel de Cervantes...," No. 4525;
Stavrou. "Love Songs of Swift...," No. 4526;
Sultan. "An Old Irish Model...," No. 4528; Sum-
merhayes. "Joyce's U and Whitman's 'Self'...,"
No. 4529; Waidner. "U by way of Culture and An-
archy," No. 3657; Senn. "Aesthetic Theories," No.
4741; Novak. "Verisimilitude and Vision...," No.
4899; Schwartz. "Eccles Street and Canterbury...,"
No. 4608; Engstrom. "A Few Comparisons...," No.
4202; Dalton. "Sources...," No. 4466; Mercier.
"Justice...," No. 4236; Prescott. "Homer's
Odyssey and...," No. 4322; Clark. "Joyce and
Blakean Vision," No. 4461; Hall. "Joyce's Use of
Da Ponte...," No. 4478; Paris. "Hamlet et ses
freres," No. 4509; Kain. "AE's Cooperative Watch
...," No. 4484; Livermore. "Carmen and U," No.
4494; Magalaner. "Layrinthine Motif...," No. 4498;
Stanford. "The Mysticism that Pleased Him," No.
4524; Strong. "Three Ghosts and...," No. 4527;
Tindall. "Dante and Mrs. Bloom," No. 4531; Whit-
aker. "Drinkers and History," No. 4534; Walsh.
"In the Name of the Father...," No. 4109; Schie-
fele. "Freuds Bedeutung...," No. 4200; Steinberg.
"Sources of the Stream," No. 4201; Paez. "Acara
de los origenes...," No. 4241; Esch. "James Joyce
und Homer," No. 4260; Mercier. "James Joyce and
Irish Tradition," No. 4265; Ellmann. "U and the
Odyssey," No. 4294; Koch. "An Approach...," No.
4309; Lord. "Heroes of Ulysses and...," No. 4312;
Nolan. Irish Writing, No. 4318; Wykes. "The Odys-
sey in U," No. 4340; Schutte. Joyce and Shakes-
peare, No. 4404; Duncan. "Unsubstantial Father..
.," No. 4414; Edwards. "Hamlet Motif in...," No.
4415; Heine. "Shakespeare in...," No. 4419; Ken-
ner. "Homer's Sticks and Bones," No. 4420; Link.
"U and...," No. 4421; Morse. "Mr. Joyce and
Shakespeare," No. 4426; Peery. "Sources of Joyce's
Shakespeare Criticism," No. 4429; Stanford.
"Joyce's First Meeting with U," No. 4433; White.
"A Note on Joyce's Esthetic," No. 3469; Prescott.
"Mosenthal's Deborah...," No. 4710; Dibble. "Vico,
Bruno and Stephen...," No. 5264; Bauerle. "Merca-
dante's 'Seven Last Words'...," No. 4758; Korg.
"Possible Source," No. 4859; II.I "Finnegans
Wake": Atherton. "Lewis Carroll and...," No.
5369; Atherton. "A Royal Divorce in...," No. 5374;
Atherton. "To Give Down...," No. 5376; Atherton.
"Lodge's The Survival of Man...," No. 5380; Ath-
erton. "French Argot in...," No. 5352; Graham.
"re'furloined notepaper...," No. 5416; Dalton.
"Kiswahili...," No. 5394; Halper. "Passage...,"
No. 5418; Atherton. "Scandinavian Elements...,"
No. 5378; Atherton. "Maunder's Praise...," No.
5379; Atherton. "Peacock...," No. 4840; Aubert.
"Notes on the French Elements...," No. 5381;
Bates. "Finnish...," No. 5382; Begnal. "Shaunspace

in...," No. 5553; Begnal. "Fables of...," No. 5383.
Benstock. "Americana in...," No. 5384; Benstock.
"Persian in...," No. 5385; Blake. "Identifications
...," No. 5564; Boldereff. Hermes..., No. 5353;
Bonheim. Lexicon of the German..., No. 5354; Broes.
"Bible in...," No. 5386; Burgess. "Mark Twain and
James Joyce," No. 5390; de Campos. "Lewis Carroll
...," No. 4916; Canby. "Gyring and Gimbling...,"
No. 5276; Carlson. "Henrik Ibsen and...," No. 5391;
Christiani. Scandinavian Elements..., No. 5356;
Cope. "From Egyptian Rubbish Heaps to...," No.
5393; Dalton. "Re 'Kiswahili words'...," No. 5394;
Faj. "La filosofia vichiana...," No. 5399; Gilman.
"Joyce and Sealsfield?," No. 5604; Glasheen. "av-
tokinatown," No. 5405; Glasheen. "Authoress of
Paradise Lost," No. 5410; Gleckner. "Byron in...,"
No. 5359; Halper. "Joyce and...Cabell," No. 5423;
Hart and Sullivan. "Australiana in...," No. 5425;
Hayman. "Tristan and Isolde...," No. 5426; Hodgart.
"Lithuanian Words...," No. 5431; Hollingdale. "A
Note on...," No. 5433; Kiralis. "Joyce and Blake,"
No. 5441; Jenkins. "A. C. Swinburne...," No. 5436;
Koch. "Giordano Bruno and...," No. 5448; Laidlaw.
"More Huck Finn in...," No. 5454; Litz. "Vico and
Joyce," No. 5360; McCarthy. "Turkish References
in...," No. 5457; Marcus. "The Wake and Piers
Plowman," No. 5462; Nagahara. "Joyce and Vico, No.
5475; Rose. "Hawthorne Allusions in ALP," No. 5482.

Books

924. ANDERSON, CHESTER G. "On the Sublime and its
      Anal-Urethal Sources on Pope, Eliot, and
      Joyce," in Modern Irish Literature: Essays
      in Honor of William York Tindall. Library
      of Irish Studies, vol. 1. Edited by Ray-
      mond J. Porter and James D. Brophy. New
      York: Iona College Press and Twayne, 1972,
      pp. 235-249.

*925. BLOCK, HASKELL M. "Theory of Language in Gus-
      tave Flaubert and James Joyce," in Langue
      et littérature: Actes du VIIIe Congres de
      la Federation des Langues et Littératures
      Modernes. Paris: Société d'édition 'Les
      belles lettres,' 1961, p. 305. [Published
      in full as "Theory of Language in Gustave
      Flaubert and James Joyce." Revue de littér-
      ature comparée, 35 (April-June 1961): 197-
      206.]

926. COLUM, MARY. From these Roots: The Ideas that
      have Made Modern Literature. New York:
      Scribner's, 1937, passim. [Reprinted Port
      Washington, New York: Kennikat, 1967.]

927. DESTAFANO, JOSÉ R. Baudelaire y otras rutas
      de la nueva literatura. Buenos Aires:
      "El Ateneo," 1945, pp. 22-24.

928. DUJARDIN, ÉDOUARD. Le monologue intérieure:
      son apparition, ses origines, sa place dans
      l'oeuvre de James Joyce. Paris: Messein,
      1931.

929. FULLER, EDMUND. "Joyce: Dedalus or Icarus?"
      in his Man in Modern Fiction. New York:
      Random House, 1958, pp. 123-132.

GENERAL STUDIES

930. GLASHEEN, ADALINE. "Joyce and the Three Ages of Charles Stewart Parnell," in A James Joyce Miscellany, Second Series, pp. 151-178, No. 1613.

931. HAMILL, ELIZABETH. These Modern Writers: An Introduction for Modern Readers. Melbourne: Georgian House, 1946, pp. 125-126.

932. HAYMAN, DAVID. Joyce et Mallarmé. 2 vols. Paris: Les Lettres Modernes, 1956. [Originally published as "Joyce et Mallarmé," La Revue des lettres modernes, 3 (January 1956): 97-128; "La Stylistique de la Suggestion." ibid., 3 (February 1956): 129-206; "Introduction à Finnegans Wake: Stylistique de la Suggestion." ibid., 3 (March 1956): 257-318; "Joyce et Mallarmé: Stylistique de la Suggestion." ibid., 3 (April 1956): 497-506.]

933. HIGHET, GILBERT. "Symbolist Poets and James Joyce," in his The Classical Tradition: Greek and Roman Influences on Western Literature. London, New York: Oxford University Press, 1949, pp. 501-519.

934. HOFFMAN, FREDERICK J. "Infroyce," in James Joyce: Two Decades of Criticism, pp. 390-435, No. 1570. [Later appeared as a chapter in his Freudianism and the Literary Mind. 2nd edition. Baton Rouge: Louisiana State University Press, 1957, pp. 116-150.]

935. HOLTZ, WILLIAM V. Image and Immortality: A Study of Tristram Shandy. Providence: Brown University Press, 1970, passim.

936. HOWARTH, HERBERT. "Whitman and the Irish Writers," in Comparative Literature: Proceedings of the Second Congress of the International Comparative Literature Association, vol. 2. Chapel Hill: University of North Carolina Press, 1959, pp. 479-488. [Reprinted as "Whitman Among the Irish." London Magazine, 7 (January 1960): 48-55.]

937. JACQUET, CLAUDE. Joyce et Rabelais: Aspects de la création verbale dans Finnegans Wake. Études anglaises: Cahiers et documents, 4. Paris: Didier, 1972.

938. LEVIN, HARRY. Contexts of Criticism. Cambridge: Harvard University Press, 1957, pp. 131-139, 269-286, et passim. [Pages 131-139 appeared as "Joyce's Sentimental Journey through France and Italy." Yale Review, 38 (June 1949): 664-672, No. 484; pages 269-286 appeared as "James Joyce: un individu dans le monde." Revue de métaphysique et de morale, 61, nos. 3-4 (July-December 1956): 346-359, No. 1166.]

939. LINDSAY, JACK. "James Joyce," in Scrutinies, vol. 2. Collected by Edgell Rickword. London: Wishart, 1931, pp. 99-122. [Excerpts reprinted in A Library of Literary Criticism, pp. 106-117, No. 250.]

940. MAGALANER, MARVIN. "James Joyce and Marie Corelli," in Modern Irish Literature: Essays in Honor of William York Tindall. Library of Irish Studies, vol. 1. Edited by J. Porter and James D. Brophy. New York: Iona College Press and Twayne, 1972, pp. 185-193.

941. MISRA, B. P. Indian Inspiration of James Joyce. Agra, India: Gaya Prasad and Sons. [n.d.].

942. MOSELEY, VIRGINIA D. Joyce and the Bible. Dekalb, Ill.: Northern Illinois University Press, 1967.

943. NOON, WILLIAM T., S.J. Joyce and Aquinas. Yale Studies in English, vol. 133. New Haven: Yale University Press, 1957. [Paperback reprint, 1963: "Epiphany" reprinted in Joyce's The Dead, pp. 82-88, No. 3138; "A Pennyworth of Thomism" reprinted in Portraits of an Artist, pp. 201-213, No. 3260; "Epiphany in 'Two Gallants'" reprinted in James Joyce's Dubliners, pp. 104-114, No. 2852; another reprint, Hamden, Conn.: Archon Books, 1970.]

944. O'FAOLAIN, SEAN. "Dante and Joyce," in his Summer in Italy. New York: Devin-Adair, 1950, pp. 113-118.

945. PEACOCK, RONALD. The Poet in the Theatre. New York: Harcourt, Brace, 1946, pp. 10-13.

946. PUNER, HELEN WALKER. Freud: His Life and His Mind. New York: Howell, Soskin, 1947, pp. 333-336.

947. ROSTVIG, MAREN-SOFIE. "The Hidden Sense: Milton and the Neoplatonic Method of Numerical Composition," in The Hidden Sense and Other Essays. Norwegian Studies in English, no. 9. Oslo: Universitetsforlaget; New York: Humanities Press, 1963, pp. 110-112.

948. SHOREY, PAUL. What Plato Said. Chicago: University of Chicago Press, 1933, p. 64.

949. STRONG, L. A. G. The Sacred River: An Approach to James Joyce. London: Methuen, 1949; London: Theodore Brun, 1949; New York: Pellegrini and Cudahy, 1951.

950. SUTHERLAND, ROBERT D. Language and Lewis Carroll. Janua linguarum, serium maior, vol. 26. The Hague: Mouton, 1970, passim.

951. TINDALL, WILLIAM YORK. The Literary Symbol. New York: Columbia University Press, 1955, passim. ["Image and Symbol in The Portrait" reprinted in Portraits of an Artist, pp. 232-240, No. 3260; reprinted in Portrait: Notes, No. 3222.]

952. TYSDAHL, BJØRN J. *Joyce and Ibsen: A Study in Literary Influence.* Norwegian Studies in English, no. 14. Oslo: Universitets-forlaget; New York: Humanities Press, 1968.

953. WAIS, KURT. "Shakespeare und die neueren Erzähler; von Bonaventura und Manzoni bis Laforgue und Joyce," in *Shakespeare, seine Welt--unsere Welt.* Edited by Gerhard Müller-Schwefe. Tübingen: Max Niemeyer, 1964, pp. 96-113.

Periodical Articles

954. AMES, VAN METER. "The Novel: Between Art and Science." *Kenyon Review,* 5 (Winter 1943): 34-48.

955. ASTRE, GEORGES-ALBERT. "Joyce et la durée." *l'Age nouveau,* no. 45 (January 1950): 29-38.

956. AUDEN, W. H. "James Joyce and Richard Wagner." *Common Sense,* 10 (March 1941): 89-90.

957. BAMBROUGH, J. R. "Joyce and Jonson." *Review of English Literature,* n.s. 2 (October 1961): 45-50.

958. BEASLAI, PIARAS. "Was Joyce Inspired by Lewis Carroll?" *Irish Digest,* 78 (July 1963): 35-38. [From the *Irish Independent*]

959. BEEBE, MAURICE. "James Joyce and Giordano Bruno: A Possible Source for Daedalus." *James Joyce Review,* 1, no. 4 (December 1957): 41-44.

960. BEHARRIELL, FREDERICK J. "Freud and Literature." *Queen's Quarterly,* 65 (Spring 1958): 118-125.

961. BENSTOCK, BERNARD. "Joyce's Swift: Synthetical But not Serene." *Dublin Magazine,* 10 (Summer 1973): 21-32.

962. BLOCK, HASKELL M. "James Joyce and Thomas Hardy." *Modern Language Quarterly,* 19 (December 1958): 337-342.

963. [BONHEIM, HELMUT?]. "Dublin's Prodigal Son." *Time,* 74 (1959): 68-69. [Flaubert and Joyce]

964. BOYLE, ALEXANDER. "Joyce's Unjust City." *Catholic World,* 181 (April 1955): 6-10.

965. BURBRIDGE, P. C. "A Joyce Source." *Times Literary Supplement,* 21 August 1953, p. 535.

966. BURGESS, ANTHONY. "Mark Twain and James Joyce." *Mark Twain Journal,* 13 (Winter 1966-67): 1-2.

967. CHURCH, MARGARET. "Joyce and Vico Panel." *James Joyce Quarterly,* 9 (Spring 1972): 311.

*968. CONNOLLY, THOMAS E. "PMLA: Parody of Scholarship." *America,* 98 (8 February 1958): 533. [Contra J. Mitchell Morse, No. 1006; see also "Joyce and the Jesuits: Morse and Remorse." *America,* 98 (8 March 1958): 662-664, including letter to the Editor from Morse.]

969. COPE, JACKSON I. "Joyce's Kabbala." *South Atlantic Bulletin,* 31 (January 1966): 5. [Abstract]

970. CURRAN, C. P. "Joyce's d'Annunzian Mask." *Studies,* 51 (Autumn 1962): 308-316. [Appeared in expanded form in his *James Joyce Remembered,* No. 304.]

971. DISKIN, PATRICK. "Joyce and Charlotte Brontë." *Notes and Queries,* n.s. 13 (March 1966): 94-95. [*Jane Eyre* and *Portrait*]

972. DONOGHUE, DENIS. "Joyce's Psychological Landscape." *Studies,* 46 (Spring 1957): 76-90.

973. _____. "Joyce and the Finite Order." *Sewanee Review,* 68 (Spring 1960): 256-273.

974. DOUGHERTY, CHARLES T. "Joyce and Ruskin." *Notes and Queries,* 198 (February 1953): 76-77.

975. DUNCAN, EDWARD. "James Joyce and the Primitive Celtic Church." *Alphabet,* no. 7 (December 1963): 17-38.

976. EPSTEIN, EDMUND L. "James Joyce and *The Way of All Flesh.*" *James Joyce Quarterly,* 7 (Fall 1969): 22-29.

977. FALQUI, ENRICO. "Marinetti, Pound e l'ulissismo." *Fiera letteraria,* 19 (1964): 1-2.

978. FANGER, DONALD. "Joyce and Meredith: A Question of Influence and Tradition." *Modern Fiction Studies,* 6 (Summer 1960): 125-130.

979. FESHBACH, SIDNEY. "Joyce Read Ruskin." *James Joyce Quarterly,* 10 (Spring 1973): 333-336. [See "Letter to the Editor." *ibid.,* 11 (Fall 1973): 77.]

980. FITZELL, L. "The Sword and the Dragon." *South Atlantic Quarterly,* 50 (April 1951): 214-232.

981. FLEMING, RUDD. "Dramatic Involution: Tate, Husserl, and Joyce." *Sewanee Review,* 60 (Summer 1952): 445-464.

982. FOWLIE, WALLACE. "Masques du héros littéraire." *Oeuvres nouvelles* (New York), 4

GENERAL STUDIES

(1944): 39-117. [Translated as "La suerte del artista como heroe: Joyce y Proust." Mercurio Peruano, no. 217 (April 1945): 143-154; appeared also in his The Clown's Grail: A Study of Love in its Literary Expressions. London: Dennis Dobson, 1948, pp. 96-109; "The Artist: Proust and Joyce" reprinted in Love in Literature. Bloomington, Ind.: Indiana University Press, Midland Book, 1965, pp. 96-109.]

983. FRITZ, HELEN M. "Joyce and Existentialism." James Joyce Review, 2, nos. 1-2 (Autumn 1958): 13-21.

984. GILBERT, STUART. "The Latin Background of James Joyce's Art." Horizon, 10 (September 1944): 178-189. [Translated by L. -E. Génissieux as "L'ambiance latine de l'art de James Joyce." Fontaine (Algiers), no. 37-40 (1944): 79-88; translated as "El fondo latino enclarte de James Joyce." Sur, no. 122 (December 1944): 11-24; reprinted in Aspects de la littérature anglaises, 1918-1945. Edited by Kathleen Raine and Max-Pol Fouchet. Paris: Fontaine, 1947, pp. 71-79.]

985. GORDON, CAROLINE. "Some Readings and Misreadings." Sewanee Review, 61 (Summer 1953): 384-407. [Appeared in her How to Read a Novel. New York: Viking Press, 1954.]

986. GREENE, DAVID. "Michael Cusack and the G. A. A." Irish Times, 27 April 1956, p. 5; 28 April 1956, p. 9.

987. HAMPSHIRE, STUART. "Joyce and Vico: The Middle Way." New York Review of Books, 18 October 1973, pp. 8, 9, 12, 14, 16, 18, 21.

988. HAYMAN, DAVID. "James Joyce and Arthur Rimbaud." South Central Bulletin, 26 (March 1966): 9. [Abstract]

989. HELSINGER, HOWARD. "Joyce and Dante." ELH: Journal of English Literary History, 35 (December 1968): 591-605.

990. HIGGINSON, FRED H. "James Joyce: Linguist." Word Study, 31 (May 1956): 1-3.

991. HOPE, A. D. "The Esthetic Theory of James Joyce." Australasian Journal of Psychology and Philosophy, 16 (December 1943): 93-114. [Reprinted in Joyce's Portrait, pp. 183-203, No. 3223.]

992. HYNES, SAM. "Catholicism of James Joyce." Commonweal, 55 (22 February 1952): 487-489.

993. JOHNSTON, DENIS. "Swift of Dublin." Éire-Ireland, 3 (Autumn 1968): 38-50.

994. KESTNER, JOSEPH A. "Tolstoy and Joyce: 'Yes.'" James Joyce Quarterly, 9 (Summer 1972): 484-486.

995. KLAWITTER, ROBERT. "Henri Bergson and James Joyce's Fictional World." Comparative Literature Studies, 3 (Winter 1966): 429-437.

996. KUNKEL, FRANK L. "Beauty in Aquinas and Joyce." Thought Patterns, 2 (1951): 61-68.

997. McHUGH, ROGER. "James Joyce's Synge-Song." Envoy, 3 (November 1950): 12-17.

998. MacLEOD, VIVIENNE K. "Influence of Ibsen on Joyce." Publications of the Modern Language Association, 60 (September 1945): 879-898; addendum, 62 (June 1947): 573-580.

999. McLUHAN, HERBERT M. "James Joyce: Trivial and Quadrivial." Thought, 28 (Spring 1953): 75-98. [Reprinted in The Interior Landscape: The Literary Criticism of Marshall McLuhan, 1943-1962. Edited by Eugene McNamara. New York, Toronto: McGraw-Hill, 1969, pp. 23-47.]

1000. _____. "Joyce, Mallarmé, and the Press." Sewanee Review, 62 (Winter 1954): 38-55. [Reprinted in The Interior Landscape. Edited by Eugene McNamara. New York, Toronto: McGraw-Hill, 1969, pp. 5-21.]

1001. MAGALANER, MARVIN. "James Joyce and the Myth of Man." Arizona Quarterly, 4 (Winter 1948): 300-309.

1002. MALLAM, DUNCAN. "Joyce and Rabelais." University of Kansas City Review, 23 (December 1956): 99-110.

1003. MARSHALL, WILLIAM H. "A Joyce-Santayana Parallel." Notes and Queries, n.s. 10 (October 1963): 379-380.

*1004. MISRA, B. P. "Sir Edwin Arnold's Role in the Artistic Development of James Joyce." Indian Journal of English Studies, 2 (1961): 108-111.

1005. MONTGOMERY, MARION. "Emotion Recollected in Tranquillity: Wordsworth's Legacy to Eliot, Joyce and Hemingway." Southern Review, 6 (July 1970): 710-721. [Reprinted in The Reflective Journey Toward Order: Essays on Dante, Wordsworth, Eliot, and Others. Athens: University of Georgia Press, 1973, pp. 283-295.]

1006. MORSE, J. MITCHELL. "The Disobedient Artist: Joyce and Loyola." Publications of the Modern Language Association, 72 (December 1957): 1018-1035. [See also No. 968; reprinted as Chapter 6 in his The Sympathetic Alien, No. 339.]

1007. _____. "Art and Fortitude: Joyce and the Summa Theologia." James Joyce Review, 1, no. 1 (February 1957): 19-30. [Chapter 7 in his The Sympathetic Alien, No. 339.]

1008. _____. "Augustine's Theodicy and Joyce's Aesthetics." ELH: Journal of English Literary History, 24 (March 1957): 30-43. [Chapters four and eight in his The Sympathetic Alien, No. 339; reprinted in Joyce's Portrait, pp. 290-303, No. 3223.]

1009. _____. "Baudelaire, Stephen Dedalus, and Shem the Penman." Bucknell Review, 7 (March 1958): 187-198.

1010. _____. "Karl Gutzkow and The Modern Novel." Journal of General Education, 15 (October 1963): 175-189. [Reprinted in James Joyce Quarterly, 2 (Fall 1964): 13-17.]

1011. NADAREISHVILI, I. SH., and YU. K. ORLOV. "Rost leksiki kak funktsilia dlini teksta na primere proizvedenii L. N. Tolstogo i D. Dzhoisa." Soobschcheniia, Akad. Nauk Gruzinskoĭ SSR (Tbilisi), 64, no. 3 (1972): 549-552.

1012. POWER, ARTHUR. "Joyce on Chekov and Dostoievsky." Irish Times, 26 November 1964.

1013. RANKIN, H. D. "Notes on the Comparison of Petronius with Three Moderns." Acta antiqua academiae scientiarum hungaricae, 18 (1970): 197-213. [Proust, Joyce, and Fitzgerald; reprinted in his Petronius the Artist. The Hague: Martinus Nijhoff, 1971, pp. 68-87.]

1014. RUBIN, LOUIS D., JR. "Joyce and Sterne: A Study in Affinity." Hopkins Review, 3 (Winter 1950): 14-22.

1015. SALERNO, GEORGE. "Santayce-Joyceana." James Joyce Quarterly, 5 (Winter 1968): 137-143.

1016. SHARPLES, SISTER MARIAN. "Hopkins and Joyce: A Point of Similarity." Renascence, 19 (Spring 1967): 156-160.

1017. SMIDT, KRISTIAN. "Joyce and Ibsen: A Study in Literary Influence." Edda, 70 (1970): 85-103.

1018. THOMSON, M. T. "James Joyce and Rimbaud's Album dit 'Zutigue.'" Revue de littérature comparée, 56 (July-September 1972): 396-400.

1019. TINDALL, WILLIAM YORK. "James Joyce and the Hermetic Tradition." Journal of the History of Ideas, 15 (January 1954): 23-39.

*1020. UNGVARI, T. "Shakespeare-Joyce-Brecht." Magyar Nemzet (Budapest), 12 September 1959.

1021. VERDIN, SIMONNE. "Mallarmé et Joyce, sumptuosités vitales et magnifique veille de la pensée." Courier du Centre International d'Études Poétiques, no. 84 (1971): 17-21.

1022. WASSERSTROM, WILLIAM. "In Gertrude's Closet." Yale Review, 48 (Winter 1958): 245-265. [Joyce and Otto Rank]

1023. WEISS, WOLFGANG. "Joyces Pastiche des Carmen Arrale." Anglia, 91 (1973): 487-492.

1024. WELLS, HENRY W. "Poetic Imagination in Ireland and India." Literary Half-Yearly, 9 (1968): 37-48.

1025. WILDI, MAX. "James Joyce and Arthur Symons." Orbis litterarum, 19, no. 4 (1964): 187-193.

1026. YEATS, J. B. "On James Joyce: A Letter," edited by Donald T. Torchiana and Glenn O'Malley. Tri-Quarterly, 1 (Fall 1964): 70-76.

REPUTATION STUDIES

See also poems by Posner (No. 3993, Purdy (No. 4577), McKinley (No. 3930), Rankin (No. 5167), Colum (No. 4919), and Boorum (No. 4989); parodies by Burgess (No. 3743), Jennings (Nos. 4943, 5106), Wells (No. 4904), and Lamb (No. 5121); II.D "Dubliners": Barr. "Footnote to...," No. 3146; II.F "Portrait": Ellmann. "The Two Faces of Edward," No. 3228; II.I "Finnegans Wake": Blish. "Prayer...," No. 4993; Aubert. "FW: pour en finir ...," No. 4975; Benstock. "Reel FW," No. 4989; Butor. "FW est...traduisible," No. 5004; Butor. "Le traduction...," No. 5005; Costanzo. "French Versions of FW," No. 5027; Eco. "My Exagmination ...," No. 4928; Hart. "FW...," No. 4934; Knuth. "The FW Translation Panel at Trieste," No. 5117; Lamb. "I Wished I had Written...," No. 5121; Senn. "The Issue is Translation," No. 5193; Spielberg. "Infant...," No. 5777; Van Laere. "Les traducteurs...," No. 5225.

General

Books

1027. BENNETT, ARNOLD. The Journal of Arnold Bennet. New York: Literary Guild, 1933, p. 1015.

1028. BROCH, HERMANN, and DANIEL BRODY. Briefwechsel, 1930-1951. Edited by Bertold Hack and Marietta Kleiss. Foreword by Herbert G. Göpfert. Frankfurt a.M.: Buchhändler-Vereinigung GMBH, 1971, passim. [Also in Archiv für Geschichte des Buchwesens, vol. 12.]

1029. BROOKS, VAN WYCK. The Opinions of Oliver Allston. New York: Dutton, 1941, passim. [See reactions by Dwight MacDonald. "Kulturbolschewismus is Here." Partisan Review, 8, no. 6 (November-December 1941):

GENERAL STUDIES

442-451, No. 1173 and Maria Jolas. Commonweal, 35 (6 February 1942): 392-393; (13 March 1942): 570-571.]

1030. CANBY, HENRY SEIDEL. Seven Years' Harvest. New York: Farrar and Rinehart, 1936, passim.

1031. CHESTERTON, G. K. "On Phases of Eccentricity," in his All I Survey. London: Methuen, 1943, pp. 62-68.

1032. COWLEY, MALCOLM. "Religion of Art," in his Exile's Return. New York: Norton, 1934, passim. [Appeared in New Republic, 77 (January 1934): 216-220.]

1033. CROSS, AMANDA. The James Joyce Murder. New York: Macmillan; London: Gollancz, 1967. [Translated by Susanne Kahn-Ackermann as In besten Kreisen. Munich: Desch, 1968.]

*1034. DUFF, CHARLES. Handrail and Wampus: Three Segments of a Polyphonic Biograd. London: Cayvie Press, 1931. [Parody]

1035. FARRELL, JAMES T. A Note on Literary Criticism. New York: Vanguard Press, 1936, pp. 83-85, 97-107, 109. [Pages 83-85 are a reply to Mirskii (No. 742); pages 97-107 are a reply to Karl Radek (No. 1059).]

1036. FREYTAG-LORINGHOVEN, ELSE von. "The Modest Woman," in The Little Review Anthology. Edited by Margaret Anderson. New York: Hermitage House, 1953, pp. 299-301.

1037. GETLEIN, FRANK. Milton Hebald. New York: Viking, 1971, pp. 122-129. [On Hebald's statues of Joyce and U.]

1038. GIEDION-WELCKER, CAROLA et al. In Memoriam James Joyce. Zürich: Fretz and Wasmuth, 1941.

1039. GILBERT, STUART. "James Joyce," in Writers of Today. Edited by Denys Van Baker. London: Sidgwick and Jackson, 1946, pp. 43-57. [Later appeared in James Joyce: Two Decades of Criticism, pp. 450-468, No. 1570.]

1040. GRIGSON, GEOFFREY and C. H. GIBBS-SMITH, eds. People. London: Grosvenor Press, 1954, p. 367.

1041. HIGHET, GILBERT. "The Personality of Joyce," in his Explorations. New York: Oxford University Press, 1971, pp. 135-146.

1042. HUNEKER, JAMES. "James Joyce," in his Unicorns. New York: Scribner's, 1917, pp. 187-194.

1043. HYMAN, STANLEY EDGAR. The Armed Vision. New York: Alfred A. Knopf, 1953, passim.

*1044. JOLAS, MARIA. "Introduction," to Pastimes of James Joyce. [New York:] Joyce Memorial Fund Committee, [1941].

1045. KELLY, BLANCHE MARY. The Voice of the Irish. New York: Sheed and Ward, 1952, pp. 291-297.

1046. KESSER, ARMIN. "James Joyce," in In Memoriam James Joyce, pp. 23-31, No. 1038. [From Neue Schweizer Rundschau, February 1941.]

1047. KIELY, BENEDICT. "The Artist on the Giant's Grave," in A Bash in the Tunnel, pp. 235-241, No. 1644.

1048. KIMPEL, BEN D. "James Joyce in Contemporary World Literature," in James Joyce: His Place in World Literature, pp. 93-102, No. 1688.

1049. LEWIS, WYNDHAM. Rude Assignment. London: Hutchinson, 1950, passim. [Disagreement with Harry Levin's James Joyce: A Critical Introduction, No. 1603.]

1050. McCARTHY, DESMOND. "James Joyce," in his Memories. New York: Oxford University Press, 1953, pp. 113-120.

1051. MARBLE, ANNIE R. A Study of the Modern Novel. New York: Appleton, 1930, pp. 44-46, et passim.

1052. NOYES, ALFRED. The Edge of the Abyss. New York: Dutton, 1942, pp. 131-133, 136-137.

1053. O'BRIEN, EDNA. "Dear Mr. Joyce," in A Bash in the Tunnel, pp. 43-47, No. 1644. [Reprinted in Times Saturday Review, 19 December 1960, p. 15 and in Audience, 1 (July-August 1971): 74-77.]

*1054. ONO, YASUKO. "Joisu Kenkyu no Keifu to Geiyo ["Contemporary Setting of the Study of James Joyce]," in Joisu Nyumon [An Introduction to James Joyce], pp. 208-216, No. 1511.

1055. ORWELL, GEORGE. "I. Letter to Brenda Salkeld (extract)," "II. The Rediscovery of Europe," "III. As I Please," in The Collected Essays, Journalism and Letters. Edited by Sonia Orwell and Ian Angus. London: Secker and Warburg, 1968, vol. 1, pp. 125-129; vol. 2, pp. 197-207; vol. 3, pp. 105-108. [Part II is from Listener, 19 March 1942, pp. 370-372; Part III is a review of Harry Levin's James Joyce, (No. 1603) from Tribune (London), 10 March 1944.]

*1056. OTA, SABURO. "The Statistical Method of Investigation in Comparative Literature," in Proceedings of the Second Congress of the International Comparative Literature Association, vol. 1. Edited by Werner P. Friederich. Chapel Hill: University of North Carolina Press, 1959, pp. 88-97.

1057. _____. "The Collective Medium: The Case of James Joyce's Introduction into Japan," in Essays on English Literature. Tokyo: Kenkyusha, 1964, pp. 251-259.

*1058. PONGS, HERMANN. "Dichter des Nihilismus," in his Im Umbruch der Zeit. Göttingen: 1952, pp. 40-59; 1956, pp. 40-49.

*1059. RADEK, KARL. "James Joyce or Socialist Realism?," in Contemporary World Literature and the Tasks of the Proletariat. A report delivered at the Congress of Soviet Writers, August 1934, pp. 151-154. [Later appeared in Problems of Soviet Literature. Edited by A. Zhdanov et al. New York: International Publishers, 1935, pp. 150-162; see response by James T. Farrell, No. 1035.]

1060. RUSSELL, GEORGE (AE). "Joyce," in his The Living Torch. Edited by Monk Gibbon. New York: Macmillan, 1938, pp. 139-140.

1061. SENN, FRITZ. "Joycean Translatitudes: Aspects of Translation," in Litters from Aloft, pp. 26-49, No. 1516.

1062. SHARE, BERNARD. "Downes's Cakeshop and Williams's Jam," in A Bash in the Tunnel, pp. 189-192, No. 1644.

1063. SITWELL, EDITH. "Notes on Innovations in Prose," in her Aspects of Modern Poetry. London: Duckworth, 1934, pp. 215-219.

1064. SLOCHOWER, HARRY. Three Ways of Modern Man. New York: International Press, 1937, pp. 150-152.

1065. _____. No Voice is Wholly Lost. New York: Creative Age Press, 1945, pp. 243-248. [Reprinted as "In Quest of Everyman: James Joyce and Eugene O'Neill," in Literature and Philosophy between Two World Wars. New York: Citadel Press, 1964, pp. 243-254.]

1066. SMITH, BERNARD. Forces in American Criticism. New York: Harcourt, 1939, passim.

1067. SPARROW, JOHN. Sense and Poetry. New Haven: Yale University Press, 1934, pp. 142-145.

1068. STRACHEY, JOHN. Literature and Dialectical Materialism. New York: Covici Friede, 1934, pp. 17-19.

1069. STRONG, L. A. G. "James and Joyce," in his Personal Remarks. London: Peter Nevill, 1953, pp. 184-189.

1070. SWINNERTON, FRANK. "Post-Freud," in his The Georgian Scene. New York: Farrar and Rinehart, 1934, pp. 415-419; The Georgian Literary Scene, 1910-1935. London: Heinemann, 1935. ["James Joyce" appeared in The Georgian Scene. 9th edition, revised. London: Radius Books-Hutchinson, 1969, pp. 324-327.]

1071. TAYLOR, ESTELLA R. The Modern Irish Writers: Cross Currents of Criticism. Lawrence, Kansas: University of Kansas Press, 1954, passim. [Reprinted New York: Greenwood Press, 1969.]

1072. TREECE, HENRY. "Prigs, the Press and James Joyce," in his How I See Apocalypse. London: Lindsay Drummond, 1946, pp. 27-30.

1073. UNTERMEYER, LOUIS. "James Joyce," in his Makers of the Modern World. New York: Simon and Schuster, 1955, pp. 586-596.

1074. WALDOCK, A. J. A. "Experiment in the Novel: With Special Reference to James Joyce," in his Some Recent Developments in English Literature: A Series of Sydney University Extension Lectures. Sydney: Printed for the University Extension Board by Australasian Medical Publishing Co., 1935, pp. 8-17. [Appeared as James, Joyce and Others. London: Williams and Norgate, 1937, pp. 30-52; reprinted Freeport, New York: Books for Libraries Press, 1967, pp. 30-52.]

1075. WHALLEY, GEORGE. Poetic Process. London: Routledge and Kegan Paul, 1953, passim.

1076. WILSON, EDMUND. A Piece of My Mind. New York: Farrar, Strauss, 1956, pp. 201-202.

Periodical Articles

1077. A., F. "Über Dublin sprechen." Die Gegenwart, 13 (1958): 501-502.

1078. ALSOP, JOSEPH W., JR. "Some Aspects of the Modern World and Four Men." Harvard Advocate, 118 (October 1931): 9-23. [Lawrence, Lewis, Eliot, and Joyce.]

1079. ANDO, ICHIRO. "Joyce Kenkyu no Fukko." Eigo, 114 (1968): 792-793.

1080. ARNETT, EARL. "An 'Amateur Joycean' Went to the Source." Baltimore Sun, 31 October 1967, p. B1. [George Leinwall.]

1081. BARANTONO, ADELCHI. "Il fenomeno Joyce." Civiltà moderna, anno 3, no. 6 (December 1931): 1159-1177.

*1082. BENNETT, ARNOLD. [n.t.]. Echo (Liverpool), 31 May 1928. [Joyce mentioned in a review of A. C. Ward's Twentieth Century Literature.]

*1083. BLACKMUR, R. P. "The Enabling Act of Criticism." American Issues, 2 (1941): 876-879.

GENERAL STUDIES

1084. BOWER-SHORE, CLIFFORD. "Modern Authors: No. 2: James Joyce." Bookfinder Illustrated, June 1932, p. 5.

1085. BUDGEN, FRANK. "James Joyce." Horizon, 4 (February 1941): 104-108. [Appeared in James Joyce: Two Decades of Criticism, pp. 19-26, No. 1570 and in his James Joyce and the Making of Ulysses, and Other Writings. Edited by Clive Hart, pp. 343-348, No. 3557.]

*1086. BÜHNER, KARL HANS. "James Joyce." Welt und Wort, 13 (November 1958): 329-330.

1087. BULLETT, GERALD. "Genius or Gibberish." Literary Guide, 71 (September 1956): 21.

1088. BUTLER, ANTHONY. "The Cult of Joyce." Sunday Press (Dublin), 18 June 1967, p. 17.

*1089. CASTIGLIANO, LUIGI. "James Joyce nella critica inglese recentissima." I libri del giorno, 30 September 1946.

1090. CHALON, JEAN. "L'Irlande à pied, à cheval... et en littérature," Figaro littéraire, 20 May 1964, p. 18.

*1091. COIGNARD, JERÔME. "James Joyce, prima maniera." Il Mattino (Pasta), 18-19 November 1926. [Reprinted in Conscienta (Rome), 27 November 1926.]

*1092. COLLIS, J. S. "Conversation Piece on Joyce." Time and Tide, 22, no. 13 (29 March 1941): 267.

1093. COPE, JACKSON I. "James Joyce: Test Case for a Theory of Style." ELH: Journal of English Literary History, 21 (September 1954): 221-236.

1094. CORRAN, H. S. "Joyce-Genghis in Ghoon for You." The Harp, Summer 1969, pp. 11-14. [Visit to Guinness Brewery using quotes from U and FW.]

1095. CROSBY, HARRY. "Observation Post." transition, no. 16-17 (June 1929): 197-204.

1096. CROWLEY, ALEISTER. "The Genius of Mr. James Joyce." New Pearson's Magazine, 49 (July 1923): 52-53.

*1097. CUNNINGHAM, LOUIS A. "Splinters from a Free Lance: XIII--The Novel." Canadian Bookman (Toronto), 10, no. 3 (March 1928): 76-79.

1098. CWIAKALA, JADWIGA. "Joyce in Poland." James Joyce Quarterly, 9 (Fall 1971): 93-98.

1099. DEVLIN, JOHN. "For Readers of James Joyce." America, 190 (10 May 1958): 195-197.

*1100. DOMENCHINA, JUAN JOSÉ. "Epilogo de James Joyce." Romance (Mexico City), 2 (15 February 1941): 4.

1101. DUYTSCHAEVER, JORIS. "James Joyce in het Nederlands: Magistrale vertaling voor loopjongensloon." Vlaamse Gids, 54 (April 1970): 20-25.

1102. EASTMAN, MAX. "The Cult of Unintelligibility." Harper's Magazine, 158 (April 1929): 632-639. [Later appeared in his The Literary Mind. New York: Scribner's, 1931; see reply by Harry Crosby, No. 1095.]

*1103. EDEL, LEON. "James Joyce." Amerikanische Rundschau, 4 (1948): 119-123.

1104. EGRI, PÉTER. "James Joyce's Works in Hungarian Translation." James Joyce Quarterly, 4 (Spring 1967): 234-236.

1105. ELIOT, T. S. "A Message to the Fish." Horizon, 3 (March 1941): 173-175. [Appeared also in James Joyce: Two Decades of Criticism, pp. 468-471, No. 1570.]

1106. ELLMANN, RICHARD. "James Joyce." Welt und Wort, 17, no. 2 (February 1962): 37-39. [From the "Introduction" to the German translation of his James Joyce, No. 308.]

1107. FEHREN, FR. HENRY. "Two Exiles." U. S. Catholic and Jubilee, 37 (September 1972): 39-41. [Dante and Joyce]

*1108. FERRANDO, GUIDO. "Divagazioni sul romanzo inglese contemporaneo." Il Mazocco (Florence), 27 December 1931.

*1109. FOUCHER, JEAN-PIERRE. "James Joyce." Horizon (Nantes), 2, no. 4 (1946?): 59-61.

*1110. FREYER, GRATTAN. "Nota di un Giovanne Irlandese su James Joyce." Letterature; revista trimestrale di letteratura contemporanea, 2, no. 4 (October 1938): 136-140.

1111. FULFORD, ROBERT. "Irish by Joyce." Toronto Daily Star, 1 December 1963. [On the Toronto James Joyce Society]

1112. GAUGEARD, JEAN. "Joyce, Demain." Les lettres françaises, 10 February 1966, p. 10.

1113. GERTSFELDE, V. "O metode Dzhoĭsa i revoliutsionnaĭ literaturĭ. Rech' nemetskogo pisatelĭa (na s'ezde pisateleĭ)." Izvestiĭa, 27 August 1936, p. 6. [Reprinted in Pervyĭ vsesoiuznyĭ s'ezd sovetskikh pisateleĭ. Moscow: 1934, pp. 358-366; translated as "A Communist on Joyce." Living Age, 347 (November 1934): 268-270.]

*1114. GIEDION-WELCKER, CAROLA. "Ein Monument für James Joyce?" Die Weltwoche (Zürich), no. 1701 (17 June 1966): 27.

1115. GILBERT, STUART. "James Joyce." Psyche, no. 20 (June 1948): 678-689.

1116. GOLDBERG, S. L. "Joyce and the Artist's Fingernails." Review of English Literature, 2 (April 1961): 59-73.

*1117. GOPALEEN, MYLES na (Flann O'Brien, Brian Nolan). "Cruiskeen Lawn." Irish Times, 29 April 1942.

*1118. _____. "Cruiskeen Lawn." Irish Times, 27 November 1942.

*1119. _____. "Cruiskeen Lawn." Irish Times, 21 March 1944.

*1120. _____. "Cruiskeen Lawn." Irish Times, 9 September 1949.

*1121. _____. "Cruiskeen Lawn." Irish Times, 12 September 1949.

*1122. _____. "Cruiskeen Lawn." Irish Times, 14 November 1949.

*1123. _____. "Cruiskeen Lawn." Irish Times, 20 March 1950.

*1124. _____. "Cruiskeen Lawn." Irish Times, 29 March 1956.

*1125. _____. "Cruiskeen Lawn." Irish Times, 10 December 1957.

*1126. _____. "Cruiskeen Lawn." Irish Times, 3 March 1958.

*1127. _____. "Cruiskeen Lawn." Irish Times, 7 August 1958.

*1128. _____. "Cruiskeen Lawn." Irish Times, 3 January 1959.

*1129. _____. "Cruiskeen Lawn." Irish Times, 30 March 1959.

*1130. _____. "Cruiskeen Lawn." Irish Times, 20 December 1961.

1131. _____. "Cruiskeen Lawn." Irish Times, 25 July 1962.

1132. _____. "Cruiskeen Lawn." Irish Times, 26 July 1962.

1133. _____. "Cruiskeen Lawn." Irish Times, 29 March 1963.

1134. _____. "Cruiskeen Lawn." Irish Times, 1 October 1965.

1135. _____. "Cruiskeen Lawn." Irish Times, 31 January 1966.

*1136. GOULD, GERALD. "1983: Television's Aged Literary Critic Looks back 50 years to 1933." Nash's Pall Mall, October 1933, pp. 26-29, 90.

*1137. GOYERT, GEORG. "James Joyce." Prisma: Kulturzeitschrift (Munich), no. 17 (1948): 17-18.

1138. GRABAU, MAX. "Are the Irish Right about Joyce?" Homiletic and Pastoral Review, 59 (May 1959): 735-743. [Reprinted in The Word, July 1959; reprinted as "What do the Irish Think of Joyce?" Irish Digest, 66 (October 1959): 51-55.]

1139. GREIG, MARGARET. "An Elizabethan Joyce." English, 9 (Summer 1953): 166-170.

*1140. HAMILTON, H. M. "Romantic Fiction." The Editor, 9 July 1927, pp. 17-21.

*1141. HENNIG, JOHN. "Books." The Bell, 2, no. 6 (September 1941): 91-94.

*1142. HERZFELDE, WIELAND. "Geist und Machet." Neue deutsche Blätter, 1, no. 12 (September 1934): 713-752. [Excerpts from the First Union Congress of Soviet Writers, Moscow, 17 August-1 September 1934; Maxim Gorki, Karl Radek, Nikolai Bucharin, W. Kirpotin, Fjodor Gladkow, Sergei Tretjakow, Linard Laizens, Jef Last, I. Babel, Ilja Ehrenberg, Wssewolod Iwanow, Lahuti, Ali-Nasin, Eric Siao, Robert Gessner, Hidsikato, Michail Kolzow, Jurij Oljescha, W. Gerassimowa, Willi Bredel, Jean-Richard Bloch, André Malraux, Germanetto, Johannes R. Becher, Theodor Plivier, Ernst Toller.]

1143. HEWITT, JAMES. "James Joyce and the Heroic Tenor." Opera, 22 (February 1971): 101-105.

1144. HOEFORT, SIGFRID. "James Joyce in East Germany." James Joyce Quarterly, 5 (Winter 1968): 132-136.

*1145. HOGAN, THOMAS. "Joyce's Countrymen." Irish Times, 21 April 1951, p. 6. [Review of Envoy, April 1951.]

*1146. HONE, JOSEPH M. "Letter from Ireland." London Mercury, 5 (January 1923): 306-308.

1147. HONIG, MILTON. "Plaque to Mark Joyce Birthplace." New York Times, 10 May 1964, p. 82. [See also New York Times, 17 June 1964, p. 45.]

1148. I., U. "Branzestatue für James Joyce." Neue Zürcher Zeitung, 18 June 1966.

1149. 'Il Vetturale.' "Scarrozzata." Il Frontespizio (Florence), May 1931, pp. 7-8.

1150. INGER, LENA. "Editorial." Joycenotes, 1 (June 1969): 2.

GENERAL STUDIES

*1151. IZQUIERDO, FRANCISCO. "Tres Vertices." Tisino delo Maina (Havanna), 13 January 1927.

1152. JALOUX, EDMOND. "James Joyce." Échanges, no. 1 (December 1929): 143-148.

1153. JAMAL, ZADEH SYED MOHAMMAD ALI. "James Joyce." Sokhan (Tehran), 5 (1953): 25-31; 5 (1953): 90-108. [In Persian]

1154. JOHNSTON, DENIS. "A Short View of the Progress of Joyceanity." Envoy, 5 (May 1951): 13-18. [Excerpts reprinted as "God's Gift to English Departments." CEA Critic, 14, no. 2 (February 1952): 4-5; reprinted in A Bash in the Tunnel, pp. 163-167, No. 1644.]

1155. JOLAS, MARIA. "Homage to James Joyce." transition, no. 21 (March 1932): 250-253.

1156. JONES, W. POWELL. "James Joyce: Master of Words." Intersection, 1 (1953): 52-69.

1157. KAIN, RICHARD M. "The Program of the James Joyce Society, New York, 1947-1968." James Joyce Quarterly, 5 (Summer 1968): 323-328.

1158. KANTERS, ROBERT. "Parmi les livres." Revue de Paris, 69 (June 1962): 126-135.

1159. KELLOG, CHARLES E. "A Joycean Holiday." American Book Collector, 17 (Summer 1967): 11, 13, 16.

1160. KELLY, P. "Literary Wake over James Joyce." America, 65 (May 1941): 103-104.

1161. KENNER, HUGH. "A Communication on James and Stanislaus Joyce." Hudson Review, 3 (Spring 1950): 157-160.

1162. KENSIK, A. C. "James Joyce." Neue Zürcher Zeitung, no. 73 (14 March 1964).

1163. KING, MARTHA. "Cesare Pavese: Reluctant Translator of James Joyce." James Joyce Quarterly, 9 (Spring 1972): 374-382.

1164. LARS, CLAUDIA. "Sombra y perspectiva de James Joyce." Hoja (San Salvador), no. 1 (January 1950): 1, 6, 9-10.

1165. LEHMANN, JOHN. "A Portrait of the Artist as an Escaper." Penguin New Writing (London), no. 33 (1948); reprinted in his The Open Night. London: Longmans, 1952, pp. 71-76.

1166. LEVIN, HARRY. "James Joyce: un individu dans le monde." Revue de métaphysique et de morale, 61, nos. 3-4 (July-December 1956): 346-359. [Reprinted in his Contexts of Criticism, pp. 269-286, No. 938.]

*1167. LIDDY, JAMES. "Coming of Age: James Joyce and Ireland." Kilkenny Magazine, no. 5 (Autumn-Winter 1961): 25-29.

*1168. LÓPEZ NARAVAEZ, FROYLÁN. "Joyce es Dublín." Diorama de la cultura (Supplement to Excelsior, Mexico City), 22 June 1969, p. 3.

*1169. LOWENFELS, WALTER. [n.t.]. Irish Statesman, 15 September 1928.

1170. LYND, ROBERT. "James Joyce and the New Kind of Fiction." John O'London's Weekly, 25 May 1935, pp. 245-246. [Appeared also in his Books and Writers. London: J. M. Dent, 1952, pp. 147-151.]

1171. LYNER, A. "Music and James Joyce." New English Weekly, 4 (19 October 1933): 16-17.

1172. MacDONAGH, DONAGH. "The Reputation of James Joyce: From Notoriety to Fame." University Review (Dublin), 3, no. 2 (1964): 12-20.

*1173. MacDONALD, DWIGHT. "Kulturbolschewismus is Here." Partisan Review, 8 (November-December 1941): 442-451. [Critique of Van Wyck Brooks' Opinions of Oliver Allston, No. 1029.]

1174. MANNING, MARY. "Mythcarriage of Joycestice." Reporter, 26 (15 March 1962): 38-39.

*1175. MARESCALCHI, GIANNINO. "Carte in Tavola." La Ossalto (Bologna), 12 March 1932.

1176. MARION, DENIS. "James Joyce." transition, no. 14 (Fall 1928): 278-279. [Appeared in Variétés (Brussels), 1, no. 3 (15 July 1928): 156-157.]

1177. De MENASCE, JEAN. "Regards." La Revue Juive, 1, no. 6 (November 1925): 756-762.

1178. MERCIER, VIVIAN. "Joyce in Gotham." Irish Times, 11 March 1953, p. 6.

1179. MORAVIA, ALBERTO. "Omaggio a Joyce." Prospettive, 4, nos. 11-12 (15 December 1940): 12-13.

1180. MOYER, ARTHUR. "Hebald on Joyce." Art Scene, 1 (April 1968): 22-26.

1181. N., M. "Gedenkstunde für James Joyce in der Universität Zürich." Neue Zürcher Zeitung, no. 170 (23 June 1966).

1182. NIEBYL, KARL H. "An Economist Considers Joyce." University of Kansas City Review, 8 (October 1941): 47-58.

1183. NICOLSON, HAROLD. "The New Spirit in Literature: The Significance of James Joyce."

Listener, 16 December 1931, p. 1062; "The Modernist Point of View." Listener, 23 December 1931, pp. 1108-1109.

1184. NIMS, JOHN FREDERICK. "The Greatest English Lyric?--A New Reading of Joe E. Skillmer's 'Therese.'" College English, 29 (January 1968): 322-331. [Parody of Joycean criticism]

1185. NOON, WILLIAM T., S.J. "James Joyce: Unfacts, Fiction, and Facts." Publications of the Modern Language Association, 76 (June 1961): 254-276.

1186. O'FAOLAIN, SEAN. "1916-1941: Tradition and Creation." The Bell, 2, no. 1 (April 1941): 5-12.

1187. O HEITHIR, BRENDAN. "Bruth Faoi thir Omos do James Joyce." Irish Times, 20 June 1964.

1188. O'NOLAN, BRIAN (Myles na Gopaleen, Flann O'Brien). "A Bash in the Tunnel," Envoy, 5 (May 1951): 5-11. [Reprinted in A Bash in the Tunnel, pp. 15-20, No. 1644; reprinted in his Stories and Plays. London: Hart-Davis, MacGibbon, 1973, pp. 201-208; translated by Serge Fauchereau in Lettres nouvelles, no. 1 (March 1973): 44-51.]

1189. _____. "Stephen Dead Loss." Irish Times, 10 April 1957, p. 6.

*1190. O'RIORDAN, CONAL. [n.t.]. New Witness (London), 16 March 1923. [Joyce mentioned in a review of Mary Butt's Speed the Plough.]

1191. P., B. C. "The Talkies: Germs of an Art Form." Morning Herald (Sydney), 28 September 1929.

1192. PASOLINI, DESIDERIA. "Gli anni giovanile di Joyce." Radio-Corriere, 28 (23-29 September 1951): 14.

*1193. PENTON, BRIAN. "The Red Page." Bulletin (Sydney), 29 February 1928.

*1194. PIÉRARD, LOUIS. "Un libro francés sobre James Joyce." La Prensa (Buenos Aires), 12 July 1942.

1195. POGLIAGHI, NORA FRANCA. "La beffa del destino di James Joyce." Porta orientale, n.s., 7, nos. 3-4 (March-April 1971).

1196. POLLOCK, HARRY J. "Fun and Names at Joyce Society." Telegram (Toronto), 30 January 1965, p. 25.

1197. _____. "An Account of the Toronto James Joyce Society." James Joyce Quarterly, 3 (Spring 1966): 213-214.

*1198. POUND, EZRA. "On Criticism in General." Criterion, 1 (January 1923): 143-156. [Reprinted in Forrest Read's Pound/Joyce, No. 725.]

1199. POWER, RICHARD. "A Literary Letter from Ireland." New York Times Book Review, 11 July 1965, pp. 44-45. [See also letter to the Editor from Mrs. Burnham Finney, ibid., 8 August 1965, p. 18.]

*1200. PRESCOTT, JOSEPH. "Dos notas sobre James Joyce y William Faulkner," translated by Alfredo Pareja Diezcanseco. Letras del Ecuador, 13, no. 110 (January-March 1958): 2.

1201. PRITCHETT, V. S. "The Comedian of Orgy." New Statesman, 78 (15 August 1969): 205-206.

1202. READ, HERBERT. "The High Priest of Modern Literature." Listener, 20 August 1930, p. 296.

1203. _____, and EDWARD DAHLBERG. "A Literary Correspondence." Sewanee Review, 67 (April-June 1959): 177-203; (July-September 1959): 422-445. [Much expanded version, "On James Joyce," in Dahlberg's Truth is More Sacred. New York: Horizon Press; London: Routledge and Kegan Paul, 1961, pp. 11-65; reprinted as "Bawds in the Beauty Parlor on Mount Ida: On James Joyce," in The Edward Dahlberg Reader. Edited by Paul Carroll. New York: New Directions, 1967, pp. 213-221.]

1204. REST, JAIME. "Actualidad crítica de Joyce." Cuadernos del sur, no. 5 (January-June 1966): 73-74.

1205. ROSENSTOCK, GEORG. "Ein Museum für James Joyce." Die Welt, 21 July 1962.

1206. ROWLAND, JOHN H. S. "James Joyce." Everyman, 5 (2 July 1931): 733.

1207. RUSSE, ELLEN. "James Joyce." Boekenschouw, 21 (1927): 305-311.

*1208. RUSSELL, DORA. "Nuestra colaboración inglesa: Literatura de desesperación." El Sol (Madrid), 16 December 1928.

1209. RUTHERFORD, ANDREW. "Joyce's Use of Correspondence." Essays in Criticism, 6 (January 1956): 123-125.

1210. S., A. G. [n.t.]. Lewiston Journal (Maine), 14 December 1926. [Review of Herbert Gorman's Longfellow study]

*1211. SCHWAB, RAYMOND. "L'illegitimate de l'art." L'Opinion, 14 August 1926, pp. 9-11.

GENERAL STUDIES

1212. SEMMLER, CLEMENT. "Solving the Problem of James Joyce." Meanjin Quarterly, 19 (Autumn 1960): 78-83.

1213. SENDER, RAMÓN J. "Speaking of Epitaphs." Books Abroad, 19 (Summer 1945): 222-227.

1214. SENN, FRITZ. "Joyce, das Scheseläuten und der Föhn." Zürcher Woche, no. 24 (17 June 1967): 7. [Reprinted in his James Joyce: Aufsätze von Fritz Senn, pp. 35-39, No. 1654.]

1215. SINGLETON, RONALD. "Are you There, Mr. Joyce?" Irish Digest, 58 (January 1957): 71-72. [Condensed from Daily Express]

*1216. SMITS, WALTER. "James Joyce." Kölnische Zeitung (Cologne), no. 707 (3 November 1927).

1217. SPEAIGHT, HUGH. "James Joyce and the Revolt from Catholicism." Period, 1929.

*1218. SQUIRE, J. C. ("Solomon Eagle"). "The Critic as Large: Irish Literature Today." Outlook (London), 16 July 1921, p. 53. [Joyce mentioned in a review of L. D'O. Walters' Irish Poets of Today.]

1219. SRINIVASA-IYENGAR, K. R. "James Joyce." New Review (London), 13 (1941): 249-260. [Reprinted in his The Adventure of Criticism. Bombay: Asia Publishing House, 1963, pp. 525-567.]

1220. STALEY, THOMAS F. "James Joyce and the Dilemma of American Academic Criticism." Dublin Magazine, 6, no. 1 (Spring 1967): 38-45.

*1221. STECHOVA, MARIA. "Slavny Joyce." Slovenské poh'lady, 47, no. 2 (1931).

*1222. THIEME, KARL. "Das Unsägliche und die Sprache: 2. James Joyce." Die christliche Welt, 43 (1929): 290-292.

1223. STRONG, L. A. G. "James Joyce: Literary Anchorite." Radio Times, 19 February 1950, p. 6.

1224. SWEENEY, JAMES J. "The Word was his Oyster." Hudson Review, 5 (Autumn 1952): 404-408.

1225. TITUS, EDWARD. "Criticism à l'Irlandaise." This Quarter, 3 (June 1931): 570-571.

*1226. VAN HUET, C. H. M. "Kattebelletjes en Apostillen: Horen Zein bij Joyce." De Gids, 117 (1940): 150-152.

1227. VIOLA, SANDRO. "Dublino non perdona allo scettico Joyce." Stampa, 3 (March 1972): 3.

1228. WEST, REBECCA. "The Strange Case of James Joyce." Bookman (New York), 68 (September 1928): 9-23. [Appeared in her The Strange Necessity: Essays. London: Jonathan Cape, 1931, pp. 13-58, 68-70, 175-194; Garden City: Doubleday, Doran, 1928, pp. 1-54, 65-67, 187-209.]

1229. WILSON, EDMUND. "James Joyce as a Poet." New Republic, 44 (November 1925): 279-280.

1230. YOUNG, FREDERIC J. "James Joyce: The Most Remarkable Man we Know." Eire-Ireland, 1 (Spring 1965-1966): 97-100.

1231. ZAREK, O. [n.t.]. Deutsches Tagebuch, 8 (1927): 963-966.

1232. ZIMMER, DIETER E. "James Joyce auf Deutsch: Der Suhrkamp Verlag bereitet eine riesige Editions-und übersetzungsaktion vor." Die Zeit (Hamburg), 17 March 1967, p. 21 (U.S. Edition, 21 March 1967, p. 11.).

1233. 'A Fellow Dubliner.' "The Veritable James Joyce According to Stuart Gilbert and Oliver St. John Gogarty." International Forum, n.s. 1 (July 1931): 13-17. [Reprinted in transition, no. 21 (March 1932): 273-282.]

*1234. Unsigned. "Chez lui." Variétés, 1, no. 6 (15 October 1928).

*1235. Unsigned. "Eine Gedenkstatte für James Joyce." Neue Zürcher Zeitung, 10 December 1965, p. 8.

*1236. Unsigned. "Great Regrets about Some of Joyce's Writings." Irish Times, 3 February 1962.

1237. Unsigned. "The Huckster who's Hooked on James Joyce." Maclean's, 82 (June 1969): 19. [About Harry Pollock]

*1238. Unsigned. "Inverse Euphuism." Paris Times, 9 June 1929.

*1239. Unsigned. "James Joyce." Neue Zürcher Zeitung, no. 343 (1 June 1961).

*1240. Unsigned. "James Joyce also Rokoko-Lyriker ...." Forum (Wein), 6 (1959): 420.

1241. Unsigned. "James Joyce steht im Mittelpunkt eines Schauspiels." Die Welt, 26 April 1963.

1242. Unsigned. "Joyce: Irish Stew." Der Spiegel, 18 (26 January 1964): 87.

*1243. Unsigned. "Joyce: Odysseus in Dublin." Der Spiegel, 15 (1 November 1961): 70-78, 84.

*1244. Unsigned. "La letteratura inglese d'oggi." Il Messaquero (Rome), 19 May 1929. [Reprinted in Egyptian Gazette (Alexandria), 4 June 1929; reprinted in Messaggero di Rodi (Rodi), 21 May 1929.]

1245. Unsigned. "L'Homme Joyce." Roman, no. 1 (January 1951): 75-78.

*1246. Unsigned. "Literature at the Cross-Roads." Irish Times, 24 January 1936, p. 8. [At a meeting of the University College English Literary Society, T. S. Eliot praises Joyce]

*1247. Unsigned. "Neues uber James Joyce." Das Antiquariat (Wien), 6 (1950): 229-230.

1248. Unsigned. "Siebenbändige Joyce-Ausgabe." Die Welt der Literatur, 6, no. 3 (1969): 2.

1249. Unsigned. "The James Joyce Society." American Book Collector, 15 (June 1965): 21-22.

*1250. Unsigned. "Was Life worth Leaving, by Another Dubliner." Iconograph, 5 (March 1942): 11-16.

*1251. Unsigned. [n.t.]. Irish News (Belfast), 25 November 1930. [Comment on Humbert Wolfe's lecture to the literary circle of the National Liberal Club on "Contemporary Poetic Tendencies."]

*1252. Unsigned. [n.t.]. Newsletter (Belfast), 5 January 1934. [Comment on speech by Sylvia Lynd]

*1253. Unsigned. [n.t.]. Observer (Ceylon), 10 November 1927.

Poems and Prose

See also Hugh McKinley. "Ulysses," No. 3930; Arthur Power. "On the Presentation...," No. 3996; Andrew Purdy. "Leopold Bloom," No. 4577; Padraic Colum. "In Memory...," No. 4919; Ted Boorum. "Finnegans Wake," No. 4999; H. D. Rankin. "After looking...," No. 5167; items are poetry unless otherwise mentioned.

*1254. ANDERSON, MARCIA LEE. "Re Joyce." Poetry, 70 August 1947): 240.

1255. ATHERTON, J. S. "For James Joyce: Let your Ghost have no Grievance." James Joyce Quarterly, 5 (Winter 1968): 166-167.

*1256. BECKETT, SAMUEL. "Home Olga." Contempo, 3, no. 13 (15 February 1934): 3.

1257. BEHAN, BRENDAN. "Buiochas do James Joyce." "Thanks to James Joyce," in Brendan Behan's Island. London: Hutchinson: New York: Bernard Geis, 1962, p. 179 (in Irish and English translation by Valentin Iremonger). [Translated as "Remerciements James Joyce" by Richard Marienstras. Lettres nouvelles, (March-April 1966): 39; translated by Ulick O'Connor in his Life Styles: Poems. Dublin: Dolmen Press; London: Hamish Hamilton, 1973, p. 36.]

1258. BORGES, JORGE LUIS. "Invocación a Joyce." Davar, 118 (July-September 1968): 3-4. [Translated by Norman Thomas de Giovanni in New Yorker, 45 (13 December 1969): 53; translation reprinted in Borges on Writing. Edited by Norman Thomas de Giovanni, Daniel Halpern, and Frank MacShane. New York: E. P. Dutton, 1973, pp. 141-143.]

1259. _____. "James Joyce." La Nación (Buenos Aires), 14 June 1968. [Reprinted in his Nueva antologia personal. Buenos Aires: Emecé, 1968, p. 60 and in his Elogia de la sombra. Buenos Aires: Emecé, 1969, p. 35; translated by Norman Thomas de Giovanni in New York Review of Books, 20 (19 July 1973): 22; translated by Robert Lima in James Joyce Quarterly, 10 (Winter 1973): 285.]

*1260. BOORUM, TED. "Finnegans Wake." Poetry, 62 (August 1943): 250.

1261. CASSOLA, CARLO. "Joyce in the Suburbs: The Unexperienced Writer," translated by Valeria Bigiaretti. Caffè, 5 (June 1960): 1-4. [Short story]

*1262. CATHERTON, L. "Portrait." Poetry, 61 (February 1943): 599-600.

1263. COLEMAN, ELLIOTT. "Joyce's Grave." Chesapeake Weekly Review, 12 June 1970, p. 7.

1264. COLUM, PADRAIC. "James Joyce at the Half-Century." transition, no. 21 (March 1932): 246.

*1265. _____. "The Artificer: James Joyce," in Irish Elegies. 2nd edition. Dublin: Dolmen Press, 1961, pp. 13-14. [Does not appear in first, 1958, edition; 3rd edition. Chester Springs, Pa.: Dufour, 1965, pp. 15-16.]

1266. DOWLING, ALBERT W. "Critic's Joyce." Georgia Review, 21 (Fall 1967): 353.

1267. FIELD, MATT. "Guidebook to Joyce." Georgia Review, 27 (Spring 1973): 108-109.

1268. FULLER, ROY. Epitaphs and Occasions. London: Lehmann, 1949, p. 50.

1269. GALLIGAN, EDWARD L. "James Joyce, Mark Twain and Alton Kurfsider." Mad River Review, 2 (Summer-Fall 1967): 61-68. [Short story]

1270. GILLON, ADAM. "A James Joyce Seminar, or Rejoyce in Ponderland." James Joyce Quarterly, 1 (Spring 1964): 51.

*1271. GOLL, YVAN. "Elegy for James Joyce." Nation, 152 (1 February 1941): 133.

1272. GREACEN, ROBERT. "James Joyce." Irish Writing, no. 10 (January 1950): 57.

GENERAL STUDIES

1273. GUINNES, BRYAN. Twenty Three Poems.
London: Duckworth, 1931.

1274. KAIN, RICHARD M. "The Fabulost Revoyager."
James Joyce Quarterly, 1 (Fall 1963): 9-
10.

1275. KAVANAGH, PATRICK. "A Wreath for Tom Moore's
Statue." Irish Times, 4 March 1944. [Re-
printed in his A Soul for Sale. London:
Macmillan, 1947 and in his Complete
Poems. Edited by Peter Kavanagh. New
York: Peter Kavanagh Hand Press, 1972,
pp. 148-149.]

1276. _____ . "The Paddiad." Horizon, 20
(1950): 80-95. [Short story]

1277. _____ . "Who Killed James Joyce?"
Envoy, 5 (May 1951): 12. [Reprinted in
A Bash in the Tunnel, pp. 49-52, No. 1644;
reprinted in Complete Poems. Edited by
Peter Kavanagh. New York: Peter Kavanagh
Hand Press, 1972, pp. 239-240; another
poem "Joyce's Ulysses," p. 246.]

1278. KELLY, SEAN. "Finnswake Again." National
Lampoon, 1, no. 34 (January 1973): 68-69.
[A parody; reprinted in This Side of Parodies. New York: Warner Paperback Library,
1974, pp. 35-39 and in James Joyce Quarterly, 11 (Summer 1974): 306-309.]

1279. KERRIGAN, ANTHONY. "Bloomsday 1965." Holy
Door, no. 2 (Winter 1965): 3-4. [Same
poem in Quest, 2 (Spring 1968): 248.]

1280. KROLL, JUDITH. "Milly Bloom's Monologue."
Quest supplement to, 3 (Summer-Fall 1968).
[i.e., Poetry Pamphlet, 1 (1969): 1.]

1281. LAWSON, JACK. "The Only God whose real Name
we Know." Colorado Quarterly, no. 15
(Winter 1967): 251-260. [Short story]

1282. LIDDY, JAMES. "Notes toward a James Joyce
Mythology." Arena, no. 2 (Autumn 1963):
5-6. [Prose poem]

1283. _____ . "Te Deum for Joyce: Imitated
from the Irish of Brendan Behan." Holy
Door, no. 3 (Spring 1966): 16.

1284. _____ , A Life of Stephen Dedalus. San
Francisco: White Rabbit Press, 1969.

1285. MacDIARMID, HUGH (C. M. Grieve). "In Memor-
ian James Joyce," in In Memoriam James
Joyce: From a Vision of World Language.
Glasgow: William McLellan, 1955, pp. 20-
73. [Reprinted in his Collected Poems.
New York: Macmillan, 1962, pp. 400-416;
reprinted in Poetry Like the Hawthorn.
Hemel Hempstead: Duncan Glen, 1962; reprinted in The Hugh MacDiarmid Anthology:
Poems in Scots and English. Edited by
Michael Grieve and Alexander Scott. London; Boston: Routledge and Kegan Paul,
1972, pp. 271-276.]

*1286. MacLEISH, ARCHIBALD. "Years of the Dog," in
his Collected Poems, 1917-1952. New York:
1952, pp. 134-135.

1287. MAURA, SISTER. "Portrait of the Artist."
Commonweal, 81 (23 October 1964): 132.

1288. MILNE, EWART. Diamond Cut Diamond. London:
Bodley Head, 1950, pp. 23, 39-45, 54-55.

1289. MONTAGUE, JOHN. [Poem], in A Bash in the
Tunnel, n.p., No. 1644.

1290. MORAVIA, ALBERTO. "Omaggio a James Joyce,
ovvero Il colpo di Stato." Nuovi Argon-
menti (1968): 23-34. [A play]

1291. MORSE, J. MITCHELL. "An Irish Medley."
James Joyce Quarterly, 4 (Fall 1966): 41.

1292. O'BRIEN, FLANN (Myles na Gopaleen, Brian
Nolan). The Dalkey Archive. London:
MacGibbon and Kee, 1964. [A novel]

1293. O'BRIEN, MAURICE N. "James Joyce." Canadian
Forum, 12 (May 1932): 294.

1294. PAYNE, BASIL. "Sunlight on a Square." Irish
Times, 8 February 1958, p. 6.

1295. PERELMAN, S. J. "Anna Trivia Pluralized."
New Yorker, 42 (26 November 1966): 53-55.
[Short story]

1296. POUND, EZRA. Pisan Cantos. London: Faber
and Faber, 1948, pp. 25, 34, 51.

1297. RATHKEY, W. A. "On James Joyce." English
Review, 62 (May 1936): 595-597.

1298. ROMAN, HOWARD. "Bloom and the Dryad." Kenyon Review, 23 (Spring 1961): 277-295.

1299. ROSENFELD, EDWARD. "Finnegans Wake," in The
Book of Highs: 250 Ways to Alter Con-
sciousness without Drugs. New York:
Quadrangle, 1973, p. 192.

1300. SAVAGE, HENRY. Long Spoon and the Devil.
London: Cecil Palmer, 1922, p. 12

1301. SHAPIRO, KARL. Essay on Rime. New York:
Reynal and Hitchcock, 1945.

1302. STEPHENS, JAMES. "Prologue" to The Joyce
Book, No. 2582.

1303. STONE, JAMES. "Lacunae: Part I (Poems)."
James Joyce Quarterly, 9 (Winter 1971):
270-277; Part II, James Joyce Quarterly,
9 (Spring 1972): 390-396.

1304. TAGLIABUE, JOHN. "Poems after Re-reading
Ulysses." Stolen Paper Review, 1 (Spring
1963): 56-57.

1305. VAN WYCK, WILLIAM. "To James Joyce, Master Builder." Contempo, 3, no. 13 (February 1934): 3.

1306. WOLFE, HUMBERT. "D. H. Lawrence and James Joyce," in his Lampoons. London: Ernest Benn, 1925, p. 35.

1307. Unsigned. "James Joyce, 1882-1941. Dos Poemas." Revue un Mexico, 17 (March 1963): 7.

Birthday and Anniversary Tributes

1308. CHRISTEN, ARNOLD. "James Joyce." Tages-Anzeiger (Zürich), 13 January 1966, p. 19. [25th anniversary of Joyce's death]

1309. COLUM, PADRAIC. "James Joyce at Half-Century," in "Hommage to James Joyce," pp. 245-246, No. 1312.

*1310. D., A. "Bergräbnis in Zürich: Vor 10 Jahren starb James Joyce." Süddeutsche Zeitung, 13 January 1951.

1311. GIEDION-WELCKER, CAROLA. "James Joyce zum 50. Geburtstag." Frankfurter Zeitung, no. 3 (3 February 1932): 9.

1312. GILBERT, STUART. "Homage to James Joyce." transition, no. 21 (March 1932): 245-255. Contents: Padraic Colum. "James Joyce at Half-Century," 245-246, No. 1309; Stuart Gilbert. "Homage to James Joyce," 247-249; Eugene Jolas. "Homage to James Joyce," 250-253, No. 1315; Thomas Mc-Greevy. "Homage to James Joyce," 254-255, No. 1318.

*1313. HAAS, WILLY. "Wüstenwander; Vor 75. Jahren wurde James Joyce geboren." Die Welt, 4 February 1957.

1314. HOHOFF, CURT. "Das Leben des James Joyce: Zum 80. Geburtstag." Süddeutsche Zeitung, 3/4 February 1962.

1315. JOLAS, EUGENE. "Homage to James Joyce," in "Homage to James Joyce," pp. 250-253, No. 1312.

1316. KRAUS, WOLFGANG. "Der Gigant aus Dublin." Saarbrücker Zeitung, 13 January 1966, p. 5. [25th anniversary of Joyce's death]

1317. LIDDY, JAMES. Esau, My Kingdom for a Drink, Homage to James Joyce on his LXXX Birthday. Dublin: Dolmen Press, 1962.

1318. McGREEVY, THOMAS. "Homage to James Joyce," in "Homage to James Joyce," pp. 254-255, No. 1312.

*1319. MAYOUX, JEAN-JACQUES. "Portrait de l'artiste 50 ans plus tard." Lettres françaises, 16-22 February 1961, pp. 1-2, 5.

1320. PRESCOTT, JOSEPH. "Homage to James Joyce." Books Abroad, 26 (Spring 1952): 156. [Reprinted in Letterature moderne, 11 (November-December 1961): 792-793; translated by Jaimé Broitmann Valdes in Sur, no. 274 (January-February 1962): 58-59.]

1321. SCHAUDER, KARLHEINZ. "Odysseus in Dublin: Zum 80. Geburtstag von James Joyce." Deutsche Post, 14 (1962): 73-74.

1322. SCHLESAK, DIETER. "Zum 25. Todestag von James Joyce." Neue Literatur (Bucharest), 27, no. 11-12 (1966): 65-66.

1323. SCHLIEN, HELMUT. "Dubliner Epopöe, Zum 50. Geburtstag von James Joyce und zu seinem Ulysses." Mannheimer Tageblatt, 3, no. 2 (1932).

1324. SCHRENK, M. "James Joyce zum 25. Todestag." Therapeutische Berichte (Leverkusen), 38 (1966): 192-197.

1325. SENN, FRITZ. "James Joyce, der Verfasser des Ulysses." Der Landbote, Winterthur, 4 February 1972, Sonntagspost, pp. 3-4. [Reprinted in his James Joyce: Aufsätze von Fritz Senn, pp. 45-51, No. 1654.]

*1326. WEISS, GERTRUD. "Die Odyssee des Grossstadt-menschen: Zum 75. Geburtstag von James Joyce am 2 Februar." Deutsche Woche (Munich), 7 (1957): 15.

*1327. WELTMANN, LUTZ. "Momentaufnahme: James Joyce: Zum 50. Geburtstag am 3. [sic] Februar 1932." Bayrische Israelitische Gemeindezeitung, 8 (February 1932): 36-37.

*1328. Unsigned. "James Joyce zum 50. Geburtstage." Die literarische Welt, 8 (1932): 5.

*1329. Unsigned. "James Joyce (Zum 50. Geburtstag)." Die literatur, 34 (April 1932): 384. [Quotes from B. Guillemin (No. 1738), Carola Giedion-Welcker (No. 1311) and Ernst Weiss (From Berliner Börsen Courier).]

Obituaries

*1330. ADAMS, J. DONALD. [n.t.]. New York Times, 26 January 1941, p. 2.

1331. CURRAN, CONSTANTINE, and ARTHUR POWER. [n.t.]. Irish Times, 14 January 1941. [Reprinted in Envoy, 5 (May 1951): 73-78; Curran piece reprinted in A Bash in the Tunnel, pp. 243-245, No. 1644.]

1332. BOWEN, ELIZABETH. "James Joyce." The Bell, 1, no. 16 (March 1941): 40-49.

1333. BYRNE, BARRY. "Flight from Eire." Commonweal, 33 (4 April 1941): 597-598.

GENERAL STUDIES

1334. HENNECKE, HANS. "James Joyce." Neue Deutsche Rundschau, 52 (February 1941): 120-
122. [Reprinted in Das Silberboot, 2
(1946): 133-138; reprinted in Dichtung
und Dasein: Gesammelte Essays. Berlin:
Henssel Vlg., 1950, pp. 160-168.]

1335. KAZIN, ALFRED. "A Man Unafraid to make
Great Mistakes." New York Herald Tribune
Books, 26 January 1941. [Reprinted as
"The Death of James Joyce," in his The
Inmost Leaf: A Selection of Essays. New
York: Harcourt, Brace and Co., 1955, pp.
3-8.]

*1336. MARICHALAR, ANTONIO. "James Joyce y sus
novelas." Revista de revistas, 30 (2
February 1941).

1337. ROWSE, A. L. "The Significance of James
Joyce's Work in English Literature."
World Review (London), March 1941, pp.
39-42.

*1338. ST. LAWRENCE, HENRY. "James Joyce." Time
and Tide, 22, no. 3 (18 January 1941):
44-45.

1339. SOFOVICH, LUISA. "Joyce el intrincado."
Alcor (Buenos Aires), no. 3 (April 1941):
50-52.

*1340. SPENDER, STEPHEN. "James Joyce: 1882-1941."
Listener, 25 (23 January 1941): 124-125.

*1341. STRAUMANN, HEINRICH. "Burial Speech for
James Joyce held at his Funeral in the
Firedhofskapelle Fluntern 15 January
1941," in In Memoriam, pp. 7-12, No. 1038.

*1342. STRONG, L. A. G. "The Art of James Joyce."
John O'London's Weekly, 24 January 1941,
pp. 428, 430.

1343. TOMKINSON, NEIL. "James Joyce." The
Adelphi, 17 (February 1941): 175-177.

*1344. Unsigned. "James Joyce Gestorben." Frank-
furter Zeitung, 15 January 1941.

*1345. Unsigned. "James Joyce Gestorben." Neue
Zürcher Zeitung, 13 January 1941.

*1346. Unsigned. "Lokales: Ein Dichter kam und
ging." Neue Zürcher Zeitung, 16 January
1941.

*1347. Unsigned. "Murky Bypath." Times Literary
Supplement, 25 January 1941, pp. 42, 45.

*1348. Unsigned. "Scientist of Letters." New
Republic, 104 (20 January 1941): 71-72.

*1349. Unsigned. "Silence, Exile, and Death."
Time, 10 February 1941, p. 72.

*1350. Unsigned. "Zum Tode von James Joyce." Neue
Zürcher Zeitung, 14 January 1941.

*1351. Unsigned. [n.t.]. New York Times, 13 Jan-
uary 1941, p. 15.

*1352. Unsigned. "James Joyce." New York Times,
14 January 1941, p. 20.

INFLUENCE STUDIES

See also II.B "Poetry: Sisson. "Verse of
James Joyce," No. 2789; II.C "Epiphanies":
Zants. "Relation of Epiphany to Description...,"
No. 2847; II.D "Dubliners: Kuehl. "à la Joyce:
The Sisters Fitzgerald...," No. 2954; Davis. "Im-
itation and Invention...," No. 2965; Hamilton.
"Between Innocence and Experience...," No. 2990;
Senn. "Reverberations," No. 3187; Ingram. "Amer-
ican Short Story Cycles...," No. 2867; Beckson.
"Moore's The Untilled Field...," No. 2892; II.F
"Portrait": Amor. "Julio Cortázar," No. 3289;
Avery. Inquiry and Testament..., No. 3215; French.
"Two Portraits...Dylan Thomas," No. 3324; Warren.
"Faulkner's 'A Portrait of the Artist,'" No. 3409;
II.H "Ulysses": Costa. "U, Lowry and The Voyage
Between," No. 4464; Fuentes. "Rayuela...," No.
4472; González. "La Novela hispanoamericano...,"
No. 4475; Lahr. "Language...," No. 4491; Lyon.
"Miguel Angel Asturias...," No. 4496; Larraya.
"Tradición y renovacion...," No. 4492; McCormick.
"James Joyce...," No. 4444; Meeuwesee. "O Atwater
ikweet...," No. 4501; Molinda. "Miguel Angel As-
turias," No. 4502; Murillo. Cyclical Night...,
No. 4448; Perez Carmona. "La ruptura...," No.
4321; Pla. "Joyce y el U," No. 3642; Poirier.
"Politics of Self-Parody," No. 4510; Reeves.
"Wolfe's Of Time and the River," No. 4515;
Schneider. "Thomas Wolfe and the Quest for Lan-
guage," No. 4518; Slabey. "Faulkner's Mosquitoes
and...," No. 4521; Sozonova. "Chilovek...," No.
4523; Stavrou. "Mr. Bloom and Nikos's Odysseus,"
No. 4585; Cohn. "Absurdity in English," No. 4462;
Palley. "Periplus of Don Pedro...," No. 4427;
Ledgard. "El torno al Ulises de Joyce," No. 4493;
Cicogna. "Preoccupazioni...," No. 3758; Patmore.
"Modern American Writers," No. 3983; Fitzgerald.
"Fitzgerald on U," No. 4470; Bienkowski. "Bodziec
...," No. 4436; Aronne. "U vs. Rayuela," No. 4435;
Varela. "James Joyce y el impacto...," No. 4452;
Unsigned. "F. Scott Fitzgerald's Copy of U," No.
4537; Gonzáles. "El U cuarenta anos despés," No.
3583; Heath. The Nouveau Roman..., No. 3592;
Boyd. "Joyce and the New Irish Writers," No. 3728;
Romera. "El monologo silente in Goldos y...," No.
4243; Rosenthal. "Sprach deformation...," No.
4273; Galloway. "Moses-Bloom-Herzog...," No. 4558;
II.I "Finnegans Wake": Burback. "Skin of our
Teeth," No. 4913; Dalton. "More Modern Instance,"
No. 5031; Dalton. "FW at large," No. 5395; Lee.
"Some Uses of FW in John Barth's The Sot Weed
Factor," No. 5455; Modic. "Eclectic...," No. 5141;
Morse. "Charles Nodier...," No. 5471; de Campos,
A. "Um lance de 'des' do Grande Sertao," No. 5013.

Books

1353. ABEL, LIONEL. "Samuel Beckett and James Joyce
in Endgame," in his Metatheatre. New York:
Hill and Wang, 1963, pp. 134-140.

1354. ALLEN, WALTER. The Modern Novel in Britain and the United States: New York: E. P. Dutton, 1964, pp. 4-14, et passim; London: Phoenix House, 1964 under the title Tradition and Dream.

*1355. ANDERSON, SHERWOOD. Dark Laughter. New York: Boni and Liveright, 1925, pp. 39, 120-121, 162.

*1356. _____. Letters. Selected with Introduction and Notes by H. M. Jones in association with W. B. Rideout. Boston: Little, Brown and Co., 1953, passim.

*1357. BERVEILLER, MICHEL. "James Joyce," in Le cosmopolitisme de Jorge Luis Borges. Publications de la Sorbonne, littéraatures, no. 4. Paris: Didier, 1973, pp. 278-280.

1358. CAMBON, GLAUCO. The Inclusive Flame: Studies in American Poetry. Bloomington: Indiana University Press, 1963, pp. 100, 160, 186ff, et passim.

1359. CARBALLO, EMMANUEL. Diecinueve protagonistas de la literatura mexicana del siglo XX. Mexico: Empresas editoriales, 1965, passim. [Discussion of J. Agustín Yáñez and his journal Bandera de Provincias in which pages of FW appeared.]

1360. CARGILL, OSCAR. Intellectual America. New York: Macmillan, 1941, pp. 346-350.

1361. CARPEAUX, OTTO MARIA. "Influência de Joyce," in Tendências contemporâneas de literatura: Um esbôço. Rio de Janeiro: Edições de Ouro, 1968, pp. 281-286.

1362. COHN, RUBY. "Joyce and Beckett, Irish Cosmopolitans," in Proceedings of the IVth Congress of the International Comparative Literature Association, vol. 1. Edited by François Jost. The Hague: Mouton, 1966, pp. 109-113. [Reprinted in James Joyce Quarterly, 8 (Summer 1971): 385-391.]

1363. COLLINS, NORMAN. The Facts of Fiction. London: Victor Gollancz, 1932, pp. 277-284.

1364. COSTA, RICHARD H. "The Literary Kinship," in Malcolm Lowry. New York: Twayne, 1972, pp. 21-44, et passim.

1365. DAICHES, DAVID. The Present Age in British Literature. Bloomington: Indiana University Press, 1958, passim.

*1366. DELATTRE, FLORIS. "L'influence de Marcel Proust et James Joyce," in Le roman psychologique de Virginia Woolf. 2nd edition. Paris: J. Vrin, 1967, pp. 142-171. [Reprint of 1932 edition]

1367. DURZAK, MANFRED. "Die Ästhetik des polyhistorischen Romans: James Joyce," in Hermann Broch: Der Dichter und seine Zeit. Stuttgart: W. Kohlhammer, 1968, pp. 76-113, et passim.

1368. EDEL, LEON. The Psychological Novel, 1900-1950. New York: Lippincott, 1955, passim. [1964 edition. The Modern Psychological Novel. New York: Grosset and Dunlap-Universal Library, includes additional section "Modes of Subjectivity."]

*1369. EVERY, GEORGE. "Impact of Joyce," in Poetry and Personal Responsibility. London: SCM Press, 1949.

1370. FEIBLEMAN, JAMES K. "The Comedy of Myth: James Joyce," in his In Praise of Comedy. London: Allen and Unwin, 1939, pp. 230-236.

1371. FRIERSON, WILLIAM C. The English Novel in Transition. Norman: Oklahoma University Press, 1942, passim.

1372. GROSSVOGEL, DAVID I. "Joyce and Robbe-Grillet," in his The Limits of the Novel: Evolutions of a Form from Chaucer to Robbe-Grillet. Ithaca: Cornell University Press, 1968, pp. 256-299.

1373. GUÉRARD, ALBERT. Literature and Society. Boston: Lothrop, Lee and Shepard, 1935, passim.

1374. HARSS, LUIS, and BARBARA DOHMANN. Into the Mainstream. New York: Harper and Row, 1967, passim.

*1375. HIDAKA, HACHIRO. "Nihou Bungaku no Baai ["Influence of Japanese Literature]," in Joisu Nyumon [An Introduction to James Joyce], pp. 186-195, No. 1511.

*1376. HOULT, NORAH. Coming from the Fair. New York: Covici Friede, 1937, pp. 158-159.

*1377. HUXLEY, ALDOUS. Eyeless in Gaza. New York: Harper and Bros., 1936, p. 106, et passim.

*1378. KENNEDY, SIGHLE. Murphy's Bed: A Study of Real Sources and Sur-real Associations in Samuel Beckett's First Novel. Lewisburg: Bucknell University Press, 1971, passim.

*1379. KOESTLER, ARTHUR. Dialogue with Death. New York: Macmillan, 1938, p. 125.

*1380. LEWIS, SINCLAIR. "The American Fear of Literature [Nobel Prize Address, 12 December 1950]," in The Man From Main Street. Edited by Harry E. Maule and Melville H. Crane. New York: Random House, 1953, p. 33.

*1381. LEWISOHN, LUDWIG. Expression in America. New York: Harper, 1932, passim.

GENERAL STUDIES

1382. McCORMICK, JOHN. The Middle Distance: A Comparative History of American Imaginative Literature: 1919-1932. New York: Free Press, 1971, passim.

*1383. McLUHAN, MARSHALL. "John Dos Passos: Technique vs Sensibility," in Dos Passos: The Critics, and the Writer's Intention. Edited by Allen Belkind. Carbondale, Edwardsville: Southern Illinois University Press; London, Amsterdam: Feffer and Simons, 1971, pp. 227-241. [Reprinted from Fifty Years of the American Novel. Edited by H. C. Gardiner (1951).]

1384. MACY, ALBERT. "James Joyce," in his The Critical Game. New York: Boni and Liveright, 1926, pp. 317-322.

1385. MAYOUX, JEAN-JACQUES. "L'Hérésie de James Joyce," in English Miscellany, No. 2. Edited by Mario Praz. Rome: 'Edizioni di Storia e Letteratura,' 1951, pp. 199-225. [Expanded in Vivants piliers, Lettres nouvelles, n.s. 6. Paris: Julliard, 1960, pp. 155-200.]

1386. MERCIER, VIVIAN. "The Greatest Precursor: Joyce," in The New Novel from Queneau to Pinget. New York: Farrar, Strauss and Giroux, 1971, pp. 23-30, et passim.

1387. MORRIS, LLOYD. Threshold in the Sun. New York: Harper, 1943, passim.

1388. MUIR, EDWIN. The Present Age, from 1914. London: Cresset Press, 1939, pp. 34, 134-139.

1389. MULLER, HERBERT J. "James Joyce," in his Modern Fiction: A Study of Values. New York: Funk and Wagnalls, 1937, pp. 288-316.

1390. MURDOCH, W. L. F. "Nihilism in Literature," in his Collected Essays. Sydney: Angus and Robertson, 1941, pp. 218-222.

1391. MYERS, WALTER L. The Later Realism. Chicago: University of Chicago Press, 1927, passim.

*1392. NORMAN, CHARLES. The Well of the Past. New York: Doubleday and Co., 1949, p. 219.

1393. NOWELL, ELIZABETH, ed. The Letters of Thomas Wolfe. New York: Charles Scribner's Sons, 1956, pp. 321-322, 566, 585-587, et passim.

*1394. OHASHI, KENZABURO. "Eibei Bungaku no Baai ["Influence on American and English Literature]," in Joisu Nyumon [An Introduction to James Joyce], pp. 180-185, No. 1511.

1395. OTA, SABURO. "Introduction to Joyce and His Influence," in A Study of Joyce, pp. 203-226, No. 1592. [In Japanese]

1396. PEYRE, HENRI. Writers and their Critics. Ithaca: Cornell University Press, 1944, passim.

1397. POWYS, JOHN COWPER. Enjoyment of Literature. New York: Simon and Schuster, 1938, passim.

1398. PROFFER, CARL R. Keys to Lolita. Bloomington, London: Indiana University Press, 1968, passim. [Also issued as Indiana University Publications, Humanities Series, no. 64.]

1399. ROSENFELD, PAUL. "James Joyce," in his Men Seen. New York: Dial Press, 1925, pp. 23-42. [Reprinted Freeport, New York: Books for Libraries Press, 1967, pp. 23-42.]

1400. ROTHMAN, NATHAN L. "Thomas Wolfe and James Joyce: A Study of Literary Influence," in A Southern Vanguard: The John Peale Bishop Memorial Volume. Edited by Allen Tate. New York: Prentice-Hall, 1947, pp. 52-77.

1401. SALINŠ, GUNARS. "Ephipanies, Old and New, in Latvian Letters," in Baltic Literature and Linguistics, publications of the Association of Baltic Studies, no. 4. Third Conference on Baltic Studies. Edited by Arvids Ziedonis, Jr. et al. Columbus: Association for the Advancement of Baltic Studies, 1973, pp. 37-43. [Influence on Imants Ziedonis and Ilze Škipsna]

1402. SARRAUTE, NATHALIE. L'Ere du soupçon: Essais sur le roman. Paris: Gallimard, 1956, passim.

1403. SCARFE, FRANCIS. Auden and After. London: Routledge, 1942, pp. 101-104.

1404. SKLAR, ROBERT. F. Scott Fitzgerald. New York: Oxford University Press, 1967, passim.

1405. SMIDT, KRISTIAN. James Joyce and the Cultic Use of Fiction. Oslo Studies in English, no. 4. Oslo: Akademisk Forlag, 1955. [Revised edition, 1959. New York: Humanities Press.]

1406. SMITH, DODIE. I Capture the Castle. Boston: Little, Brown and Co., 1948, pp. 141, 337.

1407. SPENDER, STEPHEN. "Introduction" to Malcolm Lowry's Under the Volcano. Philadelphia: Lippincott, 1965, pp. vii-xxvi.

1408. STARR, NATHAN C. The Dynamics of Literature. New York: Columbia University Press, 1945, passim.

1409. STOLTZFUS, BEN F. Alain Robbe-Grillet and the New French Novel. Carbondale: Southern Illinois University Press, 1964, passim.

1410. SULLIVAN, WALTER. "The New Faustus: The Southern Renascence and the Joycean Aesthetic," in Southern Fiction Today: Renascence and Beyond. Edited by George Core. Athens: University of Georgia Press, 1969, pp. 1-15. [Reprinted in his Death by Melancholy: Essays on Modern Southern Fiction. Baton Rouge: Louisiana State University Press, 1972, pp. 97-113.]

1411. SUMMERS, JOSEPH. After the Storm. Albuquerque: University of New Mexico Press, 1968, passim.

1412. SWIGGART, PETER. The Art of Faulkner's Novels. Austin: University of Texas Press, 1962, pp. 61-65 et passim.

1413. TAKAMURA, KATSUJI. "Joyce's Influence on English and American Literature," in A Study of Joyce, pp. 189-202, No. 1592.

1414. WEBER, BROM, ed. The Letters of Hart Crane. New York: Hermitage House, 1952, pp. 94-95 et passim.

1415. WICKHAM, HARVEY. "Cult of the Goat," in his The Impuritans. New York: Dial Press, 1929, pp. 235-258.

1416. WOLFE, THOMAS. Notebooks. Edited by Richard S. Kennedy and Paschal Reeves. Chapel Hill: University of North Carolina Press, 1970, passim.

Periodical Articles

1417. ABEL, LIONEL. "Joyce the Father, Beckett the Son." New Leader, 42 (14 December 1959): 26-27.

1418. AGGELER, GEOFFREY. "The Comic Art of Anthony Burgess." Arizona Quarterly, 25 (Autumn 1969): 234-251.

1419. BAKER, WILLIAM. "The World of Alexander Baron." Jewish Quarterly (London), 7 (Winter 1969): 17-20.

1420. BEACH, JOSEPH WARREN. "Novel from James to Joyce." Nation, 132 (10 June 1931): 634-636.

1421. BENSTOCK, BERNARD. "On William Gaddis: In Recognition of James Joyce." Wisconsin Studies in Contemporary Literature, 6 (Summer 1965): 177-189. [Summary appeared in South Central Bulletin, 25 (March 1965): 6.]

1422. BERGONZI, BERNARD. "The New Novel and the Old Book." Listener, 77 (23 March 1967): 391-392.

1423. BOULEZ, PIERRE. "'Sonate, que me veux-tu?'" translated by David Noakes and Paul Jacobs. Perspectives of New Music, 1 (Spring 1963): 32-44. [Influences of Joyce and Mallarmé on Boulez.]

1424. BROOKS, BENJAMIN G. "Shem the Penman: An Appreciation of James Joyce." Nineteenth Century and After, 129 (March 1941): 269-275.

*1425. BROWN, T. K. "Me and James Joyce." Encore, 2, no. 9 (October 1942): 438-444.

1426. BRUNO, FRANCESCO. "James Joyce et il nuova romanzo." La Giustizia (Rome), 1951.

1427. BRUSHWOOD, JOHN S. "Tradición y rebeldía en las novelas de José Augustin." Et caetera (Guadalajara), no. 14 (March 1969): 7-18.

1428. BURKE, KENNETH. "Three Definitions: The Joyce Portrait." Kenyon Review, 13 (Spring 1951): 181-192. [Reprinted in James Joyce's Dubliners, pp. 410-416, No. 2835.]

1429. CAMBON, G. GLAUCO. "La Trilogia 'USA' di John dos Passos." Le carte parlanti, n.s. 11, no. 3-4-5 (30 September 1950): 24-26.

1430. CANTWELL, ROBERT. "The Influence of James Joyce." New Republic, 77 (December 1933): 200-201.

1431. CASOTTI, FRANCESCO. "La poesia de Thomas Merton." Aevum, 39 (May-August 1965): 370-378.

1432. CISMARU, ALFRED. "Marguerite Duras and the New Novel." Dalhousie Review, 47 (Summer 1967): 203-212.

1433. CLISSMANN, ANNE. "Brian O'Nolan." Irish Times, 12 June 1973, p. 11.

1434. DAGLISH, ROBERT. "Katayev and his Critics." Anglo-Soviet Journal, 28 (January 1968): 2-5.

1435. DAVIES, WALFORD. "Imitations and Inventions: The Use of Borrowed Material in Dylan Thomas's Prose." Essays in Criticism, 18 (July 1968): 275-295.

1436. EDEL, LEON. "James and Joyce: The Future of the Novel." Tomorrow, 9 (August 1950): 53-56.

1437. EHRENBOURG, ILYA. "Entre Klebnikov et Joyce: Différences et convergencies." Esprit, n.s. 32 (July 1964): 56-62.

1438. FALQUI, ENRICO. "Da Joyce a Cassola." Fiera litteraria, 18 (1963): 1-2.

1439. FARGUE, LÉON-PAUL. "The Alchemist." transition, no. 23 (July 1935): 130-132.

GENERAL STUDIES

1440. FITTS, DUDLEY. "Two Aspects of Telemachus." Hound and Horn, 3 (April-June 1930): 445-450. [Faulkner and Thomas Wolfe]

1441. FRIEDMAN, MELVIN J. "Novels of Samuel Beckett: An Amalgam of Proust and Joyce." Comparative Literature, 12 (Winter 1960): 47-58.

1442. _____. "Anthony Burgess and James Joyce: A Literary Confrontation." Literary Criticism (University of Mysore, India), 9 (1971): 71-83.

1443. GEORGE, W. L. "Form and the Modern Novel." The Chapbook, 2, no. 8 (February 1920): 15-19.

1444. GIDLEY, M. "Some Notes on Faulkner's Reading." Journal of American Studies, 4 (July 1970): 91-102.

1445. GIDE, ANDRÉ. "Interviews imaginaires." Le Figaro, 30-31 May 1942. [Appeared as "Desperate Words call for Desperate Little Remedies" in Claybook for James Joyce, pp. 123-127, No. 1568.]

1446. GONZÁLES, MANUEL PEDRO. "Proyección infecunda de Joyce." Revista nacional de cultura, 24 (January-February 1962): 60-64. [Part of a longer article on the "Crisis de la novela en America."]

1447. HAWKES, TERRY. "Joyce and Speech." James Joyce Review, 1, no. 4 (December 1957): 33-37.

1448. HENDERSON, PHILIP. "James Joyce and Lewis Carroll: An Unsuspected Comparison." Everyman, 28 August 1930, p. 142.

1449. HENDRY, J. F. "The Element of Myth in James Joyce." Scottish Arts and Letters, no. 1 (1944): 16-20. [Appeared in James Joyce: Two Decades of Criticism, pp. 436-449, No. 1570.]

1450. HENKLE, ROGER B. "Pynchon's Tapestries on the Western Wall." Modern Fiction Studies, 17 (Summer 1971): 207-220.

1451. HICKMAN, VERA. "Waiting for Something: Samuel Beckett, Disciple of Joyce." Ante, 2, no. 3 (Summer 1966): 57-64.

1452. HOKENSON, JAN. "A Stuttering Logos: Biblical Paradigms in Beckett's Trilogy." James Joyce Quarterly, 8 (Summer 1971): 293-310.

1453. HUTCHINS, PATRICIA. "In the Wake of the Wake: Stuart Gilbert." Guardian, 2 February 1966, p. 9.

1454. IRINODA, M. "Hermann Broch no James Joyce taiken shiron." Tokyo Suisan Daigaku Ronshu (Reports of the Tokyo University of Fisheries), 1 (1966): 59-72; 2 (1967): 45-64; 4 (1969): 105-121. [With German summaries]

*1455. ISHIDA, K. "Joyce no hikaku bungaku ni okeru mondaiten." Eigoseinen (October 1961).

1456. JACK, PETER M. "Some Contemporaries: James Joyce." Manuscripts, 1 (1929): 24-27, 102-108.

*1457. JEDLICKA, GOTTHARD. "Wilhelm Gimmis 'Bildnis James Joyce.'" Neue Zürcher Zeitung, 85 (27 March 1954).

1458. JUST, GOTTFRIED. "Endstation Joyce: Werner Webers letzte Müncher Poetikvorlesung." Süddeutsche Zeitung, 13 July 1966.

1459. KAIN, RICHARD M. "Joyce notes from M.C. [i.e., C. P.] Curran's Under the Receding Wave (1970)." James Joyce Quarterly, 8 (Winter 1970): 186-188.

1460. KAPLAN, ROBERT B., and RICHARD J. WALL. "Eliot's 'Gerontion.'" Explicator, 19 (March 1961): item 36.

1461. KENNER, HUGH. "Joyce's Anti-Selves." Shenandoah, 4 (Spring 1953): 23-31.

1462. KESTING, MARIANNE. "Raymond Queneau in der Nachfolge von James Joyce." Die Zeit, 20 (1965): 31.

1463. KILGALLIN, ANTHONY R. "Eliot, Joyce and Lowry." Canadian Author and Bookman, no. 41 (Winter 1965): 3-4, 6.

1464. KRIM, SEYMOUR. "Reflections on a Ship that's not Sinking at All." London Magazine, 10 (May 1970): 26-43. [Gore Vidal]

1465. LINDSAY, JACK. "The Modern Consciousness." London Aphrodite, no. 1 (August 1928): 17-18.

1466. LITTLEJOHN, DAVID. "The Anti-Realists." Daedalus, 92 (Spring 1963): 250-264.

1467. LORIES, HECTOR-JAN. "De Wortels van de Nieuwe Roman ["Roots for a New Novel]." Nieuw Vlaams Tijdschrift, 19 (April 1966): 379-408.

1468. McMICHAEL, CHARLES T., and TED R. SPIVEY. "'Chaos--hurray!--is come again': Heroism in James Joyce and Conrad Aiken." Studies in the Literary Imagination, 3 (October 1970): 65-68.

1469. MARTIN, AUGUSTINE. "Inherited Dissent: The Dilemma of the Irish Writer." Studies, 54 (Spring 1965): 1-20.

1470. MAUROIS, ANDRÉ. "Un des saints patron de la jeune littérature." Figaro littéraire, 20 January 1966, p. 8.

1471. MELLER, HORST. "Zum literarischen Hintergund von Dylan Thomas Under Milk Wood." Neueren sprachen, 2 (February 1966): 49-58.

1472. MENTON, SEYMOUR. "Asturias, Carpentier y Yáñez: paralelismos y divergencias." Revista iberoamericana, 3 (January-April 1969): 31-52.

1473. MERCIER, VIVIAN. "Claude Simon: Order and Disorder." Shenandoah, 17 (Summer 1966): 79-92.

1474. _____. "James Joyce and the French New Novel." Tri-Quarterly, 8 (Winter 1967): 205-219.

*1475. MORRIS, LLOYD. "Modern Style and Contemporary Writers." News (Galveston, Texas), 17 February 1929.

1476. MORSE, J. MITCHELL. "The Choreography of 'The New Novel.'" Hudson Review, 16 (Autumn 1963): 396-419.

1477. _____. "The Case for Irrelevance." College English, 30 (December 1968): 201-211.

1478. NETTERVILLE, HARVEY E. "George Webber and Stephen Dedalus: Some Correspondences." South Central Bulletin, 33 (October 1973): 120, 122.

1479. NÚÑEZ, ESTUARDO. "James Joyce y Victor Llona." Revista peruana de cultura, nos. 7-8 (June 1966): 221-228.

1480. O'REILLY, JAMES P. "Joyce and Beyond Joyce." Irish Statesman, 5, no. 1 (12 September 1925): 17-18. [Reprinted in Living Age, 327 (October 1925): 250-253.]

1481. PEDEN, WILLIAM. "James Joyce en Mexico," translated by Miguel Gonzalez. La cultura en Mexico (Supplement to Siempre), 20 August 1969, pp. vii-ix.

1482. _____. "Joyce Among the Latins." James Joyce Quarterly, 7 (Summer 1970): 287-296.

1483. PENTON, BRIAN. "Note on the Form of the Novel." London Aphrodite, no. 6 (July 1929): 434-444.

1484. PETER, JOHN. "Joyce and the Novel." Kenyon Review, 18 (Autumn 1956): 619-632.

1485. POSS, STANLEY M. "Portrait of the Artist as Beginner." University of Kansas City Review, 26 (March 1960): 189-196.

1486. PRESCOTT, JOSEPH. "A Semester's Course in James Joyce." CEA Critic, 14 (February 1952): 7.

1487. QUINN, OWEN. "The Cult of the Absurd." Icarus, 3 (1953): 95-99.

1488. RECK, RIMA DRELL. "Celine and Joyce: Each Man's Journey." South Central Bulletin, 26 (March 1966): 9. [Abstract]

1489. ROCKS, JAMES E. "The Christian Myth as Salvation: Caroline Gordon's The Strange Children." Tennessee Studies in English, 16 (1968): 149-160.

1490. ROSE, MARILYN GADDIS. "More on Julien Green on James Joyce." James Joyce Quarterly, 5 (Winter 1968): 176-177.

1491. SALE, RICHARD B. "An Interview in London with Brian Moore." Studies in the Novel, 1 (Spring 1969): 67-80.

1492. SASSE, CARL. "Dichter Kampfen um ihr Augenlicht: James Joyce--Azel Munthe--Adolf von Hatzfeld." Cesra-Saule, 9 (1962): 224-228.

1493. SAUL, GEORGE BRANDON. "The Verse, Novels and Drama of Seamus O'Kelly." Éire-Ireland, 2 (Spring 1967): 48-57.

1494. SCHOLES, ROBERT. "Mithridates, He Died Old: Black Humor and Kurt Vonnegut, Jr." Hollins Critic, 3 (October 1966): 1-12.

1495. SCOTT, EVELYN. "Contemporary of the Future." Dial, 69 (October 1920): 353-367.

1496. SINKO, GRZEGORZ. "Joyce--w czterdziesci lat pozniej." Dialog (Warsaw), 9 (December 1964): 113-118.

1497. TINDALL, WILLIAM YORK. "Exiles: Rimbaud to Joyce." American Scholar, 14 (Summer 1945): 351-355.

1498. TRILLING, LIONEL. "Impersonal/Personal." Griffin, 6 (June 1957): 4-13.

1499. _____. "The Person of the Artist." Encounter, 9 (August 1957): 73-79.

*1500. TROY, WILLIAM. "Crisis in the Novel." The Figure in the Carpet, no. 1 (October 1927): 11-15.

*1501. VÁZQUEZ AMARAL, JOSÉ. "Técnica novelística de Agustin Yáñez." Cuadernos americanos, 17 (March-April 1958): 245-251.

*1502. WHITE, JOHN J. "Myths and Patterns in the Modern Novel." Mosaic, 2, no. 3 (Spring 1969): 42-55.

*1503. WILLIAMS, DOUGLAS. "Portrait of an Artist." Joycenotes, 2 (September 1969): 2-3. [Influence upon painter John Hart]

*1504. WOLFE, PETER. "Farragan's Retreat." Studies in the Twentieth Century, no. 8 (Fall 1971): 115-117.

1505. WRIGHT, DAVID. "Patrick Kavanagh." London Magazine, 8 (April 1968): 22-29.

COMPREHENSIVE STUDIES OF JOYCE'S WORKS

See also I.F "Dissertations," Nos. 2398-2428

Books

1506. ADAMS, ROBERT MARTIN. James Joyce: Common Sense and Beyond. New York: Random House, 1967. ["Study in Weakness and Humiliation" reprinted in James Joyce's Dubliners, pp. 101-104, No. 2885.]

1507. ALDRIDGE, J. W., ed. Critiques and Essays on Modern Fiction, 1920-1951. New York: Ronald Press, 1952.
    Contents: Irene Hendry. "Joyce's Epiphanies," 129-142, No. 2833; Harry Levin. "Montage," 143-159, from No. 1603; Edmund Wilson. "The Dream of H. C. Earwicker," 160-172, from No. 5530; T. S. Eliot. "Ulysses, Order and Myth," 424-426, No. 4293.

1508. ALLOTT, MIRIAM. "James Joyce: The Hedgehog and the Fox," in On the Novel: A Present for Walter Allen on his Sixtieth Birthday. Edited by B. S. Benedikz. London: J. M. Dent, 1971, pp. 161-177.

1509. ANDERSON, JOHN. Some Questions in Aesthetics. Sydney: Sydney University Literary Society, 1932, pp. 11-12, 17-18, 20-25.

1510. ANDERSON, MARGARET. My Thirty Years War. New York: Covici-Friede, 1930, pp. 174-176, 212-215, 218-227, 244-248. [New edition with preface and index added, New York: Horizon Press, 1969; reprinted New York: Greenwood, 1971.]

*1511. ARA, MASATO, and SHOICHI SAEKI, eds. Joisu Nyumon [An Introduction to James Joyce]. Tokyo: Nanun-do, 1960; enlarged edition, 1966. [In Japanese; contents below are given in English.]
    Contents: Masato Ara. "Introduction," i-ii; "The Life of James Joyce," 7-15; Study of the Works: Yasuo Deguchi. "Dubliners," 18-26, No. 2859; Yoshio Masuda. "Stephen Hero," 28-35, No. 3197; Kyoichi Ono. "A Portrait of the Artist as a Young Man," 38-45, No. 3268; Shoichi Saeki. "Composition and Technique of Ulysses," 48-64, No. 4274; Michiko Uchida. "Time and Ulysses," 65-72, No. 3667; Michiko Uchida. "On the Third Chapter," 73-77, No. 4746; Toru Tsuchiya. "On the Sixth Chapter," 78-81, No. 4767; Fumi Takano. "On the Ninth Chapter," 82-85, No. 4801; Hachiro Hidaka. "On the Eleventh Chapter," 86-93, No. 4817; Gakuji Yamakawa. "On the Fourteenth Chapter," 94-97, No. 4851; Kenzaburo Ohashi. "On the Fifteenth Chap-

ter," 98-101, No. 4863; Kenzo Suzuki. "On the Eighteenth Chapter," 102-105, No. 4901; W. R. McAlpine, Motoki Toda. "Finnegans Wake," 108-129, No. 4949; Yuji Odajima. "Chamber Music and Pomes Penyeach," 132-134, No. 2785; Takashi Sasayama. "Exiles," 135-139, No. 3489; Schoichi Saeki. "Critical Points in the Study of James Joyce," 142-153, No. 1645; Yoshio Masuda. "Bildungsroman," 154-161, No. 3259; Kenzo Suzuki. "Psychological Novel," 162-169, No. 4203; Gakuji Yamakawa. "Symbolism," 170-177, No. 4281; Influence of James Joyce: Kenzaburo Ohashi. "On American and English Literature," 180-185, No. 1394; Hachiro Hidaka. "On Japanese Literature," 186-195, No. 1375; Yasuko Ono. "Letters of James Joyce," 197-206, No. 345; Yasuko Ono. "Contemporary Setting of Study of James Joyce," 208-216, No. 1054; Yataka Haniya, Masato Ara, Yoshio Masuda, Kenzaburo Ohashi, Kenzo Suzuki, Michiko Uchida, Toru Tsuchiya, Yuji Odajima, Shoichi Saeki. "On Ulysses (Symposium)," 217-253, No. 3588; Yasuko Ono and Takezo Suzuki. "Index," 1-16; Yasuko Ono. "Chronology," 17-24; Takezo Suzuki. "Bibliography," 25-49.

1512. ARNOLD, ARMIN. James Joyce. Köpfe des XX. Jahrhunderts, 29. Berlin: Colloquium Vlg., 1963. [Translated by Armin Arnold and Judy Young. New York: Ungar, 1969.]

1513. AUBERT, JACQUES. Introduction à l'esthetique de James Joyce. Paris: Didier, 1973.

1514. BARD, JOSEPH. "Tradition and Experiment," in Transactions of the Royal Society of Literature, vol. 21. Edited by Walter de la Mare. London: Oxford University Press, 1944, pp. 103-124.

1515. BARRETT, WILLIAM. "Myth or the Museum?" in Time of Need: Forms of Imagination in the Twentieth Century. New York, London: Harper and Row; Toronto: Fitzhenry and Whiteside, 1972, pp. 312-350, et passim.

1516. BATES, RONALD, and HARRY J. POLLOCK, eds. Litters from Aloft: Papers Delivered at the Second Canadian James Joyce Seminar. University of Tulsa, Department of English Monograph Series, vol. 13. Tulsa: University of Tulsa, 1971.
    Contents: Ronald Bates. "Introduction," vii-ix; Richard M. Kain. "Treasures and Trifles in Ulysses," 1-14, No. 3606; Maurice Beebe. "Joyce and the Meanings of Modernism," 15-25, No. 3699; Fritz Senn. "Joycean Translatitudes: Aspects of Translation," 26-49, No. 1061; M. J. Sidnell. "A Daintical Pair of Accomplasses: Joyce and Yeats," 50-73, No. 810; Michael H. Begnal. "Who Speaks When I Dream?: Who

Dreams When I Speak?; A Narrational Approach to Finnegans Wake," 74-90, No. 5310; Bernard Benstock. "James Joyce and the Women of the Western World," 91-108, No. 1517.

1517. BENSTOCK, BERNARD. "James Joyce and the Women of the Western World," in Litters from Aloft, pp. 91-108, No. 1516.

1518. BERGONZI, BERNARD. The Situation of the Novel. London: Macmillan; Pittsburgh: University of Pittsburgh Press, 1970, passim.

*1519. BERTI, LUIGI. "Aspetti di Joyce," in his Boccaporto. Florence: Parenti, 1940, pp. 141-174.

1520. BLENGIO BRITO, RAÚL. Introducción a Joyce. Montevideo: Ano Internacional del Libro Biblioteca Nacional, 1972.

1521. BLISSETT, WILLIAM. "James Joyce in the Smithy of His Soul," in James Joyce Today, pp. 96-134, No. 1659.

1522. BLÖCKER, GÜNTER. "James Joyce," in his Die neuen Wirklichkeiten: Linien und Profile der modernen Literatur. Berlin: Argon Vlg., 1957, pp. 66-85. [Expanded from Neue Deutsche Hefte, no. 31 (January 1957): 535-543; reprinted Munich: Deutscher Taschenbuch Vlg., 1968, pp. 56-71; translated by Thilo Ullmann as Líneas y perfiles de la literatura moderna. Madrid: Guararrama, 1969, pp. 64-83.]

1523. _____. Literatur als Teilhabe: Kritische Orientierung zur literarischen Gegenwart. Berlin: Argon Vlg., 1966.
Contents: "Alles Joyce," 233-236, "'Das Dubliner Dagebuch' des Stanislaus Joyce," 226-228; "Stuart Gilbert 'Das Rätsel Ulysses,'" 221-223 (reviews reprinted from Frankfurter Allgemeine Zeitung, 17 September 1960, 6 January 1962, 11 July 1964).

1524. BONHEIM, HELMUT. Joyce's Benefictions. Perspectives in Criticism, vol. 16. Berkeley: University of California Press, 1964.

*1525. BONIFACINO, VICTOR. "James Joyce," in Ensayos beligerantes: Bertrand Russell-James Joyce. Montevideo: Alfa, 1960, pp. 75-96.

1526. BOREL, JACQUES et al. Joyce. Buenos Aires: Jorge Alvarez, 1969.
Contents: "Presentación," 7; Jacques Borel. "Introducción al Ulises," 11-26 (translated from Temps modernes (January 1968): 1291-1307), No. 3721; Giorgio Melchiori. "Joyce y la tradición de la novela," 27-47 (translation of No. 3629);

Edwin Berry Burgum. "El Ulises y el callejón sin salida del individualismo," 49-60 (translation of No. 3745); D. S. Savage. "James Joyce: técnicas y contendidos," 63-108 (translation from No. 1647); Edwin Berry Bergum. "Contradicciones del escepticismo en Finnegans Wake," 109-118 (translation from No. 5002); Frederick J. Hoffman. "El libro de sí mismo," 121-132 (translation from No. 4482); Hermann Broch. "James Joyce y el presente," 133-160 (translation of No. 3555); Edwin Berry Burgum. "Retrato del artista cómo hombre," 161-166 (translation of review of Ellmann's James Joyce and Stanislaus Joyce's My Brother's Keeper originally in Antioch Review (Spring 1960): 111-118); Bibliografia, 169-174; Cronología, 175-176.

1527. BOYD, ERNEST. Ireland's Literary Renaissance. Revised edition. London: Grant Richards, 1923, pp. 402-412. [Joyce is not mentioned in the 1921 edition; portions of this work appeared as "The Expressionism of James Joyce." New York Herald Tribune, 28 May 1922, p. 29 attacking Valery Larbaud (see No. 2064).]

1528. BOYLE, ROBERT. "'Astroglodynamonologos,'" in New Light on Joyce, pp. 131-140, No. 1656.

1529. BRANDABUR, EDWARD. A Scrupulous Meanness: A Study of Joyce's Early Work. Urbana: University of Illinois Press, 1971.

1530. BRASIL, ASSIS. Joyce: O romance como forma. Literatura estrangeira, vol. 1. Rio de Janeiro: Livros do Mundo Inteiro, 1971.

1531. BRENNAN, JOSEPH GERARD. Three Philosophical Novelists: James Joyce, André Gide, Thomas Mann. New York: Macmillan, 1964, pp. 3-58; London: Collier-Macmillan.

1532. BRIVIC, SHELDON R. "James Joyce: From Stephen to Bloom," in Psychoanalysis and Literary Process. Edited by Frederick C. Crews. Cambridge, Mass.: Winthrop, 1970, pp. 118-162.

1533. BURGESS, ANTHONY. Here Comes Everybody. London: Faber and Faber, 1965; Re-Joyce. New York: Norton, 1965. [Paperback edition, New York: Ballantine, 1966, translated by Gisela and Manfred Triesch as Ein Mann in Dublin. Bad Hamburg, Berlin, Zürich: Gehlen, 1968.]

1534. _____. "Giants in Those Days," in his The Novel Now. New York: W. W. Norton, 1967; Pegasus Paper, 1970, pp. 22-37.

1535. _____. "1. Dear Mr. Shame's Voice," "2. Shem the Penman," "3. Ulysses: How Well has it Worn?," in his Urgent Copy: Literary Studies. London: Jonathan Cape; New

York: W. W. Norton, 1968, pp. 74-78, 78-82, 82-84, et passim. [1. reprinted from Spectator, 27 November 1964, pp. 731-732, a review of Joyce's Portrait: Criticisms and Critiques, No. 3223; 2. reprinted from Spectator, 2 December 1966, p. 726, a review of Ellmann's Letters, No. 309; 3. reprinted from Times (London), 17 March 1966, p. 15.]

1536. _____ . Joysprick: An Introduction to the Language of James Joyce. London: André Deutsch; New York: Seminar Press, 1973. [Earlier appearance of "The Ulysses Sentence" in James Joyce Quarterly, 9 (Summer 1972): 423-435.]

1537. CALDER-MARSHALL, ARTHUR. "James Joyce," in Then and Now, 1921-1935. London: Jonathan Cape, 1935, pp. 186-188.

1538. CAMBON, GLAUCO. "Ulisse: la proteiformita del linguaggio," "Ancora su Joyce: Magia e scacco della parola," in La lotta con Proteo. Milan: Bompiani, 1963, pp. 17-38, 39-67. [Reprinted with slight changes from Aut Aut (July 1953) and (September 1953).]

1539. CAMPOS, AUGUSTO de, and HAROLDO de CAMPOS. Teoria da poesia concreta. São Paulo: Edições Invenção, 1965, passim.

1540. CHACE, WILLIAM M., compiler. Joyce: A Collection of Critical Essays. Twentieth Century Views. Englewood Cliffs, New Jersey: Prentice-Hall, 1974.
        Contents: "Introduction," pp. 1-10; Hélène Cixous. "Political Ignominy...," 11-17 (from No. 1543); Richard Ellmann. "Backgrounds of 'The Dead,'" 18-28 (from No. 308); Hugh Kenner. "The Portrait in Perspective," 29-49, No. 1600; Edmund Wilson. "James Joyce," 50-66 (from No. 1686); S. L. Goldberg. "Homer and the Nightmare of History," 67-83 (abridged from No. 1573); Anthony Cronin. "Advent of Bloom," 84-101 (from No. 4540); Richard Ellmann. "Why Molly Bloom Menstruates," 102-112 (from No. 3568); Harry Levin. "The Language of the Outlaw," 113-129 (from No. 1603); Clive Hart. "Quinet," 130-142 (from No. 5315); Lionel Trilling. "James Joyce in His Letters," 143-165, No. 2360; Robert Martin Adams. "The Bent Knife Blade: Joyce in the 1960's," 166-175, No. 62.

1541. CHATTERJEE (CHATTOPUDHYAYA), SISIR. James Joyce: A Study in Technique. Calcutta: 1957. [2nd edition, Calcutta: Das Gupta, 1970; 1957 edition reprinted Folcroft, Pa.: Folcroft Press, 1970.]

1542. CHURCH, MARGARET. "James Joyce: Time and Time Again," in her Time and Reality: Studies in Contemporary Fiction. Chapel

Hill: University of North Carolina Press, 1963, pp. 27-66, et passim.

1543. CIXOUS, HÉLÈNE. L'Exile de James Joyce: ou, l'art du remplacement. Publications de la Faculté des Lettres et Sciences Humaines de Paris-Sorbonne, sér. "Recherches," 46. Paris: Grasset, 1968. [Translated by Sally A. J. Purcell. New York: David Lewis, 1972; appendix "Thoth et l'écriture" in L'Arc, 36 (1968): 73-79; also contains earlier publication: "James Joyce et la mort de Parnell." Langues modernes, 61 (March-April 1967): 142-147.]

1544. CONNOLLY, CYRIL. "James Joyce: Portrait of the Artist," "James Joyce: Ulysses," "James Joyce: Finnegans Wake," in his The Modern Movement. London: Andre Deutsch and Hamish Hamilton; New York: Atheneum, 1966, pp. 33, 48-49, 81.

1545. COVENEY, PETER. "Joyce, Virginia Woolf, D. H. Lawrence," in his Poor Monkey: The Child in Literature. London: Rockliff, 1957, passim. [New edition, The Image of Childhood. Baltimore, Harmondsworth: Penguin, 1967, pp. 303-336.]

1546. CROSS, RICHARD K. Flaubert and Joyce: The Rite of Fiction. Princeton: Princeton University Press, 1971.

1547. D'AGOSTINO, NEMI. "Reflessioni su Joyce," in Friendship's Garland: Essays Presented to Mario Praz on his Seventieth Birthday, vol. 2. Edited by Vittorio Gabrieli. Rome: Edizioni di Storia e Letteratura, 1966, pp. 253-267.

1548. DAICHES, DAVID. "Dubliners," "Ulysses and Finnegans Wake: The Aesthetic Problem," "Ulysses: The Technical Problem," "Ulysses as Comedy: Finnegans Wake," in The Novel and the Modern World. Chicago: University of Chicago Press, 1939, pp. 80-157. [Revised edition, Chicago: University of Chicago Press, 1960, pp. 63-82, 83-97, 98-112, 113-138--second and fourth chapters substantially revised, first and third chapters substantially the same; "Dubliners" chapter reprinted in Discussions of the Short Story. Edited by Hollis Summers. Boston: D. C. Heath, 1963, pp. 80-88 and in Modern British Fiction. Edited by Mark Schorer. New York: Oxford University Press, 1961, pp. 308-321.]

1549. _____ . A Critical History of English Literature, vol. 2. New York: Ronald Press, 1960, pp. 1133-1135.

1550. DAVIES, ANEIRIN. Yr All Tud Rhagarweiniad I Weithiau James Joyce. London: Cwasg Foyle, 1944.

1551. DEBENEDETTI, GIACOMO, ed. Introduzione a
Joyce. Tutte le opere di James Joyce.
3 vols. Milan: Mondadori, 1967.
    Contents: Volume I: Excerpt from
Stanislaus Joyce. My Brother's Keeper,
No. 329; Introduction by Richard Ellmann,
Preface by T. S. Eliot, pp. 3-310, trans-
lated by Giovanni Giudici; Harry Levin.
From James Joyce: Critical Introduction,
pp. 311-559, No. 1603, translated by
Ariodante Marianni; Stuart Gilbert. From
James Joyce's Ulysses, pp. 559-1083, No.
3580, translated by Nicoletta Neri; Italo
Svevo. From James Joyce, pp. 1087-1115,
No. 781; Ernst Robert Curtius. "James
Joyce and his Ulysses," pp. 1119-1151,
No. 4259, translated by Lea Ritter San-
tini; Joseph Campbell and Henry M. Rob-
inson. From Schematic Guide to Finnegans
Wake, pp. 1155-1185, No. 5523, translated
by J. Rodolfo Wilcock; Edmund Wilson.
"Dream of H. C. Earwicker," pp. 1189-
1219, No. 5530, translated by Nemi D'Agostino; Vol. 2. Dubliners and Portrait
and Stephen Hero; Vol. 3. Ulysses and
Finnegans Wake; Vol. 4. Poems and other
writings; Vol. 5. Letters.

1552. DEMING, ROBERT H., ed. James Joyce: The
Critical Heritage. 2 vols. London:
Routledge and Kegan Paul; New York:
Barnes and Noble, 1970.

1553. DESTEFANO, JOSÉ R. "La gran aventur intel-
ectual de James Joyce," in his Ocho en-
sayes. Buenos Aires: "El Ateneo," 1943,
pp. 125-142.

1554. DONOGHUE, DENIS. The Ordinary Universe:
Soundings in Modern Literature. London:
Faber and Faber; New York: Macmillan,
1968, passim.

1555. DUFF, CHARLES C. James Joyce and the Plain
Reader. Preface by Herbert Read. London: Harmsworth, 1932. [Reprinted Folcroft, Pa.: Folcroft Press, 1969; reprinted New York: Haskell House, 1971.]

1556. DUYTSCHAEVER, JORIS. James Joyce. Ontmoet-
ingen 88. Brugge: Desclée de Brouwer,
1970.

1557. EGRI, PÉTER. "A kép tárgyszerüségének öss-
zetörése. Az ábrázolás álomszerüsége, a
belsö monolog. Az ábrázolás álombelisége.
Azalom és átomáaábrázolás változásának
dekadens végpontja Joyce," "Joyce müvészi
világképének modern valóságfedezete Mann,"
in his Alom, látomás, valóság. Budapest:
Gondolat, 1969, pp. 175-248, 249-294.
[Pages 207-215 translated as "The Place
of James Joyce's Interior Monologue in
World Literature." Umana, 20 (May-
September 1971): 32-35.]

1558. ELIOT, T. S., ed. Introducing James Joyce:
A Selection of Prose. London, Faber, 1942.

1559. FEHR, BERNHARD. "Bewusstseinsstrom und Kon-
struksion: James Joyce," in his Die englische Literatur der Gegenwart und die
Kulturfragen unserer Zeit. Leipzig:
Tauchnitz, 1930, pp. 56-68.

1560. FISCHER, THERESE. Bewusstseinsdarstellung
im Werk von James Joyce von Dubliners zu
Ulysses, Neue Beiträge zur Anglistik und
Amerikanistik, Bd. 10. Frankfurt a.M.:
Athenäum Vlg., 1973.

1561. FRIEDE, DONALD. The Mechanical Angel. New
York: Alfred Knopf, 1948, pp. 70-73, et
passim.

1562. FUKUNAGA, KAZUTOSHI. "Two Recent Discoveries
and Two Others," in A Study of Joyce, pp.
107-136, No. 1592.

1563. GANDON, YVES. "Examen de conscience litté-
aire de James Joyce Irlandais," in his
Imagéries critiques. Paris: Société
Française d'Editions littéraires et Techniques, 1933, pp. 181-192.

1564. GARCIA SABELL, D. "James Joyce i a loita
pola comunicacion total," in his Ensaios.
Vigo: Galaxio [1963], pp. 97-190. [In
Galician; translated into Castilian as
"James Joyce y la lucha por la communica-
ción total," in Tres sintomas de Europa:
James Joyce, Vincent Van Gogh, Jean-Paul
Sartre. Madrid: Ediciones de la Revista
de Occidente, 1968, pp. 9-101.]

1565. GARRETT, PETER K. "James Joyce: The Artifice
of Reality," in his Scene and Symbol from
George Eliot to James Joyce. Yale Studies
in English, no. 172. New Haven: Yale
University Press, 1969, pp. 214-271.

1566. GIEDION-WELCKER, CAROLA. Schriften, 1926-
1971: Statimen zu einer Zeitbild. Edited
by Reinhold Hohl. Cologne: M. DuMont
Schauberg, 1973.
    Contents: "Der frühe Joyce," 24-27
(reprinted from Neue Zürcher Zeitung, 5
July 1928); "Zum Ulysses von James Joyce,"
27-39, No. 3822; "Work in Progress, Ein
sprachliches Experiment von James Joyce,"
39-48, No. 5051; "James Joyce und die
Sprache," 49-51, No. 5281; "Ein beflügelter Dialog im Jahr 1938 zwichen Le Cor-
busier und James Joyce," 52-53, No. 443;
"Begegnungen mit James Joyce," 53-74, No.
1655; "Künstlerbriefe: James Joyce," 490-
493 (four items in Letters 3 and one unpublished letter of 13 February 1940 to
her from Joyce).

1567. GILLET, ERIC. "Strange Reading," in Books
and Writers. Singapore: Routledge, 1930,
pp. 21-25.

1568. GILLET, LOUIS. Stèle pour James Joyce.
Marseilles: Éditions du Sagittaire, 1941.
[Reprinted in Paris by same publisher in

COMPREHENSIVE STUDIES OF JOYCE'S WORKS

1946; translated with "Introduction" by Georges Markow-Totevy (No. 1617) as Claybook for James Joyce. Preface by Leon Edel (No. 666) and including "Desperate Words call for Desperate Little Remedies" by André Gide (No. 1445). London: Abelard-Schuman, 1958; three fragments from the first and second editions, totally by Gillet, appeared in James Joyce Yearbook, pp. 32-46, No. 1596.]
    Contents (of 1941 and 1946 editions): "Lettre à Paul Valéry," 9-10; "Avant-Propos," 11-22; "Du coté de chez Joyce," 23-42; "M. James Joyce et son nouveau roman," 43-62; "L'extraordinaire aventure de M. J. Joyce," 63-88; "Adieux à Joyce," 89-98; "Joyce vivant," 99-164; Appendix: "Lettre d'Edmund Gosse," 165-166; "Lettres de George Moore," 167-168.

1569. GIORGIANNI, ENIO. Inchiesta su James Joyce. Milan: Epiloghi di Perseo, 1934.

1570. GIVENS, SEON, ed. James Joyce: Two Decades of Criticism. New York: Vanguard Press, 1948. [Augmented edition, 1963, with addition of Givens' essay "The After Decades," pp. xv-xxxviii and additional bibliography, pp. 480-486.]
    Contents: "Introduction," pp. ix-xiii; Eugene Jolas. "My Friend James Joyce," 3-18, No. 871; Frank Budgen. "James Joyce," 19-26, No. 1085; Irene Hendry [Chayes]. "Joyce's Epiphanies," 27-47, No. 2833; Richard Levin and Charles Shattuck. "First Flight to Ithaca: A New Reading of Joyce's Dubliners," 47-94, No. 2925; James T. Farrell. "Exiles and Ibsen," 95-131, No. 3487; Hugh Kenner. "The Portrait in Perspective," 132-174, No. 3251; James T. Farrell. "Joyce's Portrait of the Artist, with a Postscript on Stephen Hero," 175-197, No. 3232; T. S. Eliot. "Ulysses, Order and Myth," 198-202, No. 4293; S. Foster Damon. "The Odyssey in Dublin, with a Postscript, 1947," 203-242, No. 3774; Philip Toynbee. "A Study of James Joyce's Ulysses," 243-284, No. 4097; Vivian Mercier. "Dublin under the Joyces," 285-301, No. 4456; William Troy. "Notes on Finnegans Wake," 302-318, No. 5221; Edmund Wilson. "The Dream of H. C. Earwicker," 319-342, No. 5530; Frank Budgen. "Joyce's Chapters on Going Forth by Day," 343-367, No. 5595; Joseph Campbell. "Finnegan the Wake," 368-389, No. 5009; Frederick J. Hoffmann. "Infroyce," 390-435, No. 934; J. F. Hendry. "James Joyce," 436-449, No. 1449; Stuart Gilbert. "James Joyce," 450-467, No. 1039; T. S. Eliot. "A Message to the Fish," 468-471, No. 1105.

1571. GLECKNER, ROBERT F. "Joyce and Blake: Notes Toward Defining a Literary Relationship," in A James Joyce Miscellany, Third Series, pp. 188-205, No. 1614.

1572. GLICKSBERG, CHARLES I. "Eros and Agape in James Joyce," in his The Sexual Revolution in Modern English Literature. The Hague: Martinus Nijhoff, 1973, pp. 73-87.

1573. GOLDBERG, S. L. The Classical Temper. New York: Barnes and Noble, 1961; London: Chatto and Windus, 1961. ["Art and Life: The Aesthetic of the Portrait" reprinted in Twentieth Century Interpretations of a Portrait of the Artist as a Young Man, pp. 64-84, No. 3273; "Art et liberté: l'esthétique d'Ulysses," reprinted in Configuration critique de James Joyce, II, pp. 93-136, No. 1584, originally in ELH, 24 (March 1957): 44-64; "Artistry of Dubliners" reprinted in Twentieth Century Interpretations of Dubliners, pp. 86-92, No. 2862; "Virtues and Limitations" reprinted in James Joyce's Dubliners, pp. 29-35, No. 2885.]

1574. _____. James Joyce. Writers and Critics. Edinburgh: Oliver and Boyd, 1962; New York: Grove Press, 1963 (reissue of 1962 title with new imprint). [Reprinted New York: Barnes and Noble, 1966; translated by Pe. Francisco de Rocha Guimarães. Rio de Janeiro: Civilizaçõa Brasileira, 1968; "Der Ulysses von James Joyce: Der gesunde und fröliche Geist," translated by Jürgen Enkemann in Englische Literatur von Oscar Wilde bis Samuel Beckett. Interpretationen, no. 9. Edited by Willi Erzgräber. Frankfurt a.M.: Fischer Bücherei, 1970, pp. 100-129.]

1575. GOLDING, LOUIS. James Joyce. London: Thornton Butterworth, 1933. [Reprinted Folcroft, Pa.: Folcroft Press, 1970; reprinted Port Washington, New York: Kennikat Press, 1972.]

1576. GOLDMAN, ARNOLD. The Joyce Paradox: Form and Freedom in His Fiction. Evanston, Ill.: Northwestern University Press; London: Routledge and Kegan Paul, 1966.

1577. _____. James Joyce. Profiles in Literature Series. London: Routledge and Kegan Paul; New York: Humanities, 1968.

1578. GOODHEART, EUGENE. "Joyce and the Career of the Artist-Hero," in his The Cult of the Ego: The Self in Modern Literature. Chicago and London: University of Chicago Press, 1968, pp. 183-200.

1579. GRIFFIN, GERALD. "James Joyce," in his Wild Geese: Pen Portraits of Famous Irish Exiles. London: Jarrolds, 1938, pp. 22-25.

1580. GROSS, JOHN. James Joyce. New York: Viking, 1970; London: Fontana, 1971. [Translated by David Léger. Paris: Seghers, 1972.]

1581. HAAN, J. den. Joyce, Mythe van Erin. Amsterdam: De Bezige Bij, 1948. [2nd edition. Literare Documenten Series, 5, 1967.]

1582. HALPER, NATHAN. The Early James Joyce. Columbia Essays on Modern Writers, no. 68. New York, London: Columbia University Press, 1973.

1583. HARMON, MAURICE, ed. The Celtic Master: Contributions to the First James Joyce Symposium Held in Dublin, 1967. Dublin: Dolmen Press, 1969.
     Contents: Maurice Harmon. "Introduction," 7; Niall Montgomery. "A Context for Mr. Joyce's Work," 9-15, No. 1622; Donagh MacDonagh. "The Lass of Aughrim or the Betrayal of James Joyce," 17-25, No. 3174; Norman Silverstein. "Evolution of the Nighttown Setting," 27-36, No. 4870; Margaret C. Solomon. "The Phallic Tree of Finnegans Wake," 37-43, No. 5302; Stanley Sultan. "A Joycean Look at The Playboy of the Western World," 45-55, No. 788; Notes on Contributors, 57.

1584. HAYMAN, DAVID, ed. Configuration critique de James Joyce, II. [La Revue des Lettres Modernes, no. 9, nos. 117-122, translated by Paul Rozenberg. Paris: Lettres Modernes, 1965. See No. 1636 for Cc de JJ, I.]
     Contents: David Hayman. "Preface," 9-10; Richard M. Kain and Robert E. Scholes. "La première version du portrait," 11-30, No. 3023; A. G. Woodward. "Technique et sentiment dans Le Portrait de l'artiste jeune," 31-48, No. 3274; David Hayman. "Dedale et Dedalus dans Portrait de l'artiste jeune," 49-72, No. 3284; Douglas Knight. "A propos de Ulysse," 73-92, No. 3682; S. L. Goldberg. "Art et liberté: l'esthétique de Ulysse," 93-136, No. 1504; William York Tindall. "Dante et Mrs. Bloom," 137-148, No. 4294; Vivian Mercier. "James Joyce et la tradition irlandaise de la parodie," 149-180, No. 4032; J. S. Atherton. "Finnegans Wake, 'la pantomime gestentielle,'" 181-199, No. 4996; Clive Hart. "Le motif 'Quinet' dans Finnegans Wake," 201-222, No. 5042; Alan M. Cohn and Phillip Herring. "Critique de James Joyce: sélection bibliographique des études générales consacrées à Joyce, suivi d'un index pour l'étude des oeuvres particulières," 223-244, No. 44.

*1585. HELSZTYŃSKI, STANISLAW. "James Joyce," in Od Szekspira do Joyce'a. 1939. [2nd edition. Warsaw: Stanislaw Cukrowski, 1948, pp. 310-323.]

1586. HIGGINS, AIDAN. "Tired Lines, or Tales my Mother Told Me," in A Bash in the Tunnel, pp. 55-60, No. 1644.

1587. HOCHMUTH, ARNO. Literatur und Dekadenz: Kritik der literarischen Entwicklung in Westdeutschland. Berlin: Dietz Vlg., 1963, passim.

1588. HODGART, MATTHEW J. C., and MABEL P. WORTHINGTON. Song in the Works of James Joyce. New York: Columbia University Press, 1959.

1589. HOWARTH, HERBERT. "James Augustine Aloysius Joyce," in his The Irish Writers, 1880-1940. New York: Hill and Wang, 1958, pp. 247-285.

1590. _____. "The Joycean Comedy: Wilde, Jonson, and Others," in A James Joyce Miscellany, Second Series, pp. 179-194, No. 1613.

1591. HUXLEY, ALDOUS, and STUART GILBERT. Joyce the Artificer: Two Studies of Joyce's Method. London: Privately Printed, 1952.

*1592. ITO, SEI, ed. Joisu Kenkyu [A Study of Joyce]. Tokyo: Eihosha, 1955, revised and enlarged edition, 1965. [In Japanese. Contents here given in English translation.]
     Contents: Sei Ito. "Preface," 5-10; Sadamu Nagamatsu. "The Life and Literature of Joyce," 11-56, No. 230; Junzaburo Nishiwaki. "On Joyce," 57-76, No. 1626; Sakae Tatsumiya. "Technique and Sentence Style of Joyce," 77-106, No. 1672; Kazutoshi Fukunage. "Two Recent Discoveries and Two Others," 107-136, No. 1562; Sei Ito. "Catholicism and Joyce's Characters," 137-168, No. 1593; Yukio Haruyama. "Joyce and His Contemporaries," 169-188, No. 612; Katsuji Takamura. "Joyce's Influence on English and American Literature," 189-202, No. 1413; Saburo Ota. "Introduction to Joyce and His Influence," 203-226, No. 1395; Yukio Suzuki. "Joyce as Seen by His Contemporaries," 227-242, No. 618; Ichiro Ando. "Joyce as Poet," 243-268, No. 2781; Shin-Ichiro Nakamura. "Decadence of 19th Century Novels and the Development of 20th Century Novels," 269-282, No. 1625; Hiroshi Noma. "The Battle Against the Subconscious," 283-298, No. 3264; Ichiro Ando. "Study of Dubliners," 299-316, No. 2849; Saiichi Maruya. "A Study of Portrait of the Artist," 317-340, No. 3258; Kazuo Nakabashi. "Study of Ulysses," 341-364, No. 3633; Shizuo Machino. "Study of Finnegans Wake," 365-406, No. 4950; Yukio Suzuki. "Study of Exiles," 407-443, No. 3490; "Chronology of Joyce's Life," 444; List of Joyce's Works, Bibliography, Contributors.

*1593. _____. "Catholicism and Joyce's Characters," in A Study of Joyce, pp. 137-168, No. 1592.

COMPREHENSIVE STUDIES OF JOYCE'S WORKS

1594. JACQUOT, JEAN. "Joyce ou l'exil de l'artiste," in Visages et perspectives de l'art moderne. Edited by Jean Jacquot. Paris: Éditions du Centre National de la Recherche Scientifique, 1956, pp. 79-112.

1595. JALOUX, EDMOND. Au pays du roman. Paris: Éditions R.-A. Corrêa, 1931, pp. 97-109, 111-122.

1596. JOLAS, MARIA, ed. A James Joyce Yearbook. Paris: Transition Press, 1949.
Contents: Maria Jolas. "Foreword"; Stuart Gilbert. "Sketch of a Scenario of Anna Livia Plurabelle," 10-19, No. 4931; Wladimir Weidlé. "On the Present State of Poetic Language," translated by M[aria] J[olas], 20-31, No. 1836; Louis Gillet. "Stèle pour James Joyce," 32-46, No. 1568; Roland von Weber. "On and About Joyce's Exiles," translated by M[aria] J[olas], 47-67, No. 3491; Hermann Broch. "Joyce and the Present Age," translated by E[ugene] and M[aria] J[olas], 68-108, No. 3555; Heinrich Straumann. "Last Meeting with Joyce," 109-116, No. 555; Paul Léon. "In Memory of Joyce," translated by M[aria] J[olas], 116-125, No. 875; Philippe Soupault. "Recollections of James Joyce," translated by M[aria] J[olas], 126-129, No. 547; Clémence Ramnoux. "The Finn Cycle: The Atmosphere and Symbols of a Legend," translated by M[aria] J[olas], 130-158, No. 5318; Unsigned. "Interview with Mr. John Stanislaus Joyce," 159-169, No. 920.

1597. KAIN, RICHARD M. "Problems of Interpretation in Symbolistic Art: The Example of James Joyce," in Literary History and Literary Criticism. Acts of the 9th Congress of the International Federation for Modern Languages and Literature. Edited by Leon Edel et al. New York: New York University Press, 1965, pp. 301-303. [An abstract; full article given in Journal of General Education, 17 (October 1965): 227-235.]

1598. KAYE, JULIAN B. "Simony, The Three Simons and Joycean Myth," in A James Joyce Miscellany, 1957, pp. 20-36, No. 1612.

1599. KELLY, ROBERT G. "Joyce Hero," in James Joyce Today, pp. 3-10, No. 1659.

1600. KENNER, HUGH. Dublin's Joyce. Bloomington: Indiana University Press, 1956. [Reprinted Gloucester, Mass.: Peter Smith, 1969; excerpt reprinted in Twentieth Century Interpretations of Dubliners, pp. 38-56, No. 2862; excerpt reprinted in Twentieth Century Interpretations of A Portrait of the Artist as a Young Man, pp. 26-37, No. 3273.]

1601. KRONEGGER, MARIA ELIZABETH. James Joyce and Associated Image Makers. New Haven: College and University Press, 1968.

1602. LARBAUD, VALÉRY. Ce vice impuni, La lecture: Domaine anglais. Paris: Gallimard, 1936, pp. 230-252. [Reprint of No. 2064.]

1603. LEVIN, HARRY. James Joyce: A Critical Introduction. Norfolk: New Directions Books, 1941; reprinted London: Faber and Faber, 1944; revised and enlarged edition, London: Faber and Faber; Norfolk: New Directions, 1960. [Includes "On First Looking into Finnegans Wake." New Directions in Prose and Poetry (1939): 253-287 and "New Irish Stew." Kenyon Review, 1 (Autumn 1939): 460-465; translated by Claude Tarnaud. Paris: R. Marin, 1950; translated by Antonio Castro Leal. Mexico City, Buenos Aires: Fondo de Cultura Economica, 1959; translated by Adiodante Marianni, edited by Amleto Lorenzini. Milan: A. Mondadori, 1972; a chapter appeared as "James Joyce: Two Keys" in Essays in Modern Literary Criticism. Edited by Ray B. West. New York: Rinehart, 1952, pp. 501-513; section 2, part 2 appeared in Critiques and Essays on Modern Fiction, 1920-1951. Selected by John W. Aldridge. New York: Ronald Press, 1952, pp. 143-149; last chapter translated by José Rodriguez as "James Joyce: Un epitatio." Origenes (Havana), 2, no. 10 (Summer 1946): 7-16; "The Artist in A Portrait" reprinted in Critical Reviews of Portrait of the Artist as a Young Man, pp. 34-47, No. 3255; same in Modern British Fiction. Edited by Mark Schorer. New York: Oxford University Press, 1961, pp. 322-335; same in Joyce's Portrait: Criticisms and Critiques, pp. 9-24, No. 3223; same in Portraits of an Artist, pp. 31-44, No. 3260; pages 42-43 reprinted in Twentieth Century Interpretations of A Portrait of the Artist as a Young Man, pp. 107-108, No. 3273; excerpts reprinted in A Library of Literary Criticism, pp. 106-117, No. 250.]

1604. LEVIN, HARRY, ed. The Portable James Joyce. New York: Viking Press, 1947; English edition as The Essential James Joyce. London: Jonathan Cape, 1948.

1605. LITZ, A. WALTON. The Art of James Joyce. New York: Oxford University Press, 1961. [Revised, paperback reprint, 1964.]

1606. _____. James Joyce. Twayne's English Author's Series, vol. 31. New York: Twayne, 1966. [Translated by A. Carbonaro. Florence: Il Castoro, 1967.]

1607. LUNDKVIST, ARTUR, ed. Europas Litteraturhistoria, 1918-1939. Stockholm: Forum, 1946, pp. 68-73.

1608. _____ . Ikarus' Flykt. Stockholm: Albert Bonniers, 1950, pp. 73-112, et passim.

*1609. LUTTER, TIBOR. James Joyce. Trodalomtörténeti kisködyvtar, no. 2. Budapest: Gondolat, 1959.

1610. LYONS, DR. J. B. "Doctors and Hospitals," in A Bash in the Tunnel, pp. 193-202, No. 1644.

1611. _____ . James Joyce and Medicine. Dublin: Dolmen, 1973; New York: Humanities Press, 1974.

1611a. McCARTHY, DESMOND. "James Joyce," in his Criticism. New York: Boni and Liveright, 1926, pp. 296-311. [Excerpts reprinted in A Library of Literary Criticism, pp. 106-117, No. 250.]

1612. MAGALANER, MARVIN, ed. A James Joyce Miscellany. New York: James Joyce Society, 1957.
Contents: Marvin Magalaner. "Editor's Note," 8; Padraic Colum. "Foreword," 9-10; Thornton Wilder. "Joyce and the Modern Novel," 11-19, No. 4969; Julian B. Kaye. "Simony, The Three Simons, and Joycean Myth," 20-36, No. 1598; Alfred Kerr. "Joyce in England," 37-43, No. 4371; Leon Edel. "James Joyce and the Academician," 44-48, No. 666; Georges Markow-Totevy. "James Joyce and Louis Gillet," 49-61, No. 667; Maria Jolas. "Joyce's Friend Jolas," 62-74, No. 4945; J. B. Yeats. "A Letter from J. B. Yeats to John Quinn," 75-76; Margaret Anderson. "Anniversary Greetings," 77.

1613. MAGALANER, MARVIN, ed. A James Joyce Miscellany, Second Series. Carbondale, Ill.: Southern Illinois University Press, 1959.
Contents: Marvin Magalaner. "Introduction," xiii-xvi; John J. Slocum and Herbert Cahoon. "Five More Pages of James Joyce's Stephen Hero," 3-8, No. 3198; H. K. Croessmann. "Joyce, Gorman and the Scheme of Ulysses: An Exchange of Letters --Paul Léon, Herbert Gorman, Bennett Cerf," 9-14, No. 4258; Joseph Prescott. "Stylistic Realism in Joyce's Ulysses," 15-66, No. 4271; Maurice Beebe. "Joyce and Stephen Dedalus: The Problem of Autobiography," 67-78, No. 3216; Julian B. Kaye. "A Portrait of the Artist as Blephen-Stoom," 79-92, No. 4545; James Stern. "James Joyce: A First Impression," 93-102, No. 591; Michael J. O'Neill. "The Joyces in the Holloway Diaries," 103-110, No. 344; Richard M. Kain. "Portraits of James Joyce, A Preliminary Checklist," 111-118, No. 48; Ruth Von Phul. "Joyce and the Strabismal Apologia," 119-132, No. 1682; John O. Lyons. "The Man in the Macintosh," 133-138, No. 3624; J. Mitchell Morse. "Molly Bloom Revisited," 139-150, No. 4603;

Adaline Glasheen. "Joyce and the Three Ages of Charles Stewart Parnell," 151-178, No. 930; Herbert Howarth. "The Joycean Comedy: Wilde, Jonson, and Others," 179-194, No. 1590; Henry Morton Robinson. "Hardest Crux Ever," 195-208, No. 5528; A. Walton Litz. "The Making of Finnegans Wake," 209-224, No. 4947; Maria Jolas. "The Little Known Paul Léon," 225-233, No. 680.

1614. MAGALANER, MARVIN, ed. A James Joyce Miscellany, Third Series. Carbondale, Ill.: Southern Illinois University Press, 1962.
Contents: Marvin Magalaner. "Introduction," xi-xx; John J. Slocum and Herbert Cahoon. "Christmas Eve: James Joyce," 3-7, No. 2887; Robert Scholes. "The Broadsides of James Joyce," 8-18, No. 2780; James R. Baker. "Ibsen, Joyce, and the Living Dead: A Study of Dubliners," 19-32, No. 2851; James R. Thrane. "Joyce's Sermon on Hell: Its Source and Its Backgrounds," 33-78, No. 3405; Joseph Prescott. "The Characterization of Molly Bloom," 79-126, No. 4607; William Empson. "The Theme of Ulysses," 127-154, No. 4416; Richard M. Kain. "The Yankee Interviewer in Ulysses," 155-157, No. 4770; Trevor Lehnam. "The Happy Hunting Ground: Shakespearean Dramatis Personae in the 'Scylla and Charybdis' Episode of James Joyce's Ulysses," 158-174, No. 4794; Morton D. Paley. "Blake in Nighttown," 175-187, No. 4449; Robert F. Gleckner. "Joyce and Blake: Notes Toward Defining a Literary Relationship," 188-225, No. 1571; Vivian Mercier. "In the Wake of the Fianna: Some Additions and Corrections to Glasheen and a Footnote or Two to Atherton," 226-238, No. 5361; Ruth Von Phul. "Circling the Square: A Study of Structure," 239-277, No. 5319; David Hayman. "Notes for the Staging of Finnegans Wake," 278-293, No. 2552.

1615. MAGALANER, MARVIN, and RICHARD M. KAIN. Joyce: The Man, The Work, The Reputation. New York: New York University Press, 1956; London: John Calder, 1957. [Reprinted New York: Collier, 1962; "The Joyce Enigma" reprinted in Portraits of an Artist, p. 3, No. 3260; "Dubliners and the Short Story" reprinted in James Joyce's Dubliners, pp. 16-28, No. 2885; "Virgin and Witch" reprinted in James Joyce's Dubliners, pp. 124-130, No. 2885; "Guest Commentary on 'The Sisters'" reprinted in The Art of Short Fiction. Edited by Barbara Pannwitt. Boston: Ginn, 1964, pp. 367-371; "Backgrounds of A Portrait" reprinted in Critical Reviews of A Portrait of the Artist, pp. 48-78, No. 3255; reprinted in Portrait: Notes, No. 3222; excerpts reprinted in A Library of Literary Criticism, pp. 106-117, No. 250.]

COMPREHENSIVE STUDIES OF JOYCE'S WORKS

1616. MAJAULT, JOSEPH. James Joyce. Classiques du XXe siècle, no. 56. Paris: Éditions Universitaries, 1963. [Translated by Anna Rosso Cattabiani. Turin: Borla, 1964; translated by Jean Stewart. London: Merlin Press; Redwood City, Calif. and Toronto: Pendragon House, 1971-- slightly revised and updated.]

1617. MARKOW-TOTEVY, GEORGES. "Introduction," in Claybook for James Joyce, pp. 13-25, No. 1568.

1618. MAYOUX, JEAN-JACQUES. "Parody and Self-Mockery in the Works of James Joyce," in English Studies Today, Third Series. Edited by G. I. Duthie. Edinburgh: Edinburgh University Press, 1964, pp. 187-198.

1619. _____. James Joyce. Paris: Gallimard, 1965. [Translated by Rudolf Wittkopf. Frankfurt a. M.: Suhrkamp, 1967; the chapter "Joyce et ses personnages" reprinted in Revue de Paris, 72 (February 1965): 39-53.]

1620. MERCANTON, JACQUES. "James Joyce," in his Poètes de l'univers. Paris: Éditions Albert Skira, 1947, pp. 13-90.

1621. MOHOLY-NAGY, LÀSZLÒ. Vision in Motion. Chicago: Paul Theobald, 1947, pp. 341-351.

1622. MONTGOMERY, NIALL. "A Context for Mr. Joyce's Work," in The Celtic Master, pp. 9-15, No. 1583.

*1623. MORSE, J. MITCHELL. "The Mephistophelian Style of James Joyce," in Langue et littérature. Actes du VIIIe Congres de la Fédération Internationale des Langues et Littératures Modernes. Paris: Societé d'Édition 'les belles lettres,' 1961, p. 308.

1624. MULTHAUP, UWE. Das Künstlerische Bewusst-sein und seine Gestaltung in James Joyces Portrait und Ulysses. Europäische Hoch-schulschriften, Reihe 14: Angelsäch-sische Sprache und literatur, Bd. 11. Bern: Herbert Lang; Frankfurt a.M.: Peter Lang, 1973.

1625. NAKAMURA, SHIN-ICHIRO. "Decadence of 19th Century Novels and the Development of 20th Century Novels," in A Study of Joyce, pp. 269-282, No. 1592.

1626. NISHIWAKI, JUNZABURO. "On Joyce," in A Study of Joyce, pp. 57-76, No. 1592.

1627. NOJIMA, HIDEKATSU. Eguzailu no Bungaku: Joisu, Eriotto, Rorensu no Ba'ai [The Literature of Exile: The Case of Joyce, Eliot, Lawrence]. Tokyo: Nan'undo, 1963.

1628. O'BRIEN, DARCY. The Conscience of James Joyce. Princeton: Princeton University Press, 1968.

1629. _____. "Some Psychological Determinants of Joyce's View of Love and Sex," in New Light on Joyce, pp. 15-27, No. 1656.

1630. OKETANI, HIDEAKI. Jeimusu Joisu. Tokyo: Kinokuniya, 1964.

1631. PACI, FRANCESCA ROMANA. Vita e opere di James Joyce. Bari: Laterza, 1968. [Translated by J. Montserrat Torrents as James Joyce: Vida y obra. Barcelona: Ediciones Peninsula, 1970.]

1632. PARIS, JEAN. James Joyce par lui-même. Écrivains de Toujours, no. 39. Paris: Éditions du Seuil, 1957. [Translated as James Joyce in Selbstzeugnissen und Bild-dokumenten by Guido G. Meister with material supplemented by Paul Raabe. Hamburg: Rowohlt, 1960; translated by Aurelio Corazon del Camino as James Joyce por el mismo. Mexico City: Compania General de Ediciones, 1959; translated by Daria Menicanti as James Joyce. Milan: Il Saggiatore, 1966.]

1633. PHILIPPIDE, AL. "Despre James Joyce," in Consideratii confortabile, vol 2. Bucharest: Editura Eminescu, 1972, pp. 47-50.

1634. PINGUENTINI, GIANNI. James Joyce in Italia. Florence: Sansoni, 1963; Verona: Linotipia Veronese di Ghidini e Fiorini, 1963.

1635. POUND, EZRA. "James Joyce: To His Memory," in his If This Be Treason. Siena: Printed for Olga Rudge, 1948, pp. 16-20. [Reprinted in Forrest Read's Pound/Joyce, No. 952.]

1636. PRESCOTT, JOSEPH, ed. Configuration critique de James Joyce, I. [La Revue des lettres modernes, 6, nos. 46-48 (Autumn 1959), nos. 49-51 (Winter 1959-1960), translations by Magali Patchett-Morsy, Marie-Claude Peugeot, and Paul Rozenberg. See No. 1584 for II.]
    Contents: Harry Levin. "Introduction à James Joyce," pp. 259-275, from No. 1604; Marvin Magalaner. "'Les Soeurs' de James Joyce," 276-287, No. 2955; Joseph Prescott. "Stephen le Héros," 288-306, No. 3207; Hugh Kenner. "Le Portrait en perspective," 307-357, No. 1570; Francis Fergusson. "Les Exilés de Joyce," 358-374, No. 3488; W. B. Stanford. "Ce mysticisme qui plaisait à Joyce: note sur la source premier d'Ulysse," 375-384, No. 4524; T. S. Eliot. "Ulysse: l'ordre et le mythe," 385-390, No. 4293; Frederick W. Sternfeld. "Ulysse: Poésie et Musique," 391-433, No. 3658; Morton D. Zabel. "Les poésies

lyriques de Joyce," 201-208, No. 2821;
William Troy. "Notes sur Finnegans Wake,"
209-228, No. 5221; John Peale Bishop.
"Finnegans Wake," 229-260, No. 5563;
Harry Levin. "Le voyage sentimental de
Joyce à travers la France et l'Italie,"
261-271, No. 484; Thornton Wilder. "Joyce
et le roman moderne," 272-282, No. 1612;
Maurice Beebe and A. Walton Litz. "Critique de James Joyce: sélection bibliographique des études générales consacrées
à Joyce, suivie d'un index pour l'étude
des oeuvres particulières," 283-332, No.
29.

1637. _____ . Exploring James Joyce. With a
Preface by Harry T. Moore. Crosscurrents/
Modern Critiques. Carbondale: Southern
Illinois University Press, 1964. [Re-
printed as James Joyce: The Man and His
Work. Toronto: Forum House, 1969; see
also Prescott's letter to editor, TLS,
29 January 1971, p. 127, disclaiming re-
sponsibility for the new title.]
Contents: "James Joyce a Study in
Words," 3-16, No. 5294, reprinted in
Portraits of an Artist, No. 3260; "Ste-
phen Hero," 17-28, No. 3207, reprinted in
Joyce's Portrait: Criticisms and Critiques,
No. 3223; "Homer's Odyssey and Joyce's
Ulysses," 29-50, No. 4322; "Local Allusions in Ulysses," 51-58, No. 4323; "The
Characterization of Stephen Dedalus in
Ulysses," 59-76, No. 4617; "The Charac-
terization of Molly Bloom," 77-105, No.
4607; "Stylistic Realism in Ulysses,"
106-134, No. 4271.

1638. RADER, RALPH W. "Defoe, Richardson, Joyce,
and the Concept of Form in the Novel,"
in Autobiography, Biography, and the
Novel: Papers Read at a Clark Library
Seminar, May 13, 1972. Los Angeles:
William Andrews Clark Memorial Library,
UCLA, 1973, pp. 31-72.

1639. REBORA, PIERO. La letteratura inglese del
novecento. Firenze: Edizioni delle Lingue
Estere, 1950, pp. 120-123.

1640. RIVOLAN, A. Littérature irlandaise contemporaine. Paris: Hachette, 1939, passim.

1641. ROHDE, PETER. "James Joyce," in Fremmede
digtere i det 20 arhundrede, vol. 2.
Edited by Sven M. Kristensen. Copenhagen:
G. E. C. Gad, 1968, pp. 67-84.

1642. ROTHE, WOLFGANG. James Joyce. Wiesbaden:
Limes Vlg., 1957.

1643. RUBIN, LOUIS D., JR. "A Portrait of a Highly
Visible Artist," in his The Teller in the
Tale. Seattle and London: University of
Washington Press, 1967, pp. 141-177.

1644. RYAN, JOHN, ed. A Bash in the Tunnel: James
Joyce by the Irish. Brighton and London:
Clifton Books, 1970.
Contents: [Starred items appear in
James Joyce Essays. Folcroft, Pa.: Fol-
croft Library Editions, 1973, a reprint
of the May 1951 issue of Envoy, No. 153.]
John Montague. "Poem," No. 1289; John
Ryan. "Introduction,"; *Brian Nolan. "A
Bash in the Tunnel," 15-20, No. 1188;
Samuel Beckett. "Dante...Bruno...Vico...
Joyce," 21-34, No. 4907; *W. B. Stanford.
"The Mysticism that Pleased Him: A Note
on the Primary Source of Joyce's Ulysses,"
35-42, No. 4524; Edna O'Brien. "Dear Mr.
Joyce," 43-47, No. 1053; *Patrick Kavan-
agh. "Who Killed James Joyce?," 49-52, No.
1277; *Joseph Hone. "A Recollection of
James Joyce," 53-54, No. 870; Aidan Hig-
gins. "Tired Lines, or Tales my Mother
Told Me," 55-60, No. 1586; *Niall Montgom-
ery. "Joyeux Quicum Ulysse...Swissairis
Dubellay Gadelice," 61-72, No. 5469; Ulick
O'Connor. "Joyce and Gogarty," 73-100, No.
234; Stanislaus Joyce. "The Bud," 101-133,
No. 331; John Jordan. "Joyce without Fears:
A Personal Journey," 135-146, No. 846; Eoin
O'Mahony. "Father Conmee and His Associ-
ates," 147-155, No. 511; Patrick Boyle.
"Drums and Guns, and Guns and Drums. Hur-
rah! Hurrah!," 157-161, No. 2857; *Denis
Johnston. "A Short View of the Progress of
Joyceanity," 163-167, No. 1154; *Andrew
Cass. "Childe Horrid's Pilgrimace," 169-
179, No. 382; Arthur Power. "James Joyce--
The Internationalist," 181-188, No. 853;
Bernard Share. "Downes's Cakeshop and
Williams's Jam," 189-192, No. 1062; Dr.
J. B. Lyons. "Doctors and Hospitals," 192-
202, No. 1610; Francis Harvey. "Stephen
Hero and A Portrait of the Artist: The
Intervention of Style in a Work of the
Creative Imagination," 203-207, No. 3245;
Monk Gibbon. "The Unraised Hat," 209-212,
No. 3578; Thomas McGreevy. "The Catholic
Element in 'Work in Progress,'" 213-219,
No. 5459; John Francis Byrne. "Diseases of
the Ox," 221-233, No. 296; Benedict Kiely.
"The Artist on the Giant's Grave," 235-
241, No. 1047; *"What the Irish Papers
Said," 243-249 (obituaries expanded from
Envoy); "Notes on Contributors," 251-254;
"Index," 255-259.

*1645. SAEKI, SHOICHI. "Joisu Kenkyu no Mondai Ten"
["Critical Points in the Study of James
Joyce]," in Joisu Nyumon [An Introduction
to James Joyce], pp. 142-153, No. 1511.

1646. SANCHEZ, LUIS ALBERTO. Panorama de la literatura actual. 3rd edition. Santiago de
Chile: Biblioteca America, 1936, pp. 109-
134.

1647. SAVAGE, D. S. "James Joyce," in his The
Withered Branch: Six Studies in the Modern

COMPREHENSIVE STUDIES OF JOYCE'S WORKS

<u>Novel</u>. London: Eyre and Spottiswoode,
1950; New York: Pellegrini and Cudahy,
1952, pp. 156-199. [Reprinted in <u>Joyce</u>,
pp. 63-108, No. 1526; reprinted Folcroft,
Pa.: Folcroft Library Editions, 1974, pp.
156-199.]

1648. SCHOLES, ROBERT, and ROBERT KELLOGG. <u>The</u>
<u>Nature of Narrative</u>. New York: Oxford
University Press, 1966, <u>passim</u>.

1649. SCHORER, MARK, ed. <u>Modern British Fiction</u>.
New York: Oxford University Press, 1961.
<u>Contents</u>: David Daiches. "<u>Dubliners</u>,"
308-321, from No. 1548; Harry Levin. "The
Artist," 322-335, from No. 1603; Philip
Toynbee. "A Study of <u>Ulysses</u>," 336-357,
from No. 4097; Edmund Wilson. "The Dream
of H. C. Earwicker," 358-375, from No.
5530.

1650. SCHULTE, EDVIGE. <u>L'eroe all'antipodo (per</u>
<u>un'interpretazione di James Joyce)</u>.
Naples: Liquori, 1973.

1651. SCOTT, NATHAN A., JR. <u>The Broken Center:</u>
<u>Studies in the Theological Horizon of</u>
<u>Modern Literature</u>. New Haven: Yale Uni-
versity Press, 1966, <u>passim</u>.

1652. SCOTT-JAMES, ROLFE. "Interior Vision," in
his <u>Fifty Years of English Literature,</u>
<u>1900-1950</u>. London: Longmans, Green, 1951,
pp. 131-137.

1653. SEMMLER, CLEMENT. <u>For the Uncanny Man:</u>
<u>Essays, Mainly Literary</u>. Melbourne:
F. W. Chesire; London: Angus and
Robertson, 1963.
<u>Contents</u>: "James Joyce in Austrailia,"
12-92 (here first published); "Notes on
the Themes and Language of <u>Finnegans</u>
<u>Wake</u>," 93-108, No. 5344; "Portrait of the
Artist as Humorist," 109-111 (from <u>Quad-</u>
<u>rant</u>, Spring 1968); "James Joyce in Zür-
ich," 112-120 (from <u>Quadrant</u>, Summer 1959-
60, pp. 41-48); "Radio and James Joyce,"
121-126, No. 2502; "Marion Bloom," 127-
132 (here first published).

1654. SENN, FRITZ. <u>James Joyce: Aufsätze von Fritz</u>
<u>Senn</u>. Zürich: Max-Geilinger-Stiftung,
1972.
<u>Contents</u>: "James Joyce über das
Schweizer Frauen Stimmrecht--ein Anweis
in <u>Finnegans Wake</u>," 10-11, No. 5190;
"Schweizerdeutsches in <u>Finnegans Wake</u>,"
12-15, No. 5485; "Hier wohnte Joyce:
<u>Ulysses</u> in Zürich," 16-21, No. 540; "Das
Besondere an Joyce: Eigenheiten im Werk
des grossen iren," 22-32, No. 1809;
"Joyce, Das Sechseläuten und der Föhn,"
35-39, No. 1214; "Der neue Joyce: Zur
Neuübersetzung des Gesamtwerkes," 40-44,
No. 1812; "James Joyce: Der Verfasser des
<u>Ulysses</u>--zu seinem neunzigsten Geburtstag,"

45-51, No. 1729; "Lebensdaten von James
Joyce," 52; "Veröffentlichungen von Fritz
Senn," 53-55.

1655. _____ . "James Joyce and Zürich." Speech
given on 4 November 1972 upon receiving
an award by the Max-Geilinger-Stiftung.
[An exhibit, "James Joyce and Zürich,"
was shown at the Zentralbibliothek Zürich,
4 November-2 December 1972; presentation
of award speech by Henri Petter; for comments on award and speeches see <u>Literatur</u>
<u>und Kunst</u> (Supplement to <u>Neue Zürcher Zei-</u>
<u>tung</u>), 19 November 1972, pp. 51-52; on
opening of exhibit see Carola Giedion-
Welcker. "Begegnung mit James Joyce in
Zürich." <u>Literatur und Kunst</u>, 19 November 1972, p. 53; for news articles on
award and exhibit see: A. S. <u>Die Tat</u>,
28 October 1972, p. 14; <u>ibid</u>., 8 November
1972, p. 5, and <u>ibid</u>., 9 November 1972, p.
5; K. O. <u>Neue Zürcher Zeitung</u>, 6 November
1972, p. 31; <u>Limmattaler Tagblatt</u>, 24 November 1972; M. Th. -P. <u>Die Tat</u>, 12 October 1972, p. 4.]

1656. _____ . <u>New Light on Joyce</u>. Bloomington:
Indiana University Press, 1972. [Thirteen
papers from the 2nd International James
Joyce Symposium, Dublin, June 1969.]
<u>Contents</u>: Fritz Senn. "Preface," vii-
xi; Philip F. Herring. "Joyce's Politics,"
3-14, No. 4830; Darcy O'Brien. "Some Psychological Determinants of Joyce's View of
Love and Sex," 15-27, No. 1629; James F.
Carens. "Joyce and Gogarty," 28-45, No.
3560; Strother B. Purdy. "Mind Your Gener-
ous: Toward a Wake Grammar," 46-78, No.
5266; Erwin R. Steinberg. "Characteristic
Sentence Patterns in Proteus and Lestry-
gonians," 79-98, No. 4743; Jack P. Dalton.
"The Text of <u>Ulysses</u>," 99-119, No. 3564;
Fred H. Higginson. "The Text of <u>Finnegans</u>
<u>Wake</u>," 120-130, No. 4939; Robert Boyle.
"'Astroglodynamonologos,'" 131-140, No.
1528; Morton P. Levitt. "The Family of
Bloom," 141-148, No. 3615; Zack Bowen.
"Libretto for Bloomusalen in Song: The
Music of Joyce's <u>Ulysses</u>," 149-166, No.
3552; Mabel P. Worthington. "The Moon and
Sidhe: Songs of Isabel," 167-179, No. 5531;
Ihab Hassan. "Joyce-Beckett: A Scenario in
Eight Scenes and a Voice," 180-194, No.
5093; Leslie Fiedler. "Bloom on Joyce; or
Jokey for Jacob," 195-208, No. 4556.

1657. SHEEHY, MICHAEL. "James Joyce," in his <u>Is</u>
<u>Ireland Dying? Culture and the Church in</u>
<u>Modern Ireland</u>. London: Hollis and Carter,
1968, pp. 88-102, <u>et passim</u>; New York:
Taplinger, 1968.

1658. SPENDER, STEPHEN. "Tradition-Bound Literature
and Traditionless Painting," in his <u>The</u>
<u>Struggle of the Modern</u>. Berkeley: Univer-
sity of California Press, 1963, pp. 189-
206.

1659. STALEY, THOMAS F., ed. James Joyce Today: Essays on the Major Works. Bloomington and London: Indiana University Press, 1966. [Paperback reprint, 1970; translated by Olga Rossi Devoto, Preface by Giulio de Angelis. Florence: Vallecchi, 1973.]
    Contents: Thomas F. Staley. "Preface," vii-viii; Robert Glynn Kelly. "Introduction: Joyce Hero," 3-10, No. 1599; Herbert Howarth. "Chamber Music and Its Place in the Joyce Canon," 11-27, No. 2784; James S. Atherton. "The Joyce of Dubliners," 28-35, No. 2850; William T. Noon. "A Portrait of the Artist as a Young Man: After Fifty Years," 54-82, No. 3265; Richard M. Kain. "The Position of Ulysses Today," 83-95, No. 3605; William Blissett. "James Joyce in the Smithy of His Soul," 96-134, No. 1521; Clive Hart. "Finnegans Wake in Perspective," 135-165, No. 4934; "Notes," 167-181; "Biographical Notes," 182-183.

1660. _____. "Some Observations on the Early Development of Joyce's Art," in Introspection: The Artist Looks at Himself. Edited by Donald E. Hayden. University of Tulsa, Department of English Monograph Series, no. 12. Tulsa: University of Tulsa, 1971, pp. 29-40.

*1661. STEGMEYER, FRANZ. "Thematik und Technik des James Joyce," in his Europäische Profile. Wiesbaden: Limes-Verlag, 1947, pp. 116-136.

1662. STEINBERG, GÜNTER. Erlebte Rede: Ihre Eigenart und ihre Formen in neuerer deutscher, französischer und englischer Erzählliteratur. Göppingen Arbeiten zur Germanistik, no. 50/51. Göppingen: Alfred Kümmerle Vlg., 1971, passim.

1663. STEPHENS, JAMES. James, Seumas and Jacques: Unpublished Writings of James Stephens. Edited by Lloyd Frankenberg. New York: Macmillan, 1964; London: Macmillan (pagination different).
    Contents: "The James Joyce I Knew," 147-155, No. 554; "Ulysses," 156-159, No. 2699 (BBC Broadcast, 1948): "Finnegans Wake," 160-162, No. 2700 (BBC Broadcast, 1947).

1664. STEWART, J. I. M. James Joyce. Writers and Their Work, no. 91. London: Longmans, Green, 1957. [Revised edition, London: Longmans, Green, 1964; with bibliography updated by J. S. Atherton; translated by Maria V. Papetti. Milan: U. Marsia, 1963; excerpt reprinted in Twentieth Century Interpretations of A Portrait of the Artist as a Young Man, pp. 15-20, No. 3273.]

1665. _____. "Joyce," in his Eight Modern Writers. Oxford History of English Literature, vol. 12. New York: Oxford University Press, 1963; Oxford: Clarendon,

1963, pp. 422-483. [Paperback reprint, London: Oxford; New York: Oxford, 1973, pp. 422-483.]

1666. STIEF, CARL, ed. Moderne Litteratur efter 1914. Copenhagen: Gyldendal, 1950, pp. 132-135.

1667. STONIER, G. W. "Gog, Magog," "Words!Words," in his Gog, Magog and Other Critical Essays. London: Dent, 1933, pp. 1-42, 156-165. [Reprinted Freeport, New York: Books for Libraries Press, 1966.]

1668. STRAUMANN, HEINRICH. "Das Zeitproblem im englischen und amerikanischen Roman: Sterne, Joyce, Faulkner und Wilder," in Das Zeitproblem im 20. Jahrhundert. Sammlung Dalp, no. 96. Edited by R. W. Meyer. Bern, Munich: Francke Vlg., 1964, pp. 140-160.

1669. STRONG, L. A. G. "James Joyce," in The English Novelists. Edited by Derek Verschoyle. London: Chatto and Windus, 1936, pp. 279-293. [Reprinted Folcroft, Pa.: Folcroft Press, 1970, pp. 301-316; excerpts reprinted in A Library of Literary Criticism, pp. 106-117, No. 250.]

1670. _____. "James Joyce and Vocal Music," in Essays and Studies, vol. 31. Oxford: Clarendon, 1946, pp. 95-106.

1671. _____. "James Joyce," in his English Novelists Today: engelsk radiokurs, hösten, 1955. Stockholm: Radiotjänst, 1955.

1672. TATSUMIYA, SAKAE. "Technique and Sentence Style of Joyce," in A Study of Joyce, pp. 77-106, No. 1592.

1673. TERY, SIMONE. L'Ile des Bardes. Paris: Flammarion, 1925, pp. 202-243.

1674. THOMPSON, LAWRENCE. A Comic Principle in Sterne, Meredith, Joyce. Oslo: British Institute, University of Oslo, 1954. [Reprinted Folcroft, Pa.: Folcroft Press, 1969.]

1675. THORNTON, WELDON. "James Joyce and the Power of the Word," in The Classic British Novel. Edited by Howard M. Harper and Charles Edge. Athens: University of Georgia Press, 1972, pp. 183-201.

1676. TINDALL, WILLIAM YORK. Forces in Modern British Literature, 1885-1956. New York: Alfred A. Knopf, 1949, passim.

1677. _____. James Joyce: His Way of Interpreting the Modern World. New York: Scribner's, 1950. [Paperback reprint, New York: Grove, 1960; paperback reprint, 1965; reprinted, London: Thames and Hudson, 1968; translated by Marcella Bassi

COMPREHENSIVE STUDIES OF JOYCE'S WORKS

with Preface by Glauco Cambon. Milan: Bompiani, 1960; "Dubliners" reprinted in Joyce's The Dead, pp. 74-81, No. 3138; excerpts reprinted in A Library of Literary Criticism, pp. 106-117, No. 250.]

1678. _____. Reader's Guide to James Joyce. New York: Noonday Press, 1959. [Reprinted London: Thames and Hudson, 1960; reprinted New York: Octagon, 1971; translated by Raquel Bengolea. Caracas: Monte Avila, 1971; "The Sisters" reprinted in Story and Critic. Edited by Myron Matlaw and Leonard Lief. New York: Harper and Row, 1963, pp. 156-159; "The Sisters" reprinted in The Art of Short Fiction. Edited by Barbara Pannwitt. Boston: Ginn, 1964, pp. 364-367; "The Boarding House" reprinted in James Joyce's Dubliners, pp. 106-107, No. 2885; "A Portrait of a Lady" reprinted in James Joyce's Dubliners, pp. 146-148, No. 2885.]

1679. VARGAS, MANUEL ARTURO. James Joyce. Madrid: EPESA, 1972.

1680. VESTDIJK, S. De poolsche Ruiter. Bussum: F. G. Kroonder, 1946, pp. 46-52.

1681. VICKERY, JOHN B. "James Joyce: From the Beginnings to Portrait," "James Joyce: Ulysses and the Anthropological Reality," "James Joyce: Ulysses and the Artist as Dying God," "James Joyce: Ulysses and the Human Scapegoat," "James Joyce: Finnegans Wake and the Rituals of Morality," in The Literary Impact of The Golden Bough. Princeton: Princeton University Press, 1973, pp. 326-345, 346-357, 358-380, 381-407, 408-423.

1682. VON PHUL, RUTH. "Joyce and the Strabismal Apologia," in A James Joyce Miscellany, Second Series, pp. 119-132, No. 1613.

1683. WALCUTT, CHARLES C., and J. EDWIN WHITESELL, eds. "James Joyce," in Explicator Cyclopedia, vol. 3: Prose. Chicago: Quadrangle Books, 1968, pp. 98-118.

1684. WALDRON, PHILIP. The Novels of James Joyce. Wellington, New Zealand: Wai-te-ata Press, 1962.

1685. WILDI, MAX. "The Joycean Paradox," in Mélanges offerts à Monsieur Georges Bonnard. Université de Lausanne, Publications de la Faculté des Lettres, no. 18. Geneva: Droz, 1966, pp. 73-79.

1686. WILSON, EDMUND. "James Joyce," in Axel's Castle. New York, London: Scribner's, 1939, pp. 191-236. [Reprinted New York: Scribner's, 1959, 1969; later appeared in Literary Opinion in America. Edited by Morton D. Zabel. New York: Harper Bros., 1951, pp. 183-206; translated by J. Salas Subirat as "James Joyce e Ulisses."

Davar (Buenos Aires), no. 1 (July-August 1945): 80-93; no. 2 (September-October 1945): 23-37; translated by Olga Humo as Akselov Zamak. Beograd: Kultura Beograd, 1964; translated by Marisa and Luciana Bulgheroni as Il castello di Axel. Milan: Il Saggiatore, 1965.]

1687. WORTHINGTON, MABEL P. "Maundy Thursday, Good Friday, The Sorrowing Mother, and the Day of Judgment," in Modern Irish Literature: Essays in Honor of William York Tindall. Library of Irish Studies, vol. 1. Edited by Raymond J. Porter and James D. Brophy. New York: Iona College Press and Twayne, 1972, pp. 143-151. [Originally "Joyce and Medievalism," a paper given at the Third International James Joyce Symposium, Trieste, June 1971.]

1688. ZYLA, WOLODYMYR T., ed. James Joyce: His Place in World Literature. Proceedings of the Comparative Literature Symposium, vol. 2. Lubbock: Texas Tech Press, 1969. Contents: Wolodymyr T. Zyla. "Preface," 1-6; William T. Noon. "The Religious Position of Joyce," 7-22, No. 341; Dounia Bunis Christiani. "The Polyglot Poetry of Finnegans Wake," 23-38, No. 5258; Thomas F. Staley. "Ulysses and World Literature," 39-52, No. 3656; William J. Handy. "Criticism of Joyce's Works: A Formalist Approach," 53-90, No. 3133; Ben D. Kimpel. "James Joyce in Contemporary World Literature," 93-102, No. 1048; William T. Noon. "Is Ulysses Immoral or All-Moral?," 103-114, No. 3635.

Periodical Articles

*1689. ALTSCHUL, CARLOS. "Hacia una interpretación del hombre James Joyce," Sur, no. 260 (September-October 1959): 24-36.

1690. ARNOLD, ARMIN. "Literatur als Rache: Überlegungen zu James Joyce." Literatur und Kunst (Supplement to Neue Zürcher Zeitung), 20 April 1969, pp. 49-50.

*1691. BECKMANN, G., and H. POLLERT. "James Joyce." Unser Egerland, 35 (1931).

1692. BEJA, MORRIS. "The Wooden Sword: Threatener and Threatened in the Fiction of James Joyce." James Joyce Quarterly, 2 (Fall 1964): 33-41.

*1693. BENNETT, ARNOLD. "Books and Persons: The Oddest Novel Ever Written." Evening Standard (London), 8 August 1929, p. 7.

1694. BENSTOCK, BERNARD. "A Covey of Clerics in Joyce and O'Casey." James Joyce Quarterly, 2 (Fall 1964): 18-32.

1695. BERGER, ALFRED P. "Wakeful Ad-venture." James Joyce Quarterly, 7 (Fall 1969): 52-60.

1696. BERINGAUSE, ARTHUR F. "James Joyce's Philosophy." Cresset, 26 (October 1963): 10-15.

1697. BIERMAN, ROBERT. "Ulysses and Finnegans Wake: The Explicit, the Implicit, and the Tertium Quid." Renascence, 11 (Autumn 1958): 14-19.

1698. BOURGEOIS, MAURICE. "A propos de James Joyce." Comoedia, 24 June 1924.

1699. BREZIANU, ANDREI. "James Joyce si Plevna." Secolul, 20, no. 5 (1969): 111-121.

1700. BRION, MARCEL. "Les grandes figures Européennes: James Joyce, romancier." La Gazette des Nations, no. 8 (3 March 1928): 4.

1701. BURGESS, ANTHONY. "Silence, Exile and Cunning." Listener, 73 (6 May 1965): 661-663.

*1702. BUTOR, MICHEL. "Petite croisière preliminaire à une reconnaissance de l'archipel Joyce," La vie intellectuelle (May 1948): 103-133. [Reprinted in his Répertoire, vol. 1. Paris: Les Editions de Minuit, 1960, pp. 195-218; reprinted in his Essais sur les modernes. Paris: Gallimard, 1964, pp. 239-281.]

*1703. _____. "Joyce et le roman modern." Lettres françaises, 16-22 February, 1961, pp. 1, 3.

*1704. C., J. [n.t.]. Post (Birmingham), 4 March 1930.

1705. CAMBON, GLAUCO. "Ancora su Joyce." Aut Aut, no. 17 (1953): 430-455. [Reprinted as "Ancora su Joyce: magia e scacco della parola" with "Ulisse: le proteiformita del linguaggio" in his La lotta con Proteo. Milan: Bompiani, 1963, pp. 39-67; second article, pp. 17-38.]

*1706. CAMERON, K. N. "The Genius of James Joyce: A Critical Tribute." The McGilliad (February-March 1931): 59-60.

1707. CANTWELL, ROBERT. "Brightness Falls from the Air." New Republic, 87 (August 1963): 375-377.

1708. _____. "Joyce and the Elizabethans." New Republic, 88 (September 1936): 131-132.

1709. CAZAMIAN, LOUIS. "L'Oeuvre de James Joyce." Revue Anglo-Américaine, 2 (December 1924): 97-113. [Appeared, revised, in Essais en deux langues. Paris: Didier, 1938, pp. 47-63.]

1710. COLLINS, BEN L. "Progression in the Works of James Joyce." Wisconsin Studies in Literature, 2 (1965): 54-59.

1711. CONNOLLY, CYRIL. "The Position of Joyce." Life and Letters, 2 (April 1929): 273-290. [Reprinted in his The Condemned Playground. New York: Macmillan, 1946, pp. 1-15; reprinted in A Library of Literary Criticism, pp. 106-117, No. 250.]

1712. CORN, MARY. "Homosexuality as a Joycean Theme." South Central Bulletin, 33 (October 1973): 122.

1713. COURTENAY, JENNIFER. "The Approach to James Joyce and Others." Everyman, 5 (9 July 1931): 765.

1714. DAVENPORT, BASIL. "The Joycean Language." Blue Pencil, 1, no. 2 (March 1934): 4-5.

*1715. DUBOIS, PAUL. "M. James Joyce, Irlandais." Revue universelle, 61 (15 June 1935): 661-687.

1716. DUFF, CHARLES. "Ulises y otros trabajos de James Joyce." Sur, no. 5 (1932): 86-127. [In English as the first two chapters of his James Joyce and the Plain Reader, No. 1555.]

*1717. ECO, UMBERTO. "Poetica ed estetica in James Joyce." Revista di estetica, no. 1 (January-April 1957).

1718. EDEL, LEON. "New Writers." Canadian Forum, 10 (June 1930): 329-330.

*1719. EGLINTON, JOHN. [W. K. McGee]. "Dublin Letter." Dial, 72 (June 1922): 619-622. [Reprinted in Dial Miscellany. Edited by William Wasserstrom. Syracuse: Syracuse University Press, 1963, pp. 113-116.]

1720. ELIOT, T. S. "The Approach to James Joyce." Listener, 30 (14 October 1943): 446-447.

*1721. ELLEGARD, ALVAR. "Estimating Vocabulary Size." Word, no. 16 (August 1960): 219-244.

1722. EMPSON, WILLIAM. "Joyce's Intentions." Twentieth Century Studies, 4 (November 1970): 26-36.

1723. EPSTEIN, EDMUND L. "King David and Benedetto Marcello in the Works of James Joyce." James Joyce Quarterly, 6 (Fall 1968): 83-86.

1724. FÁJ, ATTILA. "Probable Byzantine and Hungarian Models of Ulysses and Finnegans Wake." Arcadia (Berlin), 3 (1968): 48-72.

COMPREHENSIVE STUDIES OF JOYCE'S WORKS

*1725. FELIX, ENRIQUE. "Consideración pedagógica sobre James Joyce." Letras de Sinaloa (Mexico), 5 (15 July 1951): 7-13.

*1726. FENICHEL, ROBERT R. "A Portrait of the Artist as a Young Orphan." Literature and Psychology, 9 (Spring 1959): 19-22.

1727. FRIEND, J. H. "Joyce and the Elizabethans." New Republic, 88 (September 1936): 131.

1728. FUENTES, CARLOS. "Palabras iniciales (Conferencia inaugural en el Colegio Nacional, el Martes 17 de Octubre de 1972)." Memoria de el Colegio Nacional (Mexico City), 7, no. 3 (1972): 226-246.

1729. GIBSON, MORGAN. "Joyce's Style of Looking Inward." Arts in Society, 2, no. 3 (1963): 134-139.

*1730. GONZÁLEZ MUELA, J. "El culto a la palabra en James Joyce." Escorial (Madried), 10 (January 1943): 125-131.

1731. GONZÁLEZ y CONTRERAS, GILBERTO. "La disintegración estética en James Joyce." Claridad (Buenos Aires), 20, no. 346 (March-April 1941): 68-70.

*1732. GOPALEEN, MYLES na (Flann O'Brien, Brian Nolan). "Cruiskeen Lawn." Irish Times, 19 December 1957.

1733. GORDON, JAN B. "The Imaginary Portrait: Fin-de-siecle Icon." University of Windsor Review, 5 (Fall 1969): 81-104.

1734. GOULD, D. J. "Irish Epiphanies." Desiderata, 8 (5 August 1955): 1-3.

*1735. GOYERT, GEORG. "James Joyce." Prisma (Munich), no. 17 (1948): 17.

*1736. GRAF, ROGER. "James Joyce." Revue de belles-lettres (Geneva), 65 (1937-1938): 124-127.

1737. GUIDI, AUGUSTO. "Il primo Joyce." Idea: Settimanale di cultura 6 (9 May through 13 June, 4 July through 19 September 1954). [Appeared as Il primo Joyce. Rome: Edizioni di "Storia e Letteratura," 1954.]

1738. GUILLEMIN, BERNARD. "James Joyce." Berliner Tageblatt, 61 (2 February 1932): 2.

1739. HART, CLIVE. "James Joyce's Sentimentality." Philological Quarterly, 46 (October 1967): 516-526.

*1740. HÄUSERMANN, H. W. "Die Jungendgedichte von James Joyce." Neue Zürcher Zeitung, no. 347 (18 December 1957).

1741. HAYMAN, DAVID. "Clowns et farce chez Joyce," translated by Jean Paul Martin. Poétique, 6 (1971): 173-199.

*1742. HELWIG, WERNER. "James Joyce: Leben und Werk des irischen Dichters." Rheinischer Merkur, 21 March 1958.

1743. HENNECKE, HANS. "James Joyce." Gestalter unserer Zeit, 2 (1954): 49-59. [Reprinted in Denker und Deuter im heutigen Europa: /2./ England, Frankreich, Spanien und Portugal, Italien, Osteuropa. Edited by Hans Schwerte and Wilhelm Spengler. Oldenburg i. Oldb., 1954, pp. 49-52; reprinted as "Odyssee des XX. Jahrhunderts: James Joyce," in his Kritik: Gesammelte Essays zur modernen Literatur. Gütersloh: 1958, pp. 184-188.]

1744. HERMAN, LEWIS. "James Joyce." Book Collector's Journal (Chicago), 1, no. 4 (April 1936): 1, 4; no. 5 (May 1936): 6, 9; no. 6 (June 1936): 3; no. 7 (July 1936): 5, 6.

1745. HIGGINS, AIDAN. "Aspects of James Joyce." Fortnightly, 175 (April 1951): 264-270.

1746. HOHOFF, CURT. "James Joyce und die Einsamkeit." Wort und Wahrheit, 6 (1951): 506-516. [Reprinted in his Geist und Ursprung. Munich: Ehrenwirth Vlg., 1954, pp. 38-51.]

1747. HONIG, EDWIN. "Hobgoblin or Apollo?" Kenyon Review, 10 (Autumn 1948): 664-681.

*1748. IBARRA, JAIMÉ. "James Joyce." La gaceta literaria (Madrid), p. 5; año 3, no. 70 (15 November 1929): 5; año 3, no. 71 (1 December 1929): 4.

*1749. ISAACS, NEIL D. "The Autoerotic Metaphor in Joyce, Sterne, Lawrence, Stevens, and Whitman." Literature and Psychology, 15 (Spring 1956): 92-106.

1750. JACQUOT, JEAN. "Exégètes et interprètes de James Joyce." Études anglaises, 12 (January-March 1959): 30-46; 15 (January-March 1962): 46-63.

1751. KAIN, RICHARD M. "He Who Runes May Rede... Joyce as Philologist." Mosaic, 2 (Winter 1969): 74-85. [Incorporates his "Joyce's World View" delivered at the Opening of the Joyce Tower Museum, 16 June 1962, published in The Dubliner, 3 (Autumn 1964): 3-10.]

1752. _____. "James Joyce and the Game of Language." Studies in the Literary Imagination, 3 (October 1970): 19-25.

1753. KOEN, J. M. "Call Down Today." Angry Penguins, no. 2 (1941): 14-19.

1754. KORG, JACOB. "Language Change and Experimental Magazines, 1910-1930." Contemporary Literature, 13 (Spring 1972): 144-161.

1755. KRISTENSEN, TOM. "James Joyce." Politiken (Copenhagen), 15 October 1931; 16 October 1931.

1756. KRONEGGER, MARIA ELIZABETH. "Joyce's Debt to Poe and the French Symbolists." Revue de littérature comparée, 39 (April-June 1965): 243-254.

1757. _____. "The Theory of Unity and Effect in the Works of E. A. Poe and James Joyce." Revue de littérature comparée, 40 (April-June 1966): 226-234.

*1758. [de LESCURE, PIERRE?]. "L'homme Joyce." Roman, no. 1 (January 1951): 75-78.

1759. LESTRA, ANDRÉ. "Joyce ou la pureté reconquisse." Revue Palladienne (Paris), no. 11 (March-April 1950): 15-26.

1760. LEVENTHAL, A. J. "James Joyce." Dublin Magazine, 16 (April-June 1941): 12-21.

1761. LEVIN, HARRY. "The Essential James Joyce." Times Literary Supplement, 24 January 1950, p. 128.

1762. _____. "Due saggio su James Joyce." Inventario, 17 (1962): 1-21.

1763. LEVITT, MORTON P. "Shalt be Accurst? The Martyr in James Joyce." James Joyce Quarterly, 5 (Summer 1968): 285-296.

1764. LLOYD, P. G. "The Development of Motifs in James Joyce." Mandrake, 1, no. 6 (1949): 6-12.

1765. LOSS, ARCHIE K. "The Pre-Raphaelite Woman, The Symbolist femme-enfant, and the Girl with the Long Flowing Hair in the Earlier Work of Joyce." Journal of Modern Literature, 3, no. 1 (February 1973): 3-23.

1766. LUNDSTRÖM, BENGT. "Skarpsynoch synskärpa: Några medicinska aspekter på James Joyce." Nordisk Medicin historisk Årsbok, 1973: 1-9. [With English abstract, "Visual and Visionary Power: Some Medical Aspects of the Case of James Joyce," p. 9.]

1767. MacAONGHUSA, PROINSIAS. "Joycetown's New Boss." New Statesman, 77 (2 May 1969): 609.

1768. McHUGH, H. A. "James Joyce: Dark Angel." Redemptorist Record (Belfast), July-August 1953. [Reprinted in Irish Digest, 48 (October 1953): 25-38.]

*1769. MacKAY, L. A. "Enigmatic Novelist." Saturday Night, 55 (4 May 1940): 9.

1770. MANCAŞ, MIRCEA. "Simbol şe parodie la Joyce." Ramuri, 8, no. 1 (January 1971): 17.

*1771. MARICHALAR, ANTONIO. "James Joyce en su Labertino." Revista de Occidente (November 1924): 177-202. [Slightly revised as introduction to Dámaso Absono's (A. Donado pseud.) translation of PAYM, 1926 and later editions.]

1772. MARKS, J. "The New Humor." Esquire, 72 (December 1969): 218-220, 329, 330.

1773. MILLER, MILTON. "Definition by Comparison: Chaucer, Lawrence, and Joyce." Essays in Criticism, 3 (October 1953): 369-381.

*1774. MILLER-BUDNITSKAIA, R. "Filosofiia kultury Dzhemsa Dzhoisa." Inostrannaia literatura, no. 2 (1937): 188-209.

1775. MJÖBERG, JÖRAN. "James Joyce, Henrik Ibsens arvtagare." Samtiden, 69, no. 6 (1960): 324-331.

1776. MOCHIZUKI, MITSUKO. ["The Unconscious Progress in the Works of James Joyce."] Annual Reports of Studies: Doshisha Women's College of Liberal Arts, 23 (1972): 114-145; 24 (1973): 110-124. [In Japanese.]

1777. MONTGOMERY, JUDITH. "The Artist as Silent Dubliner." James Joyce Quarterly, 6 (Summer 1969): 306-320.

1778. MONTGOMERY, MARION. "Three Types of Novelist--And my Ideal." Discourse, 9 (Summer 1966): 359-366.

1779. MORSE, J. MITCHELL. "Joyce and the Blind Stripling." Modern Language Notes, 71 (November 1956): 497-501.

1780. NATANSON, MAURICE. "Being-in-Reality." Philosophical and Phenomenological Research, 20 (December 1959): 231-237.

1781. NOON, WILLIAM T., S.J. "Bard of the Shapeless Cosmopolis: James Joyce." Humanities Association Bulletin (Canada), 16 (1965): 45-51.

1782. _____. "'The Lion and the honeycomb: What has Scripture said': An Incarnational Perspective on Joyce and Yeats." Newsletter of the Conference on Christianity and Literature, 19 (Spring 1970): 18-24.

1783. O'BRIEN, DARCY. "Joyce and Sexuality." Twentieth Century Studies, 2 (November 1969): 32-38.

1784. O'CONNOR, FRANK. "James Joyce: A Post Mortem." The Bell, 5, no. 5 (February 1943): 363-375.

1785. ODA, MOTOI. "[Portrait of James Joyce as a Young Man: From Refusal to Acceptance]."

COMPREHENSIVE STUDIES OF JOYCE'S WORKS

Bunka, 31 (1968): 75-98, 782-783. [In Japanese with English resumee.]

1786. O'hURMOLTAIGH, SEÁN. "James Joyce agus an Ghaeilge." Innia, 14 July-22 December 1972.

*1787. OLINTO, ANTÔNIO. "Cartas de Joyce." O Globo (Rio de Janeiro), 16 April 1960.

1788. PAOLELLA, R. "Nazionidel einema in James Joyce." Filmcritica, no. 129 (1963): 8-10.

1789. PARIS, JEAN. "Un romancier d'avenir." Le nouvel Observateur (May-June 1971): 13-14.

1790. PAUL-DUBOIS, L. "M. James Joyce Irlandais." Le Revue universelle, 61 (June 1935): 661-687.

*1791. PÉREZ de AYALA, RAMÓN. "Sobre Joyce." Le Prevsc (Buenos Aires), 11 August, 15 September 1926.

1792. PITTMAN, DAN C. "James Joyce: Critic of a Dead Society." Southern Quarterly, 5 (July 1967): 471-482.

*1793. POUND, EZRA. "Storicamente Joyce (e censura)." L'Indice (September 1930): 3. [Translated with commentary by Forrest Read. "Storicamente Joyce, 1930; Ezra Pound's First Italian Essay." Tri-Quarterly, no. 15 (Spring 1969): 100-114.]

*1794. PRAZ, MARIO. "James Joyce." Terzo programma, no. 4 (1961): 91-140. [Became part of his James Joyce, Thomas Stearns Eliot: Due maestri dei moderni. Turin: Edizioni Rai Radiotelevisione Italiana, 1967, pp. 3-82.]

1795. PRESCOTT, JOSEPH. "Notes on Mencken." American Speech, 21 (October 1946): 229-231.

1796. READ, HERBERT. "The Limits of Permissiveness." Malahat Review, no. 9 (January 1969): 37-50. [Published separately as Herbert Read: A Memorial Symposium. Edited by Robin Skelton. London: Methuen, 1970; slightly different version in Resurgence, 2 (July-October 1969): 11-17 (and see letter to the editor by Christopher Booker, Resurgence, 2 (Spring 1970): 40); reprinted in The Black Rainbow: Essays on the Present Breakdown of Culture. Edited by Peter Abbs. London: Heinemann, 1975, pp. 4-18.]

1797. REED, HENRY. "James Joyce: The Triple Exile." Listener, 43 (9 March 1950): 437-439.

*1798. REES, G. E. "Editorial." Egyptian Gazette (Alexandria), 23 January 1930.

1799. RODWAY, ALLAN. "Expanding Images in the Joycian Universe." Renaissance and Modern Studies, 15 (1971): 63-69.

1800. RONSE, HENRI. "Retour à Joyce." L'Arc, 36 (1968): 1-3.

1801. SÂNDULESCU, C. G. "Joyce's Linguistic Perspectivism." Analele Universitâtii Bucuresti. Seria stiinte sociale. Filologie. 17 (1968): 449-462. [With abstract in Rumanian.]

1802. SARTRE, JEAN-PAUL. [A talk on the notion of decadence.]. Plamen (Prague), no. 2 (1964): 16-26. [French version in La Nouvelle Critique, no. 156-157 (June-July) 1964): 71-84; reprinted in Les Écrits de Sartre: Chronologie, bibliographie commentée. Edited by Michel Contat and Michel Rybalka. Paris: Gallimard, 1970, p. 407.]

1803. SCHEFFRIN, GLADYS. "Research for Meaning." New Mexico Quarterly, 25 (Spring 1955): 113-119.

1804. SCHOLES, ROBERT. "In Search of James Joyce." James Joyce Quarterly, 11 (Fall 1973): 5-16.

1805. SCHONBERG, HAROLD C. "Facing the Music." Musical Courier, 143 (15 February 1951): 6. [Similar article "He Knew His Music." New York Times, 21 January 1962, section 2, p. 11.]

*1806. SCOTT, GEORGE R. "Senescent British Fiction." New Age (10 November 1927): 18.

1807. SELL, FREDERICK C. "The Fusion of Languages: Modern Alexandrianism." Minnesota Review, 4 (Fall 1963): 51-59.

1808. SENN, FRITZ. "Joyce im Gespräch." Neue Zürcher Zeitung, 15 March 1964.

1809. _____. "James Joyce: Eigenheiten im Werk des grossen Iren." Literarische Beilage, Zolliker Bote. Zollikon no. 24 (June 1966): 9-11. [Reprinted in his James Joyce: Aufsätze von Fritz Senn, pp. 22-32, No. 1654.]

1810. _____. "'Every Word is Right...' Umgänge in Joyce's Werk." Literatur und Kunst (Supplement to Neue Zürcher Zeitung), 14 July 1968, pp. 49-50.

1811. _____. "A Throatful of Additions to Song in the Works of James Joyce." Joycenotes, 1 (June 1969): 7-17.

1812. _____. "Der neue Joyce: Zur Neuübersetzung des Gesamtwerks im Suhrkamp Verlag." Die Weltwoche, no. 6 (6 February 1970): 27. [Reprinted in his James Joyce: Aufsätze von Fritz Senn, pp. 40-44, No. 1654.]

*1813. SILVA, A. CASEMIRO da. "Libelo contra Joyce." Diário de notícias (Salvador), 17 April 1960.

1814. SOLLERS, PHILIPPE. "Une oeuvre extraordinairement réfléchie." Figaro littéraire, 20 January 1966, p. 9.

1815. SPIVEY, TED R. "The Reintegration of Modern Man: An Essay on James Joyce and Hermann Hesse." Studies in the Literary Imagination, 3 (October 1970): 49-64.

1816. SPORN, PAUL. "James Joyce: Early Thoughts on the Subject Matter of Art." College English, 24 (October 1962): 19-24.

1817. STAMIROWSKA, K. "The Conception of Character in the Works of Joyce and Beckett." Kwartalnik Neofilologiczny (Warsaw), no. 14 (1967): 443-447.

1818. STAPLES, HUGH B. "Joyce and Cryptology: Some Speculations." James Joyce Quarterly, 2 (Spring 1965): 167-173.

1819. STARKIE, WALTER. "James Joyce and Music." Saturday Review of Literature, 43 (26 March 1960): 47.

*1820. STEMMLER, WILLI. "James Joyce." Welt und Wort, 3 (1948): 329-332.

1821. SYMONS, ARTHUR. "James Joyce." Two Worlds' Monthly, 1, no. 1 (July 1926): 86-92. [Became the "Epilogue" to The Joyce Book, pp. 79-84, No. 2582.]

*1822. TARANIENKO, ZBIGNIEW. "Gzas i przestrzen Joyce'a." Studia filozoficzne (Warsaw), 69 (1961): 97-118.

1823. TAU, MAX. "James Joyce: en Stilanalyse." Samtiden, 59 (1950): 362-373.

1824. THAYER, SCOFIELD. "James Joyce." The Dial, 65, no. 773 (19 September 1918): 201-203.

1825. THORN, ERIC P. "James Joyce: Early Imitations of Structural Unity." Costerus, 9 (1973): 229-238.

1826. TRILLING, JACQUES. "James Joyce, ou l'écriture matricide." Études Freudiennes, no. 7-8 (April 1973): 7-70.

1827. UŘNOW, D. "Portret Dz. Dzojsa--pisatel ja i 'proroka." Znamia (Moscow), 35 (April 1965): 315-334. [Translated as "James Joyce, Schriftsteller und 'Prophet.'" Kunst und Literatur, 13 (1965): 1029-1055.

*1828. VALLETTE, JACQUES. "Quelques aspects du roman anglais contemporain." La quinzaine critique (Paris), 28 March 1930, pp. 477-478.

1829. VERHAEGHEN, VICTOR. "Joyce, Man van Dublin." De Periscoop, 7 (1 August 1947): 1-2.

1830. VIEBROCK, HELMUT. "James Joyce: Mensch und Werk." Akzente, 8 (April 1961): 137-145.

1831. VILLA, VITTORIANA. "Figure paterne nel Portrait e nell'Ulysses di James Joyce." Instituto Universitario Orientale (Naples). Annali: Sezione germanica, 15, no. 1 (1972): 127-144. [See also ibid., 15 (1972): 245-246 for English and German abstracts.]

1832. VISSER, G. J. "James Joyce's Prose and Welsh Cynghanedd." Neophilologus, 47 (October 1963): 305-320.

1833. WATSON, FRANCIS. "Portrait of the Artist in Maturity." Bookman (London), 85 (November 1933): 102-105.

1834. WEATHERS, WINSTON. "A Portrait of the Broken World." James Joyce Quarterly, 1 (Summer 1964): 27-40.

1835. _____. "Joyce and the Tragedy of Language." South Central Bulletin, 26 (March 1966): 9. [Abstract; published in full in Forum (Houston), 4 (Winter-Spring 1967): 16-21.]

1836. WEIDLÉ, WLADIMIR. "On the Present State of Poetic Language." Les cahiers de la Pléiade (Paris), 2 (April 1947): 127-133. [Appeared in James Joyce Yearbook, pp. 20-31, No. 1596.]

1837. WEIR, LORRAINE. "Joyce, Myth and Memory." Irish University Review, 2 (Fall 1972): 172-188.

1838. WEST, PHILIP J. "Classical Memory Culture in Joyce." Modern Language Studies, 3 (Spring 1973): LX.

1839. WHITE, TERENCE. "Joyce and Music." Chesterian, 17 (July-August 1936): 163-167.

1839a. WIBERG, B. "James Joyce i Bibliotekerne." Bogens verden, 54, no. 11 (1972): 756-757.

*1840. WOOLF, VIRGINIA. "Modern Novels." Times Literary Supplement, no. 899 (10 April 1919): 189-190. [Appeared as "Modern Fiction" in her The Common Reader. First Series. London: L. and V. Woolf, 1925 and London: Hogarth Press, 1962, pp. 184-195; also appeared in her Collected Essays, vol. 2. New York: Harcourt, Brace and World, 1967, pp. 103-110.]

1841. WORTHINGTON, MABEL P. "Gilbert and Sullivan Songs in the Works of James Joyce." Hartford Studies in Literature, 1 (1969): 209-218.

COMPREHENSIVE STUDIES OF JOYCE'S WORKS

1842. ZIPF, GEORGE K. "The Repetition of Words, Time-Perspective and Semantic Balance." Journal of General Psychology, 32 (January 1945): 127-148.

1843. ZOLLA, ELÉMIRE. "Joyce e la moderna apocalissi." Il pensiero critico, no. 6 (November 1952): 1-12.

*1844. Unsigned. "Faith and Unfaith." Daily Chronicle (London), 22 January 1926. [Report of lecture by E. M. Forster at the 1917 Club.]

*1845. Unsigned. "The Irish Revival." Cape Times (Capetown), 21 March 1929.

*1846. Unsigned. "Over the Top with the New Novelists." Current Opinion, 66 (June 1919): 387-388.

REVIEWS OF JOYCE'S WORKS

[Reviews are arranged chronologically by work and date reviewed. Reviews are only of early editions and translations of Joyce's works; for more recent editions and translations see the annual bibliography in James Joyce Quarterly.]

CHAMBER MUSIC

1847. KETTLE, THOMAS. "Review." Freeman's Journal, 1 June 1907.

1848. CLERY, ARTHUR. "Review." Leader, 22 June 1907.

1849. SYMONS, ARTHUR. "A Book of Songs." Nation, 1, no. 17 (22 June 1907): 639.

1850. Unsigned. Bookman (London), 32 (June 1907): 113.

1851. Unsigned. Egoist, 5, no. 6 (June-July 1918): 87.

1852. FIRKINS, O. V. "Assorted Poets." Nation, 107 (26 October 1918): 488.

1853. A., M. "The Lyrics of James Joyce." New Republic, 18, no. 227 (8 March 1919): 191.

1854. H[ENDERSON], A[LICE] C[ORBIN]. "Chamber Music--Old and New." Poetry, 14 (May 1919): 98-103.

1855. A., R. "Soliloquies on the Left Bank." New York Herald (Paris), 28 October 1924.

1856. W., E. New Republic, 26 October 1927.

1857. ZABEL, MORTON D. "The Lyrics of James Joyce." Poetry, 36 (July 1930): 206-213.

1858. Unsigned. Musical Opinion (London), January 1931. [Review of Eugene Goossens settings.]

1859. Unsigned. Musical Times (London), January 1931. [Review of Eugene Goossens settings.]

1860. BENÉT, WILLIAM ROSE. Saturday Review of Literature, 15 (19 December 1936): 20.

1861. TINDALL, WILLIAM YORK. "Joyce's Chambermade Music." Poetry, 80 (May 1952): 105-116.

1862. POORE, CHARLES. New York Times, 4 February 1954.

1863. GREGORY, HORACE. New York Herald Tribune Books, 30 (11 April 1954): 5.

1864. GUENTHER, CHARLES. "Joyce Without Chaos." St. Louis Post-Dispatch, 22 June 1954, part 3, p. 2.

1865. KERRIGAN, ANTHONY. "News of Molly Bloom." Poetry, 85 (November 1954): 109-112.

1866. ROSKOLENKO, HARRY. Voices, no. 156 (January-April 1955): 45-47.

1867. Press notices of CM, privately printed in Trieste, quoted in Letters, pp. 332-333, Note 3, No. 309.

DUBLINERS

1868. Unsigned. Times Literary Supplement, 18 June 1914, p. 298.

1869. Unsigned. Athenaeum, 20 June 1914, p. 875.

1870. GOULD, GERALD. New Statesman, 3 (27 June 1914): 374-375.

1871. Unsigned. Everyman, 3 July 1914, p. 380.

1872. Unsigned. Academy, 87 (11 July 1914): 49.

1873. POUND, EZRA. "Dubliners and Mr. James Joyce." Egoist, 1, no. 14 (15 July 1914): 267. [Also in Pound/Joyce, No. 752.]

1874. Unsigned. Irish Book Lover, 6, no. 4 (November 1914): 60-61.

1875. DUPLAIX, GEORGES. Revue nouvelle (Paris), 15 May 1926. [Review of French translation.]

1876. HAUER, GERARD. L'Echo de Paris, 20 May 1926. [Review of French translation.]

1877. JALOUX, EDMOND. "L'esprit des livres." Les nouvelles littéraires, 29 May 1926. [Review of French translation.]

1878. THIEBAUT, MARCEL. Revue de Paris, 1 June 1926. [Review of French translation.]

1879. RERGNER, GEORGE. Journal de l'Est (Strasbourg), 2 June 1926. [Review of French translation.]

1880. MOREMANS, VICTOR. Gazette de Liége, 3 June 1926. [Review of French translation.]

1881. TREACH, LÉON. L'Avenir (Paris), 14 July 1926. [Review of French translation.]

1882. G., Y. Vient de paraître (Paris), July-August 1926. [Review of French translation.]

1883. CHENEVIÈRE, JACQUES. "James Joyce: 'Gens de Dublin,' traduction de Yl Fernandez, H. du Pasquier, J. P. Raynaud." Bibliothèque universelle et Revue de Génève, 2 (August 1926): 267-268.

1884. Unsigned. Progrès de Lyon, 14 August 1926. [Review of French translation.]

1885. HAYWARD, FERNAND. Gazette française, 9 September 1926. [Review of French translation.]

1886. MONTALE, EUGENIO. "Cronache delle Letterature Straniere: 'Dubliners' di James Joyce." Fiera letteraria, 2, no. 38 (19 September 1926): 5.

1887. BELLY, ANDRÉ. L'Oeuvre (Paris), 5 October 1926. [Review of French translation.]

1888. Unsigned. Monde Illustré (Paris), 9 October 1926. [Review of French translation.]

1889. BOURGUET, GEORGES. Les chaiers du sud, 6 November 1926, pp. 313-315. [Review of French translation.]

1890. Unsigned. Quest-Éclair (Rennes), 25 November 1926. [Review of French translation.]

1891. Unsigned. Nouvelliste d'Alsace (Strasbourg), 27 November 1926. [Review of French translation.]

1892. LALOU, RENÉE. Revue européenne (Paris), December 1926. [Review of French translation.]

1893. PHIPPS, ALBERT. Times (St. Petersburg, Florida), 30 January 1927.

1894. Unsigned. L'Ambrosiana (Milan), 5 March 1927. [Review of French translation.]

1895. SPAINI, ALBERTO. La tribuna (Rome), 27 March 1927.

1896. SEMPLE, I. Le nouveau journal (Lyon), 9 May 1927. [Review of French translation.]

1897. R., H. Prager Presse (Prague), 4 March 1928.

1898. ARNS, KARL. "James Joyce. 'Dublin: Novellen.'" Der gral (Munster), 23 (1928-1929): 1101.

1899. C., J. "Experimentalists." Post (Birmingham), 4 March 1930.

1900. BRANDL, ALOIS. "James Joyce Dubliners." Archiv für das Studium der neueren Sprachen, 165 (1934): 145.

1901. RYKACHEV, IA. "Dublintsky." Literaturny obozrenie, no. 1 (1938): 50-53.

1902. BOROVOI, L. "Dublintsy." Literaturny gazeta, 15 February 1938.

PORTRAIT OF THE ARTIST AS A YOUNG MAN

1903. HUNEKER, JAMES. "James Joyce," in his Unicorns. New York: Scribner's, 1917, pp. 187-194. [Originally in New York Sun; extensively quoted by William Carlos Williams. "Advent in America of a New Irish Realist." Current Opinion, 62 (April 1917): 275.]

1904. GORMAN, HERBERT. Springfield Union, 1917.

1905. Unsigned. The Sphere, 1917.

1906. Unsigned. The Bookseller (London), February 1917.

1907. POUND, EZRA. "At Last the Novel Appears." Egoist, 4, no. 2 (February 1917): 21-22. [Also in Pound/Joyce, No. 725.]

1908. Unsigned. "A Study in Garbage." Everyman, 23 February 1917, p. 398.

1909. WELLS, H. G. "James Joyce." Nation, 20 (24 February 1917): 710, 712. [Same review in New Republic, 10 (10 March 1917): 158-160; excerpted in Guardian (Nassau), 16 October 1924; also in The New Republic Anthology. Edited by Groff Conklin. New York: Dodge, 1936, pp. 45-48; in Novelists on Novelists. Edited by Louis Kronenberger. New York: Doubleday-Anchor, 1962, pp. 343-346; and in New Republic, 121 (1954): 91-92; reprinted in Chester G. Anderson's edition of PAYM. New York: Viking Critical Library, 1968, pp. 329-333.]

1910. [CLUTTON-BROCK, ARTHUR]. "Wild Youth." Times Literary Supplement, no. 789 (1 March 1917): 103-104.

1911. WEAVER, HARRIET SHAW. "Views and Comments." Egoist, 3 (1 March 1916): 35.

1912. Unsigned. The Literary World (London), 83, no. 1,985 (1 March 1917): 43.

REVIEWS OF JOYCE'S WORKS

1913. M., A. "Sensitivist." Manchester Guardian, no. 22,018 (2 March 1917): 3.

1914. BOYD, ERNEST. New Ireland, 3 March 1917.

1915. HACKETT, FRANCIS. "Green Sickness." New Republic, 10, no. 122 (3 March 1917): 138-139. [Appeared in his Horizons (1918): pp. 163-168; quoted by William Carlos Williams. "Advent in America of a New Irish Realist." Current Opinion, 62 (April 1917): 275.]

1916. Unsigned. "Queer, but Honest." Brooklyn Daily Eagle, 3 March 1917, p. 6.

1917. Unsigned. The Bellman, 22 (3 March 1917): 245, 250.

1918. Unsigned. Glasgow Herald, 8 March 1917.

1919. Unsigned. "Moral though Marred." Cambridge Magazine, 10 March 1917, pp. 425-426.

1920. BOYNTON, H. W. "Outstanding Novels of the Season." Nation, 104 (5 April 1917): 403-405.

1921. Unsigned. "A Dyspeptic Portrait." Freeman's Journal (Dublin), 7 April 1917.

1922. SQUIRE, J. C. New Statesman, 9 (14 April 1917): 40. [Appeared as "Mr. James Joyce" in his Books in General (1919), pp. 245-250.]

1923. WILLIAMS, WILLIAM CARLOS. "Advent in America of a New Irish Realist." Current Opinion, 63 (April 1917): 275.

1924. Unsigned. Irish Book Lover (Dublin), 8, nos. 9-10 (April-May 1917): 113.

1925. QUINN, JOHN. "James Joyce: A New Irish Novelist." Vanity Fair, 8, no. 3 (May 1917): 48, 128.

1926. BROOKS, VAN WYCK. "New Books." Seven Arts, 2, no. 7 (May 1917): 122.

1927. Unsigned. The English Review, 24 (May 1917): 478.

1928. Unsigned. Continent (Chicago), 3 May 1917, p. 548.

1929. Unsigned. "Paths and Goals." Nation, 104 (17 May 1917): 600, 602.

1930. M., C. H. S. "The Birth of an Artist's Soul." Challenge (London), 7, no. 161 (25 May 1917): 54.

1931. Unsigned. Catholic World, 105 (June 1917): 395-397.

1932. Unsigned. The Future, June 1917, p. 237.

1933. MACY, JOHN. "James Joyce." Dial, 62, no. 744 (14 June 1917): 525-527.

1934. R[EAD], H[ERBERT]. Arts and Letters, 1 (July 1917): 26, 28, 30.

1935. Unsigned. New Age (London), 21, n.s. no. 11 (12 July 1917): 254.

1936. POUND, EZRA. "James Joyce's Novel." Little Review, 4, no. 4 (August 1917): 7-8. [Also in Pound/Joyce, No. 725.]

1937. ANGELI, DIEGO (?). "Un romanzo di Gesuiti." Il Marzocco (Florence), 22, no. 32 (12 August 1917): 2-3. [Translated by Joyce for Egoist, 5, no. 2 (February 1918): 30.]

1938. COURNOS, JOHN. Apollos (St. Petersburg), 1918.

1939. GUILLERMET, FANNY. Journal de Génève, January 1918.

1940. J., B. W. (P. S. O'Hegarty). "Mr. Joyce's Autobiography." Irish World, 15 March 1919, p. 28.

1941. MARTINDALE, C. C. "Some Recent Books." Dublin Review, 166 (January-February-March 1920): 135-138.

1942. FELS, FLORENT. "Revues." Action, no. 6 (December 1920): 63-64.

1943. JALOUX, EDMOND. "Dedalus par James Joyce." Nouvelles littéraires, 10 May 1924, p. 4. [Condensed in Chronique des lettres françaises, 2 (1924): 548-549.]

1944. LALOU, RENÉE. "Dedalus et James Joyce." Vient de paraître (Paris), June 1924.

1945. POURRAT, HENRI. "Yeats et Joyce." La Vie, 5 June 1924.

1946. GARARRY, PAUL. Radical (Marseille), 24 June 1924. [Review of Dedalus.]

1947. GREEN, JULIEN. Nouvelle revue française, 23 (August 1924): 246-249. [Review of Dedalus; reprinted in his Oeuvres complètes, vol. 1. Edited by Jacques Petit. Paris: Gallimard, 1972, pp. 1014-1017.]

1948. Unsigned. Revue mondiale (Paris), 15 September 1924. [Review of Dedalus.]

1949. Unsigned. Natal Witness (Pietermaritzburg), 22 December 1924.

1950. W., O. M. W. "Travellers." Cambridge Review, 6 March 1925, p. 325.

1951. BIRKENFELD, ERICH. "James Joyce's Jugendbildnis." Orplid, 3 (1926): 63-66. [Review of German translation.]

1952. HAAS, WILLY. "Konfessionen aus dem Inferno."
<u>Die literarische Welt</u>, 2 (May 1926): 7-8.
[Reprinted as "James Joyce's <u>Jugendbild-
nis</u>" in his <u>Gestalten der Zeit</u>. Berlin:
Gustav Kiepenheuer Vlg., 1930; reprinted
in <u>Gestalten</u>. Berlin: Propyläen Vlg.,
1962; review of Goyert's translation of
<u>PAYM</u>.]

1953. FEHR, BERNHARD. "Joyce's Jugendbildnis."
<u>Basler Nachrichten</u>, 20 June 1926. [Re-
printed in <u>Von Englands geistigen Bes-
tänden: Ausgewählte Aufsätze von Bernhard
Fehr</u>. Edited by Max Wildi. Frauenfeld:
Huber and Company, 1944, pp. 168-171.]

1954. FRISCH, EFRAIM. "Jugendbildnis eines Dichters." <u>Frankfurter Zeitung</u> and <u>Der Tag</u>
(Berlin), 12 September 1926. [Reprinted
in his <u>Die fünf Weltteile: Ein unidyl-
lisches Verlegerjahrbuch mit einem idyl-
lischen Dichter-Almanach von Francis
Jammes</u>. Basel: Rhein Vlg., 1928, pp.
47-49.]

1955. KRELL, MAX. "James Joyce: <u>Jugendbildnis</u>."
<u>Literarische Umschau</u>, 7 November 1926.
[Review of German translation.]

1956. GERÖ. "James Joyce, 'Jugendbildnis.'"
<u>Imago, Zeitschrift fur Anwendung der
Psychoanalyse auf die Natur- und Geiste-
swissenschaften</u>, 14 (1928): 535-536.

1957. BRIGHT, JOHN M. <u>Post</u> (Chicago), 25 May 1928.

1958. FRISCH, EFRAIM. "<u>Jugendbildnis</u> eines Dichters." <u>Literaturblatt der Frankfurter
Zeitung</u>, 12 September 1928. [Same as No.
1954?]

EXILES

[Reviews of the play as a published book and as performance.]

1959. <u>Record</u> of known productions: (1919) Munich,
Munchener Theater; (1925) New York, Neigh-
borhood Playhouse, 19 February 1925-22
March 1925, 41 performances; (1926) Lon-
don, Regent Theatre, The Incorporated
Stage Society, 14 February-15 February;
(1926) Boston, The Barn, Boston Stage
Society, 3 April-10 April; (1930) Berlin,
Deutsches Volkstheater, 9 March (in Ger-
man); (1930) Milan, Convegno Theatre, 30
April (in Italian); (1945) London, Torch
Theatre, 11 September-30 September; (1947)
New York, Hudson Park Branch, New York
Public Library, Equity Library Theatre, 6
January-8 January; (1948) Dublin, Gaiety
Theatre, 18 January; (1950) London, Lon-
don Q Theatre, 16 May; (1959) Vienna,
Volkstheater, October (in German); (1956)
Paris; (1958) Dublin, Trinity College;
(1970) London, Mermaid Theatre, directed
by Harold Pinter, 12 November; (1971) Lon-
don, Royal Shakespeare Company, Aldwych
Theatre, directed by Harold Pinter, 7 Oct-
ober; (1971) New York, Central Church, 22
February-27 February, 2 March-7 March;
(1971) New York, Intense Family Company,
Cubiculo Theatre, directed by John Sill-
ings, 2-4 December; (1971) Barcelona, Tea-
tro Nacional de Cámara y Ensayo, directed
by Antonio Chic, translated by Enrique
Ortenbach, 28 May-21 June 1971; (1973)
Dublin, Peacock Theatre, directed by Vincent Dowling, 21 February; (1973) Berlin,
Schlossparktheater, directed by Willi
Schmidt, translated by Klaus Reichert, 16
June; (1973) Munich, Residenz Theater,
directed by Harry Meyen, translated by
Klaus Reichert, 5 July 1973; (1973) Basle,
Basler Theater, directed by Werner Dügge-
lin, translated by Klaus Reichert, 22 December; (1973) Warsaw, Maly Theatre, directed by Andrzej Lapicki, Polish translation by Z. and L. Porembski, 10 March
1973.]

1960. Unsigned. <u>Manchester Guardian</u>, 27 May 1918.

1961. G., J. W. "Ibsen in Ireland." <u>Freeman's
Journal</u> (Dublin), 15 June 1918, p. 4.

1962. [CLUTTON-BROCK, ARTHUR]. "The Mind to Suf-
fer." <u>Times Literary Supplement</u>, 25 July
1918, p. 346.

1963. EATON, W. P. "Some Plays in Print." <u>Book-
man</u>, 47 (August 1918): 638.

1964. MacCARTHY, DESMOND. "Exiles." <u>New States-
man</u>, 11 (21 September 1918): 492-493.
[Shortened version of this review appeared as "Mr. James Joyce's Play." <u>New
Statesman</u>, 26 (20 February 1926): 581-582
at the time of the Stage Society's production; original, longer article appeared in
his <u>Humanities</u> (1953): pp. 88-93.]

1965. Unsigned. "A Subtle Play." <u>Literary World</u>,
3 October 1918, p. 150.

1966. COLUM, PADRAIC. "James Joyce as Dramatist."
<u>Nation</u>, 107 (12 October 1918): 430-431.

1967. HACKETT, FRANCIS. "Exiles." <u>New Republic</u>,
16 (12 October 1918): 318-319.

1968. Unsigned. <u>Catholic World</u>, 108 (December
1918): 404-405.

1969. Unsigned. <u>The Bellman</u>, 25 (7 December 1918):
637.

1970. DAVRAY, HENRY. "Lettres anglaises." <u>Mercure
de France</u>, 121 (1 February 1919): 514-515.

1971. 'U.' "Ein englisches Drama." <u>Neue Zürcher
Zeitung</u>, no. 471 (31 March 1919). [Review
of German production.]

1972. Unsigned. "'Verbannte': Schauspiel von James
Joyce (Uraufführung im Müncher Schauspiel-

REVIEWS OF JOYCE'S WORKS

haus)." Munchen-Augsburger-Abendzeitung, 8 August 1919.

1973. 'Eichinger.' "'Verbannte': Schauspiel von James Joyce: Uraufführung im Schauspiel-haus am. 7. August." Munchner Neueste Nachrichten, 8 August 1919.

1974. E. "Verbannte." Vossische Zeitung, 11 August 1919.

1975. MORECK, KURT. "Das 'Schauspielhaus' be-scherte uns als Uraufführung..." Allgemeine Zeitung München, 7 September 1919.

1976. B., M. "James Joyce. 'Verbannte.'" Zeitschrift für Bucherfreunde, 12 (June 1920): 114.

1977. KRUTCH, JOSEPH WOOD. "Figures of the Dawn." Nation, 120 (March 1925): 272.

1978. BENCHLEY, ROBERT. "Back to Form." Life, 82 (12 March 1925): 20.

1979. NATHAN, GEORGE J. American Mercury, 4 (April 1925): 501.

1980. Unsigned. "Echoes of the Town." Daily Sketch (London), 16 February 1926.

1981. Unsigned. Times (London), 16 February 1926, p. 12C.

1982. Unsigned. Nation (London), 28 (20 February 1926); ibid., 27 February 1926, p. 745.

1983. WALDMAN, M. London Mercury, 13 (March 1926): 535.

1984. BROWN, J. "Exiles." Saturday Review (London), 141 (1926): 223-224.

1985. ROYDE-SMITH, N. G. "Exiles." Outlook (London), 57 (March 1926): 226.

1986. ENGEL, FRITZ. "Nach Ibsen." Berliner Tageblatt, 10 March 1930.

1987. F. "James Joyce. 'Verbannte': Matinee im Deutschen Volkstheater." Deutsche Allgemeine Zeitung, 10 March 1930.

1988. ERVINE, ST. JOHN. "At the Play: Mr. Joyce and Mr. Rubenstein." Observer, 12 July 1936.

1989. REDFERN, J. Spectator, 175 (21 September 1945): 266.

1990. Unsigned. Times (London), 17 May 1950, pp. 3, 12.

1991. Unsigned. New Statesman and Nation, 39 (27 May 1950): 602-603.

1992. BREIT, HARVEY. New York Times Book Review, 16 December 1951, p. 15.

1993. McLAUGHLIN, RICHARD. Theatre Arts, 36 (February 1952): 94.

1994. Unsigned. New Yorker, 27 (2 February 1952): 79.

1995. FREEDLEY, GEORGE. Library Journal, 77 (15 February 1952): 362.

1996. HUTCHINS, PATRICIA. Irish Writing, no. 19 (June 1952): 56-57.

1997. KELLEHER, JOHN V. Furioso, 7 (September 1952): 65-67.

1998. Unsigned. "James Joyce's Exiles--First Production in Paris." Times (London), 7 May 1956, p. 3.

1999. BECKLEY, PAUL V. New York Herald Tribune, 14 March 1957.

2000. HATCH, ROBERT. Nation, 184 (30 March 1957): 281.

2001. Unsigned. "Seventeen Duologues by James Joyce." Trinity News (Dublin), 6 March 1958.

2002. RENO. T.C.D., 7 March 1958, p. 10.

2003. HOLZER, RUDOLF. "Überspitzte Gewissenser-forschung: Im Volkstheater; 'Verbannte' von James Joyce." Wiener Zeitung, 3 October 1959.

2004. Unsigned. "James Joyce also Bühnenautor: Das Drama 'Verbannte' im Wiener Volkstheater." Süddeutsche Zeitung, 15 October 1959.

2005. BRYDEN, RONALD. Observer (London), 15 November 1970, p. 29 and 29 November 1970, p. 28.

2006. DEWHURST, KEITH. Guardian (Manchester), 19 November 1970, p. 10.

2007. EXNER, JULIAN. Luzerner neuester Nachrichten (Lucerne), 30 November 1970.

2008. FIDDICK, PETER. Guardian (Manchester), 13 November 1970, p. 8.

2009. HURREN, KENNETH. Spectator, 225 (21 November 1970): 652.

2010. HOBSON, HAROLD. Sunday Times (London), 15 November 1970, p. 29.

2011. JENSE, GREGORY. UPI release (November 1970).

2012. JONES, D. A. N. Listener, 84 (26 November 1970): 760.

2013. KINGSTON, JEREMY. Punch, 259 (25 November 1970): 768-769.

2014. KRETZMER, HERBERT. _Daily Express_ (London), 13 November 1970, p. 18.

2015. NATAN, ALEX. _St. Galler Tagblatt_, 4 December 1970.

2016. Unsigned. _National-Zeitung_ (Basel), 17 December 1970.

2017. NIGHTINGALE, BENEDICT. _New Statesman_, 80 (20 November 1970): 689.

2018. 'Pit.' _Variety_, 25 (November 1970): 50.

2019. WARDLE, IRVING. _Times_ (London), 13 November 1970, p. 13.

2020. Unsigned. _New York Times_, 19 November 1970, p. 42.

2021. ASHMORE, BASIL. "Letter to the Editor." _Times_ (London), 3 December 1970, p. 11. [See response by Terence Baker _et al._, 11 December 1970, p. 13.]

2022. Unsigned. _Der Spiegel_, 24 (November 1970): 198.

2023. LAMBERT, J. W. _Drama_, 100 (Spring 1971): 21-22; 103 (Winter 1971): 22.

2024. MAIROWITZ, DAVID Z. _Village Voice_, 18 November 1971, p. 74.

2025. MANDER, GERTRUD. _Theater Heute_, 13 (January 1972): 36.

2026. WENDT, ERNST. _Theater Heute_, 13 (January 1972): 25-26.

2027. SPURLING, JOHN. _Plays and Players_, 19 (December 1971): 44-46, 88.

2028. WARDLE, IRVING. _Times_ (London), 8 October 1971, p. 20.

2029. NIGHTINGALE, BENEDICT. _Theatre 72._ Edited by Sheridan Morley. London: Hutchinson, 1972, p. 67.

2030. SAINER, ARTHUR. _Village Voice_, 2 December 1971, p. 65.

2031. BENACH, JOAN ANTON. _Reseña de literatura, arte y espectaculos_, 8 (September-October 1971): 478-479.

2032. TOMÁS, A. MARTÍNEZ. _Vanguardia espanola_, 30 May 1971, p. 58.

2033. Unsigned. _Espectador y la critica_, 14 (1971): 352.

2034. WORTH, KATHARINE J. "Joyce via Pinter," in _Revolutions in Modern English Drama_. London: G. Bell and Sons, 1973, pp. 46-54.

2035. MANNING, MARY. _Hibernia_, 37 (2 March 1973): 28.

2036. NOWLAN, DAVID. _Irish Times_, 22 February 1973, p. 12.

2037. RUSHE, DESMOND. _Irish Independent_, 22 February 1973, p. 13.

2038. GRACK, GÜNTHER. _Tagesspiegel_ (Berlin), 19 June 1973, p. 4.

2039. RISCHBIETER, HENNING. _Theater heute_, 14 (August 1973): 30-31.

2040. HENRICHS, BENJAMIN. _Süddeutsche Zeitung_, 7-8 July 1973, p. 12. [Excerpted in _Theater heute_, 14 (August 1973): 31.]

2041. NENNECKE, CHARLOTTE. _Süddeutsche Zeitung_, 5 July 1973, p. 13.

2042. DÜTSCH, ADOLF. _Reformatio_ (Schaffhausen), 23 (April 1974): 242.

2043. KUHN, CHRISTOPH. _Tages-Anzeiger_ (Zürich), 24 December 1973, p. 17.

2044. MEHREN, GÜNTHER. _Stuttgarter Zeitung_, 3 January 1974, p. 25.

2045. REICHERT, KLAUS. _Basler-Theater_, no. 6 (January 1974): 2.

2046. SEELMANN-EGGEBERT, ULRICH. _National-Zeitung_ (Basle), 24 December 1973, p. 19.

2047. MISIORNY, MICHAL. _Trybuna Ludu_ (Warsaw), 26 March 1973, p. 8.

ULYSSES

2048. ELIOT, T. S. "Contemporanea." _Egoist_, 5, no. 6 (June-July 1918): 84-85.

2049. C., R. H. (A. R. Orage). "Readers and Writers." _New Age_ (London), 28 (28 April 1921): 306-307.

2050. Unsigned. "James Joyce and his Chef d'Oeuvre." _Observer_, 11 December 1921.

2051. SELVER, PAUL. "Englischer Brief." _Das literarische Echo_, 24 (1921-1922): 1515-1516.

2052. BENCO, SILVIO. "L'_Ulisse_ du James Joyce." _La Nazione_, 5, no. 78 (1922): 1.

2053. REHM, GEORGE. _Chicago Tribune_ (Paris), 13 February 1922, p. 2.

2054. HUDDLESTON, SISLEY. "_Ulysses_." _Observer_, no. 6823 (5 March 1922): 4. [Later appeared as part of an article in _Articles de Paris_. New York: Macmillan, 1928, pp. 41-47.]

REVIEWS OF JOYCE'S WORKS

2055. SLOCOMBE, GEORGE. "The Week in Paris." Daily Herald (London), n.s. no. 921 (17 March 1922): 4.

2056. MAIS, S. P. B. "An Irish Revel: And Some Flappers." Daily Express (London), 25 March 1922.

2057. REHM, GEORGE. "Ulysses." Paris Review, 1 April 1922, p. 19.

2058. 'Aramis.' "The Scandal of 'Ulysses.'" The Sporting Times, no. 34 (1 April 1922): 4.

2059. BEVERSEN, DR. N. J. Nieuwe Rotterdamsche Courant, no. 28 (8 April 1922).

2060. Unsigned. "A New 'Ulysses.'" Evening News (London), 8 April 1922, p. 4.

2061. Unsigned. "Mr. James Joyce." Daily Mail (London), 17 April 1922.

2062. MURRAY, JOHN MIDDLETON. Nation and Athenaeum, 31 (22 April 1922): 124-125.

2063. BENNETT, ARNOLD. "James Joyce's 'Ulysses.'" Outlook, 29 April 1922, pp. 337-339. [Appeared as "Concerning James Joyce's 'Ulysses.'" Bookman, 55 (August 1922): 567-570; later appeared in his Things That Have Interested Me (1936): 185-194.]

2064. LARBAUD, VALERY. "James Joyce." Nouvelle revue français, 18 (April 1922): 385-409. [Originally a speech delivered to Les Amis des Livres, 7 December 1921; used as introduction to Gens de Dublin; translated as "The Ulysses of James Joyce." Criterion, 1 (October 1922): 94-103; translated by A. J. Battistessa. Logos (Buenos Aires), 4 (1945): 79-98; reprinted in his Ce vice impuni, la lecture, No. 1602.]

2065. Unsigned. "Could the Irish Writers Help?" Manchester Guardian, 2 May 1922, p. 5.

2066. COLLINS, JOSEPH. "James Joyce's Amazing Chronicle." New York Times Book Review, 28 May 1922, pp. 6, 17.

2067. DOUGLAS, JAMES. "Beauty-And the Beast." Sunday Express (London), 28 May 1922, p. 5.

2068. M., H. J. "The World of Books." Nation and Athenaeum, no. 4806 (10 June 1922): 377.

2069. JACKSON, HOLBROOK. "Ulysses à la Joyce." To-Day, 9 (June 1922): 47-49. [Also appeared in Bruno's Review of Two Worlds, 2, no. 4 (July-August 1922): 37-38, and as Ulysses à la Joyce. Berkeley Heights, N.J.: Oriole Press, 1961.]

2070. WILSON, EDMUND. "Ulysses." New Republic, 31, no. 396 (5 July 1922): 164-166.

[Also in Baltimore Evening Sun, 3 August 1922, p. 6.]

2071. Unsigned. Evening Transcript (Boston), 10 July 1922.

2072. COLUM, MARY. "The Confessions of James Joyce." Freeman (New York), 5, no. 123 (19 July 1933): 450-452. [Later appeared in The Freeman Book (1924), pp. 327-355; translated in part in "Auseinandersetzung mit James Joyce's Ulysses." Akzente, 12 (July 1965): 231-245.]

2073. CANBY, HENRY SEIDEL. "Crazy Literature." Literary Review, 22 July 1922.

2074. MAITLAND, CECIL. "Review." New Witness, 4 August 1922. [See reply by G. K. Chesterton. "An Extraordinary Argument." ibid., 18 August 1922 and letters to the editor, 11 August, 1, 8 and 15 September 1922.]

2075. MURRAY, J. MIDDLETON. "Reviews: Two Remarkable Novels." Nation and Athenaeum, 31 (12 August 1922): 655-656.

2076. SELDES, GILBERT. "Ulysses." Nation, 115, no. 2982 (30 August 1922): 211-212.

2077. DOMINI CANIS (Shane Leslie). "Ulysses." Dublin Review, 171 (September 1922): 112-119.

2078. JOSEPHSON, MATTHEW. "1001 Nights in a Bar-Room, or the Irish Odyseus." Broom, 3 (September 1922): 146-150.

2079. O'HEGARTY, P. S. "Mr. Joyce's Ulysses." The Separatist, 2 September 1922.

2080. LESLIE, SHANE. "Ulysses." Quarterly Review, 238 (October 1922): 219-234. [Reprinted in part in "Auseinandersetzung mit James Joyce's Ulysses." Akzente, 12 (July 1965): 231-243.]

2081. BUSS, KATE. "Ulysses." Evening Transcript (Boston), 10 October 1922.

2082. WILSON, EDMUND. "Rag-Bag of the Soul." Literary Review, 3, no. 12 (25 November 1922): 237-238.

2083. R., S. Granta (Cambridge), 1 December 1922.

2084. DEUTSCH, BABETTE. "On Ulysses." Literary Review, 2 December 1922, p. 281.

2085. O'DUFFY, EIMAR. "Ulysses." Irish Review, 9 December 1922.

2086. HUEFFER (FORD), FORD MADOX. "Ulysses and the Handling of Indecencies." English Review, 35 (December 1922): 538-548.

2087. HARWOOD, H. C. "Novels: 1922--Retrospect." Outlook, 30 December 1922.

2088. CECCHI, EMILIO. Tribuna (Rome), 2 March 1923.

2089. Unsigned. "Ulysses," and "James Joyce." Almanach des lettres françaises et étrangères (Paris), 15 March 1924, p. 300; (28 February 1924): 233; (22 March 1924): 326.

2090. GREEN, JULIEN. "'Ulysses,' par James Joyce." Philosophies, no. 2 (15 May 1924): 218-222. [Reprinted in his Oeuvres complètes, vol. 1. Edited by Jacques Petit. Paris: Gallimard, 1972, pp. 1009-1014.]

2091. FEHR, BERNHARD. Basler Nachrichten, 16 August 1925. [Reprinted as "Der roman 'Ulysses' von James Joyce," in Von Englands geistigen Reständen: Ausgewählte von Bernhard Fehr. Edited by Max Wildi. Frauenfeld: Huber and Company, 1944, pp. 162-167; reprinted in shortened form as "Die Stellungdes Ulysses im neuen englischen Schrifttum," in Der Homer unserer Zeit: Deutschland in Erwartung des Ulysses von James Joyce: Letzte Gelegenheit zur Subskription. Zürich: Rhein Vlg., 1927, pp. 10-12.]

2092. ZAREK, OTTO. "Der Ulysses des James Joyce." Das Tagebuch, 8 (1927): 1963-1966.

2093. DÖBLIN, ALFRED. "Ulysses von Joyce." Das Deutsche Buch (Leipzig), 8 (1928): 84-85. [Reprinted in his Aufsätze zur Literatur. Edited by Walter Muschg. Olten: Walter Vlg., 1963, pp. 287-290, 413; reprinted in his Die Zeitlupe: Kleine Prosa. Edited by Walter Muschg. Olten: Walter Vlg., 1962, pp. 148-152, 266; translated by Barbara L. Surowska. "Ulisses J'a." Literatura na Swiecie, no. 5 (May 1973): 188-193.]

2094. F., L. "James Joyce. Ulysses." Das Kunstblatt, 12 (1928): 63-64.

2095. GEORG, MANFRED. "Der 'Ulysses' des James Joyce." Badische Presse, Literarische umschau, no. 1 (1928).

2096. MUSCHG, WALTER. "Der Deutsche Ulysses." Annalen, 2 (1928): 19-24.

2097. SCHD., H. "Ulysses von James Joyce." Beilage: Der kleine Bund, 9, no. 2 (1928).

2098. WERNER, BRUNO E. "Der Ulysses des James Joyce." Deutsche Rundschau, 215 (1928): 268-270.

2099. ZWEIG, STEFAN. "Anmerkung zum Ulysses." Neue Rundschau, 39, no. 2 (October 1928): 476-479. [Reprinted in his Der goldene Schnitt. Edited by Christoph Schwerin. Frankfurt a.M.: Fischer, 1960, pp. 283-286.]

2100. FRISCH, EFRAIM. "'Ulysses': Zu dem Werk von James Joyce." Frankfurter Zeitung, 11 January 1928.

2101. Unsigned. Praseis (Berne), 15 February 1928.

2102. W., L. "Ulysses." Bohemia (Prague), 24 February 1928.

2103. GUILLEMIN, BERNARD. "Der Errtum des James Joyce." Magdeburgische Zeitung, 4 March 1928.

2104. GAUPP, F. "Über James Joyce, Ulysses." Badische Presse (Karlsruhe), 4 April 1928.

2105. OFFENBURG, KURT. "Joyce: Ulysses." Münchner Post, 31 May 1928. [Reprinted in Deutsche Republik (Frankfurt), 2, no. 2 (1927-1928): 1137-1139.]

2106. HENNIG, ARTUR. "Grundsätzliches zu James Joyce Ulysses." Die Tat, 20 (June 1928): 223-224.

2107. EMIÉ, LOUIS. Cahiers du sud, 15 (July 1929): 470-474.

2108. CASSOU, JEAN. "James Joyce, poète épique." Les nouvelles littéraires, 9 March 1929, p. 9. [Reprinted as "Apparition d'Ulysse," in his Pour le poésie. Paris: R. -A. Corrêa, 1935, pp. 133-139; reprinted in Revista de revistas, 19 (28 April 1929): 38, 51.]

2109. SIGUR, NICOLAS. Revue mondiale (Paris), 1 April 1929.

2110. MIOMANDRE, FRANCIS de. "Vulgarisation." Les nouvelles littéraires, 6 April 1929.

2111. IVY, WILLIAM. Journal (Atlanta), 11 April 1929.

2112. BRION, MARCEL. "Ulysse." La Revue hebdomadaire, 4 (20 April 1929): 365-367.

2113. CHADOURNE, MARC. "Un événement: Ulysse." La revue européenne, no. 5 (May 1929): 1818-1833.

2114. Unsigned. Progrès de Lyon, 3 May 1929.

2115. DONA, VICTOR. "La traduction d'Ulysse." Europe, 20 (15 June 1929): 297-299.

2116. SOUPAULT, PHILIPPE. "Sur l'Ulysse de James Joyce." Europe, 20 (15 June 1929): 292-296.

2117. Unsigned. "Aura poetica." Italia letteraria, 7 July 1929.

2118. BENNETT, ARNOLD. Evening Standard (London), 8 August 1929. [Review of French translation.]

REVIEWS OF JOYCE'S WORKS

2119. SERANDREI, MARIO. "Dall'Ulisse de J. Joyce." Cinematograph, June 1930, pp. 47-48.

2120. BURIOT-DARSILES, H. "La traduction allemande de l'Ulisse." Revue de littérature comparée, 10 (October-December 1930): 722-724.

2121. GREGORY, HORACE. New York Herald Tribune Books, 21 January 1934, pp. 1-2.

2122. MORRIS, LLOYD. Daily Eagle (Brooklyn), 21 January 1934.

2123. FADIMAN, CLIFTON. "American Debut of 'Ulysses.'" New Yorker, 9 (27 January 1934): 61.

2124. COLUM, PADRAIC. Saturday Review of Literature, 10 (27 January 1934): 433.

2125. SELDES, GILBERT. "Joyce and Lewis Share Honors of the Week." New York Evening Journal, 27 January 1934, p. 11.

2126. C[HURCH], S[AMUEL] H[ARDEN]. "A Stableboy's Book." Carnegie Magazine, 7, no. 9 (February 1934): 279-281.

2127. TROY, WILLIAM. Nation, 138 (14 February 1934): 187.

2128. FARRELL, JAMES T. Scribners, February 1934.

2129. LEARY, WILSON. Miami News, 18 February 1934.

2130. CANTWELL, ROBERT. "Outlook Book Choice." New Outlook, 163 (March 1934): 57-58.

2131. Unsigned. Booklist, 39 (March 1934): 215.

2132. Unsigned. New Outlook, 163 (March 1934): 167.

2133. BAIRD, EDWIN. "Words, Words, Words." Real America (Mount Morris, Ill.), 3, no. 2 (April 1934): 44.

2134. BRICKELL, HERSCHEL. North American Review, 237 (April 1934): 378.

2135. TALBOT, FRANCIS. America, 51 (1 September 1934): 497.

2136. SPENDER, STEPHEN. "Music and Decay." Left Review, 2, no. 15 (December 1936): 834-836.

2137. Unsigned. "Interpretations of 'Ulysses.'" Times Literary Supplement, 23 January 1937.

2138. ILLARI, PIERO. "[Review of Subirat translation]." Histonium, 7, no. 79 (December 1945): 843-844.

2139. BORGES, JORGE LUIS. "Nota sobre al Ulises en español." Anales de Buenos Aires, no. 1 (January 1946): 49.

2140. ASTURIAS, MIGUEL ANGEL. "Ulises." Suma bibliografica (Mexico City), 1 (April 1946): 17-18.

2141. C[ANO], J[OSÉ] L[UIS]. Insula, no. 24 (15 December 1947): 8.

2142. SCHMIDT, ARNO. "Ulysses in Deutschland: Kritische Anmerkungen zu einer James Joyce--Übersetzung." Frankfurter Allgemeine Zeitung, 26 October 1957.

POMES PENYEACH

2143. SLOCOMBE, GEORGE. "On the Left Bank." Daily Herald (London), 14 July 1927, p. 4.

2144. O., Y. (George Russell?). Irish Statesman, 23 July 1927, p. 478.

2145. Unsigned. Hound and Horn, 1 (September 1927): 61.

2146. ZABEL, MORTON D. "The Treasure of Dedalus." Nation, 145 (9 October 1927): 382.

2147. Unsigned. Nation, 125 (12 October 1927): 403.

2148. BRION, MARCEL. "L'Actualité littéraire à l'etranger." Les nouvelles littéraires, 12, no. 261 (15 October 1927): 7.

2149. WILSON, EDMUND. "New Poems by Joyce." New Republic, 70, no. 673 (26 October 1927): 268.

2150. Unsigned. Times Literary Supplement, 10 November 1927, p. 814.

2151. COLUM, PADRAIC. New York World, 15 January 1928. [Same review in Dublin Magazine, 3, no. 3 (July-September 1928): 68.]

2152. HILLYER, ROBERT. "Recent Poetry." New Adelphi, 1, no. 3 (March 1928): 264.

2153. Z[ABEL], M[ORTON] D. "The Lyrics of James Joyce." Poetry, 36 (July 1930): 206-213.

2154. FFRENCH, YVONNE. "Poetry." London Mercury, 28 (May 1933): 69-70.

ANNA LIVIA PLURABELLE (ALP)

2155. SCRIBE, OLIVER. "The Modern Rabelais." T. P. and Cassells's Weekly, 13 February 1926, p. 580.

2156. Unsigned. "Magazines." Irish Statesman, 10 September 1927, p. 21.

2157. Unsigned. "Querist." _Irish Statesman_, 16 April 1927.

2158. COLUM, MARY. _New York Herald Tribune_, 24 April 1927.

2159. SAGE, ROBERT. "Footnotes." _Chicago Tribune_ (Paris), 15 April 1928, p. 5.

2160. Unsigned. _Glasgow Herald_, 19 April 1928.

2161. SCHARAF, LESTER. "James Joyce the Unbounded." _The Adolescent_ (Baltimore), 1, no. 1 (Summer 1928): 17-18.

2162. SAGE, ROBERT. "Etc." _transition_, no. 14 (Fall 1928): 171-174.

2163. Unsigned. "Joyce's New Book." _New York Herald_ (Paris), 1 October 1928.

2164. GOULD, GERALD. _Observer_, 9 December 1928.

2165. Unsigned. "Mr. Joyce's Experiment." _Times Literary Supplement_, 20 December 1928, p. 1008.

2166. Unsigned. _Chronicle_ (Newcastle), 20 December 1928.

2167. O., Y. (George Russell?). "Anna Livia Plurabelle." _Irish Statesman_, 11 (29 December 1928): 339.

2168. O'FAOLAIN, SEAN. "Almost Music." _Hound and Horn_, 2 (January-March 1929): 178-180.

2169. _____. "Correspondence: 'Anna Livia Plurabelle.'" _Irish Statesman_, 11 (5 January 1929): 354-355. [See letter to Editor by Eugene Jolas, 26 January 1929; O'Faolain, 2 March 1929; and Walter Lowenfels, 16 March 1929.]

2170. Unsigned. _Irish Statesman_, 2 February 1929.

2171. Unsigned. "James Joyce and His New Prose, Polyglot Word Structures, By One Who Knows Him." _T.P.'s Weekly_, 12, no. 307 (14 September 1929): 573-574.

2172. CALMER, EDGAR. "A New Issue of 'transition.'" _Chicago Sunday Tribune_ (Paris), 17 November 1929.

2173. CORT, DAVID. "James Joyce's What-is-it?" _Vanity Fair_, 33 (December 1929): 132, 148, 150.

2174. Unsigned. _Yorkshire Post_ (Leeds), 5 February 1930.

2175. Unsigned. _Vogue_, 29 May 1930.

2176. Unsigned. _Passing Show_, 4 June 1930.

2177. Unsigned. _Post_ (Birmingham), 10 June 1930.

2178. Unsigned. _Yorkshire Herald_ (York), 11 June 1930.

2179. BENNETT, ARNOLD. "Back to Riceyman Steps." _Evening Standard_, 12 June 1930.

2180. Unsigned. _Press_ (Aberdeen), 12 June 1930.

2181. Unsigned. _Daily Herald_ (London), 12 June 1930.

2182. Unsigned. _Evening News_ (Glasgow), 13 June 1930.

2183. HEARD, GERALD. "The Language of James Joyce." _The Week-end Review_, 14 June 1930, pp. 492-493.

2184. Unsigned. _Notts Guardian_ (Nottingham), 14 June 1930.

2185. Unsigned. _Daily Sketch_ (London), 26 June 1930.

2186. Unsigned. _Yorkshire Evening Post_ (Leeds), 27 June 1930.

2187. MITCHISON, NAOMI. "Anna and the Apes." _Time and Tide_, 28 June 1930.

2188. STONIER, G. W. "Mr. James Joyce in Progress." _New Statesman_, 35, no. 896 (28 June 1930): 372-374.

2189. Unsigned. _Newsagent_ (London), 28 June 1930.

2190. HODGSON, C. H. "Clarity or Incomprehensibility? Is Vagueness a Virtue in Literature?" _Notts Journal_ (Nottingham), 2 July 1930.

2191. Unsigned. _Glasgow Herald_, 3 July 1930.

2192. Unsigned. _Evening Express_ (Liverpool), 7 July 1930.

2193. Unsigned. "Mr. Joyce's Experiment." _Times Literary Supplement_, 17 July 1930, p. 588.

2194. J., J. J. "In a New Manner--'Anna Livia Plurabelle.'" _Western Independent_ (London), 20 August 1930.

2195. MILES, HAMISH. _Criterion_, 10 (October 1930): 188-192.

2196. GRIGSON, GEOFFREY. "James Joyce Again." _Saturday Review_ (London), 150 (29 November 1930): 718.

2197. REIFENBERG, BENNO. "7 Rue de l'Odeon." _Frankfurter Zeitung_, 30 March 1931.

2198. Unsigned. "James Joyce et le snobisme." _Le Monde_, 2 May 1931, p. 4.

2199. Unsigned. "From the New Books: Not What It Seems!" _Everyman_, 7 May 1931, p. 466.

REVIEWS OF JOYCE'S WORKS

2200. CALVERT, J. "En lisant." Lettres (Paris), 3 June 1931.

2201. MEADE, NORAH. "Nonsense of New Art." New York Herald Tribune Books, 13 September 1931, pp. 1, 5, 6.

2202. TITUS, EDWARD W. "Mr. Joyce Explains." This Quarter, 4 (December 1931): 371–372.

2203. E., P. "Joyce oder die Höllenmaschine." Prager Presse (Prague), 3 March 1932.

2204. CHILTON, ELEANOR CARROL. "'Twas Brillig.'" English Review, 56 (January 1933): 107–108.

2205. OLDMEADOW, E. "Rot." Tablet, 161 (January 1933): 41–42.

2206. Unsigned. "M. James Joyce et son 'ouvrage en train.'" Le Mois, synthese de l'activité mondiale, no. 26 (February–March 1933): 185–190.

2207. REYNOLDS, HORACE. "James Joyce's Poetry does not Suggest Ulysses." New York Times Book Review, 10 October 1937, p. 4.

TALES TOLD OF SHEM AND SHAUN

2208. SALEMSON, HAROLD J. Mercure de France, 215 (1929): 746–747.

2209. OGDEN, C. K. "Current Literature." Psyche, 9 (July 1929): 86.

2210. O., Y. (George Russel?). Irish Statesman, 6 July 1929.

2211. Unsigned. Spectator, 3 August 1929.

2212. Unsigned. Spectator, 3 August 1929.

2213. MILES, HAMISH. "Tales Told of Shem and Shaun." Criterion, 19, no. 38 (October 1930): 188–192.

2214. NO ENTRY.

2215. STRONG, L. A. G. Spectator, 149 (December 1932): 844.

2216. Unsigned. Saturday Review, 154 (10 December 1932): 629.

2217. CHILTON, E. C. "'Twas Brillig." English Review, 56 (January 1933): 107–108.

2218. BARKER, GEORGE. Adelphi, 5, no. 4 (January 1933): 310–311.

2219. BRIDSON, D. G. "Views and Review." New English Weekly, 5 January 1933, pp. 281–282.

2220. OLDMEADOW, E. Tablet, 161 (14 January 1933); 41–42.

2221. Unsigned. "Mr. Eliot and Mr. Joyce." Everyman, 28 January 1933.

HAVETH CHILDERS EVERYWHERE

2222. COLUM, PADRAIC. "From a 'Work in Progress.'" New Republic, 64 (17 September 1930): 131–132. [Same article appeared in Dublin Magazine, 6, no. 3 (July–September 1931): 33–37.]

2223. Unsigned. Courier (Inverness), 19 May 1931.

2224. HOULT, NORAH. Yorkshire Evening Post (Leeds), 15 May 1931.

2225. CARGEEGE, F. B. "The Mystery of James Joyce." Everyman, 11 June 1931.

2226. COOKE, GREVILLE. "Musical Notes. Ulta Modernism in Art, Literature and Music." Kettering Leader, 12 June 1931.

2227. COURTENAY, JENNIFER. "The Approach to James Joyce." Everyman, 9 July 1931, p. 765.

2228. RUSHTON, G. WYNNE. "The Case Against James Joyce." Everyman, 9 July 1931, pp. 765–766.

2229. GILBERT, STUART. "The Joycean Protagonist." Échanges, no. 5 (December 1931): 154–157.

2230. Unsigned. Times Literary Supplement, 17 July 1930, p. 588.

2231. MATTHEWS, HERBERT L. New York Times Book Review, 11 January 1931, p. 11.

2232. R., L. Daily Telegraph (London), 7 May 1931.

2233. GORDON, W. R. News Chronicle (London), 7 May 1931.

2234. Unsigned. Post (Birmingham), 19 May 1931.

2235. Unsigned. Herald (Glasgow), 25 May 1931.

2236. M., T. M. Guardian (Manchester), 1 June 1931.

2237. WATSON, FRANCIS. Yorkshire Daily Post (Leeds), 2 June 1931.

2238. Unsigned. Dorset Daily Echo (Weymouth), 6 June 1931.

2239. H., I'A. F. Guardian (Manchester), 7 August 1931.

MIME OF MICK, NICK, AND THE MAGGIES

2240. STONIER, G. W. "Joyce without End." New Statesman and Nation, 8 (22 September 1934): 364.

COLLECTED POEMS

2241. GREGORY, HORACE. "Fifty Lyrics by the Author of <u>Ulysses</u>." <u>New York Herald Tribune Books</u>, 13 December 1936, p. 8.

2242. BÉNET, WILLIAM ROSE. "Contemporary Poetry." <u>Saturday Review of Literature</u>, 15 (19 December 1936): 20.

2243. REYNOLDS, HORACE. "James Joyce's Poetry does not Suggest <u>Ulysses</u>." <u>New York Times Book Review</u>, 10 October 1937, p. 4.

2244. HENDRY, IRENE. "Joyce's Alter Ego." <u>Washington Square College Review</u>, 2, no. 2 (January 1938): 17.

FINNEGANS WAKE

2245. LEVIN, HARRY. "On First Looking into 'Finnegans Wake.'" <u>New Directions in Prose and Poetry</u> (1939): 253-287.

2246. FEENEY, L. J. "James Joyce." <u>America</u>, 61 (May 1939): 139.

2247. MERCANTON, JACQUES. "Finnegans Wake (notes pour une 'Introduction à la methode de Joyce')." <u>Nouvelle revue française</u>, 27, no. 308 (1 May 1939): 858-864.

2248. DAVIS, ELRICK B. <u>Press</u> (Cleveland), 2 May 1939.

2249. GANNETT, LEWIS. <u>New York Herald Tribune</u>, 4 May 1939.

2250. HANSEN, HARRY. "The First Reader." <u>World Telegram</u> (New York), 4 May 1939. [Also in <u>News</u> (Greensboro, North Carolina), 6 May 1939; <u>Virginian Pilot</u> (Norfolk), 8 May 1939.]

2251. LYND, ROBERT. <u>News Chronicle</u> (London), 4 May 1939.

2252. McFEE, WILLIAM. "James Joyce's New Work and a Key to its Significance." <u>New York Sun</u>, 4 May 1939.

2253. SELBY, JOHN. <u>Journal-Courier</u> (Lafayette, Ind.), 29 April 1939. [Syndicated also in: <u>Nonpareil</u> (Council Bluff, Iowa), 29 April 1939; <u>Register</u> (New Haven), 30 April 1939; <u>Record</u> (Bristow, Oklahoma), 2 May 1939; <u>Press</u> (Newport News), 3 May 1939; <u>Register</u> (Sandusky, Ohio), 3 May 1939; <u>Courier-Journal</u> (Louisville), 4 May 1939; <u>Telegram</u> (Worcester), 4 May 1939; <u>Times Dispatch</u> (Richmond), 4 May 1939; <u>Intelligencer</u> (Wheeling), 4 May 1939; <u>Gazette</u> (Niagara Falls), 4 May 1939; <u>Leader</u> (Staunton, Virginia), 4 May 1939; <u>Leader-Republican</u> (Gloversville, New York), 4 May 1939; <u>News Bulletin</u> (Bristol, Virginia), 4 May 1939; <u>Republican Times</u> (Ottawa, Illinois), 4 May 1939; <u>Standard Sentinel</u> (Hazelton, Pa.), 4 May 1939; <u>Star</u> (Rockford, Illinois), 4 May 1939; <u>Telegram</u> (Bridgeport), 4 May 1939; <u>Tribune</u> (Hornell), 4 May 1939; <u>Union Sun Journal</u> (Lockport), 4 May 1939; <u>World-News</u> (Roanoke), 4 May 1939; <u>Spokesman Review</u> (Spokane), 5 May 1939; <u>Argus</u> (Rock Island), 6 May 1939; <u>Express</u> (Portland), 6 May 1939; <u>News</u> (Galveston), 7 May 1939; <u>Observer</u> (Charlotte), 7 May 1939; <u>Herald</u> (Miami), 14 May 1939; <u>Vindicator</u> (Youngstown), 14 May 1939; <u>Union</u> (San Diego), 21 May 1939; <u>Bee</u> (Sacramento), 27 May 1939; <u>Times</u> (Toledo), 16 July 1939.]

2254. THOMPSON, RALPH. "Books of the Times." <u>New York Times</u>, 4 May 1939, p. 21.

2255. WAGNER, CHARLES. "Books." <u>Daily Mirror</u> (New York), 4 May 1939.

2256. MARCH, MICHAEL. "Page after Page." <u>Citizen</u> (Brooklyn), 5 May 1939, 12 May 1939.

2257. NICOLSON, HAROLD. "The Indecipherable Mystery of Mr. James Joyce's Allegory." <u>Daily Telegraph</u> (London), 5 May 1939.

2258. STRONG, L. A. G. "James Joyce's Dream World." <u>John O'London's Weekly</u>, 41, no. 1147 (5 May 1939): 168. [See also letters to the Editor about review from Elliott Whitfield, 19 May 1939; W. B. Howell, 30 June 1939.]

2259. Unsigned. "Ancient and Modern." <u>Irish Times</u>, 5 May 1939.

2260. BOGAN, LOUISE. "Proteus, or Vico's Road." <u>Nation</u>, 138 (6 May 1939): 533-535. [Appeared in her <u>Selected Criticism: Prose and Poetry</u> (1955), pp. 142-148.]

2261. FADIMAN, CLIFTON. "Don't Shoot the Reviewer: He's Doing the Best he Can." <u>New Yorker</u>, 15 (6 May 1939): 88.

2262. ROSENFELD, PAUL. "James Joyce's Jabberwocky." <u>Saturday Review of Literature</u>, 6 May 1939, pp. 10-11. [Another review appeared as "James Joyce: Charlatan or Genius?" <u>American Mercury</u>, 47 (July 1939): 367-371; letter to the Editor concerning the former by Ford Madox Ford. "Finnegans Wake." <u>ibid.</u>, 20 (3 June 1939): 9, also in his <u>The Letters of Ford Madox Ford</u>. Edited by Richard M. Ludwig. Princeton: Princeton University Press, 1965, pp. 320-323; Rosenfeld's reply in <u>Saturday Review</u>, 20 (10 June 1939): 9, 20.]

2263. Unsigned. "The Progress of James Joyce." <u>Times Literary Supplement</u>, 6 May 1939, pp. 265-266. [Reprinted in <u>Sunday Union and Republican</u> (Springfield), 4 May 1939.]

REVIEWS OF JOYCE'S WORKS

2264. W., J. D. Star (Kansas City), 6 May 1939.

2265. WALPOLE, SIR HUGH. "Read Joyce Aloud." Daily Sketch (London), 6 May 1939, p. 12.

2266. COLUM, PADRAIC. "A New Work by James Joyce." New York Times Book Review, 7 May 1939, pp. 1, 14.

2267. GOGARTY, OLIVER ST. JOHN. "Roots in Resentment: James Joyce's Revenge." Observer (London), 7 May 1939, p. 4. [See also letter to the Editor by Harold Binns. ibid., 18 June 1939.]

2268. RASCOE, BURTON. "Finnegans Wake." Newsweek, 13 (8 May 1939): 36.

2269. MUIR, KENNETH. Yorkshire Post (Leeds), 10 May 1939.

2270. B., B. Schoolmaster and Woman Teachers' Chronicle (London), 11 May 1939.

2271. BINGAY, MALCOLM W. Free Press (Detroit), 11 May 1939.

2272. MUIR, EDWIN. "James Joyce's New Novel." Listener, 21, no. 539 (11 May 1939). [See the letter to the Editor by Reginald A. Wilson, 25 May 1939.]

2273. EVANS, B. IFOR. "In Lieu of Review." Manchester Guardian, 12 May 1939, p. 8.

2274. HUDIS, NORMAN. "Mr. James Joyce's 'Eyrawyggla Saga.'" Hampstead and Highgate Express, 12 May 1939.

2275. VERSCHOYLE, DEREK. "A Private Document." Spectator, 162 (12 May 1939): 820.

2276. BUTCHER, FANNY. Chicago Tribune, 13 May 1939.

2277. THOMPSON, MORTON. Citizen-News (Hollywood), 13 May 1939.

2278. BECKWITH, ETHEL. Sunday Herald (Bridgeport), 14 May 1939.

2279. GRAY, JAMES. Pioneer-Press (St. Paul), 14 May 1939.

2280. HUGHES, ELIZABETH. World (Tulsa), 14 May 1939.

2281. M., B. K. Journal (Providence), 14 May 1939.

2282. S., P. J. Times (Los Angeles), 14 May 1939.

2283. W., L. "In the Limelight." Truth (Elkhart, Ind.), 15 May 1939.

2284. WICKHOLM, CARRIE K. "Letter to the Editor." Evening Post (New York), 15 May 1939.

2285. 'The Booktaster.' "On the Table." Daily Post (Liverpool), 17 May 1939.

2286. F., S. Daily Herald (London), 18 May 1939.

2287. McINTYRE, WILLIAM T. Times (Ardmore, Pa.), 18 May 1939.

2288. SINZ, WILLIAM. Midwest Daily Record (Chicago), 18 May 1939.

2289. BERTRAM, ANTHONY. "Views on Mr. Joyce." Spectator, 162 (19 May 1939): 858-859.

2290. LYND, ROBERT. "Why Authors Write." John O'London's Weekly, 19 May 1939, p. 236. [See Margaret Brash. "Letter to the Editor." ibid., 9 June 1939.]

2291. DAVIS, ELRICK B. Press (Cleveland), 20 May 1939.

2292. STONIER, G. W. "Joyce's Airy Plume Flights." New Statesman and Nation, n.s. 17 (20 May 1939): 788, 790. [See letters to the Editor from: Desmond MacCarthy, 27 May 1939, pp. 824-825 and Stonier's reply p. 825; J. W. Hartley, 3 June 1939, p. 861; J. H. Eggleshaw, 3 June 1939, p. 961; John Stewart Collis, 17 June 1939, p. 938; Percy Blocker, 24 June 1939, p. 980.]

2293. LIND, L. ROBERT. Boston Transcript, 20 May 1939, p. 2.

2294. MUGGERIDGE, MALCOLM. "Men and Books." Time and Tide, 20 May 1939, pp. 654-655.

2295. ZIMMER, CARL E. "The Reading Lamp." Tribune (South Bend), 21 May 1939.

2296. MULDER, ARNOLD. Press Gazette (Green Bay), 20 May 1939. [Also in Chronicle (Musketon), 29 May 1939.]

2297. PELORSON, GEORGE. "Finnegans Wake of James Joyce, or the Book of Man." Aux écoutes, 23, no. 1096 (20 May 1939): 29. [Also appeared in expanded form in Revue de Paris, 46 (September 1939): 227-235.]

2298. KAZIN, ALFRED. "The Strange Dream World of James Joyce." New York Herald Tribune Books, 21 May 1939. [Also in Mail (Charleston, West Virginia), 28 May 1939.]

2299. LAKE, TALBOT. Enterprise (Riverside, Calif.), 21 May 1939. [Also in Independent (Stockton, Calif.), 1 June 1939; Morning-Times-Herald (Vallejo, Calif.), 2 May 1939; News (Washington, D.C.), 22 May 1939; Tribune (Madera, Calif.), 27 June 1939.]

2300. KINCAID, BEATRICE. People's World (San Francisco), 23 May 1939.

2301. 'Northerner.' "This World of Ours." York-shire Post (Leeds), 25 May 1939.

2302. V. "Diary of a Bookworm." Bon-Accord (Aberdeen), 25 May 1939.

2303. McAREE, J. V. Globe and Mail (Toronto), 26 May 1939.

2304. CALLAGHAN, MORLEY. "Into the Dream World." Saturday Night (Toronto), 27 May 1939.

2305. CONROY, JACK. "Mr. Finnegan Weird Hero of Joyce's Dublin Nightmare." New York Daily Worker, 28 May 1939.

2306. LALLEY, JOSEPH M. "Joys of Bejabbers." Post (Washington, D.C.), 28 May 1939.

2307. W., H. A. Sunday Times Advertiser (Trenton), 28 May 1939.

2308. TROY, WILLIAM. "Finnegans Wake." Partisan Review, 6 (Summer 1939): 97–110.

2309. ADLINGTON, RICHARD. Atlantic Bookshelf, June 1939.

2310. LYND, SYLVIA. Harper's Bazaar, June 1939.

2311. WADE, SARAH. Journal-Courier (New Haven), 2 June 1939.

2312. DOHN, JOHN. Pantagraph (Bloomington, Illinois), 4 June 1939.

2313. L., W. News Observer (Raleigh, North Carolina), 18 June 1939.

2314. WILSON, EDMUND. "H. C. Earwicker and Family: Review of Finnegans Wake." New Republic, 99 (28 June 1939): 203–206; (12 July 1939): 270–274.

2315. BIRNEY, EARLE. "Foolosall Choredomm." Canadian Forum, 19 (July 1939): 125.

2316. GLENDINNING, ALEX. "Commentary: Finnegans Wake." Nineteenth Century and After, 126 (July 1939): 73–82.

2317. RICHARDSON, DOROTHY M. "Finnegans Wake Review." Life and Letters Today, 22 (July 1939): 45–52.

2318. DOBRÉE, BONAMY. "Work Concluded." New English Weekly, 6 July 1939, pp. 189–190.

2319. BYRNE, BARRY. "Finnegans Wake." Commonweal, 30 (7 July 1939): 279.

2320. D., F. "Classic or Hoax?" Post-Dispatch (St. Louis), 19 July 1939.

2321. BOWEN, ELIZABETH. "Reviews, Fiction." Purpose, 11, no. 3 (July-September 1939): 177–179.

2322. C., A. Dublin Magazine, n.s. 14 (July-September 1939): 71–74.

2323. ROBERTS, LYNETTE. "Finnegans Wake." La Nación (Buenos Aires), 27 August 1939, section 2, p. 1.

2324. LEWIS, WYNDHAM. "Standing by One Thing and Another." The Bystander, 143 (30 August 1939): 316, 318.

2325. LEVIN, HARRY. "New Irish Stew." Kenyon Review, 1 (Autumn 1939): 460–465.

2326. McQUIRE, OWEN B. "Finnegans Wake." Commonweal, 30 (September 1939): 436–437.

2327. COLUM, MARY. "The Old and the New." Forum and Century, 102 (October 1939): 158–163.

2328. EDEL, LEON. "James Joyce and His New Work." University of Toronto Quarterly, 9 (October 1939): 68–81.

2329. HILL, ARCHIBALD. "A Philologist Looks at Finnegans Wake." Virginia Quarterly Review, 15 (October 1939): 650–656.

2330. ROSATI, SALVATORE. "Finnegans Wake." Nuova antologia, 406 (1 November 1939): 102–104.

2331. KHEZLOP, G. "Pominki po Finneganu Dzhemsa Dzhoisa." International Literature, no. 1 (1940): 185–188.

2332. W., R. "Finnegans Wake Deutsch." Neue Zürcher Zeitung, no. 168 (21 June 1961).

2333. Unsigned Reviews: Advance (Dover, New Jersey), May 1939; Advertiser (Boston), 21 May 1939; Book of the Month Club News, July 1939; 'Bookseller's Almanac.' Retail Bookseller (New York), May 1939; Bulletin (Providence), 11 May 1939; Centre Times (State College, Pa.), 5 May 1939; Church of England Newspaper, 19 May 1939; Citizen (Brooklyn), 22 May 1939; Commercial News (San Francisco), 13 May 1939; County Gazette and Guardian (Alnwick), 12 May 1939; Courier Express (Buffalo), 7 June 1939; Courant (Hartford), 31 May 1939; Courier Magazine (England), Summer 1939; Daily Express (London), 11 May 1939; Daily Worker (London), 31 May 1939; Democrat-Chronicle (Rochester), 20 May 1939; Eagle (Lawrence, Mass.), 17 May 1939; Eagle (Brooklyn), 24 May 1939; Evening Journal (Ottawa, Canada), 27 May 1939; Evening News (Glasgow), 8 May 1939; Evening Post (New York), 9 May 1939; Examiner (Launceston), 27 May 1939; Gazette (Montreal), 13 May 1939; Globe and Mail (Toronto), 13 May 1939; Herald (Boston), 7 June 1939; Herald (Glasgow), 4 May 1939; Herald (Rutland, Vermont), 9 May 1939; Independent (Dublin), 9 May 1939; Independent (Wilkes-Barre), 7 May 1939; Inquirer (Philadelphia), 10 May

REVIEWS OF JOYCE'S WORKS

1939; Irish Times, 6 May 1939; John Ball (London), 13 May 1939; Journal (Knoxville), 14 May 1939; Journal (Providence), 24 May 1939; Midwest Record (Chicago), 12 May 1939; Morning News Press (Santa Barbara), 28 May 1939; New English Weekly (London), 8 June 1939, see James Donaghy. "Letter to the Editor." ibid., 22 June 1939, 'Pontifex.' "Letter to the Editor." ibid., 29 June 1939; News (Amarillo), 11 June 1939; News (Red Bluff), 13 May 1939; News (Charlotte, South Carolina), 14 May 1939; News (Detroit), 14 May 1939; News (Greensboro, North Carolina), 21 May 1939; News (Miami), 24 May 1939; News (Millerton), 14 May 1939; News (Washington, D.C.), 6 May 1939; News Chronicle (London), 19 May 1939; News Observer (Raleigh, North Carolina), 21 May 1939; News-Press (St. Joseph, Missouri), 21 May 1939; News-Republican (Boone, Iowa), 27 May 1939; News Review (London), 18 May 1939; Observer (London), 30 April 1939; Post (Bridgeport), 10 May 1939; Post (Liverpool), 2 May 1939; Post (West Palm Beach), 21 May 1939; Progress Index (Petersburg, Virginia), 15 May 1939; Publisher's Weekly, 13 May 1939; Rocky Mountain News (Denver), 7 May 1939; Scotsman (Edinburgh), 11 May 1939; Spectator (London), 5 May 1939; Sun (Baltimore), 14 May 1939; Schoolmaster (London), 15 June 1939; Sun (New York), 8 May 1939; Telegram (Worcester), 5 May 1939; Time, 33 (8 May 1939): 78, 80-82 and letters to the Editor by Joseph H. Lafferty, 29 May 1939, p. 6 and J. S. van Meter Hinman, 29 May 1939, p. 6; Times (Chattanooga), 21 May 1939; Times (Crestfield, Maryland), 9 May 1939; Times-Union (Rochester), 27 May 1939; Tribune (Altoona, Pa.), 15 May 1939; Tribune (Tampa), 28 May 1939; Union (Manchester, New Hampshire), 10 May 1939; Union Sun Journal (Lockport), 26 May 1939; Virginian Pilot (Norfolk), 26 May 1939; Weekly Review (Darien), 25 May 1939; World's Press News (London), 29 June 1939; Yorkshire Post (Leeds), 25 May 1939.

STEPHEN HERO

2334. STONIER, G. W. "The Young Joyce." New Statesman and Nation, 28 (29 July 1944): 74-75.

2335. O'BRIEN, KATE. The Spectator, 173 (4 August 1944): 112, 114.

2336. Unsigned. Manchester Guardian, 16 August 1944, p. 3.

2337. Unsigned. Times Literary Supplement, 14 October 1944, p. 501; "Second Thoughts." ibid., 14 October 1944, p. 499.

2338. WILSON, EDMUND. "Stephen Hero." New Yorker, 20 (6 January 1945): 63-64.

2339. REYNOLDS, HORACE. New York Times Book Review, 21 January 1945, p. 10.

2340. SCHWARTZ, DELMORE. "The Early Joyce." Nation, 160 (27 January 1945): 106.

2341. WARREN, ROBERT PENN. "Rare Insight into Genesis of Joyce's Work." Chicago Sunday Tribune, 4 February 1945, section 6, p. 10.

2342. POST, ROBERT. "A Tale of Youthful Tribulations." Saturday Review of Literature, 28 (10 February 1945): 12.

2343. TROY, WILLIAM. New York Times Book Review, 11 February 1945, p. 6.

2344. HANLEY, MILES L. Book Week, 11 February 1945, p. 7.

2345. BYRNE, BARRY. Commonweal, 41 (16 February 1945): 450.

2346. Unsigned. Times, 45 (26 February 1945): 199.

2347. Unsigned. College English, 6, no. 6 (March 1945): 358.

2348. SCHAWLOW, R., and C. WEIN. Canadian Forum, 24 (March 1945): 290.

2349. WATTS, RICHARD. New Republic, 112 (16 April 1945): 518.

2350. MERCIER, VIVIAN. The Bell, 10, no. 2 (May 1945): 172-174.

2351. MONTAGUE, CLIFFORD. "Stephen Hero." Poet Lore, 51, no. 2 (Summer 1945): 180-182.

2352. BRADLEY, JOHN L. Books Abroad, 30 (Summer 1956): 333.

2353. Unsigned. "Stephen Hero." Nation and Athenaeum (1968): 353-362.

CRITICAL WRITINGS

2354. CAHOON, HERBERT. Library Journal, 84 (1 March 1959): 758.

2355. LEVIN, HARRY. "The Rest is Literature." The Griffin, 8 (May 1959): 5-11. [Reprinted as "Joyce as Critic" in his Grounds for Comparison. Harvard Studies in Comparative Literature, vol. 32 (1972), pp. 358-364.

2356. HICKS, GRANVILLE. "Joyce as Critic." Saturday Review of Literature, 42 (9 May 1959): 13.

2357. CASSIDY, THOMAS E. Commonweal, 70 (August 1959): 427-428.

2358. EGRI, PÉTER. "Jegyzetek James Joyce kritikajhoz." Vilagirodalmi Figyelo (Budapest), 7 (1961): 259-264.

2359. CRESSET, MICHEL. Nouvelle revue française, 14 (September 1966): 510-514.

DISSERTATIONS

BIBLIOGRAPHICAL STUDIES: BIBLIOGRAPHY OF BIBLIOGRAPHIES, CHECKLISTS, SURVEYS OF JOYCEANA, EXHIBITIONS, COLLECTIONS, SPECIAL JOYCE ISSUES, AND INTERNATIONAL JAMES JOYCE SYMPOSIA

2360. HOWARD, PATSY C., compiler. "James Joyce." Theses in English Literature, 1894-1970. Ann Arbor, Mich.: Pierian Press, 1973, pp. 155-159. [International Bibliography of M.A. Theses.]

2361. MacKENDRICK, LOUIS KING DeGRAFF. "The Life and Times of the Egoist: The History of a British Little Magazine." Ph.D. Dissertation, University of Toronto. Dissertation Abstracts International, 32 (June 1972): 6985-6986.

2362. McMILLAN, DOUGALD. "James Joyce and transition," "Eugene and Maria Jolas in Finnegans Wake," in "transition: A Critical and Historical Account." Ph.D. Dissertation, Northwestern University. Dissertation Abstracts International, 30 (January 1970): 3017-3018.

2363. SCHOLES, ROBERT E. "The Cornell Joyce Collection: A Catalogue." Ph.D. Dissertation, Cornell University. Dissertation Abstracts, 20 (1959): 1794-1795. See No. 16.

2364. SPIELBERG, PETER. "An Annotated Catalogue of the James Joyce Manuscripts in the Lockwood Memorial Library of the University of Buffalo." Ph.D. Dissertation, University of Buffalo. Dissertation Abstracts, 22 (January 1962): 2401. See No. 20.

2365. TURNER, SUSAN JANE. "A Short History of The Freeman, A Magazine of the Early Twenties, with Particular Attention to the Literary Criticism." Ph.D. Dissertation, Columbia University. Dissertation Abstracts, 16 (1956): 1258. See No. 3666.

GENERAL CRITICAL AND BIOGRAPHICAL

2366. SCHERBACHER, WOLFGANG. "Der Künstler im modernen englischen Roman, 1916-1936." Ph.D. Dissertation, Universität of Tubingen, 1954.

MILIEU STUDIES

2367. ANDREACH, ROBERT JOSEPH. "The Spiritual Life in Hopkins, Joyce, Eliot, and Hart Crane." Ph.D. Dissertation, New York University. Dissertation Abstracts International, 25 (1964): 467. See No. 3214.

2368. ANGHINETTI, PAUL W. "Alienation, Rebellion, and Myth: A Study of the Works of Nietzsche, Jung, Yeats, Camus, and Joyce." Ph.D. Dissertation, Florida State University. Dissertation Abstracts International, 30 (1969): 1974-1975.

2369. BYRNE, SISTER MARY E. "From Tradition to Technique." Ph.D. Dissertation, University of Southern Mississippi. Dissertation Abstracts, 29 (1969): 3091.

2370. COLLINS, ROBERT GEORGE. "Four Critical Interpretations in the Modern Novel." Ph.D. Dissertation, University of Denver. Dissertation Abstracts, 22 (1962): 3642.

2371. CROSS, RICHARD K. "By Obstinate Isles: A Study in the Craft of Flaubert and Joyce." Ph.D. Dissertation, Stanford University. Dissertation Abstracts, 28 (1968): 2678. See No. 1546.

2372. EBERLY, RALPH S. "Joyce Cary's Theme of Freedom and a Comparison with James Joyce and Graham Greene." Ph.D. Dissertation, University of Michigan. Dissertation Abstracts International, 31 (1971): 6601.

2373. FARROW, ANTHONY. "Currents in the Irish Novel: George Moore, James Joyce, Samuel Beckett." Ph.D. Dissertation, Cornell University. Dissertation Abstracts International, 33 (April 1973): 5719-5720.

2374. FOX, CHARLES JAY. "James Joyce and Arthur Symons in Transition." Ph.D. Dissertation, Purdue University. Dissertation Abstracts International, 32 (February 1972): 4609.

2375. FRANKE, ROSEMARIE. "James Joyce und der Deutsche Sprachbereich: Übersetzung, Verbreitung und Kritik in der Zeit von 1919-1967." Ph.D. Dissertation, Freie Universität, 1969. [For English abstract see "English and American Studies in German," supplement to Anglia (1970): 88-90.]

2376. GARRETT, PETER K. "Scene and Symbol: Changing Mode in the English Novel from George Eliot to Joyce." Ph.D. Dissertation, Yale University. Dissertation Abstracts, 27 (1967): 4251. See No. 1565.

2377. GARZILLI, ENRICO F. "Paths to the Discovery and the Creation of Self in Contemporary Literature." Ph.D. Dissertation, Brown University. Dissertation Abstracts International, 31 (1971): 6604. See No. 5314.

2378. GOLDFARB, RICHARD L. "Arnold Bennett and James Joyce on the Art of Fiction: Realism and Symbolism in Modern English

DISSERTATIONS

Theories of the Novel." Ph.D. Dissertation, Northwestern University. <u>Dissertation Abstracts International</u>, 30 (January 1970): 3008.

2379. HANDLER, PHILLIP LEONARD. "Joyce in France, 1920-1959." Ph.D. Dissertation, Columbia University. <u>Dissertation Abstracts</u>, 27 (August 1966): 476.

2380. KELLY, ROBERT G. "The Premises of Disorganization." Ph.D. Dissertation, Stanford University. <u>Stanford University Abstracts of Dissertations</u> (1952): 226.228.

2381. KERSHNER, RICHARD B. "Joyce and Queneau as Novelists: A Comparative Study." Ph.D. Dissertation, Stanford University. <u>Dissertation Abstracts International</u>, 32 (June 1972): 6981.

2382. KRONEGGER, MARIA ELIZABETH. "James Joyce and Associated Image Makers." Ph.D. Dissertation, Florida State University. <u>Dissertation Abstracts</u>, 20 (1960): 4398. See No. 1601.

2383. LYNGSTAD, SVERRE. "Time in the Modern British Novel: Conrad, Woolf, Joyce, and Huxley." Ph.D. Dissertation, New York University. <u>Dissertation Abstracts</u>, 27 (1966): 1374-1375.

2384. O HEHIR, DIANA F. "Ibsen and Joyce: A Study of Three Themes." Ph.D. Dissertation, Johns Hopkins University. <u>Dissertation Abstracts International</u>, 31 (January 1971): 3515.

2385. PEDERSEN, BERTEL S. "The Theory and Practice of Parody in the Modern Novel: Mann, Joyce, and Nabokov." Ph.D. Dissertation, University of Illinois (Champaign-Urbana). <u>Dissertation Abstracts International</u>, 33 (July 1972): 322.

2386. PETERSON, RICHARD FRANK. "Time as Character in the Fiction of James Joyce and William Faulkner." Ph.D. Dissertation, Kent State University. <u>Dissertation Abstracts International</u>, 31 (September 1970): 1285-1286.

2387. THEALL, DONALD F. "Communication Theories in Modern Poetry: Yeats, Pound, Eliot, and Joyce." Ph.D. Dissertation, University of Toronto, 1955.

2388. SOLOMON, ALBERT J. "James Joyce and George Moore: A Study of a Literary Relationship." Ph.D. Dissertation, Pennsylvania State University. <u>Dissertation Abstracts International</u>, 31 (October 1970): 1814.

2389. TOTH, ALEXANDER S., JR. "Joyce-Bergson Correspondences in the Theory and Time Structure of <u>Dubliners</u>, <u>A Portrait</u>, and <u>Ulysses</u>." Ph.D. Dissertation, University of Southern California. <u>Dissertation Abstracts International</u>, 30 (1969): 738-739.

PROVENIENCE: INFLUENCES UPON JOYCE

2390. ALBERT, LEONARD. "Joyce and the New Psychology." Ph.D. Dissertation, Columbia University. <u>Dissertation Abstracts</u>, 18 (1957): 1424-1425.

2391. CALLAHAN, EDWARD F., JR. "James Joyce's Early Esthetic: A Study of its Origins and Function." Ph.D. Dissertation, University of Wisconsin. <u>Dissertation Abstracts</u>, 17 (1957): 141.

2392. MOSELY, VIRGINIA D. "Joyce and the Bible." Ph.D. Dissertation, Columbia University. <u>Dissertation Abstracts</u>, 19 (1958): 328. See No. 942.

2393. NOON, WILLIAM T., S.J. "Joyce and Aquinas." Ph.D. Dissertation, Yale University, 1954. See No. 943.

2394. STALEY, HARRY C. "James Joyce and the Catechism." Ph.D. Dissertation, University of Pennsylvania. <u>Dissertation Abstracts</u>, 29 (1968): 275.

2395. SULLIVAN, KEVIN. "Joyce's Jesuit Schooling." Ph.D. Dissertation, Columbia University, 1957. See No. 357.

INFLUENCE STUDIES: JOYCE'S INFLUENCE UPON OTHERS

2396. HIRSCHMANN, JACK AARON. "The Orchestrated Novel: A Study of Poetic Devices in Novels of Djuna Barnes and Hermann Broch, and the Influence of the Works of James Joyce upon Them." Ph.D. Dissertation, Indiana University. <u>Dissertation Abstracts</u>, 22 (1962): 3220.

2397. O'DONNELL, THOMAS DANIEL. "Joycean Themes and Techniques in the Works of Michel Butor." Ph.D. Dissertation, University of Wisconsin. <u>Dissertation Abstracts International</u>, 32 (1971): 3321.

COMPREHENSIVE STUDIES OF JOYCE'S WORKS

2398. BATES, R. G. "The Trivial Joyce: Studies in the Compositional Method of James Joyce." Ph.D. Dissertation, University of Toronto, 1960.

2399. BENSON, EUGENE P. "James Joyce: Orthodoxy and Heterodoxy." Ph.D. Dissertation, University of Toronto. <u>Dissertation Abstracts</u>, 28 (1967): 1426.

2400. BLOCK, HASKELL M. "Theorie et technique du roman chez Flaubert et Joyce." Ph.D. Dissertation, University of Paris, 1948. See No. 925.

2401. BONHEIM, HELMUT. "Anti-Authoritarianism in the Works of James Joyce." Ph.D. Dissertation, University of Washington. Dissertation Abstracts, 20 (1959): 295. See No. 1524.

2402. BROWN, HOMER O. "The Early Fiction of James Joyce: The Biography of a Form." Ph.D. Dissertation, Johns Hopkins University. Dissertation Abstracts, 27 (1966): 1813-1814. See No. 3219.

2403. BRYER, JACKSON ROBERT. "A Trial-Track for Racers: Margaret Anderson and the Little Review." Ph.D. Dissertation, University of Wisconsin. Dissertation Abstracts, 25 (1965): 6616-6617.

2404. DANIEL, MARY L. "João Guimarães Rosa: travessis literária." Ph.D. Dissertation, University of Iowa, 1967. [Published in the series "Coleção documentos brasileiros," 133 in Rio de Janeiro: Livraria Jose Olympio Editora, 1968.]

2405. EATON, EDWARD E. "Reality-Construction and the New Novel." Ph.D. Dissertation, University of Michigan. Dissertation Abstracts International, 31 (1971): 6545.

2406. FINE, DONALD F. "The Style of Alienation: A Study of 'Paralysis' in Joyce's Dublin, and of the Consequent Effects of this on Joyce's Development as Prose Stylist." Ph.D. Dissertation, University of Toronto. Dissertation Abstracts International, 32 (1972): 6972.

2407. FINKE, WILHELM. "Der Ausdruck seelischer Wirklichket im Werk des James Joyce: Versuch einer Deutung von Inhalt, Form und Entwicklung." Ph.D. Dissertation, Kiel Universität, 1953.

2408. FITZPATRICK, WILLIAM PATRICK. "Myth and Maternity: A Study of James Joyce's Mythopoeia." Ph.D. Dissertation, University of Maryland. Dissertation Abstracts International, 34 (1973): 767-768.

2409. GOLDMAN, ARNOLD. "Development in the Fiction of James Joyce to 1922: Techniques, Themes, Criticisms, and Analogues." Ph.D. Dissertation, Yale University, 1964. See No. 1577.

2410. GULLETTE, DAVID G. "Linguistic Dualism in the Works of James Joyce." Ph.D. Dissertation, University of North Carolina (Chapel Hill). Dissertation Abstracts, 29 (1969): 4488.

2411. HERMAN, WILLIAM. "'Within His Handiwork': Self-Conscious Artistry in the Fiction of James Joyce." Ph.D. Dissertation, Fordham University. Dissertation Abstracts International, 30 (1970): 5445-5446.

2412. HORWATH, WILLIAM F. "The Ache of Modernism: Thomas Hardy, Time, and the Modern Novel." Ph.D. Dissertation, University of Michigan. Dissertation Abstracts International, 31 (1971): 4164-4165.

2413. KENNER, WILLIAM H. "James Joyce: Critique in Progress." Ph.D. Dissertation, Yale University, 1950.

2414. KLUG, MICHAEL A. "Comic Structure in the Early Fiction of James Joyce." Ph.D. Dissertation, University of Illinois. Dissertation Abstracts, 28 (1968): 3188.

2415. KREKELER, ELIZABETH MARIE. "The Archetypal Dimensions of Joyce's Dedalian Novels." Ph.D. Dissertation, St. Louis University. Dissertation Abstracts International, 33 (1972): 1173.

2416. LAMEYER, GORDON A. "The Automystic and the Cultic Twalette: Spiritual and Spiritualistic Concerns in the Works of James Joyce." Ph.D. Dissertation, Columbia University. Dissertation Abstracts International, 30 (1970): 4455-4456.

2417. LISS, ARCHIE K. "Joyce's Visible Art: The Earlier Work of Joyce and the Visual Arts of the '90's and the Turn of the Century: A Comparative Study." Ph.D. Dissertation, Pennsylvania State University. Dissertation Abstracts International, 32 (1971): 441.

2418. LIST, ROBERT NELSON. "Investigation of the Effects of the Matriarchal Family Structure and the Effects of Political and Economic Oppression of James Joyce, His Works, and his Society." Ph.D. Dissertation, University of Illinois (Urbana). Dissertation Abstracts International, 34 (1973): 781-782.

2419. LITTLE, SHERRY B. "The Relationship of the Woman Figure and Views of Reality in Three Works by James Joyce." Ph.D. Dissertation, Arizona State University. Dissertation Abstracts International, 32 (1971): 1518-1519.

2420. LITZ, A. WALTON. "The Evolution of James Joyce's Style and Technique from 1918 to 1932." Ph.D. Dissertation, Oxford University (Merton), 1954. See No. 1605.

2421. O'BRIEN, DARCY G. "The Conscience of James Joyce." Ph.D. Dissertation, University of California (Berkeley). Dissertation Abstracts, 26 (1966): 7323. See No. 1628.

2422. POSS, STANLEY HORN. "Joyce: The Immobilized Act." Ph.D. Dissertation, University of Washington. Dissertation Abstracts, 20 (1959): 1028-1029.

DISSERTATIONS

2423. RUBIN, DAVID I. "The Free Voice: A Study of the Relationship between Parodic Voices and the Liberation of Animate Voices in the Work of James Joyce." Ph.D. Dissertation, Brandeis University. Dissertation Abstracts International, 32 (1971): 983.

2424. SCARRY, JOHN M. "Shem and Shaun: John McCormack in the Works of James Joyce." Ph.D. Dissertation, New York University. Dissertation Abstracts International, 32 (1972): 4022.

2425. SNYDER, R. L. "The Artifice of James Joyce: His Way as Writer." Ph.D. Dissertation, Trinity-Dublin University, 1962.

2426. SOMERVILLE, ELIZABETH S. "The Application of an Ontological Perspective to the Literary Interpretation of Works Drawn from Several Periods." Ph.D. Dissertation, Ohio University. Dissertation Abstracts, 28 (1968): 3158.

2427. SWINSON, HENRY W. "Joyce and the Theater." PH.D. Dissertation, University of Illinois. Dissertation Abstracts International, 30 (1969): 1184-1185.

2428. THOMSON, ALLAN. "Space-Time in James Joyce's Thought: A Study of the Role of the Artist in History." Ph.D. Dissertation, Syracuse University. Dissertation Abstracts, 22 (1961): 265.

EPIPHANIES

2429. SHERWIN, JANE KING. "The Literary Epiphany in Some Early Fiction of Flaubert, Conrad, Proust and Joyce." Ph.D. Dissertation, University of Michigan. Dissertation Abstracts, 23 (1963): 3902.

2430. ZANIELLO, THOMAS A. "The Moment of Perception in Nineteenth and Twentieth Century Literature." Ph.D. Dissertation, Stanford University. Dissertation Abstracts International, 33 (February 1973): 4373.

DUBLINERS

2431. BRANDABUR, EDWARD JAMES. "Quest and Flight: A Study of Fact and Symbol in Dubliners." Ph.D. Dissertation, University of Cincinnati. Dissertation Abstracts, 22 (1962): 3197-3198. See No. 1529.

2432. CORRINGTON, J. W. "The Themes of Corruption, Escape and Frustration in James Joyce's Dubliners." Ph.D. Dissertation, University of Sussex, 1964.

2433. CREIGHTON, JOANNE VANISH. "Dubliners and Go Down Moses: The Short Story Composite." Ph.D. Dissertation, University of Michigan. Dissertation Abstracts International, 31 (1970): 1792-1793.

2434. GRAY, PAUL EDWARD. "James Joyce's Dubliners: A Study of the Narrator's Role in Modern Fiction." Ph.D. Dissertation, University of Virginia. Dissertation Abstracts, 26 (1966): 6042.

2435. JEDYNAK, STANLEY LOUIS. "Epiphany and Dantean Correspondences in Joyce's Dubliners: A Study in Structure." Ph.D. Dissertation, Syracuse University. Dissertation Abstracts, 23 (1962): 1018-1019.

2436. MAGALANER, MARVIN. "James Joyce's Dubliners." Ph.D. Dissertation, Columbia University. Dissertation Abstracts, 11 (1951): 1037.

2437. RISTKOK, TUULI-ANN. "A Study of Joyce's Narrative Technique in Dubliners." Ph.D. Dissertation, University of Chicago, 1970.

A PORTRAIT OF THE ARTIST AS A YOUNG MAN

2438. ANDERSON, CHESTER G. "A Portrait of the Artist as a Young Man, by James Joyce: Critically Edited with an Introduction and Textual Notes." Ph.D. Dissertation, Columbia University, 1962. See No. 3213.

2439. BEEBE, MAURICE. "The Alienation of the Artist: A Study of Portraits of the Artist by Henry James, Marcel Proust, and James Joyce." Ph.D. Dissertation, Cornell University, 1953. See No. 3216.

2440. BRIVIC, SHELDON R. "James Joyce from Stephen to Bloom: A Psychoanalytic Study." Ph.D. Dissertation, University of California (Berkeley). Dissertation Abstracts International, 31 (1971): 3539-3540.

2441. COLLINS, BEN L. "The Created Conscience: A Study of Technique and Symbol in James Joyce's A Portrait of the Artist as a Young Man." Ph.D. Dissertation, University of New Mexico. Dissertation Abstracts, 23 (1963): 2523.

2442. EPSTEIN, EDMUND L. "The Ordeal of Stephen Dedalus: The Father-Son Conflict and the Process of Maturing, in James Joyce's Portrait of the Artist as a Young Man." Ph.D. Dissertation, Columbia University. Dissertation Abstracts International, 31 (1971): 4766-4767. See No. 3229.

2443. FORTUNA, DIANE D. "The Labyrinth of the Art: Myth and Ritual in James Joyce's A Portrait of the Artist as a Young Man." Ph.D. Dissertation, Johns Hopkins University. Dissertation Abstracts, 28 (1967): 1817.

2444. GOLDBERG, GERALD J. "Artist as Hero in British Fiction, 1890-1930." Ph.D. Dissertation, University of Minnesota. Dissertation Abstracts, 20 (1959): 2289.

2445. NAGEL, RAYMOND P. "Romantic Reality in the Edwardian-Georgian Novel." Ph.D. Dissertation, University of New Mexico. _Dissertation Abstracts International_, 34 (November 1973): 2644-2645.

2446. OSBORNE, MARIANNE MUSE. "The Hero and Heroine in the British 'Bildungsroman': 'David Copperfield,' and 'A Portrait of the Artist as a Young Man,' 'Jane Eyre' and 'The Ranibow.'" Ph.D. Dissertation, Tulane University. _Dissertation Abstracts International_, 32 (1972): 4013-4014.

2447. PASKOFF, LOUIS. "The Artist-Hero in the Works of Six Modern Novelists." Ph.D. Dissertation, University of Michigan. _Dissertation Abstracts International_, 33 (1973): 5192.

2448. REECE, SHELLEY C. "_A Portrait of the Artist as a Young Man_: Its Narrative Art and Its Origins." Ph.D. Dissertation, University of Nebraska. _Dissertation Abstracts_, 28 (1968): 2693.

2449. ROTH, ROCHELLE L. "James Joyce and Stephen Dedalus: A Portrait of the Aesthetic." Ph.D. Dissertation, University of Nebraska. _Dissertation Abstracts International_, 32 (1971): 2706.

2450. RYF, ROBERT S. "A Study of James Joyce's _A Portrait of the Artist as a Young Man_." Ph.D. Dissertation, Columbia University, 1956. See No. 3271.

2451. SCHOW, HOWARD W. "Genre in Transition: Studies of _L'Education Sentimentale_, _Niels Lyhne_, _Tonio Kröger_, and _A Portrait of the Artist as a Young Man_." Ph.D. Dissertation, University of Iowa. _Dissertation Abstracts International_, 31 (1971): 4793-4794.

2452. SCOTTO, ROBERT M. "Self-Portraits of the Apprentice Artist: Walter Pater's _Marius_, George Moore's _Confessions_, and James Joyce's _A Portrait of the Artist as a Young Man_." Ph.D. Dissertation, City University of New York. _Dissertation Abstracts International_, 31 (1970): 2939.

2453. SMITH, JOHN B. "A Computer Assisted Analysis of Imagery in Joyce's _A Portrait of the Artist as a Young Man_." Ph.D. Dissertation, University of North Carolina (Chapel Hill), _Dissertation Abstracts International_, 31 (1971): 6072.

2454. SPRAGUE, JUNE ELIZABETH. "Strategy and the Evolution of Structure in the Early Novels of James Joyce." Ph.D. Dissertation, Bryn Mawr College. _Dissertation Abstracts_, 25 (1964): 2501.

2455. STERN, BARBARA BERGENFELD. "Entrapment and Liberation in James Joyce's Dedalus Fiction." Ph.D. Dissertation, City University

sity of New York. _Dissertation Abstracts_, 26 (1966): 6726-6727.

2456. YARON, MARK S. "The War Games of James Joyce: A Study of an Aspect of the Personality, Life and Works of a Great Artist." Ph.D. Dissertation, Temple University. _Dissertation Abstracts International_, 33 (1973): 6380.

2457. YOUNG, CALVIN E. "A Critical Explication of Irony as a Thematic Structure." Ph.D. Dissertation, Indiana University. _Dissertation Abstracts International_, 30 (1970): 5007-5008.

2458. ZINGRONE, FRANK D. "The Thematic Structure of James Joyce's _A Portrait of the Artist as a Young Man_." Ph.D. Dissertation, State University of New York (Buffalo). _Dissertation Abstracts_, 27 (1966): 1845.

ULYSSES

2459. AUSTIN, AVEL. "_Ulysses_ and the Human Body." Ph.D. Dissertation, Columbia University. _Dissertation Abstracts_, 27 (1966): 1778.

2460. BAAKE, JOSEF. "Sinn und Zweck der Reproduktionstechnik im _Ulysses_ von James Joyce." Ph.D. Dissertation, Universität of Bonn, 1937.

2461. BARROW, CRAIG WALLACE. "Montage in James Joyce's _Ulysses_." Ph.D. Dissertation, University of Colorado. _Dissertation Abstracts International_, 33 (1972): 1713.

2462. BENNETT, JOHN Z. "Detail, Allusion, and Theme in the 'Telemachus' Episode of James Joyce's _Ulysses_." Ph.D. Dissertation, University of North Carolina (Chapel Hill). _Dissertation Abstracts_, 28 (1968): 3663.

2463. BOWEN, ZACK R. "An Analysis of the Music in James Joyce's _Ulysses_ as it Pertains to the Stream of Conscious Thought and Activity of Leopold Bloom." Ph.D. Dissertation, State University of New York (Buffalo). _Dissertation Abstracts_, 28 (1967): 1387-1388.

2464. CARD, JAMES VAN DYCK. "A Textual and Critical Study of the 'Penelope' Episode of James Joyce's _Ulysses_." Ph.D. Dissertation, Columbia University. _Dissertation Abstracts_, 26 (1965): 1037.

2465. CIERPIAL, LEO JOSEPH. "Degeneration and the Religion of Beauty: A Traditional Pattern in Coleridge's _The Rime of the Ancient Mariner_, Pater's _The Renaissance_, Maugham's _Of Human Bondage_, and Joyce's _Ulysses_." Ph.D. Dissertation, University of Denver. _Dissertation Abstracts_, 13 (1962): 1361.

DISSERTATIONS

2466. CLEMENS, THOMAS CRAINE. "M'Intosh as a Key to the Role of the Artist in James Joyce's *Ulysses*." Ph.D. Dissertation, Northern Illinois University. *Northern Illinois University Abstracts of Selected Qualifying Papers*, 26 (1966): 38.

2467. DEBOO, KITAYUN E. "The Principle of the Cycle in James Joyce's *Ulysses* and William Blake's *The Mental Traveller*." Ph.D. Dissertation, State University of New York (Buffalo). *Dissertation Abstracts*, 28 (1967): 623.

2468. DUNCAN, IRIS JUNE AUTRY. "The Theme of the Artist's Isolation in Works by Three Modern British Novelists." Ph.D. Dissertation, University of Oklahoma. *Dissertation Abstracts*, 26 (1965): 3332.

2469. FITCH, NOEL R. "An American Bookshop in Paris: The Influence of Sylvia Beach's Shakespeare and Company on American Literature." Ph.D. Dissertation, Washington State University. *Dissertation Abstracts International*, 39 (1970): 3005-3006.

2470. HENKE, SUZETTE ANN. "Joyce's Moraculous Sindbook: A Study of *Ulysses*." Ph.D. Dissertation, Stanford University. *Dissertation Abstracts International*, 33 (1973): 4415-4416.

2471. HENTZE, RUDOLF. "Die Proteische Wandlung im *Ulysses* von James Joyce und Ihre Spiegelung im Stil." Ph.D. Dissertation, Marburg Universität, 1933.

2472. HERRING, PHILLIP F. "A Critical Edition of James Joyce's Notesheets for *Ulysses* in the British Museum." Ph.D. Dissertation, University of Texas. *Dissertation Abstracts*, 27 (1967): 3049. See No. 3602.

2473. HOFFMAN, FREDERICK J. "Freudianism: A Study of Influences and Reactions, Especially as Revealed in the Fiction of James Joyce, D. H. Lawrence, Sherwood Anderson, and Waldo Frank." Ph.D. Dissertation, Ohio State University, 1942. See No. 934.

2474. HURLEY, ROBERT EDWARD. "The Proteus Episode of James Joyce's *Ulysses*." Ph.D. Dissertation, Columbia University. *Dissertation Abstracts*, 24 (1964): 3338.

2475. JANUSKO, ROBERT J. "The Source and Structure of the 'Oxen of the Sun' Episode of James Joyce's *Ulysses*." Ph.D. Dissertation, Kent State University. *Dissertation Abstracts*, 28 (1968): 4632.

2476. KEENER, ULYSSES GRANT. "Joyce's 'Scylla and Charybdis.'" Ph.D. Dissertation, Columbia University. *Dissertation Abstracts International*, 33 (1972): 276.

2477. KILBURN, PATRICK E. "*Ulysses* in Catawba: A Study of the Influence of James Joyce on Thomas Wolfe." Ph.D. Dissertation, New York University. *Dissertation Abstracts*, 17 (1958): 2267-2268.

2478. KINTANAR, THELMA B. "The Significance of the Comic in James Joyce's *Ulysses*." Ph.D. Dissertation, Stanford University. *Dissertation Abstracts*, 29 (1968): 1541.

2479. KIREMIDJIAN, GARABED D. "A Study of Parody: James Joyce's *Ulysses*, Thomas Mann's *Doktor Faustus*." Ph.D. Dissertation, Yale University. *Dissertation Abstracts*, 29 (1969): 3976.

2480. KREUTZER, EBERHARD. "Sprach und Spiel im *Ulysses*." Ph.D. Dissertation, Bonn Universität, 1969. See No. 3611.

2481. KULEMEYER, GUENTHER. "Studien zur Psychologie im Neuen Englischen roman: Dorothy Richardson und James Joyce." Ph.D. Dissertation, Greifswald Universität, 1933.

2482. LEWIS, JANET ELIZABETH O'BRIEN. "The Wasteland Theme in James Joyce's *Ulysses*." Ph.D. Dissertation, University of Toronto. *Dissertation Abstracts International*, 32 (1972): 5796-5797.

2483. LINK, VICTOR. "Bau und Funktion der Circe-Episode im *Ulysses* von James Joyce." Ph.D. Dissertation, Bonn Universität. See No. 4421.

2484. MADTES, RICHARD EASTMAN. "A Textual and Critical Study of the 'Ithaca' Episode of James Joyce's *Ulysses*." Ph.D. Dissertation, Columbia University. *Dissertation Abstracts*, 25 (1964): 1213.

2485. MASON, ELLSWORTH. "James Joyce's *Ulysses* and Vico's *Cycle*." Ph.D. Dissertation, Yale University, 1948.

2486. McELHANEY, JAMES H. "The Irish Cyclist: An Inquiry into the Theme of Death and Rebirth in James Joyce's *Ulysses*." Ph.D. Dissertation, Pennsylvania State University, 1966.

2487. McMAHON, DOROTHY E. P. "James Joyce's *Ulysses*: Its Menippean Mood and Mode." Ph.D. Dissertation, Vanderbilt University. *Dissertation Abstracts International*, 32 (1971): 1519.

2488. McNELLY, WILLIS E. "The Use of Catholic Elements as an Artistic Source in James Joyce's *Ulysses*." Ph.D. Dissertation, Northwestern University. *Dissertation Abstracts*, 17 (1957): 3020.

2489. MANGLAVITI, LEO M. J. "The Consistency of Multi-Perspectival Narration in James Joyce's Ulysses." Ph.D. Dissertation, Johns Hopkins University. Dissertation Abstracts International, 34 (1973): 3413.

2490. MONAHAN, MARY J. "The Position of Molly Bloom in Ulysses." Ph.D. Dissertation, Kent State University. Dissertation Abstracts International, 32 (1971): 2699-2700.

2491. MOORE, FREDERIC L. "Blickpunkt: Ulysses and the Changing German Perspective: A Translation and Evaluation of German Criticism from Three Decades." M.A. Thesis, Northern Illinois University. Northern Illinois University Abstracts of Selected Qualifying Papers, no. 25 (1966): 49-50.

2492. OBRADOVIC, ADELHEID B. "Die Behandlung der Räumlichkeit im spaeteren Werk des James Joyce." Ph.D. Dissertation, Marburg Universität, 1934.

2493. PRESCOTT, JOSEPH. "James Joyce's Ulysses as Work in Progress." Ph.D. Dissertation, Harvard University, 1944.

2494. RISTER, GENE. "The Odyssean Backgrounds of Ulysses: Joyce's Sources and his Development of the Homeric Motif." Ph.D. Dissertation, University of Wisconsin. Dissertation Abstracts International, 33 (1972): 325.

2495. SCHECHNER, MARK E. "Joyce's Ulysses: A Psychoanalytic Investigation." Ph.D. Dissertation, University of California at Berkeley. Dissertation Abstracts International, 32 (1972): 984-985.

2496. SCHIEFELE, HANS. "Erlebte Vergangenheit und Ihre Dauer: Ein Beitrag zur Psychologie Menschl, Zeitlichkeit, Kasuist, Entwichelt an James Joyce's Ulysses and Marcel Proust's A la Recherche du Temps Perdu." Ph.D. Dissertation, Muenchen Universität, 1957.

2497. SCHNEIDER, ULRICH. "Die Funktion der Zitate im Ulysses von James Joyce." Ph.D. Dissertation, Bonn Universität, 1970.

2498. SCHOONBROODT, JEAN. "Point of View and Expressive Form in James Joyce's Ulysses." Ph.D. Dissertation, Eugen (Belgium), 1967.

2499. SCHUTTE, WILLIAM M. "James Joyce's Use of Shakespeare in Ulysses." Ph.D. Dissertation, Yale University, 1954. See No. 4404.

2500. SILVERSTEIN, NORMAN. "Joyce's Circe Episode: Approaches to Ulysses through a Textual and Interpretative Study of Joyce's Fif-teenth Chapter." Ph.D. Dissertation, Columbia University. Dissertation Abstracts, 21 (1960): 904.

2501. SMITH, JAMES PENNY. "Musical Allusions in James Joyce's Ulysses." Ph.D. Dissertation, University of North Carolina (Chapel Hill). Dissertation Abstracts, 29 (1969): 2724-2725.

2502. SOLMECKE, GERT. "Funktion und Bedeutung der Parodie im Joyce's Ulysses." Ph.D. Dissertation, Köln Universität, 1970.

2503. STEINBERG, ERWIN R. "The Stream of Consciousness Technique in James Joyce's Ulysses." Ph.D. Dissertation, New York University, 1956. See No. 4202.

2504. STOKER, RICHARD J. "Fiction: The Search for Friendship." Ph.D. Dissertation, State University of New York at Buffalo. Dissertation Abstracts International, 34 (1973): 792-793.

2505. SULTAN, STANLEY. "Ulysses as an English Novel." Ph.D. Dissertation, Yale University, 1955. See No. 3662.

2506. SURVANT, JOSEPH W. "Tristram Shandy and Ulysses: A Study in the Use of Time." Ph.D. Dissertation, University of Delaware. Dissertation Abstracts International, 32 (1972): 6395.

2507. THOMAS, VLAD IVAN. "Narrative Types and Techniques in James Joyce's Ulysses." Ph.D. Dissertation, University of Wisconsin. Dissertation Abstracts, 23 (1963): 4692.

2508. THORNTON, WELDON ELIJAH. "Some Uses of Allusions in James Joyce's Ulysses." Ph.D. Dissertation, University of Texas. Dissertation Abstracts, 22 (1961): 2008. See No. 4406.

2509. VAN COURT, ANN FISHER. "The Druidic Tradition in Joyce's Ulysses." Ph.D. Dissertation, Rensselaer Polytechnic Institute. Dissertation Abstracts International, 33 (1973): 6935-6936.

2510. WACHTEL, ALBERT. "The Cracked Lookingglass: The Aesthetic Basis of James Joyce's Ulysses." Ph.D. Dissertation, State University of New York (Buffalo). Dissertation Abstracts, 29 (1968): 1908.

2511. WARD, DAVID F. "The Use and Function of Irish History in James Joyce's Ulysses." Ph.D. Dissertation, University of Tulsa. Dissertation Abstracts International, 31 (1970): 2944.

2512. WHITE, PATRICK THOMAS. "James Joyce's Ulysses and Vico's 'Principles of Humanity.'"

DISSERTATIONS

Ph.D. Dissertation, University of Michigan. Dissertation Abstracts, 24 (1963): 2492.

2513. WOODBERY, WILLIAM P., JR. "James Joyce's Ulysses: An Index and Guide to the Dramatic Characters." Ph.D. Dissertation, Emory University. Dissertation Abstracts International, 31 (1970): 772.

2514. ZEMELMAN, STEVEN A. "The Way Ulysses is Told." Ph.D. Dissertation, Brandeis University. Dissertation Abstracts International, 32 (1971): 992.

FINNEGANS WAKE

2515. BEECHHOLD, HENRY F. "Early Irish History and Mythology in Finnegans Wake." Ph.D. Dissertation, Pennsylvania State University, 1956.

2516. BEGNAL, MICHAEL H. "'The Problem Passion Play of the Millentury': Some Aspects of Narrative Technique in Finnegans Wake." Ph.D. Dissertation, University of Washington. Dissertation Abstracts, 29 1969): 3604.

2517. BEJA, MORRIS. "Evanescent Moments: The Epiphany in the Modern Novel." Ph.D. Dissertation, Cornell University. Dissertation Abstracts, 24 (1964): 2903. See No. 2826.

2518. BENSTOCK, BERNARD. "Ironic Alchemy: A Study of Language, Humor, and Significance in James Joyce's Finnegans Wake." Ph.D. Dissertation, Florida State University. Dissertation Abstracts, 17 (1958): 1795. See No. 4909.

2519. BROES, ARTHUR T. "Jonathan Swift in Finnegans Wake." Ph.D. Dissertation, University of Pittsburg. Dissertation Abstracts International, 31 (1971): 6592.

2520. CHRISTIANI, DOUINA B. "Scandinavian Elements in Finnegans Wake." Ph.D. Dissertation, Columbia University. Dissertation Abstracts, 27 (1967): 3449. See No. 5356.

2521. ECKLEY, GRACE E. W. "Anna Livia Plurabelle, the Continuum of Finnegans Wake." Ph.D. Dissertation, Kent State University. Dissertation Abstracts International, 31 (1971): 4156-4157.

2522. FLEMING, WILLIAM SAMUEL. "The Proteiform Graph: Some Aspects of Style in James Joyce's Finnegans Wake." Ph.D. Dissertation, Kent State University. Dissertation Abstracts International, 31 (1970): 2383.

2523. HART, CLIVE. "Structure and Motive in Finnegans Wake." Ph.D. Dissertation, Cambridge University (Fitzwilliam), 1961. See No. 5315.

2524. HENSELER, DONNA L. "Vico's Doctrine of Ricorso in James Joyce's Finnegans Wake." Ph.D. Dissertation, Michigan State University. Dissertation Abstracts International, 32 (1971): 1475.

2525. HIGGINSON, FRED H. "James Joyce's Revisions of Finnegans Wake: A Study of the Published Versions." Ph.D. Dissertation, University of Minnesota. Dissertation Abstracts, 14 (1954): 525. See No. 4938.

2526. JAY, MAURICE LaVERNE. "The Montage of the Malt Dream: A Systems Study of Basic Images in Finnegans Wake." Ph.D. Dissertation, University of Michigan. Dissertation Abstracts International, 31 (1970): 2347-2348.

2527. KOPPER, EDWARD A., JR. "A Study of the Catholic Allusions in Finnegans Wake. Ph.D. Dissertation, Temple University. Dissertation Abstracts, 24 (1964): 5410-5411.

2528. MANCINI, SHARON G. BROOKS. "Finnegans Wake as Dante's Purgatorio." Ph.D. Dissertation, Kent State University. Dissertation Abstracts International, 32 (1972): 6435.

2529. MANNING, WALTER J. "Athletic Allusions in Finnegans Wake." Ph.D. Dissertation, Temple University. Dissertation Abstracts International, 33 (1973): 5734.

2530. MURPHY, JAMES J. "The 'Hen' Chapter (I,v) of Finnegans Wake: Annotation and Thematic Analysis." Ph.D. Dissertation, Temple University. Dissertation Abstracts International, 32 (1972): 6993.

2531. NORRIS, MARGOT CHRISTA. "The Decentered Universe of Finnegans Wake: A Structuralist Analysis." Ph.D. Dissertation, State University of New York (Buffalo). Dissertation Abstracts International, 33 (1973): 4428-4429.

2532. PHILLIPS, JOSEPH M. "The Use of Scientific and Philosophical Concepts of Space and Time in James Joyce's Finnegans Wake." Ph.D. Dissertation, Temple University. Dissertation Abstracts International, 32 (1972): 6999.

2533. SOLOMON, MARGARET CLAIRE. "The Sexual Universe of Finnegans Wake." Ph.D. Dissertation, Claremont Graduate School and University Center. Dissertation Abstracts, 29 (1968): 615-616. See No. 4962.

2534. SPEAR, ROLFE M. "The Argument of Finnegans Wake." Ph.D. Dissertation, Syracuse University. Dissertation Abstracts International, 31 (1971): 6073.

2535. WOLLESEN, CHARLES A. "Fabulous Joyce." Ph.D. Dissertation, University of Washington. Dissertation Abstracts International, 31 (1971): 3570.

MUSICAL SETTINGS, THEATRICAL PRODUCTIONS, FILMS, RADIO AND TELEVISION BROADCASTS, AND RECORDINGS

MUSICAL SETTINGS

Abbreviations used are CM for Chamber Music, PP for Pomes Penyeach, PAYM for A Portrait of the Artist, U for Ulysses, FW for Finnegans Wake, c. for copyright.

General

2536. COHN, ALAN M. "Musical Settings of Texts by James Joyce: A Further Supplement." Longroom, no. 6 (Autumn 1972): 17-21.

2537. DALLAPICCOLA, LUIGI. "Sulla Strada della Dodecafonia." Aut Aut, 1 (January 1951): 30-45. [Translated by Deryck Cooke as "On the Twelve-Note Road." Music Survey, 5 (October 1951): 323-325.]

2538. FEEHAN, FANNY. "Chjoyce Words." Hibernia, 35 (22 January 1971): 18. [Review of concert of works on Joyce texts by Hoddinut, Moerans, Sweeney, and Stockhausen.]

2539. HILL, S. "Musical Settings of Texts by James Joyce." Longroom, no. 2 (Autumn-Winter 1970): 12-17.

Settings

2540. ALLEN, CREIGHTON. Lay of Solitude. New York: G. Schirmer, 1929. 6pp. c. 30 October 1929. [CM XXXV]

2541. ANTHEIL, GEORGE. [Extract] Mr. Bloom and the Cyclops. Opera upon the "Cyclops" episode in U. This Quarter Antheil Musical Supplement. Milan. 26pp. Published as supplement to This Quarter (Autumn-Winter 1925/26).

2542. BARBER, SAMUEL. Rain Has Fallen. New York: G. Schirmer, 1939. 8pp. c. 15 September 1939. [CM XXXII]

2543. _____. Sleep Now. New York: G. Schirmer, 1939. 6pp. c. 15 September 1939. [CM XXXIV]

2544. _____. I Hear an Army. New York: G. Schirmer, 1939. 10pp. c. 15 September 1939. [CM XXXVI]

2545. _____. Nuvoletta. New York: G. Schirmer, 1952. 12pp. c. 1952. [FW 157-159, extracts only]

2546. _____. "Solitary Hotel," Despite and Still: Song Cycle. New York: G. Schirmer, 1969, pp. 14-18. [from "Ithaca" U]

2547. BATE, STANLEY. Five Songs. London: Ricordi. c. 1951. 16pp. [from PP]

2548. BERIO, LUCIANO. Chamber music per voce femminile, clarinetto in sib, violoncello ed arpa. Milan: Suvini Zerboni. c. 1954. 18pp. [CM I, XXXV, IX]

2549. _____. Epifanie (1959-1961); revision 1965. London: Universal. c. 1969. 13 parts. [13 sections of which "d" is setting of words from PAYM]

2550. _____. Thema (Omaggio a Joyce). Milan: Suvini Zerboni. Tape recording. 7 minutes. [see No. 2714]

2551. BONNER, EUGENE. From Dewy Dreams. London: J. W. Chester, 1924. 10pp. c. 13 September 1924. [CM XV]

2552. BOYDELL, BRIAN. She Weeps Over Rahoon. 1936. [from PP]

2553. _____. Watching the Needleboats at San Sabba. 1936, 1937. [from PP]

2554. _____. Sleep Now. 1944. [CM XXXIV]

2555. _____. Five Settings of Poems by James Joyce. 1946. [CM I, XXVIII, XXXI, XXXII, XXXVI]

2556. _____. Arrangement for baritone and chamber orchestra available in photostat copies from the Cultural Relations Department of the Department of External Affairs (Dublin).

2557. _____. Because Your Voice was at my Side. 1948. [CM XVII]

2558. BRIDGE, FRANK. Goldenhair. London: Chappell, 1925. 8pp. c. 21 December 1925. [CM V]

2559. CAGE, JOHN. The Wonderful Widow of Eighteen Springs. New York, London, Frankfurt: Peters. c. 1961. 6pp. [FW 556]

2560. CITKOWITZ, ISRAEL. Five Songs for Voice and Piano from 'Chamber Music' by James Joyce. New York: Cos Cob Press, 1930. 18pp. c. 11 November 1930. [CM I, IV, XXXI, XI, VII]

2561. Cos Cob Song Volume. Ten Songs by American Composers. New York: Cos Cob Press, 1935. 36pp. c. 15 April 1935. [Contains Roger Sessions. "On the Beach at Fontana," 3-6; Israel Citkowitz. "Gentle Lady," 11-13, from PP and CM XXVIII]

2562. DALLAPICCOLA, LUIGI. Tre Poemi per Una Voce e Orchestra da Camera (Variazioni sopra una serie di dodici note). Zürich: Hermann Scherchen-Ars Viva, 1949. [c. 1950.] 28pp. [from PP]

DRAMATIC AND MUSICAL PRODUCTIONS

2563. _____ . "Dingdong. The Castle Bell!,"
     Requiescat, no. 5. Milan: Edizioni Su-
     vini Zerboni, 1960, pp. 45-57. ['Brigid's
     Song' (PAYM)]

2564. DIAMOND, DAVID. Three Madrigals. New York:
     Edwin F. Kalmus, 1938. 8pp. c. 15 Sep-
     tember 1938. [CM XXI, XXVIII, XI]

2565. _____ . A Flower Given to My Daughter.
     New York: Arrow Music Press, 1942. 4pp.
     c. 7 July 1942. [from PP]

2566. _____ . Brigid's Song. New York: Music
     Press, 1947. 4pp. c. 5 November 1947.
     [from PAYM]

2567. FELMAN, HAZEL. Anna Livia Piurabelle.
     Chicago: Argus Book Shop, 1935. 24pp.
     c. 2 January 1936. Also in Martin Ross.
     Music and James Joyce. Chicago: Argus
     Book Shop, 1936. [Reprinted Folcroft,
     Pa.: Folcroft Library Editions, 1973.]
     [ALP, FW 215, 11. 3-216]

2568. FERRIS, JOAN. Six Songs. New York: Carl
     Fischer, 1967. 19pp. [CM I, XVI, XXV,
     IX, XXIII, X]

2569. FETLER, PAUL. All Day I Hear. New York:
     Lawson-Gould; London: Curwen. c. 1962.
     4pp. [CM XXXV]

2570. FOX, J. BERTRAM. Strings in the Earth. New
     York: J. Fischer and Bros., 1926. 8pp.
     c. 31 December 1926. [CM I]

2571. GENZMER, HARALD. Irische Harfe. Frankfurt,
     London, New York: Peters. c. 1965.
     14pp. [CM XXXVI]

2572. GOOSSENS, EUGÈNE. Chamber Music. Six Songs
     for Medium Voice. London: J. Curwen and
     Sons, 1930. 30pp. c. 22 July 1930.
     [CM XXXIII, XXVIII, XXIX, XVI, XXXV,
     XXXVI]

2573. GRAYSON, RICHARD. All Day I Hear the Noise
     of Waters. [n.p.]: Curlew Music Publish-
     ers, 1972. [CM XXXV]

2574. GRIFFIS, ELLIOT. Goldenhair. New York:
     Composers Music Corp., 1922. 8pp. c.
     24 August 1922; renewed 9 September 1949.
     [CM V]

2575. HARRISON, SIDNEY. I Hear an Army. London:
     J. B. Cramer, 1927. 8pp. [CM XXXVI]

2576. HARTMANN, THOMAS de. Six Commentaires pour
     Ulysse de James Joyce. Paris: M. P. Bel-
     aieff, 1948. 36pp. c. 2 January 1949;
     published 1948. [French text taken from
     translation published by Adrienne Monnier
     in 1929.]

2577. HEAD, MICHAEL. Lean out of the Window. Lon-
     don: Boosey and Hawkes. c. 1961. 4pp.
     [CM V]

2578. HODEIR, ANDRÉ. Anna Livia Plurabelle. New
     York: MJQ Music. [For 2 voices, jazz-
     band, and "clapping section."]

2579. HOPKINS, BILL. Two Pomes. London: Universal.
     c. 1967. 8pp. [from PP]

2580. HUGHES, HERBERT, ed. The Joyce Book. Lon-
     don: Sylvan Press, 1933.
         Contents: Editor's Note, p. 9; James
     Stephens. "Prologue," 11, reprinted in his
     James, Seumas and Jacques. Edited by
     Lloyd Frankenberg. New York: Macmillan,
     1964; Padraic Colum. "James Joyce as Poet,"
     13-15; Arthur Symons. "Epilogue," 79-84;
     portrait of Joyce by Augustus John, 5;
     the thirteen poems of PP set to music:
     'Tilly' by E. J. Moeran, 16-19; 'Watching
     the Needleboats at San Sabba," by Arnold
     Bax, 20-23; 'A Flower Given to My Daugh-
     ter,' by Albert Roussel, 24-27; 'She Weeps
     over Rahoon,' by Herbert Hughes, 28-31;
     'Tutto è Sciolto,' by John Ireland, 32-35;
     'On the Beach at Fontana,' by Roger Ses-
     sions, 36-41; 'Simples,' by Arthur Bliss,
     42-47; 'Flood,' by Herbert Howells, 48-53;
     'Nightpiece,' by George Antheil, 54-57;
     'Alone,' by Edgardo Carducci, 58-61; 'A
     Memory,' by Eugene Goossens, 62-67; 'Bahn-
     hofstrasse,' by C. W. Orr, 68-71; 'A Pray-
     er,' by Bernard Van Dieren, 72-77. [See
     also H.E.W. "13 Composers and James Joyce,"
     Daily Telegraph (London), 17 March 1932,
     p. 8.]

2581. JARRETT, JACK. Bright Cap and Streamers.
     New York: Lawson-Gould, 1964. 7pp.
     [CM X]

2582. _____ . Lean out of the Window. New York:
     Lawson-Gould, 1964. 7pp. [CM V]

2583. _____ . Strings in the Earth. New York:
     Lawson-Gould, 1964. 4pp. [CM I]

2584. KAGEN, SERGIUS. All Day I Hear. New York:
     Weintraub Music Company, 1950. 6pp.
     c. 1950. [CM XXXV]

2585. _____ . Sleep Now. New York: Leeds
     Music Corp., 1951. 4pp. c. 1951. [CM
     XXXIV]

2586. KAUDER, HUGO. Ten Poems from James Joyce's
     Chamber Music. From Music Foundation, 2.
     New York: Boosey and Hawkes, 1955. 27pp.
     [CM I, III, V, VIII, IX, XIV, XVI, XXXII,
     XXXIV, XXXV]

2587. KLOTZMAN, DOROTHY HILL. Three Songs from
     Chamber Music. New York: Mercury Music,
     1963. 11pp. [CM X, IX, V]

2588. KOEMMENICH, LOUIS. O Cool is the Valley Now. New York: J. Fischer and Bros., [1919]. 6pp. c. 24 May 1919. [CM XVI]

2589. KUNZ, ALFRED. "O Cool is the Valley Now," Three Works for Male Chorus. Waterloo, Ont.: Waterloo Music, 1972, pp. 2-4. [CM XVI]

2590. LeFLEMING, CHRISTOPHER. Strings in the Earth and Air. London: Elkin, 1955. 3pp. [CM I]

2591. LINN, ROBERT. Three Madrigals. New York: Mills Music, 1953. 15pp. [CM IX, XXIV, VIII]

2592. MANN, ADOLPH. Out by Donnycarney. Song. Words by James Joyce. Cincinnati: John Church, [1910]. 8pp. c. 19 January 1910. [CM XXXI]

2593. MARTINO, DONALD. Three Songs. [n.p.]: Ione Press, 1970. 11pp. [from PP]

2594. MENGELBERG, RUDOLF. Chamber Music. Amsterdam: Broekmans and Van Poppel, 1960. 23pp. [CM I, V, IX, XIV, XVII, XXXI, XXXII, XXXIV, XXXVI]

2595. MOERAN, E. J. Seven Poems by James Joyce. London: Oxford University Press, 1930. 28pp. c. 27 November 1930. [CM I, VIII, X, XVI, XXXI, XXXII, XXXIII]

2596. _____. Rosefrail. London: Augener, 1931. 4pp. c. 22 October 1931. [PP]

2597. _____. Rahoon. London: Oxford University Press, 1947. 8pp. c. 3 July 1947. [from PP]

2598. NABOKOV, NICHOLAS. Alone. New York: Associated Music Publishers, 1957. 3pp. [from PP]

2599. _____. Sleep Now. New York: Associated Music Publishers, 1957. 4pp. [CM XXXIV]

2600. NAYLOR, BERNARD. "Ecce Puer," in Sing Nowell: 51 Carols New and Arranged. Compiled by Louis Halsey and Basil Ramsey. London: Novello, 1963, pp. 46-47.

2601. ORR, CHARLES WILFRED. Four Songs for High Voice and Piano. London: Oxford University Press, c. 1959. 16pp. [from PP]

2602. PATTISON, LEE. Sleep Now. New York: G. Schirmer, 1926. 4pp. c. 23 April 1926. [CM XXXIV]

2603. PENDLETON, EDMUND. Bid Adieu. Paris: Ars Musica, 1949. 8pp. c. [CM XI]

2604. PERSICHETTI, VINCENT. James Joyce Songs, op. 74. Philadelphia Composers' Forum,

pub. ser. no. 1. Philadelphia: Elkan-Vogel, 1959. 3, 3, 5pp. [CM XXXIV, 'Brigid's Song' (PAYM), CM XXXV]

2605. READ, GARDNER. All Day I Hear. New York: Boosey and Hawkes, 1950. 8pp. c. 1950. [CM XXXV]

2606. REED, ALFRED. Rahoon. New York: Piedmont Music Co., [n.d.]. 26 pp. [from PP]

2607. REUTTER, HERMANN. Chamber Music. Mainz, London, New York: Schott, 1973. [CM I, V, XIV, XXXIV]

2608. RICHARDS, HOWARD. Rain. New York: Lawson-Gould, c. 1960. 8pp. [CM XXXII]

2609. _____. Who Goes Amid the Green Wood. New York: Lawson-Gould, c. 1960. 10pp. [CM VIII]

2610. ROUSSEL, ALBERT. A Flower Given to My Daughter. Paris: Durand, 1948. 4pp. c. 30 April 1948. French translation by Rollo H. Myers. [from PP]

2611. SEARLE, HUMPHREY. The riverrun, op. 20. London: Schott, 1951. 54pp. MS score. [FW 619-620, 625-626, 628-conclusion]

2612. SEIBER, MÁTYÁS. Ulysses. Cantata for Tenor Solo, Chorus and Orchestra. London: Schott, 1948. 84pp. c. 9 September 1948.

2613. _____. Three Fragments from "A Portrait of the Artist as a Young Man" by James Joyce: A Chamber Cantata for Speaker, Mixed Chorus (wordless) and Instrumental Ensemble. London: Schott, c. 1958. 42pp. [from PAYM]

2614. SESSIONS, ROGER. On the Beach at Fontana. London: British and Continental Music Agencies, c. 1964. 4pp. [from PP]

2615. SMITH, WILLIAM R. Rain Has Fallen all the Day. Philadelphia: Elkan-Vogel, 1948. 6pp. c. 17 September 1948. [CM XXXII]

2616. SPENCER, WILLIAMETTA. Bright Cap and Streamers. Marquette, Mich.: Fostco Music Press, 1972. [CM X]

2617. _____. In the Dark Pine-Wood. Marquette, Mich.: Fostco Music Press, 1972. [CM XX]

2618. _____. Winds of May. Marquette, Mich.: Fostco Music Press, 1972. [CM IX]

2619. STERNE, COLIN. Dear Heart. New York: Peer International, 1953. 3pp. [CM XXIX]

2620. _____. Gentle Lady. New York: Peer International, 1953. 3pp. [CM XXVIII]

DRAMATIC AND MUSICAL PRODUCTIONS

2621. _____ . My Love is in a Light Attire. New York: Peer International, 1953. 3pp. [CM VII]

2622. STRICKLAND, WILLIAM. A Flower Given to My Daughter. New York: Galaxy Music, 1961. 3pp. [from PP]

2623. _____ . She Weeps over Rahoon. New York: Galaxy Music, 1961. 3pp. [from PP]

2624. SUSA, CONRAD. Chamber Music: Six Joyce Songs. Boston: E. C. Schirmer Music, 1973. [CM XIV, XXI, XXXVI, XVI, XXV, I]

2625. SZYMANOWSKI, KAROL. 4 Pieśni. 4 Songs. Cracow: Polskie Wydawnictwo Muzyczne, 1949. 12pp. c. 15 August 1949. [CM XXVIII, XXXIV, V, XIV]

2626. TREACHER, GRAHAM. Bright Cap and Streamers. London: Schott, c. 1963. 4pp. [CM X]

2627. _____ . The Dove. London: Schott, c. 1963. 4pp. [CM XIV]

2628. _____ . Winds of May. London: Schott, c. 1963. 4pp. [CM IX]

2629. TRIGGS, HAROLD. She Weeps Over Rahoon. New York: Galaxy Music Corp., 1935. 6pp. c. 13 July 1935. [from PP]

2630. VICTORY, GERARD. Five Songs by James Joyce. 1954. [CM XV, X, XXIV, V, XXXIV]

2631. WARD, ROBERT. Rain Has Fallen all the Day. New York: Peer International Corp., 1951. 4pp. c. 1951. [CM XXXII]

2632. WOOD, HUGH. Three Choruses, op. 7. London: Universal, c. 1967. 16pp. ["Sirens" from U]

THEATRICAL PRODUCTIONS

2633. ABRAHAMI, IZZY. "The Joyce-Theatre Affair." Levende Talen, no. 269 (June–July 1970): 453-455. [Theatrical adaptations of Joyce's works.]

2634. BARKENTIN, MARJORIE. Ulysses in Nighttown, with "Introduction" by Padraic Colum, "Nighttown: A City and a Search" [reprinted in Scene (Toronto), 3 (20-26 February 1966): 18]. New York: Ramdon House, 1958. [Also in The Off-Broadway Theatre. Edited by R. A. Cordell and L. Matson. New York: Random House, 1959, pp. 335-405; La nuit d'Ulysse adapted by George Auclair from the translation of Auguste Morel et al. Paris: Editions Gallimard, 1959; extract from Act I appears in Lettres nouvelles, 7 (July 1959): 16-26; La notte di Ulisse, translated by Gianfranco Corsini. Milan: Il Saggiatore, 1962.] [Rooftop Theatre production, Burgess Meredith directing, June 1958; Arts Theatre (London) production, May 1959; Equity Library Theatre (New York) production, May 1964; Poor Alex Theatre (Toronto) production, February 1966; Peacock Theatre (Dublin), 30 August 1971, directed by Thomas MacAnna; Compagnie du Bois Lacte (Paris) production, Theatre Gaite Montparnasse, opened 10 May 1973.]

2635. Passages from James Joyce's Finnegans Wake, by Mary Ellen Bute, Mary Manning, and Jean Merrill. New York: Gotham Book Mart, 1965. [Scenario of the film]

2636. "Coach with Six Insides." Adapted from Finnegans Wake by Jean Erdman. [Village South Theatre (New York), 26 November 1962-17 March 1963, then on tour; for cast, etc., see Theatre World, 19 (1962/63): 149; touring production of above, including a booking 23-28 September 1963 at Eblana Theatre (Dublin) as part of the Dublin Theatre Festival; Philadelphia Production, November 1965; college tour (see New York Times, 15 October 1965, p. 51); East 74th Street Theatre (New York) production, 11 May-25 June 1967; for cast, etc., see Theatre World, 23 (1966/67): 145.]

2637. "A Portrait of the Artist as a Young Man," adapted by Frederic Ewen, Phoebe Brand, and John Randolph. [Opened Martinique Theatre (New York) 28 May 1962, closed 17 February 1963. For cast, etc., see Theatre World, 19 (1962/63): 131.]

2638. GALLACHER, TOM. Mr. Joyce is Leaving Paris. Playscript 64. London: Calder and Boyars, 1972. [Quipu Basement Theater (London), 16 November 1970; Dublin Theatre Festival at Eblana Theatre (Dublin), directed by Robert Gillespie; production at King's Head, Islington (1972).]

2639. HAYMAN, DAVID. "Notes for the Staging of Finnegans Wake." A James Joyce Miscellany. Third series, pp. 278-293, No. 1614.

2640. Finnegans Wake. Adapted by David Kerry Heefner, Thresholds Theatre (New York) production, 24 April-25 May 1969.

2641. "Dublin One," adapted from Dubliners by Hugh Leonard (1963). [At the Gate Theatre as part of the Dublin Theatre Festival, November 1963; Telefis Eireann production, featuring Abbey Theatre players and shown on NET, December 1967.]

2642. Stephen D, by Hugh Leonard, a play in two acts, adapted from Portrait of the Artist and Stephen Hero. London, New York: Evans Bros., 1964; New York: Dramatists Play Service, 1968; Arabic translation by Amin al'Atiwi as "Stiphin Didalis." Al-Masrah (Cairo), 71 (April 1970): 65-81; Hugh Leonard. "Half the Agony." Plays and

Players, 10 (March 1963): 18-19. [Opened Gate Theatre (Dublin), 24 September 1962; St. Martin's Theatre (London) production, opened 12 February 1963; for cast, photos, etc., see Theatre World Annual (1964), no. 14, pp. 74-77; Das Deutsche Schauspielhaus (Hamburg) production, February 1964; Theatre des Nations (Paris) production, June 1965; Olney, Maryland Theatre production, August 1966; opened East 74th Street Theatre (New York) 24 September 1967, closed 12 November 1967; Burgtheater (Vienna), beginning 3 November 1971, directed by Hans Schweikart; on BBC "Play of the Month," 20 February 1972.]

2643. "Bloomsday," adapted from Ulysses by Allan McClelland. [Bloomsdag, translated by Gerardine Franken, afterword by John Vandenbergh. Amsterdam: De Bezige Bij, 1965; Unity Theatre (London) production, January 1960.]

2644. Unsigned. "Stage Version of Ulysses Dropped." Irish Times, 15 February 1958. [Decision of Dublin Theatre Festival Council not to produce Allan McClelland's adaptation; see also Irish Times, 19 February 1958; Padriac Colum's letter, Irish Times, 21 February 1958; Manchester Guardian, 24 February 1958; Father A. O'Rahilly's defense, Standard (Dublin), 28 February 1958.]

2645. Here are Ladies, with Siobhan McKenna, directed by Sean Kenny. [Part 2 adapted from FW and U.] At the Criterion (London), 28 July-8 August 1970; opened at the Public Theater (New York), 22 February 1971 for 67 performances.

2646. MANNING, MARY. Passages from Finnegans Wake by James Joyce: A Free Adaptation for the Theatre. Poet's Theatre Series, no. 3. Cambridge: Harvard University Press, 1957; London: Faber and Faber, 1958, as The Voice of Shem, with "Introduction" by Denis Johnston. [Poet's Theatre, Cambridge, Mass., Spring 1955; New York Poetry Center, December 1955; Voice of Shem. Eblana Theatre (Dublin) as part of the Dublin Theatre Festival, November 1961; Theatre de Nations (Paris) production, June 1962.]

2647. "Bloomsday," selections from Portrait and Ulysses, read by Moral Pub People, opened White Horse Pub, New York, 16 June 1972.

2648. ROCCO-BERGERA, NINY. "Ulysses by Joyce in a Modern Performance at Palazzo Grassi in Venice." James Joyce Quarterly, 9 (Spring 1972): 397-399.

2649. Ulises, translated and adapted by Maciej Słomczyński, directed by Zygmunt Hubner. [Teatr Wybrzeze (Gdnask, Poland), 14 February 1970.]

2650. TAUBMAN, HOWARD. "Joyce is a '67 Festival." New York Times, 31 October 1967, p. 37. [Recent stage and film versions of Joyce's works.]

2651. Finnegans Wake. Adapter anonymous; reading by Gateway Theatre Company at City Art Museum, St. Louis, 6 September 1964. [For cast, etc. see St. Louis Globe-Democrat, 29-30 August 1964, p. 5F.]

FILMS

2652. BURGESS, ANTHONY. "Silence, Exile, and Cunning." London: BBC-TV, 1971 (dist. in U.S. by Time-Life Films). 30 min., 16mm, b & w film.

2653. 'Candida,' "An Irishwoman's Diary," Irish Times, 26 September 1966, p. 9. [Film by Jean Paul Aubert on James Joyce, Dublin, Joseph Strick, etc.]

2654. COHN, ALAN M. "Joyce in the Movies." James Joyce Quarterly, 2 (Summer 1965): 317-319.

2655. Ulysses. 20 min., 16mm. Color film, directed and produced by Saul Field, based on his engravings, written by Jeniva Berger, narrated by Nuala Fitzgerald, distributed by Haida Films, Willowdale, Canada. [For description, see Éire-Ireland, 6 (Spring 1971): 144-145; see also his A Storyboard of the Film Ulysses. Toronto: Haida Films, a 4' x 9-1/4" x 3" scroll of rough sketches.]

2656. Faithful Departed. 10 min., 16mm, b & w film, written and produced by Des Hickey, still photos by William Laurence, narrated by Jack MacGowan, distributed by Contemporary/McGraw-Hill Films (1968).

2657. MACKSEY, RICHARD. "The Ineluctable Modality of the Verbal." Chesapeake Weekly Review, 12 June 1970, p. 6. [Joyce films.]

2658. NATHAN, PAUL. "Rights and Permissions." Publishers' Weekly, 188 (16 August 1965): 35. [U, FW and PAYM films.]

2659. O'CONNOR, ULICK. "JJ's Dublin," directed by Michael O'Connor. Dublin: Milick Productions, 1967 (dist. in U.S. by Carousel Films). 22 min., 16mm, color film.

2660. Ulysses, film produced by Joseph Strick, August 1966.

RADIO AND TELEVISION BROADCASTS

2661. BLOCH, JEAN-JACQUES and ROLAND BERNARD, with Marcel Brion. "James Joyce." French TV program, 10 May 1973.

2662. BBC Broadcast. "Portrait of James Joyce," by Maurice Brown (13 February 1950).

DRAMATIC AND MUSICAL PRODUCTIONS

2663. CBS Broadcast. Ulysses, by Lyman Bryson, Clifton Fadiman, Christopher la Farge (28 December 1947).

2664. CBS Broadcast. Ulysses, by Lyman Bryson, William G. Rodgers, William York Tindall (2 March 1952).

2665. BBC Broadcast. "Irish Writers, No. 15: James Joyce," by George Buchanan (15 December 1948).

2666. "Araby," a reading by C. Cusack. BBC Broadcast (13 June 1948).

2667. BBC Broadcast. "A Portrait of the Artist as a Young Man," reading from Joyce's autobiography, Gerard Fay and Bill Shine (17 May 1946).

2668. "Paris in the Twenties," narrated by Janet Flanner. CBS "Twentieth Century Series" (16 April 1960). [Uses 16mm home movies shot in 1930 and 1937 by Robert Kastor, brother of Helen Joyce.]

2669. BBC Radio 3. "Send Him Canorius, Long to Lung over Us," by Arnold Goldman, with interview with Mme. Paul Léon (28 May 1972).

2670. Ulysses, radio broadcast (Berlin), adaptation prepared by Ivan Goll (1932).

2671. James Joyce's Dublin, by Miles Hanley. [22 minute silent film, shot in the 1940's; available on rental from the University of Wisconsin's Bureau of Audio-Visual Instruction.]

2672. "Der Dichter und Sein Stadt: James Joyce und Dublin," filmed program by Kurt Heinrich Hansen and Claus Simon (Summer 1964). [German Television.]

2673. HIGHET, GILBERT. The Personality of Joyce. New York: Book-of-the-Month Club, 1959. [Transcript of a radio talk.]

2674. HIGHET, GILBERT. Ulysses. New York: Book-of-the-Month Club, 1958. [Transcript of radio talk.]

2675. "Hemingway," narrated by Chet Huntley. NBC Documentary (1961). [Uses 16mm home movies shot by Robert Kastor.]

2676. BBC Broadcast. "James Joyce Exhibition in London," by Patricia Hutchins (21 June 1950).

2677. BBC Broadcast. Anna Livia Plurabelle, as recorded by James Joyce (14 May 1949).

2678. BBC Broadcast. "James Joyce," by Stanislaus Joyce (11 May 1949).

2679. BBC Broadcast. "Ibsen and Joyce," talk by Vivienne Koch (21 February 1950).

2680. BBC TV Production. "Bloomsday," adapted by Allan McClelland (10 June 1964).

2681. BBC Broadcast. Exiles, produced by D. MacWhinnie (19 February 1950).

2682. "Two Gallants," co-produced by Gavin Millar and Melvyn Bragg. BBC-2 TV adaptation (1972).

2683. "The Dead," a reading by Nathalie Moya. BBC Broadcast (9 May 1948).

2684. NBC Theatre. "A Portrait of the Artist as a Young Man," dramatized on 23 April 1950 in a full-hour version.

2685. BBC Broadcast. "Writers and Music, No. 4: James Joyce," by Sean O'Faolain (10 March 1949).

2686. O hAODHA, MICHAEL. "Joyce and the Loudspeaker." RTV Guide (Dublin), 10 June 1966, p. 6. [Joyce and radio.]

2687. OLDEN, G. A. Irish Times, 12 October 1956. [Review of BBC dramatization, Stephen Dedalus.]

2688. _____. "Salute to Bloom." Irish Times, 24 June 1954. [Review of radio broadcast.]

2689. "Eveline," read by Nelson Olmstead. NBC. Stories by Olmstead (5 December 1941).

2690. PASOLINI, DESIDERIA. "Gli Anni Giovanile di Joyce." Radio-Corriere, 28 (23-29 September 1951): 14. [Script of program presented on Radio Italy.]

2691. "Eveline," adapted by Jeremy Paul. BBC 2 Thirty Minute Theatre (6 March 1968).

2692. BBC Broadcast. "The English Novel, No. 8: James Joyce," by Henry Reed (28 February 1950).

2693. CBS Broadcast. Finnegans Wake, by Henry Morton Robinson, William York Tindall, Mark Van Doren (22 January 1950).

2694. RODGERS, W. R. "Joyce's Wake." Explorations, no. 5 (June 1955): 19-25. [Portion of BBC program, "The Portrait of James Joyce," edited by W. R. Rodgers and produced by Maurice Brown.]

2695. _____. "James Joyce: A Portrait of Joyce as a Young Man," "James Joyce: A Portrait of the Artist in Maturity." London: BBC, 1972, pp. 22-47, 48-74. [Transcriptions from BBC broadcasts of February 1950; discussants include: Nial Sheridan, George

Roberts, Richard Best, Oliver St. John Gogarty, W. K. Magee, Constantine Curran, Stanislaus Joyce, Eileen Joyce Schaurek, Eva Joyce, James Stephens, Maria Jolas, Carola Giedion-Welcker, Harriet Weaver, Sylvia Beach, Adrienne Monnier, Frank Budgen, Nino Frank, Lucie Léon, Arthur Power, Austin Clarke, Frank O'Connor; for errors in the transcription see TLS, 29 September 1972, p. 1148.]

2696. SEMMLER, CLEMENT. "Radio and James Joyce." BBC Quarterly, 9, no. 2 (1954): 92-96. [Reprinted in his For the Uncanny Man, pp. 121-126, No. 1653.]

2697. SMIDT, KRISTIAN. "Joyce i togenrer: Exiles og Ulysses." Norsk Rikskringkasting (1972). [Reprinted in Kongstfuglen og natlergalen: Essays orn diktning og Kritikk. Oslo: Gyldendal Norsk Forlag, 1972, pp. 139-148.]

2698. BBC Broadcast. "Ulysses from Homer to Joyce," talk by Professor W. B. Stanford (3 November 1949).

2699. BBC Broadcast. Ulysses, reviewed in "Books and Authors" by James Stephens (10 January 1948).

2700. BBC Broadcast. Finnegans Wake, talk by James Stephens (25 January 1947).

2701. BBC Broadcast. Finnegans Wake, No. 1, talk by Walter Taplin (19 June 1947).

2702. BBC Broadcast. Finnegans Wake, No. 2, talk by Walter Taplin (22 August 1947).

2703. Unsigned. "Dublin Solicitor's Suit Against BBC." Evening Mail (Dublin), 8 October 1954. [Suit by Reuben J. Dodd; see also Irish Press, 7 July 1954; Evening News (Dublin), 8 October 1954; Evening Herald (Dublin), 8 October 1954; Times (London), 8 October 1954; Irish Independent, 24 June 1955; Julia Monks. "Ulysses--9 Hour Version by BBC." Irish Press, 24 October 1953; Unsigned. "Maria Duce says 'No' to BBC Ulysses." Irish Times, 7 November 1953.]

2704. VANDENBERGH, JOHN, PETER van GESTEL, and anonymous announcer. "Voorrang: Ulysses van James Joyce." Levende Talen, no. 269 (June-July 1970): 416-425. [Script of N.C.R.V. radio broadcast of 27 October 1969.]

2705. BBC Broadcast. "James Joyce and Italo Svevo in Trieste," by Bernard Wall (21 May 1950).

RECORDINGS

2706. ANDERSON, CHESTER. Form in Ulysses. University of Minnesota 100-73-747. 44 min. tape.

2707. "Anna Livia Plurabelle," in a number of different pressings: (1) Orthological Institue, London, the first pressing, made for C. K. Ogden; (2) His Master's Voice; (3) Argus Book Shop, Chicago; (4) Gotham Book Mart, New York.

2708. ARCHIBALD, R. C. "James Joyce: Phonograph Records." Notes and Queries, 198 (April 1953): 173; (September 1953): 408; (December 1953): 545.

2709. BARBER, SAMUEL. Nuvoletta. Eleanor Steber, soprano; Edwin Bitcliffe, piano, in Songs of American Composers, Desto, D 412 (or D 7412, stereo). 12", 33 1/3 RPM record. [S-C F 37.]

2710. BEACH, SYLVIA. Writers of the Left Bank. Center for Cassette Studies, 020, 5227M. 28 min. cassette (1970).

2711. BEARD, M. C. "The Firesign Theatre: A Review." College English, 33 (December 1971): 379-382. [On the Firesign Theatre phonorecord "Don't Crush that Dwarf, Hand me the Pliers." Columbia, C30102.]

2712. Brendan Behan on Joyce. Folkways, FL 9826. 12", 33 1/3 RPM record. [At a meeting of the James Joyce Society at the Gotham Book Mart, 1961.]

2713. BERIO, LUCIANO. Epifanie. Cathy Berberian, mezzo-soprano; BBC Symphony Orchestra, conducted by Berio; liner notes by Paul Moor. RCA Victor, LSC-3189. British Issue, SB6850. 12", 33 1/3 RPM record. [Somewhat different version from published score; also includes a passage from U.]

2714. _____. "Thema (Omaggio a Joyce)," on Electronic Music/Musique Concrete. Mercury, SR 29123. 12", 33 1/3 RPM record. [Also on Electronic Music, Phillips Forefront (England), 4FE8503; on Electronic Music III, Turnabout-Vox TV 32177.]

2715. "The Boarding House." Read by Carol Mitchell. American Foundation for the Blind, CR 315. Tape cassette (1972).

2716. BUDGEN, FRANK. My Friend James Joyce. London, LK4400. 12", 33 1/3 RPM record (c. 1964).

2717. BURGESS, ANTHONY. James Joyce's Dublin: A Documentary on the Work and World of a Masterful Writer. Motivational Programming Corp., 020 5330. 27 min. 1 7/8 ips tape. Center for Cassette Studies, 5330. 27 min. cassette.

2718. CAMPBELL, JOSEPH. Readings from James Joyce: Ulysses. Big Sur Recordings, S-411-90. 90 min. 3 3/4 ips tape.

DRAMATIC AND MUSICAL PRODUCTIONS

2718a. _____ . Readings from James Joyce: Finnegans Wake. Big Sur Recordings, S-442-
90. 90 min. 3 3/4 ips tape.

2719. CLARKE, LAURENCE. Chamber Music: Five Poems
by James Joyce. Dorothy Renzi, soprano;
Nathan Schwartz, piano. Fantasy, 5010
(1960). 12", 33 1/3 RPM record. [CM I,
VI, VIII, XXV, XXVIII]

2720. Coach with the Six Insides: A Musical Play,
adapted by and directed by Jean Erdman,
music by Teisi Ito. ESP-Disk, ESP 1019.
12", 33 1/3 RPM record.

2721. COLUM, PADRAIC. Golden Treasury of Irish
Verse. Spoken Arts, 706. 12", 33 1/3
RPM record.

2722. CUSACK, CYRIL. Portrait of the Artist as a
Young Man. Caedmon, TC 1110. 12",
33 1/3 RPM record.

2723. DEL TREDICI, DAVID. Night Conjure-Verse.
Benita Valente, soprano; Mary Burgess,
mezzo; orchestra conducted by David del
Tredici. On Composers Recordings, Inc.,
CRI SD 243. 12", 33 1/3 RPM record.
["Simples," "A Memory of the Players."]

2724. _____ . Syzgy. Phyllis Bryn-Julson,
soprano; Festival Chamber Orchestra, conducted by Richard Duffalo. On Commis-
sioned by the Koussevitzky Music Foundation. Columbia, MS 7281. 12", 33 1/3
RPM record.

2725. _____ . I Hear an Army. Phyllis Bryn-
Julson, soprano, Composers Quartet. On
Composers Recordings, Inc., CRI-SD-294.
12", 33 1/3 RPM phonorecord.

2726. DIAMOND, DAVID. Brigid's Song. Mildred
Miller, mezzo; Edwin Bitcliffe, piano, in
Songs of American Composers. Desto, D411
(or D7411, stereo). 12", 33 1/3 RPM
record (1964). [S-C F25.]

2727. Dubliners. Made available for the blind in
Talking Books, 7 records, with an introduction by Padraic Colum.

2728. Finnegans Wake, selections read by Patrick
Bedford. Spoken Arts, SA 854. 12",
33 1/3 RPM record. [For contents see
Schwann Long Playing Record Catalogue,
May 1963, p. 141.]

2729. GREGOR, IAN and MARK KINKEAD-WEEKES. "Approach to the Twentieth-Century Novel."
Approach to Literary Criticism, Series
A8. BFA Educational Media F12008. Tape
cassette.

2730. HAYES, HAROLD. "Notes on This Bloomsday:
Listening to James Joyce." Esquire, 54
(July 1960): 22-24. [Survey of five Joyce
recordings: McKenna's and Marshall's

"Soliloquies of Molly and Leopold Bloom,"
No. 2745; Frank O'Connor's "James Joyce,"
No. 2750; C. Cusack's "Portrait of the
Artist as a Young Man," No. 2722; "Bren-
dan Behan on Joyce," No. 2712; McKenna's
and Cusack's "Finnegans Wake," No. 2746.]

2731. HODEIR, ANDRÉ. Anna Livia Plurabelle. Monique Aldebert, Nichole Croisille, sopran-
os; orchestra conducted by Hodeir; liner
notes by John Lewis. Philips, PHS-900-
255; also issued as EPIC, 64 695. 12",
33 1/3 RPM phonorecord.

2732. James Joyce Birthday Celebration. Cinema,
956. 12", 33 1/3 RPM record. [Meeting
of the James Joyce Society (2 February
1962), Joseph Campbell presiding.]
   Contents: Leonie Adams. "A Tribute to
Vivienne Koch"; Samuel Rosenberg. "The
Irismanx: Word Game with James Joyce";
Mary Manning. "Mythcarriage of Joyces-
tice," see No. 1174; Matthew Josephson.
"Memories of 1920"; William York Tindall.
"Announcement of Joyce Tour"; Jean Erdman.
"Dance Theatre Production Report"; Nathan
Halper. "Comments on James Joyce's Ear
Trouble."

2733. James Joyce Spricht, selections read by Joyce
and (in German) by Gert Westphal. Rhein
Vlg., 478. 12", 33 1/3 RPM record (1960).
[Reissued Gunther Neske NV 11, 1970.]
   Contents: Joyce reading from "Aeolus"
and from ALP; Westphal reading from Goy-
ert's translation of "Lestrygonians" and
ALP.

2734. JOYCE, JAMES. "O'Molloy's Speech," a recording of Joyce reading the speech from Ulysses. Random House Edition, pp. 140-141;
Paris: H. M. V., 1923.

2735. James Joyce Reading from Ulysses and Finnegans Wake. Caedmon, TC 1340. 12", 33 1/3
RPM recording. [Joyce reading from U and
FW and Cyril Cusack reading from CM, PP,
and "Ecce Puer."]

2736. James Joyce's Ulysses-"Calypso," dramatic
reading by students and faculty of the
State University College, Fredonia, New
York, produced and directed by Zack R.
Bowen. Folkways, FL 9835. 12", 33 1/3
RPM record.

2737. James Joyce's Ulysses-"Hades," dramatic reading, produced and directed by Zack R. Bow-
en and J. Tyler Dunn. Folkways, FL 9814.
12", 33 1/3 RPM record.

2738. James Joyce's Ulysses-"Lestrygonians," dramatic reading with the original music per-
formed by students and faculty of the State
University College, Fredonia, New York,
produced and directed by Zack R. Bowen.
Folkways, FL 9562. 2 12", 33 1/3 RPM
records.

2739. James Joyce's Ulysses--"Lotus Eaters," dramatic reading by students and faculty of the State University College, Fredonia, New York, produced and directed by Zack R. Bowen. Folkways, FL 9836. 12", 33 1/3 RPM record.

2740. James Joyce's Ulysses--"Sirens," dramatic reading, produced by Zack R. Bowen, directed by Zack R. Bowen and Oscar Brownstein. Folkways, FL 9563. 2 12", 33 1/3 RPM records.

2741. KREINER, PAUL G. "Joyce and Music." Chesapeake Weekly Review, 12 June 1970, p. 9.

2742. LERDAHL, FRED. Wake. Bethany Beardslee, soprano; Boston Symphony Chamber Players, conducted by David Epstein; liner notes by Donald Sur. Deutsche Grammophon, 0654 083. 12", 33 1/3 RPM recording. [From FW, Bk. 1, Chapter 8.]

2743. McHUGH, ROGER. "Joyce, gesprochen." Neue Zürcher Zeitung, 15 March 1964, p. 5. [In the Fernausgabe, appears 14 March 1964, p. 14.]

2744. McKENNA, SIOBHAN. Irish Ballads and Lyrics. Spoken Arts, 707. 12", 33 1/3 RPM record. [Includes "I Hear an Army," "On the Beach at Fontana," "She Weeps over Rahoon."]

2745. _____, and E. G. MARSHALL. Ulysses: Soliloquies of Molly and Leopold Bloom. Caedmon, TC 1063. 12", 33 1/3 RPM record. [See Notes, ser. 2, 14 (September 1957): 522 for contents.]

2746. _____, and CYRIL CUSACK. Finnegans Wake. Caedmon, TC 1086. 12", 33 1/3 RPM record.

2747. Meeting of the Joyce Society. Folkways, FP 93-94. Two 12", 33 1/3 RPM records. [Meeting of 23 October 1951.]

2748. Meeting of the James Joyce Society. Expanding Cinema, 956. 12", 33 1/3 RPM record. [Meeting of 9 November 1961.]
      Contents: Padraic Colum. "The Tower Joyce Left to the World"; Mary Ellen Bute. "A Report on the Filming of Finnegans Wake"; Padraic Colum reading the "Tower Scene" from Ulysses.

2749. MEYERS, STANLEY. Ulysses, orchestra conducted by Stanley Meyers. RCA Victor, LOC 1138 (mono), LSO 1138 (stereo). 12", 33 1/3 RPM recording. [Original soundtrack recording of the score for the film.]

2750. O'CONNOR, FRANK. James Joyce. Folkways, FL 9834. 12", 33 1/3 RPM record. [Includes introduction, excerpts from PAYM, U and FW.]

2751. _____. The Irish Literary Tradition. Folkways, FL 9825. 12", 33 1/3 RPM record.

2752. O'TUAMA, SEAN. James Joyce's The Dead and Ireland's "Split Little Pea." University of Minnesota 100-71-796. 66 min. tape.

2753. Passages from Finnegans Wake, from the soundtrack of Mary Ellen Bute's film. RCA Victor, VDM 118 (mono), VDS (stereo). 12", 33 1/3 RPM record.

2754. PAWLE, IVAN. "Strings in the Earth and Air." Dr. Strangely Strange combo. On Kip of the Serenes. Island (Ireland), LPIS 9106. 12", 33 1/3 RPM record (1969).

2755. PISK, PAUL. Songs from Chamber Music by James Joyce, op. 101. Leslie Chabay, tenor; Evelyn Mitchell, piano. On (Washington University), T4RM-5570. 12", 33 1/3 RPM record (1965). [CM V, XV, XIX, XXXII, XXV.]

2756. Portrait of the Artist as a Young Man. Center for Cassette Studies, 055 3141. 55 min. cassette. ["Dramatic highlights."]

2757. PRESCOTT, JOSEPH. James Joyce. World Tapes for Education, 44. 7.5 ips tape recording. [Recording of his "James Joyce's Stephen Hero," No. 1637.]

2758. ROACH, HELEN. Spoken Records. New York: Scarecrow Press, 1963, pp. 80-82, 151-153; 2nd edition. New York, London: Scarecrow Press, 1966. [Appendix I, pp. 175-177 reprints Sylvia Beach's "Two Records" from No. 3544, pp. 170-173.]

2759. SCHICKELE, PETER. "Of the Dark Past," from Portrait of the Artist as a Young Man. Joan Baez, soprano; orchestra conducted by Peter Schickele. In On Baptism: A Journey Through Our Time. Vanguard, VRS 9275 (mono), VSD 79275 (stereo). 12", 33 1/3 RPM record. [A setting of "Ecce Puer" and a reading of first two pages of Portrait with musical background.]

2760. SEIBER, MÁTYÁS. Three Fragments from A Portrait of the Artist as a Young Man: A Chamber Cantata. Peter Pears, speaker Melos Ensemble, Dorian Singers, conducted by Mátyás Seiber. London, CM 9625. 12", 33 1/3 RPM record.

2761. SERLY, TIBOR. Four Songs from Chamber Music. Carolyn Stanford, mezzo-soprano; Kundstmaand Chamber Orchestra, conducted by Tibor Serly. On the Music of Tibor Serly (1967). [CM XXXIV, XXVIII, XXXV, XXIV.]

DRAMATIC AND MUSICAL PRODUCTIONS

2762. Songs to Texts by James Joyce. Patricia
       Neway, sporano; Robert Colston, piano.
       Lyrichord, LL 83. 12", 33 1/3 RPM
       record (1960):
           Contents: Settings from CM by Israel
       Citkowitz and Seymour Barab; from PP by
       John Gruen; from U by Thomas de Hartmann;
       from FW by Samuel Barber and Hazel Felman
       Buchbinder.

2763. Ulysses. Described in Sylvia Beach's cata-
       logue of 1935, no. 4 as: "Phonograph
       record of a reading by James Joyce from
       'Ulysses,' pages 136-137 ["Aeolus" epi-
       sode], recorded by His Master's Voice on
       one side only; with parchment label on
       which is printed: Ulysses (pp. 136-137),
       Shakespeare and Company, 12, rue de
       l'Odeon, Paris. Signed: James Joyce,
       Paris, 17 November 1926 (date of record-
       ing). Only remaining copy of the 30 that
       were made. Paris 1936."

2764. Ulysses, from the soundtrack of Joseph
       Strick's film. Caedmon, TRS 328. 2 12",
       33 1/3 RPM records.

Studies of the Separate Works

CRITICAL ARTICLES WRITTEN BY JOYCE

See "Reviews of Joyce's Works," I.E., Nos. 2354-2359; S. Benco. "James Joyce in Trieste," No. 329; Bruno. "James Joyce in Italia," No. 342; Francini-Bruni. "Ricordi Personali...," No. 395; Meenan. Centenary History, passim, No. 306.

Books

2765. JOYCE, STANISLAUS, and ELLSWORTH MASON, eds. The Early Joyce, The Book Reviews, 1902-1903. Colorado Springs: Mamalujo Press, 1955.

2766. LOMBARDO, AGOSTINO. "Saggi di James Joyce." Ritratto di Enobarbo: Saggi sulla letteratura inglese. Saggi di varia umanita, n.s. 13. Pisa: Nistri-Lischi, 1971, pp. 287-299. [Appeared in part in a review in Il Mondo, 22 September 1959.]

2767. MASON, ELLSWORTH, and RICHARD ELLMAN, eds. The Critical Writings of James Joyce. New York: Viking Press, 1959. [Translated by Hiltrud Marschall. Frankfurt a.M.: Suhrkamp, 1973.]

2768. PRESCOTT, JOSEPH, ed. Daniel Defoe. Edited from Italian manuscripts and translated. Buffalo Series 1, i. Buffalo: State University of New York at Buffalo, 1964.

2769. PRITCHETT, V. S., ed. "James Joyce." Turnstile One. London: Turnstile Press, 1948, pp. 10-13.

Periodical Articles

*2770. EGRI, PÉTER. "Jegyzetek Joyce kritakáihoz ["Notes on Joyce's Critiques]." Világirodalmi Figyeló (A Review of World Literature, Budapest), 7 (1961): 259-264.

*2771. EGRI, PÉTER. "James Joyce kritikája Munkácsy Mihály Ecce Homojárol ["A Review by James Joyce on Mihaly Munkacsy's Painting Ecce Homo]." Müvészet [Art] (Budapest), 2, no. 1 (1961): 18-21.

2772. KAIN, RICHARD M. "Two Book Reviews by James Joyce." Publications of the Modern Language Association, 67 (March 1952): 291-294.

2773. KUBOTA, SHIGEYOSHI. ["A Study of Joyce's Essays on James Clarence Mangan"]. Kwansei gakuin daigaku eibei bungaku, 16 (December 1971): 69-70. [In Japanese.]

*2774. MASON, ELLSWORTH, ed. "William Blake." Criticism, 1 (Summer 1959): 181-189.

2775. MASON, ELLSWORTH, ed. "Joyce's Shrill Note: The Piccolo Della Sera Articles." Twentieth Century Literature, 2 (October 1956): 115-139.

2776. MASON, ELLSWORTH, and RICHARD ELLMANN, eds. "From a Banned Writer to a Banned Singer." Analyst, no. 14 (September 1957): 1-13. [Also appeared in The Critical Writings of James Joyce, No. 2767.]

2777. MASON, ELLSWORTH, and RICHARD ELLMANN, eds. "From a Banned Writer to a Banned Singer." Analyst, no. 15 (1958): 1-8.

2778. MERCHANT, W. M. "From a Banned Writer to a Banned Singer: Some Further Notes." Analyst, no. 16 (1959): 23.

2779. O'NEILL, MICHAEL J. "The Date of 'The Holy Office.'" James Joyce Review, 3, nos. 1-2 (February 1959): 50-51.

2780. SCHOLES, ROBERT. "The Broadsides of James Joyce." A James Joyce Miscellany, Third Series, pp. 8-18, No. 1614.

STUDIES OF JOYCE'S POETRY

See also Brasil. Joyce..., 47-56, No. 1530; Curran. James Joyce Remembered, 76-77, et passim, No. 304; Ellmann. Letters, passim, No. 307; Ellmann. James Joyce, passim, No. 308; Gogarty. It Isn't This Time..., No. 319; Goldberg. James

STUDIES OF JOYCE'S POETRY

Joyce, passim, No. 1574; Golding. James Joyce, 9-21, No. 1575; Guidi. Il Primo Joyce, 105-117, No. 1737; Hughes. The Joyce Book, No. 2582; Kenner. Dublin's Joyce, 27-35, 39-44, 95-105, No. 1600; Levin. Critical Introduction, No. 1603; Litz. James Joyce, passim, No. 1606; Magalaner and Kain. Joyce: The Man..., 47-52, No. 1615; Majault. James Joyce, 59-61, No. 1616; Misra. Indian..., 26-27, No. 941; Mosely. Joyce and the Bible, 12-18, No. 942; Naganowski. Telemach..., 41-44, No. 3632; Pinguentini. James Joyce in Italia, passim, No. 1634; Pound. Pound/Joyce, 136-139, et passim, No. 725; Ryf. New Approach..., 37-41, No. 3271; Stewart. Eight Modern..., 428-430, No. 1665; Sullivan. Joyce Among..., passim, No. 357; Tysdahl. Joyce and Ibsen, passim, No. 952. [See Section I.E "Reviews of Joyce's Works," Nos. 1847-1867, 2143-2154, 2241-2244; see I.G "Musical Settings" and "Recordings."]

Books

2781. ANDO, ICHIRO. "Joyce as Poet," in A Study of Joyce, pp. 243-268, No. 1592.

2782. COLUM, PADRAIC. "James Joyce as Poet," in The Joyce Book, pp. 13-15, No. 2582.

2783. DOYLE, PAUL A., ed. A Concordance of the Collected Poems of James Joyce. New York: Scarecrow, 1966.

2784. HOWARTH, HERBERT. "Chamber Music and Its Place in the Joyce Canon," in James Joyce Today, pp. 11-27, No. 1659.

*2785. ODAJIMA, YUJI. "Chamber Music and Pomes Penyeach," in Joisu Nyumon [An Introduction to James Joyce], pp. 132-134, No. 1511.

2786. PUCCINI, DARIO. "Neruda traduttore di Joyce." Studi di letteratura spagnola. Rome: Facoltà di Magistero e Facoltà di Lettere dell 'Univ. di Roma, 1965, pp. 234-241. [On Neruda's translation of XXXV and XXXVI; first published in Poesía (Buenos Aires), 1933.]

*2787. ROSSI, ALBERTO. "James Joyce e la poesia," in Poesia da un soldo. Milan: Cederna, 1949.

*2788. SAXER, JOHANN ULRICH. "Vorwort des Übersetzers," in James Joyce's Chamber Music. Zürich (1958), pp. 5-6.

*2789. SISSON, C. H. "The Verse of James Joyce," "The Influence of the Prose of James Joyce and D. H. Lawrence," in English Poetry 1900-1950: An Assessment. London: Rupert Hart-Davis, 1971, pp. 68-70, 197-201.

2790. STALEY, THOMAS F. "The Poet Joyce and the Shadow of Swift," in Jonathan Swift: Tercentenary Essays. University of Tulsa Department of English Monograph Series, no. 3. Edited by Winston Weathers and Thomas F. Staley. Tulsa, Oklahoma (1967), pp. 39-52.

2791. STEPHENS, JAMES. "Prologue," in The Joyce Book, p. 11, No. 2582. [Also in James, Seumas and Jacques. Edited by Lloyd Frankenberg. New York: Macmillan, 1964.]

2792. SYMONS, ARTHUR. "Epilogue," in The Joyce Book, pp. 79-84, No. 2582.

2793. TINDALL, WILLIAM YORK. "Introduction," "The Texts of Chamber Music," and "Notes," in Joyce's Chamber Music. New York: Columbia University Press, 1954.

*2794. WILDI, MAX. "The Lyrical Poems of James Joyce," in Language and Society: Essays presented to Arthur M. Jensen on his Seventieth Brithday. Copenhagen: Det Berlingske Bogtrykkeri, 1961, pp. 169-186.

Periodical Articles

2795. ANDERSON, CHESTER G. "James Joyce's 'Tilly.'" Publications of the Modern Language Association, 73 (June 1958): 285-298.

2796. BAKER, JAMES R. "Joyce's Chamber Music: The Exile of the Heart." Arizona Quarterly, 15 (Winter 1959): 349-356.

2797. BOREL, JACQUES. "Joyce et la poésie." L'Arc, 36 (1968): 6-12.

2798. BOWEN, ZACK. "Goldenhair: Joyce's Archetypal Female." Literature and Psychology, 17 (1967): 219-228.

2799. BREMER, RUDY. "The Poetry of James Joyce." Levende Talen, no. 269 (June-July 1970): 447-453.

2800. COHN, ALAN M. "Corrigendum to Slocum and Cahoon: Joyce's Chamber Music." Papers of the Bibliographical Society of America, 67 (3rd Quarter 1973): 341.

2801. DOYLE, PAUL A. "Joyce's Miscellaneous Verse." James Joyce Quarterly, 2 (Winter 1965): 90-96; [Addenda] James Joyce Quarterly, 4 (Fall 1967): 71.

2802. FALLON, PADRAIC. "The Light Tenor of His Ways." Irish Times, 16 June 1962, p. 11.

2803. FISHER, MARVIN. "James Joyce's 'Ecce Puer': The Return of the Prodding Gaul." University of Kansas City Review, 25 (June 1959): 265-271.

2804. GOLDING, LOUIS. "A Sidelight on James Joyce." Nineteenth Century and After, 113 (April 1933): 491-497.

2805. GRECO LOBNER, CORINNA del, "James Joyce's 'Tilly' and Gabriele D'Annunzio's 'I Pastori d'Abruzzo.'" James Joyce Quarterly, 9 (Spring 1972): 383-389.

2806. GYSLING, FRITZ. "A Doctor's Look at a Neglected Poem." James Joyce Quarterly, 7 (Spring 1970): 251-252. ['Bahnhofstrasse']

2807. HERVIEU, ANNIE, and AUGUSTE MOREL. "Poèmes." Mercure de France, 309 (May 1950): 5-11.

2808. HOLMES, LAWRENCE R. "Joyce's 'Ecce Puer.'" Explicator, 13 (November 1954): item 12. [Reprinted in The Explicator Cyclopedia, vol. 1. Edited by C. C. Walcutt and J. E. Whitesell. Chicago: Quadrangle, 1966, pp. 200-201.]

2809. _____. "The Mystery of 'The Simple' in Poetry." Mankato State College Studies, 3 (December 1968): 27-52.

2810. HOWARTH, HERBERT. "James Joyce between the Troubadours and the Liebestod." South Central Bulletin, 26 (March 1966): 9. [Abstract.]

2811. HUNTER, J. STEWART. "Collected Poems." Fantasy, 3 (1939): 69-70.

*2812. KAESTLIN, JOHN. "Joyce by Candlelight." Contemporaries, 2 (Summer 1933): 47-54.

2813. KAIN, RICHARD M. "Joyce's 'Ecce Puer.'" Explicator, 14 (February 1956): item 29. [Reprinted in The Explicator Cyclopedia, vol. 1. Edited by C. C. Walcutt and J. E. Whitesell. Chicago: Quadrangle, 1966, p. 201.]

2814. MOSELEY, VIRGINIA. "The 'Perilous Theme' of Chamber Music." James Joyce Quarterly, 1 (Spring 1964): 19-24.

2815. PERRINE, LAURENCE. "Interpreting Poetry: Two Ways of Going Wrong." California English Journal, 1 (Winter 1965): 49-52. ['I Hear an Army.']

2816. SCHOLES, ROBERT. "James Joyce, Irish Poet." James Joyce Quarterly, 2 (Summer 1965): 255-270. [See reply by John T. Shawcross. "'Tilly' and Dante," ibid., 7 (Fall 1969): 61-64; answer by Scholes. ibid., 7 (Spring 1970): 281-282; reply by Shawcross. ibid.: 282-283; "Letter to the Editor" by Scholes. ibid., 8 (Winter 1970): 192-193.]

2817. SEN, MIHIR KUMAR. "The Poetry of James Joyce." Modern Review (Calcutta), 118 (November 1965): 398-406.

2818. TANIGUCHI, SATOJO. [Joyce and Lyric]. Daitō bunka daigaku eibei bungaku ronsō, no. 3 (1972): 13-29. [In Japanese]

2819. TINDALL, WILLIAM YORK. "Joyce's Chambermade Music." Poetry, 80 (May 1952): 106-116.

2820. WILLIAMS, MARTIN T. "Joyce's Chamber Music." Explicator, 10 (May 1952): item 44. [Reprinted in The Explicator Cyclopedia, vol. 1. Edited by C. C. Walcutt and J. E. Whitesell. Chicago: Quadrangle, 1966, p. 199.]

2821. ZABEL, MORTON D. "Lyrics of James Joyce." Poetry, 36 (July 1930): 206-213. [Translated in Configuration critique I, pp. 201-208, No. 1636.]

2822. ZAVALETA, C. E. "La Poesia de Joyce." Letras Peruanas (Lima), 1, no. 1 (June 1951): 18-19.

*2823. Unsigned. "La Jeune Poesie Irlandaise." Chronique des lettres françaises (March 1931).

EPIPHANIES

See Luciana Berio. Epifanie, No. 2713; Stanislaus Joyce. "The Backgrounds to Dubliners," No. 2921; Paul C. Doherty. "Words as Idols," No. 2948.

2824. AGRAWAL, I. N. "Epiphanies in Portrait of the Artist as a Young Man." Indian Journal of English Studies, no. 8 (1967): 72-78.

2825. BECKSON, KARL, and JOHN H. MUNRO. "Symons, Browning, and the Development of the Modern Aesthetic." Studies in English Literature, 10 (Autumn 1970): 687-699.

2826. BEJA, MORRIS. Epiphany in the Modern Novel. Seattle: University of Washington Press, 1971. [Joyce, Virginia Woolf, Thomas Wolfe, William Faulkner.]

2827. _____. "Mau-Mauing the Epiphany Catchers." Publications of the Modern Language Association, 87 (October 1972): 1131-1132. [Reply to Sidney Feshbach. PMLA, 87 (March 1972): 304-305, No. 2829.]

2828. ECO, UMBERTO. "Joyce et d'Annunzio: Les sources de la notion d'Epiphanie," translated by Elisabeth Hollier. L'Arc, 36 (1968): 29-38.

2829. FESHBACH, SIDNEY. "Hunting Epiphany-Hunters." Publications of the Modern Language Association, 87 (March 1972): 304-305. [Answer to Scholes. PMLA, 82 (March 1967): 152-154, No. 2842; see reply by Beja, No. 2827.]

2830. FRIEDMAN, MELVIN J. "The Cracked Vase." Romance Notes, 7 (Spring 1966): 127-129. [Use of cracked vase as epiphany in Le

EPIPHANIES

Rouge et le Noir, The Idiot, The Egoist,
Set This House on Fire.]

2831. HARRISON, KATE. "The Portrait Epiphany."
James Joyce Quarterly, 8 (Winter 1970):
142-150.

2832. HELSZTYŃSKI, STANISLAW. "James Joycea arty-
styczne epifanie." Zycie i mysl, 13
(March-April 1963): 130-148.

2833. HENDRY [CHAYES], IRENE. "Joyce's Epiphanies." Sewanee Review, 54 (July 1946):
449-467. [Appeared in James Joyce: Two
Decades of Criticism, pp. 27-46, No. 1570;
reprinted in Joyce's Portrait: Criticisms
and Critiques, pp. 204-220, No. 3223; in
Portraits of an Artist: A Casebook on
James Joyce's A Portrait of the Artist as
a Young Man, pp. 153-167, No. 3260; in
Chester G. Anderson, ed. Portrait of the
Artist as a Young Man, pp. 358-370, No.
3213; in Twentieth Century Interpretations of A Portrait of the Artist as a
Young Man, pp. 117-118, No. 3273.]

2834. HEYEN, WILLIAM. "Toward the Still Point:
The Imagist Aesthetic." Ball State University Forum, 9 (Winter 1968): 44-48.

2835. HÜLLERER, WALTER. "Die Epiphanie als Held
des Romans." Akzente, 8 (April 1961):
125-136; (June 1961): 275-285. [Trans-
lated by Anne LeRoy as "L'epiphanie, personnage principal du roman." Meditations,
no. 4 (Winter 1961-1962): 25-40; original
reprinted in James Joyces Portrait: Das
≪Jugendbildnis≫ im Lichte neurer deutschen Forschung, pp. 65-74, No. 3236.]

2836. HOWELL, EDWARD. "Epiphany and the Short
Story." Mexico Quarterly Review, 1
(December 1962): 233-236.

2837. KUMAR, SHIV K. "Joyce's Epiphany and Bergson's l'Intuition Philosophique." Modern
Language Quarterly, 20 (March 1950): 27-
30. [Reprinted in his Bergson and the
Stream of Consciousness Novel, No. 4194.]

2838. MARCUS, PHILLIP. "George Moore's Dublin
'Epiphanies' and Joyce." James Joyce
Quarterly, 5 (Winter 1968): 157-161.
[Moore's Confessions of a Young Man
(1888).]

2839. PRESCOTT, JOSEPH. "James Joyce's Epiphanies." Modern Language Notes, 64 (May
1949): 346.

2840. SANDULESCU, C. G. "Epifanie si Structură la
Joyce." Secolul 20, no. 6 (1968): 20-28.

2841. SCHOLES, ROBERT. "Joyce and the Epiphany:
The Key to the Labyrinth?" Sewanee Review, 72 (Winter 1964): 65-77.

2842. _____ , and FLORENCE L. WALZL. "The Epiphanies of Joyce." Publications of the
Modern Language Association, 82 (March
1967): 152-154. [See reply to Feshbach,
No. 2829.]

2843. SILVERMAN, O. A. "Introduction" and notes
to Joyce's Epiphanies. Buffalo: Lockwood
Memorial Library, 1956.

2844. WALZL, FLORENCE L. "The Liturgy of the Epiphany Season and the Epiphanies of Joyce."
Publications of the Modern Language Association, 80 (September 1965): 436-450.
[Reprinted in Twentieth Century Interpretations of A Portrait of the Artist as a
Young Man, pp. 115-117, No. 3273.]

2845. WIEHL, INGA. "Johannes V. Jenson's Myte and
James Joyce's Epiphany." Orbis litterarum, 23 (1968): 225-232.

2846. ZANIELLO, THOMAS. "The Epiphany and the
Object-Image Distinction." James Joyce
Quarterly, 4 (Summer 1967): 286-288.

2847. ZANTS, EMILY. "The Relation of Epiphany to
Description in the Modern French Novel."
Comparative Literature Studies, 5 (Spring
1968): 317-328.

*2848. ZIOLKOWSKI, THEODORE. "James Joyces Epiph-
anie und die Überwindung der empirischen
Welt in der modernen deutschen Prosa."
Deutsche Vierteljahrsschrift für Litera-
turwissenschaft und Geistgeschichte, 35
(December 1961): 594-616.

STUDIES OF DUBLINERS

See also Adams. James Joyce..., 63-90, No.
1506; Beja. "The Wooden Sword," No. 1693; Benstock. "A Covey of Clerics," No. 1695; Brandabur.
Scrupulous..., 55-126, No. 1529; Brasil. Joyce...,
57-78, No. 1530; Burgess. Joyceprick, passim,
No. 1536; Burgess. Re-Joyce, 35-48, No. 1533;
Church. Time..., 27-30, No. 1542; Collins. "Progression in...," No. 1710; Coveney. Poor Monkey,
passim, No. 1545; Crosse. Flaubert and Joyce, 17-
19, 29-32, No. 1546; Curran. James Joyce Remembered, passim, No. 304; Daiches. Critical History..., No. 1549; Daiches. Novel and..., 63-82,
No. 1548; Eliot. After Strange Gods, 35-38, No.
696; Ellmann. Letters, passim, No. 307; Ellmann.
James Joyce, passim, No. 308; Garrett. Scene and
Symbol..., 214-218, 230-240, No. 1565; Gilbert.
Letters, 55, 60-64, No. 317; Goldberg. James
Joyce, passim, No. 1574; Golding. James Joyce,
22-33, No. 1575; Goldman. Joyce Paradox,
1-21, No. 1576; Gorman. James Joyce..., 26-64,
No. 321; Gross. James Joyce, 32-37, No. 1580;
Guidi. Il primo Joyce, 7-40, No. 1737; Hodgart
and Worthington. Song in..., No. 1588; Hone. "A
Recollection of James Joyce," No. 870; Jacquot.
"Exegetes...," No. 1750; Jaloux. Au Pays du Ro-
man, 97-109, No. 1595; Jones. James Joyce..., 9-

23, No. 3602; Joyce, S. My Brother's Keeper, No. 331; Joyce, S. "Background of...," No. 2921; Kenner. Dublin's Joyce, 46-48, No. 1600; Kenner. "James Joyce: Comedian...," No. 4443; Kiely. Modern Irish Fiction, passim, No. 334; Levin. Critical Introduction, 27-37, No. 1603; Litz. James Joyce, 47-59, No. 1606; Magalaner. "James Joyce and the Uncommon Reader," passim, No. 2926; Magalaner and Kain. Joyce: The Man..., 53-101, No. 1615; Majault. James Joyce, 61-66, No. 1616; Mayoux. James Joyce, passim, No. 1619; Mercanton. Poetes..., 70-76, No. 1620; Miller. "Definition by Comparison...," No. 1773; Misra. Indian..., 27-29, No. 941; Moseley. Joyce and the Bible, 19-30, No. 942; Naganowski. Telemach..., 45-49, No. 3632; O'Brien. Conscience..., 14-16, No. 1628; O'Connor. "Joyce and Dissociated Metaphor," No. 2878; Pinguentini. James Joyce..., No. 1634; Ryf. New Approach..., 59-76, No. 3271; Sanchez. Panorama..., 109-112, No. 1646; Stewart. James Joyce, 10-15, No. 1646; Stewart. Eight..., 431-435, No. 1665; Stief. Moderne..., 132-135, No. 1666; Strong. Sacred River, 17-23, 29-31, No. 949; Walzl. "Liturgy of the Epiphany...," No. 2844; Zhantieva. Dzhiems Dzhois, 6-20, No. 257; see Section I.E "Reviews of Joyce's Works," Nos. 1868-1902; I.F "Dissertations," Nos. 2431-2437.

GENERAL STUDIES

Books

2849. ANDO, ICHIRO. "A Study of Dubliners." A Study of Joyce, pp. 299-316, No. 1592.

2850. ATHERTON, JAMES S. "The Joyce of Dubliners," in James Joyce Today, pp. 28-35, No. 1659.

2851. BAKER, JAMES R. "Ibsen, Joyce and the Living Dead: A Study of Dubliners," in James Joyce Miscellany, Third Series, pp. 18-32, No. 1614. [Reprinted in James Joyce's Dubliners: A Critical Handbook, pp. 62-71, No. 2852; in Joyce's The Dead, pp. 64-70, No. 3138.]

2852. _____, and THOMAS F. STALEY, eds. James Joyce's Dubliners: A Critical Handbook. Belmont, Calif.: Wadsworth, 1969.
Contents: "Editors' Preface"; "The Author's Theories and the Short Story Genre," with materials from Joyce: "Drama and Life," PAYM, "Epiphany"; Theodore Spencer. "Introduction," 10-11, No. 1615; from Letters, 12-15; "Dubliners and the Short Story," 16-28 (from No. 1615); S. L. Goldberg. "Virtues and Limitations," 29-35 (from No. 1573); Brewster Ghiselin. "The Unity of Joyce's Dubliners," 35-62, No. 2914; James R. Baker. "Ibsen, Joyce and the Living Dead: A Study of Dubliners," 63-70, No. 1614; Gerhard Friedrich. "The Perspective of Joyce's Dubliners," 71-78, No. 2912; Thomas E. Connolly. "Joyce's 'The Sisters': A Pennyworth of Snuff," 79-86, No. 2946; Julian B. Kaye. "The Wings of Daedalus: Two Stories in Dubliners," 87-92, No. 2968; Cleanth Brooks and

Robert Penn Warren. 93-96 (from No. 2978); Martin Dolch. "'Eveline,'" 96-101, No. 3008; Robert M. Adams. (from No. 1506); William T. Noon. "'Epiphany' in 'Two Gallants,'" 104-106 (from No. 943); William York Tindall. 106-107 (from No. 1678); James Ruoff. "'A Little Cloud,'" 107-120, No. 3043; John V. Hagopian. "'Counterparts,'" 120-124, No. 3051; Marvin Magalaner and Richard M. Kain. 124-130 (from No. 1615); John William Corrington. "Isolation as Motif in 'A Painful Case,'" 130-139, No. 3088; Joseph L. Blotner. "'Ivy Day in the Committee Room,'" 139-146 (revised version of No. 3098); William York Tindall. 146-148 (from No. 1678); Carl Niemeyer. "'Grace' and Joyce's Method of Parody," 148-154, No. 3124; Lionel Trilling. 154-158 (from No. 3144); Jack Barry Ludwig. "James Joyce's Dubliners," 159-162, No. 3135; "Chronology," "Bibliography."

2853. BEACHCROFT, T. S. The Modest Art: A Survey of the Short Story in English. London, New York: Oxford University Press, 1968, passim.

2854. BECK, WARREN. Joyce's Dubliners: Substance, Vision, and Art. Durham, N.C.: Duke University Press, 1969.

2855. BEJA, MORRIS, ed. James Joyce, Dubliners and A Portrait of the Artist as a Young Man: A Selection of Critical Essays. London: Macmillan, 1973.
Contents: "Introduction," 15-32; "Background and Early Responses," 35-80; Harry Levin. "The Artist," 83-99, No. 1603; Brewster Ghiselin. "The Unity of Dubliners," 100-116, No. 2914; Frank O'Connor. "Joyce and Dissociated Metaphor," 117-123, No. 2878; Hugh Kenner. "Portrait in Perspective," 124-150, No. 1600; Maurice Beebe. "Joyce and Aquinas," 151-171, No. 3431; Richard Ellmann. "The Backgrounds of 'The Dead,'" 172-187, No. 308; Wayne C. Booth. "The Problem of Distance in Portrait," 188-201, No. 3218; J. I. M. Stewart. "Dubliners," 202-207, No. 1665; Morris Beja. "The Wooden Sword: Threatener and Threatened in the World of James Joyce," 208-223, No. 1693; Anthony Burgess. "A Paralysed City," 224-240, No. 1533; John Gross. "The Voyage Out," 241-244, No. 1580; "Select Bibliography," "Notes on Contributors."

2856. BOOTH, WAYNE C. "How to Use Aristotle," "Pluralism and Its Rivals," in his Now Don't Try to Reason with Me. Chicago, London: University of Chicago Press, 1970, pp. 117-129, 131-149. [With discussions of "Clay" and "Araby."]

2857. BOYLE, PATRICK. "Drums and Guns, Guns and Drums. Hurrah!, Hurrah!, in A Bash in the Tunnel, pp. 157-161, No. 1644.

119

STUDIES OF DUBLINERS

2858. COLUM, PADRAIC. "Dublin in Literature."
Bookman (London), 63 (July 1926): 555-
561; became the "Introduction" in Joyce's
Dubliners. New York: Modern Library,
1926, pp. v-xiii.

*2859. DEGUCHI, YASUO. "Dabuvin no Hito Bito"
["Dubliners"], in Joisu Nyumon [Introduc-
tion to James Joyce], pp. 18-26, No. 1511.

2860. DIAZ SOLIS, GUSTAVO. "James Joyce: La
'quidditas' en Dublineses," in Explora-
ciones críticas. Coleccion avance, 19.
Caracas: University Central de Venezuela,
1968, pp. 87-104.

2861. ENGEL, MONROE. "Dubliners and Erotic Expec-
tation," in Twentieth-Century Literature
in Retrospect. Harvard English Studies,
no. 2. Edited by Reuben A. Brower.
Cambridge, Mass.: Harvard University
Press, 1971, pp. 3-26.

2862. GARRETT, PETER, ed. Twentieth Century In-
terpretations of Dubliners: A Collection
of Critical Essays. Englewood Cliffs,
N.J.: Prentice-Hall, 1968.
Contents: Peter Garrett. "Introduc-
tion," pp. 1-17; Frank O'Connor. "Work in
Progress," 18-26, No. 2879; David Daiches.
"Dubliners," 27-37 (from No. 1548); Hugh
Kenner. 38-56 (from No. 1600); Brewster
Ghiselin. "The Unity of Joyce's Dublin-
ers," 57-85, No. 2914; S. L. Goldberg.
"The Artistry of Dubliners," 86-92, No.
1574; Ben L. Collins. "Joyce's 'Araby'
and the 'Extended Simile,'" 93-99, No.
2981; Robert Boyle. "'Two Gallants' and
'Ivy Day in the Committee Room,'" 100-
106, No. 3099; Florence L. Walzl. "Joyce's
'Clay,'" 107-109, No. 3083; C. C. Loomis.
"Structure and Sympathy in Joyce's 'The
Dead,'" 110-114, No. 3172.

2863. GIFFORD, DON, with the assistance of Robert
J. Seidman. Notes for Joyce: Dubliners
and Portrait of the Artist. New York:
E. P. Dutton; Toronto: Clarke, Irwin,
1967.

2864. GOULD, GERALD. "A Review of Dubliners," in
Joyce's The Dead, pp. 71-73, No. 3138.
[See also No. 3138.]

2865. HALTER, PETER. "Die epiphanien in James
Joyce's Dubliners," in Katherine Mansfield und die Kurzgeschichte. Schweizer
anglistische Arbeiten, Bd. 71. Zürich:
Francke Vlg., 1972, pp. 56-73.

2866. HART, CLIVE, ed. James Joyce's Dubliners:
Critical Essays. New York: Viking;
London: Faber and Faber, 1969.
Contents: Clive Hart. "Preface," 9-
11; John William Corrington. "'The Sis-
ters,'" 13-25, No. 2947; Fritz Senn. "'An
Encounter,'" 26-38, No. 2969; J. S. Ather-
ton. "'Araby,'" 39-47, No. 2973; Clive

Hart. "'Eveline,'" 48-52, No. 3009; Zack
Bowen. "'After the Race,'" 53-61, No.
3021; A. Walton Litz. "'Two Gallants,'"
62-71, No. 3028; Nathan Halper. "'The
Boarding House,'" 72-83, No. 3031; Robert
Boyle. "'A Little Cloud,'" 84-92, No.
3035; Robert Scholes. "'Counterparts,'"
93-99, No. 3052; Adaline Glasheen.
"'Clay,'" 100-106, No. 3068; Thomas E.
Connolly. "'A Painful Case,'" 107-114, No.
3087; M. J. C. Hodgart. "'Ivy Day in the
Committee Room,'" 115-121, No. 3102; David
Hayman. "'A Mother,'" 122-133, No. 3108;
Richard M. Kain. "'Grace,'" 134-152, No.
3119; Bernard Benstock. "'The Dead,'" 153-
169, No. 3126; "Appendix," 171-179; "Notes
on Contributors," 181-183.

2867. INGRAM, FORREST L. "American Short Story
Cycles: Foreign Influences and Parallels,"
in Proceedings of the Comparative Literature Symposium, vol. 5. Edited by Wolodymyr T. Zyla and Wendell M. Aycock. Lubbock, Texas: Texas Tech Press, 1971, pp.
19-37.

2868. _____. Representative Short Story Cycles
of the Twentieth Century: Studies in a
Literary Genre. Hague: Mouton, 1971, pp.
21-23, 26-34, et passim.

2869. KILCHENMANN, RUTH J. Die Kurzgeschichte:
Formen und Entwicklung. Sprache und Literatur, Bd. 37. Stuttgart: W. Kohlhammer,
1967, passim.

2870. KORNINGER, SIEGFRIED. "Artistic Integration
in Joyce's Dubliners," in Festschrift
Prof. Dr. Herbert Koziol zum siebzigsten
Geburtstag. Wiener Beiträge zur englis-
chen Philologie, no. 75. Vienna: Wilhelm
Braumüller, 1973, pp. 147-168.

2871. LANE, GARY, ed. A Word Index to James
Joyce's Dubliners. Programmed by Roland
Dedekind. New York: Haskell House, 1972.

2872. LaVALLEY, ALBERT J. "'Doublin Their Mamper':
Some Thoughts on the Symbolist Drama of
Joyce's Dubliners," in Literary Studies:
Essays in Memory of Francis A. Drumm.
Edited by John H. Dorenkamp. Worcester,
Mass.: College of the Holy Cross, 1973,
pp. 172-190.

*2873. LUDWIG, JACK BARRY. "James Joyce's Dublin-
ers," in Stories: British and American.
Edited by J. B. Ludwig and W. Richard
Poirier. Boston: Houghton Mifflin, 1953,
pp. 384-391.

*2874. MACY, JOHN. The Critical Game. New York:
Boni and Liveright, 1922, p. 322.

2875. MAGALANER, MARVIN. Time of Apprenticeship:
The Fiction of Young James Joyce. New
York: Abelard-Schuman, 1959. [Re-

printed Freeport, New York: Books for Libraries, 1970.]

2876. MARX, PAUL. Instructor's Manual for Twelve Short Story Writers. New York: Holt, Rinehart, Winston, 1970, pp. 10-13. [On "Araby," "The Boarding House," "The Dead."]

2877. MURPHY, GERALDINE. The Study of Literature in High School. Waltham, Mass.: Blais-dell, 1968, passim.

2878. O'CONNOR, FRANK (Michael O'Donovan). "Joyce and Dissociated Metaphor," in his The Mirror in the Roadway: A Study of the Modern Novel. New York: Knopf, 1956, pp. 295-312. [Reprinted in Joyce's The Dead, pp. 89-92, No. 3138; reprinted by Free-port, New York: Books for Libraries, 1970, pp. 295-312.]

2879. _____. "Work in Progress," in his The Lonely Voice: A Study of the Short Story. Cleveland: World Publishing Co., 1963; London: Macmillan, 1966, pp. 113-127. [Reprinted in Twentieth Century Interpre-tations of Dubliners, pp. 18-26, No. 2862; in James Joyce's Dubliners, pp. 304-315, No. 2885.]

2880. QUASHA, GEORGE. James Joyce's Dubliners and A Portrait of the Artist as a Young Man. Monarch Notes and Study Guides. New York: Monarch Press, 1965.

2881. REICHERT, KLAUS, FRITZ SENN, and DIETER E. ZIMMER, eds. Materialien zu James Joyces Dubliner. Frankfurt a. M.: Suhrkamp, 1969. Supplement to the Frankfurter Ausgabe translation.
    Contents: German translation of early Joyce items and letters; from Stanislaus Joyce's My Brother's Keeper and Dublin Diary (Nos. 329, 330); from early reviews; from articles by Michael J. O'Neill (No. 3109) and Richard Ellmann (No. 3157); "Anmerkungen," pp. 233-272; "Bibliogra-phie," pp. 273-290. All material trans-lated into German.

2882. RUBINSTEIN, JOSEPH, and EARL FARLEY. He who destoyes a good Booke, kills reason it selfe: an exhibition of books which have survived Fire, the Sword, and the Censors. Lawrence, Kansas: University of Kansas Library, 1955, p. 10.

2883. SAN JUAN, EPIFANIO. James Joyce and the Craft of Fiction: An Interpretation of Dubliners. Rutherford, N.J.: Farleigh Dickinson University Press, 1972.

2884. SAUL, GEORGE BRANDON. "James Joyce," in Rushlight Heritage: Reflections on Se-lected Irish Short-Story Writers of the Yeatsian Era. Philadelphia: Walton Press, 1969, pp. 55-61.

2885. SCHOLES, ROBERT, and A. WALTON LITZ, eds. James Joyce's Dubliners: Text, Criticism, and Notes. New York: Viking, 1969.
    Contents: Editors' "Preface"; "Dub-liners" in the Scholes-Ellmann text, with "further corrections...based on sugges-tions by Jack P. Dalton"; "Dubliners: Background," with sections entitled "Chronology," "The Composition and Revi-sion of the Stories," "Epiphanies and Epicleti," "The Evidence of the Letters"; Frank O'Connor. "Work in Progress," 304-315 (from No. 2879); Brewster Ghiselin. "The Unity of Dubliners," 316-322, No. 2914; Edward Brandabur. "'The Sisters,'" 333-343 (first published); Harry Stone. "'Araby,'" 344-367, No. 3004; A. Walton Litz. "'Two Gallants,'" 368-378 (from No. 3028); Robert Scholes. "'Counterparts,'" 379-387 (from No. 3052); Richard Ellmann. "Backgrounds of 'The Dead,'" 388-403 (from No. 308); Allen Tate. "'The Dead,'" 404-409, No. 3131; Kenneth Burke. "'Stages' in 'The Dead,'" 410-416, No. 1428; C. C. Loomis. "Structure and Sympathy in 'The Dead,'" 417-422, No. 3172; Florence L. Walzl. "Gabriel and Michael: The Conclu-sion of 'The Dead,'" 423-444, No. 3193.

2886. SKLARE, ARNOLD B., and WILLIAM E. BUCKLER. "Questions for Discussion and Writing." Stories from Six Authors, 2nd series. New York: McGraw-Hill, 1966, pp. 154-158. [On 'A Little Cloud,' 'A Mother,' 'An Encounter,' 'A Painful Case,' 'Grace.']

2887. SLOCUM, JOHN J., and HERBERT CAHOON. "Intro-duction," in A James Joyce Miscellany, Third Series, pp. 3-5, No. 1614. [Intro-ductory notes to "Christmas Eve" previ-ously unpublished short story fragment by Joyce, pp. 5-7.]

*2888. THURSTON, JARVIS et al. "James Joyce." Short Fiction Criticism: A Checklist of Interpretation. Denver: Alan Swallow, 1960, pp. 115-120.

*2889. WALKER, WARREN S. "James Joyce." Twentieth-Century Short Story Explication. Hamden, Conn.: Shoe String Press, 1961, pp. 206-215; Supplement, 1963, pp. 68-71. [Sec-ond edition, 1967, pp. 358-374; supple-ment to second edition, 1973, vol. 2, pp. 76-80.]

2890. WHITE, ALISON. "The Devil Has a Dublin Ac-cent," in Children's Literature: The Great Excluded, vol. 2. Edited by Francelia Butler. Storrs, Conn.: Children's Liter-ature Association, 1973, pp. 139-141.

Periodical Articles

2891. ADICKS, RICHARD. "The Unconsecrated Euchar-ist in Dubliners." Studies in Short Fic-tion, 5 (Spring 1968): 295-296.

STUDIES OF DUBLINERS

2892. BECKSON, KARL. "Moore's The Untilled Field and Joyce's Dubliners: The Short Story's Intricate Maze." English Literature in Transition, 15, no. 4 (1972): 291-304.

2893. BOYLE, ROBERT. "'Two Gallants' and 'Ivy Day in the Committee Room.'" James Joyce Quarterly, 1 (Fall 1963): 3-9.

*2894. BUDRECKI, LECH. "Poczatek Ulissesa ["The Beginnings of Ulysses]." Tworczosc (Warsaw), 15 (June 1959): 136-141. [Review article based on Polish translation of Dubliners.]

*2895. BUSCH, GÜNTHER. "Einspruch gegen das Hauptwerk: Zur Neuauflage des 'Jugendbildnesses' und der Novellen 'Dublin' von James Joyce." Wort in der Zeit, 5 (1959): 45-48.

2896. CAMERON, K. N. [n.t.]. McGilliad (February-March 1931).

2897. CARRIER, WARREN. "Dubliners: Joyce's Dantean Vision." Renascence, 17 (Summer 1965): 211-215.

2898. CHATMAN, SEYMOUR. "New Ways of Analyzing Narrative Structure, with an Example from Joyce's Dubliners." Language and Style, 2 (1969): 3-36.

2899. CHURCH, MARGARET. "Dubliners and Vico." James Joyce Quarterly, 5 (Winter 1968): 150-156.

2900. COOKE, M. G. "From Comedy to Terror: On Dubliners and the Development of Tone and Structure in the Modern Short Story." Massachusetts Review, 9 (Spring 1968): 331-343.

2901. COPE, JACKSON I. "An Epigraph for Dubliners." James Joyce Quarterly, 7 (Summer 1970): 362-364.

2902. DAVIS, JOSEPH K. "The City as Radical Order: James Joyce's Dubliners." Studies in the Literary Imagination, 3 (October 1970): 79-96.

2903. DAVIS, WILLIAM V. "Point of View in Joyce's Dubliners." CEA Critic, 31 (April 1969): 6.

2904. DELANY, PAUL. "Joyce's Political Development and the Aesthetic of Dubliners." College English, 34 (November 1972): 256-266. [See Gaylord C. LeRoy, "Comment," pp. 266-268.]

*2905. de PIERREFEU, JEAN. "Les Oeuvres de James Joyce: Ontelles Mérité d'Être Brûlées?" Le quotidien (Paris), 7 June 1926, p. 2.

2906. DUFFY, JOHN J. "Ernest Dowson and the Failure of Decadence." University of Kansas City Review, 34 (October 1967): 45-49.

2907. _____. "The Stories of Frederick Wedmore: Some Correspondences with Dubliners." James Joyce Quarterly, 5 (Winter 1968): 144-149.

2908. EGRI, PÉTER. "Thomas Mann és James Joyce elsö vilaghaboru elötti novellai." Filologiai Kazlony (Budapest), 9 (January-June 1963): 71-86.

2909. FREYER, GRATTAN. "A Reader's Report on Dubliners." James Joyce Quarterly, 10 (Summer 1973): 455-457.

2910. FRIEDRICH, GERHARD. "The Gnomonic Clue to James Joyce's Dubliners." Modern Language Notes, 62 (June 1957): 421-424.

2911. _____. "Joyce's Pattern of Paralysis in Dubliners." College English, 22 (April 1961): 519-520. [Reply to Walzl, No. 2941.]

2912. _____. "The Perspective of Joyce's Dubliners." College English, 26 (March 1965): 421-426. [Reprinted in James Joyce's Dubliners: A Critical Handbook, pp. 71-78, No. 2852.]

*2913. FRYE, NORTHROP. "Four Forms of Prose Fiction." Hudson Review, 2 (Winter 1950): 582-595.

2914. GHISELIN, BREWSTER. "The Unity of Joyce's Dubliners." Accent, 16 (Spring 1956): 75-88; (Summer 1956): 196-213. [Reprinted in Twentieth Century Interpretations of Dubliners, pp. 57-85, No. 2862; in James Joyce's Dubliners: A Critical Handbook, pp. 35-62, No. 2852; in James Joyce's Dubliners: Text, Criticism and Notes, pp. 316-332, No. 2885.]

2915. GIBBONS, T. H. "Dubliners and the Critics." Critical Quarterly, 9 (Summer 1967): 179-187.

2916. HAAS, WILLY. "Konfessionen aus dem Inferno." Die literarische Welt, 21 (May 1926): 7-8. [Reprinted as "James Joyces Jugendbildnis," in his Gestalten. Berlin: Propylaen Vlg., 1962, pp. 159-162.]

*2917. HARMON, MAURICE. "The Early Joyce." Northwest Review, 3 (Fall-Winter 1959): 60-66.

2918. HART, JOHN RAYMOND. "Moore on Joyce: The Influence of The Untilled Field on Dubliners." Dublin Magazine, 10 (Summer 1973): 61-76.

2919. HASEGAWA, KAZUO. ["Dubliners by James Joyce." Joyce"]. Shosen Koto senmon gakko kiyo, no. 3 (March 1971): 334-344. [In Japanese.]

2920. JEDYNAK, STANLEY L. "Epiphany as Structure in Dubliners." Greyfriar, 12 (1971): 29-56.

2921. JOYCE, STANISLAUS. "The Backgrounds to Dubliners." Listener, 51 (March 1954): 526-527.

2922. KENNEDY, SISTER EILEEN. "Moore's Untilled Field and Joyce's Dubliners." Éire-Ireland, 5 (Autumn 1970): 81-89.

2923. LACHTMAN, HOWARD. "The Magic-Lantern Business: James Joyce's Ecclesiastical Satire in Dubliners." James Joyce Quarterly, 7 (Winter 1969): 82-92.

2924. LESTER, JOHN A. "Joyce, Yeats, and the Short Story." English Literature in Transition, 15, no. 4 (1972): 305-314.

2925. LEVIN, RICHARD, and CHARLES SHATTUCK. "First Flight to Ithaca: A New Reading of Joyce's Dubliners." Accent, 4 (Winter 1944): 75-99. [Reprinted in James Joyce: Two Decades of Criticism, pp. 47-94, No. 1570.]

2926. MAGALANER, MARVIN. "James Joyce and the Uncommon Reader." South Atlantic Quarterly, 52 (April 1953): 267-276.

2927. MURPHY, MICHAEL W. "Darkness in Dubliners." Modern Fiction Studies, 15 (Spring 1969): 97-104.

2928. NAGAHARA, KAZUO. ["Dubliners--The Centre of Paralysis"]. Otaru shoka daigaku jinmon kenkyu, no. 43 (November 1971): 217-248. [In Japanese.]

2929. OSTROFF, ANTHONY. "The Moral Vision in Dubliners." Western Speech, 20 (Fall 1956): 196-209.

2930. PETERSON, RICHARD F. "Joyce's Use of Time in Dubliners." Ball State University Forum, 14 (Fall 1973): 43-51.

2931. PRITCHARD, WILLIAM H. "Related Exercise on Joyce and Faulkner." Exercise Exchange, 10 (November 1962): 3-5.

2932. PRITCHETT, V. S. "Current Literature: Books in General." New Statesman and Nation, 21 (15 February 1941): 162.

2933. RUSSELL, JOHN. "James Joyce's Sentences (Dubliners)." Style, 6 (Fall 1972): 260-293.

2934. RYAN, MARJORIE. "Dubliners and the Stories of Katherine Anne Porter." American Literature, 31 (January 1960): 464-473.

2935. SCHOLES, ROBERT. "Grant Richards to James Joyce." Studies in Bibliography, 16 (1963): 139-160.

2936. _____. "Further Observations on the Text of Dubliners." Studies in Bibliography, 17 (1964): 107-122.

2937. TORCHIANA, DONALD T. "The Opening of Dubliners: A Reconsideration." Irish University Review, 1 (Spring 1971): 149-160.

2938. VERHAEGHEN, VICTOR. "Capriolen on Joyce." De Periscoop, 8 (1 September 1958): 7. [Discussion of Magalaner's theory of the foundation of Dubliners upon Homer's Odyssey, No. 2875.]

2939. W., D. "Die Dubliner--Übersetzung als Liebsmüh; Gespräch mit Dieter E. Zimmer." Die Weltwoch (Zürich), 6 February 1970, p. 27.

2940. WALSH, RUTH M. "That Pervasive Mass-in Dubliners and Portrait of the Artist." James Joyce Quarterly, 8 (Spring 1971): 205-220. [Complements earlier article, "In the Name of the Father and of the Son...Joyce's Use of the Mass in Ulysses," No. 4109.]

2941. WALZL, FLORENCE L. "Pattern of Paralysis in Joyce's Dubliners: A Study of the Original Framework." College English, 22 (January 1961): 221-228. [See response by Gerhard Friedrich, No. 2911, and Walzl's reply College English, 22 (April 1961): 520.]

2942. WIGGINTON, B. ELIOT. "Dubliners in Order." James Joyce Quarterly, 7 (Summer 1970): 297-314.

"THE SISTERS"

2943. BENSTOCK, BERNARD. "Joyce's 'The Sisters.'" Explicator, 24 (September 1965): item 1.

2944. _____. "'The Sisters' and the Critics." James Joyce Quarterly, 4 (Fall 1966): 32-35.

2945. BRANDABUR, EDWARD. "'The Sisters,'" in James Joyce's Dubliners: Text, Criticism, and Notes, pp. 333-343, No. 2885.

2946. CONNOLLY, THOMAS E. "Joyce's 'The Sisters': A Pennyworth of Snuff." College English, 27 (December 1965): 189-195. [Reprinted in James Joyce's Dubliners: A Critical Handbook, pp. 79-86, No. 2852.]

2947. CORRINGTON, JOHN WILLIAM. "'The Sisters,'" in James Joyce's Dubliners: Critical Essays, pp. 13-25, No. 2866.

2948. DOHERTY, PAUL C. "Words as Idols: The Epiphany in James Joyce's 'The Sisters.'" CEA Critic, 32 (October 1969): 10-11.

2949. FABIAN, DAVID R. "Joyce's 'The Sisters': Gnomon, Gnomic, Gnome." Studies in Short Fiction, 5 (Winter 1968): 187-189.

STUDIES OF DUBLINERS

2950. FAHEY, WILLIAM. "Joyce's 'The Sisters.'" Explicator, 17 (January 1959): item 26.

2951. FISCHER, THERESE. "From Reliable to Unreliable Narrator: Rhetorical Changes in Joyce's 'The Sisters.'" James Joyce Quarterly, 9 (Fall 1971): 85-92.

2952. GLEESON, W. F., JR. "Joyce's 'The Sisters.'" Explicator, 22 (December 1963): item 30.

2953. KRUSE, HORST. "Joyce: 'The Sisters,'" in Die englische Kurzgeschichte. Edited by Karl Heinz Göller and Gerhard Hoffmann. Düsseldorf: August Bagel Vlg., 1973, pp. 147-161, 368-372.

2954. KUEHL, JOHN. "A la Joyce: The Sisters Fitzgerald's Absolution." James Joyce Quarterly, 2 (Fall 1964): 2-6. ['The Sisters' and 'Absolution.']

2955. MAGALANER, MARVIN. "'The Sisters' of James Joyce." University of Kansas City Review, 18 (Summer 1952): 255-261. [Also in Configuration critique I, pp. 276-287, No. 1636.]

2956. REYNOLDS, MICHAEL S. "The Feast of the Most Precious Blood and Joyce's 'The Sisters.'" Studies in Short Fiction, 6 (Spring 1969): 336.

2957. SAN JUAN, EPIFANIO. "Method and Meaning in Joyce's 'The Sisters.'" Die neuren Sprachen, 20 (1971): 490-496. [Also in his James Joyce and the Craft of Fiction, No. 2883.]

2958. SENN, FRITZ. "'He was too scrupulous always': Joyce's 'The Sisters.'" James Joyce Quarterly, 2 (Winter 1965): 66-72.

2959. SPIELBERG, PETER. "'The Sisters': No Christ at Bethany." James Joyce Quarterly, 3 (Spring 1966): 192-195.

2960. STEIN, WILLIAM B. "Joyce's 'The Sisters.'" Explicator, 20 (March 1962): item 61; 21 (September 1962): item 2.

2961. WALZL, FLORENCE L. "A Date in Joyce's 'The Sisters.'" Texas Studies in Literature and Language, 4 (Summer 1962): 183-187.

2962. _____. "Joyce's 'The Sisters': A Development." James Joyce Quarterly, 10 (Summer 1973): 375-421.

2963. WEST, MICHAEL. "Old Cotter and the Enigma of Joyce's 'The Sisters.'" Modern Philology, 67 (May 1970): 370-372.

"AN ENCOUNTER"

2964. BLUEFARB, SAM. "Quest, Initiation, and Escape: 'American' Themes in James Joyce's 'An Encounter.'" Dublin Magazine, 10 (Summer 1973): 53-60.

2965. DAVIES, WALFORD. "Imitation and Invention: The Use of Borrowed Material in Dylan Thomas' Prose." Essays in Criticism, 18 (July 1968): 275-295. [Thomas' 'Who do you wish was with us' and 'An Encounter.']

2966. DEGNAN, JAMES P. "The Reluctant Indian in Joyce's 'An Encounter.'" Studies in Short Fiction, 6 (Winter 1969): 152-156.

2967. FESHBACH, SIDNEY. "Death in 'An Encounter.'" James Joyce Quarterly, 2 (Winter 1965): 82-89.

2968. KAYE, JULIAN B. "The Wings of Daedalus: Two Stories in Dubliners." Modern Fiction Studies, 4 (Spring 1958): 31-41. [Reprinted in James Joyce's Dubliners: A Critical Handbook, pp. 87-92, No. 2852.]

2969. SENN, FRITZ. "'An Encounter,'" in James Joyce's Dubliners: Critical Essays, pp. 26-38, No. 2866.

2970. THORNBURN, DAVID. "Reading Fiction: Joyce's 'An Encounter.'" Report of the Yale Conference on the Teaching of English, 14 (April 1968): 51-63.

2971. VAN VOORHIS, JOHN W. "The Smoothing Iron: A Topographical Note to 'An Encounter.'" James Joyce Quarterly, 10 (Winter 1973): 266.

"ARABY"

2972. apROBERTS, ROBERT P. "'Araby' and the Palimpset of Criticism; or, Through a Glass Eye Darkly." Antioch Review, 26 (Winter 1966/67): 469-489. [Reply to Harry Stone, No. 3004.]

2973. ATHERTON, J. S. "'Araby,'" in James Joyce's Dubliners: Critical Essays, pp. 39-47, No. 2866.

2974. BACON, WALLACE A. The Art of Interpretation. Second edition. New York: Holt, Rinehart and Winston, 1972, pp. 44-47, 422-425.

2975. BARROLL, J. LEEDS, III, and AUSTIN M. WRIGHT. "Thought and Feeling," in The Art of the Short Story: An Introductory Anthology. Boston: Allyn and Bacon, 1969, pp. 25-27.

2976. BENSTOCK, BERNARD. "Arabesques: Third Position of Concord." James Joyce Quarterly, 5 (Fall 1967): 30-39.

2977. BONAZZA, BLAZE O., and EMIL ROY, eds. Studies in Fiction. New York: Harper and Row, 1965, pp. 24-28. [Instructor's Manual to Accompany Studies in Fiction. New York: Harper and Row, 1965, pp. 1-2.]

2978. BROOKS, CLEANTH, and ROBERT PENN WARREN. "An Interpretation of 'Araby,'" in Understanding Fiction. New York: Crofts, 1944, pp. 420-423. [Reprinted as The Scope of Fiction. New York: Appleton-Century-Crofts, 1960, pp. 169-172; reprinted in Prose and Criticism. Edited by John Hamilton McCallum. New York: Harcourt, Brace and World, 1966, pp. 674-676 from 2nd edition; reprinted in James Joyce's Dubliners: A Critical Handbook, pp. 73-76, No. 2852.]

2979. _____ , and JOHN T. PURSER. An Approach to Literature. Third edition. New York: Appleton-Century-Crofts, 1952, pp. 188-191.

2980. BURTO, WILLIAM. "Joyce's 'Araby.'" Explicator, 25 (April 1967): item 67.

2981. COLLINS, BEN L. "Joyce's 'Araby' and the 'Extended Simile.'" James Joyce Quarterly, 4 (Winter 1967): 84-90. [Reprinted in Twentieth Century Interpretations of Dubliners, pp. 93-99, No. 2862.]

2982. DADUFALZA, CONCEPCION D. "The Quest of the Chalice Bearer in James Joyce's 'Araby.'" Diliman Review, 7 (July 1959): 317-325.

2983. FREIMARCK, JOHN. "'Araby': A Quest for Meaning." James Joyce Quarterly, 7 (Summer 1970): 366-368.

2984. FRIEDMAN, STANLEY. "Joyce's 'Araby.'" Explicator, 24 (June 1966): item 43.

2985. FULLER, JAMES A. "A Note on Joyce's 'Araby.'" CEA Critic, 20 (February 1958): 8.

2986. GARRISON, JOSEPH M., JR. "The Adult Consciousness of the Narrator in Joyce's 'Araby." Studies in Short Fiction, 10 (Fall 1973): 416-417.

2987. GOING, WILLIAM T. "Joyce's 'Araby.'" Explicator, 26 (January 1968): item 39.

2988. GROSS, THEODORE, and NORMAN KELVIN. An Introduction to Fiction. New York: Random House, 1967, pp. 173-179.

2989. GUERIN, WILFRED L, et al. Manual for Mandala. New York: Harper College Books, 1970, pp. 17-19.

2990. HAMILTON, ALICE. "Between Innocence and Experience: From Joyce to Updike." Dalhousie Review, 49 (Spring 1969): 102-109. ['Araby' and 'You'll Never Know, Dear, How Much I Love You.']

2991. HIRSCH, DAVID H. "Linguistic Structure and Literary Meaning." Journal of Literary Semantics, 1 (1972): 80-88. [Response to Ohmann, No. 2999.]

2992. LaHOOD, MARVIN J. "A Note on the Priest in Joyce's 'Araby.'" Revue des langues vivantes, 34, no. 1 (1968): 24-25.

2993. LYONS, JOHN O. "James Joyce and Chaucer's Prioress." English Language Notes, 2 (December 1964): 127-132.

2994. MALE, ROY R. "The Story of the Sensitive Young Man: A Brief Comparative Analysis," in Types of Short Fiction. Belmont, Calif.: Wadsworth, 1962, pp. 31-34. ['Araby,' Willa Cather's 'Paul's Case,' Sherwood Anderson's 'I Want to Know Why.']

2995. MANDEL, JEROME. "The Structure of 'Araby.'" Modern Language Studies, 3 (Spring 1973): 48.

2996. MARCUS, FRED H. Manual for Perception and Pleasure. Boston: Heath, 1968, pp. 27-28.

2997. MELLARD, JAMES M. Four Modes: A Rhetoric of Modern Fiction. New York: Macmillan, 1973, pp. 335-337.

2998. MIZENER, ARTHUR. A Handbook to Modern Short Stories: The Use of the Imagination. New York: W. W. Norton, 1971, pp. 138-140.

2999. OHMANN, RICHARD. "Literature as Sentences." College English, 27 (January 1966): 261-267. [See comment by John Russell, No. 3002 and David Hirsch, No. 2991.]

3000. PETERS, MARGOT. "The Phonological Structure of James Joyce's 'Araby.'" Language and Style, 6 (Spring 1973): 135-144.

3001. ROHRBERGER, MARY, SAMUEL H. WOODS, and BERNARD F. DUKORE. "For Comment," in An Introduction to Literature. New York: Random House, 1968, pp. 181-182.

3002. RUSSELL, JOHN. "From Style to Meaning in 'Araby.'" College English, 28 (November 1966): 170-171. [Reply to Richard Ohmann, No. 2999; Ohmann's rebuttal, pp. 171-173.]

3003. STEIN, WILLIAM B. "Joyce's 'Araby': Paradise Lost." Perspective, 12 (Spring 1962): 215-222.

3004. STONE, HARRY. "'Araby' and the Writings of James Joyce." Antioch Review, 25 (Fall 1965): 375-410. [Reprinted in James Joyce's Dubliners: Text, Criticism, and Notes, pp. 344-367, No. 2885.]

3005. TURAJ, FRANK. "'Araby' and Portrait: Stages of Pagan Conversion." English Language Notes, 7 (1970): 209-213.

3006. WALDHORN, ARTHUR, and HILDA K. "'Araby,'" in The Rite of Becoming: Stories and Studies of Adolescence. Cleveland: World, 1966, pp. 145-146, 150-152.

STUDIES OF DUBLINERS

3007.   WEST, RAY B. "The Use of Theme in 'Araby,'"
        in Reading the Short Story. New York:
        Thomas Y. Crowell, 1968, pp. 123-128.

"EVELINE"

3008.   DOLCH, MARTIN. "'Eveline,'" in Insight II:
        Analyses of Modern British Literature.
        Edited by John V. Hagopian and Martin
        Dolch. Frankfurt a. M.: Hirschgraben
        Vlg., 1964, pp. 193-200. [Reprinted in
        James Joyce's Dubliners: A Critical Hand-
        book, pp. 96-101, No. 2852.]

3009.   HART, CLIVE. "Eveline,'" in James Joyce's
        Dubliners: Critical Essays, pp. 48-52,
        No. 2866.

3010.   HEDBERG, JOHANNES. "'Derevaun Seraun'--A
        Joycean Puzzle." Moderna Språk, 60
        (1966): 109-110.

3011.   MOSELEY, VIRGINIA. "The 'Dangerous' Paradox
        in Joyce's 'Eveline.'" Costerus, 1
        (1972): 169-182.

3012.   PIRA, GISELA. "James Joyce: 'Eveline.'"
        Neuren sprachen, n.s. 16 (November 1967):
        552-554.

3013.   POOLEY, ROBERT C., GEORGE K. ANDERSON, PAUL
        FARMER, and HELEN THORNTON. "James Joyce's
        'Eveline.'" Teacher's Resource Book to
        Accompany England in Literature. Chicago:
        Scott, Foresman, 1965, pp. 187-188.

3014.   SAN JUAN, EPIFANIO. "'Eveline': Joyce's
        Affirmation of Ireland." Éire-Ireland,
        4 (Spring 1969): 46-52. [Also in his
        James Joyce and the Craft of Fiction,
        No. 2883.]

3015.   SOLOMON, ALBERT J. "The Backgrounds of
        'Eveline.'" Éire-Ireland, 6 (Fall 1971):
        23-28.

3016.   _____ . "The Sound of Music in 'Eveline':
        A Long Note on a Barrel-Organ." Costerus,
        9 (1973): 187-194.

3017.   STEIN, WILLIAM B. "The Effects of Eden in
        Joyce's 'Eveline.'" Renascence, 15
        (Winter 1962): 124-126.

3018.   TAUBE, MYRON. "Joyce and Shakespeare: 'Eve-
        line' and Othello." James Joyce Quarter-
        ly, 4 (Winter 1967): 152-153.

3019.   TORCHIANA, DONALD T. "Joyce's 'Eveline' and
        the Blessed Margaret Mary Alacoque."
        James Joyce Quarterly, 6 (Fall 1968): 22-
        28.

3020.   WILDING, MICHAEL. "James Joyce's 'Eveline'
        and The Portrait of a Lady." English
        Studies, 49 (December 1968): 552-556.

"AFTER THE RACE"

3021.   BOWEN, ZACK. "'After the Race,'" in James
        Joyce's Dubliners: Critical Essays, pp.
        53-61, No. 2866.

3022.   _____ . "Hungarian Politics in 'After the
        Race,'" James Joyce Quarterly, 7 (Winter
        1969): 138-139.

3023.   TORCHIANA, DONALD T. "Joyce's 'After the
        Race,' The Race of Castlebar, and Dun
        Laoghaire." Éire-Ireland, 6 (Fall 1971):
        119-128.

3024.   WARD, DAVID F. "The Race Before the Story:
        James Joyce and the Gordon Bennett Cup
        Automobile Race." Éire-Ireland, 2
        (Summer 1967): 27-35.

"TWO GALLANTS"

3025.   BOGORAD, SAMUEL N. "Saved or Stolen? the
        Gold Coin in 'Two Gallants.'" Éire-
        Ireland, 7 (Summer 1972): 62-66.

3026.   CINIGLIO, ADA V. "'Two Gallants': Joyce's
        Wedding Guests." James Joyce Quarterly,
        10 (Winter 1973): 264.

3027.   EPSTEIN, EDMUND L. "Hidden Imagery in James
        Joyce's 'Two Gallants.'" James Joyce
        Quarterly, 7 (Summer 1970): 369-370.

3028.   LITZ, A. WALTON. "'Two Gallants,'" in James
        Joyce's Dubliners: Critical Essays, pp.
        62-71, No. 2866. [Reprinted in James
        Joyce's Dubliners: Text, Criticism, and
        Notes, pp. 368-378, No. 2885.]

3029.   TORCHIANA, DONALD T. "Joyce's 'Two Gallants':
        A Walk Through the Ascendancy." James
        Joyce Quarterly, 6 (Winter 1968): 115-127.

3030.   WALZL, FLORENCE L. "Symbolism in Joyce's
        'Two Gallants.'" James Joyce Quarterly,
        2 (Winter 1965): 73-81.

"THE BOARDING HOUSE"

3031.   HALPER, NATHAN. "'The Boarding House,'" in
        James Joyce's Dubliners: Critical Essays,
        pp. 72-83, No. 2866.

3032.   KENNER, HUGH. Studies in Change: A Book of
        of the Short Story. Englewood Cliffs,
        N.J.: Prentice-Hall, 1965, pp. 7-11.

3033.   ROSENBERG, BRUCE A. "The Crucifixion in 'The
        Boarding House.'" Studies in Short Fic-
        tion, 5 (Fall 1967): 44-53.

3034.   SAN JUAN, EPIFANIO. "Joyce's 'The Boarding
        House.'" University Review, 35 (March
        1969): 229-236. [Also in his James Joyce
        and the Craft of Fiction, No. 2883.]

"A LITTLE CLOUD"

3035. BOYLE, ROBERT. "'A Little Cloud,'" in James Joyce's Dubliners: Critical Essays, pp. 84-92, No. 2866.

3036. BRODBAR, HAROLD. "A Religious Allegory: Joyce's 'A Little Cloud.'" Midwest Quarterly, 2 (Spring 1961): 221-227.

3037. CASTY, ALAN. Teaching Suggestions and Examples for the Shape of Fiction. Boston: Raytheon, 1967, pp. 1-2, 18-20.

*3038. COX, SIDNEY, and EDMUND FREEMAN, eds. Prose Preferences. New York, London: Harper and Bros., 1924, pp. 115-130.

3039. HARMON, MAURICE. "Little Chandler and Byron's 'First Poem.'" Threshold, no. 17 (1962): 59-61.

3040. HEILMAN, ROBERT B., ed. Modern Short Stories: A Critical Anthology. New York: Harcourt, Brace, 1950, pp. 133-147.

3041. JAFFE, ADRIAN H., and VIRGIL SCOTT. Instructor's Manual for Studies in the Short Story. Third edition. New York: Holt, Rinehart and Winston, 1968, pp. 87-90.

3042. PERRINE, LAURENCE, ed. Story and Structure, Second edition. New York: Harcourt, Brace, 1966, pp. 88-99.

3043. RUOFF, JAMES. "'A Little Cloud': Joyce's Portrait of the Would-be Artist." Research Studies of the State College of Washington, 25 (September 1957): 256-271. [Reprinted in James Joyce's Dubliners: A Critical Handbook, pp. 107-120, No. 2852.]

3044. SCHORER, MARK, ed. The Story: A Critical Anthology. New York: Prentice-Hall, 1950, pp. 288-305.

3045. SHORT, CLARICE. "Joyce's 'A Little Cloud.'" Modern Language Notes, 72 (April 1957): 275-278.

3046. SOLOMON, ALBERT J. "'The Celtic Note' in 'A Little Cloud.'" Studies in Short Fiction, 9 (Summer 1972): 269-270.

"COUNTERPARTS"

3047. BROWN, WENTWORTH K., and STERLING P. OLMSTEAD. Language and Literature. New York: Harcourt, Brace and World, 1962, pp. 240-255, 359-361.

3048. DAVIS, WILLIAM V. "The Loss of Time in 'Counterparts.'" James Joyce Quarterly, 10 (Spring 1973): 336-339.

3049. FOFF, ARTHUR, and DANIEL KNAPP. "Analysis," in Story: An Introduction to Prose Fiction. Belmont, Calif.: Wadsworth, 1964, pp. 142-145.

3050. GOPALEEN, MYLES na (Flann O'Brien, Brian Nolan). "Cruiskeen Lawn." Irish Times, 20 July 1955.

3051. HAGOPIAN, JOHN V. "'Counterparts,'" in Insight II: Analyses of Modern British Literature. Edited by John V. Hagopian and Martin Dolch. Frankfurt a. M.: Hirschgraben Vlg., 1964, pp. 201-206; in slightly different form in Studies in Short Fiction, 1 (Summer 1964): 272-276. [Reprinted in James Joyce's Dubliners: A Critical Handbook, pp. 120-124, No. 2852.]

3052. SCHOLES, ROBERT. "'Counterparts' and the Method of Dubliners," in James Joyce's Dubliners: Critical Essays, pp. 93-99, No. 2866. [Reprinted in James Joyce's Dubliners: Text, Criticism, and Notes, pp. 379-387, No. 2885.]

3053. SCOTT, VIRGIL. "James Joyce: 'Counterparts'; 'The Boarding House,'" in Instructor's Manual for Studies in the Short Story. Alternate edition. New York: Holt, Rinehart, and Winston, 1971, pp. 67-69, 94-96.

3054. SIDER, DAVID. "'Counterparts' and the Odyssey." James Joyce Quarterly, 8 (Winter 1970): 182-184.

3055. SKAGGS, CALVIN, and MERRILL M. SKAGGS. Instructor's Manual for Galaxy. New York: Harcourt, Brace and World, 1967, pp. 23-25.

3056. STEIN, WILLIAM B. "'Counterparts': A Swine Song." James Joyce Quarterly, 1 (Winter 1964): 30-32.

"CLAY"

3057. BROOKS, CLEANTH. "The Criticism of Fiction: The Role of Close Analysis," in A Shaping Joy: Studies in the Writer's Craft. New York: Harcourt, Brace, Jovanovich, 1971, pp. 143-165.

3058. _____, JOHN T. PURSER, and ROBERT PENN WARREN, eds. An Approach to Literature. Third edition. New York: Appleton-Century-Crofts, 1952, pp. 137-140. [Fourth edition, changed and expanded. New York: Appleton-Century-Crofts, 1964, pp. 63-65.]

3059. CARPENTER, RICHARD, and DANIEL LEARY. "The Witch Maria." James Joyce Review, 3, nos. 1-2 (February 1959): 3-7.

3060. CONNOLLY, FRANCIS. The Types of Literature. New York: Harcourt, Brace, 1955, pp. 127-130, 709-710.

STUDIES OF DUBLINERS

3061. CONNOLLY, THOMAS E. "Marriage Divination in Joyce's 'Clay.'" Studies in Short Fiction, 3 (Spring 1966): 293-299.

3062. COWAN, S. A. "Joyce's 'Clay.'" Explicator, 23 (March 1965): item 50.

3063. _____ . "Celtic Folklore in 'Clay'; Maria and the Irish Washerwoman." Studies in Short Fiction, 6 (Winter 1969): 213-215.

3064. DAVIES PHILLIPS, GEORGE. "Maria's Song in Joyce's 'Clay.'" Studies in Short Fiction, 1 (Winter 1964): 153-154.

3065. DENEAU, DANIEL P. "Joyce's 'Minute' Maria." Journal of Narrative Technique, 2 (January 1972): 26-45.

3066. DIETRICH, R. F., and ROGER H. LUNDELL. [Instructor's Manual for] The Art of Fiction. New York: Holt, Rinehart and Winston, 1967, pp. 58-64.

3067. EASSON, ANGUS. "Parody as Comment in James Joyce's 'Clay.'" James Joyce Quarterly, 7 (Winter 1969): 75-81.

3068. GLASHEEN, ADALINE. "'Clay,'" in James Joyce's Dubliners: Critical Essays, pp. 100-106, No. 2866.

3069. HUDSON, RICHARD B. "Joyce's 'Clay.'" Explicator, 6 (March 1948): item 30.

3070. KIECKHEFER, PATRICIA. "Maria's Plants in 'Clay.'" James Joyce Quarterly, 11 (Fall 1973): 55-57.

3071. LYNSKEY, WINIFRED, ed. Reading Modern Fiction. Third edition. New York: Scribner's, 1962, pp. 311-317.

3072. McFATE, PATRICIA A. "'A Letter to Rome' and 'Clay': Similarities in Character and Conclusion." Studies in Short Fiction, 9 (Summer 1972): 277-279.

3073. MADDEN, DAVID. "James Joyce's 'Clay.'" University Review, 33 (March 1967): 229-233.

3074. MAGALANER, MARVIN. "The Other Side of James Joyce." Arizona Quarterly, 9 (Spring 1953): 5-16.

3075. MATHEWS, F. X. "Punchestime: A New Look at 'Clay.'" James Joyce Quarterly, 4 (Winter 1967): 102-106.

3076. MIZENER, ARTHUR. Handbook to Accompany Modern Short Stories. Revised edition. New York: Norton, 1967, pp. 118-120.

3077. NOON, WILLIAM T. "Joyce's 'Clay'; An Interpretation." College English, 17 (November 1955): 93-95.

3078. PEARSON, NORMAN H. "Joyce's 'Clay.'" Explicator, 7 (October 1948): item 9.

3079. SCHOLES, ROBERT. "A Commentary on 'Clay,'" in his Elements of Fiction. New York: Oxford University Press, 1968, pp. 66-77.

3080. SHORT, RAYMOND W., and RICHARD B. SEWALL. A Manual of Suggestions for Teachers Using Short Stories for Study. Third edition. New York: Holt, 1956, pp. 4-5.

3081. SMITH, G. RALPH, II. "A Superstition of Joyce's 'Clay.'" James Joyce Quarterly, 2 (Winter 1965): 133-134.

3082. STALEY, THOMAS F. "Moral Responsibility in Joyce's 'Clay.'" Renascence, 18 (Spring 1966): 124-128.

3083. WALZL, FLORENCE L. "Joyce's 'Clay.'" Explicator, 20 (February 1962): item 46. [Reprinted in Twentieth Century Interpretations of Dubliners, pp. 107-109, No. 2862.]

3084. _____ . "A Social Note on Joyce's 'Clay.'" James Joyce Quarterly, 9 (Fall 1971): 119-121.

3085. WEBER, ROBERT. "'Clay,'" in Insight II: Analyses of Modern British Literature. Edited by John V. Hagopian and Martin Dolch. Frankfurt a. M.: Hirschgraben Vlg., 1964, pp. 206-212.

"A PAINFUL CASE"

3086. BARROWS, HERBERT. Suggestions for Teaching Fifteen Stories. Boston: D. C. Heath, 1950, pp. 19-22.

3087. CONNOLLY, THOMAS E. "'A Painful Case,'" in James Joyce's Dubliners: Critical Essays, pp. 107-114, No. 2866.

3088. CORRINGTON, JOHN WILLIAM. "Isolation as Motif in 'A Painful Case.'" James Joyce Quarterly, 3 (Spring 1966): 182-191. [Reprinted in James Joyce's Dubliners: A Critical Handbook, pp. 130-139, No. 2852.]

3089. DUFFY, JOHN J. "The Painful case of M'Intosh." Studies in Short Fiction, 2 (November 1964): 183-185.

3090. GETTMAN, ROYAL A., and BRUCE HARKNESS, eds. Teacher's Manual for A Book of Stories. New York: Rinehart, 1955, pp. 7-9.

3091. KRANIDAS, THOMAS. "Mr. Duffy and the Song of Songs." James Joyce Quarterly, 3 (Spring 1966): 220.

3092. MAGALANER, MARVIN. "Joyce, Nietzsche, and Hauptmann in James Joyce's 'A Painful Case.'" Publications of the Modern Language Association, 68 (March 1953): 95-102.

3093. MILLER, JAMES E., and BERNICE SLOTE. "'A Painful Case,'" in Notes for Teaching the Dimensions of the Short Story. New York: Dodd, Mead, 1964, pp. 22-23.

3094. REID, STEPHEN. "'The Beast in the Jungle' and 'A Painful Case': Two Different Sufferings." American Imago, 20 (Fall 1963): 221-239.

3095. SAN JUAN, EPIFANIO. "From Contingency to Probability: Joyce's 'A Painful Case.'" Research Studies, 37 (June 1969): 139-144. [See also his James Joyce and the Craft of Fiction, No. 2883.]

3096. SLOAN, BARBARA L. "The d'Annunzian Narrator in 'A Painful Case.'" James Joyce Quarterly, 9 (Fall 1971): 26-36.

3097. WRIGHT, CHARLES D. "Melancholy Duffy and Sanguine Sinico: Humors in 'A Painful Case.'" James Joyce Quarterly, 3 (Spring 1966): 171-180.

"IVY DAY IN THE COMMITTEE ROOM"

3098. BLOTNER, JOSEPH L. "'Ivy Day in the Committee Room.'" Perspective, 9 (Summer 1957): 210-217. [Revised version in James Joyce's Dubliners: A Critical Handbook, pp. 139-146, No. 2852.]

3099. BOYLE, ROBERT. "'Two Gallants' and 'Ivy Day in the Committee Room.'" James Joyce Quarterly, 1 (Fall 1963): 3-9. [Reprinted in Twentieth Century Interpretations of Dubliners, pp. 100-106, No. 2862.]

3100. _____. "A Note on Hynes's 'The Death of Parnell.'" James Joyce Quarterly, 2 (Winter 1965): 133.

3101. BURGESS, C. F. "A Note on 'The Death of Parnell' in Joyce's 'Ivy Day in the Committee Room.'" James Joyce Quarterly, 9 (Fall 1971): 123-125.

3102. HODGART, M. J. C. "'Ivy Day in the Committee Room,'" in James Joyce's Dubliners: Critical Essays, pp. 115-121, No. 2866.

3103. ORMSBY, FRANK, and JOHN CRONIN. "'A Very Fine Piece of Writing': 'Ivy Day in the Committee Room.'" Éire-Ireland, 7 (Summer 1972): 84-94.

3104. SAN JUAN, EPIFANIO. "Form and Meaning in Joyce's 'Ivy Day in the Committee Room.'" Archiv, 207 (September 1970): 185-191.

3105. STEGNER, WALLACE et al. The Writer's Art. Boston: D. C. Heath, 1950, pp. 78-95.

3106. STERN, FREDERICK C. "'Parnell is Dead': 'Ivy Day in the Committee Room.'" James Joyce Quarterly, 10 (Winter 1973): 228-239.

"A MOTHER"

3107. COLLINS, BEN L. "Joyce's Use of Yeats and of Irish History: A Reading of 'A Mother.'" Éire-Ireland, 5 (September 1970): 45-66.

3108. HAYMAN, DAVID. "'A Mother,'" in James Joyce's Dubliners: Critical Essays, pp. 122-133, No. 2866.

3109. O'NEILL, MICHAEL J. "Joyce's use of Memory in 'A Mother.'" Modern Language Notes, 74 (March 1959): 226-230.

3110. SCARRY, JOHN. "The 'First Tenor' in James Joyce's 'A Mother.'" Éire-Ireland, 7 (Winter 1972): 67-69.

"GRACE"

3111. ABBOTT, H. PORTER. "The Importance of Martin Cunningham." James Joyce Quarterly, 5 (Fall 1967): 47-52.

3112. BAKER, JOSEPH E. "The Trinity in Joyce's 'Grace.'" James Joyce Quarterly, 2 (Summer 1965): 299-303.

3113. BOYLE, ROBERT. "Swiftian Allegory and Dantean Parody in Joyce's 'Grace.'" James Joyce Quarterly, 7 (Fall 1969): 11-21.

3114. CUNNINGHAM, FRANK R. "Joyce's 'Grace': Gracelessness in a Lost Paradise." James Joyce Quarterly, 6 (Spring 1969): 219-223.

3115. DUFFY, CHARLES F. "The Seating Arrangement in 'Grace.'" James Joyce Quarterly, 9 (Summer 1972): 487-489.

3116. FRAKES, JAMES R., and ISADORE TRASCHEN, eds. "Critical Comments." Short Fiction: A Critical Collection. Second edition. Englewood Cliffs, N.J.: Prentice-Hall, 1968, pp. 368-371.

3117. GOZZI, FRANCESCO. "Dante nell'inferno di Joyce." English Miscellany, no. 23 (1972): 195-229.

*3118. JACKSON, ROBERT S. "A Parabolic Reading of James Joyce's 'Grace.'" Modern Language Notes, 76 (December 1961): 719-724.

3119. KAIN, RICHARD M. "'Grace,'" in James Joyce's Dubliners: Critical Essays, pp. 134-152, No. 2866.

3120. KAUVER, ELAINE M. "Swift's Clothing Philosophy in A Tale of A Tub and Joyce's 'Grace.'" James Joyce Quarterly, 5 (Winter 1968): 162-165.

3121. MAGALANER, MARVIN. "Leopold Bloom Before Ulysses." Modern Language Notes, 68 (February 1953): 110-112.

STUDIES OF DUBLINERS

3122. MOSELEY, VIRGINIA. "The 'Coincidence' of 'Contrarieties' in 'Grace.'" James Joyce Quarterly, 6 (Fall 1968): 3-21.

3123. NEWMAN, F. X. "The Land of Ooze: Joyce's 'Grace' and the Book of Job." Studies in Short Fiction, 4 (Fall 1966): 70-79.

3124. NIEMEYER, CARL. "'Grace' and Joyce's Method of Parody." College English, 27 (December 1965): 196-201. [Reprinted in James Joyce's Dubliners: A Critical Handbook, pp. 148-154, No. 2852.]

"THE DEAD"

Books

3125. BATES, H. E. The Modern Short Story: A Critical Survey. London: Thomas Nelson, 1943, pp. 154-156.

3126. BENSTOCK, BERNARD. "'The Dead,'" in James Joyce's Dubliners: Critical Essays, pp. 153-169, No. 2866. [See John P. McKenna. "An Ill-Starred Magus." James Joyce Quarterly, 9 (Fall 1971): 126-128.]

3127. BRANDABUR, EDWARD. "Arrayed for the Bridal: The Embodied Vision of 'The Dead,'" in Joyce's The Dead, pp. 108-119, No. 3138.

3128. DAVIS, ROBERT GORHAM. Ten Modern Masters. New York: Harcourt, Brace, 1959, pp. 43-45.

3129. DOLAN, PAUL J. Modes of Fiction (Manual). New York: Free Press, 1970, pp. 40-43.

3130. ENROTH, C. A. Joyce and Lawrence. New York, Toronto: Holt, Rinehart and Winston, 1969. [For grades 10-12.]

3131. GORDON, CAROLINE, and ALLEN TATE. "Commentary on 'The Dead,'" in their The House of Fiction. New York: Scribner, 1950, pp. 279-282. [Reprinted in James Joyce's Dubliners: Text, Criticism, and Notes, pp. 404-409, No. 2885.]

3132. GRACE, WILLIAM J. "Art Form in Joyce's 'The Dead,'" in his Response to Literature. New York: McGraw-Hill, 1965, pp. 149-152, et passim.

3133. HANDY, WILLIAM J. "Criticism of Joyce's Works: A Formalist Approach," in Proceedings of the Comparative Literature Symposium, vol. 2. Edited by Wolodymyr T. Zyla. Lubbock, Texas: Texas Tech Press, 1969; and in Modern Fiction: A Formalist Approach. Carbondale and Edwardsville: Southern Illinois University Press; London: Feffer and Simons, 1971, pp. 29-61.

3134. HEDBERG, JOHANNES, ed. James Joyce: The Dead. Stockholm: Almqvist and Wiksell, 1968.

3135. LUDWIG, JACK B. "James Joyce's Dubliners," in Stories British and American. Edited by Jack B. Ludwig and W. R. Poirier. Boston: Houghton, Mifflin, 1953, pp. 384-391. [Reprinted in James Joyce's Dubliners: A Critical Handbook, pp. 159-162, No. 2852.]

3136. MAGALANER, MARVIN, and EDMOND L. VOLPE. "Introduction," in their Twelve Short Stories. New York: Macmillan, 1961.

3137. MANNIN, ETHEL. "Contemporary Irish Fiction," in Modern British Writing. Edited by Denys Val Baker. New York: Vanguard Press, 1947, pp. 165-177.

3138. MOYNIHAN, WILLIAM T., ed. Joyce's The Dead. Boston: Allyn and Bacon, 1965.
Contents: William T. Moynihan. "Preface," pp. 5-7; "Joyce's 'The Dead,'" pp. 3-35; Richard Ellmann. "A Chronology of the Life of James Joyce," 39-45; Richard Ellmann. "The Backgrounds of 'The Dead,'" 46-57 (from No. 308); Stanislaus Joyce. "Recollections of James Joyce," 58-59 (from No. 476); James Joyce. "She Weeps over Rahoon," pp. 60-61; James Joyce. "Letter to Henrik Ibsen," 62-63; James R. Baker. "Ibsen, Joyce and the Living-Dead," 64-70 (from No. 1614); Gerald Gould. "A Review of Dubliners," 71-73, No. 1870; William York Tindall. "Dubliners," 74-81 (from No. 1678); William T. Noon. "Epiphany," 82-88, No. 943; Frank O'Connor. "Joyce and Dissociated Metaphor," 89-92, No. 2878; Kenneth Burke. "Stages in 'The Dead,'" 95-99, No. 3151; C. C. Loomis, Jr. "Structure and Sympathy in Joyce's 'The Dead,'" 100-104, No. 3172; George Knox. "Michael Furey: Symbol-Name in Joyce's 'The Dead,'" 105-107, No. 3169; Edward Brandabur. "Arrayed for the Bridal: The Embodied Vision of 'The Dead,'" 108-119, No. 3127; Brendan P. O Hehir. "Structural Symbol in Joyce's 'The Dead,'" 120-132, No. 3179; "Further Suggestions for Writing," 133-134.

3139. NEIDER, CHARLES. "James Joyce," in Short Novels of the Masters. New York: Rinehart, 1948, pp. 37-40.

3140. RAUTER, HERBERT. "Joyce: 'The Dead,'" in Die englische Kurzgeschichte. Edited by Karl Heinz Göller and Gerhard Hoffmann. Düsseldorf: August Bagel Vlg., 1973, pp. 137-146, 366-368.

3141. SALE, WILLIAM M., JR., JAMES HALL, and MARTIN STEINMANN. Short Stories: Tradition and Direction. Norfolk: New Directions Books, 1949, pp. 178-224.

3142. SKLARE, ARNOLD B. Art of the Novella. New York: Macmillan, 1965, pp. 182-183.

3143. SPINNER, KASPAR. "Vorwort," in James Joyce: Die Toten: Erzählungen. Diogenes. Erzähler-Bibliothek. Zürich, 1966, pp. 7-25.

3144. TRILLING, LIONEL. "Characterization in 'The Dead,'" in his The Experience of Literature. New York: Holt, Rinehart, and Winston, 1967, pp. 228-231. [Reprinted in James Joyce's Dubliners: A Critical Handbook, pp. 155-159, No. 2852.]

Periodical Articles

3145. BĂLĂIȚĂ, GEORGE. "O nuvelă de Joyce: 'Cei morti' [A Short Story by Joyce: 'The Dead']." Ateneu, 7, no. 3 (1970): 3, 13.

3146. BARR, ISABELLE H. "Footnote to 'The Dead.'" A.D., 2 (Autumn 1951): 112.

3147. BATES, H. E. "Is this the Greatest Short Story?" Irish Digest, 55 (January 1956): 103.

3148. BIERMAN, ROBERT. "Structural Elements in 'The Dead.'" James Joyce Quarterly, 4 (Fall 1966): 42-45.

3149. BLUM, MORGAN. "The Shifting Point of View: Joyce's 'The Dead' and Gordon's 'Old Red.'" Critique, 1, no. 1 (1956): 45-66.

3150. BOGORAD, SAMUEL N. "Gabriel Conroy as 'Whited Sepulchre'; Prefiguring Imagery in 'The Dead.'" Ball State University Forum, 14 (Fall 1973): 52-58.

3151. BOYD, JOHN D., and RUTH A. "The Love Triangle in Joyce's 'The Dead.'" UTQ, 42 (Spring 1973): 202-217.

3152. BURKE, KENNETH. "Three Definitions." Kenyon Review, 13 (Spring 1951): 181-192. [Reprinted in James Joyce's Dubliners: Text, Criticism, and Notes, pp. 410-416, No. 2885.]

3153. COX, ROGER L. "Johnny the Horse in Joyce's 'The Dead.'" James Joyce Quarterly, 4 (Fall 1966): 36-41.

3154. DAMON, PHILIP. "A Symphasis of Antipathies in 'The Dead.'" Modern Language Notes, 74 (February 1959): 111-114.

3155. DEANE, PAUL. "Motion Picture Techniques in James Joyce's 'The Dead.'" James Joyce Quarterly, 6 (Spring 1969): 231-236.

3156. DETONI, GIANANTONIO. "Su una Pagina di Joyce." Aut Aut, 2, no. 8 (1952): 138-147.

3157. ELLMANN, RICHARD. "Backgrounds of 'The Dead.'" Kenyon Review, 20 (Autumn 1958): 507-528.

3158. FOSTER, JOHN W. "Passage Through 'The Dead.'" Criticism, 15 (Spring 1973): 91-108.

3159. FRIEDRICH, GERHARD. "Bret Harte as a Source for James Joyce's 'The Dead.'" Philological Quarterly, 33 (October 1954): 442-444.

3160. H., U. "Kurzkritik: James Joyce: 'Die Toten.'" Die Welt der Literatur, 3 (1966): 8.

3161. HASEGAWA, KAZUO. ["James Joyce's 'The Dead'"]. Mie daigaku eibunkaishi, no. 11 (1972): 39-51. [In Japanese.]

3162. HEDBERG, JOHANNES. "The Dangers of Criticism: An Example from Richard Ellmann's James Joyce." Moderna Språk, 63 (1969): 24-25.

3163. HUMMA, JOHN B. "Gabriel and the Bedsheets: Still Another Reading of the Ending of 'The Dead.'" Studies in Short Fiction, 10 (Winter 1973): 207-209.

3164. HUNTER, ROBERT. "Joyce's 'The Dead.'" James Joyce Quarterly, 7 (Summer 1970): 365.

3165. HUTTON, VIRGIL. "James Joyce's 'The Dead.'" East-West Review, 2 (Winter 1965-1966): 124-139.

3166. KAYE, JULIAN B. "The Wings of Dedalus: Two Stories in Dubliners." Modern Fiction Studies, 4 (Spring 1958): 31-41. [See also No. 2968.]

3167. KELLEHER, JOHN V. "Irish History and Mythology in James Joyce's 'The Dead.'" Review of Politics, 27 (July 1965): 414-433. [Reprinted as Irish History and Mythology in James Joyce's 'The Dead.' Reprints in Irish Studies, Literature Series, no. 2. Chicago: American Committee for Irish Studies, 1971.]

3168. KENNELLY, BRENDAN. "The Irishness of 'The Dead' by James Joyce." Moderna Språk, 61 (1967): 239-242.

3169. KNOX, GEORGE. "Michael Furey: Symbol-Name in Joyce's 'The Dead.'" Western Humanities Review, 13 (Spring 1959): 221-222. [Reprinted in Joyce's The Dead, pp. 105-107, No. 3138.]

3170. KOPPER, EDWARD A. "Joyce's 'The Dead.'" Explicator, 26 (February 1968): item 46.

3171. LOGAN, DOROTHY. "Joyce's 'The Dead.'" Explicator, 32 (January 1973): item 16.

3172. LOOMIS, C. C., JR. "Structure and Sympathy in Joyce's 'The Dead.'" Publications of the Modern Language Association, 75 (March 1960): 149-151. [Reprinted in Joyce's

STUDIES OF <u>DUBLINERS</u>

<u>The Dead</u>, pp. 100-104, No. 3138; in <u>Twen-tieth Century Interpretations of Dublin-ers</u>, pp. 110-114, No. 2862; in <u>James Joyce's Dubliners: Text, Criticism, and Notes</u>, pp. 417-422, No. 2885.]

3173. LYTLE, ANDREW. "A Reading of Joyce's 'The Dead.'" <u>Sewanee Review</u>, 77 (Spring 1969): 193-216.

3174. MacDONAGH, DONAGH. "Joyce and 'The Lass of Aughrim.'" <u>Hibernia</u>, no. 31 (June 1967): 21. [Expanded as "The Lass of Aughrim or the Betrayal of James Joyce," in <u>The Celtic Master</u>, pp. 17-25, No. 1583; re-printed in <u>Hibernia</u>, 33 (6-26 June 1969): 18.]

3175. McKENNA, JOHN P. "An Ill-Starred Magus." <u>James Joyce Quarterly</u>, 9 (Fall 1971): 126-128. [See Benstock, No. 3126.]

3176. _____. "Joyce's 'The Dead.'" <u>Explica-tor</u>, 30 (1971): item 1.

3177. MOSELEY, VIRGINIA. "'Two Sights for Ever a Picture' in Joyce's 'The Dead.'" <u>College English</u>, 26 (March 1965): 426-433.

3178. O'CONNOR, FRANK (Michael O'Donovan). "At the Microphone." <u>The Bell</u>, 3, no. 6 (March 1942): 415-419.

3179. O HEHIR, BRENDAN P. "Structural Symbol in Joyce's 'The Dead.'" <u>Twentieth Century Literature</u>, 3 (April 1957): 3-13. [Re-printed in <u>Joyce's The Dead</u>, pp. 120-132, No. 3138.]

3180. ROBINSON, ELEANOR M. "Gabriel Conroy's Cooked Goose." <u>Ball State University Forum</u>, 11 (Spring 1970): 25.

3181. SCARRY, JOHN. "'Poor Georgina Burns' in Joyce's 'The Dead.'" <u>English Language Notes</u>, 10 (December 1972): 123-126.

3182. _____. "The 'Negro Chieftan' and Dis-harmony in Joyce's <u>The Dead</u>." <u>Revue des langues vivantes</u>, 39 (1973): 182-183.

3183. _____. "William Parkinson in Joyce's <u>The Dead</u>." <u>Journal of Modern Literature</u>, 3 (February 1973): 105-107.

3184. SCHEUERLE, WILLIAM H. "'Gabriel Hounds' and Joyce's 'The Dead.'" <u>Studies in Short Fiction</u>, 2 (Summer 1965): 369-371.

3185. SCHMIDT, HUGO. "Hauptmann's Michael Kramer and Joyce's 'The Dead.'" <u>Publications of the Modern Language Association</u>, 80 (March 1965): 141-142.

3186. SCHOLES, ROBERT E. "Some Observations on the Text of <u>Dubliners</u>: 'The Dead.'" <u>Studies in Bibliography</u>, 15 (1962): 191-205.

3187. SENN, FRITZ, "Reverberations." <u>James Joyce Quarterly</u>, 3 (Spring 1966): 222.

3188. _____. "Not too Scrupulous Always." <u>James Joyce Quarterly</u>, 4 (Spring 1967): 244.

3189. SMITH, THOMAS F. "Color and Light in 'The Dead.'" <u>James Joyce Quarterly</u>, 2 (Sum-mer 1965): 304-313.

3190. STONE, WILLIAM B. "Teaching 'The Dead': Literature in the Composition Class." <u>College Composition and Communication</u>, 19 (October 1968): 229-231.

3191. TATE, ALLEN. "Three Commentaries: Poe, James, and Joyce." <u>Sewanee Review</u>, 58 (Winter 1950): 1-15. [Appeared in his <u>The House of Fiction</u>, No. 3131.]

3192. WALZL, FLORENCE L. "Ambiguity in the Struc-tural Symbols of Gabriel's Vision in Joyce's 'The Dead.'" <u>Wisconsin Studies in Literature</u>, 2 (1965): 60-69.

3193. _____. "Gabriel and Michael: The Con-clusion of 'The Dead.'" <u>James Joyce Quarterly</u>, 4 (Fall 1966): 17-31. [Re-printed in <u>James Joyce's Dubliners: Text, Criticism, and Notes</u>, pp. 423-444, No. 2885.]

3194. WARE, THOMAS C. "A Miltonic Allusion in Joyce's 'The Dead.'" <u>James Joyce Quarterly</u>, 6 (Spring 1969): 273-274.

STEPHEN HERO

See also Burgess. <u>Re-Joyce</u>, 48-50, No. 1533; Curran. <u>James Joyce Remembered</u>, 51-53, No. 304; Eco. "Le moyen age...," No. 3316; Ellmann. <u>James Joyce</u>, No. 308; Ellmann. "Portrait...," 63-66, No. 421; Forster. "Joyce, <u>Stephen Hero</u>, et...," No. 3322; Goldberg. <u>Joyce</u>, passim, No. 1574; Goldman. <u>Joyce Paradox</u>, 120-125, No. 1576; Guidi. <u>Il Primo...</u>, 41-46, No. 1737; Harvey. "<u>Stephen Hero</u> and...," No. 3245; Hackett. <u>On Juding Books</u>, 251-254, No. 4932; Henning. "<u>Stephen Hero</u> and <u>Wilhelm Meister</u>," No. 3202; Hodgart and Worthing-ton. <u>Song in...</u>, 60-61, No. 1588; Kaye. "Simony ...," No. 1598; Levin. <u>Critical Introduction</u>, 46-48, No. 1603; MacLeod. "Influence of Ibsen...," No. 998; Magalaner. <u>Time...</u>, passim, No. 2875; Mayoux. <u>Joyce</u>, passim, No. 1619; Moseley. <u>Joyce and the Bible</u>, 1-11, No. 942; Naganowski. <u>Tele-mach...</u>, 59-62, No. 3632; Pinguentini. <u>James Joyce in Italia</u>, passim, No. 1634; Prescott. <u>Exploring...</u>, 17-28, No. 1636; Ryf. <u>New Approach</u> ..., 42-58, No. 3271; Scholes and Kain. <u>Workshop</u> ..., No. 3272; Stewart. <u>Eight...</u>, 438-442, 445-447, No. 1665; Sullivan. <u>Joyce Among...</u>, passim, No. 357; Tysdahl. <u>Joyce and Ibsen</u>, 50-55, No. 952; Ziolkowski. "James Joyce's Epiphanie...," No. 2848; see Section I.E "Reviews of Joyce's Works," Nos. 2334-2353.

Books

3195. ANDERSON, CHESTER G. Word Index to James
Joyce's Stephen Hero. Ridgefield, Conn.:
Ridgebury Press, 1958.

3196. FARRELL, JAMES T. "Postscript on Stephen
Hero," in James Joyce: Two Decades of
Criticism, pp. 190-197, No. 1570.

*3197. MASUDA, YOSHIO. "Stibun Hiro" [Stephen
Hero], in Joisu Nyumon [Introduction to
James Joyce], pp. 28-35, No. 1511.

3198. SLOCUM, JOHN J., and HERBERT CAHOON. "Five
More Pages of James Joyce's Stephen Hero,"
in A James Joyce Miscellany, Second series, pp. 3-8, No. 1613. [Five pages
which did not appear in Theodore Spencer's
revised (1955) edition, No. 3200.]

3199. SPENCER, THEODORE. "Introduction and Editorial Note" in Joyce's Stephen Hero.
Norfolk: New Directions Books, 1944, pp.
7-19. [Reprinted in James Joyce's Dubliners: A Critical Handbook, pp. 10-11,
No. 2852; in Portraits of an Artist: A
Casebook on James Joyce's Portrait of the
Artist as a Young Man, pp. 151-152, No.
3260.]

3200. SPENCER, THEODORE. "Introduction and Editorial Note" in Joyce's Stephen Hero. A
new edition incorporating the additional
manuscript pages...edited by John J. Slocum and Herbert Cahoon. New York: New
Directions Books, 1955, pp. 7-19; London:
New English Library, 1966; London: Cape,
1969.

Periodical Articles

3201. CONNOLLY, THOMAS E. "Stephen Hero Revisited." James Joyce Review, 3, nos. 1-2
(February 1959): 40-46.

*3202. HENNING, JOHN. "Stephen Hero and Wilhelm
Meister: A Study of Parallels." German
Life and Letters, 5 (October 1951): 22-29.

3203. KAIN, RICHARD M., and ROBERT E. SCHOLES.
"The First Version of Joyce's Portrait."
Yale Review, 49 (March 1960): 355-369.
[Reprinted in Configuration critique de
James Joyce, II, pp. 11-30, No. 1584.

3204. LEVIN, HARRY. "James Joyce." Atlantic
Monthly, 178 (December 1946): 125-129.

3205. McLUHAN, HERBERT M. "Joyce, Aquinas, and
the Poetic Process." Renascence, 4
(Autumn 1951): 3-11. [Reprinted in
Joyce's Portrait: Criticisms and Critiques, pp. 249-265, No. 3223.]

3206. MOSELEY, VIRGINIA. "Stephen Hero: 'The Last
of the First.'" James Joyce Quarterly,
3 (Summer 1966): 278-287.

3207. PRESCOTT, JOSEPH. "James Joyce's Stephen
Hero." Journal of English and Germanic
Philology, 53 (April 1954): 214-223.
[Reprinted in his Exploring James Joyce,
pp. 17-28, No. 1630.]
    Translations: Letterature Moderne
(Bologna), 6 (November-December 1956):
679-688; Sur (Buenos Aires), no. 250
(January-February 1958): 39-50, translated by Jaime Rest. Armas y Letras, Second
series, 1 (October-December 1958): 64-76;
Joseph Prescott, ed. Configuration critique de James Joyce, I, pp. 48-66, No.
1636; La revue des lettres modernes, 6
(Autumn 1959): 288-306; Moznaim (Tel
Aviv), 14, no. 2 (January 1962): 137-143;
De Vlaamse Gids, 48 (1964): 663-673,
translated by Ben Cami; Kultura (Paris),
no. 10/204 (October 1964): 136-145, translated by Maria Danielwicz; Caldernos brasileiros, 7 (March-April 1965): 14-20;
Nuova antologia, 103 (November 1968):
353-362.
    Reprinted: The Bell (Dublin), 19 (Nov-
ember 1954): 27-35; Diliman Review (Quezon
City), 7 (October 1959): 373-385; in
Joyce's Portrait: Criticisms and Critiques,
pp. 77-88, No. 3223; Rising Generation
(Tokyo), 111 (1 September 1965): 604-607;
(1 October 1965): 602-665; Phoenix (Korea),
2 (Spring 1967): 11-22; in Twentieth Century Interpretations of A Portrait of the
Artist as a Young Man, pp. 21-25, No. 3273.

3208. SPENCER, THEODORE. "A Proposito di Stephen
Hero." Inventario, Ano 1, num. 2 (Summer 1946): 47-54.

3209. STERN, RICHARD G. "Proust and Joyce Under-
way: Jean Santeuil and Stephen Hero."
Kenyon Review, 18 (Summer 1956): 486-496.

3210. TOBIN, PATRICIA. "A Portrait of the Artist
as Autobiographer: Joyce's Stephen Hero."
Genre, 6 (June 1973): 189-203.

3211. WALDRON, PHILLIP. "A Note on the Text of
Stephen Hero." James Joyce Quarterly,
3 (Spring 1966): 220-221.

STUDIES OF *A PORTRAIT OF THE ARTIST AS A YOUNG MAN*

See also Adams. James Joyce, 91-116, No.
1506; Agrawal. "Epiphanies in...," No. 2824;
Bell. The English Novel, 71-86, No. 28; Benstock.
"A Covey of Clerics...," No. 1695; Bourgeois.
"Apropos de James Joyce," No. 1698; Boyd. Ire-
land's Literary..., 402-408, No. 1527; Brandabur.
Scrupulous..., 159-174, No. 1529; Brivic. "James
Joyce...," No. 1532; Brasil. Joyce..., 79-90, No.
1530; Burgess. Re-Joyce, 50-69, No. 1533; Burgess.
Joycesprick, 62-65, No. 1536; Busch. "Einspruch..
.," No. 1903; Byrne. Silent Years, passim, No.
296; Chatterjee. James Joyce..., 1-18, No. 1541;
Collins. "Progression in...," No. 1710; Cixous.
L'Exile..., No. 1543; Coveney. Poor Monkey, No.

STUDIES OF A PORTRAIT OF THE ARTIST AS A YOUNG MAN

1545; Crosse. Flaubert and Joyce, 44-53, 58-67, No. 1546; Curran. James Joyce Remembered, passim, No. 304; Daiches. Forms of..., 61-71, No. 410; Daiches. Novel and the Modern World, 101-110, No. 1548; Diskin. "Joyce and...Bronte," No. 971; Donoghue. "Joyce and Finite Order," No. 973; Eliot. After Strange Gods, 35-38, No. 696; Ellmann. James Joyce, No. 308; Ellmann. Letters, passim, No. 309; Foran. "A Mirror held up to Stephen," No. 4610; Friedman. Stream of..., 214-220, No. 4189; Frierson. English Novel..., 200-203, No. 1371; Garrett. Scene and Symbol..., 218-230, No. 1565; Gifford. Notes for Joyce, passim, No. 2863; Gilbert. "James Joyce...," No. 1039; Glasheen. "Joyce and the Three Ages...," No. 930; Goldberg. Classical Temper, 41-65, No. 1573; Goldberg. James Joyce..., 47-63, No. 1574; Golding. James Joyce, 34-68, No. 1575; Goldman. Joyce Paradox, 22-73, No. 1576; Goldman. James Joyce, 4-6, 11-29, No. 1577; Gorman. James Joyce, 65-100, No. 321; Goodheart. Cult of the Ego, 183-191, No. 1578; Griffin. Wild Geese, 22-30, No. 1579; Gross. James Joyce, 37-41, No. 1580; Guidi. Il Primo Joyce, 57-104, No. 1737; Harrison. "Portrait Epiphany," No. 2831; Halter. "Die Epiphanien...," No. 2865; Harmon. "The Early Joyce," No. 2917; Hodgart and Worthington. Song in the Works of..., No. 1588; Hollerer. "Die Epiphanie ...," No. 2835; Honig. "Hobgoblin...," No. 1747; Jaloux. Au Pays..., 111-122, No. 1595; John. "Fragment of an...," No. 473; Jones. James Joyce and the Common Reader, 24-38, No. 3602; Joyce, S. My Brother's Keeper, No. 331; Kaye. "Simony, the Three Simons...," No. 1598; Kenner. Dublin's Joyce, 109-157; No. 1600; Kulemeyer. Studien zur..., 12-15, No. 2484; Levin. Critical Introduction, 41-62, No. 1603; Levitt. "Shall be Accurst...," No. 1763; Litz. James Joyce, 60-72, No. 1606; Lundkvist. Ikarus' Flykt, 73-112, No. 1608; Magalaner. Time of..., 97-115, No. 2875; Magalaner and Kain. Joyce: The Man..., 102-129, No. 1615; Majault. James Joyce, 66-71, No. 1616; Mayoux. Joyce, passim, No. 1619; Misra. Indian..., 29-32, No. 941; More. On Being Human, 70-74, No. 697; Morse. "Baudelaire, Stephen Dedalus...," No. 1009; Morse. Sympathetic Alien, passim, No. 339; Moseley. Joyce and the Bible, 31-44, No. 942; Naganowski. Telemach..., 62-77, No. 3632; Noon. Joyce and Aquinas, 18-39, No. 943; O'Brien. Conscience..., passim, No. 1628; O'Connor. "Joyce and Dissociated Metaphor," No. 2878; O'Mahony. "Father Conmee...," No. 511; Paris. James Joyce ..., No. 1632; Prescott. Exploring..., passim, No. 1637; Quasha. James Joyce's Dubliners and..., passim, No. 2880; Roberts. "James Joyce, from...," No. 4015; Rubin. "Joyce and Sterne...," No. 1014; Sanchez. Panorama..., 113-118, No. 1646; Savage. Withered Branch, 160-168, No. 1647; Schutte. Joyce and Shakespeare, 80-84, No. 4170; Smidt. James Joyce and the Cultic..., 35-42, 53-61, No. 1405; Stewart. James Joyce, 15-22, No. 1664; Stewart. Eight..., 442-450, No. 1665; Stief. Moderne literatur..., 132-135, No. 1666; Strong. Sacred River..., 23-27, No. 949; Sypher. "Portrait...," No. 3403; Tindall. James Joyce..., 16-22, No. 1677; Tindall. Literary Symbol..., 76-86, 239-246, No. 951; Turaj. "'Araby' and Portrait ...," No. 3005; Tysdahl. Joyce and Ibsen, 59-86,

No. 952; Walsh. "That Pervasive Mass...," No. 2940; Waldron. Novels of..., 1-5, No. 1684; Ziolkowski. "James Joyce's Epiphanies...," No. 2848; Hart. James Joyce's Ulysses, 28-36, No. 3590; Sultan. Argument of..., 62-88, No. 3662; O Hehir. Gaelic Lexicon..., 335-336, No. 5363. [See Section I.E "Reviews of Joyce's Works," Nos. 1903-1958; I.F "Dissertations," Nos. 2438-2458.]

GENERAL STUDIES

Books

3212. ALOYSE, SISTER M. "The Novelist as Popularizer: Joyce and Psychological Fiction," in Dedalus on Crete, pp. 31-42, No. 3233.

3213. ANDERSON, CHESTER G., ed. A Portrait of the Artist as a Young Man: Text, Criticism and Notes. New York: Viking, 1968.
    Contents: Editor's Preface; A Portrait of the Artist as a Young Man in the Anderson-Ellmann text; "Related Texts by Joyce"; Ezra Pound. "Letter to Joyce" (September 1915--from Pound/Joyce, edited by Forrest Read, No. 725); Edward Garnett. "Reader's Report"; Ezra Pound. "At Last the Novel Appears," No. 1907; Diego Angeli. Review from Il Marzocco (Florence), 12 August 1917, translated by Joyce, No. 1937; H. G. Wells. "James Joyce's A Portrait of the Artist as a Young Man," No. 1909; "Extracts from First Press Notices," Egoist (April 1917); "James Joyce and His Critics: Some Clasified Comments," from Egoist (June 1917); Maurice Beebe. From Ivory Towers and Sacred Founts, No. 3216; Irene Hendry Chayes. "Joyce's Epiphanies," No. 2833; Frank O'Connor. "Joyce and Dissociated Metaphor," No. 2878; William York Tindall. "Image and Symbol in The Portrait," No. 951; Richard Ellmann. From James Joyce, No. 308; Harry Levin. From James Joyce: A Critical Introduction, No. 1603; Hugh Kenner. From Dublin's Joyce, No. 1600; Kenneth Burke. "Three Definitions: The Joyce Portrait," No. 3151; Wayne C. Booth. From Rhetoric of Fiction, No. 3218; Robert Scholes. "Stephen Dedalus, Poet or Aesthete?," No. 3389; Explanatory Notes, pp. 481-550; Chronology, Topics for Discussion and Papers; Selected Bibliography.

3214. ANDREACH, ROBERT J. "James Joyce," in his Studies in Structure. London: Burns and Oates, 1965; New York: Fordham University Press, 1964, pp. 40-71.

3215. AVERY, GEORGE C. Inquiry and Testament: A Study of the Novels and Short Prose of Robert Walser. Philadelphia: University of Pennsylvania Press, 1968, pp. 242-246.

3216. BEEBE, MAURICE. "James Joyce: The Return from Exile," in his Ivory Towers and Sacred Founts: The Artist as Hero in Fiction from Goethe to Faust. New York: New York

University Press, 1964, pp. 260-295.
[Contains his "James Joyce: Barnacle
Goose and Lapwing," and "Joyce and Stephen Dedalus: The Problem of Autobiography," which first appeared in A James
Joyce Miscellany, Second series, pp. 67-
78, No. 1613.]

3217. BEJA, MORRIS, ed. James Joyce, Dubliners
and A Portrait of the Artist as a Young
Man. [See No. 2855 for contents.]

*3218. BOOTH, WAYNE C. "The Problem of Distance in
A Portrait," in his The Rhetoric of Fic-
tion. Chicago: University of Chicago
Press, 1961, pp. 323-336. [Reprinted in
Twentieth Century Interpretations of A
Portrait of the Artist as a Young Man,
pp. 85-95, No. 3273.]

3219. BROWN, HOMER OBED. James Joyce's Early Fiction: The Biography of a Form. Cleveland
and London: Press of Case Western Reserve
University, 1972.

3220. BROWN, RICHARD K. Joyce's A Portrait of the
Artist as a Young Man. Bar-Notes Literature Study and Examination Guides,
5563-5572. New York: Barrister, 1966.

3221. CAMPBELL, JOHN W. A Portrait of the Artist
as a Young Man: An Appreciation. Sydney:
Sydney University Literary Society, 1933.

3222. COLLINGWOOD, FRANK. Portrait: Notes. Tor-
onto: Coles Notes, 1970.
Contents: Frank Collingwood. "Intro-
duction," 5-48; "Critical Reviews," 49-
109; Grant H. Redford. "The Role of
Structure in Joyce's Portrait," No. 3382;
Melvin Friedman. "Stream of Consciousness
in The Portrait," No. 4189; William York
Tindall. "Image and Symbol in The Por-
trait," No. 951; Marvin Magalaner. "Back-
grounds of A Portrait," No. 1615; Joseph
Prescott. "James Joyce: A Study in Words,"
No. 5294; Elizabeth F. Boyd. "James
Joyce's Hell-Fire Sermons," No. 3301;
Julian B. Kaye. "Who is Betty Byrne?,"
No. 3346; Chester G. Anderson. "The Sac-
rificial Butter," No. 3471.

3223. CONNOLLY, THOMAS E., ed. Joyce's Portrait:
Criticisms and Critiques. New York:
Appleton-Century-Crofts, 1962; London:
Owen, 1964.
Contents: Thomas E. Connolly. "In-
troduction," 1-6; Harry Levin. "The Art-
ist," 9-24 (from No. 1603); Hugh Kenner.
"The Portrait in Perspective," 25-60
(from No. 3251); Dorothy Van Ghent. "On A
Portrait," 60-74 (from No. 3422); Joseph
Prescott. "James Joyce's Stephen Hero,"
77-88 (from No. 3207); Richard Ellmann.
"A Portrait of the Artist as Friend," 88-
101, No. 421; Grant Redford. "The Role of
Structure in Joyce's Portrait," 102-114,
No. 3382; Eugene M. Waith. "The Calling

of Stephen Dedalus," 114-123, No. 3407;
Chester G. Anderson. "The Sacrificial But-
ter," 123-136, No. 3471; Caroline Gordon.
"Some Readings and Misreadings in Joyce's
Portrait," 136-156, No. 3331; Jane H.
Jack. "Art and A Portrait," 156-167, No.
3341; Barbara Seward. "The Artist and the
Rose," 167-180, No. 3483; A. D. Hope. "The
Esthetic Theory of James Joyce," 183-203,
No. 991; Irene Hendry Chayes. "Joyce's
Epiphanies," 204-220, No. 2833; Geddes
MacGregor. "Artistic Theory in James
Joyce," 221-230, No. 3456; Haskell M.
Block. "The Critical Theory of James
Joyce," 231-249, No. 3433; H. Marshall
McLuhan. "Joyce, Aquinas, and the Poetic
Process," 249-265, No. 3205; Thomas E.
Connolly. "Joyce's Aesthetic Theory," 266-
271, No. 3436; Maurice Beebe. "Joyce and
Aquinas," 272-289, No. 3431; J. Mitchell
Morse. "Augustine's Theodicy and Joyce's
Aesthetics," 290-303, No. 1008; Dorothy
Van Ghent. "Problems for Study and Dis-
cussion for A Portrait," 307-318, No.
3422; Peter Spielberg. "James Joyce's
Errata for American Editions of A Por-
trait," 318-328 (here first published);
"Selective Bibliography," 329-335.

3224. COWLEY, MALCOLM, and HOWARD E. HUGO. "Por-
trait (1961)," The Lesson of the Masters:
An Anthology of the Novel from Cervantes
to Hemingway: Texts with Commentaries.
New York: Scribner's, 1971, pp. 425-440.
[With last part of Chapter 4.]

3225. DREW, ELIZABETH. "James Joyce: A Portrait of
the Artist as a Young Man," in her The
Novel: A Modern Guide to Fifteen English
Masterpieces. New York: Dell, 1963, pp.
245-261.

3226. DREWS, JÖRG. Enzyklopädisches Stichwort:
Joyce's《Portrait》," in James Joyce's
《Portrait》: Das《Jugendbildnis》im Lichte
neuerer deutschen Forschung, pp. 187-190,
No. 3236.

3227. ELLIS, CHARLES R., project editor; BERTRAM
LIPPMAN, CAROL Z. ROTHKOPF, series consult-
ants. A Portrait: A Critical Commentary.
Study Master Publication, no. 415. New
York: R. D. M. Corporation, 1963, new
edition, 1966.

*3228. ELLMANN, RICHARD, ed. "Two Faces of Edward,"
in his Edwardians and Late Victorians:
English Institute Essays, 1959. New York:
Columbia University Press, 1960, pp. 188-
210. [Revised in his Golden Codgers:
Biographical Speculations. New York, London: Oxford University Press, 1973, pp.
132-154; also reprinted in Literary Criticism: Idea and Act. The English Institute,
1939-1972: Selected Essays. Edited by W.
K. Wimsatt. Berkeley: University of California Press, 1974, pp. 560-575.]

STUDIES OF <u>A PORTRAIT OF THE ARTIST AS A YOUNG MAN</u>

3229. EPSTEIN, EDMUND L. <u>The Ordeal of Stephen Dedalus: The Conflict of Generations in James Joyce's A Portrait of the Artist as a Young Man</u>. Carbondale, Ill.: Southern Illinois University Press, 1971; paperback reprint, 1973.

3230. ERZGRABER, WILLI. "James Joyce: <u>A Portrait of the Artist as a Young Man</u>," in <u>Der moderne englische Roman: Interpretationen</u>. Edited by Horst Oppel. Berlin: Erich Schmidt, 1965, pp. 78-114.

3231. EVANS, FALLON. "The <u>Portrait</u> as a Literary Work," in <u>Dedalus on Crete</u>, pp. 11-28, No. 3233.

3232. FARRELL, JAMES T. "Joyce's <u>A Portrait of the Artist as a Young Man</u>," in his <u>The League of Frightened Philistines</u>. New York: Vanguard Press, 1946, pp. 45-59. [Also appeared in <u>James Joyce: Two Decades of Criticism</u>, pp. 175-197, No. 1570.]

3233. FEEHAN, JOSEPH, ed. <u>Dedalus on Crete: Essays on the Implications of Joyce's Portrait</u>. Los Angeles: St. Thomas More Guild, Immaculate Heart College, 1956; paperback reprint, 1964.
    Contents: Joseph Feehan. "Introduction"; Fallon Evans. "The <u>Portrait</u> as a Literary Work," 11-28, No. 3231; Sister M. Aloyse. "The Novelist as Popularizer: Joyce and Psychological Fiction," 31-42, No. 3212; James P. Reilly. "Non Ego--Non Serviam: The Problem of Artistic Freedom," 45-52, No. 3426; Kenneth Pratt. "History on the Loose," 55-60, No. 3269; Alois Schardt. "The Mission of the Artist," 63-74, No. 3427; John F. Nims. "Dedalus in Crete," 77-88, No. 3263.

3234. FRANKE, ROSEMARIE. "Die Rezeption des ≪Portrait≫ im Deutschen Sprachbereich: Übersetzung, Verbreitung und Kritik," in <u>James Joyce's ≪Portrait≫: Das ≪Jugendbildnis≫ im Lichte neuerer Deutschen Forschung</u>, pp. 39-64, No. 3236.

3235. FREYRE, GILBERTO. "Reminiscências Católicas en James Joyce," <u>Retalhos de jornais</u>. Second edition, revised and enlarged. Rio de Janeiro: José Olypio, 1964, pp. 43-44. [First published 1925; collection published as <u>Artigos de jornal</u>. Recife, 1935.]

3236. FUGER, WILHELM, ed. <u>James Joyce's ≪Portrait≫ Das ≪Jugendbildnis≫ im Lichte neuerer deutschen Forschung</u>. Munich: Wilhelm Goldmann Vlg., 1972.
    Contents: Hans Walter Gabler. "Sur Textgeschichte und Textkritik des ≪Portrait≫" 20-38, No. 3237; Rosemarie Franke. "Die Rezeption des ≪Portrait≫ im deutschen Sprachbereich: Übersetzung, Verbreitung und Kritik," 39-64, No. 3234; Walter Höllerer. "Die Epiphanie also Held

des Romans," 65-74, No. 2835; Fränzi Maierhöffer. "Die fledermausähnliche Seele des Stephen Dedalus," 75-94, No. 3256; Ludwig W. Kahn. "Der Künstler als Luzifer und Heiland," 95-101, No. 3450; Ortwin Kuhn. "Zur Rolle des Nationalismus im Fruhwerk von James Joyce," 102-164, No. 3252; Wilhelm Fuger. "Türsymbolik in Joyce's ≪Portrait≫" 165-186 and in <u>Germanische-Romanische Monatsschrift</u>, n.F. 22 (1972): 39-57, No. 3478; Jörg Drews. "Enzyklopädisches Stichwort: Joyce's ≪Portrait≫," 187-190, No. 3226.

3237. GABLER, HANS WALTER. "Sur Textgeschichte und Textkritik des ≪Portrait≫" in <u>James Joyce's ≪Portrait≫: Das ≪Jugendbildnis≫ im Lichte neuerer deutschen Forschung</u>, pp. 20-38, No. 3236.

3238. GILLIE, CHRISTOPHER. "Human Subject and Human Substance: Stephen Dedalus of <u>A Portrait of the Artist</u>, Rupert Birkin of <u>Women in Love</u>," in <u>Character in English Literature</u>. London: Chatto and Windus; New York: Barnes and Noble, 1965, pp. 177-202.

3239. GOLDBERG, M. A. "Joyce, Freud, and the Internalization of Order," in his <u>The Poetics of Romanticism: Toward a Reading of John Keats</u>. Yellow Springs, Ohio: Antioch Press, 1969, pp. 151-160.

3240. GORMAN, HERBERT. "Introduction," in Joyce's <u>A Portrait of the Artist as a Young Man</u>. New York: Modern Library, 1928, pp. v-xii.

3241. HACKETT, FRANCIS. "Green Sickness." <u>New Republic</u>, 10 (3 March 1917): 138-139. [Reprinted in his <u>Horizons</u>. New York: B. W. Huebsch, 1918, pp. 163-168.]

3242. HANCOCK, LESLIE. <u>Word Index to James Joyce's Portrait of the Artist</u>. Carbondale, Ill.: Southern Illinois University Press; London: Feffer and Simons, 1967.

3243. HANSON, CHRISTOPHER. <u>Portrait as a Young Man (Joyce)</u>. Oxford: Blackwell, 1969.

3244. HARDY, JOHN EDWARD. "Joyce's <u>Portrait</u>: The Flight of the Serpent," in his <u>Man in the Modern Novel</u>. Seattle: University of Washington Press, 1964, pp. 67-81.

3245. HARVEY, FRANCIS. "<u>Stephen Hero</u> and <u>Portrait of the Artist</u>: The Intervention of Style in a Work of the Creative Imagination," in <u>A Bash in the Tunnel</u>, pp. 203-207, No. 1644.

3246. HELLYAR, RICHMOND H. <u>W. N. P. Barbellion</u>. London: Leonard Parsons, 1926, pp. 55, 82-89, 130.

3247. HESTON, LILLA. "The Interpreter and the Structure of the Novel," in <u>Studies in

Interpretation. Edited by Esther M.
Doyle and Virginia Hastings Floyd. Amsterdam: Rodopi, 1972, pp. 137-152.

3248. HOPPER, J. L. A Comprehensive Outline of
Joyce's Portrait of the Artist. East
Longmeadow, Mass.: Harvard Outline Co.,
1965.

*3249. JAFFE, ADRIAN, and HERBERT WEISINGER. The
Laureate Fraternity: An Introduction to
Literature. Evanston, Ill.: Row, Peter-
son, 1960, pp. 272-273.

3250. JOHNSON, ROBERT G. "The Daedalus Myth in
Joyce's Portrait," in Studies in the
Humanities, no. 3. Edited by John
Freund. Indiana, Pa.: Indiana Univer-
sity of Pa., 1973, pp. 17-19.

3251. KENNER, HUGH. "The Portrait in Perspective,"
in James Joyce: Two Decades of Criticism,
pp. 132-174, No. 1570; differs greatly
from the chapter with the same title in
his Dublin's Joyce, No. 1600. [Appeared
in Kenyon Review, 10 (Summer 1948): 361-
381; reprinted in Joyce's Portrait: Criticisms and Critiques, pp. 25-60, No. 3223
and in Portraits of an Artist: A Casebook
on James Joyce's A Portrait, pp. 45-64,
No. 3260.]

3252. KUHN, ORTWIN. "Zur Rolle des Nationalismus
im Früwerk von James Joyce," in James
Joyce's ≪Portrait≫ Das ≪Jugendbildnis≫
im Lichte neuerer deutscher Forschung,
pp. 102-164, No. 3236.

3253. LASS, ABRAHAM H., ed. "Portrait of the Artist by James Joyce," in A Student's Guide
to 50 British Novels. New York: Washington Square, 1966, pp. 277-284.

3254. LILLY, KATHERINE A. A Portrait of the Artist as a Young Man by James Joyce: Notes.
Lincoln, Nebr.: Cliff's Notes, 1964.

3255. MAGALANER, MARVIN, ed. Critical Reviews of
A Portrait of the Artist as a Young Man
by James Joyce. New York: Simon and
Schuster, 1966. [New York: Selected
Academic Readings, 1965; preliminary
edition.]
  Contents: Marvin Magalaner. "Intro-
duction," 7-9; Robert Ryf. "Patterns in
A Portrait," 11-33 (from No. 3271); Harry
Levin. "The Artist in A Portrait," 34-47
(from No. 1603); Marvin Magalaner and
Richard M. Kain. "Backgrounds of A Por-
trait," 48-78 (from No. 1615); Julian
Kaye. "Who is Betty Byrne?," 79-81, No.
3346; Chester G. Anderson. "The Sacrifi-
cial Butter," 82-92, No. 3471; "Selected
Bibliography," 93-94.

3256. MAIERHÖFFER, FRÄNZI. "Die fledermausähnliche Seele des Stephen Dedalus," in
James Joyce's ≪Portrait≫: Das ≪Jugend-

bildnis≫ im Lichte neuerer deutscher Forschung, pp. 75-94, No. 3236.

3257. MARKOVIC, VIDA E. "Stephen Dedalus," in
The Changing Face: Disintegration of Personality in the Twentieth-Century British
Novel, 1900-1950. Carbondale and Edwardsville: Southern Illinois University Press;
London and Amsterdam: Feffer and Simons,
1970, pp. 38-53.

3258. MARUYA, SAIICHI. "A Study of Portrait of
the Artist as a Young Man," in A Study
of Joyce, pp. 317-340, No. 1592.

*3259. MASUDA, YOSHIO. "Kyoyo Shosetsu" [Bildungs-
roman], in Joisu Nyumon [An Introduction
to James Joyce], pp. 154-161, No. 1511.

3260. MORRIS, WILLIAM E., and CLIFFORD A. NAULT,
eds. Portraits of an Artist: A Casebook
on James Joyce's A Portrait. New York:
Odyssey Press, 1962.
  Contents: Richard M. Kain. "The Joyce
Enigma," 3 (from No. 1615); Richard Ellmann. "A Chronology of the Life of James
Joyce," 4-11 (from No. 308); William Powell Jones. "Themes, Styles, and Episodes,"
12-18 (from No. 3602); Edward Garnett.
"Rejection by a Publisher's Reader," 19-
21 (from No. 308); Marvin Magalaner.
"Early Reviews and Notices," 22-27 (from
No. 1615); Harry Levin. "Joyce's Portrait,"
31-44 (from No. 1603); Hugh Kenner. "The
Portrait in Perspective," 45-64 (from No.
3251); Dorothy Van Ghent. "On A Portrait,"
65-76 (from No. 3422); Eugene M. Waith.
"The Calling of Stephen Dedalus," 77-84
(from No. 3407); John V. Kelleher. "The
Perceptions of James Joyce," 85-94, No.
3418; Richard Ellmann. "Ten Passages from
the Life of the Artist," 97-119 (from No.
308); Kevin Sullivan. "Clongowes Wood and
Belvedere," 120-142 (from No. 357); James
Joyce. "Limerick for Ezra Pound," 143
(from No. 317); James Joyce. "The 'Eagle'
Epiphany," 147 (from No. 2843); James
Joyce. "Passing through Eccles Street,"
148-150 (from Stephen Hero, 1955); Theodore Spencer. "Introduction," 151-152, No.
3200; Irene Hendry Chayes. "Joyce's Epi-
phanies," 153-167, No. 2833; Rudd Fleming.
"Quidditas in the Tragi-Comedy of Joyce,"
168-178 (from No. 3443); James R. Baker.
"James Joyce: Esthetic Freedom and Dra-
matic Art," 179-190, No. 3430; Ellsworth
Mason. "Joyce's Categories," 191-195, No.
3457; Shiv K. Kumar. "Bergson and Stephen
Dedalus' Aesthetic Theory," 196-200, No.
3454; William T. Noon. "A Pennyworth of
Thomism," 201-213 (from No. 943); Grant H.
Redford. "The Role of Structure in Joyce's
Portrait," 217-227, No. 3382; Melvin
Friedman. "Stream of Consciousness in the
Portrait," 228-232 (from No. 4189); Wil-
liam York Tindall. "Image and Symbol in
the Portrait," 232-240 (from No. 951);
Marvin Magalaner. "Motif in the Portrait,"

STUDIES OF A PORTRAIT OF THE ARTIST AS A YOUNG MAN

241-247 (from No. 1615); Joseph Prescott. "James Joyce: A Study in Words," 248-252, No. 5294; Elizabeth F. Boyd. "Joyce's Hell-Fire Sermons," 253-263, No. 3301; Julian B. Kaye. "Who is Betty Byrne?," 264-266 (from No. 3346); Chester G. Anderson. "The Sacrificial Butter," 267-277, No. 3471; "Suggestions for Individual Interpretation, Class Discussions, and Themes," 281-290; "Some Suggested Research Paper Topics," 291-292; "A One-Hundred Item Checklist of Publications Relevant to the Portrait," 293-298.

3261. MUELLER, WILLIAM R. "The Theme of Vocation: James Joyce's Portrait of the Artist," in his The Prophetic Voice in Modern Fiction. New York: Association Press, 1959, pp. 27-55; paperback reprint. New York: Doubleday-Anchor, 1966, pp. 15-45.

3262. _____. "James Joyce: Genesis of an Artist," in his Celebration of Life: Studies in Modern Fiction. New York: Sheed and Ward, 1972, pp. 9-29.

3263. NIMS, JOHN F. "Dedalus in Crete," in Dedalus on Crete, pp. 77-88, No. 3233.

3264. NOMA, HIROSHI. "The Battle against the Subconscious," in A Study of Joyce, pp. 283-298, No. 1592.

3265. NOON, WILLIAM T. "A Portrait of the Artist as a Young Man: After Fifty Years," in James Joyce Today, pp. 54-82, No. 1659.

3266. O'FAOLAIN, SEAN. "Introduction" in A Portrait of the Artist as a Young Man. New York: New American Library, 1954.

3267. OLFSON, LEWY, ed. "Portrait of the Artist," in Plot Outlines of 100 Famous Novels: The Second Hundred. Garden City, New York: Dolphin-Doubleday, 1966, pp. 110-115.

*3268. ONO, KYOICHI. "Wakaki Geijutsuka no Shozo" [Portrait], in Joisu Nyumon [An Introduction to James Joyce], pp. 38-45, No. 1511.

3269. PRATT, KENNETH. "History on the Loose," in Dedalus on Crete, pp. 55-60, No. 3233.

*3270. PRAZ, MARIO. "Ritratto dell'artista giovane," Cronache letterarie anglosassoni. Letture di Pensiero e de'arte, no. 16. Rome: Edizioni di Storia e Letteratura, 1950, pp. 223-226. [Reprint of 1933 review of Pavese's translation of PAYM.]

3271. RYF, ROBERT S. A New Approach to Joyce. Berkeley: University of California Press, 1962. [Contains "Joyce's Visual Imagination." Texas Studies in Literature and Language, 1 (Spring 1959): 30-43; "Patterns in A Portrait," reprinted in Crit-ical Reviews of A Portrait of the Artist, pp. 11-33, No. 3255.]

3272. SCHOLES, ROBERT, and RICHARD M. KAIN, eds. The Workshop of Daedalus: James Joyce and the Materials for A Portrait of the Artist as a Young Man. Evanston, Ill.: Northwestern University Press, 1965. [Part I, Manuscript Materials; Part II, Biographical Materials; Part III, Milieu and Influences.]

3273. SCHUTTE, WILLIAM M., ed. Twentieth Century Interpretations of A Portrait of the Artist as a Young Man. Englewood Cliffs, New Jersey: Prentice-Hall, 1968.
Contents: "Introduction," 1-14; J. I. M. Stewart. "A Portrait of the Artist as a Young Man," 15-20 (from revised edition of No. 1664); Joseph Prescott. "Stephen Hero," 21-25 (from No. 3207); Hugh Kenner. "The Portrait in Perspective," 26-37 (from 3251); Richard Ellmann. "The Structure of the Portrait," 38-40 (from No. 308); Lee T. Lemon. "A Portrait of the Artist as a Young Man: Motif as Motivation and Structure," 41-52, No. 3356; Barbara Seward. "The Artist and the Rose," 53-63 (from No. 3483); S. L. Goldberg. "Art and Life: The Aesthetic of the Portrait," 64-84 (from No. 1574); Wayne C. Booth. "The Problem of Distance in A Portrait of the Artist," 85-95 (from No. 3218); F. Parvin Sharpless. "Irony in Joyce's Portrait: The Stasis of Pity," 96-106, No. 3396; Harry Levin. 107-108 (from No. 1603); Eugene M. Waith. "The Calling of Stephen Dedalus," 108-110, No. 3407; Richard Ellmann. "The Growth of Imagination," 110 (from No. 308); James Naremore. "Style as Meaning in A Portrait of the Artist," 110-111, No. 3371; Dorothy Van Ghent. "On A Portrait of the Artist," 112-114 (from No. 3422); Ernest Bernhardt-Kabisch. "Joyce's Portrait of the Artist," 114-115, No. 3299; Florence L. Walzl. "The Liturgy of the Epiphany Season and the Epiphanies of Joyce," 115-117, No. 2844; Irene Hendry Chayes. "Joyce's Epiphanies," 117-118, No. 2833.

3274. SENN, FRITZ. "Nawoord," to Stephen Dedalus, translated by John Vandenbergh. Amsterdam: De Bezige Bij, 1968, pp. 91-108.

3275. SHANKS, EDWARD. First Essays on Literature. London: Collins, 1923, pp. 23-45, 139, 180-182.

3276. SMITH, JOHN B. "Image and Imagery in Joyce's Portrait: A Computer-Assisted Analysis," in Directions in Literary Criticism: Contemporary Approaches to Literature [Festschrift for Henry W. Sams]. Edited by Stanley Weintraub and Philip Young. University Park and London: Pennsylvania State University Press, 1973, pp. 220-227.

3277. SPIELBERG, PETER. "James Joyce's Errata for American Editions of A Portrait of the Artist," in Joyce's Portrait: Criticisms and Critiques, pp. 318-328, No. 3223.

3278. SPRINCHORN, EVERT. "A Portrait of the Artist as Achilles," in Approaches to the Twentieth-Century Novel. Edited by John Unterecker. New York: Crowell, 1965, pp. 9-50.

3279. STALEY, THOMAS F. A Critical Study Guide to James Joyce's A Portrait of the Artist as a Young Man. Totowa, New Jersey; Los Angeles: Littlefield, Adams, 1968; Philadelphia: Educational Research Associates, 1968.

3280. SUCKSMITH, HARVEY PETER. James Joyce: Portrait. Studies in English Literature, no. 52. London: Edward Arnold, 1973.

3281. URANGA, EMILIO. Astucias Literarias. Mexico City: FEM, 1971, pp. 233-237. [An untitled dialogue, taking off from Joyce's question and answer about a man "lacking in Fury," etc. from Paris Notebooks (Workshop of Daedalus), p. 55, No. 3272.]

*3282. VIEBROCK, HELMUT. "Nachwort" to James Joyce, Jugendbildnis des Dichters. Exempla Classica, 11. Frankfurt a.M.: Fischer Bücherei, 1960, pp. 199-201.

3283. WOODS, SAMUEL H. "Style and Point of View in A Portrait of the Artist," in An Introduction to Literature. Edited by Mary Rohrberger, Samuel H. Woods, and Bernard F. Dukore. New York: Random House, 1968, pp. 342-345.

3284. Unsigned. A Critical Commentary: A Portrait of the Artist as a Young Man. New York: American R. D. M. Corporation, 1963.

3285. Unsigned. Notes on James Joyce's Portrait of the Artist as a Young Man. London: Methuen Educational, 1971; Cape Town: College of Careers, 1971.

Periodical Articles

3286. ABERNETHY, F. W. "Stephen's Passage Through the Wilderness." South Central Bulletin, 26 (March 1966): 14; published in New Orleans Review, 1 (Winter 1969): 162-165.

3287. ADAMS, ROBERT M. "Letters." James Joyce Quarterly, 6 (Fall 1968): 98-99. [Reply to review of Adams' James Joyce: Common Sense and Beyond, No. 1506, by Chester G. Anderson. James Joyce Quarterly, 5 (Spring 1968): 245-256 (especially pp. 250-256 concerning Anderson's text of Portrait).]

3288. ALTIERI, CHARLES. "Organic and Humanist Models in Some English Bildungsroman." Journal of General Education, 23 (October 1971): 220-240. [Oscar Wilde, James Joyce, John Barth.]

3289. AMOR, JOSÉ BLANC. "Julio Cortázar." Cuadernos Americanos, 160 (September-October 1968): 219.

3290. ANDERSON, CHESTER G. "The Text of James Joyce's A Portrait of the Artist as a Young Man." Neuphilologische mitteilungen, 65 (1964): 160-200.

3291. _____. "Note." James Joyce Quarterly, 5 (Spring 1968): 255. [Suggests "Edward Garnett's 'reader's report'" to Duckworth and Company was by Herbert J. Cape, an employee, and sent to J. B. Pinker, Joyce's agent.]

*3292. ANGELI, DIEGO. "Extract from 'Il Marzocco' Florence, August 12, 1917." The Egoist, 5, no. 2 (February 1918): 30. [Translated, if not in fact written, by Joyce.]

3293. AUBERT, JACQUES. "Letter to the Editor." James Joyce Quarterly, 8 (Winter 1970): 273. [On Synopsis philosophiae scholasticae in Portrait.]

3294. AUGUST, EUGENE R. "Father Arnall's Use of Scripture in A Portrait." James Joyce Quarterly, 4 (Summer 1967): 275-279.

3295. BACH, ROBYN. "If a Tuckoo Meet a Moocow Coming Through the Green, Which Jumps Over the Moon." Wake Newslitter, 6 (December 1969): 83-91.

3296. BALOTA, NICOLAE. "Resurectia lui Joyce: Portretul artistului in tinerete." România Literară, 1 (May 1969): 12.

3297. BERGER, HÉLÈNE. "L'avant-portrait ou la bifurcation d'une vocation." Tel quel, no. 22 (Summer 1965): 69-76.

3298. _____. "Portrait de sa femme par l'artiste." Lettres nouvelles, 15 (March-April 1966): 41-67.

3299. BERNHARDT-KABISCH, ERNEST. "Joyce's A Portrait of the Artist as a Young Man." Explicator, 18 (January 1960): item 24. [Reprinted in The Explicator Cyclopedia, Vol. 3. Edited by C. C. Walcutt and J. E. Whitesell. Chicago: Quadrangle, 1966; reprinted in Twentieth Century Interpretations of A Portrait of the Artist as a Young Man, pp. 114-115, No. 3273.]

3300. BIDERSON, ELLIS. "Joyce Without Fear." English Journal, 57 (February 1968): 200-202. [See reply by Hazel E. Cohen, ibid., 57 (November 1968): 1203-1204.]

STUDIES OF <u>A PORTRAIT OF THE ARTIST AS A YOUNG MAN</u>

3301. BOYD, ELIZABETH F. "James Joyce's Hell-Fire Sermons." <u>Modern Language Notes</u>, 75 (November 1960): 561-571. [Reprinted in <u>Portraits of an Artist: A Casebook on James Joyce's A Portrait of the Artist as a Young Man</u>, pp. 253-263, No. 3260; reprinted in <u>Portrait: Notes</u>, No. 3222.]

3302. BRANDABUR, EDWARD. "Stephen Dedalus and Paul Morel." <u>Revista de letras</u>, 2 (September 1970): 358-370.

3303. BULLOUGH, GEOFFREY. "Science and Literature: Influences in the Modern Novel." <u>Scotsman</u> (Edinburgh), 31 August 1933.

3304. BURROWS, JOHN. "A Sketch of Joyce's <u>Portrait</u>." <u>Balcony</u> (Sydney), no. 3 (Spring 1965): 23-29.

3305. BURTON, DOLORES M. "Intonation Patterns of Sermons in Seven Novels." <u>Language and Style</u>, 3 (Summer 1970): 205-218.

3306. CASTAGNA, BARBARA. "Boine e <u>Dedalus</u>: Une proposta di lettura." <u>Resine</u>, 2 (June 1973): 59-67.

3307. COHEN, HAZEL E. "To the Editor." <u>English Journal</u>, 57 (November 1968): 1203-1204. [Reply to Biderson, No. 3300.]

3308. COHN, ALAN M. "The Spanish Translation of <u>A Portrait of the Artist as a Young Man</u>." <u>Revue de littérature comparée</u>, 37 (July-September 1963): 405-409.

3309. COLLINS, R. G. "The Second Dedalus: Simon the Testifier." <u>James Joyce Quarterly</u>, 8 (Spring 1971): 233-235.

3310. CRANE, HART. "Joyce and Ethics." <u>Little Review</u>, 5, no. 3 (July 1918): 65. [Also appeared in <u>Twice a Year</u>, no. 12-13 (1945): 427-428; in <u>The Little Review Anthology</u>, pp. 298-299, No. 4356; reprinted in <u>Complete Poems and Selected Letters and Prose</u>. Edited by Brom Weber. New York: Liveright, 1966, pp. 199-200.]

3311. CURRAN, STUART. "'Bous Stephanoumenos': Joyce's Sacred Cow." <u>James Joyce Quarterly</u>, 6 (Winter 1968): 163-170.

3312. DESNOES, EDMONDO. "La mirada de Joyce." <u>Edita</u> (Havana), 1 (October 1964): 1-4.

3313. DIBBLE, BRIAN. "A Brunonian Reading of Joyce's <u>A Portrait of the Artist</u>." <u>James Joyce Quarterly</u>, 4 (Summer 1967): 280-285.

3314. DOHERTY, JAMES. "Joyce and <u>Hell Opened to Christians</u>: The Edition He Used for His 'Hell Sermons.'" <u>Modern Philology</u>, 61 (November 1963): 110-119. [See also James R. Thrane, No. 3405 and Elizabeth Boyd, No. 3301.]

3315. DYRKØB, JAN ULRIK. "En analyse af James Joyces <u>A Portrait of the Artist as a Young Man</u> med saerligt henblik på forholdet mellem fortaeller og hovedpersonen.'" <u>Extracta</u>, 2 (1969): 71-79.

3316. ECO, UMBERTO. "Le moyen age de James Joyce." <u>Tel quel</u>, 11 (Autumn 1962): 39-52.

*3317. EGRI, PÉTER. "James Joyce: Ifjukori önarckep." <u>Filologiai kozlony</u> (Budapest), 6 (1960): 261-266.

3318. _____. "The Function of Dreams and Visions in <u>A Portrait</u> and <u>Death in Venice</u>." <u>James Joyce Quarterly</u>, 5 (Winter 1968): 86-102.

3319. FARRELL, JAMES T. "Joyce and His Self-Portrait." <u>New York Times Book Review</u>, 31 December 1944, pp. 6, 16; "Joyce and the Tradition of the European Novel." <u>ibid.</u>, 21 January 1945, pp. 4, 18.

3320. FESHBACH, SIDNEY. "A Slow and Dark Birth: A Study of the Organization of <u>A Portrait of the Artist as a Young Man</u>." <u>James Joyce Quarterly</u>, 4 (Summer 1967): 289-300.

3321. FORAN, DONALD J. "A Mirror Held up to Stephen." <u>James Joyce Quarterly</u>, 4 (Summer 1967): 301-309.

3322. FORSTER, JEAN-PAUL. "Joyce, Stephen Hero et Stephen Dedalus." <u>Études des lettres</u>, s. 2, 9 (July-September 1966): 149-164.

3323. FRANKEN, GERARDINE. "Een portret van de kunstenaar als jongeman." <u>Levende Talen</u>, no. 269 (June-July 1970): 443-447.

3324. FRENCH, WARREN. "Two Portraits of the Artist: James Joyce's <u>Young Man</u>; Dylan Thomas's <u>Young Dog</u>." <u>University Review</u> (Dublin), no. 33 (June 1967): 261-266.

3325. FÜGER, WILHELM. "Joyce's <u>Portrait</u> und Nietzsche." <u>Arcadia</u>, 7 (1972): 231-259.

3326. GECKLE, GEORGE L. "Stephen Dedalus and W. B. Yeats: The Making of the Villanelle." <u>Modern Fiction Studies</u>, 15 (Spring 1969): 87-96.

3327. GILLAM, DOREEN M. E. "Joyce's <u>A Portrait of the Artist as a Young Man</u>." <u>Explicator</u>, 30 (February 1972): item 47.

*3328. GILLET, LOUIS. "Shakespeare: Les Tragedies: <u>Hamlet</u>." <u>Revue Hebdomadaire</u>, 39, no. 10 (8 March 1930): 147-[165]-174.

3329. GODIN, HENRI. "Variations Littéraires sur le Thème de la Confession." <u>French Studies</u>, 5 (July 1951): 197-216.

3330. GOLDMAN, ARNOLD. "Stephen Dedalus's Dream of Parnell." James Joyce Quarterly, 6 (Spring 1969): 262-264.

3331. GORDON, CAROLINE. "Some Readings and Misreadings." Sewanee Review, 61 (Summer 1953): 384-407. [Appeared in her How to Read a Novel, No. 985; reprinted in Joyce's Portrait: Criticisms and Critiques, pp. 136-156, No. 3223.]

3332. GORDON, JAN B. "The Dialogue of Life and Art in Arthur Symons' Spiritual Adventures." English Literature in Transition, 12 (1969): 105-117.

3333. HARRIS, JOHN F. "A Note on James Joyce." Today, 2, no. 15 (May 1918): 88-92.

3334. HAYMAN, DAVID. "A Portrait of the Artist as a Young Man and L'Éducation sentimentale: The Structural Affinities." Orbis litterarum, 19 (1964): 161-175.

*3335. HEAP, JANE. "James Joyce." Little Review, 3, no. 10 (April 1917): 8-9.

3336. HEDBERG, JOHANNES. "'Smugging.'" Moderna språk, 66, no. 1 (1972): 19-25. [See also article by Rynell, No. 3387.]

3337. HEIMER, JACKSON W. "The Betrayer as Intellectual: Conrad's Under Western Eyes." Polish Review, 12 (Autumn 1967): 57-68.

3338. HELMS, DENISE M. "A Note on Stephen's Dream in Portrait." James Joyce Quarterly, 8 (Winter 1970): 151-156.

3339. HERMANN, WALTER M. "Deutsche Erstaufführung im Schauspielhaus: 'Ich will nicht dienen': 'Stephen Daedalus'--erfolgreiche Dramatisierung einer James Joyce Biographie." Hamburger Abendblatt, 13 February 1964.

3340. HUEFFER [FORD], FORD MADOX. "A Haughty and Proud Generation." Yale Review, 11 (July 1922): 714-717.

3341. JACK, JANE H. "Art and The Portrait of the Artist." Essays in Criticism, 5 (October 1955): 354-364. [Reprinted in Joyce's Portrait: Criticisms and Critiques, pp. 156-167, No. 3223.]

3342. JANIK, DEL IVAN. "Flann O'Brien: The Novelist as Critic." Éire-Ireland, 4 (Winter 1969): 64-72. [At Swim-Two-Birds and PAYM.]

3343. JARNES, BENJAMIN. "James Joyce's 'El Artista Adolescente.'" Revista de occidente (Madrid), 13, no. 39 (September 1926): 383-386.

3344. KAIN, RICHARD M. "New Perspectives on the Portrait: A Prefactory Note." James Joyce Quarterly, 4 (Summer 1967): 251-254.

3345. _____. "Why is 'The Best English' Spoken in Lower Drumcondre? A Note on the Portrait." James Joyce Quarterly, 11 (Fall 1973): 51-52.

3346. KAYE, JULIAN B. "Who is Betty Byrne?" Modern Language Notes, 71 (February 1956): 93-95. [Reprinted in Portraits of an Artist: A Casebook on James Joyce's A Portrait of the Artist as a Young Man, pp. 264-266, No. 3260; in Critical Reviews of A Portrait of the Artist as a Young Man, pp. 79-81, No. 3255; reprinted in Portrait: Notes, No. 3222.]

3347. KELL, RICHARD. "The Goddess Theme in Portrait." Dublin Magazine, 9 (Summer 1972): 100-108.

3348. KELLY, EDWARD H. "Joyce's A Portrait of the Artist as a Young Man, Chapter II. Conclusion." Explicator, 27 (January 1969): item 32.

3349. KELLY, RICHARD. "The Lost Vision in Dylan Thomas's 'One Warm Saturday.'" Studies in Short Fiction, 6 (Winter 1969): 205-209.

3350. KELLY, ROBERT G. "James Joyce: A Partial Explanation." Publications of the Modern Language Association, 64 (March 1949): 26-39.

3351. KENNER, HUGH. "Joyce's Portrait--A Reconsideration." University of Windsor Review, 1 (1965): 1-15.

3352. _____. "The Counterfeiters." Virginia Quarterly Review, 42 (Winter 1966): 72-88.

3353. KLEIN, JAMES R. "Lotts, Horse Piss, and Rotted Straw." College English, 34 (April 1973): 952-958, 967-974.

3354. KOLJEVIĆ, SVETOZAR. "Roman o rečima: Ogled o Džojsovom portretu umetnika u mladosti." Knji, no. 22 (1967): 1-16.

3355. KURZWEIL, BARUCH. "Al shlosha sippurei hitbagrut mereshit ha-me'ah ha-essrim [Three Early Twentieth Century Stories Dealing with Maturing of the Personality of the Hero]." Bikoret u-Parshanut, 1 (1970): 7-11. [Robert Musil's The Pupil Törless, Joyce's PAYM and Franâ Sramek's Silvery Wind.]

3356. LEMON, LEE T. "Portrait of the Artist as a Young Man: Motif as Motivation and Structure." Modern Fiction Studies, 12 (Winter 1966/67): 439-450. [Reprinted in Twentieth Century Interpretations of A Portrait of the Artist as a Young Man, pp. 41-52, No. 3273.]

3357. LEONARD, HUGH. "Half the Agony." Plays and Players, 10 (March 1963): 18-19.

STUDIES OF A PORTRAIT OF THE ARTIST AS A YOUNG MAN

3358. LITTLE, GEORGE A. "James Joyce and the Boy Called Little." Irish Digest, 76 (November 1962): 53-57.

3359. _____ . "James Joyce and Little's Death." James Joyce Quarterly, 4 (Summer 1967): 258-262.

3360. McCAUGHEY, G. S. "Stephen Ego." Humanities Association Bulletin (of Canada), 13 (1962-1963): 5-9.

*3361. MacMANUS, FRANCIS. "Portrait of the Reader as a Young Man." Irish Press, 27 October 1962, p. 4.

3362. MAGALANER, MARVIN. "Reflections on A Portrait of the Artist." James Joyce Quarterly, 4 (Summer 1967): 343-346.

3363. MANSO, PETER. "The Metaphoric Style of Joyce's Portrait." Modern Fiction Studies, 13 (Summer 1967): 221-236.

3364. MARCUS, PHILIP L. "In Defense of Mr. Deasy." James Joyce Quarterly, 4 (Fall 1966): 49.

*3365. MAREN, VALERIE. "Des Mystikers James Joyce Weltruhm." Borsen Courier (Berlin), 417 (8 September 1926): 5.

*3366. MARIATEGUI, JOSÉ CARLOS. "Figuras y aspectos de la vida mundial: Dedalus o la adolescenci de James Joyce." Variedades, 22, no. 952 (29 May 1926).

3367. MERCER, CAROLINE G. "Stephen Dedalus's Vision and Synge's Peasant Girls." Notes and Queries, 205 (December 1960): 473-474.

3368. MIYATA, KYOKO. ["A Study of Joyce's Portrait"]. Hikaku bungaku kenkyu (January 1971): 76-103. [In Japanese.]

3369. MOLEN, SVEN ERIC. "A Method for Analyzing Novels." Exercise Exchange, 11 (November 1963): 7-9.

*3370. MORSE, J. MITCHELL. "Study Guide to A Portrait." Exercise Exchange, 9 (November 1961): 13-16.

3371. NAREMORE, JAMES. "Style as Meaning in A Portrait of the Artist." James Joyce Quarterly, 4 (Summer 1967): 331-342. [Reprinted in Twentieth Century Interpretations of A Portrait of the Artist as a Young Man, pp. 110-111, No. 3273.]

3372. NEWMAN, FRANCIS X. "A Source for the Name 'Dedalus.'" James Joyce Quarterly, 4 (Summer 1967): 271-274.

3373. NOON, WILLIAM T., S.J. "Three Young Men in Rebellion." Thought, 38 (Winter 1963): 560-577.

3374. O'NEILL, BRIDGET. "Joyce and Lemon Plat." American Notes and Queries, 3 (April 1965): 117-118.

3375. PASSANANTE, JEAN. "The Role of Woman in Joyce's Portrait." Crescendo (Horton Watkins High School, Ladue, Mo.), 10 (Spring 1971): 19-23.

3376. PEARCE, DONALD R. "My Dead King: The Dinner Quarrel in Joyce's Portrait of the Artist." Modern Language Notes, 66 (April 1951): 249-251.

3377. PLUMMER, JOACHIM. "The Secular City and the Sacred Countryside: A Reflection on James Joyce's Portrait of the Artist." Dominicana, 53 (Summer 1968): 128-135.

3378. POSS, STANLEY H. "Stephen's Words, Joyce's Attitude." Washington State University Research Studies, 28 (December 1960): 156-161.

*3379. POUND, EZRA. "Editorial." Little Review, 4, no. 1 (May 1917): 3-6.

3380. PRATT, ANNIS. "Women and Nature in Modern Fiction." Contemporary Literature, 13 (Fall 1972): 476-490. [Sarah Orne Jewett's "A White Heron" and PAYM.]

3381. REDDICK, BRYAN. "The Importance of Tone in the Structural Rhythm of Joyce's Portrait." James Joyce Quarterly, 6 (Spring 1969): 201-218.

3382. REDFORD, GRANT H. "The Role of Structure in Joyce's Portrait." Modern Fiction Studies, 4 (Spring 1958): 21-30. [Reprinted in Joyce's Portrait: Criticisms and Critiques, pp. 102-114, No. 3223; reprinted in Portraits of an Artist: A Casebook on James Joyce's Portrait of the Artist as a Young Man, pp. 217-227, No. 3260; reprinted in Portrait: Notes, No. 3222.]

*3383. REYES, PEDRO A. "A Difference of Grammar." Diliman Review, 9 (January 1961): 117-123. [Huck Finn and PAYM.]

3384. RHIND, NEIL. "Letter to the Editor." Times Literary Supplement, 28 December 1967, p. 1259. [About Leslie Hancock's Word Index to James Joyce's Portrait of the Artist, No. 3242.]

*3385. RILEY, SR. MARY GERALDINE. "The Verbal Ritual of James Joyce." Greyfriar, 3 (1960): 13-21.

3386. ROBINSON, K. E. "The Stream of Consciousness Technique and the Structure of Joyce's Portrait." James Joyce Quarterly, 9 (Fall 1971): 63-84.

3387. RYNELL, ALARIK. "On the Etymology of James Joyce's 'Smugging.'" Moderna Språk, 66 (1972): 366-369. [See article by Hedberg, No. 3336.]

3388. SCHOLES, ROBERT E. "Stephen Dedalus: Eiron and Alazon." Texas Studies in Literature and Language, 3 (Spring 1961): 8-15.

3389. _____. "Stephen Dedalus, Poet or Aesthete?" Publications of the Modern Language Association, 79 (September 1964): 484-489.

3390. SCHORER, MARK. "Technique as Discovery." Hudson Review, 1 (Spring 1948): 67-87. [Reprinted in his The World We Imagine. New York: Farrar, Straus and Giroux, 1968, pp. 3-23.]

3391. SCHWARTZ, EDWARD. "Joyce's A Portrait of the Artist as a Young Man, V." Explicator, 11 (February 1953): item 27.

*3392. SCOTT, ROBERT IAN. "Modern Theories of Communication and Types of Literature." James Joyce Review, 1 (December 1957): 18-32.

3393. SCOTTO, ROBERT M. "'Visions' and 'Epiphanies': Fictional Technique in Pater's Marius and Joyce's Portrait." James Joyce Quarterly, 11 (Fall 1973): 41-50.

3394. SENN, FRITZ. "Portrait of the Artist as a Young Man: Goodness Gracious." Joycenotes, 3 (December 1969): 13. [On Third Chapter.]

3395. _____. "Latin Me That." James Joyce Quarterly, 4 (Spring 1967): 241-243.

3396. SHARPLESS, F. PARVIN. "Irony in Joyce's Portrait: The Stasis in Pity." James Joyce Quarterly, 4 (Summer 1967): 320-330. [Reprinted in Twentieth Century Interpretations of A Portrait of the Artist as a Young Man, pp. 96-106, No. 3273.]

3397. SINGH, V. D. "Versions of Joyce's Portrait." Rutgers University Studies in English, 5 (1971): 59-67.

3398. SOLE, J. L. "Structure in Joyce's A Portrait." The Serif, 5 (1968): 9-13.

*3399. SPIELBERG, PETER. "A Portrait of the Artist as a Young Man: A Novel for Reading in Freshman English." Exercise Exchange, 7 (April 1960): 5-7.

3400. SQUIRE, J. C. "Mr. James Joyce." New Statesman, 9 (14 April 1917): 40. [Reprinted in his Books in General. New York: Knopf, 1919, pp. 225-230; reprinted Freeport, New York: Books for Libraries, 1971, pp. 245-250.]

3401. STALEY, THOMAS F. "James Joyce's Portrait of the Artist and the Bildungsroman." South Central Bulletin, 24 (February 1964): 8.

3402. SUZUKI, KENZO. "...logumque perosus exilium tactusque loci natalis amore-A Portrait of the Artist Shiron." Eigo Seinen (Tokyo), 118 (1972): 16-19.

*3403. SYPHER, WYLIE. "Portrait of the Artist as John Keats." Virginia Quarterly Review, 25 (Summer 1949): 420-428.

3404. TARBOX, RAYMOND. "Auditory Experience in Joyce's Portrait." American Imago, 27 (Winter 1970): 301-328.

3405. THRANE, JAMES R. "Joyce's Sermon on Hell: Its Source and its Backgrounds." Modern Philology, 57 (February 1960): 172-198. [Reprinted in A James Joyce Miscellany, Third Series, pp. 33-78, No. 1614.]

3406. VAN LAAN, THOMAS F. "The Meditative Structure of Joyce's Portrait." James Joyce Quarterly, 1 (Spring 1964): 3-13.

3407. WAITH, EUGENE M. "The Calling of Stephen Dedalus." College English, 18 (February 1957): 256-261. [Reprinted in Joyce's Portrait: Criticisms and Critiques, pp. 114-123, No. 3223; in Portraits of an Artist: A Casebook on James Joyce's A Portrait of the Artist as a Young Man, pp. 77-84, No. 3260; in Twentieth Century Interpretations of A Portrait of the Artist as a Young Man, pp. 108-110, No. 3273.]

3408. WALCOTT, WILLIAM O. "The Paternity of James Joyce's Stephen Dedalus." Journal of Analytical Psychology, 10 (January 1965): 77-95.

3409. WARREN, JOYCE W. "Faulkner's 'A Portrait of the Artist.'" Mississippi Quarterly, 19 (Summer 1966): 121-131. ["Mosquitoes."]

*3410. WEAVER, HARRIET SHAW. "Views and Comments." Egoist, no. 3 (March 1916): 35.

3411. WILDS, NANCY G. "Style and Auctorial Presence in Portrait." Style, 7 (Winter 1973): 39-55.

*3412. WILHELM, WOLFGANG. "Das Literarische Porträt bei James Joyce: Betrachtung über ein Fruhwerk des irischen Dichters." Zeitschrift für Ästhetik und Allgemeine Kunstwissenschaft, 36 (1942): 166-173.

3413. WILSON, DON A. "Joyce's A Portrait of the Artist as a Young Man." Explicator, 28 (1970): item 84.

3414. WOODBERY, POTTER. "The Irrelevance of Stephen Dedalus: Some Reflections on Joyce and the Student Activist Movement."

STUDIES OF <u>A PORTRAIT OF THE ARTIST AS A YOUNG MAN</u>

<u>Studies in the Literary Imagination</u>, 3 (October 1970): 69-78.

3415. WORTHINGTON, MABEL P. "The Song Simon Sang." <u>James Joyce Quarterly</u>, 4 (Winter 1967): 159-160.

3416. Unsigned editorial. <u>Bookfinder Illustrated</u>, (May 1932).

A PORTRAIT OF THE ARTIST AS AUTOBIOGRAPHY

3417. GWYNN, STEPHEN. "Modern Irish Literature." <u>Manchester Guardian</u>, 15 March 1923, pp. 36-40. [Reprinted in his <u>Irish Literature and Drama in the English Language: A Short History</u>. London: Nelson, 1936, pp. 192-202; reprinted, Folcroft, Pa.: Folcroft Press, 1969, pp. 183-206.]

3418. KELLEHER, JOHN V. "The Perceptions of James Joyce." <u>Atlantic Monthly</u>, 201 (March 1958): 82-90. [Reprinted in <u>Portraits of an Artist: A Casebook on James Joyce's A Portrait of the Artist As a Young Man</u>, pp. 85-94, No. 3260.]

3419. LIND, ILSE DUSIOR. "<u>The Way of All Flesh</u> and <u>A Portrait of the Artist as a Young Man</u>: A Comparison." <u>Victorian Newsletter</u>, 9 (Spring 1956): 7-10.

3420. MAGALANER, MARVIN. "James Mangan and Joyce's Dedalus Family." <u>Philological Quarterly</u>, 31 (October 1952): 363-371.

3421. PASCAL, ROY. "The Autobiographical Novel and the Autobiography." <u>Essays in Criticism</u>, 9 (April 1959): 134-150.

3422. VAN GHENT, DOROTHY. "On <u>A Portrait of the Artist as a Young Man</u>," in her <u>The English Novel: Form and Function</u>. New York: Rinehart, 1953, pp. 263-276. [Reprinted in <u>Joyce's Portrait: Criticisms and Critiques</u>, pp. 60-74, No. 3223; in <u>Portraits of an Artist: A Casebook on James Joyce's A Portrait of the Artist as a Young Man</u>, pp. 65-76, No. 3260; in <u>Twentieth Century Interpretations of A Portrait of the Artist as a Young Man</u>, pp. 112-114, No. 3273.]

JOYCE'S AESTHETIC THEORY IN A PORTRAIT OF THE ARTIST

<u>Books</u>

3423. BRANDABUR, EDWARD. "Stephen's Aesthetic in <u>A Portrait of the Artist</u>," in <u>The Celtic Cross</u>. Edited by Ray B. Browne, William John Roscelli, and Richard Loftus. Lafayette, Ind.: Purdue University Studies, 1964, pp. 11-21. [Followed by "Comment" by Maurice Beebe, pp. 22-25.]

3424. HOFFMAN, FREDERICK J. "The Hardness of Reality: Joyce's Stephen Dedalus," in <u>The Imagination's New Beginning: Theology and Modern Literature</u>. University of

Notre Dame, Ward-Phillips Lectures in English Language and Literature, no. 1. South Bend, Ind.: University of Notre Dame Press, 1967, pp. 20-47. [Slightly revised version of essay in <u>Barat Review</u>, 1 (June 1966): 129-137.]

3425. JACQUOT, JEAN. <u>Mèlanges Georges Jamati</u>. Paris: Editions du Centre National da la Recherche Scientifique, 1956, pp. 135-159.

3426. REILLY, JAMES P. "Non Ego-Non Serviam: The Problem of Artistic Freedom," in <u>Dedalus on Crete</u>, pp. 45-52, No. 3233.

3427. SCHARDT, ALOIS. "The Mission of the Artist," in <u>Dedalus on Crete</u>, pp. 63-74, No. 3233.

<u>Periodical Articles</u>

3428. ARNOLD, ALLEN D. "A Consideration of James Joyce's Aesthetic Theory and His Indebtedness to Gustave Flaubert." <u>Horizontes</u>, 25 (1971): 27-35.

3429. BAKER, JAMES R. "James Joyce: Affirmation after Exile." <u>Modern Language Quarterly</u>, 18 (December 1957): 275-281.

3430. _____ . "James Joyce's Esthetic Freedom and Dramatic Art." <u>Western Humanities Review</u>, 5 (Winter 1950-1951): 29-42. [Reprinted in <u>Portraits of an Artist: A Casebook on James Joyce's A Portrait of the Artist as a Young Man</u>, pp. 179-190, No. 3260.]

3431. BEEBE, MAURICE. "Joyce and Aquinas: The Theory of Aesthetics." <u>Philological Quarterly</u>, 36 (January 1957): 20-35. [Reprinted in <u>Joyce's Portrait: Criticisms and Critiques</u>, pp. 272-289, No. 3223.]

3432. BLAKE, FORRESTER. "Conceptualizing." <u>Rendevous</u>, 1 (Winter 1966): 29-31.

3433. BLOCK, HASKELL M. "The Critical Theory of James Joyce." <u>Journal of Aesthetics and Art Criticism</u>, 8 (March 1950): 172-184. [Reprinted in <u>Joyce's Portrait: Criticism and Critiques</u>, pp. 231-249, No. 3223.]

3434. BREDIN, HUGH. "Applied Aquinas: James Joyce's Aesthetics." <u>Éire-Ireland</u>, 3 (Spring 1968): 61-78.

3435. _____ . "Joyce e l'Aquinate." <u>Il Verri</u>, 31 (December 1969): 96-112.

3436. CONNOLLY, THOMAS E. "Joyce's Aesthetic Theory." <u>University of Kansas City Review</u>, 23 (October 1956): 47-50. [Reprinted in <u>Joyce's Portrait: Criticisms and Critiques</u>, pp. 266-271, No. 3223.]

3437. _____ . "Kinesis and Stasis: Structural Rhythm in Joyce's <u>Portrait of the Artist</u>." <u>University Review</u> (Dublin), 3 (1966): 21-30.

Joyce's Aesthetic Theory in <u>A Portrait of the Artist</u>

3438. DAICHES, DAVID. "James Joyce: The Artist as Exile." <u>College English</u>, 2 (December 1940): 197-206. [Appeared, with slight revision, in <u>Forms of Modern Fiction</u>. Edited by William Van O'Connor. Minneapolis: University of Minnesota Press, 1948, pp. 61-71.]

3439. FACKLER, HERBERT V. "Stephen Dedalus Rejects Forgotten Beauty: A Yeats Allusion in <u>Portrait of the Artist</u>." <u>College Language Association Journal</u>, 12 (December 1968): 164-167.

3440. FARKAS, PAUL D. "The Irony of the Artist as a Young Man: A Study in the Structure of Joyce's <u>Portrait</u>." <u>Thoth</u>, 11 (1971): 22-32.

3441. FERNANDO, LLOYD. "Language and Reality in <u>A Portrait of the Artist</u>: Joyce and Bishop Berkeley." <u>Ariel</u>, 2 (1971): 78-93.

3442. FESHBACH, SIDNEY. "A Dramatic First Step: A Source for Joyce's Interest in the Idea of Daedalus." <u>James Joyce Quarterly</u>, 8 (Spring 1971): 197-204.

3443. FLEMING, RUDD. "<u>Quidditas</u> in the Tragic-comedy of Joyce." <u>University of Kansas City Review</u>, 15 (Summer 1949): 288-296. [Reprinted in <u>Portraits of an Artist: A Casebook on James Joyce's A Portrait of the Artist as a Young Man</u>, pp. 168-178, No. 3260.]

3444. FORREST, BARBARA. "The Writer's Craft (A Dialogue)." <u>Mexico Quarterly Review</u>, 4 (1971): 15-17. [Between Joyce and Aristotle.]

3445. GERARD, ALBERT. "Le Dédale de James Joyce." <u>Revue nouvelle</u>, 27 (1958): 493-501.

*3446. GOLDBERG, S. L. "Joyce and the Artist's Fingernails." <u>Review of English Literature</u>, 2 (April 1961): 59-73.

3447. GRAYSON, THOMAS W. "James Joyce and Stephen Dedalus: The Theory of Aesthetics." <u>James Joyce Quarterly</u>, 4 (Summer 1967): 310-319.

3448. HANLON, JAMES. "Reality in James Joyce's <u>A Portrait of the Artist as a Young Man</u>." <u>Shippensburg State College Review</u> (October 1968): 31-34.

3449. JONES, DAVID E. "The Essence of Beauty in James Joyce's Aesthetics." <u>James Joyce Quarterly</u>, 10 (Spring 1973): 291-311.

3450. KAHN, LUDWIG. "James Joyce: Der Künstler als Luzifer und als Heiland." <u>Literature und Glaubenskrise, Sprache und Literatur</u>, 17 (1964): 109-113. [Reprinted in <u>James</u> <u>Joyces «Portrait»: Das «Jugendbildnis» im Lichte neuerer deutscher Forschung</u>, pp. 95-101, No. 3236.]

3451. KARPOWITZ, STEPHEN. "A Psychology of the Joycean Artist and Aesthetic." <u>University of Windsor Review</u>, 7 (Fall 1971): 56-61.

3452. KELLEHER, V. M. K. "'The Fingernails of God': A Comment on Joyce's Aesthetic." <u>Unisa English Studies</u>, 9 (March 1971): 14-17.

3453. KIM, CHONG-KEON. "Sin iyŏ, Kyosuja yŏ! Han chŏlm ŭn yesulg ŭi yesul sekye sangso wa sin-ang ["Oh, God! the Hangman! The Creed and Creative World of a Young Artist]." <u>Yŏng-o yŏng munhak: The English Language and Literature</u> (Seoul), no. 26 (Summer 1968): 58-81.

3454. KUMAR, SHIV K. "Bergson and Stephen Dedalus's Aesthetic Theory." <u>Journal of Aesthetics and Art Criticism</u>, 16 (September 1957): 124-127. [Reprinted in <u>Bergson and the Stream of Consciousness Novel</u>, No. 4194; reprinted in <u>Portraits of an Artist: A Casebook on James Joyce's A Portrait of the Artist as a Young Man</u>, pp. 196-200, No. 3260.]

3455. LINK, FREDERICK M. "The Aesthetics of Stephen Dedalus." <u>Papers on Language and Literature</u>, 2 (Spring 1966): 140-149.

3456. MacGREGOR, GEDDES. "Artistic Theory in James Joyce." <u>Life and Letters</u>, 54 (July 1947): 18-27. [Reprinted in <u>Joyce's Portrait: Criticisms and Critiques</u>, pp. 221-230, No. 3223.]

3457. MASON, ELLSWORTH. "Joyce's Categories." <u>Sewanee Review</u>, 61 (Summer 1953): 427-432. [Reprinted in <u>Portraits of an Artist: A Casebook on James Joyce's A Portrait of the Artist as a Young Man</u>, pp. 191-195, No. 3260.]

3458. MORIN, EDWIN. "Joyce as Thomist." <u>Renascence</u>, 9 (Spring 1957): 127-131.

3459. MORSE, J. MITCHELL. "A Personal Postscript." <u>James Joyce Review</u>, 1, no. 2 (June 1957): 39-40.

3460. O'CONNOR, FRANK. "James Joyce." <u>American Scholar</u>, 35 (Summer 1967): 466-490. [Reprinted from <u>A Short History of Irish Literature</u>. New York: 1967, pp. 195-211; <u>PAYM</u> based on Aristotle's <u>De Anima</u>.]

3461. O'CONNOR, WILLIAM VAN. "Aristotle and Modern Criticism." <u>CEA Critic</u>, 24 (January 1962): 1, 4-5.

3462. O'DEA, RICHARD J. "The Young Artist as Archangel." <u>Southern Review</u>, 3 (1967): 106-114.

STUDIES OF <u>A PORTRAIT OF THE ARTIST AS A YOUNG MAN</u>

3463. PALIWAL, B. B. "The Artist as Creator in <u>Portrait</u>." <u>Literary Criterion</u>, 10 (Winter 1971): 44-49.

3464. POSS, STANLEY H. "A Portrait of the Artist as Hard-Boiled Messiah." <u>Modern Language Quarterly</u>, 27 (March 1966): 68-79.

3465. RANALD, MARGARET L. "Stephen Dedalus' Vocation and the Irony of Religious Ritual." <u>James Joyce Quarterly</u>, 2 (Winter 1965): 97-102.

*3466. REILLY, JAMES P. "Aesthetics as a Way of Life: A Study of Joyce." <u>Fresco</u>, 10 (Fall 1959): 37-47.

*3467. VIDAN, IVO. "Ravnodusnost tvorac." <u>Izraz</u> (Sarajevo), 8 (December 1960): 515-523. ["The Indifferent Creator."]

3468. WEINSTOCK, DONALD J. "Dedalus as the Great Oscar." <u>American Notes and Queries</u>, 8 (October 1969): 22-23.

3469. WHITE, PATRICK T. "A Note on Joyce's Esthetic: Vico's Laws of History as Aquinian <u>Quidditas</u>." <u>Wisconsin Studies in Literature</u>, 1 (1964): 44-53.

3470. WOODWARD, A. G. "Technique and Feeling in James Joyce's 'A Portrait of the Artist as a Young Man.'" <u>English Studies in Africa</u>, 4 (March 1961): 39-53. [Reprinted in <u>Configuration critique de James Joyce</u>, II, pp. 31-48, No. 1584.]

STUDIES OF THE SYMBOLISM OF A PORTRAIT OF THE ARTIST

3471. ANDERSON, CHESTER G. "The Sacrificial Butter." <u>Accent</u>, 12 (Winter 1952): 3-13. [Reprinted in <u>Joyce's Portrait: Criticisms and Critiques</u>, pp. 124-136, No. 3223; in <u>Portraits of an Artist: A Casebook on James Joyce's A Portrait of the Artist as a Young Man</u>, pp. 267-277, No. 3260; in <u>Critical Reviews of A Portrait of the Artist as a Young Man</u>, pp. 82-92, No. 3255; reprinted in <u>Portrait: Notes</u>, No. 3222.]

3472. ASPELL, JOSEPH. "Fire Symbolism in <u>A Portrait of the Artist as a Young Man</u>." <u>University of Dayton Review</u>, 5 (1968-69): 29-39.

3473. BATES, RONALD. "The Correspondence of Birds to Things of Intellect." <u>James Joyce Quarterly</u>, 2 (Summer 1965): 281-290.

3474. BECKSON, KARL. "Stephen Dedalus and the Emblematic Cosmos." <u>James Joyce Quarterly</u>, 6 (Fall 1968): 95-96.

3475. CAMPBELL, JOSEPH. <u>The Masks of God: Creative Mythology</u>. New York: Viking, 1968, <u>passim</u>.

3476. CAROTHERS, ROBERT L. "The Hand and Eye in Joyce's <u>Portrait</u>." <u>Serif</u>, 4 (1967): 17-29.

3477. FORTUNA, DIANE. "The Labyrinth as Controlling Image in Joyce's <u>Portrait</u>." <u>New York Public Library Bulletin</u>, 76 (1972): 120-180.

3478. FUGER, WILHELM. "Türsymbolik in Joyce's Portrait," in <u>James Joyces ≪Portrait≫: Das ≪Jugendbildnis≫ im Lichte neuerer deutscher Forschung</u>, pp. 165-186, No. 3236; in <u>Germanisch-Romanische Monatsschrift</u>, n.F. 22 (1972): 39-72.]

3479. GILLAM, DOREEN M. E. "Stephen Kouros." <u>James Joyce Quarterly</u>, 8 (Spring 1971): 221-232. [Jane Harrison's <u>Themis</u> (1912).]

3480. HAYMAN, DAVID. "Daedalian Imagery in <u>A Portrait of the Artist as a Young Man</u>," in <u>Hereditas: Seven Essays on the Modern Experience of the Classical</u>. Edited by Frederic Will. Austin: University of Texas Press, 1964. [Translated in <u>Configuration critique de James Joyce</u>, II, pp. 49-71, No. 1584.]

3481. MOSELEY, VIRGINIA D. "James Joyce's 'Grave of Boyhood.'" <u>Renascence</u>, 13 (Autumn 1960): 10-20.

3482. SENN, FRITZ. "Symbolic Juxtaposition," <u>James Joyce Quarterly</u>, 5 (Spring 1968): 276-278.

3483. SEWARD, BARBARA. "The Artist and the Rose." <u>University of Toronto Quarterly</u>, 26 (January 1957): 180-190. [Expanded in her <u>The Symbolic Rose</u>. New York: Columbia University Press, 1960, pp. 187-221; reprinted in <u>Joyce's Portrait: Criticisms and Critiques</u>, pp. 167-180, No. 3223; in <u>Twentieth Century Interpretations of A Portrait of the Artist as a Young Man</u>, pp. 53-63, No. 3273.]

3484. SMITH, JOHN B. "A Computational Analysis of Imagery in James Joyce's <u>Portrait</u>," in <u>Information Processing 71: Proceedings of IFIP Congress, 1971</u>, volume 2. Edited by C. V. Freiman. Amsterdam and London: North-Holland, 1972, pp. 1443-1447. [See also his "National Language Analysis: <u>Portrait</u>." <u>Computers and the Humanities</u>, 6 (May 1972): 308.]

3485. WASSON, RICHARD. "Stephen Dedalus and the Imagery of Sight: A Psychological Approach." <u>Literature and Psychology</u>, 15 (Fall 1965): 195-209.

EXILES

See also Beebe. Ivory Towers...., 290-293, No. 3216; Brasil. Joyce...., 91-98, No. 1530; Brandabur. Scrupulous...., 127-158, No. 1529; Cohn, Ruby. "Absurdity in English....," No. 4462; Ellmann. "Portrait....," No. 421; Ellmann. James Joyce, No. 308; Goldberg. Joyce...., 63-67, No. 1574; Golding. James Joyce, 69-82, No. 1575; Gorman. James Joyce, 101-115, No. 321; Gorman. James Joyce: First...., 69-94, No. 3585; Jacquot. Mélanges Georges Jamati, 135-159, No. 3425; Kenner. "Joyce and Ibsen's Naturalism," No. 671; Kenner. Dublin's Joyce, 69-94, No. 1600; Levin. Critical Introduction, 37-40, No. 1603; Litz. James Joyce, 73-76, No. 1606; Magalaner and Kain. Joyce: The Man...., 130-145, No. 1615; Majault. Joyce, 61, No. 1616; Misra. Indian...., 24-25, No. 941; Moseley. Joyce and the Bible, 45-56, No. 942; O'Brien. Conscience...., 60-64, No. 1628; Read. Pound/Joyce, 49-56, No. 725; Stewart. Eight...., 436-437, No. 1665; Tindall. Reader's Guide...., 104-122, No. 1678; Tysdahl. Joyce and Ibsen, 87-122, No. 952; Goldberg. Classical Temper, 111-113, No. 1513. [See Section I.E "Review of Joyce's Works," Nos. 1959-2004.]

Books

3486. COLUM, PADRAIC. "Introduction," in Joyce's Exiles. New York: Viking Press, 1951; London: Cape, 1972.

3487. FARRELL, JAMES T. "Exiles and Ibsen," in James Joyce: Two Decades of Criticism, pp. 95-131, No. 1570. [Later, changed version, reprinted as "Joyce and Ibsen" in his Reflections at Fifty and Other Essays. New York: Vanguard Press, 1954, pp. 66-96; this later version reprinted in his Selected Essays. Edited by Luna Wolf. New York: McGraw-Hill, 1964, pp. 119-149.]

3488. FERGUSSON, FRANCIS. "A Reading of Exiles," in Joyce's Exiles. Norfolk: New Directions Books, 1945, pp. v-xviii. [Also in Configuration critique I, pp. 358-374, No. 1636.]

*3489. SASAYAMA, TAKASHI. "Exiles," in Joisu Nyumon [An Introduction to James Joyce], pp. 135-139, No. 1511.

3490. SUZUKI, YUKIO. "A Study of Exiles," in A Study of Joyce, pp. 407-443, No. 1592.

3491. VON WEBER, ROLAND. "On and About Joyce's Exiles," in James Joyce Yearbook, pp. 47-67, No. 1596.

Periodical Articles

3492. ADAMS, ROBERT M. "Light on Joyce's Exiles? A New Ms, A Curious Analogue, and Some Speculations." Studies in Bibliography, 17 (1964): 83-105.

3493. _____ . "The Manuscript of James Joyce's Play." Yale University Library Gazette, 39 (1964): 30-41.

3494. AITKIN, D. J. F. "Dramatic Archetypes in Joyce's Exiles." Modern Fiction Studies, 4 (Spring 1958): 42-52.

3495. ATKINSON, BROOKS. "Joyce's Credo." New York Times, 24 March 1957, sec. 2, p. 1.

3496. BANDLER, BERNARD. "Joyce's Exiles." Hound and Horn, 6 (January-March 1933): 266-285.

3497. BARNES, A. C. "On Joyce's Exiles." The Little Review, 5, nos. 10-11 (February-March 1919): 44, 49.

3498. BAUERLE, RUTH. "Two Unnoted Musical Allusions." James Joyce Quarterly, 9 (Fall 1971): 140-142. [See also "Some Mots on a Quickbeam in Joyce's Eye." James Joyce Quarterly, 10 (Spring 1973): 346-348.]

3499. BENSTOCK, BERNARD. "Exiles: 'Paradox Lust' and 'Lost Paladays.'" ELH: Journal of English Literary History, 36 (December 1969): 739-756.

3500. _____ . "Exiles, Ibsen and the Play's Function in the Joyce Canon." Ball State University Forum, 11 (Spring 1970): 26-37.

3501. BRIVIC, SHELDON R. "Structure and Meaning in Joyce's Exiles." James Joyce Quarterly, 6 (Fall 1968): 29-52.

3502. CLARK, EARL JOHN. "James Joyce's Exiles." James Joyce Quarterly, 6 (Fall 1968): 69-78.

3503. COLUM, PADRAIC. "Ibsen in Irish Writing." Irish Writing, no. 7 (February 1949): 66-70.

3504. CUNNINGHAM, FRANK R. "Joyce's Exiles: A Problem of Dramatic Stasis." Modern Drama, 12 (February 1970): 399-407.

3505. DEV, AMIYA. "The Artist in Ibsen and Joyce." Jadavpur Journal of Comparative Literature, 7 (1967): 85-101.

3506. DOUGLASS, JAMES W. "James Joyce's Exiles: A Portrait of the Artist." Renascence, 15 (Winter 1963): 82-87.

*3507. ENGEL, FRITZ. "Nach Ibsen." Berliner Tageblatt, 10 March 1930.

3508. FERGUSSON, FRANCIS. "Exiles and Ibsen's Work." Hound and Horn, 5 (April-June 1932): 345-353.

3509. FERRIS, WILLIAM R. "Rebellion Matured: Joyce's Exiles." Éire-Ireland, 4 (Winter 1969): 73-81.

EXILES

*3510. FRIEDERICHS, KARL WILHELM. "Fremde Literatur: /u.a./James Joyce, 'Verbannte.'" Literarisches Centralblatt für Deutschland, Beiblatt, Die Schöne Literatur, 22 (1921): 249-252.

3511. GENIEVA, E. IU. "Dzhois i Ibsen." Vestnik Moskovskogo Universiteta, no. 10 (Filologiia), no. 3 (May-June 1971): 32-41.

*3512. GOPALEEN, MYLES na (Flann O'Brien, Brian Nolan). "Cruiskeen Lawn." Irish Times, 4 June 1945.

*3513. _____. "Cruiskeen Lawn." Irish Times, 4 March 1958.

3514. HARMON, MAURICE. "Richard Rowan, His Own Scapegoat." James Joyce Quarterly, 3 (Fall 1965): 34-40.

*3515. HEAP, JANE. [Editorial Note] Little Review, 5, no. 10-11 (February-March 1919): 49.

3516. JACQUOT, JEAN. "Réflexions sur les Exiles de Joyce." Études anglaises, 9 (October-December 1956): 337-343.

3517. KELLER, DEAN H. "Linati's Translation of Exiles: An Unnoticed Appearance." James Joyce Quarterly, 10 (Winter 1973): 265.

3518. KENNER, HUGH. "Joyce's Exiles." Hudson Review, 5 (Autumn 1952): 389-403.

3519. KLIESS, WETNER. "Kann man Joyce dramatisieren?" Theater heute, 5 (1964): 52.

3520. LEMARCHAND, JACQUES. "Un disciple égare d'Ibsen." Figaro littéraire, 20 January 1966, p. 9.

3521. McCARTHY, DESMOND. "Exiles." New Statesman, 11 (21 September 1918): 492-493. [Shortened version appeared as "Mr. James Joyce's Play." New Statesman, 26 (20 February 1926): 581-582 at the time of the Stage Society's production; original appeared in his Humanities. London: MacGibbon and Kee, 1953, pp. 88-93.]

3522. MacNICHOLAS, JOHN. "Joyce's Exiles: The Argument for Doubt." James Joyce Quarterly, 11 (Fall 1973): 33-40.

3523. MAHER, R. A. "James Joyce's Exiles: The Comedy of Discontinuity." James Joyce Quarterly, 9 (Summer 1972): 461-474.

3524. METZGER, DEENA P. "Variations on a Theme: A Study of Exiles by James Joyce and The Great God Brown by Eugene O'Neill." Modern Drama, 8 (September 1965): 174-184.

3525. MOSELEY, VIRGINIA D. "Joyce's Exiles and the Prodigal Son." Modern Drama, 1 (Spring 1959): 218-227.

3526. POUND, EZRA. "Mr. James Joyce and the Modern Stage." Drama, 6, no. 21 (February 1916): 122-132.

3527. REICHERT, KLAUS. "Der nicht aufhebba re Lweiful: ...über den Stellenwert der Verbannten im Gesamtwerk von Joyce." Theater heute, 14 (August 1973): 32. [Reprinted from the Programm-Heft for the Munich production; his 1968 translation follows, pp. 33-52.]

3528. RODKER, JOHN, ISRAEL SOLON, SAMMUEL A. TANNENBAUM, JANE HEAP. "Exiles, A Discussion of James Joyce's Play." Little Review, 5, no. 9 (January 1919): 20-27. [A symposium of critics.]

3529. TANIGUCHI, SATOJI. [Drama in Joyce with Special Reference to Exiles and Ulysses.] Daitō Bunka University Bulletin, 10 (1972): 1-38. [In Japanese.]

3530. TYSDAHL, BJØRN. "Joyce's Exiles and Ibsen." Orbis litterarum, 19 (1964): 176-186.

3531. WHITE, WILLIAM. "GBS on Joyce's Exiles." Times Literary Supplement, 4 December 1959, p. 709. [See reply by Stephen Winsten. Ibid., 18 December 1959, p. 741, quoting from his book Days with Bernard Shaw (New York 1949), p. 129 and White's reply, "Irish Antithesis: Shaw and Joyce." The Shavian, 2, no. 3 (February 1961): 27 and comment on "Winsten's known inaccuracy" in ibid., 1 (September 1954): 9.]

3532. WILLIAMS, RAYMOND. "The Exiles of James Joyce." Politics and Letters, 1 (Summer 1948): 13-21. [Much changed version in his Drama from Ibsen to Brecht. London: Chatto and Windus, 1968; New York: Oxford University Press, 1969, pp. 141-146.]

3533. WORSLEY, T. C. "Comment." New Statesman and Nation, 29 (27 May 1950): 602-603.

ULYSSES

See also Acton. Memoirs...., No. 818; Adams. James Joyce, No. 1506; Adams. Censorship...., No. 290; Alberes. Histoire...., No. 168; Allen. Modern Novel...., passim, No. 1354; Alcott. "James Joyce....," 170-177, No. 1508; Anderson. My Thirty Years' War, passim, No. 1510; Arnold. James Joyce, 35-54, No. 1512; Astre. "Joyce et la durée," passim, No, 955; Bacca. "Edmund Husserl and James Joyce," passim, 4455; Barnes. "James Joyce," No. 596; Beach. Catalogue of a Collection, No. 132; Beaslai. "Joyce among the Journalists," No. 857; Beebe. Ivory Towers...., passim, No. 3216; Bell. The English Novel, 71-86, No. 29; Berger. "Wakeful Ad-venture," No. 1696; Bierman. "Ulysses and Finnegans Wake....," No. 1692; Blöcker. Die Neuen Wirklichkeiten...., 66-85, No. 1522; Bonheim. Joyce's Benefictions, passim, No. 1524; Boyd.

Ireland's Literary...., 408-412, No. 1527; Brandabur. Scrupulous...., 159-174, No. 1529; Brasil. Joyce...., 99-164, No. 1530; Brick. "Madman in his Cell," No. 3733; Brivic. "James Joyce....," No. 1532; Broch. James Joyce und die...., No. 3555; Brooks, B. G. "Shem the Penman....," No. 1424; Burgess. Re-Joyce, 70-176, No. 1533; Burgess. Joycesprick, 21-44, 163-178, No. 1536; Burgess. The Novel Now, 22-37, No. 1534; Burgess. Urgent Copy, 82-84, No. 1535; Burgum. Novel and the World's Dilemma, 95-108, No. 3745; Butor. "Joyce et le roman modern," No. 1703; Byrd. "Joyce's Method of Philosophic Fiction," No. 3746; Cambon. "Ancora su Joyce," No. 1705; Cazamian. Essays...., passim, No. 180; CEA Critic, passim, No. 151; Chatterjee. James Joyce, 19-62, 72-85, No. 1541; Collins. "Progression in the....," No. 1710; Colum, M. Life and the Dream, passim, No. 297; Connolly, Cyril. Condemned Playground, 1-7, No. 1711; Crosse. Flaubert and Joyce, 95-99, 100-149, No. 1546; Curran. James Joyce Remembered...., passim, No. 304; Dahlberg and Read. Truth is...., passim, No. 1203; Debenedetti. Il romanzo...., 594-616, No. 757; Daiches. Novel and the Modern...., 110-147, No. 1548; Daiches. Critical History...., 1134-1135, No. 1549; Deakin. "D. H. Lawrence's Attacks....," No. 733; Duff. James Joyce...., 33-62, No. 1555; Dujardin. Le Monologue...., passim, No. 928; Eco. Poetiche ..., 59-111, No. 5259; Edel. Psychological Novel, 115-139, No. 1368; Egri. Álom, látomás...., 206-248, No. 1557; Ellmann. James Joyce, passim, No. 308; Evans, B. I. English Literature...., 40-48, No. 193; Fáj. "Probable Byzantine....," No. 1724; Fehr. Die Englische...., 56-58, No. 1559; Frierson. English Novel...., 234-236, No. 1371; Foran. "A Mirror Held up....," No. 4610; Friedman. Stream of...., No. 4189; Garrett. Scene and Symbol...., 245-271, No. 1565; Gillet. "Recuerdos de James Joyce," No. 444; Gillet. Claybook...., 23-42, No. 1568; Gilbert. "Wanderings of Ulysses," No. 7; Glasheen. "Joyce and the Three Ages ....," No. 1033; Gogarty. It Isn't this Time...., passim, No. 319; Godwin. "Rushlight for the....," No. 3827; Golding. James Joyce, 84-141, No. 1575; Goldman. James Joyce, passim, No. 1577; Goodheart. Cult of the Ego, 192-200, No. 1578; Gorman. James Joyce: His First...., 116-229, No. 3585; Griffin. Wild Geese, 30-39, No. 1579; Gross. James Joyce, 43-70, 7-15, No. 1580; Haan. Joyce, Mythe..., No. 1581; Hayman. Joyce et Mallarmé, volume 1, 76-117, No. 932; Highet. Classical Tradition...., 501-519, No. 933; Hodgart and Worthington. Song in the Works of...., passim, No. 1588; Hoffman. Freudianism...., 132-139, No. 934; Howarth. Irish Writers, 247-285, No. 1589; Hutchins. "James Joyce's Tower," No. 470; Jacquot. "Exegetes....," No. 1750; Jones. James Joyce and the Common Reader, 39-148, No. 3602; John. "Fragment....," No. 473; Kain. "Problems....," No. 1597; Kelleher. "Notes....," No. 5438; Kenner. Dublin's Joyce, 19-26, 158-162, No. 1600; Kulemeyer. Studien...., 16-34, No. 2484; Larbaud. Ce vice...., 230-252, No. 1602; Lestra. "Joyce ou la pureté....," No. 1759; Levin. Contexts...., 277-280, No. 938; Levin. Critical Introduction...., 65-135, No. 1603; Litz. Art of...., 1-75, No. 1605; Litz. James Joyce, 77-98, No. 1606; Lundkvist. Icarus

...., 73-112, No. 1608; McCarthy. Criticism...., No. 1611a; Magalaner. "James Joyce and Marie....," No. 940; Magalaner and Kain. Joyce: The Man...., 146-215, No. 1615; Majault. Joyce, 72-84, No. 1616; Mallam. "Joyce and Rabelais," No. 1002; Markow-Totevy. "James Joyce and Louis Gillet," No. 1568; Marriott. No. 115; Mayoux. Joyce, passim, No. 1619; Mercanton. Poètes de...., 13-46, No. 1620; Mercier. "Joyce and Irish....," No. 4265; Misra. Indian...., 32-42, No. 941; Moody. History of English...., 431-434, No. 229; More. On Being Human, 74-96, No. 697; Morse. Sympathetic...., No. 339; Moseley. Joyce and the Bible, 57-143, No. 942; Muir. Transition, No. 3965; Niebyl. "Economist considers....," No. 1182; Noon. Joyce and...., 86-125, No. 943; Orwell. Collected Essays, 125-129, No. 1055; Paris. James Joyce...., passim, No. 1632; Pinguentini. James Joyce in...., 240-275, No. 1634; Pound. If This be...., 16-20, No. 1635; Prescott. Exploring...., passim, No. 1636; Read. Pound/Joyce, No. 725; Rebora. La letteratura inglese...., 121-122, No. 1639; Roberts. "Bibliographical....," No. 15; Roberts. "James Joyce: From Religion to Art," No. 4015; Russell. "Joyce and Alexandria," No. 5300; Ryf. New Approach...., 77-97, No. 3271; Sanchez. Panorama...., 118-129, No. 1646; Savage. Withered Branch, 169-191, No. 1647; Schoeck. "Catholicism of....," No. 4042; Sell. "Fusion of Languages," No. 1807; Semmler. For the Uncanny Man, 127-132, No. 1653; Sergeant. "A Study of....," No. 4246; Smidt. James Joyce and...., 81-99, No. 1405; Soupault. Souvenirs de...., 35-56, No. 547; Spender. Destructive Element, passim, No. 672; Stavrou. "Gulliver's Voyage....," No. 784; Stewart. James Joyce, 23-32, No. 1664; Stewart. Eight Modern...., 451-465, No. 1665; Stief. Moderne...., 132-135, No. 1666; Spivey. "Reintegration....," No. 1815; Straumann. "Das Zeitproblem....," No. 1668; Strong. Sacred River, 27-28, 31-38, No. 949; Svevo, L. "Svevo et Joyce," No. 782; Tanselle. "Samuel Roth's....," No. 22; Thompson. A Comic Principle...., No. 1674; Tindall. Literary Symbol, passim, No. 951; Tindall. James Joyce: His Way...., 22-51, No. 1677; Tindall. Reader's Guide, No. 1678; Tysdahl. Joyce and Ibsen, 103-122, No. 952; Waldock. James, Joyce and...., 30-52, No. 1074; West, R. Strange Necessity...., No. 1228; Wilson. Axel's Castle, 192-225, No. 1686; Woolmer, No. 60; Zhantieve. Dzheims Dzhois, passim, No. 257. [See Section I.E "Reviews of Joyce's Works," Nos. 2048-2142; I.F "Dissertations," Nos. 2459-2514.]

GENERAL STUDIES

Books

3534. ADAMS, ROBERT MARTIN. "Ipso Translators (Mostly Joyce)," in his Proteus, His Lies, His Truth. New York: W. W. Norton, 1973, pp. 136-150.

3535. ALBERES, R. M. (René Marill). L'Aventure Intellectuelle du XXe siècle, 1900-1950. Paris: La Nouvelle Edition, 1950, pp. 163-164.

ULYSSES

*3536. ANDERSON, JOHN. "Ulysses...An Address," Australian English Association Offprint, no. 3. Sydney: Australasian Medial Publishing Co., 1930. [Reprinted from Union Recorder (1930).]

3537. ANGIOLETTI, G. B. "Aura Poetica," in Servizio di Guardia. Lanciano: Giuseppe Carabba, 1933, pp. 63-73.

3538. ARNS, KARL. "James Joyce," in Jüngstes England: anthologie und einführung. Leipzig: E. Kuner, 1925, pp. 43-47.

3539. ASHCROFT, EDWARD. "Ulysses," in 100 Great Books: Masterpieces of All Time. Edited by John Canning. London: Odhams, 1966, pp. 488-493.

3540. BAAKE, JOSEF. Das Riesenscherzbuch "Ulysses." Bonner Studien zu Englischen Philologie, no. 32. Bonn: Peter Hanstein, 1937. [The first section, and the first chapter of the second section, appeared in Sinn und Zweck der Reproduktionstechnik in Ulysses von James Joyce. Bonn: Hagen, 1937.]

3541. BAJARLIA, JUAN JACOBO. Literatura de vanguardia del Ulysses de Joyce y las escuelas poéticas. Buenos Aires: Editorial Araujo, 1946, pp. 13-57.

3542. BALOTĂ, NICOLAE. "Impasul lui Ulise," in Euphorion: eseuri. Bucharest: Editura Pentru Literatură, 1969, pp. 451-463.

3543. BEACH, JOSEPH WARREN. "Post-Impressionism: Joyce," in his Twentieth Century Novel. New York, London: Century Co., 1932, pp. 403-424.

3544. BEACH, SYLVIA. Shakespeare and Company. New York: Harcourt, Brace, 1959; London: Faber and Faber, 1960. [The first chapter appeared in Mercure de France, 309 (May 1950): 12-29; Ulysses in Paris, printed by Harcourt, Brace Co., in 1956 was for Miss Beach's friends and represents pp. 34-47 of the complete book; excerpts in Figaro littéraire, 3 February 1962, p. 4; excerpt with comments by Gilbert Sigaux in Nouvelles littéraires, 19 July 1962, p. 10; French translation by George Adam. Paris: Mercure de France, 1962; Treffpunkt--ein Buchladen in Paris, German translation by Lilly von Sauter. Munich: Paul List Vlg., 1962, paperback reprint 1970; Italian translation by Elena Spagnol Vaccari. Milan: Rizzoli, 1962; paperback reprint by Harcourt, Brace and World, 1966; recording discussed in Spoken Records by Helen Roach, 2nd edition. New York, London: Scarecrow, 1966, pp. 170-173.]

3545. BENJAMIN, JUDY-LYNN, editor. The Celtic Bull: Essays on Joyce's Ulysses. University of Tulsa, Department of English, Monograph Series, no. 1. Tulsa: University of Tulsa (1966). [By students of Leonard Albert's honors seminar in Ulysses at Hunter College.]
    Contents: Leonard Albert. "A Pastor's Pupil Bull," 7-9; Judy-Lynn Benjamin. "The Tale of The Celtic Bull," 10-11; Maryann Nichols. "An Epochal Palimpset," 1-23, No. 3634; Rochelle Petta. "From Corpus to Corpse: 'Lotus Eaters' to 'Hades,'" 24-31, No. 4760; Axel Mundigo. "Decussated Keys in Dublin," 33-38, No. 4774; Axel Mundigo. "Bloom's Litany: Sacred and Profane," 39-44, No. 4780; Joann Medioli. "Sabellian Shakespeare: Bull, Ba'al, or Bard?," 45-53, No. 4797; Judy-Lynn Benjamin. "'The Wandering Rocks': The Heart of Ulysses," 54-61, No. 4804; Judy-Lynn Benjamin. "A Symphony for Calliope," 62-69, No. 4813; Sandra Hartley. "Bloom's Dilemma: Odysseus Versus the Cyclops," 70-73, No. 4829; Carol Meskin. "The Paralleled Virgin and the Unparalleled Mother," 74-76, No. 4602; Rosemary Price. "Nighttown: Lethartic Cathargy," 77-82, No. 4867; Joanne Kolbe. "Parallel/Parallax," 83-95, No. 4877; Joanne Kolbe. "A Protean Mollylogue," 96-100, No. 4601.

3546. BENSTOCK, BERNARD. "Ulysses: The Making of an Irish Myth," in Approaches to Ulysses, pp. 199-234, No. 3657.

3547. BIRĂESCU, TRAIAN LIVIU. "Margina lii la Ulysse," in Condita romanului. Cluj: Dacia, 1971, pp. 140-167.

3548. BLACKMUR, R. P. Anni Mirabiles, 1921-1925: Reason in the Madness of Letters. Washington, D.C.: Library of Congress, 1956, pp. 24-25, 42-46. ["Contemplation" reprinted in A Primer of Ignorance. Edited by Joseph Frank. New York: Harcourt, Brace and World, 1967, pp. 59-80.]

3549. BLAMIRES, HARRY. The Bloomsday Book: A Guide through Joyce's Ulysses. London: Methuen, 1966.

3550. BODELSEN, CARL A. Moderne Engelsk Skønlitteratur. Copenhagen: Gyldendal, 1929, pp. 130-137.

3551. BONNEFOY, YVES. "Un rêve fait à Mantoue," in Un rêve fait à Mantoue. Paris: Mercure de France, 1967, pp. 41-49. [Meetings with Sylvia Beach.]

3552. BOWEN, ZACK. "Libretto for Bloomusalem in Song: The Music of Joyce's Ulysses," in New Light on Joyce, pp. 149-166, No. 1656.

3553. BOYLE, ROBERT. "The Priesthoods of Stephen and Buck," in Approaches to Ulysses, pp. 29-60, No. 3657.

3554. BREWSTER, DOROTHY, and ANGUS BURRELL. "James Joyce and Ulysses," in their Modern Fiction. New York: Columbia University Press, 1934, pp. 155-217.

3555. BROCH, HERMAN. James Joyce und die Gegenwart. Wien: Reichner, 1936. [Reprinted in Dichten und Erkennen, volume 6 of his Gesammelte Werke. Zürich: Rhein Vlg., 1955, pp. 183-210; original translated by Eugené and Maria Jolas as "Joyce and the Present Age" in James Joyce Yearbook, pp. 68-108, No. 1596; also translated by H. Hildenbrand and A. Lindenberg as "Joyce et son temps," Lettres nouvelles, n.s. 13 (April 1961): 65-93; in Création littéraire et connaissance. Translated by Albert Kohn. Introduction by Hannah Arendt. Paris: Gallimard, 1966, pp. 185-213; in Eco (Bogotá), 17 (May 1968): 7-46; reprinted in Revista de Bellas artes, 22 (July-August 1968): 4-18; translated in Joyce, pp. 133-160, No. 1526, paperback reprint. Frankfurt a.M.: Jahrkamp Vlg., 1972.]

3556. BROOKS, CLEANTH. "Joyce's Ulysses: Symbolic Poem, Biography, or Novel?," in Imagined Worlds: Essays on Some English Novels and Novelists in Honor of John Butt. Edited by Maynard Mack and Ian Gregor. London: Methuen, 1968, pp. 419-439. [Also appeared in Brooks' A Shaping Joy. New York: Harcourt, Brace, Jovanovich, 1971, pp. 66-86.]

3557. BUDGEN, FRANK. James Joyce and the Making of Ulysses. London: Grayson, 1934; 2nd edition, 1937; new edition, with introduction by Hugh Kenner. Bloomington, Ind.: Midland Books, 1960; new edition, with introduction by Clive Hart. London: Oxford University Press, 1972, James Joyce and the Making of Ulysses, and Other Writings, including his "Joyce's Chapters of Going Forth by Day," 323-342, No. 5575; "James Joyce," 343-348, No. 1085; "Further Recollections of James Joyce," 349-366, No. 3530.

3558. BULHOF, FRANCIS. Transpersonalismus und Synchronizität: Wiederholung also strukturelement in Thomas Manns Zauberberg. Groningen: Van Denderen, 1966, passim. [Der Zauberberg and U compared.]

3559. CAMERINO, ALDO. "L'Ulisse di Joyce dopo un quarto di secolo," "Le traduzioni da Joyce," "'Arriva Ulisse,'" "Una chiave per Ulisse," in his Scrittori di lingua inglese. Milan, Naples: Riccardo Ricciardi, 1968, pp. 234-238, 239-241, 242-245, 246-247. [Reprints of essays and reviews from 1943, 1955, 1960, and 1964.]

3560. CARENS, JAMES F. "Joyce and Gogarty," in New Light on Joyce, pp. 28-45, No. 1656.

3561. CHARQUES, R. D. Contemporary Literature and Social Revolution. London: Martin Secker, 1933, pp. 90-95.

3562. COLLINS, JOSEPH. "Ireland's Latest Literary Antinomian: James Joyce," in his The Doctor Looks at Literature. New York: Doran, 1923, pp. 35-60. [Reprinted Port Washington, New York: Kennikat Press, 1972.]

3563. DAICHES, DAVID. "The Importance of Ulysses," in his New Literary Values. Edinburgh: Oliver and Boyd, 1936, pp. 69-82. [Reprinted Freeport, New York: Books for Libraries, 1968, pp. 69-82.]

3564. DALTON, JACK P. "The Text of Ulysses," in New Light on Joyce, pp. 99-119, No. 1656. [Delivered three times as (1) lecture 6-7 December 1966 at Cornell University; (2) on 10 May 1969 at Marquette University, Seventh Annual American Committee for Irish Studies Conference; (3) Second International James Joyce Symposium (13 June 1969); also in Éire-Ireland, 7 (Summer 1972): 67-83.]

3565. DeANGELIS, GIULIO. Guida alla lettura dell' Ulisse di J. Joyce. Milan: Lerici, 1961; second edition revised and enlarged, 1964.

3566. DIMES, L. T. Plain Talk on Ulysses. Melbourne: E. Malvern, 1942.

3567. ELLIS, HAVELOCK. The Dance of Life. Boston, New York: Houghton Mifflin, 1923, pp. 175-177.

3568. ELLMANN, RICHARD. Ulysses on the Liffey. New York: Oxford University Press; London: Faber and Faber, 1972. [A chapter, "Why Molly Bloom Menstruates" appeared in New York Review of Books, 18 (23 March 1972): 25-30; paperback edition, New York: Oxford University Press, 1973.]

3569. ESCH, ARNO. James Joyce und sein Ulysses. Veröffentichungen der Arbeitsgemeinschaft für Forschung des Landes Nordrhein-Westfalen. Geisteswissenschaft, Heft 164. Cologne, Opladen: Westdeutsche Vlg., 1970.

*3570. FADIMAN, CLIFTON. "James Joyce (1882-1941) Ulysses," in The Lifetime Reading Plan. Cleveland: World, 1960, pp. 106-108.

3571. FIELD, SAUL, and MORTON P. LEVITT. Bloomsday: An Interpretation of James Joyce's Ulysses. Greenwich, Conn.: New York Graphic Society, 1972; London: Bodley Head, 1973. [Color engravings, with text by Levitt; the graphics are reproduced from embossed color engravings originally issued in a limited edition of 25 by the Upstairs Gallery, Toronto.]

ULYSSES

3572. FINKELSTEIN, SIDNEY. Art and Society. New York: International Publishers, 1947, pp. 204-209.

3573. FLORA, FRANCESCO. Poesia e impoesia nell' Ulisse di Joyce. Milan: Nuova accademia, 1962.

*3574. FORD, FORD MADOX. Thus to Revisit. London: Chapman and Hall, 1921, pp. 64-65.

3575. _____ . The Letters of.... Edited by Richard M. Ludwig. Princeton: Princeton University Press, 1965, passim.

3576. FORSTER, E. M. Aspects of the Novel. New York: Harcourt, Brace, 1927, pp. 177-189, 199.

3577. FRIEDMAN, MELVIN J. "Three Experiences of the War: A Triptch," in The Promise of Greatness: The War of 1914-1918. Edited by George A. Panichas. New York: John Day, 1968, pp. 541-555. [Joyce, Wyndham Lewis, Virginia Woolf.]

3578. GIBBON, MONK. "The Unraised Hat," in A Bash in the Tunnel, pp. 209-212, No. 1644.

*3579. GIEDION-WELCKER, CAROLA. "Einführung," in James Joyce, Ulysses. Rhein Vlg., 1956, pp. 813-836; reprinted in James Joyce, Ulysses. Munich: 1966, pp. 817-840.

3580. GILBERT, STUART. James Joyce's Ulysses: A Study. London: Faber and Faber, 1930. [First American edition. New York: Alfred A. Knopf, 1931; Second revised edition. London: Faber and Faber, 1952; First Vintage edition. New York: Vintage Books, 1956; translated by Georg Goyert, Das Rätsel Ulysses. Zurich: Rhein Vlg., 1932, reprinted 1960; translated by Manuel de la Escalera. El Ulises de James Joyce. Foreword by Juan Benet. Madrid: Siglo XXI de España Editores, 1971; Penguin edition, 1963; reprinted Frankfurt a.M.: Suhrkamp, 1969.]

3581. _____ . "Introduction," in Joyce's Ulysses. New York: Limited Editions Club, 1935, pp. v-xvi.

3582. GINDIN, JAMES. "James Joyce," in his Harvest of a Quiet Eye: The Novel of Compassion. Bloomington and London: Indiana University Press, 1971, pp. 222-236.

3583. GONZALEZ, MANUEL PEDRO. "El Ulysses cuarenta años después," in Ensayos critcos. Caracas: Universidad Central de Venezuela, 1963, pp. 5-21. [Also in Cuadernos Americanos (May-June 1963).]

3584. GORJAN, ZLATKO. "On Translating Joyce's Ulysses," in The Nature of Translation: Essays on the Theory and Practice of Literary Translation. Approaches to Trans-

lation Studies, no. 1. Edited by James S. Holmes. Hague: Mouton; Bratislava: Publishing House of the Slovak Academy of Sciences, 1970, pp. 201-207.

3585. GORMAN, HERBERT. James Joyce, His First Forty Years. New York: B. W. Huebsch, 1924; London: Geoffrey Bles, 1924. [Translated by Maximo Siminovich as James Joyce, el hombre que escribió "Ulises." Buenos Aires: Santiago Rueda, 1945; reprinted Folcroft, Pa.: Folcroft Press, 1969.]

*3586. GOTTGETREU, ERICH. "James Joyce, der Spiesserschreck," Neues Wiener Journal, 30 November 1926; Neue Leipziger Zeitung, 30 December 1926; Müncher Post, 23 March 1927; reprinted in Der Homer unserer Zeit, pp. 7-9, No. 3599.

3587. HAHN, FRIEDRICH. "Eros." Bibel und moderne Literatur: Grosse Lebensfragen in Textvergleichen. Second edition. Stuttgart: Quell Vlg., 1967, pp. 108-111. [First edition, 1966.]

*3588. HANIYA, YATAKA et al. "Urisizu o megute (Zadau Kai) ["On Ulysses (Symposium)]," in Joisu Nyumon [An Introduction to James Joyce], pp. 217-253, No. 1511.

3589. HANLEY, MILES (and others). A Word Index to James Joyce's Ulysses. Madison: University of Wisconsin Press, 1937. [Revised edition appeared in 1951.]

3590. HART, CLIVE. James Joyce's Ulysses. University Park: Pennsylvania State University Press; Sydney University Press; London: Methuen, 1968. ["Select Bibliography" reprinted in Levende Talen, 269 (June-July 1970): 481-483.]

3591. HAYMAN, DAVID. Ulysses: The Mechanics of Meaning. Englewood Cliffs, N.J.: Prentice-Hall, 1970; paperback reprint, 1972.

3592. HEATH, STEPHEN. The Nouveau Roman: A Study in the Practice of Writing. London: Elek, 1972, passim.

*3593. HENDERSON, ARCHIBALD. The Table-Talk of GBS. New York, London: Harper and Bros., 1925, pp. 129-134.

3594. HENDERSON, PHILIP. Literature and a Changing Civilization. London: John Lane, 1935, pp. 147-151.

3595. HERRING, PHILIP F. Joyce's Ulysses Notesheets in the British Museum. Charlottesville: Published for the Bibliographical Society of the University of Virginia by the University Press of Virginia, 1972. ["Ulysses Notesheets," in Intellectual Digest (February 1972).]

3596. HESELTINE, PHILIP. Merry Go Down: A Gallery of Gorgeous Drunkards in Literature from Genesis to Joyce. London: Mandrake Press, 1929.

*3597. HEWETT, R. P. "James Joyce: From Ulysses," in Reading Response. London: Harrap, 1960, pp. 147-154.

3598. HODGART, MATTHEW. Satire. London: Weidenfeld and Nicholson; New York, Toronto: McGraw-Hill, 1969, pp. 232-237.

3599. Der Homer Unserer Zeit: Deutschland in Erwartung des Ulysses von James Joyce: Letzte Gelegenheit zur Subskription. Zürich: Rhein Vlg., 1927.
Contents: Ivan Goll. "Über James Joyce," pp. 2-6, No. 3832; Erich Gottgetreu. "Joyce der Spiesserschreck," 7-9, No. 3586; Bernhard Fehr. "Die deutsche Wissenschaft zum Ulysses," 12-13, No. 4296; Bernhard Fehr. "Die Stellung des Ulysses im neuen englischen Schriftum," 10-12, No. 2091.

3600. ISER, WOLFGANG. "Indeterminacy and the Reader's Response in Prose," in Aspects of Narrative: English Institute Essays, 1970. Edited by J. Hillis Miller. New York: Columbia University Press, 1971, pp. 1-45.

3601. JANSCHLEA, FRITZ. [Twenty-Six etchings based on U.] Berlin: Propyläen Vlg., 1972? [Also issued in a limited edition by Newman Contemporary Gallery; an exhibit of etchings and related drawings shown at the Eidg. Technischen Hochschule, Zürich, 4 November-22 December 1972; catalogue with six reproductions and a brief introduction by Charles Mitchell also issued.]

3602. JONES, W. POWELL. James Joyce and the Common Reader. Norman, Okla.: University Press, 1955. [First chapter appeared in American Scholar, 21 (April 1952): 161-171; "Themes, Styles and Episodes," reprinted in Portraits of an Artist, pp. 12-18, No. 3260; excerpted as "James Joyce: Master of Words," Intersection (Cleveland), 1 (Spring 1953): 52-69.

3603. JUNG, CARL GUSTAV. "Ulysses: Ein Monolog," Europaische Revue, 8 (September 1932): 547-566. [Reprinted in Wirklichkeit der Seele. Anwendungen und Fortschritte der Neueren Psychologie. Zürich: Rascher Vlg., 1934, 132-169; appeared in Realidad del alma (Buenos Aires), 1946; in Spring Nineteen Forty-Nine. New York: 1949, pp. 1-20; translated by Stanley Dell as Ulysses, A Monologue. New York: Analytical Psychology Club of New York, 1949, reprinted Folcroft, Pa.: Folcroft Press, 1972; translated by Stanley Dell in Nimbus, 2 (June-August 1953): 7-20; appeared as ¿Quien es Ulises? Buenos Aires: Rueda,

1944; reviewed by Cesar Fernandez Moreno in Sur, no. 120 (October 1944): 79-92; reprinted in Hidden Patterns: Studies in Psychoanalytic Literary Criticism. Edited by Leonard and Eleanor Manheim. New York: Macmillan; London: Collier-Macmillan, 1966, pp. 192-219; translated by Yves Lelay as "Ulysse," in Problèmes de l'âme moderne. Paris: Buchet Chastel-Correa, 1960, pp. 407-439; a part of Collected Work of C. G. Jung as volume 15, The Spirit in Man, Art, and Literature. Edited by Sir Herbert Read, Michael Fordham, and Gerhard Adler. Translated by R. F. C. Hull. New York: Pantheon; London: Routledge and Kegan Paul, 1966, pp. 109-134.]

3604. KAIN, RICHARD M. Fabulous Voyager: James Joyce's Ulysses. Chicago: University of Chicago Press, 1947; revised edition, New York: Viking, 1959; University of Chicago Press, 1959.

3605. _____. "The Position of Ulysses Today," in James Joyce Today, pp. 83-95, No. 1659.

3606. _____. "Treasures and Trifles in Ulysses," in Litters from Aloft, pp. 1-14, No. 1516.

3607. KAISER, GERHARD R. "Joyce, Ulysses," in Proust, Musil, Joyce: Zum Verhältnis von Literatur und Gesellschaften Paradigma des Zitats. Frankfurt a.M.: Athenäum Vlg., 1972, pp. 145-225, et passim.

3608. KAPLAN, HAROLD J. "Stoom: The Universal Comedy of James Joyce," in his The Passive Voice: An Approach to Modern Fiction. Athens: Ohio University Press, 1966, pp. 43-92.

3609. KERMODE, FRANK. "Puzzles and Epiphanies," in Puzzles and Epiphanies. London: Routledge and Kegan Paul, 1962, pp. 86-90. [Originally in Spectator, 13 November 1959.]

3610. KOT, JOZEF. "James Joyce dnes (niekol'ko okrajovych poznamok)," in O svetovom romane. Edited by Mikulas Bakos and Jozef Felix. Bratislava: Vydavatel'stvo Slovenskej Academie Vied, 1967, pp. 157-174.

3611. KREUTZER, EBERHARD. Sprach und Spiel im Ulysses von James Joyce. Studien zur englischen Literatur, Bd. 2. Bonn: H. Bouvier, 1969. [Also as Ph.D. dissertation, Bonn; abstract in English and American Studies in German, supplement to Anglia (1969): 76-77.]

3612. LAGERCRANTZ, OLOF. Att finnas til: En studie i James Joyces Roman Odysseus. Stockholm: Wahlström and Widstraud; Helsinki: Söderström, 1970. [Essays originally in Dagens Nyheter (Stockholm).]

ULYSSES

3613. LANEY, AL. Paris Herald. New York: Appleton-Century, 1947, pp. 159, 162.

3614. LANGBAUM, ROBERT. The Modern Spirit: Essays on the Continuity of Nineteenth and Twentieth Century Literature. New York: Oxford University Press, 1970, pp. 81-82, et passim.

3615. LEVITT, MORTON P. "The Family of Bloom," in New Light on Joyce, pp. 141-148, No. 1656.

3616. LEWIS, WYNDHAM. The Letters of....Edited by W. K. Rose. Norfolk: New Directions, 1963, passim.

3617. _____. Men Without Art. First published 1934, reissued 1964. New York: Russell and Russell, pp. 166-168, et passim.

3618. _____. "The Period of Ulysses, Blast, The Wasteland," "First Meeting with James Joyce," in Blasting and Bombardiering. London: Eyre and Spottiswoode, 1937, pp. 271-272, et passim; Second edition, revised. Berkeley and Los Angeles: University of California Press, 1967, pp. 252-256, 265-270.

*3619. LILJEGREN, STEN BODVAR. "Irish Studies in Sweden," Irish Essays and Studies, 6. Upsala: A.-B. Lundequistska; Copenhagen: Ejnar Munksgaard, 1961, pp. 24-29.

3620. LOEHRICH, ROLF RUDOLF. The Secret of Ulysses: An Analysis of James Joyce's Ulysses. McHenry, Illinois: Compass Press, 1953. [Reprinted Folcroft, Pa.: Folcroft Press, 1971.]

3621. LOVETT, ROBERT M. "Post-Realistic Novel," in his Preface to Fiction. Chicago: Rockwell, 1931, pp. 113-127.

*3622. LUKÁCS, GEORG. "A polgár nyomában ["In the Wake of the Bourgeois]," in Nemet realisták [German Realists]. Budapest: Szépirodalmi Könyvkiadó, 1955, pp. 254-255, 309-310, 394.

3623. LUZI, MARIO. "Poesie di Joyce," in Aspetti della Generazione Napoleonica ed altri Saggi di Letteratura Francese. Parma: Guanda, 1956, pp. 235-239.

3624. LYONS, JOHN O. "The Man in the Macintosh," in A James Joyce Miscellany. Second Series, pp. 133-138, No. 1613.

*3625. MARIE, ARISTIDE. Le Forêt Symboliste. Paris: Firmin-Didot et Cie., 1936, pp. 136-137. [Quotes George Moore on U.]

3626. MARIÑO PALACIO, ANDRES. "Para una dimension del Ulises," in his Ensayos, Biblioteca popular venezola, 110. Edited by Rafael Pineda. Caracas: Inst. Nacional de Cultura y Bellas Artes, 1967, pp. 287-293. [Also contains No. 3938.]

3627. MARTINSON, MOA. "En bok av James Joyce," in her Kärlek mellan Krigen: Noveller och Skisser. Stockholm: Tidens förlag, 1947, pp. 203-210.

3628. MASON, MICHAEL. James Joyce: Ulysses. Studies in English Literature, no. 50. London: Edward Arnold, 1972.

3629. MELCHIORI, GIORGIO. "Joyce and the Eighteenth Century Novelists," in English Miscellany, no. 2. Edited by Mario Praz. Rome: Edizioni di "Storia e Letteratura," 1951, pp. 227-245. [Appeared in his The Tightrope Walkers. London: Routledge and Kegan Paul, 1956, pp. 34-52; translated by Ruggero Bianchi. Turin: Giulio Einaudi, 1963, pp. 49-108; translated in Joyce, pp. 27-47, No. 1526; contains his "The Waste Land and Ulysses." English Studies, 35 (April 1954): 56-68.]

3630. MORTON, RICHARD. Ulysses. Lincoln, Neb.: Cliff's Notes, 1972.

3631. MOZLEY, CHARLES. Concerning Ulysses and the Bodley Head. Barnet, England: Stellar Press, 1961.

3632. NAGANOWSKI, EGON. Telemach w labiryncie swiata: o tworczosci Jamesa Joyce'a. Warsaw: Czytelnik, 1962. [One chapter appears as "La nuit au bord du flewe de la vie; essai d'interprétation de Finnegans Wake," translated by Erik Veaux. Lettres nouvelles, n.s. 11 (February-March 1964): 80-94; n.s. 12 (April-May 1964): 127-142; book reprinted 1967; Third revised edition, 1972.]

3633. NAKABASHI, KAZUO. "A Study of Ulysses," in A Study of Joyce, pp. 341-364, No. 1592.

3634. NICHOLS, MARYANN. "An Epochal Palimpset," in The Celtic Bull, pp. 1-23, No. 3545.

3635. NOON, WILLIAM T., S.J. "Is Ulysses Immoral or All-Moral?," in James Joyce: His Place in World Literature, pp. 103-114, No. 1688.

3636. NOYES, ALFRED. Some Aspects of Modern Poetry. New York: Stokes, 1924, pp. 333-336.

3637. ORAGE, ALFRED R. Readers and Writers. New York: Knopf, 1922, pp. 31-33, 171-173.

3638. _____. Selected Essays and Critical Writings. Edited by Herbert Read and Denis Saurat. London: Nott, 1935, pp. 184-185.

3639. PANICHAS, GEORGE A. Mansions of the Spirit: Essays in Literature and Religion. New York: Hawthorn, 1967, passim.

3640. PEARL, CYRIL. Dublin in Bloomtime. New York: Viking; London: Angus and Robertson, 1969.

3641. PIMENTEL, OSMAR. "James Joyce (cá entre nós)," in A lâmpada e o passado: Estudios de literatura e psicologia. Coleção ensaio, 56. São Paulo: Conselho Estadual de Cultura, Commisão de Literatura, 1968, pp. 63-78. [On the occasion of Housiss's translation of U; reprinted from literary supplement to daily, O Estado de São Paulo.]

3642. PLA, ROGER. "Joyce y el Ulises," in Proposiciones: Novela nueva y narrativa argentina. Rosario: Editorial Biblioteca, 1969, pp. 31-44.

3643. QUASHA, GEORGE. James Joyce's Ulysses: A Critical Commentary. Monarch Notes and Study Guides, no. 564-565. New York: Monarch Press, 1965.

3644. RAUTER, HERBERT. "Ulysses," in Der englische Roman von Mittelater zur Moderne, vol. 2. Edited by Franz K. Stanzel. Düsseldorf: August Bagel Vlg., 1969, pp. 317-355.

3645. READ, HERBERT. Reason and Romanticism: Essays in Literary Criticism. London: Faber and Gwyer, 1926, pp. 207-223.

3646. REICHERT, KLAUS. "Reise ans Ende der Möglichen: James Joyce," in Romananfänge: Versuch zu einer Poetik des Romans. Edited by Norbert Miller. Berlin: 1965, pp. 317-343.

3647. REVOL, ENRIQUE LUIS. "1922, Annus mirabilis," "James Joyce," in Literatura inglesa del siglo XX. Nuevos esquemas, no. 29. Buenos Aires: Editorial Columba, 1973, pp. 231-240, 269-311.

*3648. RUSSELL, GEORGE (AE). The Living Torch. Edited by Monk Gibbon. New York: Macmillan, 1938, pp. 139-140.

3649. RYAN, DESMOND. Remembering Sion. London: Arthur Barker, 1934, pp. 41-48, et passim.

3650. RYCHNER, M. "Concerning the Ulysses of James Joyce, Reality in the Novel," in In Memoriam James Joyce, pp. 32-36, No. 1038. [Appeared as "Wirklichkeit im Roman. Zum 'Ulysses' von James Joyce," Die Tat, 18/19 January 1941.

3651. SERVOTTE, HERMAN. "Ulysses: De triomf van de Kunst," in De verteller in de Engelse roman: Een studie over romantechniek. Hasselt, Belgium: Uitgeverij Heideland, 1965, pp. 133-164. [With English summary, pp. 195-198.]

3652. SIMON, IRENE. Formes du Roman Anglais de Dickens à Joyce. Liege: Faculté de Philosophie et Lettres, Fasc. 118, 1949, pp. 388-437.

3653. SMITH, PAUL JORDAN. "Ulysses," in his On Strange Altars. New York: Albert and Charles Boni, 1924, pp. 14-34.

3654. _____. A Key to the Ulysses of James Joyce. Chicago: Covici, 1934. [Reprinted New York: Haskell House, 1965; Folcroft, Pa.: Folcroft Press, 1969; San Francisco: City Lights, 1970.]

3655. SPEARS, MONROE K. Dionysus and the City: Modernism in Twentieth Century Poetry. New York: Oxford University Press, 1970, pp. 66-68, 94-99, 102-104, 201-202, et passim.

3656. STALEY, THOMAS F. "Ulysses and World Literature," in James Joyce: His Place in World Literature, pp. 39-52, No. 1688.

3657. _____, and BERNARD BENSTOCK, editors. Approaches to Ulysses: Ten Essays. Pittsburgh: University of Pittsburgh Press, 1970.
  Contents: Thomas F. Staley and Bernard Benstock. "Introduction," ix-xi; Thomas F. Staley. "Stephen Dedalus and the Temper of the Modern Hero," 3-28, No. 4618; Robert Boyle. "The Priesthoods of Stephen and Buck," 29-60, No. 3553; Richard M. Kain. "Motif as Meaning: The Case of Leopold Bloom," 61-101, No. 4544; David Hayman. "The Empirical Molly," 103-135, No. 4595; Darcy O'Brien. "Some Determinants of Molly Bloom," 137-155, No. 4604; William M. Schutte and Erwin R. Steinberg. "The Fictional Technique of Ulysses," 157-178, No. 4276; H. Frew Waidner. "Ulysses by Way of Culture and Anarchy," 179-197, No. 3670; Bernard Benstock. "Ulysses: The Making of an Irish Myth," 199-234, No. 3546; Weldon Thornton. "The Allusive Method in Ulysses," 235-248, No. 4407; Fritz Senn. "Ulysses in Translation," 249-286, No. 4055; "Biographical Notes," 287-289.

3658. STERNFELD, FREDERICK W. "Poetry and Music--Joyce's Ulysses," in Sound and Poetry: English Institute Essays, 1956. Edited by Northrop Frye. New York: Columbia University Press, 1957, pp. 16-54. [Translated in Configuration critique I, pp. 391-433, No. 1636.]

*3659. STEWART, DOUGLAS. "James Joyce's "Apocalypticism," in The Ark of God. London: Carey Kingsgate Press, 1961, pp. 17-43.

*3660. STRONG, L. A. G. Personal Remarks. London: Peter Nevill, 1953, pp. 184-189.

ULYSSES

3661. STRUVE, GLEB. "Socialist Realism versus James Joyce," in Russian Literature under Lenin and Stalin, 1917-1953. Norman: University of Oklahoma Press, 1971, pp. 268-275.

3662. SULTAN, STANLEY. The Argument of Ulysses. Columbus: Ohio State University Press, 1964.

3663. SZLADITS, LOLA L. 1922: A Vintage Year. New York: New York Public Library, 1972.

3664. TILLYARD, E. M. W. "Joyce's Ulysses," in his The Epic Strain in the English Novel. London: Chatto and Windus, 1958, pp. 187-196.

3665. TIMPE, EUGENE P. "Ulysses and the Archetypal Feminine," in Perspectives in Literary Symbolism. Yearbook of Comparative Criticism, no. 1. Edited by Joseph Strelka. University Park; London: Pennsylvania State University, 1968, pp. 199-213.

3666. TURNER, SUSAN J. A History of the Freeman. New York, London: Columbia University Press, 1963, pp. 148-158.

*3667. UCHIDA, MICHIKO. "Urisize to Jika ["Time and Ulysses]," in Joisu Nyumon [Introduction to James Joyce], pp. 65-72, No. 1511.

3668. VANDENBERGH, JOHN. Aantekeningen bij James Joyce's Ulysses. Introduction by Leo Knuth. Amsterdam: De Bezige Bij; New York: Lambert Oliemeulen, 1969. [Companion volume to his translation.]

3669. VELA, ARQUELES. Evolución Histórica de la Literatura Universal. Mexico, D. F.: Ediciones Fuente Cultural, 1941, pp. 338-346.

3670. WAIDNER, H. FREW. "Ulysses by way of Culture and Anarchy," in Approaches to Ulysses, pp. 179-197, No. 3657.

3671. WARD, A. C. The Nineteen Twenties. London: Methuen, 1930, pp. 55-60.

3672. WEBER, J. SHERWOOD et al. From Homer to Joyce: A Study Guide to Thirty-Six Great Books. New York: Holt, 1959, pp. 262-275.

3673. WILD, FRIEDRICH. Die Englische Literatur der Gegenwart seit 1870: Drama und Roman. Wiesbaden: Im Dioskuren Vlg., 1928, pp. 334-336.

3674. WILSON, COLIN. "The Existential Temper of the Modern Novel," in Christian Faith and the Contemporary Arts. Edited by Finley Eversole. New York: Abingdon Press, 1962, pp. 115-120.

*3675. WOOD, JOHN H. "James Joyce: Genius or Sewer Rat?," in Through the Window: A Window Cleaner Views the World. Melbourne: Fraser and Jenkinson, 1937, pp. 449-481.

3676. WOOLF, LEONARD. Beginning Again. London: Hogarth Press, 1964, pp. 245-247. [The Woolfs' plan to publish U in 1918.]

3677. WOOLF, VIRGINIA. A Writer's Diary: Being Extracts from the Diary of Virginia Woolf. New York: Harcourt, Brace and Co., 1953; London: Hogarth Press, 1965 (pagination differs from American edition), pp. 8, 22, 27, 48, 49, 349. [Entries for 6, 7, 26 September 1922 on U.]

3678. YEATS, W. B. The Voice of Ireland. Edited by William G. Fitzgerald. Dublin: Virtue, 1924, pp. 460-465.

3679. ZHANTIEVA, B. [i.e., D] G. "Joyce's Ulysses," translated by Anne White, in Preserve and Create: Essays in Marxist Literary Criticism. AIMS Monogram Series, no. 4. Edited by Gaylord C. LeRoy and Ursula Beitz. New York: Humanities Press, 1973, pp. 138-172. [From her Angliiskii roman XX veka, 1965.]

3680. ZOLLA, ELÉMIRE. "Joyce o l'apoteosi del fantasticare," in Storia del fantasticare. Milan: Bompiani, 1964, pp. 177-191.

3681. Unsigned. James Joyce's Ulysses: A Critical Commentary. Monarch Notes and Study Guides. New York: Thor Publications, 1965.

Periodical Articles

3682. A, E. L. "James Joyce to his Literary Agents." More Books (Bulletin of the Boston Public Library), 18, no. 1 (January 1943): 22.

3683. 'Affable Hawk' (Desmond MacCarthy). "Books in General." New Statesman, 20, no. 520 (31 March 1923): 751.

*3684. AHEARN, EDWARD J. "Religious Values in Joyce's Ulysses." Christian Scholar, 44 (Summer 1961): 139-145.

*3685. ALDINGTON, RICHARD. "A Forbidden Masterpiece." Sunday Referee (London), 29 June 1930.

3686. ALLEN, WALTER. "New Wine that Tastes like Old." New York Times Book Review, 25 December 1960, pp. 1, 13. [Review article on Dwight Macdonald's Parodies (1960).]

3687. ANCESCHI, LUCIANO. "Tre Lettere di Ezra Pound al Dottor Rouse sul Tradurre Poesia, e una Lettera a Joyce." Letterature Moderne, 1 (September 1950): 220-226. [Also in Pound/Joyce, No. 725.]

3688. ANDRADE, RAUL. "Destierro y amnistia de Ulises." Excelsior (Mexico City), 4 July 1962, p. 7A.

*3689. ARCIENIEGA, ROSA. "Ulises en español." La Cronica (Lima), 24 November 1945.

3690. "Auseinandersetzung mit James Joyces Ulysses." Akzente, 12 (July 1965): 231-243. [Part of special section of 'Literatur vor Gericht'.]
    Contents: Arnold Bennett, translation from No. 3704; James Douglas review from Sporting Times; Shane Leslie review No. 2080; Mary Colum review, No. 2072; Valery Larbaud letter of protest of 2 February 1927; part of Morris Ernst's foreword to Ulysses; Judge Woolsey's decision, No. 4392.

*3691. B., S. S. "What Joyce is up Against." Little Review, 5, no. 2 (June 1918): 54.

*3692. BALTZELL, E. D. "Bell Telephone's Experiment in Education." Harper's Magazine, 210 (March 1955): 73-77. [Account of liberal arts program for business executives, study of U most controversial part of course.]

3693. BARUCCA, PRIMO. "Sogni di Dublino nel divenire della coscienza: L'Ulisse di J. Joyce." L'Italia che scrive, 44 (January 1961): 7-8.

3694. BASSOFF, BRUCE. "The Mummer as Epic Hero." Forum (Houston), 9, no. 2 (Summer 1971): 17-20.

*3695. BAUMANN, LISE. "Irlands Anteil an der Englischen Literatur." Vossische Zeitung (Berlin), 24 August 1928.

3696. BEACH, SYLVIA. "Ulysses a Paris." Mercure de France, 309 (May 1950): 12-29. [Appeared in Inventario, 3, no. 2 (Summer 1950): 77-87; in her Shakespeare and Company, No. 3544.]

*3697. _____. "Shakespeare and Co., Paris: Sylvia Beach Recalls How She Published Ulysses." Listener, 62 (2 July 1959): 27-28.

3698. _____. "Joyce sème le désordre à l'Opéra...et s'attire des scenes de ménage: Souvenirs inédits." Figaro littéraire, 3 February 1962, p. 4.

3699. BEEBE, MAURICE. "Joyce and the Meanings of Modernism." Umana, 20 (May-September 1971): 29-31. [Reprinted in expanded form in Litters from Aloft, pp. 15-25, No. 1516; reprinted as "Ulysses and the Age of Modernism." James Joyce Quarterly, 10 (Fall 1972): 172-188.]

3700. BEGNAL, MICHAEL H. "The Mystery Man of Ulysses." Journal of Modern Literature, 2 (November 1972): 565-568.

*3701. BELLAMANN, HENRY. "The Literary Highway." Record (Columbia, S.C.), 25 November 1928.

*3702. BENCO, SILVIO. "Un Ulisse Irlandese." Il Secolo, 18 November 1921, p. 3.

*3703. BENEDIT, M. A. "El Ulisse." [Revista?] Fiesta, 2 (30 July 1927): 18-20.

3704. BENNETT, ARNOLD. "Concerning James Joyce's Ulysses." Bookman (New York), 55 (August 1922): 567-579. [Appeared in Outlook, 49 (29 April 1922): 29, 337-339; in his Things That Have Interested Me. New York: Doran, 1936, pp. 185-194; reprinted in The Author's Craft and Other Critical Writings. Edited by Samuel Hynes. Lincoln: University of Nebraska Press, 1968, pp. 211-217; reprinted in translation in "Auseinandersetzung mit James Joyces Ulysses," pp. 231-243, No. 3690.]

*3705. _____. "The Progress of the Novel." The Realist, 1 (April 1929): 3-11.

*3706. _____. "Books and Persons." Evening Standard (London), 23 January 1930. [Reply to a "Letter" by E. S. Jones, ibid., 22 January 1930.]

*3707. _____. "Le Roman." Figaro littéraire, 11 April 1931.

3708. BENSTOCK, BERNARD. "Ulysses without Dublin." James Joyce Quarterly, 10 (Fall 1972): 90-117.

3709. BERETTA, ALBERTO. "Ulysses: Ecclesia diabili e socialismo." Paragone, 22 (August 1971): 117-128.

3710. BIEŃKOWSKI, ZBIGNIEW. "Nad Ulissessem." Tworczose (Warsaw), 14 (1958): 57-68. [Reprinted in his Piekfa: c Orfersze. Warsaw: Zytelnic, 1960.]

3711. BILLINGS, ROBERT, and DONALD ZOCHERT. "Ulysses and The Hog Butchers." James Joyce Quarterly, 11 (Fall 1973): 27-32.

3712. BINI, LUIGI. "James Joyce esule ribelle." Letture, 16 (March 1961): 163-182.

*3713. BINZ, ARTUR F. "Der Abstruse Ulysses." Saarbrücker Zeitung, 21 April 1928.

3714. BLACKMUR, R. P. "The Jew in Search of a Son." Virginia Quarterly Review, 24 (Winter 1948): 96-116. [Appeared in his Eleven Essays on the European Novel. New York: Harcourt, Brace, and World, 1964, pp. 27-47.]

ULYSSES

3715. BLASS, ERNEST. "James Joyce und der Dulder Ulysses." Unterhaltungsblatt der Vossischen Zeitung, no. 229 (18 August 1932): 396.

3716. BLODGETT, HARRIET. "Joyce's Time Mind in Ulysses: A New Emphasis." James Joyce Quarterly, 5 (Fall 1967): 22-29.

3717. BLOEM, REIN. "Brief Encounters in Ulysses." Levende Talen, no. 269 (June-July 1970): 438-443. [In Dutch.]

3718. BOISEN, MOGENS. "Translating Ulysses." James Joyce Quarterly, 4 (Spring 1967): 165-169.

3719. BONDY, FRANCOIS. "Abschied von Sylvia Beach." Die Welt, 15 October 1962.

3720. BOREL, JACQUES. "Ulysse et l'éternel retour." Figaro littéraire, 20 January 1966, p. 8.

3721. _____. "Petite introduction à l'Ulysse de Joyce." Temps modernes (1968): 1291-1307. [Also in Joyce, pp. 11-26, No. 1526.]

*3722. BORGES, JORGÉ LUIS. "El Ulises de Joyce." Proa, no. 6 (January 1925): 3-6; "La ultima hoja del Ulises," pp. 8-9. [Reprinted in his Inquisiciones. Buenos Aires: Proa, 1925.]

*3723. _____. "Fragmento sobre Joyce." Sur, 10, no. 77 (February 1941): 60-62.

*3724. _____. "Noto sobre el Ulises en español." Annales de Buenos Aires, no. 1 (January 1946): 49.

3725. BOYD, ERNEST. "A Propos de Ulysses." Nouvelle revue francaise, 24 (March 1925): 309-313. [Response to Valery Larbaud, No. 3905.]

*3726. _____. "Readers and Writers." New York, 6 August 1927.

3727. _____. "Clue to Ulysses." Saturday Review of Literature, 10 (3 March 1934): 520. [Random House advertisement, 'How to Read Ulysses.']

*3728. _____. "Joyce and the New Irish Writers." Current History, 39 (March 1934): 699-704.

3729. BOYLE, PATRICK. "Bloomsday: A Sloppy Balance Sheet." Hibernia, 36 (1 December 1972): 14.

3730. BRADBURY, MALCOLM. "Passencore Rearrived from North America." Punch, 251 (27 July 1966): 155-156. [Answer to article by Alan Pryce-Jones in New York Review of Books.]

3731. BREZIANU, ANDREI. "Mediterana si Anglia. Ulise-Crîmpeie dintr-o reversiune metaforică ["The Mediterranean and Great Britain. U-Smithereens from a Metaphorical Revision]." Secolul 20, nos. 7-8 (1970): 276-282.

3732. _____. "Ulise, parodie si rodnicie." Secolul 20, nos. 10-12 (1971): 99-108.

3733. BRICK, ALLAN. "The Madman in His Cell: Joyce, Beckett, Nabokov, and the Stereotypes." Massachusetts Review, 1 (October 1959): 40-55.

3734. BRIVIC, SHELDON R. "Time, Sexuality and Identity and Joyce's Ulysses." James Joyce Quarterly, 7 (Fall 1969): 30-51.

*3735. BROMFIELD, LOUIS. "The New Yorker." Bookman (New York), July 1925.

3736. BROWN, ALEC. "Joyce's Ulysses and the Novel." Dublin Magazine, 9 (January-March 1934): 41-50.

3737. BRYER, JACKSON R. "Pound to Joyce on Ulysses: A Correction." American Notes and Queries, 4 (April 1966): 115.

3738. _____. "Joyce, Ulysses, and the Little Review." South Atlantic Quarterly, 66 (Spring 1967): 148-164.

3739. BUCKLEY, VINCENT. "Leavis and his 'Line.'" Critical Review, 8 (1965): 110-120.

3740. BUDGEN, FRANK. "Further Recollections of Joyce." Partisan Review, 23 (Fall 1956): 530-544. [Additional notes to his James Joyce and the Making of Ulysses, No. 3557.]

3741. BURGESS, ANTHONY. "How Well Have they Worn? Ulysses." Times (London), 17 March 1966, p. 15. [Reprinted in his Urgent Copy. London: Jonathan Cape; New York: Norton, 1968, pp. 82-84.]

3742. _____. "The Reticence of Ulysses." Spectator, 222 (7 June 1969): 748.

3743. _____. "Mulligan Stew: Irving Wallace Rewrites Ulysses." New York Times Book Review, 6 June 1971, pp. 5-6. [Parody.]

3744. _____. "The Ulysses Sentence." James Joyce Quarterly, 9 (Summer 1972): 423-435. [Reprinted in his Joysprick, No. 1536.]

3745. BURGUM, EDWIN B. "Ulysses and the Impasse of Individualism." Virginia Quarterly Review, 17 (Autumn 1941): 561-573. [Appeared in his The Novel and the World's Dilemma. New York: Oxford University Press, 1947, pp. 95-108; reprinted in Joyce, pp. 49-60, No. 1526.]

3746. BYRD, DON. "Joyce's Method of Philosophic Fiction." James Joyce Quarterly, 5 (Fall 1967): 9-21.

*3747. C., R. H. "Readers and Writers." New Age, 28 April 1921, p. 89.

3748. CALLADO, A. C. "Odyssey in Dublin." Americas, 4 (July 1952): 33-35.

3749. CAMPBELL, JOSEPH. "Contransmagnificandjew-bangtantiality." Studies in the Literary Imagination, 3, no. 2 (October 1970): 3-18.

3750. CAMPBELL, KENNETH. "Tour of Landmarks from Ulysses." New York Times Book Review, 2 November 1958, p. 5.

3751. CARD, WILLIAM, and VIRGINIA McDAVID. "English Words of Very High Frequency." College English, 27 (May 1966): 596-604.

*3752. CECCHI, EMILIO. "Incontro con Ulysses." La Tribuna (Rome), 2 March 1923. [Published under pseud. 'Il Tarlo'; reprinted as "Sull'Ulysses; il primo giudizio italiano: 1923." Europa letteraria, 2 (October 1961): 9-12; reprinted in his Scrittori inglesi e americani, volume 2, fourth edition, revised and augmented. Milan: Il Saggiatore, 1964, pp. 59-63.]

3753. CELA, CAMILO JOSE. "A los cuarenta y cinco años del Ulises." Papeles de son armadans, no. 12 (December 1967): 227-230. [Preface to Catalonian translation.]

3754. CERF, BENNETT. "Publishing Ulysses." Contempo, 3, no. 13 (February 1934): 1-2.

3755. CHAMSON, ANDRÉ. "Quand la république des lettres fêtait le poète d'Ulysse." Figaro littéraire, 20 January 1966, pp. 9, 13.

3756. CHARLTON, LINDA. "New Yorker's Ulysses Inching Along." Times (New York), 4 May 1970, p. 44.

3757. CHESTERTON, G. K. "The Spirit of the Age in Literature." The Bookman, 72 (October 1930): 97-103.

*3758. CICOGNA, O. "Preoccupazioni Letterarie Americane." Augustea-Roma, 28 February 1929, pp. 121-122.

3759. CLARKE, AUSTIN. "James Joyce." Everyman, 3, no. 68 (15 May 1930): 486.

3760. CLEMENT-JANIN. "L'amour du livre les gangsters de l'Edition." Candide, 25 February 1932, p. 4. [On Pirated ninth edition.]

3761. COLLINS, R. G. "Admiring a Bouquet of Blooms." Mosaic, 6 (Fall 1972): 103-112.

3762. COLUM, MARY M. "Modernists." Literary Review, 3, no. 18 (6 January 1923): 361-362.

*3763. COMMON, JACK. "James Joyce and the Making of Ulysses." Adelphi, 8 (1934): 68-70.

*3764. CONSIGLIO, ALBERTO. "Ulisse Terrestre." Il Giornale d'Italia (Rome), 12 October 1927.

*3765. _____. "Un Giorno di Vita." Mattino (Naples), 5 July 1929.

3766. COWLEY, MALCOLM. "James Joyce." Bookman (New York), 59 (July 1924): 518-521.

3767. CRONIN, ANTHONY. "A Note on Ulysses." The Bell, 18, no. 4 (July 1952): 221-227.

3768. _____. "A Question of Modernity." X:A Quarterly Review, 1 (October 1960): 283-292.

3769. _____. "U and The Waste Land." Irish Times, 16 June 1972, p. 10. [Interview with T. S. Eliot.]

3770. CROSS, GUSTAV. "Joyeux Quicum Ulysse...." Essays in Criticism, 8 (October 1955): 420.

*3771. CURTNESSE, D. M. "The English Novel Since 1914." New Age, 34 (29 November 1923): 55.

*3772. D., H. E. [n.t.]. Evening Post (New York), 30 April 1927.

3773. DALTON, JACK P. "Ulysses X 2. A New Conversion Table." James Joyce Quarterly, 1 (Summer 1964): 52-55.

3774. DAMON, S. FOSTER. "The Odyssey in Dublin." Hound and Horn, 3 (October-December 1929): 7-44. [Appeared with "Postscript 1947" in James Joyce: Two Decades of Criticism, pp. 203-242, No. 1570.]

3775. DANINOS, PIERRE. "Les snobs et la littérature." Figaro littéraire, 20 May 1964, pp. 1, 7.

3776. DASSEN, J. M. H. "Ulysses." Utopia, 8 (June 1969): 16-19.

3777. DAWSON, N. P. "The Cuttlefish School of Writers." Forum, 69 (January 1923): 1174-1184.

3778. DeCASTRESANA, LUIS. "Ulises, en Dublin," photo by Jaime Balleste. Blanco y negro, 81 (12 June 1971): 90-92.

*3779. DELLING, MANFRED. "Ulysses." Frankfurter Allgemeine Zeitung, 2 February 1957.

*3780. DEUTSCH, BABETTE. "On Ulysses." Literary Review, 2 December 1922, p. 281.

ULYSSES

*3781. de WALEFFE, MAURICE. "Un Ulysse Irlandais ou le Bonheur d'être Latin." Paris-Midi, 16 June 1930.

3782. DREW, ELIZABETH. "The Difficulties of Joyce's Ulysses." CEA Critic, 14 (February 1952): 1, 6.

3783. DUFFY, JOHN J. "The Painful Case of M'Intosh." Studies in Short Fiction, 2 (Winter 1965): 183-185.

*3784. DUJARDIN, ÉDOUARD. "Der roman stirbt nicht-- in Frankreich." Vossische Zeitung (Berlin), 31 January 1929, p. 1.

3785. DUNDES, ALAN. "Re:Joyce--No In at the Womb." Modern Fiction Studies, 8 (Summer 1962): 137-147.

3786. DUPLAIX, GEORGES. "Joyce à la 'Revue des Deux Mondes.'" La Revue nouvelle, no. 10-11 (September-October 1925): 23-29.

*3787. DUWELL, BERNHARD. "Ulysses oder: Der Bolschewismus der Kultur." Sachsisches Volkblatt (Zwickau), 20 August 1931.

3788. DUYTSCHAEVER, JORIS. "James Joyce's Ulysses in Dutch." Revue des langues vivantes, 37, no. 6 (1971): 701-711.

3789. EHRENSTEIN, ALBERT. "James Joyce." Berliner Tageblatt, no. 163 (5 April 1928): 8. [Reprinted in Ostseezeitung (Stettin), 9 May 1928.]

3790. EISENSTEIN, SERGEI M. "An American Tragedy." Close-up, 10, no. 2 (June 1933): 109-124.

3791. ELEKTOROWICZ, LESZEK. "Dookola Ulissesa." Kultura (Warsaw), 3 (7 November 1965): 1-2. [Reprinted in his Zwierciadlo w okruchach: Szkice o powiesci amerykanskiej i angielskie. Warsaw: Panstowowy Instytut Wydawniczy, 1966, pp. 26-40.]

*3792. ELIOT, T. S. "Contemporanea." Egoist, 5, no. 6 (June-July 1918): 84-85.

3793. ELIZONDO, SALVADOR. "En torno al Ulises de Joyce." Estaciones, 4 (Spring 1959): 98-111.

3794. ELLMANN, RICHARD. "The Backgrounds of Ulysses." Kenyon Review, 16 (Summer 1954): 337-386. [Became part of his James Joyce, No. 308.]

3795. _____. "The Limits of Joyce's Naturalism." Sewanee Review, 63 (Autumn 1955): 567-575.

3796. _____. "James Joyce's Ulysses." Inventario, 17 (1962): 22-23.

3797. _____. "Odyssey of a Unique Book." New York Times Magazine, 14 November 1965, pp.

56-57, 92, 94, 96, 102, 104, 106. [See letter to the editor by David Lawson. Ibid., 28 November 1965, p. 75.]

3798. _____. "Why Does Stephen Pick His Nose?" Times Literary Supplement, 21 May 1971, pp. 591-593; became a chapter in his Ulysses on the Liffey (1972), No. 3568. [Exchange of "Letters to the Editor" summarized in James Joyce Quarterly, 9 (Fall 1971): 3-5; Arthur Frewen. TLS, 11 June 1971, p. 677; Ellmann's reply, 11 June 1971, p. 677; Ruth Hedger, 18 June 1971, n.p.; J. Cunningham, 25 June 1971, p. 737; Arthur Frewen, 7 July 1971, p. 780; J. Cunningham, 16 July 1971, p. 835; Edward Caulfield, 23 July 1971, p. 861; Wilbur Gafney, 6 August 1971, p. 945; Karl Beckson, 16 July 1971, p. 835.]

3799. EMERY, LAURENCE K. "The Ulysses of Mr. James Joyce." Claxon: An Irish International Quarterly (Winter 1923-24): 14-20.

*3800. EMETH, OMER [pseudonym of Emilio Vaisse]. "Un gran escritor irlandes: James Joyce y su Ulisse, Paris, 1925." Crónica literaria, 14 March 1926, p. 3. [Reprinted in Repertorio Americano, 7 November 1936, pp. 264, 276.]

3801. EPSTEIN, EDMUND L. "Cruxes in Ulysses: Notes Toward an Edition and Annotation." James Joyce Review, 1, no. 3 (September 1957): 25-36.

3802. _____. "The Irrelevant Narrator: A Stylistic Note on the Place of the Author in Contemporary Technique of the Novel." Language and Style, 2 (Winter 1969): 92-94.

3803. FAVERTY, FREDERICK E. "Ulysses: One of the Most Arresting Books of All Time." Chicago Sunday Tribune Magazine of Books, 21 October 1956, p. 3. [Appeared in his Your Literary Heritage. Philadelphia: Lippincott, 1959, pp. 195-197.]

*3804. FECHTER, PAUL. "Der Ulysses des James Joyce." Deutsche Allgemeine Zeitgeblatt (Berlin), 22 January 1928; Die Schöne Literatur (Leipzig), 29 (May 1928): 239-243.

*3805. FEHR, BERNHARD. "Ulysses von James Joyce." Frankfurter Zeitung, 8 June 1930.

3806. FERRANDINO, JOSEPH. "Joyce and Phenomenology." Telos, 1 (Fall 1968): 84-92.

3807. FERRIS, WILLIAM R. "Ulysses: A Reexamination of Artistic Rebellion." Jackson [Mississippi] State College Review, 4, no. 1 (1972): 1-12.

3808. FIOL, J. M., and J. C. SANTOYO. "Joyce, Ulisse y Espana." Papeles de son armadans, 67 (August 1972): 121-140.

*3809. FISCHER, ADOLF JOHANNES. "James Joyce in Salzburg." Salzburger Volksblatt, 25 August, 1928, p. 5.

3810. FISHMAN, JOANNE. "Robert Kastor of West Long Branch Aided in Publication of Ulysses Here." Red Bank [New Jersey] Daily Register, 23 February 1966, p. 3.

3811. FLANNER, JANET (GENÊT). "The Great Amateur Publisher." Mercure de France, 347 (August-September 1963): 46-51.

3812. FLORA, FRANCESCO. "Da un Saggio sull'Ulisse di Joyce." Letterature moderne, 11 (March-April 1961): 149-178.

3813. FLORES, OLAGUE. "James Joyce, a cincuenta años de Ulises." Comunidad, 8 (April 1973): 228-233.

*3814. FLUCHERE, HENRI. "Ulysse." Le foyer Universitaire, 2, no. 5 (May 1931): 1-6.

*3815. FORD, FORD MADOX. "Literary Causeries: VIII: So She Went Into the Garden." Chicago Tribune Sunday Magazine, 6 April 1924, pp. 3, 11.

*3816. FORSTER, E. M. "The Book of the Age? James Joyce's Ulysses." New Leader (London), 13, no. 24 (12 March 1926): 13-14.

*3817. FRANZEN, ERICH. "Zum Ulysses von Joyce." Die literarische Welt, 4 (1928): 5-6.

*3818. FRIIS-MOLLER, KAI. "Skribenter og Bøger: 'Det unge England.'" Politiken (Copen- hagen), 20 August 1928.

*3819. GARNETT, DAVID. "Jacob's Room." Dial, 75 (July 1923): 83-86. [Ulysses discussed in review of Virginia Woolf's Jacob's Room.]

3820. GAYA NUÑO, JUAN ANTONIO. "En el cincuenten- ario del Ulises: Relieves críticos." El Urogallo, 3 (July-August 1972): 99-105.

3821. GERSTENBERG, JOACHIN. "Six Photographs of the Backgrounds of Ulysses." Envoy, 3 (November 1950): 56ff.

3822. GIEDION-WELCKER, CAROLA. "Zum Ulysses von James Joyce." Neue Schweizer Rundschau, 21 (January 1928): 18-32.

*3823. _____. "Die Funktion der Sprache in der Heutigen Dichtung." transition, no. 22 (February 1933): 90-100.

*3824. GILBERT, BERNARD. "The Tragedy of James Joyce." G. K.'s Weekly, 1, no. 3 (4 April 1925): 36-38.

3825. GILLET, LOUIS. "Du Côté de Chez Joyce." Revue des deux mondes, 28 (August 1925): 686-697. [Appeared in his Claybook for

James Joyce, No. 1568, and in his Esquis- ses anglaises. Paris, 1930, pp. 118-133.]

3826. GLASGOW, ELLEN. "Impressions of the Novel." New York Herald Tribune, 20 May 1928, pp. 1, 5.

3827. GODWIN, MURRAY. "A Rushlight for the Laby- rinth." Pacific Spectator, 6 (Winter 1952): 84-96.

3828. GOLD, ED. "Bloom Becoming." Chesapeake Weekly Review, 12 June 1970, p. 6.

*3829. GOLDBERG, S. L. "The Conception of History in Joyce's Ulysses." Present Opinion, 2 (1947): 62-65.

3830. GOLDKNOPF, DAVID. "Realism in the Novel." Yale Review, 60 (Autumn 1970): 69-84.

3831. GOLDMAN, ARNOLD. "Some Proposed Emendations in the text of Joyce's Ulysses." Notes and Queries, 10 (April 1963): 148-150.

3832. GOLL, YVAN. "Der Homer unserer Zeit: James Joyce." Die literarische Welt, 3 (17 June 1927): 1-2. [Reprinted in Living Age, 333 (1927): 316-320; reprinted as "Über James Joyce," in Der Homer unserer Zeit: Deutschland in Erwartung des Ulysses von James Joyce, pp. 2-6, No. 3599; re- printed in Zeitgemässess aus der Literar- ischen Welt von 1925-1932. Edited by Willy Haas. Stuttgart: J. G. Cottasche Buchhand- lung Nacht, 1963, pp. 98-101.]

*3833. _____. "La nueva Literatura, James Joyce." La Gaceta Literaria (Madrid), 1 November 1927, p. 3.

3834. _____. "Ulysses: Sub Specie Aeternita- tis." Die Weltbühne, 23, no. 2 (27 Dec- ember 1927): 960-963.

*3835. _____. "Joycuv Ulysses: pro a proti." Pritomnost (Prague), 1928, pp. 105-107. ["Proti" by Peter Panter.]

*3836. _____. "James Joyce." Die Weltbühne, 28, no. 1 (1932): 216-218.

*3837. GOPALEEN, MYLES na (Flann O'Brien, Brian Nolan). "Cruiskeen Lawn." Irish Times, 5 April 1944.

*3838. _____. "Cruiskeen Lawn." Irish Times, 28 May 1945.

*3839. _____. "Cruiskeen Lawn." Irish Times, 1 June 1949.

*3840. _____. "Cruiskeen Lawn." Irish Times, 10 February 1953.

*3841. _____. "Cruiskeen Lawn." Irish Times, 1 June 1955.

ULYSSES

*3842. _____ . "Cruiskeen Lawn." Irish Times, 9 February 1956.

*3843. _____ . "Cruiskeen Lawn." Irish Times, 15 August 1956.

*3844. _____ . "Cruiskeen Lawn." Irish Times, 22 August 1956.

*3845. _____ . "Cruiskeen Lawn." Irish Times, 7 June 1957.

*3846. _____ . "Cruiskeen Lawn." Irish Times, 19 February 1958.

*3847. _____ . "Cruiskeen Lawn." Irish Times, 5 March 1958.

*3848. _____ . "Cruiskeen Lawn." Irish Times, 12 January 1959.

*3849. _____ . "Cruiskeen Lawn." Irish Times, 18 April 1959.

*3850. _____ . "Cruiskeen Lawn." Irish Times, 23 December 1961.

3851. _____ . "Cruiskeen Lawn." Irish Times, 19 June 1962.

3852. _____ . "Enigma." Irish Times, 16 June 1962, p. 10.

3853. _____ . "Cruiskeen Lawn." Irish Times, 9 December 1965.

*3854. GOTTGETREU, ERICH. "Die Abenteuer des Ulysses." Montag Morgen (Berlin), 27 June 1927.

3855. GOULD, GERALD. "The English Novel." Observer, 6 April, 13 April, 9 December 1924. [Appeared in his The English Novel Today. New York: Dial Press, 1925, pp. 19-23; reprinted Freeport, New York: Books for Libraries, 1971, pp. 19-27.]

*3856. GOYERT, GEORG. "Noch Einmal: Ulysses in Deutschland: Antwort des übersetzers Georg Goyert." Frankfurter Allgemeine Zeitung, 6 December 1957.

*3857. GREEN, LAURENCE. [n.t.]. Morning Sun (Baltimore), 14 May 1939.

*3858. GREGORY, HORACE. [n.t.]. Herald Tribune (New York), 21 January 1934.

*3859. GRINLING, A. H. "On Smollett, Sailor and Surgeon." Press (Christchurch, N.Z.), 4 May 1929.

*3860. HALL, DOUGLAS KENT. "James Joyce at 71, Rue du Cardinal Lemoine." Brigham Young University Studies, 3 (Spring-Summer 1961): 43-49.

3861. HAMALIAN, LEO. "The Secret Careers of Samuel Roth." Journal of Popular Culture, 1 (Spring 1968): 317-338. [Appeared in 3X3. Saratoga Springs: Harian Press, 1969, pp. 69-110 in enlarged and corrected version.]

3862. HAMMERTON, J. A. "The Literary Show: What I Think of James Joyce." The Bystander, 23 April 1930, pp. 194, 197.

3863. HARRISON, JOSEPH B. "Literature and the Current Crisis." Interim (Seattle), 1, no. 3 (1945): 12-18.

*3864. HARTMANN, W. "Setkání s Jamesem Joycem." Pravo Lidu (Praha), 9 September 1929.

3865. HARWOOD, H. C. "The Post-War Novel in England." Outlook (7 May 1927). [Reprinted Living Age, 333, no. 4309 (1 July 1927): 67-69.]

*3866. HATFIELD, THEODORE. [n.t.]. Capital (Annapolis, Maryland), 8 March 1928. [News report of lecture on 'The Modern Novel' by Professor Theodore Hatfield of St. John's College.]

3867. HAYMAN, DAVID. "Forms of Folly in Joyce: A Study of Clowning in Ulysses." ELH: Journal of English Literary History, 34 (June 1967): 260-283.

3868. HENIG, SUZANNE. "Ulysses in Bloomsbury." James Joyce Quarterly, 10 (Winter 1973): 203-208. [See Christine St. Peter Breech. "Letter to the Editor." James Joyce Quarterly, 11 (Fall 1973): 75-76.]

*3869. 'Der Herausgeber'. "Ulysses und die Deutsche Literatur-Kritik." Deutsche Bücherschau, 6, no. 2 (February 1928): 87-89.

3870. HERMAN, LEWIS. "The Problem of the Tsk." American Spectator, 3, no. 29 (March 1935): 13.

3871. HERRING, PHILIP F. "Ulysses Notebook VIII. A.5 at Buffalo." Studies in Bibliography, 22 (1969): 287-310.

*3872. HOHOFF, CURT. "Die Odyssee des James Joyce." Süddeutsche Zeitung, 15/16 February 1958.

3873. _____ . "Neues zur James Joyce--Saga." Neue Zürcher Zeitung, no. 196 (18 July 1964).

3874. HULL, WILLIAM. "Shaw on the Joyce he Scarcely Read." Shaw Bulletin, 1, no. 6 (September 1954): 16-20.

3875. JACKSON, HOLBROOK. "Ulysses a la Joyce." Today, 9 (June 1922): 47-49. [Appeared in Bruno's Review of Two Worlds (New

York), 2, no. 4 (July-August 1922): 37-38, reprinted Berkeley Heights, New Jersey: Oriole Press, 1961.]

*3876. JALOUX, EDMOND. "L'Inspiration poétique et l'Aridité.'" Études Carmélitaines, 22 no. 2 (October 1937): 31-45.

3877. JAMESON, F. R. "Seriality in Modern Literature." Bucknell Review, 18 (Spring 1970): 63-80.

3878. JENKINS, WILLIAM D. "It Seems There Were Two Irishmen...." Modern Fiction Studies, 15 (Spring 1969): 63-71.

*3879. JOLAS, EUGENE. "Rambles Through Literary Paris." Chicago Tribune (Paris), 11 January 1925. [Account of the Larbaud-Boyd Feud.]

3880. JOLAS, EUGENE, ELIOT PAUL, and ROBERT SAGE. "First Aid to the Enemy." transition, no. 9 (December 1927): 161-176. [Answer to Wyndham Lewis' attacks on Joyce, see No. 3915.]

3881. JONES, ALUN. "Portrait of the Artist as Himself." Critical Quarterly, 2 (Spring 1960): 40-46.

3882. JOSEPHSON, MATTHEW. "1001 Nights in a Bar-Room, or the Irish Odysseus." Broom, 3 (September 1922): 146-150.

3883. KAIN, RICHARD M. "Joyce's World View." Dubliner, 3 (Autumn 1964): 3-10.

3884. _____. "Footnotes to Ulysses from Shane Leslie's Memoirs." James Joyce Quarterly, 4 (Summer 1967): 354.

3885. _____. "Ulysses as a Classic: Some Anniversary Reconsiderations." Mosaic, 6 (Fall 1972): 57-62.

3886. _____. "The Significance of Stephen's Meeting Bloom: A Survey of Interpretations." James Joyce Quarterly, 10 (Fall 1972): 147-160.

*3887. KARLING, KARIN. "En Bannlyst Bok och dess Forfattare." Posten (Goteborgs), 20 June 1928.

3888. KAVANAGH, PATRICK. "Diary." Envoy, 5 (May 1951): 70-72. [Reprinted in A Bash in the Tunnel, pp. 49-52, No. 1644.]

3889. KAWAGUCHI, KYOICHI. "Ulysses ni okeru Jinbutsu Saigen no Mondai." Eigo Seinen (Tokyo), 116 (1970): 314-315.

3890. _____. "[Double Vision in Ulysses]." Eigo Seinen, 118 (August 1971): 300-302.

3891. KENNEDY, SISTER EILEEN. "Another Root for Bloomsday?" James Joyce Quarterly, 6 (Spring 1969): 271-272.

3892. KILEEN, A. "Ulysse." Revue de littérature comparée, 10 (April-June 1930): 323-327.

3893. KILLHAM, JOHN. "'Ineluctable Modality' in Joyce's Ulysses." University of Toronto Quarterly, 34 (April 1965): 269-289.

3894. KIMBALL, JEAN. "The Hypostasis in Ulysses." James Joyce Quarterly, 10 (Summer 1973): 422-438.

3895. KITTREDGE, SELWYN. "Richard Aldington's Challenge to T. S. Eliot: The Background of their James Joyce Controversy." James Joyce Quarterly, 10 (Spring 1973): 339-341.

*3896. KNAPP, OTTO. "Das Bild des Menschen im neuen englischen Roman." Hochland, 30 (September 1933): 532-544.

3897. KNIGHT, DOUGLAS. "The Reading of Ulysses." ELH: Journal of English Literary History, 19 (March 1952): 64-80. [Reprinted in Configuration critique de James Joyce, II, pp. 73-92, No. 1584.]

3898. KNUTH, LEO. "Joyce's Verbal Acupuncture." James Joyce Quarterly, 10 (Fall 1972): 61-71.

3899. KOLJEVIC, SVETOZAR. "Igra svesti i postojanja u Džojsovom Ulisu." Izraz, 10, no. 5 (1966): 429-433.

3900. KOPPER, EDWARD A. "Ulysses and James Joyce's Use of Comedy." Mosaic, 6 (Fall 1972): 45-56.

*3901. LAMBERTO, LATTANZI. "El Ulises de Joyce y su condena." Heroica (Revista para la Juventud), December 1945.

3902. LANGBAUM, ROBERT. "The Mysteries of Identity: A Theme in Modern Literature." American Scholar, 34 (Autumn 1965): 569-586.

*3903. LANGER, FELIX. "Der Ulysses von Joyce." Berliner Tageblatt, 26 November 1927.

3904. LARBAUD, VALERY. "James Joyce." Nouvelle revue français, 18 (April 1922): 385-409. [Speech delivered to Les Amis des Livres, 7 December 1921; used as introduction to Gens de Dublin (Paris, 1926); translated as "The Ulysses of James Joyce." Criterion, 1 (October 1922): 94-103; translated by A. J. Battistessa. Logos (Buenos Aires), 4 (1945): 79-98; reprinted in his Ce vice impuni, la lecture, No. 1602.]

ULYSSES

3905. _____ . "A Propos de James Joyce et de Ulysse." Nouvelle revue française, 24 (January 1925): 1-17. [Criticism of statements made by Ernest Boyd in his Ireland's Literary Renaissance (No. 1527) on Larbaud and U.]

3906. _____ . "Sur 'Ulysses.'" Mercure de France, 347 (August-September 1963): 99-101. [Two letters written to Sylvia Beach in 1921, translated by Marcelle Sibon.]

3907. LASSON, ROBERT. "Happy 36." Book World, 25 January 1970, p. 6. [36th anniversary of Random House edition of U.]

3908. LECOMTE, MARCEL. "L'Esthétique Joycienne." Le Journal des Poètes, 23 (December 1953): 4.

*3909. LESTER, LEIGH. "Nuevos Libros Ingleses." La Nacion (Buenos Aires), 10 July 1927, p. 16.

*3910. LEVIN, HARRY. "What was Modernism?" Massachusetts Review, 1, no. 4 (August 1960): 609-630. [Translated in Inventario (January-December 1963); reprinted in Varieties of Literary Experience. Edited by Stanley Burnshaw. New York: New York University Press, 1962, pp. 307-329; reprinted in Levin's Refractions: Essays in Comparative Literature. New York: Oxford University Press, 1966, pp. 271-295.]

*3911. LEWERS, CONSTANCE E. "The Red Page." The Bulletin (Sydney).

3912. LEWICKI, ZBIGNIEW. "Sceniczny Ulisses Slomczyńskiego." Literatura na świecie, no. 5 (May 1973): 218-240.

3913. L[EWICKI], Z[BIGNIEW?]. "Ulisses na świecie." Literatura na świecie, no. 5 (May 1973): 286-289.

3914. LEWICKI, ZBIGNIEW, and DANIEL C. GEROULD. "Ulysses in Gdansk." James Joyce Quarterly, 9 (Fall 1971): 99-116.

3915. LEWIS, WYNDHAM. "The Revolutionary Simpleton." The Enemy (London), 1 (January 1927): 95-130. [Appeared in expanded version as "An Analysis of the Mind of James Joyce," in his Time and Western Man. London: Chatto and Windus, 1927, pp. 91-130; New York: Harcourt, Brace, 1928, pp. 75-113. Attacked by Harry Levin in James Joyce, No. 1603 which led to Lewis' rebuttal in his Rude Assignment, No. 1049.]

3916. LIDDERDALE, J. H. "Harriet Weaver and James Joyce." Book Collector, 15 (Winter 1966/67): 439-450.

*3917. LINDNER, G. "Über James Joyce, Ulysses." Königsberger Hartungsche Zeitung, 22 March 1931.

3918. LIPPMAN, BERT. "Literature and Life." Georgia Review, 25 (Summer 1971): 145-158.

3919. LITZ, A. WALTON. "Joyce's Notes for the Last Episodes of Ulysses." Modern Fiction Studies, 4 (Spring 1958): 3-20.

3920. _____ . "The Last Adventures of Ulysses." Princeton University Library Chronicle, no. 28 (Autumn 1966): 63-75.

3921. _____ . "Pound and Eliot on Ulysses: The Critical Tradition." James Joyce Quarterly, 10 (Fall 1972): 5-18.

3922. LOEPPERT, ELSBETH. "The Prophecy of Ulysses." Cresset, 35 (March 1972): 10-12.

3923. LORENZINI, AMLETO. "Tearslations." James Joyce Quarterly, 9 (Spring 1972): 353-373.

*3924. LOW, STEPHEN. "Current Literature: This Generation--." London Weekly, 1 (5 March 1927): 300-301.

3925. LYONS, J. B. "Anatomy in James Joyce's Ulysses." The Practitioner, 209 (September 1972): 374-379. [From his James Joyce and Medicine, No. 1611.]

*3926. McCAFFREY, JOHN. "Barney Kiernan's." Irish Times, 29 October 1959.

*3927. MacCARTHY, DESMOND. "Le roman anglais d'après-guerre (1919-1929)." Revue de Paris, 39, no. 9 (May 1932): 129-152.

3928. McCOLE, CAMILLE. "Ulysses." Catholic World, 138 (March 1934): 722-728.

3929. McHUGH, ROGER. "The Passing of Barney Kiernan's." Envoy, 1, no. 1 (December 1949): 9-14.

3930. McKINLEY, HUGH. "Ulysses." Dublin Magazine, 9 (Summer 1972): 9. [Poem.]

3931. McLAIN, EVELYN N. "'Alle Schiffe Brücken': Joyce's Ulysses Resolved." South Central Bulletin, 30 (1970): 209-211.

3932. McLEAN, ANDREW M. "Joyce's Ulysses and Döblin's Alexanderplatz Berlin." Comparative Literature, 25 (Winter 1973): 97-113.

3933. McNELLY, WILLIS E. "Twenty Years in Search of a Footnote." James Joyce Quarterly, 9 (Summer 1972): 452-459. [Praise of U by Msgr. Ennio Francia. "Letteratura irlandese contemporanea." l'Osservatore Romano, no. 245 (20 October 1937): 3.]

3934. MACIAS, RAUL. "Ulisse: Mito y realidad."
Union (Havana), 2 (January-April 1963):
101-110.

3935. MAITLAND, CECIL. "Mr. Joyce and the Catholic Tradition." New Witness, 20 (August
1922): 70-71.

*3936. MARCU, VALERIU. "Des Mystikers James Joyce
Weltruhm." Hamburger Fremdenblatt, 22
January 1927.

3937. MARICHALAR, ANTONIO. "James Joyce en su
Labertino." Revista de Occidente
(Madrid), 11 (1924): 177-202.

3938. MARIÑO-PALACIO, ANDRIS. "Le Estetica Moderna in Ulisses." Revista Nacional de
Cultura, no. 65 (November-December 1947):
73-80. [Reprinted in his Ensayos, Biblioteca popular venezola, 110. Edited by
Rafael Pineda. Caracas: Inst. Nacional
de Cultura y Bellas Artes, 1967, pp. 295-
307.]

*3939. MARMON, C. "Tehisla." La revue littéraire
russe, 4 (1931): 225-229. [In Russian.]

3940. MASON, ELLSWORTH. "Ulysses, the Hair Shirt,
and Humility." CEA Critic, 14, no. 2
(February 1952): 6.

3941. _____. "James Joyce: Moralist." Twentieth Century Literature, 1 (January
1956): 196-206.

3942. MASON, MICHAEL YORK. "Ulysses the Sequel to
Portrait? Joyce's Plans for the Two Works."
English Language Notes, 8 (June 1971):
296-300. [Replies by A. Walton Litz,
Robert Scholes, Richard M. Kain, pp. 301-
305.]

*3943. MATHEWS, JACKSON. "Conversations with Syl-
via Beach and Company." Kenyon Review,
22 (Winter 1960): 137-150.

3944. MATHEWS, JACKSON, and MAURICE SAILLET, editors. "Sylvia Beach (1887-1962)." Mercure de France, 349 (August-September
1963): 5-170. [Special issue dedicated
to Miss Beach; for Contents, see No. 156.]

3945. MATLACK, DAVID. "On Reading James Joyce's
Ulysses." Tanager (June 1946): 77-78.

3946. MAYO, W. K. "Los 50 Años de Ulisses."
Letura, 200 (1-15 November 1972): 25-28.

*3947. MAZZI, LIBERO. "L'Ulysses approdo in Ital-
ia." Piccolo (Trieste), 24 November 1960.

3948. MEAGHER, JAMES A. "A Dubliner Reads Ulysses." Australasian Quarterly, 17 (June
1945): 74-86.

3949. _____. "Two Joyous Dactyls." Meanjin
(Melbourne), 7 (Autumn 1948): 57-58.

3950. MEGRET, FREDERIC. "Au pays d'Ulysse et des
cavaliers de la mer." Figaro littéraire,
26 June-2 July 1967, pp. 32-33.

3951. MENENDEZ, ALDO. "James Joyce." Islas (Santa
Clara, Cuba), 5 (January-June 1963): 331-
335.

3952. MERCANTON, JACQUES. "James Joyce." Europe,
46 (15 April 1938): 433-471.

3953. MERKLING, FRANK. "This Week." Opera News,
37 (3 March 1973): 4. [Ulysses and Don
Giovanni.]

3954. MIKHALSKAYA, N. P. "Roman Ulios Dzheimsa
Dzhoisa." Uchenye Zapiski, Moskovskii
Gosudarstvennyi Pedagogicheskii Institut
Imeni Lenina, 304 (1968): 3-33.

3955. MILLER-BUDNITSKAYA, R. "Uliss Dzheimsa
Dzhoisa." Literaturnyi Kritik (1934):
also in International Literature, no. 4
(1935): 106-116; translated in Dialectics,
no. 5 (1938): 6-26. [Reprinted Folcroft,
Pa.: Folcroft Press, 1972, translated by
N. J. Nelson.]

*3956. MIOMANDRE, FRANCIS de. "Vulagrisation."
Les nouvelles littéraires, no. 338 (6
April 1929): 2.

3957. MITCHELL, BREON. "A Note on the Status of
the Authorized Translation." James Joyce
Quarterly, 4 (Spring 1967): 202-205.

3958. _____. "Joyce and Döblin: At the Cross-
roads of Berlin Alexanderplatz." Contemporary Literature, 12 (Spring 1971): 173-
187.

3959. MOHRT, MICHEL. "Sylvia Beach: Une Americaine
à Paris." Figaro littéraire, 13 October
1962, p. 15.

*3960. MONNIER, ADRIENNE. "Lectures chez Sylvia."
Nouvelle revue française, 274 (1 August
1936): 250-252. [Reprinted in Mercure de
France, special Sylvia Beach Issue, pp.
133-135, No. 156.]

3961. _____. "L'Ulysse de Joyce et le Public
francais." La Gazette des Amis des Livres
(Paris), 3, no. 10 (May 1940): 50-64.
[Translated by Sylvia Beach in Kenyon Review, 8 (Summer 1946): 430-444; later appeared in Kenyon Critics: Studies in Modern Literature. Edited by John Crowe
Ransom. New York: World Publishing Co.,
1951, pp. 75-88; reprinted Port Washington, New York: Kennikat Press, 1967, pp.
75-88.]

3962. _____. "La Traduction d'Ulysse." Mercure de France, 309 (May 1959): 30-37.
[Reprinted in Rue de l'Odeon. Paris: Editions Albin Michel, 1960, pp. 159-170.]

ULYSSES

3963. MORRISEY, FRANCIS J., JR. "Joyce v. Carr--
The Artist as Litigant." The Shingle
(Philadelphia Bar Association), 35 (Feb-
ruary 1972): 32-36. [See also Alfred L.
Wolf. "Joyce's Ghost Still Confronts Lo-
cal Lawyers." The Shingle, 35 (November
1972): 171-173, reprinted in James Joyce
Quarterly, 10 (Spring 1973): 330-332.]

3964. MUIR, EDWIN. "A Note on Ulysses." New Republic, 41, no. 523 (10 December 1924):
4-6. [See next item, No. 3965.]

3965. _____. "James Joyce: The Meaning of
Ulysses." Calendar of Modern Letters, 1
no. 5 (July 1925): 347-355. [Same article
appeared as "James Joyce." Nation, 121,
no. 3145 (14 October 1925): 421-423.
Former version, plus a revised version of
"A Note on Ulysses," No. 3964, appeared
in his Transition. New York: Viking
Press, 1926, pp. 19-36; reprinted Freeport, New York: Books for Libraries,
1972, pp. 19-45.]

3966. MULLEN, SISTER M. ST. IGNATIUS. "Dublin Em-
balmed in Joyce's Ulysses." Daedalian
Quarterly, 47 (Fall 1966): 13-20.

3967. MURRAY, JOHN MIDDLETON. "Mr. Joyce's Ulysses." Nation and Athenaeum, 31 (22 April
1922): 124-125.

3968. NAGANOWSKI, ÉGON. "Problemów Ulyssesa."
Wspołczesność, no. 18 (1962).

3969. _____. "Structura czasu, przestrzeni i
postaci w Ulissessie Jamesa Joyce'a."
Umana, 20 (May-September 1971): 49-51.
["On Time, Space and Form in Ulysses,"
with English abstract.]

3970. NÜHBAUER, HANS. "Ulysses: Die grossen Romane
unseres Jahrhunderts (VIII)." Epoca (Munich), 8 (September 1968): 74-75, 97.

3971. NOON, WILLIAM T., S.J. "Bard of the Shapeless Cosmopolis." Humanities Association
Bulletin (Canada), 16 (Fall 1965): 45-51.

*3972. NOYES, ALFRED. "Rottenness in Literature."
Evening-Standard (London), 28 October
1922; Sunday Chronicle (Manchester), 29
October 1922, p. 2. [Account of lecture
given at Royal Society of Literature.]

3973. O'BRIEN, DARCY. "Cod be with You." Umana,
20 (May-September 1971): 27-28.

*3974. O'CALLAGHAN, J. "Letter." Irish Statesman,
22 August 1925.

*3975. O'C [O'Connor], F[rank]. Irish Statesman, 8
June 1929, pp. 276-277. [Attack on Wyndham Lewis' Time and Western Man, No.
3915.]

3976. OLDEN, G. A. "R. E. Should Tackle Joyce's
Ulysses." Irish Times, 25 February 1954,
p. 4.

3977. OPFERMANN, H. C. "Uber den Ulysses von James
Joyce aus deutscher Sicht." Lion (German
edition), no. 11 (November 1965): 527-531.

*3978. ORNSTEIN, WILLIAM. "Joyce's Ulysses sans
Those Words: Cardiff's Credo." Variety,
21 June 1961, pp. 2, 66.

*3979. OTTEN, J. F. "Shakespeare and Company."
Neusse Rotterdam Courant, 27 April 1932.

3980. PASTOR, BERNARD. "Le cri de l'homme: Cin-
quantenaire d'Ulysses de Joyce." Nouvelles littéraires, no. 2361 (25-31 December 1972): 4.

3981. PASTORE, ANNIBALE. "L'Interpretazione filo-
sofica della Vita nell'Ulisse di James
Joyce." L'Indagine: Quaderni di Critica
e Filosofia (Rome), no. 1 (1947): 75-89.

3982. PATERAKIS, DEBORAH T. "Keylessness, Sex and
The Promised Land: Associated Themes in
Ulysses." Éire-Ireland, 8 (Spring 1973):
97-108.

*3983. PATMORE, DEREK. "Modern American Writers."
Nineteenth Century (January 1931).

*3984. PAUL, ELLIOT. "From a Litterateur's Note-
book." Chicago Tribune (Paris), 16 January 1927.

*3985. PEAKE, CHARLES. "Ulysses and Some Modern
Criticism." Gymnasium Helviticum, 15
(June 1960): 289-304; Literary Half-
Yearly, 2 (January 1961): 26-40.

3986. PEIGNOT, JÉROME. "Ulysse, ou de l'inattendu
considéré comme l'un des beaux-arts."
Cahiers des saisons, 10 (Spring 1965): 45-
56.

3987. PENDER, R. H. "James Joyce." Deutsche Rundschau, 203 (June 1925): 285-286.

3988. PENUELAS, MARCELINO. "James Joyce tras el
Interrogante." Cuadernos Americanos, 16
(March-April 1957): 183-200.

*3989. PILLEMENT, GEORGES. [n.t.]. La Nacion (San-
tiago), 5 November 1931.

3990. PLEBE, ARMANDO. "L'Ulysses di Joyce e l'estetica dell'arte al quadrato." Giornale
critico della filosofia italiana, 41,
series 3, 16 (April-June 1962): 219-237.

3991. POIRIER, RICHARD. "A Literature of Law and
Order." Partisan Review, 36 (Spring 1969):
189-204.

3992. POMERANZ, VICTORY. "Leonardo of Pisa." James Joyce Quarterly, 7 (Winter 1969): 148-150.

3993. POSNER, DAVID. "Two Poems from the Voices of Ulysses." James Joyce Review, 1, no. 4 (15 December 1957): 46-48.

3994. POWELL, LAWRENCE C. "The Enjoyment of Joyce." Hoja Volante, no. 19 (May 1948): 3-5.

3995. POWER, ARTHUR. "Bloomsday." Irish Tatler and Sketch, 63 (July 1954): 29.

3996. _____. "On the Presentation of Ulysses to Nora." Dublin Magazine, 9 (Summer 1972): 10-13.

*3997. POWYS, JOHN COWPER. "James Joyce's 'Ulysses'--An Appreciation." Life and Letters, 2, no. 2 (October 1923): 16, 18, 20, 22.

*3998. PRAZ, MARIO. "Commento a Ulysses." La Stampa, 5 August 1930. [Reprinted in Cronache letterarie anglosassoni, vol. 1. Letture di pensiero e d'arte, 16. Rome: Edizioni di Storia e letteratura, 1950, pp. 227-231.]

3999. _____. "Notes on James Joyce." Translated by Wallace Sillanpoa from Radiot's Italian lectures. Mosaic, 6 (Fall 1972): 85-102.

4000. PRESCOTT, JOSEPH. "Notes on Joyce's Ulysses." Modern Language Quarterly, 13 (June 1952): 149-162. [See his Exploring James Joyce, No. 1637.]

4001. _____. "A Song in Joyce's Ulysses." Notes and Queries, 197 (5 January 1952): 15-16.

4002. PRESTON, HAYTER. "Bloomsday." Courier, 22, no. 6 (June 1954): 30-33.

4003. PRITCHETT, V. S. "Joyce's Ulysses." New Statesman and Nation, 51 (21 January 1956): 75-76.

4004. _____. "The Comedian of Orgy." New Statesman, 15 August 1969, pp. 205-206.

*4005. PUCCINI, MARIO. "Altri pensieri sull'Ulisse di Joyce." L'Ambrosiano (Milan), 10 February 1930; "Incontri con l'Ulisse di Joyce." Ibid., 3 February 1930.

4006. RALEIGH, JOHN HENRY. "Who was M'Intosh?" James Joyce Review, 3, nos. 1-2 (February 1959): 59-62. [See response by Hugh B. Staples, No. 4072 and Raleigh's Letter to the Editor, James Joyce Quarterly, 10 (Winter 1973): 283-284.]

4007. _____. "'Afoot in Dublin in Search of the Habitations of Some Shades.'" James Joyce Quarterly, 8 (Winter 1970): 129-141.

4008. READ, HERBERT. "James Joyce: Romantic or Classic." Cambridge Review, 51 (13 June 1930): 488-489. [Reprinted in his A Coat of Many Colors. London: Routledge, 1945, pp. 145-148.]

4009. RECK, RIMA DRELL. "Julien Green on James Joyce." James Joyce Quarterly, 2 (Winter 1965): 138-139.

*4010. REES, G. E. "The Post-War Novel." Egyptian Gazette (Alexandria), 16 August 1928.

4011. REID, MARJORIE. "Shopkeeper of Shakespeare and Company." New York Times Book Review, 3 December 1922, pp. 7, 12.

*4012. RENDA, AGOSTINO. "La letteratura Inglese di Oggi." Mezzogiorno (Naples), 6 July 1929; same article with different title, "Scrittori editori e lettori," Popolo (Trieste), 10 July 1929.

4013. RICHARDSON, DOROTHY M. "A Few facts for you...." Mercure de France, 347 (August-September 1963): 127-128. [Letter written to Sylvia Beach, 15 January 1935.]

*4014. RIDDELL, JOHN. "The People's Joyce." Vanity, 42 (June 1934): 57, 72.

4015. ROBERTS, JOHN H. "James Joyce: From Religion to Art." New Humanist, 7 (May-June 1934): 7-13.

4016. RODGERS, WILLIAM G., WILLIAM YORK TINDALL, and LYMAN BRYSON. "Joyce's Ulysses." Invitation to Learning, 2 (Spring 1952): 63-70. [Reprinted in Invitation to Learning: English and American Novels. Edited by George D. Crothers. New York, London: Basic Books, 1966, pp. 198-207; see No. 2546.]

4017. RODGERS, W. R. "The Dublin of James Joyce." Harper's Bazaar, 96 (February 1963): 92-93, 167, 169; Meanjin Quarterly, 22 (June 1963): 184-191.

4018. ROED, ARNE. "James Joyce." Vinduet (Copenhagen), 4 (September 1950): 419-424, 522-530.

*4019. ROEDDER, KARSTEN. "The Book Parade." Citizen (Brooklyn), 29 May 1927.

4020. ROMAINS, JULES. "'Aussi peu Anglais que possible.'" Figaro littéraire, 20 January 1966, p. 9. [On the Monnier translation.]

ULYSSES

4021. ROOT, WAVERLY L. "King of the Jews." transition, no. 9 (December 1927): 178-184. [Samuel Roth's pirating of U.]

4022. ROSENBERG, KURT. "James Joyce: Ein wanderer ins Reich des Unbewussten." Geist und Zeit, no. 4 (1959): 114-127.

*4023. ROSSI, ALBERTO. [Review]. Pecaso (Firenze), August 1931, pp. 125-128. [Joyce mentioned in review of Léon Paul Fargue's Sous le lampe.]

4024. ROTH, SAMUEL. "Prelude." Two Worlds' Monthly, 1, no. 1 (September 1927).

*4025. _____. "The Black Fountain." Two Worlds' Monthly, 3 no. 4 (1927): 237-239.

*4026. _____. "Joyce, 'Ulysses,' Roth, The Van Dorens, Villard's 'Nation.'" Two Worlds' Monthly, 3, no. 2 (May-June 1927): 119-122.

*4027. _____. "An Offer to James Joyce." Two Worlds' Monthly, 3, no. 3 (September 1927): 181-182.

4028. [RYAN, JOHN]. "Editorial: The Year of Ulysses." Dublin Magazine, 9 (Summer 1972): 6-8.

4029. [RYAN, JOHN]. "Rosevean: Ulysses' Silent Ship." Dublin Magazine, 10 (Summer 1973): 42-52.

4030. RYF, ROBERT S. "James Joyce." Nation, 191 (10 September 1960): 138-139.

*4031. S., A. Z. "Joyceov Ulysses i njegov štampar [Dusan] Popović." Globus (Zagreb), no. 148, 2, 1 (1957): 7.

*4032. S., M. "The Mysterious Author of Ulysses." Press and Journal (Aberdeen), 12 April 1926.

*4033. SABARD, NOEL. "Ma Semaine Littéraire." Paris-Midi, 17 March 1929.

4034. SACKS, SHELDON. "Golden Birds and Dying Generations." Comparative Literature Studies, 6 (September 1969): 274-291.

4035. SAHL, HANS. "Das Dublin von James Joyce: Adäquat getroffen: 'Ulysses' auf der Leinwand." Die Welt, 1 April 1967.

4036. SAMILOWITZ, HAZEL. "James Joyce's Ulysses." Psychiatric Communications, 10 (1968): 21-31.

*4037. SANDGREN, GUSTAV. "Den Moderna Romanen." Tidningen (Stockholm), 9 October 1931.

4038. SANTIAGO, LUCIANO P. R. "The Ulysses Complex." American Imago, 28 (Summer 1971): 158-187.

4039. SCHECHNER, MARK. "Ulysses at Fifty: Fiftieth Anniversary of the Publication of Ulysses." SUNYAB Reporter, 3, no. 18 (3 February 1972).

4040. _____. "The Song of the Wandering Aengus: James Joyce and His Mother." James Joyce Quarterly, 10 (Fall 1972): 72-89.

*4041. SCHNEIDERS, HEINZ-LUDWIG. "Der bedeutendste Roman unseres Jahrhunderts? James Joyce: 'Ulysses.'" aachener prisma, 9, no. 1 (1960-61): 21-22.

4042. SCHOECK, R. J. "Catholicism of Joyce." Commonweal, 56 (May 1952): 143-145.

4043. SCHOLES, ROBERT. "Ulysses: A Structuralist Perspective." James Joyce Quarterly, 10 (Fall 1972): 161-171.

4044. SCHOONBROODT, JEAN. "Sheminant avec Ulysse." L'Arc, 36 (1968): 80-87.

*4045. SCRIBE, OLIVER. "The Modern Rabelais." T. P. and Cassell's Weekly, n.s. 5, no. 121 (13 February 1926): 580.

*4046. SEIBER, MATYAS. "A Note on Ulysses." Music Survey, 4 (April 1951): 263-270.

*4047. SELVER, PAUL. "Englischer Brief." Das literarische Echo, 26 (1923/24): 425.

*4048. SENN, FRITZ. "Joyce: Odysseus in Dublin." Der Spiegel, 15 (1961): 70-80.

4049. _____. "When one reads...." James Joyce Quarterly, 1 (Summer 1964): 65.

4050. _____. "Ulysses in Zürich." Zürcher Woche, 20 August 1965, p. 15.

4051. _____. "Tiens, Tiens." James Joyce Quarterly, 4 (Spring 1967): 201.

4052. _____. "Seven Against Ulysses." James Joyce Quarterly, 4 (Spring 1967): 170-193. [Based in part on his "Ulysses in der übersetzung." Sprache im Technischen Zeitalter, 28 (October-December 1968): 346-375; slightly changed reprint in Levende Talen, no. 270 (August-September 1970): 512-535; reprinted as "Zeven tegen Ulysses." Raam, 63 (1970): 6-35, translated by B. Wijffels-Smulders.]

4053. _____. "Wilderness." James Joyce Quarterly, 4 (Spring 1967): 245.

4054. _____. "Ex unque Leopold." English Studies, 48, no. 6 (December 1967): 537-543.

4055. _____. "Ulysses in der übersetzung." Sprache im technischen Zeitalter, 28

(October-December 1968): 346-375. [Translated in Approaches to Ulysses, pp. 249-286, No. 3657.]

4056. _____ . "James Joyce en zijn Ulysses," translated into Dutch by B. Wijffels-Smulders. Utopia, 6 (June 1969): 23-26.

4057. _____ . "Book of Many Turns." James Joyce Quarterly, 10 (Fall 1972): 29-46.

4058. SHAW, GEORGE BERNARD. "Letter" (11 June 1921); in Sylvia Beach. Shakespeare and Company, p. 53, No. 3544. [Translated by Sylvia Beach for Mercure de France, 309 (May 1950): 23; also in David Dempsey. "G. B. S. on Joyce: Joyce on G. B. S." New York Times Book Review, 23 July 1950, p. 8, with four sentences missing; William Hull. "Shaw on the Joyce He Scarcely Read." Shaw Bulletin, 1, no. 6 (September 1954): 16-20; in William White. "Irish Antitheses: Shaw and Joyce." Shavian, 2, no. 3 (February 1961): 24-34; also in Letters, vol. 3. Edited by Richard Ellmann, p. 50, No. 309.]

*4059. _____ . "Letter." Picture Post (London), 3 June 1939.

4060. _____ , and ARCHIBALD HENDERSON. "Literature and Science." Fortnightly Review, n.s. 116 (October 1924): 518-521.

4061. SILVERSTEIN, NORMAN. "Toward A Corrected Text of Ulysses." James Joyce Quarterly, 6 (Summer 1969): 348-356.

4062. _____ . "Committee on the Text of Ulysses." James Joyce Quarterly, 11 (Fall 1973): 60-61.

4063. SINKO, GRZEGORZ. "Ulisses jakim go znamy ["What is Significant in Ulysses]." Miesiecznik literacki, 5 (July 1970): 53-61.

*4064. SITWELL, EDITH. "Readers and Writers." New Age, 31 (10 August 1922): 184.

4065. SODUMS, DZINTARS. "Dzeims Dzoiss un Vina Uliss." Cela Zimes, no. 20 (1954): 274.

*4066. SORANI, ALDO. "Anglicisti Francesi." Marzocco, 9 August 1925.

4067. SPIEGEL, ALAN. "Flaubert to Joyce: Evolution of a Cinematographic Form." Novel, 6 (1973): 229-243.

4068. SPOERRI, JAMES F. "The Odyssey Press Edition of James Joyce's Ulysses." Papers of the Bibliographical Society of America, 50 (Second Quarter 1956): 195-198.

4069. STALEY, HARRY C. "The Spheretual Exercises of Dedalus and Bloom." James Joyce Quarterly, 10 (Winter 1973): 209-214.

4070. STALEY, THOMAS F. "Ulysses in England: Some British Joyceana." James Joyce Quarterly, 3 (Spring 1966): 223-224.

4071. _____ . "Ulysses: Fifty Years in the Joycean Conundrum." Mosaic, 6 (Fall 1972): 69-76.

4072. STAPLES, HUGH B. "Our Exagmination Round His Perambulations in Exploration of Habitations." James Joyce Quarterly, 9 (Fall 1971): 157-160. [See No. 4007.]

*4073. STARTSEV, A. "Dzhois pered Ulissom." International Literature, no. 1 (1937): 196-202.

4074. STEIN, SOL. "The Aesthetics of James Joyce's Ulysses." University of Kansas City Review, 18 (Summer 1952): 241-254.

4075. STEINBERG, ERWIN R. "A Book with a Molly in It." James Joyce Review, 2, nos. 1-2 (June 1958): 55-62.

*4076. STEMPORSKI, JERZY. "Ulisses. Joyces jaki proba psychoanalisy stosowaney." Wiadomosci Literackie (Warsaw), 7 February 1932.

4077. STERN, FREDERICK C. "The Other Parnell." Éire-Ireland, 7 (Autumn 1972): 3-12. [John Howard Parnell in U.]

*4078. STRAUMANN, HEINRICH. "Mängel der übersetzungen." Frankfurter Allgemeine Zeitung, 16 November 1957.

*4079. STRONG, L. A. G. "The Novel: Assurances and Perplexities." The Author, Playwright, and Composer, 45, no. 4 (Summer 1935): 112-115.

*4080. STRUNSKY, SIMEON. "About Books, More or Less." New York Times Book Review, 16 October 1927, p. 4.

4081. SÜHNEL, RUDOLF. "Die literarischen Voraussetzungen von Joyces Ulysses." Germanisch-romanische Monatsschrift, 12 (1962): 202-211.

4082. SULLIVAN, PHILIP B. "Los Toros in Ulysses." Wake Newslitter, no. 11 (March 1963): 3-4.

4083. SZBOTKA, TIBOR. "James Joyce's Ulysses." Umana, 20 (May-September 1971): 43-45. [In Hungarian with English abstract.]

*4084. 'Il Tarlo.' "Libri, Nuovi e Usati." La Tribuna (Rome), 2 March 1923.

4085. TAU, MAX. "James Joyce." Die Neuren Sprachen, 40 (August 1932): 344-354.

4086. TELLEGEN, A. O. H. "Ja, nee en geen van beide." Levende Talen, no. 269 (June-July 1970): 427-432.

ULYSSES

4087. TEMPLE, MICHAEL. "New Tendencies in Fiction." The Referee (London), 12 October 1924.

*4088. THEILE, HARALD. "Credo der Ausgestoszenheit zu James Joyces Ulysses." Edart, 9, no. 2 (February 1933): 70-78.

4089. THIEBAUT, MARCEL. "Ulysse et James Joyce." Revue de Paris, 3 (15 June 1929): 944-958.

4090. THOMPSON, ALAN R. "Farewell to Achilles." Bookman, 70 (January 1930): 465-471.

4091. THORNTON, WELDON. "Joyce's Ulysses, 1922." Book Collector, 11 (Spring 1962): 85-86.

4092. TITUS, EDWARD W. "Sartor Resartus: Being Comment Upon Commentary." This Quarter, 3, no. 1 (July-September 1930): 120-141.

4093. TODOROV, TZVETAN. "Le récit primitif." Tel Quel, no. 30 (Summer 1967): 47-55.

4094. TOMASI, BARBARA R. "The Fraternal Theme in Joyce's Ulysses." American Imago, 30 (1973): 177-191.

4095. TOMPKINS, PHILLIP K. "The Rhetoric of James Joyce." Quarterly Journal of Speech, 54 (April 1968): 107-114.

4096. TOYNBEE, PHILIP. "The Decline and Future of the English Novel." New Writing and Daylight (Winter 1943-1944): 35-45. [Appeared in Penguin New Writing, 23 (1945): 127-139.]

4097. _____. "A Study of James Joyce's Ulysses." Polemic, no. 7 (March 1947): 34-43; no. 8, 28-39. [Appeared in James Joyce: Two Decades of Criticism, pp. 243-284, No. 1570; reprinted in Modern British Fiction. Edited by Mark Schorer. New York: Oxford University Press, 1961, pp. 336-357.]

4098. TROY, WILLIAM. "Stephen Dedalus and James Joyce." Nation, 138 (February 1934): 187-188. [Reprinted in his Selected Essays. Edited by Stanley Edgar Hyman. New Brunswick, New Jersey: Rutgers University Press, 1967, pp. 89-93.]

4099. TUCHOISKY, KARL. "Ulysses." Die Weltbühne, 23, 2 (1927): 788. [Reprinted in Gessammelte Werke, vol. 2. Edited by Mary Gerold-Tuchoisky and Fritz J. Raddatz. Hamburg: Rowohlt Vlg., 1961, pp. 949-955; also reprinted in Ausgewahlte Werke, vol. 2. Edited by Fritz J. Raddatz. Hamburg: Rowohlt, 1965, pp. 381-389.]

*4100. UZANNE, OCTAVE. "Hommes et choses: James Joyce." Dépêche de Toulouse, 17 March 1930.

*4101. UZZELL, THOMAS R. "Try These on your Next Story." Writer's Digest (June 1939).

4102. VANE, HENRY. "Dublin's Odyssey." Twentieth Century, 162 (November 1957): 480-483.

4103. VAN VOORHIS, JOHN W., and FRANCIS C. BLOODGOOD. "Ulysses: Another Pirated Edition?" James Joyce Quarterly, 9 (Summer 1972): 436-444.

4104. VON ABELE, RUDOLPH. "Film as Interpretation: A Case Study of Ulysses." Journal of Aesthetics and Art Criticism, 31 (Summer 1973): 487-500.

4105. VREESWIJK, A. "Introduction to an Imperfect, Incomplete Ulysses-Commentary." Levende Talen, no. 269 (June-July 1970): 432-438. [From his Notes on Joyce's Ulysses, Part I (Chapter 1-3): A Very First Draft. Amsterdam: Van Gennep, 1971.]

4106. WALBANK, ALAN. "Stephen Hero's Bookshops." Book Collector, 14 (Summer 1965): 194-199.

4107. WALCOTT, WILLIAM. "Notes by a Jungian Analyst on Dreams in Ulysses." James Joyce Quarterly, 9 (Fall 1971): 37-48. [See David L. McCarroll. "Stephen's Dream and Bloom's." James Joyce Quarterly, 6 (Winter 1969): 174-176.]

4108. WALDRIP, CARL. "'Names Change, that's All': A Broadened View of Christianity as Seen in James Joyce's Ulysses." Proceedings of Conference of College Teachers of English of Texas, 36 (September 1971): 16-22.

4109. WALSH, RUTH M. "In the Name of the Father and of the Son...Joyce's Use of the Mass in Ulysses." James Joyce Quarterly, 6 (Summer 1969): 321-347. [Complemented by later article: "That Pervasive Mass--in Dubliners and Portrait of the Artist." James Joyce Quarterly, 8 (Spring 1971): 205-220.]

4110. WASSON, RICHARD. "Notes on a New Sensibility." Partisan Review, 36 (Summer 1969): 460-477.

4111. WAUGH, ALEC. "The Neo-Georgians." Fortnightly, n.s. 115 (January 1924): 126-137.

4112. WAZYK, ADAM. "Pierwsza lektura." Dialog (Warsaw), 9 (December 1964): 91-92. [From his book Kwestia Gustu.]

*4113. WELLS, H. G., and BERNARD SHAW. "Modern Novels and Sex." Evening Standard (London), 26 May 1922.

*4114. WEST, JOHN ALEXANDER. "Über den'Ulysses.'" Annalen, 1 (1926/27): 510-516.

4115. WHITE, PATRICK. "Vico's Institution of Burial in Ulysses." Ball State University Forum, 14 (Summer 1973): 59-68.

*4116. WHITE, WILLIAM. "Press Copies of Joyce's Ulysses." Book Collector, 10 (Spring 1961): 72.

*4117. WILLIAMS, WILLIAM CARLOS. "Readers and Writers." New English Weekly, 2, no. 4 (10 November 1932): 90-91.

4118. WILSON, EDMUND. "James Joyce." New Republic, 61 (December 1929): 84-93. [Later appeared in his Axel's Castle, No. 1686.]

4119. _____. "The Literary Writer's Polonius." Atlantic Monthly, 155 (June 1935): 674-682.

4120. WLASSICS, TIBOR. "Nota su Dane nell'Ulisse." Rivista di Letterature moderne e comparate (Florence), 24 (1971): 151-154.

*4121. WOOD, CLEMENT. "The World's Worst Books." Books Abroad, 15 (January 1941): 51.

*4122. WOOLF, VIRGINIA. "Character in Fiction." Criterion, 2, no. 8 (July 1924): 427.

*4123. YOUNG, B. A. "Joyce in Space." Punch, 239 (7 December 1960): 816-818. [Parody of U.]

*4124. ZAREK, OTTO. "Der Ulysses des James Joyce." Tagebuch (1927).

4125. SWEIG, STEFAN. "Anmerkung zum Ulysses." Die Neue Rundschau, 39 (October 1928): 476-479 [Reprinted in Begegnung mit Menschen, Büchern, Städten. Vienna: Reichner, 1937, pp. 418-421; reprinted in Der goldene Schnitt: Grosse Essayisten der Neuen Rundschau, 1890-1960. Edited by Christoph Schwerin. Frankfurt a.M.: Fischer Vlg., 1960, pp. 283-286.]

4126. Unsigned. "Ateneo." Hispanoamericano, 60 (21 February 1972): 57. [Fiftieth Anniversary of U.]

*4127. Unsigned. "Aus den Revuen." Prager Presse (Prague), 27 September 1927.

*4128. Unsigned. "Comment." Dial, 72, no. 6 (June 1922): 662-663.

*4129. Unsigned. "Das Rätsel Joyce." Neue Schweizer Rundschau, n.F. 18 (1950/51): 378-381.

*4130. Unsigned. "De Vertaling van Ulysses: Interview met J. Vandenbergh." Utopia, 8 (June 1969): 9-12.

*4131. Unsigned. "Der 'Homer' James Joyce." Prager Tagblatt (Prague), 26 June 1927.

*4132. Unsigned. "Diversions of a Poet." News (Harrisburg, Pa.), 12 August 1927.

4133. Unsigned. [n.t.]. New York Times, 20 May 1928, p. 12. [On U and Samuel Roth piracy.]

*4134. Unsigned. "Gli esuli di J. Joyce: al Convegno." Corriere della Sera (Milan), 30 April 1930.

*4135. Unsigned. "Irish Writers. Scholarship. Fiction and Poetry. Tailteann Awards." Irish Times, 11 August 1924, p. 7.

4136. Unsigned. "James Joyce i København: Skal Ulysses oversoettes til Dansk?" Berlingske Aftenavis, 3 September 1936, p. 3.

*4137. Unsigned. "James Joyce Makes Deposition Against Roth for Pirating Work." Chicago Tribune (Paris), 20 March 1928, p. 8.

*4138. Unsigned. "James Joyce's Ulysses." New Statesman and Nation, 12, no. 295 (17 October 1936): 597.

*4139. Unsigned. "James Joyce's Ulysses." Bookseller (London), no. 1610 (7 October 1936): 365.

*4140. Unsigned. "Joyce im Funk: Ein Hörspiel nach dem 'Ulysses.'" Frankfurter Allegemeine Zeitung, 21 September 1960.

*4141. Unsigned. "Joyce's Ulysses Sets a New Standard in Fiction." Current Opinion, 73 (July 1922): 101-103.

*4142. Unsigned. "Kleine Chronik: 'James Joyce in Frankreich.'" Neue Zürcher Zeitung, no. 613 (1 April 1931): 5.

*4143. Unsigned. "Letteratura Inglese Odierna." Il Nuovo Cittadino (Geneva), 18 April 1929.

*4144. Unsigned. "Lewis Portrays Dome 'Kultur': Gopher Prairie Discusses Paris Intellectuals." Chicago Tribune (Paris), 4 October 1925, p. 3.

*4145. Unsigned. "Letters to the Editor." Egyptian Gazette (Alexandria): J. K. 24 August 1928; "Roland," A. A. Maudlin, G. E. Rees, 25 August 1928; R. Bell. 28 August 1928; Isabel MacDermott. 29 August 1928; J. T. Hardcastle. "Old Guard," R. Bell, A. A. Maudlin, S. Weston. "Oliver," 31 August 1928; "Mystic," "Churchman," "Bohemian." 1 September 1928; "Churchman," G. E. Rees, Editor, 10 September 1928; G. E. Rees, Editor, 20 September 1928.

*4146. Unsigned. "Letters to the Editor." Evening Chronicle (Newcastle-on-Tyne), 29 September 1930. [On the subject of Professor

ULYSSES

Morrison's resignation from Newcastle Literary and Philosophical Society because of Lecture to be given by Mr. Louis V. Wilkinson on D. H. Lawrence, Aldoux Huxley, and James Joyce.]; "Miss Modern," Mary Muriel Hayes, John Sweet, "Student," J. W. Heslop Harrison.

*4147. Unsigned. "Letters to the Editor." Times (London), 14, 16, 19, 21, 24 December 1931. [In connection with Harold Nicholson's Broadcast on BBC.]

*4148. Unsigned. "Literature, Criticism, and Psycho-Analysis." New York Herald Tribune Books, 24 April 1927.

*4149. Unsigned. "The Modern Novel: An Irish Author Discussed." Irish Times, 9 November 1923, p. 4. [Meeting of Dublin University Philosophical Society at which Mr. W. Beare presented a paper, "The Modern Novel," and W. B. Yeats responded.]

*4150. Unsigned. "Moderni Irska Literatura." Ceskoslovensky Dennik, 24 March 1929.

*4151. Unsigned. "Nieren für ein nasses Buch." Blick (Yverson), 19 June 1964, p. 3. [Winner of contest to find copy of U thrown into Zurichsee on Bloomsday; see also Blick, 17 June 1964, p. 2; Tages-Anzeiger (Zürich), 18 June 1964, p. 18; Fritz Senn letter to editor, ibid., 8 July 1964.]

*4152. Unsigned. "Notes and Comments." Irish Statesman, 7, no. 26 (5 March 1927): 611-614. [Pirating of U and protest.]

*4153. Unsigned. "Nowoczesna Odyseja." Dialog (Warsaw), 9 (December 1964): 135-137.

*4154. Unsigned. "Odysseus in Dublin." Der Spiegel, 15, no. 51 (13 December 1961): 70-84.

4155. Unsigned. "The Playboy Advisor." Playboy, no. 14 (September 1967): 67.

*4156. Unsigned. "Pour L'Ulysses de James Joyce." Europe, 13, no. 49 (15 January 1927): 128. [Two Worlds' controversy.]

*4157. Unsigned. "S. Roth's Payments to James Joyce." New York Times, 26 May 1928, p. 14.

4158. Unsigned. "Signed Copy of Ulysses brings $1,050 at Auction." New York Times, 11 January 1967, p. 53. [Limited 1932 Odyssey Press edition inscribed to Paul Léon.]

4159. Unsigned. "Sur les pas de James Joyce." Figaro littéraire, 5 May 1962, p. 6.

*4160. Unsigned. "Two Views of Ulysses." Chicago Daily News, 2 August 1922.

4161. Unsigned. "Ulises tiene cuarenta años." Cal, no. 4 (8 June 1962).

*4162. Unsigned. "Ulises, un desconcertante soliloquis de James Joyce." Caras y caretas (Buenos Aires), 29 (5 June 1926).

4163. 'Ulysses,' "Algo Sobra Joyce." Atenea, 25, no. 91 (November-December 1948): 156-158.

*4164. Unsigned. "'Ulysses,'" "James Joyce." Almanach des lettres françaises et etrangeres (Paris), 15 March 1924, p. 300; 28 February 1924, p. 233.

*4165. Unsigned. "Ulysses in Omaha." World Herald (Omaha), 7 August 1927.

4166. Unsigned. "Ulysses Map of Dublin." Ireland of the Welcomes, 11 (July-August 1962): five page insert without pagination.

*4167. Unsigned. "Ulysses Protest." The Humanist, 4, no. 4 (April 1927): 173.

4168. Unsigned. "Ulysses Returns: A Day in Edwardian Dublin." Times Literary Supplement, 24 June 1960, pp. 393-394.

4169. Unsigned. "Ulysses the 3,000 Penguin: First Printing of 250,000 copies." Bookseller, 29 (March 1969): 1896-1897.

4170. Unsigned. "Ulysses von James Joyce." Frankfurter Allgemeine Zeitung, 14 September 1965.

*4171. Unsigned. "World's Worst Comment on 'Ulysses' Appears." Chicago Tribune (Paris), no. 6, 934 (12 March 1934): 2. [Lambastes an article by S. H. C. in Carnegie Magazine, February 1934.]

*4172. Unsigned. "Writers Protest Publication of 'Ulysses' by Roth." Chicago Tribune (Paris), no. 3, 488 (2 February 1927): 2.

*4173. Unsigned. [n.t.]. Aberdeen Journal, 30 June 1922. [Review of Today, 9 (June 1922) with emphasis upon Holbrook Jackson's article on U, pp. 47-49.]

*4174. Unsigned. [n.t.]. The Bookseller, no. 1614 (4 November 1936): 540.

*4175. Unsigned. [n.t.]. Catholic Bulletin (Dublin), June 1927. [U piracy.]

*4176. Unsigned. [n.t.]. Chicago Sunday Tribune (Paris), 5 January 1930. [Interview with Paul Souday.]

*4177. Unsigned. [n.t.]. Journal (Grantham), 15 February 1930. [News report of Bruce Beddow's lecture "Ulysses and the Realistic Modern Novel."]

*4178. Unsigned. [n.t.]. Mail (Oxford), 28 October 1933. [News report on Alec Waugh's lecture on the modern novel.]

*4179. Unsigned. [n.t.]. New York Times, 20 May 1928, p. 12. [On Roth and the Two Worlds' Monthly controversy.]

*4180. Unsigned. [n.t.]. Staffs English Sentinel (London), 18 October 1929. [News report on Alec Waugh's lecture on "The Modern Novel."]

*4181. Unsigned. [n.t.]. Times (Middlesex County), 6 June 1931. [News report of lecture by Rev. A. T. G. Hunt to the Bankside Theatre and Literary Club.]

*4182. Unsigned. [n.t.]. T. P.'s and Cassell's Weekly, 11 September 1926. [Interview with Sylvia Beach.]

*4183. Unsigned. [n.t.]. Wiadomosci Literackie (Warsaw), 27 November 1931.

INNER MONOLOGUE: STREAM OF CONSCIOUSNESS

Books

4184. ALBERES, R. M. "Le lyrisme et le mythe: De Joyce à Malcolm Lowry," "Joyce et la naissance du monolgue intérieur," in Metamorphoses du roman. Paris: Albin Michel, 1966, pp. 119-131, 177-198, et passim.

*4185. ARNS, KARL. "Die Bewusstseinskunst in modernen roman," in Grundriss der Geschichte der englischen literatur. Paderborn: Ferninand Schönigh, 1941, pp. 146-149. [Joyce, Virginia Woolf, Dorothy Richardson.]

4186. DAHL, LIISA. Linguistic Features of the Stream-of Consciousness Techniques of James Joyce, Virginia Woolf, and Eugene O'Neill. Turun Yliopiston julkaisuja, series B, 116. Turku: Turun Yliopisto, 1970.

4187. DUJARDIN, ÉDOUARD. Les Lauriers Sont Coupés. "Preface" by Valery Larbaud. Paris: Messein, 1925, pp. 5-16. [Later translated by Stuart Gilbert as We'll to the Woods No More. Includes essay by James Laughlin, "Joyce's New Direction," pp. 149-157. Norfolk: New Directions Books, 1938, pp. 148-157; reprinted 1957 with "Introduction" by Leon Edel, pp. vii-xxviii.]

4188. EDGAR, PELHAM. "Psycho-Analysis and James Joyce," in his The Art of the Novel. New York: Macmillan, 1933, pp. 301-319. [Reprinted New York: Russell and Russell, 1965, pp. 301-319.]

4189. FRIEDMAN, MELVIN. "James Joyce: The Full Development of the Method," in his Stream of Consciousness: A Study of Literary Method. New Haven: Yale University Press, 1955, pp. 210-243. ["Stream of Consciousness in the Portrait" reprinted in Portraits of an Artist, pp. 228-232, No. 3260, reprinted in Portrait: Notes, No. 3222.]

4190. HENDERSON, PHILIP. "Stephen Dedalus versus Bloom," in his The Novel Today. London: John Lane, 1936, pp. 81-87. [Reprinted Folcroft, Pa.: Folcroft Press, 1969, 1973.]

*4191. HEPPENSTALL, RAYNER. "Streams of Consciousness," in The Fourfold Tradition. London: Barrie and Rockliff, 1961, pp. 132-159.

4192. HORIA, VINTILA. "James Joyce o la novela como 'Consciencia Pura,'" in Mester de novelista. Madrid: Editorial Prensa Espanola, 1972, pp. 57-66.

4193. HUMPHREY, ROBERT. Stream of Consciousness in the Modern Novel. Berkeley: University of California Press, 1954, passim.

4194. KUMAR, SHIV K. "James Joyce," in his Bergson and the Stream of Consciousness Novel. London: Blackie and Son, 1962; New York: New York University Press, 1963, pp. 103-138. [Contains "Bergson and Stephen Dedalus's Aesthetic Theory." Journal of Aesthetics and Art Criticism, 16 (September 1957): 124-127, No. 3454, and "Joyce's Epiphany and Bergson's l'Intuition Philosophique." Modern Language Quarterly, 20 (March 1949): 27-30, No. 2837, and "Joyce and Bergson's 'memoire pure.'" Osmania Journal of English Studies, no. 1 (1961): 55-60.]

4195. LEWIS, WYNDHAM. The Art of Being Ruled. New York: Harper, 1926, passim.

4196. MACAULEY, ROBIE, and GEORGE LANNING. Technique in Fiction. New York: Harper and Row, 1964, pp. 88-94.

4197. McCOLE, C. JOHN. Lucifer at Large. London: Longmans, Green, 1937, pp. 85-104.

4198. MORO, KŌCHI. "Monolog and Dialog: The Distance Between J. Joyce and S. Bellow," in Jōsai Jinbun Kenkyu [Studies in the Humanities]. Sakado, Iruma-Gun, Saitama, Japan: Jōsai University, 1973, pp. 102-131. [In Japanese.]

4199. RIAMOND, MICHEL. "Le monologue intérieur," in La crise du Roman. Paris: José Corti, 1966, pp. 258-263, et passim.

4200. SCHIEFELE, HANNES. "Freuds Bedeutung für die Kunst Betrachtung: Marcel Proust, James Joyce, Thomas Mann," in Lebendige Psychoanalys: Die Bedeutung Sigmund Freud für das Verstehen des Menschen. Edited by Fritz Rieman. Munich: Beck, 1956, pp.

ULYSSES

136-159. [Translated by Irene Garfeldt-Klever de Leal as El psicoanalisis vivi-ente. Buenos Aires: Fabril, 1961, pp. 167-192.]

4201. STEINBERG, ERWIN R. "The Sources of the Stream," in In Honor of Austin Wright. Carnegie Mellon Series in English, no. 12. Edited by Joseph Baim, Ann L. Hayes, and Robert J. Gangewere. Pittsburgh: Carnegie-Mellon University, 1972, pp. 87-101.

4202. _____ . The Stream of Consciousness and Beyond in Ulysses. Pittsburgh: University of Pittsburgh Press, 1972.

*4203. SUZUKI, KENZO. "Shinrich Shosetsu ["Psychological Novel]," in Joisu Nyumon [An Introduction to James Joyce], pp. 162-169, No. 1511.

4204. THRALL, WILLIAM F., and ADDISON HIBBARD. A Handbook to Literature. Revised and enlarged by C. Hugh Holman. New York: Odyssey, 1960, pp. 243, 471-472.

*4205. UZZELL, THOMAS H. "The Interior Monologue," "Character without Incident," in Technique of the Novel. Revised Edition. New York: Citadel Press, 1959, pp. 186-187, 242-247, et passim.

4206. VIDAN, IVO. Romani struje svijesti: James Joyce Uliks, William Faulkner Buka i bejes [Stream of Consciousness Novels: James Joyce's Ulysses, William Faulkner's Sound and the Fury]. Zagreb: Skolska Knjiga, 1971.

4207. WAGENKNECHT, E. C. "Stream of Consciousness," in his Cavalcade of the English Novel. New York: Holt, 1943, pp. 505-522.

Periodical Articles

4208. BICKERTON, DEREK. "Modes of Interior Monologue: A Formal Definition." Modern Language Quarterly, 28 (June 1967): 229-239.

4209. _____ . "James Joyce and the Development of the Interior Monologue." Essays in Criticism, 18 (January 1969): 32-46.

*4210. BOWLING, LAWRENCE E. "What is the Stream of Consciousness Technique?" Publications of the Modern Language Association, 65 (June 1950): 333-345.

4211. CLUNY, CLAUDE-MICHEL. "Les lourds lauriers d'Ulysse." Lettres françaises, no. 1242 (24 July 1968): 9.

4212. DAHL, LIISA. "The Attributive Sentence Structure in the Stream-of-Consciousness technique with Special Reference to the Interior Monologue used by Virginia Woolf, James Joyce, and Eugene O'Neill." Neuphilologische Mitteilungen, no. 68 (15 December 1967): 440-454.

4213. _____ . "The Linguistic Presentation of the Interior Monologue in James Joyce's Ulysses." James Joyce Quarterly, 7 (Winter 1969): 114-119.

4214. _____ . "A Comment on Similarities between Édouard Dujardin's Monologue intérieur and James Joyce's Interior Monologue." Neuphilologische Mitteilungen, 73 (1972): 45-54. ["Studies Presented to Tauno F. Mustanoja on the occasion of his Sixtieth Birthday."]

4215. DANIEL-ROPS, HENRY. "Une technique nouvelle: le Monologue intérieur." Le Correspondent, no. 1664 (January 1932): 281-305.

4216. DECKER, HEINZ. "Der innere Monolog: Zur analyse des Ulysses." Antösse: Berichte, aus der Arbeit der Evangelischen Hotgeismar, no. 5 (November 1959): 127-143. [Reprinted in Akzente, 8 (April 1961): 99-125.]

4217. EDEL, LEON. "Criticism and Psychoanalysis: Notes on Two Disciplines." Chicago Review, 15 (Autumn 1961): 100-109.

4218. EGRI, PÉTER. "Parallelen zwischen der Mannschen und Joyceschen Form der inneren Monologs, der Truam- and Phantasiehaftigkeit im Spiegel des Romans Lotte in Weimar." Német Filológiai Tanulmányok, 3 (1968): 131-142. [Appeared in Avantgardism and Modernity: A Comparison of James Joyce's Ulysses with Thomas Mann's Der Zauberberg and Lotte in Weimar. Joint edition by the Akademiaia Kiado, Budapest and University of Tulsa. Translated by Paul Aston. Edited with Introduction by H. Frew Waidner. University of Tulsa Monograph Series, no. 14. 1972.]

4219. _____ . "The Place of James Joyce's Interior Monologue in World Literature." Umana, 20, no. 5-8 (1971): 32-35.

4220. FAAS, EGBERT. "Formen der Bewusstseindarstellung in der dramatischen Lyrik Pounds und Eliots." Germanisch-Romanische Monatsschrift, n.s. 18 (April 1968): 172-191.

*4221. FEHR, BERNHARD. "Neukrafte des Englischen Gegenwartrmans." Neue Zürcher Zeitung, no. 1539 (1926).

*4222. FISCHER, EMERIC. "Le monologue intérieur dans l'Ulysse de James Joyce." La Revue française, 28, no. 3 (25 March 1933): 445-453.

4223. FRANKE-HEILBRONN, H. "Das Ende des Psychologischen Romans der Burgerlichen Dekadenz:

James Joyce und die Aufgaben der Jungen Deutschen Epic." Geist der Zeit, 16 (1938): 156-165.

*4224. FRIEDMAN, NORMAN. "Point of View in Fiction: The Development of the Critical Concept." Publications of the Modern Language Association, 70 (December 1955): 1160-1184.

4225. GILBERT, STUART. "We'll to the Woods no More." Contempo, 3 (February 1934): 1, 6.

4226. GLIKIN, GLORIA. "Variations on a Method." James Joyce Quarterly, 2 (Fall 1964): 42-49.

4227. HANDLER, PHILIP. "The Case for Édouard Dujardin." Romanic Review, 56 (October 1965): 194-202.

4228. HARTLEY, L. G. "The Sacred River, Stream of Consciousness: The Evolution of a Method." Sewanee Review, 39 (January-March 1931): 80-89.

*4229. HEPPENSTALL, RAYNER. "The Bays are Sere." London Magazine, 7 (August 1960): 47-53. [Influence of Dujardin on Joyce.]

*4230. HOOPS, REINALD. "Der Einfluss der Psychoanalyse auf die englische Literatur." Anglistische Forschungen, 77 (1934).

4231. JEREMIC, LJUBIŠA. "Unutrašnj monolog kod Tolstoja i Džojsa." Delo, 12 (1966): 1242-1260, 1390-1406.

4232. KELLY, H. A. "Consciousness in the Monologues of Ulysses." Modern Language Quarterly, 24 (March 1963): 3-12.

4233. KING, C. D. "Édouard Dujardin, Inner Monologue, and the Stream of Consciousness." French Studies, 7 (April 1953): 116-128.

4234. LILLYMAN, W. J. "The Interior Monologue in James Joyce and Otto Ludwig." Comparative Literature, 23 (Winter 1971): 45-54. [Ludwig's Zwischen Himmel und Eerde (1956).]

4235. LINCECUM, J. B. "A Victorian Precursor of the Stream-of-Consciousness Novel: George Meredith." South Central Bulletin, 31 (Winter 1971): 197-200.

4236. MERCIER, VIVIAN. "Justice for Édouard Dujardin." James Joyce Quarterly, 4 (Spring 1967): 209-213.

4237. MIROIU, MIHAI. "The Makers of the Stream of Consciousness Novel." Analele Universitatii Bucuresti (Limbi germanice, 19), (1970): 137-149.

4238. _____ . "In the Stream: James Joyce and Virginia Woolf." Analele Universitatii

Bucuresti (Limbi germanice, 20) (1971): 145-157.

4239. MITCHELL, BREON. "Hans Henry Jâhn and James Joyce: The Birth of the Inner Monologue in the German Novel." Arcadia, 6 (1971): 44-71.

4240. O'NEILL, SAMUEL J. "Interior Monologue in Al Filo de Agus." Hispania, 51 (September 1968): 447-456.

4241. PAEZ URDANETA, IRASET. "Acera de los orígenes del monólogo interior." Imagen, no. 44 (25 April-2 May 1972): part 2, pp. 12-13.

4242. READDY, CORAL ANN. "An Approach to the Stream of Consciousness in Ulysses." Galmahra (Brisbane), 1963, pp. 14-16.

*4243. ROMERA, ANTONIO R. "El monólogo silente en Galdós y en Joyce." Atenea, no. 257/258 (November-December 1946): 373-379.

4244. SALLENAVE, DANIELE. "A Propos du 'monologue intérieur': Lecture d'une théorie." Littérature, no. 5 (February 1972): 69-87.

4245. SCHAARSCHMIDT, G. "Interior Monologue and Soviet Literary Criticism." Canadian Slavonic Papers, 8 (1966): 143-152.

*4246. SERGEANT, HOWARD. "A Study of James Joyce." Aryan Path, 30 (September 1959): 407-411.

4247. SPENCER, JOHN. "A Note on the 'Steady Monologue of the Interiors.'" Review of English Literature, 6 (April 1965): 32-41.

4248. STEINBERG, ERWIN R. "Introducing the Stream-of-Consciousness Technique in Ulysses." Style, 2 (Winter 1968): 49-58.

4249. _____ . "'...the steady monologue of the interiors; the pardonable confusion...'" James Joyce Quarterly, 6 (Spring 1969): 185-200.

4250. UZZELL, THOMAS H. "Modern Innovations." College English, 7 (November 1945): 59-65.

*4251. YANKWICH, LEON R. Record (Los Angeles), 20 January 1926. [On the republication of Dujardin's Les Lauriers sont Coupés.]

*4252. Unsigned. "Der Stumme Monolog bei Joyce." Neue Zürcher Zeitung, 13 January 1932.

4253. Unsigned. "Im Vorgeld: zu Joyce: Hinweis auf Dujardins Roman 'Les Lauriers sont Coupés.'" Neue Zürcher Zeitung, no. 194, 17 July 1966.

*4254. Unsigned. "Joyce: Ohne Monologe." Der Spiegel, 11 (1957): 48-49.

ULYSSES

*4255. Unsigned. "Proust, Joyce and Miss Richard-
        son." Spectator, 30 June 1923.

STUDIES OF TECHNIQUE AND STRUCTURE

Books

4256. ADAMS, ROBERT M. Surface and Symbol: The
       Consistency of James Joyce's Ulysses.
       New York: Oxford University Press, 1962.
       [Paperback reprint, Galaxy, 1967.]

4257. AQUIN, HUBERT. "Considération sur la forme
       romanesque d'Ulysse de James Joyce," in
       L'Oeuvre littéraire et ses significations.
       Cahiers de Univ. du Québec, no. 24; Re-
       cherches en symbolique, no. 2; Edited by
       Renée Legris and Pierre Pagé. Montréal:
       Presses de l'Univ. du Québec, 1970, pp.
       53-66.

4258. CROESSMANN, H. K. "Joyce, German and the
       Schema of Ulysses: An Exchange of Let-
       ters," in A James Joyce Miscellany, Sec-
       ond Series, pp. 9-14, No. 1613.

4259. CURTIUS, ERNST ROBERT. James Joyce und sein
       Ulysses. Zürich: Neue Schweizer Rund-
       schau, 1929. [Contains his "James Joyce."
       Die Literatur, 31 (December 1928/29): 121-
       128, and "Technik und Thematic von James
       Joyce." Neue schweizer Rundschau, 22 (1
       January 1929): 47-68; latter essay trans-
       lated by Eugene Jolas in transition, no.
       16-17 (June 1929): 310-325; whole entry
       reprinted in his Kritische Essays zu
       europäischen Literatur, second enlarged
       edition. Bern: A. Francke Vlg., 1954;
       third edition, 1963, pp. 290-314; short-
       ened version, "James Joyce and his Ulys-
       ses," translated from the latter by
       Michael Kowal. Princeton: Princeton Uni-
       versity Press, 1973, pp. 327-354.]

4260. ESCH, ARNO. "James Joyce und Homer: Zur
       Frage der Odyssee-Korrespondenzen im
       Ulysses," in Lebende Antike, pp. 423-
       432, No. 644.

4261. HENTZE, RUDOLFE. Die Proteische Wandlung im
       Ulysses von James Joyce und ihre Spiege-
       lung im Stil. Marburg: Elwert, 1933.

4262. HOCHMAN, BARUCH. "Joyce's Ulysses and Ho-
       mer's Odyssey," in Further Studies in
       English Language and Literature, scripta
       hierosolymitona, vol. 25. Edited by A.
       A. Mendilow. Jerusalem: At the Magnes
       Press, Hebrew University, 1973, pp. 214-
       226.

4263. HONIG, EDWIN. Dark Conceit: The Making of
       Allegory. Evanston: Northwestern Univer-
       sity Press, 1959, pp. 174-176, et passim.

4264. ISER, WOLFGANG. "Der Archetyp als Leerform:
       Erzählschablonen und Kommunikation in
       Joyce's Ulysses," in Terror und Spiel:

Probleme der Mythenrezeption. Edited by
Mandred Fuhrmann. Munich: Fink, 1971,
pp. 369-408. [Reprinted in Der implizite
Leser: Kommunikationsformen des Romans
von Bunyan bis Beckett, vol. 1. Theorie
und Geschichte der Literatur und erschön-
en Künste, no. 31. Munich: Fink, 1972,
pp. 300-358.]

4265. MERCIER, VIVIAN. "James Joyce and Irish Tra-
       dition," in Society and Self in the Novel:
       English Institute Essays, 1955. Edited
       by Mark Schorer. New York: Columbia Uni-
       versity Press, 1956, pp. 78-116. [Ap-
       peared in Studies, 45 (1956): 194-218;
       revised as "Joyce and the Irish Tradition
       of Parody." in The Irish Comic Tradition.
       Oxford: Clarendon Press, 1962, pp. 210-
       236; paperback reprint, 1969; reprinted
       in Configuration critique de James Joyce,
       II, pp. 149-180, No. 1584.]

4266. MÜHLHEIM, ULRIKE. "Mythos und Struktur in
       James Joyces Ulysses: Die Verarbeitung
       des Klassischen Mythos als Beispiel für
       die Darstellungstechnik von James Joyce."
       English and American Studies in German
       (Supplement to Anglia), 1973, pp. 115-116.

4267. MUIR, EDWIN. The Structure of the Novel.
       London: Hogarth Press, 1928, pp. 126-133.

*4268. NEUBERT, ALBRECHT. Die Stilformen der 'Er-
       lebten Rede' im neueren englischen roman.
       Hall: Saale, 1957.

4269. NICHOLSON, NORMAN. "James Joyce and T. F.
       Powys," in his Man and Literature. Lon-
       don: S. C. M. Press, 1944, pp. 144-151.

4270. PARR, MARY. James Joyce: The Poetry of Con-
       science. Milwaukee: Inland Press, 1961.

*4271. PRESCOTT, JOSEPH. "Stylistic Realism in
       Joyce's Ulysses," in A James Joyce Mis-
       cellany, Second Series, pp. 15-66, No.
       1613. [Also in abbreviated form in Stil-
       und Formprobleme in der Literatur. Vor-
       trage des VII. Kongresses der Interna-
       tionalen Vereinigung für moderne Sprachen
       und Literaturen. Edited by Paul Böck-
       mann. Heidelberg: Carl Winter Universi-
       tatsverlag, 1959, pp. 427-429.]

4272. _____ . "The Language of James Joyce's
       Ulysses," in Langue et littérature:
       Actes du VIIIe Congres de la Fédération
       Internationale des Langues et Littéra-
       tures Modernes. Paris: 1961, pp. 306-307.

4273. ROSENTHAL, ERWIN THEODOR. "Sprachdeformation
       als Gestaltungsmittel der schwebenden
       Wirklichkeit: Joyce, [Martin] Walser,
       [João Guimarães] Rosa," in Das fragmen-
       tarische universum. Munich: Nymphen-
       burger Verlagshandlung, 1970, pp. 39-54,
       et passim.

*4274. SAEKI, SHOICHI. "Urisize no Kozo to Giho ["Ulysses: Composition and Technique]," in Joisu Nyumon [Introduction to James Joyce], pp. 48-64, No. 1511.

4275. SCHOONBROODT, JEAN. Point of View and Expressive Form in James Joyce's Ulysses. Eupen, Belgium: The Author, 1967.

4276. SCHUTTE, WILLIAM M., and ERWIN R. STEINBERG. "The Fictional Technique of Ulysses," in Approaches to Ulysses, pp. 157-178, No. 3657.

4277. SETTANNI, ETTORE. "Aria di Joyce," in his Romanzo e Romanzieri d'Oggi. Naples: Guida, 1933, pp. 55-61.

4278. SHAPIRO, KARL. Essays on Rime. New York: Reynal and Hitchcock, 1945, pp. 17-18, 38-39.

4279. STANZEL, FRANZ. "Ulysses," in his Die Typischen Erzählsituationem im Roman, dargestellt an Tom Jones, Moby-Dick, The Ambassadors, Ulysses, u. a. Wiener Beiträge zur englischen Philologie, vol. 63. Vienna: W. Braumüller, 1955, pp. 122-124. [Translated by James P. Pusack as Narrative Situations in the Novel: Tom Jones, Moby Dick, The Ambassadors, Ulysses. Bloomington, Ind.; London: Indiana University Press, 1971, pp. 121-144, et passim.

*4280. WINTERS, IVOR. In Defense of Reason. Denver: University of Denver Press, 1947, pp. 56, 341, et passim.

*4281. YAMAKAWA, GAKUJI. "Shocho Shugi [Symbolism]," in Joisu Nyumon [An Introduction to James Joyce], pp. 170-177, No. 1511.

Periodical Articles

*4282. BELL, CLIVE. "Plus de Jazz." New Republic, 28 (21 September 1921): 92-96.

4283. BOYLE, ROBERT. "Ulysses as Frustrated Sonata Form." James Joyce Quarterly, 2 (Summer 1965): 247-254.

4284. BRION, MARCEL. "The Idea of Time in the Work of James Joyce." transition, no. 12 (March 1928): 163-170. [Appeared in Our Exagmination, pp. 25-33, No. 4906; translated by Robert Sage in Revista d'Italia (Milan), 26, no. 7 (July 1928): 403-408.]

*4285. _____. "La technique et la Thématique de James Joyce." Les nouvelles littéraires, no. 337 (30 March 1929): 6.

*4286. CELATI, GIANNI. "Orientamenti technici per una analisi non introspettiva dello Ulysses di James Joyce." Marcatre, nos. 23/24/25 [n.d.].

4287. COPE, JACKSON I. "The Rhythmic Gesture: Image and Aesthetic in Joyce's Ulysses." ELH: Journal of English Literary History, 29 (March 1962): 67-89.

4288. CWIAKALA, JADWIGA. "Homeric Parody in James Joyce's Ulysses." Kwartalnik Neofilologiczny (Warsaw), 18 (1971): 57-68.

4289. DeMARCO, CONCHA. "Gestación del Ulises." El Urogallo, 3 (July-August 1972): 106-112.

4290. DiPIETRO, ROBERT J. "A Transformational Note on a Few Types of Joycean Sentences." Style, 3 (Spring 1969): 156-167. [An earlier report appeared as "Joycean Sentences and Transformational Rules." Linguistic Society of America, Meeting Handbook, 41st (1966): p. 79; translated by Marie Jo Renard and Jean Paris in Change, no. 11 (May 1972): 34-46, No. 150.]

4291. DUNCAN, JOSEPH E. "The Modality of the Audible in Joyce's Ulysses." Publications of the Modern Language Association, 72 (March 1957): 286-295.

4292. EDWARDS, PHILIP. "Ulysses and the Legends." Essays in Criticism, 5 (April 1955): 118-128.

4293. ELIOT, T. S. "Ulysses, Order and Myth." Dial, 75 (November 1923): 480-483. [Appeared in Criticism: The Foundation of Modern Literary Judgment. Edited by Mark Schorer, Josephine Miles, and Gordon McKenzie. New York: Harcourt, Brace, 1948; and in James Joyce: Two Decades of Criticism, pp. 198-202, No. 1570; translated in Configuration critique I, pp. 385-390, No. 1636.]

4294. ELLMANN, RICHARD. "Ulysses and the Odyssey." English Studies, 43 (October 1962): 439-443.

4295. EPSTEIN, EDMUND L. "The Jewel of Asia." James Joyce Review, 3, nos. 1-2 (September 1959): 47-49.

4296. FEHR, BERNHARD. "James Joyce's Ulysses." Englische Studien, 60 (1925/26): 180-205. [Reprinted as "Die deutsche Wissenschaft zum Ulysses," in Der Homer unserer Zeit, pp. 12-13, No. 3599.]

4297. FLYNN, BRIAN. "Form and Technique in James Joyce's Ulysses." Zenith (Maynooth), 2 (1972): 25-30.

4298. FRANK, JOSEPH. "Spatial Form in Modern Literature." Sewanee Review, 53 (April 1945): 233-235. [Slightly changed version as "Flaubert and Joyce," in his The Widening Gyre. New Brunswick: Rutgers

ULYSSES

University Press, 1963, pp. 16-19; appeared in Critiques and Essays on Modern Fiction. Edited by John Aldridge. New York: Ronald Press, 1952, pp. 44-46; translated by M. Zurowski as "Forma przestrzenna w literaturze nowoczesnej." Przeglad Humanistyczny, 15, no. 2 (1971): 115-137.]

4299. GILL, RICHARD. "The 'Corporal Works of Mercy' as a Moral Pattern in Joyce's Ulysses." Twentieth Century Literature, 9 (April 1963): 17-21.

4300. GORMAN, HERBERT. "Joyce Today and Tomorrow." New Republic, 50 (April 1927): 197-199.

4301. GREENWAY, JOHN. "A Guide Through James Joyce's Ulysses." College English, 17 (November 1955): 67-78.

4302. HARDY, BARBARA. "Form as End and Means in Ulysses." Orbis litterarum, 19 (1964): 194-200.

*4303. IREMONGER, V. [n.t.]. The Bell, 8 (1944): 260-263.

4304. ISAACS, NEIL D. "Autoerotic Metaphor in Joyce, Sterne, Lawrence, Stevens, and Whitman." Literature and Psychology, 15 (Spring 1965): 92-106.

4305. ISER, WOLFGANG. "Historische Stilformen in Joyce's Ulysses." Mitteilungsblatt des Allgemeinen Deutschen Neuphilologenverbandes, 18 (1964): 167-177. [Reprinted as "Historische Stilformen in Joyce's Ulysses: Zur Interpretation des Kapitels 'The Oxen of the Sun,'" in Lebende Antike, pp. 433-450, No. 644; reprinted in Der implizite Leser: Kommunikationsformen des Romans von Bunyan bis Beckett, vol. 1. Theorie und Geschicht der Literatur und der schönen Künste, no. 31. Munich: Fink, 1972, pp. 276-299.]

4306. KENNER, HUGH. "Joyce's Ulysses: Homer or Hamlet?" Essays in Criticism, 2 (January 1952): 85-104.

4307. KIM, CHONG-KEON. "Joyce's Ashplant Symbolism." Yŏng-ŏ yŏng munhak: The English Language and Literature, no. 30 (Summer 1969): 64-78.

4308. KNUTH, LEO. "Joyce's Verbal Acupuncture." James Joyce Quarterly, 10 (Fall 1972): 61-71.

4309. KOCH, VIVIENNE. "An Approach to the Homeric Context of Joyce's Ulysses." Maryland Quarterly, 1 (1944): 119-130.

4310. LEE, ROBIN. "Patterns of Sympathy and Judgment in Ulysses." English Studies in Africa, 14 (1971): 37-48.

4311. LITZ, A. WALTON. "Early Vestiges of Joyce's Ulysses." Publications of the Modern Language Association, 71 (March 1956): 51-60.

4312. LORD, GEORGE de F. "Heroes of Ulysses and their Homeric Prototypes." Yale Review, 62 (Autumn 1972): 43-58.

4313. MACURA, VLADIMIR. "Polysemantization as a Constructional Principle in James Joyce's Novel." Umana, 20 (May-September 1971): 36-37.

4314. MARTINDALE, C. C. "Ulysses." Dublin Review, 171 (1922): 273-276.

4315. MASON, ELLSWORTH. "The Difficulties of Joyce's Ulysses." CEA Critic, 14 (February 1952): 1, 6.

4316. MIRKOVIC, RADOSLAVA. "Tehnika toka svesti u Dzojsovom Ulisu." Delo (Belgrade), 17 (1971): 1102-1120.

4317. MORSE, J. MITCHELL. "More Early Vestiges of Ulysses." Publications of the Modern Language Association, 71 (December 1956): 1173.

*4318. NOLAN, BRIAN (Myles na Gopaleen, Flann O'Brien). Irish Writing, no. 10 (1950): 71-72. [U. and the Book of Kells.]

4319. PARIS, JEAN. "Ulysses et la mer." Lettres nouvelles, 5 (June 1957): 841-859.

4320. PERADOTTO, J. J. "Liturgical Pattern in Ulysses." Modern Language Notes, 75 (April 1960): 321-326.

4321. PEREZ CARMONA, ANTONIO. "La ruptura del orden tradicional en la poesia y la novela." Revista nacional de cultura, 25 (January-April 1963): 146-149.

4322. PRESCOTT, JOSEPH. "Homer's Odyssey and Joyce's Ulysses." Modern Language Quarterly, 3 (September 1942): 427-444. [Also in his Exploring James Joyce, pp. 29-50, No. 1637.]

4323. _____. "Local Allusions in Joyce's Ulysses." Publications of the Modern Language Association, 68 (December 1953): 1223-1228. [Reprinted with slight changes in Letterature moderne, 12 (October-December 1962): 613-618; also in his Exploring James Joyce, pp. 51-58, No. 1637.]

4324. ROGERS, HOWARD E. "Irish Myth and the Plot of Ulysses." ELH: Journal of English Literary History, 15 (December 1948): 306-327.

4325. ROUTH, H. V. "The Quest for Currents in Contemporary English Literature." College English, 8 (January 1947): 169-178.

4326. RUSSELL, H. K. "The Incarnation in <u>Ulysses</u>." <u>Modern Fiction Studies</u>, 4 (Spring 1958): 53-61.

4327. SCHNEIDER, DANIEL. "Techniques of Cognition in Modern Fiction." <u>Journal of Aesthetics and Art Criticism</u>, 26 (Winter 1967): 317-328.

4328. SLAVOV, ATANAS. "Ideyna nasochenost i kompositsionna tekhnika v <u>Az Chukam Na Vratata</u>, na Shon O'Keysi i Odisey na Dzheyms Dzhoys (Kum vuprosa za proletarski i burzhoanznata partiymost v novata angliyska literatura) ["Ideological Thrust and Technique of Composition in Sean O'Casey's <u>I Knock at the Door</u> and James Joyce's <u>Ulysses</u> (On the Question of Proletarian and Bourgeois Party Spirit in Modern English Literature)]." <u>Literaturna Misul</u>, 14 (1970): 72-83. [In Bulgarian.]

4329. SMITH, DON NEAL. "Musical Form and Principles in the Scheme of <u>Ulysses</u>." <u>Twentieth Century Literature</u>, 18 (Spring 1972): 79-92.

4330. SOLMECKE, GERT. "Funktion und Bedeutung der Parodie im Joyce's <u>Ulysses</u>." <u>Anglia</u> (1969): 78-89. [Supplement, English and American Studies in German: University of Cologne, 1969, Ph.D. Dissertation.]

4331. STANFORD, W. B. "Studies in the Characterization of <u>Ulysses</u>--IV." <u>Hermathena</u>, 77 (May 1951): 52-64; 78 (November 1951): 67-82. [The first two chapters of his <u>The Ulysses Theme: A Study in the Adaptability of a Traditional Hero</u>. Oxford: Blackwell, 1954; second edition, 1963, pp. 211-240; paperback edition, University of Michigan Press, 1968, pp. 211-240.]

4332. TARANIENKO, ZBIGNIEW. "Poworty <u>Ulissesa</u>." <u>Literatura na świecie</u>, no. 5 (May 1973): 194-216.

4333. VAN CASPEL, P. P. J. "The Theme of the Red Carnation in James Joyce's <u>Ulysses</u>." <u>Neophilologus</u>, 38 (July 1954): 189-198.

4334. VISSER, G. J. "James Joyce's <u>Ulysses</u> and Anglo-Irish." <u>English Studies</u>, 24 (April 1942): 45-56; (June 1942): 79-90.

4335. VIZIOLI, PAULO. "'Dogsbody' e 'Godsbody' no simbologia do <u>Ulisses</u>." <u>Letras</u> (Curbita, Brazil), 15 (1966): 19-28.

4336. VON ABELE, RUDOLPH. "<u>Ulysses</u>: The Myth of Myth." <u>Publications of the Modern Language Association</u>, 69 (June 1954): 358-364.

4337. WARD, DAVID F. "James Joyce, <u>The Book of Kells</u>, and the Structure of <u>Ulysses</u>."

<u>South Central Bulletin</u>, 32 (October 1972): 160.

4338. WEATHERS, WINSTON. "Joyce and the Tragedy of Language." <u>Forum</u> (Houston), 4, no. 12 (Winter-Spring 1967): 16-21.

4339. WHITE, JOHN. "<u>Ulysses</u>: The Metaphysical Foundations and Grand Design." <u>Modern Fiction Studies</u>, 15 (Spring 1969): 27-34.

4340. WYKES, DAVID. "The <u>Odyssey</u> in <u>Ulysses</u>." <u>Texas Studies in Literature and Language</u>, 10 (Summer 1968): 301-316.

ULYSSES IN COURT: CENSORSHIP

Books

4341. BLANSHARD, PAUL. <u>The Right to Read: The Battle Against Censorship</u>. Boston: Beacon Press, 1955, pp. 149-151.

4342. BOYER, PAUL S. <u>Purity in Print: The Vice-Society Movement and Book Censorship in America</u>. New York: Scribner's, 1968, <u>passim</u>.

4343. ERNST, MORRIS L. <u>The Censor Marches On</u>. New York: Doubleday, Doran, 1940, pp. 20-22, 281-290. [Later appeared in his <u>The Best is Yet</u>. New York: Harpers, 1945, pp. 112-119.]

4344. _____, and ALAN U. SCHWARTZ. "Four-letter Words and the Unconscious," in <u>Censorship</u>. New York, London: Macmillan, 1964, pp. 93-107.

4345. GERBER, ALBERT B. "F--- Becomes Legal," in <u>Sex, Pornography, and Justice</u>. New York: Lyle Stuart, 1965, pp. 99-103, <u>et passim</u>.

4346. HAIGHT, ANNE L. "James Joyce," "Excerpts from the Opinion of Judge John Woolsey..., Judge Augustus N. Hand," in her <u>Banned Books</u>, 2nd edition. New York: R. R. Bowker, 1955, pp. 145-146; 3rd edition. New York, London: R. R. Bowker, 1970, pp. 75-77, 136-137.

*4347. HANEY, ROBERT W. "From <u>Ulysses</u> to <u>Howl</u>," in <u>Comstockery in America</u>. Boston: Beacon Press, 1960, pp. 26-35.

*4348. KILPATRICK, JAMES J. <u>The Smut Peddlers</u>. New York: Doubleday, 1960; London: Elek, 1961, pp. 119-125.

4349. McCOY, RALPH E. <u>Freedom of the Press: An Annotated Bibliography</u>. Carbondale and Edwardsville: Southern Illinois University Press; London and Amsterdam: Feffer and Simons, 1968, <u>passim</u>.

4350. MICHELSON, PETER. <u>The Aesthetics of Pornography</u>. New York: Herder and Herder, 1971, <u>passim</u>.

ULYSSES

4351. MURPHY, TERRENCE J. "Obscenity, the Law, and the Courts," in Censorship: Government and Obscenity. Baltimore, Dublin: Helicon, 1963, pp. 3-11.

4352. REMBAR, CHARLES. The End of Obscenity. New York: Random House, 1968, passim.

4353. ST. JOHN-STEVAS, NORMAN. "The Ulysses Case," in his Obscenity and the Law. London: Secker and Warburg, 1956, pp. 95-96, 162-166.

4354. WITTENBERG, PHILIP. The Protection and Marketing of Literary Property. New York: Julian Messner, 1937, pp. 148-151.

Periodical Articles

*4355. ANDERSON, MARGARET. "An Obvious Statement." Little Review, 7, no. 3 (September-December 1920): 8-16.

4356. _____. "Ulysses in Court." Little Review, 7 (January-March 1921): 22-25. [Appeared in her The Little Review Anthology. New York: Hermitage House, 1953, pp. 297-298, 305-308; reprinted New York: Horizon Press, 1970.]

4357. ATLAS, NICHOLAS. "James Joyce." Scraps, 9, no. 11 (12 December 1933): 12-28.

4358. BENSTOCK, BERNARD. "Redhoising James Joyce: USSR/11." James Joyce Quarterly, 6 (Winter 1968): 177-180.

*4359. BRASH, MARGARET M. "The Censor Again." Author, Playwright and Composer, 44, no. 4 (Summer 1934): 131.

4360. DAVIDSON, DONALD. "Decorum in the Novel." Modern Age, 9 (Winter 1964-65): 34-48.

*4361. de ROBECK, E. O. "The Censor Again?" Author, Playwright and Composer, 45, no. 1 (Autumn 1934): 21.

4362. DOBSON, J. L. "Against Anti-Censorship Propaganda." The Bookseller (London), 4 March 1936, p. 209.

4363. DODSON, DANIEL B. "Ulysses in America." Columbia Library Columns, 21 (February 1972): 12-19.

4364. ERNST, MORRIS L. "Reflections on the Ulysses Trial and Censorship." James Joyce Quarterly, 3 (Fall 1965): 3-11.

4365. FORSTER, E. M. "The Censor Again?" Author, Playwright and Composer, 44, no. 3 (Spring 1934): 78-79.

*4366. GANNETT, LEWIS. [n.t.]. New York Herald Tribune, 12 May 1932.

*4367. GIEDION-WELCKER, CAROLA. "Ulysses in Amerika freigegeben." Neue Zürcher Zeitung, 17 December 1933.

*4368. GOPALEEN, MYLES na (Flann O'Brien, Brian Nolan). "Cruiskeen Lawn." Irish Times, 19 December 1961.

4369. HEAP, JANE. "James Joyce," "Art and Law." Little Review, 7 (September-December 1920): 5-7. [Appeared in The Little Review Anthology, pp. 129-131, 329-330, No. 4356.]

*4370. HICKEY, WILLIAM. "These Names Make News: UXXXXXs by JXXXs JXXXe." Daily Express (London), 20 October 1936, p. 6.

4371. KERR, ALFRED. "Joyce en Angleterre." Les nouvelles littéraires (Paris), no. 691 (11 January 1936): 6-12. [Translated by Joseph Prescott as "James Joyce in England," in A James Joyce Miscellany, 1957, pp. 37-43, No. 1612; reprinted in Diliman Review, 7 (October 1959): 386-392; reprinted in Writers Workshop Miscellany (Calcutta), 10 (January-April 1962): 39-42.]

*4372. 'L.' [n.t.]. Post (Birmingham), 8 May 1928.

4372a. LEAVIS, F. R. "Freedom to Read." Times Literary Supplement, 3 May 1963, p. 325.

*4373. LESLIE, SHANE. "The Suppression of a Book." Bookman (New York), October 1927.

*4374. LINDSAY, NORMAN. "The Sex Synonym in Art: Ulysses and the Conquest of Disgust." Vision, no. 1 (May 1923): 22-28.

*4375. MARSHALL, BEATRICE. "Nazi Purging of Literature." Author, Playwright and Composer, 45, no. 1 (Autumn 1934): 22.

4376. MONROE, HARRIET. "Sumner versus James Joyce." Little Review, 7 (January-March 1921): 346.

4377. POLLOCK, JOHN. "Ulysses and the Censorship." Author, Playwright and Composer, 44, no. 4 (Summer 1934): 115-117.

4378. POUND, EZRA. "Historically Joyce (and Censorship)," translated by Forrest Read. Tri-Quarterly, no. 15 (Spring 1969): 108-114.

4379. PRESTON, HAROLD P. "Ulysses." Modern Review, 1, no. 1 (Autumn 1922): 40-42.

*4380. PRIESTLEY, J. B. "This Banned Book Nonsense." Clarion, 28 April 1934.

4381. REDMAN, BEN R. "Obscenity and Censorship." Scribner's, 95, no. 5 (May 1934): 341-344.

*4382. SCOTT, GEORGE RYLEY. "State Censorship." New Age, 43 (13 September 1928): 233.

4383. SHEED, WILFRED. "Pornography and Literary Pleasure." Catholic World, 194 (January 1962): 222-229.

4384. SILVA, JOSÉ ENRIQUE. "Nueva absolución de Ulises." Criminalia (Mexico City), 29 (December 1963): 920-922.

4385. SILVEIRA, ALCÁNTARA. "Una Sentencia Judicial Sobre Ulysses," translated by José Anibal. Universidad de Antioquia, 30 (1954): 265-270.

4386. SOUPAULT, PHILIPPE. "Le Public les livres; Injustices, Indifferences." L'Intransigeant, 22 October 1929, p. 4.

4387. TALBOT, FRANCIS. "Ulysses the Dirty." America, 51 (September 1934): 497-498.

4388. THOMAS, DONALD. "Ulysses and the Attorney-General 1936." Library, series 5, no. 24 (December 1969): 343-345.

4389. WHITE, JACK. "The Bloomsday Book." Spectator, 192 (11 June 1954): 702-704.

4390. WOLFE, HUMBERT. "The Limits of Obscenity." This Quarter, 4 (June 1932): 622-629.

4391. WOOLSEY, F. W. "Term Paper in New Terms." Louisville Courier-Journal and Times Magazine, 8 September 1968, pp. 42-43.

4392. WOOLSEY, JOHN. "Judge Woolsey on Ulysses." Saturday Review of Literature, 16 December 1933, p. 356. [Appeared in Voices in Court. Edited by William Davenport. New York: Macmillan, 1958, pp. 218-223; translated in Revista mexicana de literatura, n.s., no. 5/8 (May-August 1961): 78-84; reprinted as "Censorship" in Law in American Society. Reference Shelf, vol. 35, no. 2. Edited by Sara Toll East. New York: H. W. Wilson, 1963, pp. 70-74; reprinted in part in "Auseinandersetzung mit James Joyce Ulysses," pp. 231-243, No. 3690; reprinted as "Ein Buch namens Ulysses." Eckart-Jahrbuch 1964/1965 (1968): 225-231; reprinted with Augustus N. Hand's "United States v. Ulysses" in First Freedom. Edited by Robert B. Downs. Chicago: American Library Association, 1960, pp. 83-89; John Hand's decision on the appeal taken from 72 Federal Reporter, 2nd series. (1934): 706-709.]

*4393. Unsigned. "A Commentary." Criterion (December 1928): 187-188. [Reference to Sean O'Faolain's "Censorship in America." Irish Statesman, 6 October 1928.]

*4394. Unsigned. "Another Repeal." Nation, 137 (20 December 1933): 693.

*4395. Unsigned. "Around New York with a Newfoundlander." Telegram (St. John's, Newfoundland) [n.d.].

*4396. Unsigned. "James Joyce's Ulysses Seized in Morality Squad Raid Here." St. Louis Post-Dispatch, 1 July 1959, p. 1A.

*4397. Unsigned. "Verboten!" The Clique (London), no. 1708 (21 July 1923).

*4398. Unsigned. "What is Poetry?" New Britain, 8 November 1933, p. 784.

*4399. Unsigned. [n.t.]. Catholic Bulletin (Dublin), February 1927.

*4400. Unsigned. [n.t.]. New York Evening Post, 15 March 1934.

*4401. Unsigned. "Editorial." New York Herald Tribune, 16 December 1933.

*4402. Unsigned. "Editorial." Saturday Review of Literature, 10 (16 December 1933): 3-6.

ALLUSIONS

Books

[See also Marcus No. 4796 and Schutte No. 4404.]

4403. HARTT, JULIAN N. "The Death of the Epic Image," in The Lost Image of Man. Baton Rouge: Louisiana State University Press, 1963, pp. 12-37.

4404. SCHNEIDER, ULRICH. Die Funktion der Zitate im Ulysses von James Joyce. Studien zur englischen Literatur, no. 3. Bonn: H. Bouvier, 1970.

4405. SCHUTTE, WILLIAM M. Joyce and Shakespeare: A Study in the Meaning of Ulysses. Yale Studies in English, vol. 134. New Haven: Yale University Press, 1957; reprinted Hamden, Conn.: Archon, 1971.

4406. THORNTON, WELDON. Allusions in Ulysses: An Annotated List. Chapel Hill: University of North Carolina Press, 1968. [Paperback reprint New York: Simon and Schuster, 1973.]

4407. _____. "The Allusive Method in Ulysses," in Approaches to Ulysses, pp. 235-248, No. 3657.

4408. WHITE, JOHN. Mythology in the Modern Novel: A Study of Prefigurative Techniques. Princeton: Princeton University Press, 1971, passim.

Periodical Articles

*4409. ARIAS, AUGUSTO. "¿Ha regresada Ulises?" Letras (Lima), no. 6 (1937): 110-117.

ULYSSES

4410. BASS, RICHARD K. [See No. 4872, "Eumaeus."]

4411. BAUERLE, RUTH. "Two Unnoted Musical Allusions." James Joyce Quarterly, 9 (Fall 1971): 140-142.

4412. BIER, JEAN-PAUL. "James Joyce et Karl Bleibtreau: Sens et fonction d'une allusion littéraire dans Ulysses." Revue de littérature comparée, 44 (April-June 1970): 215-223.

4413. COPE, JACKSON I. "Ulysses: Joyce's Kabbalah." James Joyce Quarterly, 7 (Winter 1969): 93-113.

4414. DUNCAN, EDWARD. "Unsubstantial Father: A Study of the Hamlet Symbolism in Joyce's Ulysses." University of Toronto Quarterly, 19 (January 1950): 126-140.

4415. EDWARDS, CALVIN R. "The Hamlet Motif in Joyce's Ulysses." Western Review, 15 (Autumn 1950): 5-13. [See No. 4418.]

4416. EMPSON, WILLIAM. "The Theme of Ulysses." Kenyon Review, 18 (Winter 1956): 26-52. [Also in A James Joyce Miscellany, Third Series, pp. 127-154, No. 1614; translated by Roger Giroux in Les lettres nouvelles, 5 (June 1957): 801-826; reprinted in Twentieth Century Studies, 1 (November 1969): 39-40.]

4417. _____. "Humanism and Mr. Bloom." New Statesman and Nation, 52 (11 August 1956): 163-164.

4418. GODWIN, MURRAY. "Three Wrong Turns in Ulysses." Western Review, 15 (Spring 1951): 221-225. [Reply to Edwards, No. 4415.]

4419. HEINE, ARTHUR. "Shakespeare in James Joyce." Shakespeare Association Bulletin, 24 (January 1949): 56-70.

4420. KENNER, HUGH. "Homer's Sticks and Stones." James Joyce Quarterly, 6 (Summer 1969): 285-298.

4421. LINK, VICTOR. "Ulysses and the 'Eighth and Ninth Book of Moses.'" James Joyce Quarterly, 7 (Spring 1970): 199-203.

4422. LITTMANN, MARK E., and CHARLES A. SCHWEIGHAUSER. "Astronomical Allusions, their Meaning and Purpose in Ulysses." James Joyce Quarterly, 2 (Summer 1965): 238-246.

4423. MARCUS, PHILIP L. "Three Irish Allusions in Ulysses." James Joyce Quarterly, 6 (Summer 1969): 299-305.

4424. MAYHEW, GEORGE. "Joyce on Shakespeare." Southwestern Journal, 5 (Summer 1950): 109-126.

*4425. MILNER, IAN. "The Heroic and the Mock-Heroic in James Joyce's Ulysses." Philologica Pragensia, 2 (1959): 37-45.

4426. MORSE, B. J. "Mr. Joyce and Shakespeare." Englische studien, 65, no. 3 (1931): 367-381.

*4427. MUNZER, KURT. "Homer aus Dublin." Prager Tagblatt (Prague), 13 November 1927.

4428. PALLEY, JULIAN. "The Periplus of Don Pedro: Tiemp de Silencio." Bulletin of Hispanic Studies, 48 (July 1971): 239-254. [U, Odyssey, and Luis Martin-Santos' Tiempo de Silencio.]

4429. PEERY, WILLIAM. "The Sources of Joyce's Shakespeare Criticism." Shakespeare Newsletter, 1 (November 1951): 23.

4430. PEERY, WILLIAM. "The Hamlet of Stephen Dedalus." Studies in English (University of Texas), 31 (1952): 109-119.

4431. POMERANZ, VICTORY. "When McCarthy Took the Floor." James Joyce Quarterly, 11 (Fall 1973): 52-54.

4432. SOLOMAN, ALBERT J. "A [George] Moore in Ulysses." James Joyce Quarterly, 10 (Winter 1973): 215-227.

4433. STANFORD, W. B. "Joyce's First Meeting with Ulysses." Listener, 46 (10 July 1951): 99, 105. [Lamb's Adventures of Ulysses.]

4434. VAN der VAT, D. G. "Paternity in Ulysses." English Studies, 19 (August 1937): 145-158.

STUDIES OF INFLUENCE AND COMPARISON

Books

4435. ARONNE AMESTOY, LIDA. "Ulysses vs. Rayuela: Dos etapas en la Odisee del siglo XX," in Cortázar: La novela mandalo. Buenos Aires: Fernando García Cambeiro, 1972, pp. 17-31.

4436. BIENKOWSKI, ZBIGNIEW. "Bodziec," in Modelunki: Skzice literackie. Warsaw: Czytelnik, 1966, pp. 381-390, et passim.

4437. CARRUTHERS, JOHN (John Young Thomson Grieg). Scheherazade: or, the Future of the English Novel. London: Kegan Paul, 1927, pp. 12-13, 62-66, 73-76.

4438. EGRI, PÉTER. James Joyce es Thomas Mann. Budapest: Akadémiai, 1967. [Later published as Avantgardism and Modernism: A Comparison of James Joyce's Ulysses with Thomas Mann's Der Zauberberg and Lotte in Weimar. University of Tulsa Monograph Series, no. 14. Translated by Paul Aston. Edited by H. Frew Waidner. Tulsa, Budapest: University of Tulsa and Akadémiai Kiadb, 1972; see also No. 4218.]

4439. ENGSTROM, ALFRED G. "A Few Comparisons and Contrasts in the Word-Craft of Rabelais and James Joyce," in Renaissance and Other Studies in Honor of William Leon Wyley. University of North Carolina Studies in Romance Languages and Literatures, no. 72. Edited by George B. Daniel. Chapel Hill: University of North Carolina Press, 1968, pp. 65-82.

*4440. GOLWARZ, SERGIO. "Jung y Ulises," in 126 ensayos de bolsillo y 126 gotas toxicas. Mexico City: Libro Mex., 1961, pp. 128-129. [Reprinted from Novedades.]

4441. GRABO, CARL H. The Technique of the Novel. New York: Scribners, 1928, pp. 219-220.

*4442. JAUSS, HANS ROBERT. "Die Ausprägung des Zeits Romans in Thomas Manns Zauberberg and James Joyces Ulysses," in Zeit und Errinerung in Marcel Prousts A la recherche du temps perdu: Ein Beitrag zu Theorie des Romans. Heidelberger Forschungen, no. 3. Heidelberg: Carl Winter, 1955; second edition, revised, 1970, pp. 35-53.

4443. KENNER, HUGH. Flaubert, Joyce and Beckett: The Stoic Comedians. London: W. H. Allen, 1964; Boston: Beacon Press, 1963. [Contains his "Art in a Closed Field." Virginia Quarterly Review, 38 (Autumn 1962): 597-613; his "The Book as Book" appeared in Christianity and Culture. Edited by J. Stanley Murphy. Baltimore: Helicon Press, 1960, pp. 158-171, incorporated as "James Joyce: Comedian of the Inventory," pp. 3-66; latter essay reprinted in Perspectives on Fiction. Edited by James L. Calderwood and Harold E. Toliver. New York, London: Oxford University Press, 1968, pp. 38-54.]

4444. McCORMICK, JOHN. "James Joyce and Hermann Broch: From Influence to Originality," in Proceedings of the IVth Congress of the International Comparative Literature Association, vol. 2. Edited by François Jost. The Hague: Mouton, 1966, pp. 1344-1352.

4445. McKAY, CLAUDE. A Long Way Home. New York: Lee Furman, 1937, pp. 246-249.

4446. MERCIER, VIVIAN. "Dublin under the Joyces," in James Joyce: Two Decades of Criticism, pp. 285-301, No. 1570.

4447. MONROE, N. ELIZABETH. The Novel and Society. Chapel Hill: University of North Carolina Press, 1941, pp. 205-206.

4448. MURILLO, L. A. "James Joyce: The Way of Irony to the Threshhold of Myth," in The Cyclical Night: Irony in James Joyce and Jorge Luis Borges. Cambridge: Harvard University Press, 1968, pp. 1-115.

4449. PALEY, MORTON D. "Blake in Nighttown," in A James Joyce Miscellany, Third Series, pp. 175-187, No. 1614.

4450. PESCH, LUDWIG. "Das Ulysses-Phanomen," in Die romantische Rebellion in der modernen literatur und Kunst. Munich: C. H. Beck, 1962, pp. 115-124, et passim.

4451. RASCOE, BURTON. Titans of Literature. New York: Putnam, 1932, passim.

4452. VARELA JACOME, BENITO. "James Joyce y el impacto del Ulises," in Renovacion de la novela en el siglo XX. Barcelona: Ediciones Destino, 1967, pp. 144-171.

Periodical Articles

*4453. AIKEN, CONRAD. "The Dead 'Novel.'" Dial, 79 (July 1925): 60-63. [Review of Jules Romains' Lucienne.]

4454. ALDINGTON, RICHARD. "Mr. James Joyce's Ulysses." English Review, 32 (April 1921): 333-341. [Expanded in his Literary Studies and Reviews. London: Unwin Brothers, 1924, pp. 192-207; New York: Dial Press, 1924, pp. 192-207, which includes "The Influence of Mr. James Joyce." English Review, 32 (April 1921): 333-341 (same article as above with different title): Russian translation as "Uliss mistera Dzheimsa Dzhoisa." Inostrannaia literatura, no. 8 (August 1963): 221-223.]

4455. BACCA, JUAN DAVID GARCIA. "E. Husserl and James Joyce, or Theory and Practice of the Phenomenal Attitude." Philosophical and Phenomenological Research, 9 (March 1949): 588-594.

4456. BEARDSLEY, HARRY M. "James Joyce vs. Gertrude Stein." Real America, 6, no. 5 (February 1936): 43, 76-77.

*4457. BEDDOW, BRUCE. Teacher's World, 19 May 1926. [Review of Radcliffe Hall's Adam's Breed and Christopher Morley's Thunder on the Left.]

4458. BELGION, MONTGOMERY. "Mr. Joyce and Mr. Gilbert." This Quarter, 3, no. 11 (July-August-September 1930): 122-128.

4459. BIHALJI-MERIA, OTTO. "Faustus und Ulysses: Gespräch mit Tomas Mann." Nedeljne informativne novine-Wochen-Zeitung, 9 August 1953.

4460. CABIBBE, GIORGIO, and EUGENIO MONTALE. "Francesco Flora et l'Ulisse." Revista di studi Crociani, 5 (January-March 1968): 1212.

4461. CLARKE, JOHN. "Joyce and Blakean Vision." Criticism, 5 (Spring 1963): 173-180.

ULYSSES

4462. COHN, RUBY. "Absurdity in English: Joyce and O'Neill." Comparative Drama, 3 (1969): 56-61.

4463. COLEMAN, ELLIOTT, "A Note on Joyce and Jung." James Joyce Quarterly, 1 (Fall 1963): 11-16.

4464. COSTA, RICHARD H. "Ulysses, Lowry's Volcano and the Voyage Between: A Study of an Un-acknowledged Literary Kinship." University of Toronto Quarterly, 36 (July 1967): 335-352.

4465. CUNNINGHAM, EVERETT V. "Bleitbreau in Joyce's Ulysses." Names, 1 (1953): 203-204.

4466. DALTON, JACK P. "Sources: A Cautionary Note." James Joyce Quarterly, 6 (Fall 1968): 96-97.

4467. DAY, ROBERT ADAMS. "Joyce's Waste Land and Eliot's Unknown God." Literary Monographs, 4 (1971): 139-210, 218-226.

4468. DEANE, SEAMUS. "Ulysses: Fifty Years After." Journal of the [Irish] Association of Teachers of English, no. 3 (Easter 1972): 6-21. [Also as "The Joycean Triumph: Ulysses 50 Years Later." Encounter, 39, no. 5 (November 1972): 42-51.]

4469. DURZAK, MANFRED. "Hermann Broch und James Joyce: Zur Äethetik des modernen Romans." Deutsche Vierteljahresschrift für Literaturwissenschaft und Geistesgeschichte, 40 (October 1966): 391-433.

4470. FITZGERALD, F. SCOTT. "Fitzgerald on Ulysses: A Previously Unpublished Letter to Bennett Cerf." Fitzgerald/Hemingway Annual (1972): 3-4.

*4471. FRANKE, HANS. "Das Ende des psychologischen Romans der bürgerlichen Dekadenz: James Joyce und die Aufgaben der jungen deutschen Epik." Geist der Zeit, 16 (1938): 156-165.

4472. FUENTES, CARLOS. "Rayuela: la novela como caja de Pandora." Mundo nuevo, 9 (1966): 68. [Cortázar and U.]

4473. GLASHEEN, ADALINE. "Another Face for Proteus." James Joyce Review, 1, no. 2 (June 1957): 308.

4474. GONZALEZ, MANUEL PEDRO. "Crisis de la novela in America." Revista Nacional de Cultura, no. 150 (January-February 1962): 50-69. ["Proyeccion Infecundade Joyce," 60-64.]

4475. _____ . "La novela hispanoamericana en el contexto de la internacional." Coloquio sobre la novela hispanoamericano (Fondo de Cultura Economica) (1967): 92.

4476. GUIGUET, JEAN. "Un-American Considerations on Frost's Poetry." Travaux du Centre d'Études anglaises et americaines, 1 (1962): 105-117.

4477. HALL, VERNON. "Joyce's Ulysses." Explicator, 10 (June 1952): item 59.

4478. _____ . "Joyce's Use of Da Ponte and Mozart's Don Giovanni." Publications of the Modern Language Association, 66 (March 1951): 78-84.

4479. HARSS, LUIS. "Cortázar, o la cachetada metaficica." Mundo nuevo, no. 7 (1966): 73.

4480. HARTLEY, LODWICK. "'Swiftly Sterneward': The Question of Sterne's Influence on Joyce." Studies in the Literary Imagination, 3 (October 1970): 37-47. [See also James Joyce Quarterly, 10 (Winter 1973): 264-265.]

4481. HENKE, SUZETTE. "James Joyce and Philip James Bailey's Festus." James Joyce Quarterly, 9 (Summer 1972): 445-451.

*4482. HOFFMAN, FREDERICK J. "The Authority of the Commonplace: Joyce's Bloomsday." Kenyon Review, 22 (Spring 1960): 316-323. [Became part of Part 3 of chapter 12 of The Mortal No: Death and the Modern Imagination. Princeton: Princeton University Press, 1964, pp. 393-423; first part translated in Joyce, pp. 121-132, No. 1526.]

*4483. JOSEPHSON, MATHEW. "Virginia Woolf and the Modern Novel." New Republic, 66 (15 April 1931): 239-241.

4484. KAIN, RICHARD M. "AE's Cooperative Watch in Ulysses and in Moore's Salve." James Joyce Quarterly, 9 (Winter 1971): 278.

4485. KENNER, HUGH. "Baker Street to Eccles Street: The Odyssey of a Myth." Hudson Review (Autumn 1948): 481-499.

4486. _____ . "Joyce's Ulysses." Explicator, 10 (June 1952): item 58.

4487. _____ . "Note." Shenandoah, 3 (Autumn 1952): 3-8.

4488. KILEEN, J. F. "Joyce's Roman Prototype." University Review, 1 (1955): 34-47. [Later appeared in Comparative Literature, 9 (Summer 1957): 193-203.]

4489. KOHLER, DAYTON. "Time in the Modern Novel." College English, 10 (October 1948): 15-24.

4490. KRUSE, HORST. "Hemingway's 'Cat in the Rain' and Joyce's Ulysses." Literatur in Wissenschaft und Unterricht (Kiel), 3 (1970): 28-30.

4491. LAHR, JOHN. "The Language of Silence." Evergreen Review, 13 (March 1969): 53-55, 82-90.

4492. LARRAYA, ANTONIO PAGES. "Tradición y renovación en la novela hispanoamericana." Mundo nuevo, 34 (April 1969): 81.

4493. LEDGARD, RUDOLFO. "El torno al Ulises de Joyce." 3 [Tres], no. 3 (December 1939): 83-91. [On Joyce's influence upon Pablo de Rokha; rejections of this position by: Oscar Chávez. El poeta crucificado y la jauria... Santiago: Dirección General de Prisiones, 1940, also in Multitud, no. 33 (January-March 1940): 19-72; Antonio de Undurraga. "De Joyce a de Rokha." Atenea, no. 242/243 (August-September 1945): 200-222, part of a longer article, "El arte poética de Pablo de Rokha," also issued in book form. Santiago: Editorial Nascimento, 1945.]

4494. LIVERMORE, ANN. "Carmen and Ulysses." Music Review, no. 28 (November 1967): 300-310.

4495. LORCH, THOMAS M. "The Relationship between Ulysses and The Waste Land." Texas Studies in Literature and Language, 6 (Summer 1964): 123-133.

4496. LYON, THOMAS E. "Miguel Angel Asturias: Timeless Fantasy." Books Abroad, 42 (Spring 1968): 183-189.

4497. McMILLAN, DOUGALD. "Influences of Gerhardt Hauptmann in Joyce's Ulysses." James Joyce Quarterly, 4 (Winter 1967): 107-119.

4498. MAGALANER, MARVIN. "Labyrinthine Motif: James Joyce and Leo Taxil." Modern Fiction Studies, 2 (Winter 1956-57): 167-182.

4499. MAGNY, CLAUDE EDMONDE. "Note conjointe sur T. S. Eliot et James Joyce." Esprit, 16 (August 1948): 232-240. [Translated by M. M. J. as "El tiempo de la reflexion." Moradas, 2 (October 1948): 292-297; translated by Sonia Brownell as "Double Note on T. S. Eliot and James Joyce," in T. S. Eliot: A Symposium from Conrad Aiken. Compiled by Richard March and M. J. Tambimuttu. Chicago: Henry Regnery, 1949, pp. 208-217; reprinted as "Le temps de la réflexion: Note conjointe sur T. S. Eliot et James Joyce ou le point de vue de Tiresias." Littérature et critique. Paris: Payot, 1971, pp. 185-192.]

4500. MANGLAVITI, LEO M. J. "Joyce and St. John." James Joyce Quarterly, 9 (Fall 1971): 152-155.

4501. MEEUWESSE, KAREL. "O Awater ik weet waarvan gij peinst." Raam, no. 34 (1967): 43-65;

"Aantekeningen bij Awater, II." Nieuwe Taalgids, 60 (1967): 171-176. [Nijhoff's Awater and U.]

4502. MOLINA, A. VANDARES. "Miguel Angel Asturias." Mundo Hispánico, no. 243 (June 1968): 23.

4503. MORSE, J. MITCHELL. "Augustine, Ayenbite, and Ulysses." Publications of the Modern Language Association, 70 (December 1955): 1143-1159. [Appeared as chapter 2 of his Sympathetic Alien, No. 339.]

4504. MOSS, HOWARD. "Tom Swift in Hell." New Yorker, 44 (28 September 1968): 174-180. [O'Brien's Third Policeman and U.]

4505. MOUCHERON, ANDRÉE. "Joyce and Shakespeare." Revue des langues vivantes, 30 (1964): 342-346.

*4506. MUIR, EDWIN. "The Zeit Geist." The Calendar (October 1925). [Huxley and Joyce's U.]

4507. NATHAN, MONIQUE. "James Joyce et T. S. Eliot: conjonctions et divergences." Cahiers du Monde nouveau, 6, no. 43 (1950): 94-102.

4508. ORWELL, GEORGE. "Rediscovery of Europe." Listener, 37 (19 March 1942): 370-372. [Reprinted in his Collected Essays, Journalism and Letters, vol. 1. Edited by Sonia Orwell and Ian Angus. London: Secker and Warburg, 1968, pp. 125-129.]

4509. PARIS, JEAN. "Hamlet et ses frères." Cahiers Renaud-Barrault, 57 (November 1966): 63-89.

4510. POIRIER, RICHARD. "Politics of Self-Parody." Partisan Review, 35 (Summer 1968): 339-353. [Joyce, Nabokov, Barth, Murdoch, Borges.]

4511. POUND, EZRA. "James Joyce et Pécuchet." Mercure de France, 156 (June 1922): 307-320. [Appeared in his Polite Essays. London: Faber, 1937, pp. 82-97; translated by Fred Bornhauser in Shenandoah, 3 (Autumn 1952): 9-20, with accompanying note by Hugh Kenner; reprinted in L'Herne, no. 6 (?): 54-61; reprinted in L'Arc, 36 (1968): 44-48; reprinted in Forrest Read's Pound/Joyce, No. 725.]

4512. PRESCOTT, JOSEPH. "NED Supplement: 'Sherlock (Holmes) v. int.'" Modern Language Notes, 58 (March 1943): 203.

4513. PRITCHARD, WILLIAM H. "On Wyndham Lewis." Partisan Review, 35 (Spring 1968): 253-267.

4514. PURDY, STROTHER B. "On the Psychology of Erotic Literature." Literature and Psychology, 20, no. 1 (1970): 23-29. [Phallic fallacy in U and Lady Chatterly's Lover.]

ULYSSES

4515. REEVES, PASCHAL. "Wolfe's Of Time and the River." Explicator, 26 (October 1967): item 18.

4516. REYNOLDS, MARY T. "Joyce's Planetary Music: His Debt to Dante." Sewanee Review, 76 (Summer 1968): 450-477.

4517. RIDGEWAY, ANN. "Two Authors in Search of a Reader." James Joyce Quarterly, 1 (Summer 1964): 41-51. [Sterne and Joyce.]

4518. SCHNEIDER, DUANA. "Thomas Wolfe and the Quest for Language." Ohio University Review, 11 (1969): 5-18.

4519. SCHOOLFIELD, G. C. "Broch's Sleepwalker: Aeneas and the Apostles." James Joyce Review, 2, nos. 1-2 (June 1958): 21-38.

4520. SÉGUR, NICHOLAS. "James Joyce: Ulysse." La revue Mondiale, 189 (April 1929): 295-299.

4521. SLABEY, ROBERT M. "Faulkner's Mosquitoes and Joyce's Ulysses." Revue des langues vivantes, 28 (1962): 435-437.

4522. SMOOT, JEAN JOHANNESSEN. "Variations in Water Imagery in James Joyce and Bousseut." Romance Notes, 9 (Spring 1968): 252-257.

4523. SOZONOVA, I. "Chelovek i khod istorii. (Ie nabliudenii nad Tikhim Donom Sholokhova)." Voprosy literatury, 6 (January 1962): 179-192.

4524. STANFORD, W. B. "The Mysticism that Pleased Him: A Note on the Primary Source of Joyce's Ulysses." Envoy, 5 (May 1951): 62-69. [Lamb's Adventures of Ulysses in Andrew Lang's or John Cooke's edition; reprinted in A Bash in the Tunnel, pp. 35-42, No. 1644; translated in Configuration critique I, pp. 375-384, No. 1636.]

4525. STARKIE, WALTER T. "Miguel de Cervantes and the English Novel." Transactions of the Royal Society of Literature, 34 (1966): 159-179.

4526. STAVROU, C. N. "The Love Songs of J. Swift, G. Bernard Shaw, and J. A. A. Joyce." Midwest Quarterly, 6 (1964): 135-162.

*4527. STRONG, L. A. G. "Three Ghosts and Stephen Dedalus." Penguin New Writing, no. 22 (1944): 121-134. [Shakespeare, Swift, Blake.]

4528. SULTAN, STANLEY. "An Old-Irish Model for Ulysses." James Joyce Quarterly, 5 (Winter 1968): 103-109. ["Voyage of Maelduin."]

4529. SUMMERHAYES, DON. "Joyce's Ulysses and Whitman's 'Self': A Query." Wisconsin Studies in Contemporary Literature, 4 (Spring-Summer 1963): 216-224.

4530. TINDALL, WILLIAM YORK. "Many-Leveled Fiction: Virginia Woolf to Ross Lockridge." College English, 10 (November 1948): 65-71.

4531. _____. "Dante and Mrs. Bloom." Accent, 11 (Spring 1951): 85-92. [Reprinted in Configuration critique de James Joyce, I, pp. 137-147, No. 1636.]

*4532. VISHNEVSKY, VSEVOLOD. "Znat Napad! ["We Must Know the West!]." Literaturny Kritik, no. 7 (1933): 80-95.

4533. WETZEL, HEINZ. "Spuren des Ulysses in The Waste Land." Germanisch-Romanische Monatsschrift, n.s. 20 (November 1970): 442-466.

4534. WHITAKER, T. R. "Drinkers and History: Rabelais, Balzac, Joyce." Comparative Literature, 11 (Spring 1959): 157-164. [U and Rabelais' Discourse of the Drinkers.]

4535. WHITE, ANDREW. "Labyrinths of Modern Fiction." Arcadia, 2 (1967): 288-304. [Max Frisch's Gandenbein, Joyce's U, and Kafka's Joseph K.]

4536. WITT, MARION. "A Note on Joyce and Yeats." Modern Language Notes, 63 (December 1948): 552-553.

4537. Unsigned. "F. Scott Fitzgerald's Copy of Ulysses." Fitzgerald/Hemingway Annual, (1972): 5-7.

4538. Unsigned. "Marxism and the Arts." Arena, 1, no. 3 (October-December 1937): 195-198.

LEOPOLD BLOOM, MOLLY BLOOM, STEPHEN DEDALUS AND OTHERS

Leopold Bloom

Books

4539. BROPHY, JOHN. The Human Face. New York: Prentice-Hall, 1946, pp. 176-178.

4540. CRONIN, ANTHONY. "The Advent of Bloom," in A Question of Modernity. London: Secker and Warburg, 1966, pp. 58-96, et passim. [Reprinted in Joyce: A Collection of Critical Essays, pp. 84-101, No. 1540.]

4541. FISCH, HAROLD. The Dual Image: The Figure of the Jew in English and American Literature. Revised and enlarged edition. London: World Jewish Congress, British Section; New York: Ktav, 1971, passim. [1959 edition omits Joyce and Bloom.]

4542. HORNIK, MARCEL. Studies in James Joyce: Leopold-Bloom-Candaules. Boars Hill, Oxford: Loncombe Lodge Research Library, 1959?

4543. HYMAN, LOUIS. "Some Aspects of the Jewish Backgrounds of Ulysses," in The Jews of Ireland from Earliest Times to the Year 1910. Shannon: Irish University Press, 1972, pp. 167-192, et passim.

4544. KAIN, RICHARD M. "Motif as Meaning: The Case of Leopold Bloom," in Approaches to Ulysses, pp. 61-101, No. 3657.

4545. KAYE, JULIAN B. "A Portrait of the Artist as Blephen-Stoom," in A James Joyce Miscellany, Second Series, pp. 79-92, No. 1613.

4546. KETTLE, ARNOLD. "James Joyce: Ulysses," in his An Introduction to the English Novel, vol. 2. London: Hutchinson's University Library, 1953, pp. 135-151. [Translated as "James Joyce et Ulysse." Recherches internationales à la lumière du marxisme, no. 50 (November-December 1965): 68-84.]

*4547. SACHS, JOSEPH. "The Jew in James Joyce," in his Beauty and the Jew. London: Edward Gosdston: 1937, pp. 155-172.

4548. WEST, ALICK. "James Joyce: Ulysses," in his Crisis and Criticism. London: Lawrence and Wishart, 1937, pp. 143-180.

Periodical Articles

4549. ANDERSON, CHESTER G. "Leopold Bloom as Dr. Sigmund Freud." Mosaic, 6 (Fall 1972): 23-44.

4550. BEAUSANG, MICHAEL. "Seeds for the Planting of Bloom." Mosaic, 6 (Fall 1972): 11-22.

4551. BENNETT, JOHN Z. "Unposted Letter: Joyce's Leopold Bloom." Bucknell Review, 14 (March 1966): 1-13.

*4552. CONSIGLIO, ALBERTO. "L'uomo di Joyce." Il Mattino (Naples), 13 March 1929.

4553. DAVIS, RODERICK. "The Fourfold Moses in Ulysses." James Joyce Quarterly, 7 (Winter 1969): 120-131.

4554. ELLENBOGEN, EILEEN. "Leopold Bloom--Jew." Changing World, no. 3 (Winter 1947-1948): 79-86.

4555. EPSTEIN, EDMUND L. "The Religion of Leopold Bloom." Ethos (Spring 1957): 19-21.

4556. FIEDLER, LESLIE. "Bloom on Joyce: or, Jokey for Jacob." Journal of Modern Literature, 1 (First Issue, 1970): 19-29. [Reprinted in New Light on Joyce, pp. 195-208, No. 1656.]

4557. FISHER, FRANKLIN. "James Joyce and the Misfortunes of Mr. Bloom." Spectrum, 8 (Winter 1965): 76-83.

4558. GALLOWAY, DAVID D. "Moses--Bloom--Herzog: Bellow's Everyman." Southern Review, n.s. 2 (January 1966): 61-76.

4559. GIBSON, GEORGE H. "The Odyssey of Leopold Bloom's Bar of Soap." Furman Studies, n.s. 13 (May 1966): 15-19.

4560. GONZALEZ MADRIZ, ZUNILDA. "El espacio y el tiempo en el Ulysses: Leopoldo Bloom, eje de la obra." Imagen, 2 (October 1972): 9-12.

4561. GRIFFITH, BENJAMIN W. "Bloom + Molly 'Carried Westward': An Alternate Reading." James Joyce Quarterly, 9 (Fall 1971): 122.

4562. GROSS, HARVEY. "From Barabas to Bloom: Notes on the Figure of the Jew." Western Humanities Review, 11 (Spring 1957): 149-156.

4563. HIGGINS, BERTRAM. "The Natural Pander: Leopold Bloom and Others." Calendar of Modern Letters, 1, no. 2 (April 1925): 139-146.

4564. HOLMES, THEODORE. "Bloom, the Father." Sewanee Review, 79 (April 1971): 236-255.

4565. KNIGHT, G. WILSON. "Lawrence, Joyce, and Powys." Essays in Criticism, 11 (October 1961): 403-417.

4566. KUEHN, ROBERT E. "Mr. Bloom and Mr. Joyce: A Note on 'Heroism' in Ulysses." Wisconsin Studies in Contemporary Literature, 4 (Spring-Summer 1963): 209-215.

4567. LEVENTHAL, A. J. "The Jew Errant." Dubliner, 2 (Spring 1963): 11-24.

4568. LEVITT, MORTON P. "A Hero for our Time: Leopold Bloom and the Myth of Ulysses." James Joyce Quarterly, 10 (Fall 1972): 132-146.

*4569. McALEER, EDWARD C. "The Ignorance of Mr. Bloom." Tennessee Studies in Literature: Special Number [1]. (1961): 121-129. [Studies in honor of John C. Hodges and Alwin Thuler. Edited by Richard Behle Davis and John Leon Lievsay.]

4570. MAGALANER, MARVIN. "The Anti-Semitic Limerick Incidents in Joyce's 'Bloomsday.'" Publications of the Modern Language Association, 68 (December 1953): 1219-1223.

4571. MARKSON, DAVID. "James Joyce's Jew." Symposium (Union College), 3 (Fall 1964): 10-12.

4572. MASON, ELLSWORTH. "Bloom on Rye." Hofstra Review, no. 2 (Summer 1967): 1-6.

4573. MOSS, JUDITH P. "Elijah Ben Bloom." Massachusetts Studies in English, 2 (1969): 19-21.

ULYSSES

4574. O'CONNELL, DANIEL. "Bloom and the Royal Astronomer." James Joyce Quarterly, 5 (Summer 1968): 299-302.

4575. OSSOTT, HANNI. "El cuarto reloj del Señor Bloom." Papeles, no. 17 (December 1972): 89-103.

4576. PRESCOTT, JOSEPH. "The Characterization of Leopold Bloom." Literature and Psychology, 9 (Winter 1959): 3-4.

4577. PURDY, ANDREW. "Leopold Bloom." Carolina Quarterly, 24 (Winter 1972): 14. [Poem]

4578. RUSSELL, STANLEY C. "A Baedeker to Bloom." James Joyce Quarterly, 3 (Summer 1966): 226-235.

4579. SCHUTTE, WILLIAM M. "Leopold Bloom: A Touch of the Artist." James Joyce Quarterly, 10 (Fall 1972): 118-131.

4580. SHAPIRO, LEO. "The Zion Motif in Joyce's Ulysses." Jewish Frontier, 13 (September 1946): 14-16. [Reprinted in Jewish Frontier Anthology, 1945-1967. New York: Jewish Frontier Association, 1967, pp. 315-321.]

4581. SHAPIRO, STEPHEN A. "Leopold Bloom and Gulley Jimson: The Economic of Survival." Twentieth Century Literature, 10 (April 1964): 3-11.

4582. SHERWOOD, JOHN C. "Bloom and the Left-Handed Adulterer." James Joyce Quarterly, 4 (Winter 1967): 151-152.

4583. STALEY, THOMAS F. "The Search for Leopold Bloom: James Joyce and Italo Svevo." James Joyce Quarterly, 1 (Summer 1964): 59-63.

4584. STANFORD, W. B. "Ulyssean Qualities in Joyce's Leopold Bloom." Comparative Literature, 5 (Spring 1953): 125-136.

4585. STAVROU, C. N. "Mr. Bloom and Nikos' Odysseus." South Atlantic Quarterly, 62 (Winter 1963): 107-118.

4586. STERN, FREDERICK C. "Pyrrhus, Fenians And Bloom." James Joyce Quarterly, 5 (Spring 1968): 211-228.

4587. TINDALL, WILLIAM YORK. "Mosaic Bloom." Mosaic, 6 (Fall 1972): 3-10.

4588. TOMKINSON, NEIL. "Bloom's Job." James Joyce Quarterly, 2 (Winter 1965): 103-107. [Followed by Patrick F. Byrne of the Dublin Evening Herald.]

4589. _____. "A Reply to 'Bloom's Job.'" James Joyce Quarterly, 3 (Fall 1965): 72-74.

4590. TRACY, ROBERT. "Leopold Bloom Fourfold: A Hungarian-Hebraic-Hellenic-Hibernia Hero." Massachusetts Review, 6 (Spring-Summer 1965): 523-538.

4591. WOLLMAN, MAURICE. "Jewish Interest in James Joyce's Ulysses." Jewish Chronicle Supplement, no. 176 (June 1937): 3-4.

Molly Bloom

4592. ELLMANN, RICHARD. "Why Molly Bloom Menstruates." New York Review of Books, 18 (23 March 1972): 25-30. [Became a chapter in his Ulysses on the Liffey, No. 3568.]

4593. FERRARA, PETER. "Why Molly Menstruates: The Language of Desire." Sub-stance, no. 4 (Fall 1972): 51-62.

4594. HARRIS, WENDELL V. "Molly's 'Yes': The Transvaluation of Sex in Modern Fiction." Texas Studies in Literature and Language, 10 (Spring 1968): 107-118.

4595. HAYMAN, DAVID. "The Empirical Molly," in Approaches to Ulysses, pp. 103-135, No. 3657.

4596. _____. "'So They Think They Know Molly.'" James Joyce Quarterly, 9 (Summer 1972): 492-494. [Reply to O'Brien, No. 4604.]

4597. HERRING, PHILIP F. "The Bedfastness of Molly Bloom." Modern Fiction Studies, 15 (Spring 1969): 49-61.

4598. KAPLAN, FRED. "Dickens' Flora Finching and Joyce's Molly Bloom." Nineteenth Century Fiction, 23 (December 1968): 343-346.

4599. KENNER, HUGH. "Molly's Masterstroke." James Joyce Quarterly, 10 (Fall 1972): 19-28.

4600. KIM, CHONG-KEON. "T'ŭkhi Molly Bloom ŭi sexuality ye tae hayo." Yŏng-ŏ yŏng munhak: The English Language and Literature, no. 36 (Winter 1970): 55-62.

4601. KOLBE, JOANNE. "A Protean Mollylogue," in The Celtic Bull, pp. 96-100, No. 3545.

4602. MESKIN, CAROL. "The Paralleled Virgin and the Unparalleled Mother," in The Celtic Bull, pp. 74-76, No. 3545.

4603. MORSE, J. MITCHELL. "Molly Bloom Revisited," in A James Joyce Miscellany, Second Series, pp. 139-149, No. 1613.

4604. O'BRIEN, DARCY. "Some Determinants of Molly Bloom," in Approaches to Ulysses, pp. 137-155, No. 3657.

STUDIES OF THE SEPARATE WORKS

4605. _____. "A Note on Molly." James Joyce Quarterly, 9 (Summer 1972): 490-491. [See reply by David Hayman, No. 4596.]

4606. PHILLIPS, ROBERT S. "A Note on Molly Bloom as Queen of Tubber Tintye." Western Humanities Review, 16 (Summer 1962): 275-276.

4607. PRESCOTT, JOSEPH. "The Characterization of Molly Bloom," in A James Joyce Miscellany, Third Series, pp. 79-126, No. 1614.

4608. SCHWARTZ, LEWIS M. "Eccles Street and Canterbury: An Approach to Molly Bloom." Twentieth Century Literature, 15 (October 1969): 155-165.

4609. WILLIAMS, BRUCE. "Molly Bloom: Archetype or Stereotype." Journal of Marriage and the Family, 33 (August 1971): 545-546.

Stephen Dedalus

4610. FORAN, DONALD J. "A Mirror Held up to Stephen." James Joyce Quarterly, 4 (Summer 1967): 301-309.

4611. GECKLE, GEORGE L. "Stephen Dedalus as Lapwing: A Symbolic Center of Ulysses." James Joyce Quarterly, 6 (Winter 1968): 104-114.

4612. KAIN, RICHARD M. "The Significance of Stephen's Meeting Bloom: A Survey of Interpretations." James Joyce Quarterly, 10 (Fall 1972): 147-160.

4613. LEE, JAE-HO. ["Hamlet and Stephen Dedalus"]. English Language and Literature (Seoul), 19 (Autumn 1966): 20-28.

4614. McCARROLL, DAVID L. "Stephen's Dream--and Bloom's." James Joyce Quarterly, 6 (Winter 1964): 174-176.

4615. MAGALANER, MARVIN. "The Humanization of Stephen Dedalus." Mosaic, 6 (Fall 1972): 63-68.

4616. MAIERHÖFER, FRÄNZI. "Die Fledermausähnliche Seele des Stephen Dädalus: Zum Werk von James Joyce." Stimmen der Zeit (1968): 39-53.

4617. PRESCOTT, JOSEPH. "The Characterization of Stephen Dedalus in Ulysses." Lettérature moderne, 9 (March-April 1959): 145-164. [Also in his Exploring James Joyce, pp. 59-76, No. 1637.]

4618. STALEY, THOMAS F. "Stephen Dedalus and the Temper of the Modern Hero," in Approaches to Ulysses, pp. 3-28, No. 3657.

4619. STEINBERG, ERWIN R. "Rogues Tum Lingo: The Language of Stephen, Bloom, and Molly."

Carnegie Studies in English, 11 (1970): 21-30.

*4620. TELLO QUIJANO, JAIME (Jaime Tello). "Presentacion de 'Dedalus' Joyce y de 'Ulysses' Bloom. Revista de las Indias, series 2, no. 24 (June 1945): 347-360.

4621. VOGEL, JANE. "The Consubstantial Family of Stephen Dedalus." James Joyce Quarterly, 2 (Winter 1965): 108-132.

4622. WALCOTT, WILLIAM O. "The Paternity of James Joyce's Stephen Dedalus." Journal of Analytical Psychology, 10 (January 1965): 77-95.

4623. WASSON, RICHARD. "Stephen Dedalus and the Imagery of Sight: A Psychological Approach." Literature and Psychology, 15 (Fall 1965): 195-209.

And Others

4624. DALTON, JACK P. "Stately, Plump Buck Mulligan, in Djoytsch." James Joyce Quarterly, 4 (Spring 1967): 206-208.

4625. KNUTH, LEO. "How Stately was Plump Buck Mulligan?" James Joyce Quarterly, 7 (Spring 1970): 204-209.

MARTELLO TOWER, JAMES JOYCE MUSEUM

4626. BRYDEN, RONALD. "All Sons of Kings," Spectator, 22 June 1962, p. 823. [See also Ewart Milne's letter to the Editor, 6 July 1962, p. 16.]

4627. ELLMANN, RICHARD. James Joyce's Tower. Dun Loaghire: Eastern Regional Tourism Organization, 1969.

4628. GARVIN, JOHN. "Martellomache." Ireland of the Welcomes, 21 (July-August 1972): 7-10.

4629. GOGARTY, OLIVER ST. JOHN. "The Tower: Fact and Fiction." Irish Times, 16 June 1962, p. 11.

4630. GRAHAM, RIGBY. "Joyce's Tower, Sandycove." American Book Collector, 22 (November-December 1971): 16-19.

4631. IGOE, VIVIEN. "The Tower." Joycenotes, 1 (June 1969): 22-25. [List of items displayed in museum.]

4632. _____. "The Joyce Tower." Joycenotes, 2 (September 1969): 10-12.

4633. _____. "The Joyce Tower." Joycenotes, 3 (December 1969): 10-12.

4634. KAIN, RICHARD M. "James Joyce Slept Here: The Opening of the Joyce Tower Museum." James Joyce Quarterly, 1 (Summer 1964): 3-6.

ULYSSES

4635. MacNEICE, LOUIS. "Under the Sugar Loaf."
       New Statesman, 63 (29 June 1962): 948-949.

*4636. NICHOLS, LEWIS. "Tower." New York Times
       Book Review, 10 December 1961, p. 8.

4637. RUSSELL, FRANCIS. "Ulysses's Tower."
       Horizon, 11 (Summer 1969): 48-51.

4638. SENN, FRITZ. "The Tower." Joycenotes, 1
       (June 1969): 20-21.

4639. SUTCLIFFE, SHEILA. Martello Towers. New-
       ton Abbot: David and Charles, 1972;
       Rutherford, Madison, Teaneck, New Jersey:
       Farleigh Dickinson University Press, 1973.

4640. VEALE, VIVIEN. "The Martello Tower." James
       Joyce Quarterly, 3 (Summer 1966): 276-277.

4641. VERBER, RICH EARED. "Hommidge to mistra
       germ's choice." Dubliner, no. 3 (May-
       June 1962): 36-37.

4642. Unsigned. "Martello Tower Sold for £4700."
       Evening Press (Dublin), 1 December 1954.
       [See also Evening Herald (Dublin), 1
       December 1954; Irish Times, 2 December
       1954; Observer (London), 5 December 1954.]

4643. Unsigned. "Dublin ReJoyces." Newsweek, 60
       (2 July 1962): 80.

4644. Unsigned. "Home at Last to Dublin." St.
       Louis Post-Dispatch, 18 June 1962, p. 2C.

4645. Unsigned. "James Joyce Comes Home." New
       York Times, 16 June 1962, p. 18.

4646. Unsigned. "Martello Tower to be Joyce
       Museum." Irish Times, 3 February 1962.

4647. Unsigned. "Martello Tower to be Joyce
       Museum." Irish Independent, 5 February
       1962, p. 6.

4648. Unsigned. "Topics." New York Times, 22
       April 1962, section 4, p. 10.

4649. Unsigned. "Publisher of Ulysses Opens Joyce
       Museum." Eire, no. 579 (25 June 1962):
       4-5.

4650. Unsigned. "Ulysses Tower to be Joyce Muse-
       um." Times (London), 7 June 1962, p. 13;
       (18 June 1962): 7.

4651. Unsigned. "Will Establish Joyce Museum in
       Martello Tower." Irish Press, 3 February
       1962.

4652. Unsigned. Time, 79 (22 June 1962): 38.

"BLOOMSDAY"

4653. ALEXANDER, SIDNEY. "Bloomsday in Italy."
       The Reporter, 24 (13 April 1961): 38-42.

4654. BEACH, SYLVIA. "Portrait of the Artist."
       Irish Times, 16 June 1962, p. 10.

4655. BEURNIQUEL, CAMILLE. "Le retour d'Ulysse."
       Figaro littéraire, 30 June 1962, p. 21.

4656. GOPALEEN, MYLES na (Flann O'Brien, Brian
       Nolan). "J-Day." Irish Times, 16 June
       1954, p. 6.

*4657. HAYES, HAROLD. "Notes on this Bloomsday:
       Listening to James Joyce." Esquire, 54
       (July 1960): 22-24.

4658. JOHNSTON, DENIS. "Pleasurable Pilgrimages."
       Irish Times, 16 June 1962, p. 11.

4659. KENNER, HUGH. "Bloomsday in Trieste." Life,
       71 (8 October 1971).

4660. KONER, MARVIN. "Bloomsday in Dublin." Hol-
       iday, 45 (June 1969): 40-45.

4661. LAUGHLIN, ROBERT E. "Dublin to Mark Blooms-
       day." New York Times, 7 June 1964, sec-
       tion 10, p. 63.

4662. LEINWALL, GEORGE. "Bloomsday '70." Chesa-
       peake Weekly Review, 12 June 1970, p. 5.

*4663. McCAFFREY, JOHN. "A Joycean Pilgrimage to
       No. 7 Eccles Street." Irish Times, 14
       July 1959.

4664. MacDONAGH, DONAGH. "In the Steps of Leopold
       Bloom." Irish Times, 15 June 1954, p. 6;
       (16 June 1954): 6.

4665. MERCIER, VIVIAN. "Bloomsday in Gotham."
       New York Herald Tribune Magazine, 14
       June 1964, pp. 10-11.

4666. MITCHELL, CAROLINE. "Dress Show for Joyce
       Week." Irish Times, 16 June 1962, p. 11.

4667. MONTGOMERY, NIALL. "Dublin's Dublin." Irish
       Times, 16 June 1962, p. 10 [Bloomsday ar-
       ticles by Sylvia Beach, Flann O'Brien,
       and Quidnunc (Seamus Kelly).]

4668. MOULTON, HERBERT. "Bloomsday by Bus." Ire-
       land of the Welcomes, 21 (May-June 1963):
       13-18.

4669. MURPHY, TERRENCE J. "Bloomsday." New York
       Times, 16 June 1963, section 4, p. 10.

4670. O'FLAHERTY, GERRY. "Bloomsday in Dublin."
       James Joyce Quarterly, 4 (Fall 1966):
       50-51.

4671. PEARL, CYRIL. "Dublin 'Re-Joyce's' in
       Spring." Sydney Morning Herald, 21 May
       1966, p. 16.

4672. _____. "If Mr. Bloom went back to Dub-
       lin." Sydney Morning Herald, 11 June
       1966, p. 18.

4673. RONAN, THOMAS P. "Dublin to Honor Joyce Tomorrow." New York Times, 15 June 1962, pp. 29, 55.

4674. SCHECHNER, MARK. "City Walker: in Dublin or Buffalo: Bloomsday, 1972." Buffalo Evening News, 17 June 1972, p. B-7.

4675. WALD, RICHARD C. "Back to Dublin Town." New York Herald Tribune Books, 24 June 1962, pp. 3, 10.

4676. WEBB, W. L. "Bloomsday in Joycetown." Guardian, 16 June 1962, p. 5.

4677. Unsigned. "Bloomsday." Irish Times, 16 June 1954, p. 5.

4678. Unsigned. "Bloomsday." Die Welt, 16/17 June 1966.

4679. Unsigned. "Cab Trip to Joyce-Land, 'on the way to Finnegans Wake.'" Irish Press, 17 June 1954, p. 8.

4680. Unsigned. "An Irishman's Diary." Irish Times, 14 June 1954, p. 5.

4681. Unsigned. "The Anniversary." Irish Times, 16 June 1972, p. 11.

EXPLICATIONS

4682. ATHERTON, JAMES S. "'Snap!' in Ulysses." Wake Newslitter, 8 (August 1971): 53.

4683. BASS, RICHARD N. "Joyce's Ulysses." Explicator, 24 (February 1966): item 55.

4684. BENSTOCK, BERNARD. "Arthur Griffith in Ulysses: The Explosion of a Myth." English Language Notes, 4 (December 1966): 123-128.

4685. BERGER, ALFRED PAUL. "James Joyce, Adman." James Joyce Quarterly, 3 (Fall 1965): 25-33.

4686. BOWEN, ZACK. "Lizzie Twigg: Gone but not Forgotten." James Joyce Quarterly, 6 (Summer 1969): 368-370.

4687. BOYLE, ROBERT. "A Note on Reuben as 'a Dirty Jew.'" James Joyce Quarterly, 3 (Fall 1965): 64-66.

4688. _____. "Miracle in Black Ink: A Glance at Joyce's Use of his Eucharistic Image." James Joyce Quarterly, 10 (Fall 1972): 47-60.

4689. BRIAND, PAUL L. "The Catholic Mass in James Joyce's Ulysses." James Joyce Quarterly, 5 (Summer 1968): 312-322. [See also Patrick McCarthy, JJQ, 7 (Winter 1969): 132-137.]

4690. [BURGOS, ROGER]. "James Joyce and Tauromaquia." La Busca (Newsletter of the Taurine Bibliophiles of America), n.s. 1 (September 1966): 1-2. [Bullfighters in U; see also (October 1966): p. 8.]

4691. BUSS, RICHARD K. "James Joyce's Ulysses." Explicator, 24 (February 1966): item 55.

4692. CASTRONOVO, DAVID. "'Touching the Much Vexed Question of Stimulants': Drinkers and Drinking in James Joyce's Ulysses." November Review, no. 3 (Fall 1966): 20-45.

4693. DALTON, JACK P. "Two Notes." Joycenotes, 2 (September 1969): 2.

4694. DANO, FINN. "A Note on 'Eleven.'" James Joyce Quarterly, 5 (Spring 1968): 275-276.

4695. EVANS, WILLIAM A. "Wordagglutionations in Joyce's Ulysses." Studies in the Literary Imagination, 3 (October 1970): 27-36.

4696. GARVIN, JOHN. "The Trial of Festy King." Dublin Magazine, 9 (Autumn 1972): 36-43.

4697. GOLDMAN, ARNOLD. "Two Errors in Ulysses." Notes and Queries, 10 (April 1963): 146-148.

4698. HAMALIAN, LEO. "The 'Gift of Guild' in Ulysses." Renascence, 19 (Fall 1966): 21-29.

4699. JACOBSON, HOWARD. "Joyce and the Iliad: A Suggestion." James Joyce Quarterly, 7 (Winter 1969): 141-142.

4700. LYONS, J. B. "James Joyce and the Mirus Bazaar." Dublin Magazine, 7, nos. 2, 3, 4 (Autumn-Winter 1968): 40-42. [From his James Joyce and Medicine, No. 1611.]

4701. McALEER, JOHN. "The 'Father of Thousands' Image in Ulysses." Notes and Queries, 9 (August 1962): 306-307.

4702. McCARTHY, PATRICK A. "Further Notes on the Mass in Ulysses." James Joyce Quarterly, 7 (Winter 1970): 132-137. [See Paul L. Briand, No. 4689.]

4703. McNELLY, WILLIS E. "Liturgical Deviations in Ulysses." James Joyce Quarterly, 2 (Summer 1965): 291-298.

4704. MAXWELL, J. C. "An Echo of Niels Lyhne in Ulysses." Wake Newslitter, 9 (June 1972): 35.

4705. MICKELSON, ANNE. "Joyce's Ulysses." Explicator, 26 (March 1968): item 58.

4706. MOSELEY, VIRGINIA. "The Mary-Martha Theme in Ulysses." Midwest Quarterly, 4 (Winter 1963): 165-178.

ULYSSES

4707. NEUFELD, MARTHA R. "Mirrors and Photographs in James Joyce's Ulysses." November Review, 1 (November 1964): 11-33.

4708. O HEHIR, BRENDAN. "An Unnoticed Textual Crux in Ulysses." James Joyce Quarterly, 5 (Summer 1968): 296-298.

4709. PATERAKIS, DEBORAH TANNEN. "Mananaan MacLir in Ulysses." Éire-Ireland, 7 (Autumn 1972): 29-35. [See correction in 8 (Spring 1973): 131.]

4710. PRESCOTT, JOSEPH. "Mosenthal's Deborah and Joyce's Ulysses." Modern Language Notes, 67 (May 1952): 334-336.

4711. _____ . "Leopold Bloom's Memory Concerning Cormac's Death." Notes and Queries (London), 196 (29 September 1951): 434. [Bloom quotes Samuel Ferguson's "The Burial of King Cormac."]

4712. ROEFFEN, NELLY. "'Built on Bread and Onions.'" James Joyce Quarterly, 10 (Winter 1973): 263-264. [U 164.33.]

4713. RYAN, STEPHEN P. "Joyce's Father Cowley." Notes and Queries, 9 (August 1962): 305-306.

4714. SCHEURLE, WILLIAM. "Joyce's Ulysses." Explicator, 20 (April 1962): item 70.

4715. SENN, FRITZ. "The Duke of Beaufort's Ceylon." James Joyce Quarterly, 1 (Summer 1964): 64-65.

4716. _____ . "Breslin's Hotel." Joycenotes, 1 (June 1969): 6.

4717. _____ . "Chaste Delights." James Joyce Quarterly, 7 (Spring 1970): 253-254. ["Conjugal" or "conjugial" in U.]

4718. SILVERSTEIN, NORMAN. "Bruno's Particles of Reminiscence." James Joyce Quarterly, 2 (Summer 1965): 271-280.

4719. STAPLES, HUGH B. "Ribbonmen: Signs and Passwords in Ulysses." Notes and Queries, 13 (March 1966): 95-96.

4720. TOOR, DAVID. "Joyce's Ulysses." Explicator, 24 (April 1966): item 65.

4721. WHALEY, HELEN R. "The Role of the Blind Piano Tuner in Joyce's Ulysses." Modern Fiction Studies, 16 (Winter 1970-71): 531-535.

4722. WHITE, PATRICK. "The Key in Ulysses." James Joyce Quarterly, 9 (Fall 1971): 10-25. [See "Letter" by R. Danis O'Hanlon. JJQ, 10 (Winter 1973): 281-283.]

4723. WORTHINGTON, MABEL P. "Irish Folksongs in Joyce's Ulysses." Publications of the Modern Language Association, 71 (June 1956): 321-339. [Later appeared in Song in the Works of James Joyce, No. 1588.]

STUDIES OF THE INDIVIDUAL EPISODES

Telemachus

4724. GOGARTY, OLIVER ST. JOHN. "James Joyce: A Portrait of the Artist," in his Mourning Became Mrs. Spendlove. New York: Creative Age Press, 1948, pp. 39-61. [Originally in Tomorrow (1947).]

4725. KLEIN, A. M. "The Black Panther, A Study in Technique." Accent, 10 (Summer 1950): 139-155. [Very brief summary of this article appeared in College English, 12 (October 1950): 49.]

4726. LEVENSTON, E. A. "Narrative Technique in Ulysses: A Stylistic Comparison of 'Telemachus' and 'Eumaeus.'" Language and Style, 5 (Fall 1972): 260-275.

4727. McALEER, EDWARD. "James Joyce and Dr. Kuno Meyer." Notes and Queries, 204 (1959): 49-50.

4728. MAUGERI, ALDO. "Joyce e il preludio di Ulisse." Letterature moderne, 7 (January-February 1957): 52-59.

4729. MORSE, J. MITCHELL. "Another Goethe Allusion." James Joyce Quarterly, 3 (Winter 1966): 163. ["milkwoman's reckoning her bill" with Faust I, lines 2540-2552: "witch's hocus-pocus over her elixer of youth."]

4730. SOLOMON, ALBERT J. "Another Broken Mirror." James Joyce Quarterly, 5 (Spring 1968): 206-210. ["cracked lookinglass of a servant" and Wilde's The Decay of Living and Summa Theologica III. 76. 3.]

4731. THORNTON, WELDON. "An Allusion List for James Joyce's Ulysses: Part I. 'Telemachus.'" James Joyce Quarterly, 1 (Fall 1963): 17-25. [In his Allusions in Ulysses, No. 4406.]

Nestor

4732. CHURCH, MARGARET. "Joyce's Ulysses." Explicator, 19 (June 1961): item 66.

4733. DIBBLE, BRIAN. "Vico, Bruno, and Stephen Dedalus in Dalkey: An Analysis of the Nestor Episode of James Joyce's Ulysses." Barat Faculty Review, 1 (January 1966): 40-48.

4734. DUNDES, ALAN. "The Study of Folklore in Literature and Culture: Identification and Interpretation." Journal of American Folklore, 78 (April-June 1965): 136-142.

4735. KLEIN, A. M. "Shout in the Street: An Analysis of the Second Chapter of Joyce's Ulysses," in New Directions 13. Norfolk: New Directions Books, 1951, pp. 327-345.

4736. SENN, FRITZ. "Notes." James Joyce Quarterly, 1 (Summer 1964): 64-65. [U 33.12-13; 41.37-38.]

4737. THORNTON, WELDON. "An Allusion List for James Joyce's Ulysses; Part 2, 'Nestor.'" James Joyce Quarterly, 1 (Winter 1964): 2-9. [In his Allusions in Ulysses, No. 4406.]

Proteus

4738. EGRI, PÉTER. "Natura Naturans: An Approach to the Poetic Reflection of Reality. The Aspect of Poetry in the Proteus Episode of James Joyce's Ulysses." Acta litteraria academiae scientiarum hungaricae, 15, nos. 3-4 (1973): 379-417.

4739. GILBERT, STUART. "Prote: Ulysse." Échanges, no. 2 (March 1930): 118-134. [In his James Joyce's Ulysses, No. 3580.]

4740. KAIN, RICHARD M. "A Note on Frank Budgen's Sketch of the Proteus Episode." American Book Collector, 15 (June 1965): 6.

4741. SENN, FRITZ. "Aesthetic Theories." James Joyce Quarterly, 2 (Winter 1965): 134-136.

4742. STEINBERG, ERWIN R. "The Proteus Episode: Signature of Stephen Dedalus." James Joyce Quarterly, 5 (Spring 1968): 187-198.

4743. _____. "Characteristic Sentence Patterns in Proteus and Lestrygonians," in New Light on Joyce, pp. 79-98, No. 1656. [In his The Stream of Consciousness and Beyond in Ulysses, No. 4202.]

4744. SWANSON, WILLIAM J. "Les deux morte de Felix Faure." James Joyce Quarterly, 9 (Fall 1971): 129-130. [U 43-44.]

4745. THORNTON, WELDON. "An Allusion List for James Joyce's Ulysses--Part 3: 'Proteus.'" James Joyce Quarterly, 1 (Spring 1964): 25-41. [In his Allusions in Ulysses, No. 4406.]

*4746. UCHIDA, MICHIKO. "Daisan Sowa Tsuite ["On the Third Chapter]," in Joisu Nyumon [An Introduction to James Joyce], pp. 73-77, No. 1511.

4747. VON PHUL, RUTH. "The Beast of Heraldry in the 'Proteus' Episode of Ulysses." Journal of Modern Literature, 1 (March 1971): 399-405.

4748. WEISS, WOLFGANG. "James Joyce und Joachim von Fiore." Anglia, 85 (1967): 58-63.

Calypso

4749. BULHOF, FRANCIS. "Agendath Again." James Joyce Quarterly, 7 (Summer 1970): 326-332. [See also Charles Parish. "Agenbite of Agendath Netaim." JJQ, 6 (Spring 1969): 237-241.]

4750. GRANIER, MARIE-DANIÈLE. "Le Métonymie dans l'épisode 'Calypso' d'Ulysse." Univ. de Saint-Étienne, Travaux de linguistique et littérature, 3 (1971-72?): 67-80?.

4751. MOCHIZUKI, MITSUKO. "The Meanings of Episodes 4, 5, 6, in Joyce's Ulysses." Doshisha Women's College of Liberal Arts. Annual Reports of Studies, 21 (1970): 338-365. [In Japanese.]

4752. PARISH, CHARLES. "Agenbite of Agendath Netaim." James Joyce Quarterly, 6 (Spring 1969): 237-241. [See Francis Bulhof, No. 4749.]

4753. SCHWEGEL, DOUGLAS M. "Joyce's Ulysses, Calypso Episode." Explicator, 27 (March 1969): item 49.

4754. SENN, FRITZ. "Mulligan Heifer." James Joyce Quarterly, 2 (Winter 1965): 136-137. [See also Nos. 4755, 4756.]

4755. SOLOMON, AL. "Letter to the Editor." James Joyce Quarterly, 9 (Summer 1972): 496.

4756. THOMPSON, GEORGE. "Two More on 'Beef to the Heel.'" James Joyce Quarterly, 9 (Summer 1972): 495-496.

4757. THORNTON, WELDON. "An Allusion List for James Joyce's Ulysses--Part 4--'Calypso.'" James Joyce Quarterly, 1 (Summer 1964): 7-13. [In his Allusions in Ulysses, No. 4406.]

Lotus Eaters

4758. BAUERLE, RUTH. "Mercadante's 'Seven Last Words.'" Wake Newslitter, 8 (December 1971): 91.

4759. CORBEILLIER, PHILIPPE. "Explication u'une ligne de Ulysses." Revue Anglo-Americaine, 9 (December 1931): 145.

4760. PETTA, ROCHELLE. "From Corpus to Corpse: 'Lotus Eaters' to 'Hades,'" in The Celtic Bull, pp. 24-31, No. 3545.

4761. POMERANZ, VICTORY. "The Frowning Face of Bethel." James Joyce Quarterly, 10 (Spring 1973): 342-344.

ULYSSES

Hades

4762. BALDWIN, PETER, F.S.C. "Joyce's Ulysses, pp. 95-96." Explicator, 24 (December 1965): item 38.

4763. GILBERT, STUART. "Irish Ulysses: Hades Episode." Fortnightly, 132 (July 1929): 46-58. [Chapter 6 in his James Joyce's Ulysses, No. 3580.]

4764. HALLAM, CLIFFORD. "Mr. Bloom's Visit to Hell: A Withdrawal and a Return." Dickinson Review, 1 (Winter 1968): 16-21.

4765. HUNTER, JIM. "James Joyce," in The Modern Novel in English Studied in Extracts. London: Faber and Faber, 1966, pp. 32-47.

4766. POMERANZ, VICTORY. "O'Callaghan on His Last Legs." James Joyce Quarterly, 9 (Fall 1971): 136-138. [U 92]

*4767. TSUCHIYA, TORU. "Dairoku Sowa in Tsuite [On the Sixth Chapter]," in Joisu Nyumon [An Introduction to James Joyce], pp. 78-81, No. 1511.

Aeolus

4768. BRISKIN, IRENE ORGEL. "Some New Lights on 'The Parable of the Plums.'" James Joyce Quarterly, 3 (Summer 1966): 236-251.

4769. GILBERT, STUART. "The Aeolus Episode of Ulysses." transition, no. 18 (November 1929): 129-146. [Appeared as Chapter 7 in his James Joyce's Ulysses, No. 3580; translated by Nina Ferrer in Solaria (Florence), 5, no. 3 (March 1930): 30-46.]

4770. KAIN, RICHARD M. "The Yankee Interviewer in Ulysses," in A James Joyce Miscellany, Third Series, pp. 155-157, No. 1614.

4771. KEOGH, J. G. "Ulysses: 'Parable of the Plums' as Parable and Paraplum." James Joyce Quarterly, 7 (Summer 1970): 377-378.

4772. LEITCH, VINCENT B. "Myth in Ulysses: The Whirlwind and Hosea-Bloom." James Joyce Quarterly, 10 (Winter 1973): 267-269.

*4773. MARKS, LESTER. "The Theme of Loyalty to Lost Causes in the Episode of the Newspaper Office in James Joyce's Ulysses." Thoth, 1 (Spring 1959): 34-36.

4774. MUNDIGO, AXEL. "Decussated Keys in Dublin," in The Celtic Bull, pp. 32-38, No. 3545.

4775. PHELAN, FRANCIS. "A Source for the Headlines of 'Aeolus?'" James Joyce Quarterly, 9 (Fall 1971): 146-151.

4776. SULTAN, STANLEY. "Joyce's Irish Politics: The Seventh Chapter of Ulysses." Massachusetts Review, 2 (Spring 1961): 549-556.

4777. TOMPKINS, PHILLIP K. "James Joyce and the Enthymeme: The Seventh Episode of Ulysses." James Joyce Quarterly, 5 (Spring 1968): 199-205.

Lestrygonians

4778. ALBERT, LEONARD. "Ulysses, Cannibals, and Freemasons." A.D., 2 (Autumn 1951): 265-283.

4779. BAUERLE, RUTH. "Ambly Ulysses. Pia." James Joyce Quarterly, 9 (Fall 1971): 117-118. [U 158.12.]

4780. MUNDIGO, AXEL. "Bloom's Litany: Sacred and Profane," in The Celtic Bull, pp. 39-44, No. 3545.

4781. STEINBERG, ERWIN R. "'Lestrygonians,' A Pale 'Proteus?'" Modern Fiction Studies, 15 (Spring 1969): 73-86.

4782. SWANSON, ROY ARTHUR. "Edible Wandering Rocks: The Pun as Allegory in Joyce's 'Lestrygonians.'" Genre, 5 (December 1972): 385-403.

Scylla and Charybdis

See under "Allusions" sections, supra: Schutte. Joyce and..., No. 4404; Duncan. "Unsubstantial Father...," No. 4414; Edwards. "Hamlet Motif...," No. 4415; Heine. "Shakespeare...," No. 4419; Mayhew. "Joyce on...," No. 4424; Morse. "Mr. Joyce...," No. 4426; Peery. "Hamlet...," No. 4430; Bienkowski. "Bodziec," No. 4436.

4783. BASALLA, GEORGE. "Joyce's Ulysses." Explicator, 11 (December 1952): item 19.

4784. BERGER, HÉLÈNE. "Stephen, Hamlet, Will: Joyce par delà Shakespeare." Études anglaises, 17 (October-December 1964): 571-585.

4785. CHATTERJEE (or CHATTOPADHYAYA), SISIR. "A Joycean Formulation of a Ghoststory," in Shakespeare: A Book of Homage. Calcutta: Jadavpur University, 1965, pp. 66-79.

4786. COLUM, PADRAIC. "Dublin's Library and Joyce's Ulysses." New Republic, 132 (16 May 1955): 33-35.

4787. FESHBACH, SIDNEY. "About 'Autontimerumenos' (U 210.19)." James Joyce Quarterly, 9 (Summer 1972): 475-478.

4788. GILBERT, ALLAN. "Joyce's Ulysses." Explicator, 12 (1953): item 7.

4789. JENKINS, RALPH. "Theosophy in 'Scylla and Charybdis.'" Modern Fiction Studies, 15 (Spring 1969): 35-48.

4790. KAIN, RICHARD M. "James Joyce's Shakespeare Chronology." Massachusetts Review, 5 (Winter 1964): 342-355.

4791. _____. "Anne Hathaway's Puritan Tracts, U 204, 206." James Joyce Quarterly, 4 (Winter 1967): 150.

4792. _____. "Shakespeare in Ulysses: Additional Annotations." James Joyce Quarterly, 8 (Winter 1970): 176-177.

4793. _____. "'Your Dean of Studies' and His Theory of Shakespeare (U 205.15)." James Joyce Quarterly, 10 (Winter 1973): 262-263.

4794. LEHNAM, TREVOR. "The Happy Hunting Ground: Shakespearean Dramatis Personae in the 'Scylla and Charybdis' Episode of James Joyce's Ulysses." University of Toronto Quarterly, 29 (April 1960): 386-397. [Appeared in A James Joyce Miscellany, Third Series, pp. 158-174, No. 1614.]

4795. MARCUS, PHILLIP L. "A Possible Anachronism in 'Scylla and Charybdis.'" James Joyce Quarterly, 3 (Summer 1966): 294-295.

4796. _____. "Notes on Irish Elements in 'Scylla and Charybdis.'" James Joyce Quarterly, 10 (Spring 1973): 312-320.

4797. MEDIOLI, JOANN. "Sabellian Shakespeare: Bull, Ba'al, or Bard?," in The Celtic Bull, pp. 45-53, No. 3545.

4798. RADFORD, F. L. "'Christfox in Leather Trews': The Quaker in the Library in Ulysses." ELH: Journal of English Literary History, 39 (September 1972): 441-458.

4799. SCHUTTE, WILLIAM M. "Allusions in 'Scylla and Charybdis': A Supplement to Weldon Thornton's List." James Joyce Quarterly, 7 (Summer 1970): 315-325.

4800. SHARPE, GAROLD. "The Philosophy of James Joyce." Modern Fiction Studies, 9 (Summer 1963): 120-126.

*4801. TAKANO, FUMI. "Daiku Sowa in Tsuite ["On the Ninth Chapter]," in Joisu Nyumon [An Introduction to James Joyce], pp. 82-85, No. 1511.

4802. WALCUTT, CHARLES C. "Joyce's Ulysses." Explicator, 14 (March 1956): item 37.

4803. WOODBERY, POTTER. "The Blueribboned Hat: A Possible Reference to Emma Clery in Ulysses." James Joyce Quarterly, 7 (Winter 1969): 151-152.

Wandering Rocks

4804. BENJAMIN, JUDY-LYNN. "'The Wandering Rocks': The Heart of Ulysses," in The Celtic Bull, pp. 54-61, No. 3545.

4805. ELLIOTT, JOHN R. "Father Conmee and the Number of the Elect." James Joyce Review, 3, nos. 1-2 (February 1959): 62-64.

4806. GUIDACCI, MARGHERITA. "Sul capitolo X dell 'Ulisse." Humanitas, 17 (February 1962): 130-137.

4807. KNUTH, LEO. "James Joyce's Ulysses, Chapter X: 'Wandering Rocks.'" Language and Literature (Copenhagen), 1 (Winter 1972): 30-54.

4808. _____. "A Bathymetric Reading of Joyce's Ulysses, Chapter X." Dutch Quarterly Review, 2 (1972): 49-64. [Reprinted in James Joyce Quarterly, 9 (Summer 1972): 405-422.]

4809. OBLER, PAUL C. "Joyce's Numerology." James Joyce Review, 3, nos. 1-2 (February 1959): 53-56.

4810. SENN, FRITZ. "Cabbage Leaves." James Joyce Quarterly, 2 (Winter 1965): 137-138.

4811. _____. "No Trace of Hell." James Joyce Quarterly, 7 (Spring 1970): 255-256.

4812. SMITH, LESLIE. "Homer and Apollonius on the Wandering Rocks." James Joyce Quarterly, 9 (Summer 1972): 479-481.

Sirens

4813. BENJAMIN, JUDY-LYNN. "A Symphony for Callipe," in The Celtic Bull, pp. 62-69, No. 3545.

4814. BOWEN, ZACK. "The Bronzegold Sirensong: A Musical Analysis of the Sirens Episode of Joyce's Ulysses." Literary Monographs I. Edited by Eric Rothstein and Thomas K. Dunseath. Madison: University of Wisconsin Press, 1967, pp. 255-298, 319-320.

4815. COLE, DAVID W. "Fugal Structure in the Sirens Episode of Ulysses." Modern Fiction Studies, 19 (Summer 1973): 221-226.

4816. HARDY, ANNE. "A Fugal Analysis of the Sirens Episode in Joyce's Ulysses." Massachusetts Studies in English, 2 (Spring 1970): 59-67.

*4817. HIDAKA, HACHIRO. "Daijuichi Sowa in Tsuite ["On the Eleventh Chapter]," in Joisu Nyumon [An Introduction to James Joyce], pp. 86-93, No. 1511.

ULYSSES

4818. KAPLAN, MARIAN. "The Search for the 'Song of the Sirens.'" James Joyce Review, 3, nos. 1-2 (February 1959): 51-53.

4819. KOEGLER, HORST. "James Joyce oder die Literarische Metamorphose der Musik." Schweizerische Musikzeitung und Sängerblatt, 93 (1953): 257-260.

4820. LEVIN, LAWRENCE. "The Sirens Episode as Music: Joyce's Experiment in Prose Polyphony." James Joyce Quarterly, 3 (Fall 1965): 12-24.

4821. NOON, WILLIAM T., S.J. "Song the Syrens Sange." Mosaic, 6 (Fall 1972): 77-84.

4822. OGAWA, YOSHIHIKO. "Three Allusions in 'The Sirens.'" James Joyce Quarterly, 10 (Winter 1973): 269-270.

4823. PRESCOTT, JOSEPH. "A Song in Joyce's Ulysses." Notes and Queries, 197 (5 January 1952): 15-16.

4824. SALUS, PETER H. "Joyce's Ulysses, II, viii." Explicator, 23 (May 1965): item 67.

4825. SULTAN, STANLEY. "Sirens at the Ormond Bar: Ulysses." University of Kansas City Review, 26 (December 1959): 83-92.

Cyclops

4826. BIRO, DIANA. "Leopold in Norman's Land: The 5:00 Chapter of Ulysses." Thoth, 11 (1971): 9-21.

4827. COHN, ALAN M. "Douglas Hyde in Ulysses." English Studies, 43 (August 1962): 255-256.

4828. FINHOLT, RICHARD D. "Methods in the Cyclops Episode: Joyce on the Nature of Epic Heroes in the Modern World." University of Dayton Review, 9 (Summer 1972): 3-13.

4829. HARTLEY, SANDRA. "Bloom's Dilemma: Odysseus versus the Cyclops," in The Celtic Bull, pp. 70-73, No. 3545.

4830. HERRING, PHILIP F. "Joyce's Politics," in New Light on Joyce, pp. 3-14, No. 1656.

4831. HODGART, MATTHEW. "A Viconian Sentence in Ulysses." Orbis litterarum, 19 (1964): 201-204. [U 338.30-40.]

4832. POMERANZ, VICTORY. "Letter to the Editor." James Joyce Quarterly, 11 (Fall 1973): 76-77.

4833. RANKIN, H. D. "Joyce's Satyr-Play: The 'Cyclops' Episode in Ulysses." Agora, 2 (Winter 1973): 3-12.

4834. SUGGS, JON C. "Joyce's Deadwood Dick." James Joyce Quarterly, 10 (Spring 1973): 344-345.

Nausicaa

4835. HOHOFF, CURT. "Die Schwarze Summa des James Joyce." Hochland, 51 (August 1959): 534-544. [Reprinted in Schnittpunkte Gesammelte Aufsätze. Stuttgart: Deutsche Vlgs-Anstalt, 1963, pp. 206-221.]

4836. KÖHLER, ERICH. "Nausikaa, Danae, und Gerty McDowell: Zur Literaturgeschichte des Feuerwerkes," in Lebende Antike, pp. 451-472, No. 644.

4837. MESKIN, CAROL. "The Paralleled Virgin and the Unparalleled Mother," in The Celtic Bull, pp. 74-76, No. 3545.

4838. RASBRIDGE, W. J. "Giltrap and Garryowen." Times Literary Supplement, 9 January 1964, p. 27; (19 March 1971): 325.

4839. SENN, FRITZ. "Symbolic Juxtaposition." James Joyce Quarterly, 5 (Spring 1968): 276-278.

Oxen of the Sun

4840. ATHERTON, JAMES S. "The Peacock in the Oxen." Wake Newslitter, 7 (October 1970): 77-78.

4841. _____. "Still More Peacock in the Oxen." Wake Newslitter, 8 (August 1971): 53.

4842. BAUERLE, RUTH. "A Sober Drunken Speech: Stephen's Parodies in 'The Oxen of the Sun.'" James Joyce Quarterly, 5 (Fall 1967): 40-46.

4843. COHN, ALAN M. "Joyce's Notes on the end of 'The Oxen of the Sun.'" James Joyce Quarterly, 4 (Spring 1967): 194-201.

4844. HERRING, PHILIP F. "More Peacock in the Oxen." Wake Newslitter, 8 (August 1971): 51-53.

*4845. HOHOFF, CURT. "Die Ochsen der Sonne: Zu briefen von James Joyce." Suddeutsche Zeitung, 26/27 April 1958. [Later reprinted as "Ezra Pounds irischer Zögling: in London wurde der Briefwechsel James Joyce--Ezra Pound Veröffentlicht." Der Tagesspiegel (Berlin), 22 June 1958.]

4846. ISER, WOLFGANG. "Historische Stilformen in Joyce's Ulysses: Zur Interpretation des Kapitels 'The Oxen of the Sun,'" in Lebende Antike, pp. 433-450, No. 644.

4847. KLEIN, A. M. "'The Oxen of the Sun.'" Here and Now, 1 (January 1949): 28-48.

*4848. LENNON, MICHAEL J. "The End of the 'Oxen of the Sun.'" Analyst, 15 (March 1958): 14-16.

4849. MASON, ELLSWORTH. "The Oxen of the Sun." Analyst, 10 (March 1956): 10-18.

4850. WEISS, DANIEL. "The End of the 'Oxen of the Sun.'" Analyst, 9 (1956): 1-16.

*4851. YAMAKAWA, GAKUJI. "Daijushi Sowa in Tsuite ["On the Fourteenth Chapter]," in Joisu Nyumon [An Introduction to James Joyce], pp. 94-97, No. 1511.

Circe

4852. ARNERI, GABRIJELA. "Les travestissements de Saint Antoine." Studia romanica et anglica Zagrabiensia, no. 13-14 (July-December 1962): 31-42. [Comparison of 'Circe' with Flaubert's Tentation de Saint Antoine.]

4853. BOLDEREFF, FRANCES MOTZ. A Blakean Translation of Joyce's Circe. Woodward, Pa.: Classic Non-Fiction Library, 1965.

4854. COHN, RUBY. "Absurdity in English: Joyce and O'Neill." Comparative Drama, 3 (Fall 1969): 156-161.

4855. ELLENBOGEN, EILEEN. "Examination of Joyce." Times Litterary Supplement, 6 November 1948, p. 625.

4856. GLASHEEN, ADALINE. "Another Note on Ulysses." James Joyce Quarterly, 7 (Summer 1970): 379. [Controversy over Aristotle and Phyllis in U 432; see Ruth von Phul. JJQ, 8 (Winter 1970): 180-181; Glasheen. JJQ, 8 (Winter 1970): 185; Alan M. Cohn. JJQ, 9 (Fall 1971): 131-133; Louis O. Mink. JJQ, 9 (Fall 1971): 134-135.]

4857. HERRING, PHILIP F. "Some Corrections and Additions to Norman Silverstein's 'Magic on the Notesheets of the Circe Episode.'" James Joyce Quarterly, 2 (Spring 1965): 217-226. [See No. 4869.]

4858. JARRELL, MACKIE L. "Joyce's Use of Swift's Polite Conversation in the 'Circe' Episode of Ulysses." Publications of the Modern Language Association, 72 (June 1957): 545-554.

4859. KORG, JACOB. "A Possible Source of the Circe Chapter of Joyce's Ulysses." Modern Language Notes, 71 (February 1956): 96-98.

4860. LINK, VIKTOR. Bau und Funktion der Circe-Episode im Ulysses von James Joyce. Bonn: Rheinische Friedrich-Wilhelms-Univ., 1970.

4861. MERTON, THOMAS. "Correspondence." Sewanee Review, 76 (Autumn 1968): 694.

4862. NASSAR, EUGENE PAUL. "'Nighttown': Joyce's Ulysses," in The Rape of Cinderella: Essays in Literary Continuity. Bloomington, London: Indiana University Press, 1970, pp. 58-70.

*4863. OHASHI, KENSABURO. "Daijugo Sowa in Tsuite ["On the Fifteenth Chapter]," in Joisu Nyumon [An Introduction to James Joyce], pp. 98-101, No. 1511.

4864. PARIS, JEAN. "Joyce au Bordel." Cahiers de la Compagnie Madeleine Renaud-Jean Louis Barrault, no. 37 (February 1962): 32-36.

4865. PIWINSKA, MARTA. "Drogi z nocnego miasta." Dialog (Warsaw), 9 (December 1964): 93-103.

4866. POSS, STANLEY. "Ulysses and the Comedy of Immobilized Art." ELH: Journal of English Literary History, 24 (March 1957): 65-83.

4867. PRICE, ROSEMARY. "Nighttown: Lethartic Cathargy," in The Celtic Bull, pp. 77-82, No. 3545.

4868. SCHNEIDER, ULRICH. "Freemasonic Signs and Passwords in the 'Circe' Episode." James Joyce Quarterly, 5 (Summer 1968): 303-311.

4869. SILVERSTEIN, NORMAN. "Magic on the Notesheets of the 'Circe' Episode." James Joyce Quarterly, 1 (Summer 1964): 19-26. [See reply by Herring, No. 4857.]

4870. _____. "Evolution of the Nighttown Setting," in The Celtic Master, pp. 27-36, No. 1583.

4871. WIRPSZA, WITOLD. "Matnia i siec." Dialog (Warsaw), 9 (December 1964): 104-112.

Eumaeus

4872. BASS, RICHARD K. "Joyce's Ulysses." Explicator, 24 (February 1966): item 55.

4873. _____. "Additional Allusions in 'Eumaeus.'" James Joyce Quarterly, 10 (Spring 1973): 321-329.

4874. FEENEY, WILLIAM J. "Ulysses and the Phoenix Park Murder." James Joyce Quarterly, 1 (Summer 1964): 56-58.

4875. HALL, VERNON. "Joyce's Ulysses, XVI." Explicator, 12 (February 1954): item 25.

4876. KAIN, RICHARD M. "A Possible Source for the Galway Bay Accident in Ulysses." James Joyce Quarterly, 6 (Fall 1968): 82-83.

4877. KOLBE, JOANN. "Parallel/Parallax," in The Celtic Bull, pp. 83-95, No. 3545.

ULYSSES

4878. WORTHINGTON, MABEL P. "Joyce's Ulysses, XVI." Explicator, 13 (December 1954): item 20.

Ithaca

4879. CHURCH, MARGARET. "Joyce's Ulysses." Explicator, 19 (June 1961): item 66.

4880. COPLAND, R. A., and G. W. TURNER. "The Nature of James Joyce's Parody in 'Ithaca.'" Modern Language Review, 64 (October 1969): 759-763.

4881. CROSMAN, ROBERT. "Who was M'Intosh?" James Joyce Quarterly, 6 (Winter 1968): 128-136.

4882. DeCURTIS, ANTHONY. "An Error in Ulysses." James Joyce Quarterly, 11 (Fall 1973): 54-55.

4883. DOXEY, WILLIAM S. "'Ithaca's' Westward-Turning Earth: A New Portal of Discovery in Ulysses." James Joyce Quarterly, 7 (Summer 1970): 371-374. [See Benjamin W. Griffith, No. 4886.]

4884. FLEISHMAN, AVROM. "Science in Ithaca." Wisconsin Studies in Contemporary Literature, 8 (Summer 1967): 377-391.

4885. GOLDMAN, ARNOLD. "Stephen's Parleyvoce: Ulysses, pp. 672-674." James Joyce Quarterly, 8 (Winter 1970): 157-162.

4886. GRIFFITH, BENJAMIN W. "Bloom and Molly 'Carried Westward': An Alternate Reading." James Joyce Quarterly, 9 (Fall 1971): 122. [Reply to William S. Doxey, No. 4883.]

4887. HALL, VERNON. "Joyce's Ulysses." Explicator, 10 (June 1952): item 57.

4888. MADTES, RICHARD E. "Joyce and the Building of Ithaca." ELH: Journal of English Literary History, 31 (December 1964): 443-459.

4889. MILGATE, W. "Joyce's Scientific Dialogue." James Joyce Quarterly, 9 (Fall 1971): 143-145.

4890. SENN, FRITZ. "Wilderness." James Joyce Quarterly, 4 (Spring 1967): 245. [Translation of U 682.15.]

4891. SMITH, GROVER. "The Cryptogram in Joyce's Ulysses: A Misprint." Publications of the Modern Language Association, 73 (September 1958): 446-447.

4892. WATSON, EDWARD A. "Stoom--Bloom: Scientific Objectivity versus Romantic Subjectivity in the Ithaca Episode of Joyce's Ulysses." University of Windsor Review, 2 (Fall 1966): 11-25.

4893. WORTHINGTON, MABEL P. "Joyce's Ulysses." Explicator, 21 (January 1963): item 37.

Penelope

4894. CARD, JAMES VAN DYCK. "The Misleading Mr. McAlmon and Joyce's Typescript." James Joyce Quarterly, 7 (Winter 1969): 143-147.

4895. _____. "A Gibralter Sourcebook for 'Penelope.'" James Joyce Quarterly, 8 (Winter 1970): 163-175.

4896. _____. "'Contradicting': The Word for Joyce's 'Penelope.'" James Joyce Quarterly, 11 (Fall 1973): 17-26.

4897. GOLDSTONE, HERBERT. "Not so Puzzling Pinter: 'The Homecoming.'" Theatre Annual, 25 (1969): 20-27.

4898. MOSELEY, VIRGINIA. "Joyce's Ulysses (Epilogue)." Explicator, 22 (March 1964): item 60.

4899. NOVAK, JANE. "Verisimilitude and Vision: Defoe and Blake as Influences on Joyce's Molly Bloom." Carrell, no. 8 (1967): 7-20.

4900. RICHARDSON, ROBERT O. "Molly's Last Words." Twentieth Century Literature, 12 (January 1967): 177-185.

*4901. SUZUKI, KENZO. "Daijuhachi Sowa in Tsuite ["On the Eighteenth Chapter]," in Joisu Nyumon [An Introduction to James Joyce], pp. 102-105, No. 1511.

4902. TINDALL, WILLIAM YORK. "Dante and Mrs. Bloom." Accent, 11 (Spring 1951): 85-92.

4903. TOLOMEO, DIANE. "The Final Octagon of Ulysses." James Joyce Quarterly, 10 (Summer 1973): 439-454.

4904. WELLS, JOEL. "The Night Thoughts of Cinderella, by J*M*S J*Y*E," in Grim Fairy Tales for Adults. New York: Macmillan; London: Collier-Macmillan, 1967, pp. 5-10. [Parody.]

FINNEGANS WAKE

See also Adams. James Joyce..., 172-213, No. 1506; Arnold. James Joyce, 55-86, No. 1512; Astre. "James Joyce et la durée," No. 955; Barrett. "Myth or the Museum," 312-350, No. 1515; Beaslai. "Was Joyce Inspired by...," No. 958; Bell. The English Novel, 71-86, No. 29; Bierman. "Ulysses and...," No. 1692; Bonheim. Joyce's Benefictions, passim, No. 1524; Budgen. James Joyce and the Making..., 282-313, No. 3557; Burbridge. "A Joyce Source...," No. 965; Burgess. Re-Joyce, 177-272, No. 1533; Burgess. Joycesprick, 135-178, No. 1536; Burgess. The Novel Now, 22-37, No. 1534; Burgum. The Novel and the World's..., 109-119, No. 3745; Cambon.

"Ancora su Joyce," No. 1705; Carbello. Dieeinueve..., No. 1359; Collins. "Progression...," No. 1710; Colum, M. Life and the Dream, passim, No. 297; Colum, P. "Working with Joyce," No. 395; Connolly, Cyril. Condemned Playground, 7-15, No. 1711; Crosse. Flaubert and Joyce, 186-191, No. 1546; Daiches. Novel and the Modern..., 147-157, No. 1548; Daiches. Critical History..., 1135, No. 1549; Duncan. "James Joyce and the Primitive...," No. 975; Eastman. Literary Mind..., 97-102, No. 581; Eco. Poetice..., 113-163, No. 5259; Eglinton. Irish Literary..., 131-158, No. 307; Evans. English Literature..., 40-48, No. 193; Faj. "Probable Byzantine...," No. 1724; Fehr. Die Englische Literatur..., 56-58, No. 1559; Fowlie. Clown's Grail..., 96-109, No. 982; Gilbert. Letters, 213, 224-225, 247-248, 263, No. 317; Gillet. Claybook..., 43-85, No. 1568; Golding. James Joyce, 142-156, No. 1575; Goldman. Joyce Paradox, passim, No. 1576; Goldman. James Joyce, 8-10, 73-102, No. 1577; Griffin. Wild Geese..., 40-45, No. 1579; Gross. James Joyce, 75-89, No. 1580; Hackett. On Judging Books, 51-60, No. 4932; Halper. "James Joyce and Rebecca West," No. 793; Hayman. Joyce et Mallarmé, 121-181, No. 932; Hendry, J. F. "James Joyce...," No. 1449; Hodgart and Worthington. Song in the Works of..., No. 1588; Hoffman. Freudianism..., 122-215, 139-146, No. 934; Hollingdale. "A Note on Joyce and Bruno...," No. 5433; Hutchins. James Joyce's World, 214-230, No. 326; Hutchins. "James Joyce and the Cinema," No. 471; Jacquot. Melanges..., 135-159, No. 3425; Jones. James Joyce and the Common Reader, 149-158, No. 3602; Kelleher. "Notes...," No. 5438; Kenner. Dublin's Joyce, 265-270, No. 1600; Larbaud. Ce Vice..., 230-252, No. 1602; Lestra. "Joyce ou la purete ...," No. 1759; Levin. Contexts..., 280-285, No. 938; Levin. Critical Introduction, 139-205, No. 1603; Litz. Art of..., 76-128, No. 1605; Litz. James Joyce, 99-111, No. 1606; McAlmon. Being Geniuses..., passim, No. 336; McLuhan. "James Joyce: Trivial...," No. 999; McCarthy. Criticism..., 296-311, No. 1611a; Magalaner. "James Joyce and the Myth of Man," No. 1001; Magalaner. "James Joyce and Marie Corelli," No. 940; Magalaner and Kain. Joyce: The Man..., 216-255, No. 1615; Majault. Joyce, No. 1616; Mallam. "Joyce and Rabelais," No. 1002; Mason. "Mr. Stanislaus Joyce...," No. 496; Mayoux. Joyce, No. 1619; Mercanton. Poetes..., 57-69, No. 1620; Mercanton. "Les Heures...," No. 880; Mercier. Joyce and Irish..., 226-236, No. 4265; Misra. Indian..., 42-57, No. 941; Moholy-Nagy. Vision in Motion, 344-351, No. 1621; Moody. History..., No. 229; Morse. Sympathetic Alien..., 38-67, No. 339; Moseley. Joyce and the Bible, 144-150, No. 942; Naganowski. Telemach..., 137-167, No. 3632; Neill. Short History..., 319-324, No. 231; Noon. Joyce and Aquinas, 126-160, No. 943; O'Brien. Conscience..., 217-228, No. 1628; O'Faolain. "Style...," No. 5152; Paris. James Joyce..., No. 1632; Peter. "Joyce and the Novel," No. 1484; Pinguentini. James Joyce in Italia, 276-313, No. 1634; Prescott. "Two Manuscripts...," No. 5164; Ponce. "Musil and Joyce," No. 702. Raleigh. "My Brother's Keeper...," No. 522; Rivolain. Litterature..., passim, No. 1640; Ross. Music and Joyce,

No. 2425; Rowland. "James Joyce...," No. 1206; Rubin. "Joyce and Sterne...," No. 1014; Russel. "Joyce and Alexandria...," No. 5300; Ryf. New Approach..., 98-105, No. 3271; Sanchez. Panorama ..., 130-134, No. 1646; Sell. "Fusion of...," No. 1807; Semmler. For the Uncanny Man, 93-108, 121-126, No. 1653; Sergeant. "A Study of James Joyce," No. 4246; Soupault. Souvenirs..., 57-91, No. 547; Spender. Struggle of the Modern, 189-206, No. 1658; Spoerri. Finnegans Wake by James Joyce, No. 125; Staples. "Joyce and Cryptology," No. 1818; Stewart. Eight..., 465-483, No. 1665; Stewart. James Joyce, 32-37, No. 1664; Spivey. "Reintegration...," No. 1815; Stief. Moderne literatur..., 132-135, No. 1666; Straumann. "Das Zeitproblem...," No. 1668; Strong. Sacred River..., passim, No. 949; Svevo. "Svevo et Joyce," No. 782; Sweeney. "The Word was his Oyster," No. 1224; Tindall. James Joyce: His Way..., 51-94, No. 1677; Tindall. Reader's Guide..., 237-296, No. 1678; Tysdahl. Joyce and Ibsen, 123-210, No. 952; Ussher. Three Great..., 115-118, 139-150, No. 4967; Waldron. The Novels of..., 11-15, No. 1684; Wilson. Axel's Castle, 225-236, No. 1686; Zhantieve. Dzheims Dzhois. 87-90, No. 257. [See Section I.E "Reviews of Joyce's Works," Nos. 2245-2333, 2155-2207, 2208-2221, 2222-2240; I.F "Dissertations," Nos. 2515-2535.]

GENERAL STUDIES

Books

4905. ADAMS, J. DONALD. The Shape of Books to Come. New York: Viking Press, 1944, pp. xii, 12-15, 62. [Appeared, in abbreviated form, as "Speaking of Books." New York Times Book Review, 16 February 1944, p. 2.]

4906. BECKETT, SAMUEL et al. Our Exagmination Round His Factification for Incamination of Work in Progress. Paris: Shakespeare and Co., 1929. [Appeared in London: Faber and Faber, 1936; appeared as An Exagmination of James Joyce. Norfolk: New Directions Books, 1939; translated by Francesco Saba Sardi, "Preface" by Sylvia Beach, as Introduzione a Finnegans Wake. Milan: Sugar, 1964; reprinted London: Faber and Faber; New York: New Directions, 1972, with introduction by Sylvia Beach, pp. vii-viii, paperback reprint.]
  Contents: Samuel Beckett. "Dante... Bruno. Vico...Joyce," 1-22, No. 4907; Marcel Brion. "The Idea of Time in the Work of James Joyce," 25-33, No. 4284; Frank Budgen. "James Joyce's 'Work in Progress' and Old Norse Poetry," 37-46, No. 5355; Stuart Gilbert. "Prolegomena to 'Work in Progress,'" 49-75, No. 4930; Eugene Jolas. "The Revolution of Language and James Joyce," 79-92, No. 5261; Victor Llona. "I Don't Know What to call it but it's Mighty Unlike Prose," 95-102, No. 5264; Robert McAlmon. "Mr. Joyce Directs an Irish Word Ballet," 105-116, No. 5265; Thomas McGreevy. "The Catholic Element in 'Work in Progress,'" 119-127, No. 5459; Elliot Paul. "Mr. Joyce's Treatment of Plot," 131-137,

FINNEGANS WAKE

No. 5317; John Rodker. "Joyce and His Dy-
namic," 141-146, No. 5297; Robert Sage.
"Before Ulysses--and After," 149-170, No.
4957; William Carlos Williams. "A Point
for American Criticism," 173-185, No.
4970; G. V. L. Slingsby. "Writes a Common Reader," 189-191, No. 4961; Vladimir
Dixon. "A Letter to Mr. James Joyce,"
193-194, No. 4926.

4907. BECKETT, SAMUEL. "Dante...Bruno. Vico...
Joyce," in Our Exagmination, pp. 1-22,
No. 4906. [Reprinted in A Bash in the
Tunnel, pp. 21-34, No. 1644.]

4908. BEGNAL, MICHAEL H. "James Joyce and the
Mythologizing of History," in Directions
in Literary Criticism: Contemporary Approaches to Literature. [Festschrift for
Henry W. Sams.] University Park and London: Pennsylvania State University Press,
1973, pp. 211-219.

4909. BENSTOCK, BERNARD. Joyce-Again's Wake: An
Analysis of Finnegans Wake. Seattle:
University of Washington Press, 1965.

4910. BOUCHET, ANDRE du. James Joyce: Finnegans
Wake. Introduction by Michel Butor.
Suivis de ALP. Paris: Gallimard, 1962.

4911. BRANDEIS, IRMA. "Finn Again!," in Jiggery
Pokery. Edited by Anthony Hecht and John
Hollander. New York: Antheneum Press,
1967, p. 109. [Reprinted with a note by
Ruth Von Phul. Wake Newslitter, 5 (Feb-
ruary 1968): 3.]

4912. BROWN, NORMAN O. Closing Time. New York:
Random House, 1973.

*4913. BURBANK, REX. "The Skin of our Teeth," in
his Thornton Wilder. Twayne's United
States Authors Series, no. 5. New York:
Twayne, 1961, pp. 101-104.

4914. BURGESS, ANTHONY. A Shorter Finnegans Wake.
New York: Viking, 1966.

4915. CAMPOS, AUGUSTO de, and HAROLDO, eds. Panaroma do Finnegans Wake. Coleção Ensaio,
no. 23. São Paulo: Conselho Estadual de
Cultura, Comissão de Literature, 1962.
   Contents: Haroldo de Campos. "Panaroma em Portugues," 7-12, No. 4918; "Finnegans Wake/Ficcicius Revém--fragmentos,"
13-56; Lewis Carroll. "Jabberwock/Jaguad-
arte," translated by Augusto de Campos,
58-59, No. 4916; Campbell and Robinson.
"Introdução a um assunto estranho," translated by Augusto de Campos, 61-73 (from
No. 5523); Augusto de Campos. "O lance de
dados do Finnegans Wake," 75-80, No. 4917;
"James Joyce: Síntese biobibliografica,"
81-82; "Bibliografia consultada," 83-85.

4916. CAMPOS, AUGUSTO de, translator. "Lewis Carroll, Jabberwocky/Jaguadarte," in Pano-
roma do Finnegans Wake, pp. 58-59, No.
4915.

4917. _____. "O lance de dados do Finnegans
Wake," in Panaroma do Finnegans Wake, pp.
75-80, No. 4915. [Reprinted from O Estado
de São Paulo, "Supplemento literario," 29
November 1958.]

4918. CAMPOS, HAROLDO de. "Panaroma em Portugues,"
in Panaroma do Finnegans Wake, pp. 7-12,
No. 4915.

4919. COLUM, PADRAIC. "In Memory of James Joyce,"
in Twelve and a Tilly, pp. 9-10, No. 4923.
[Poem; slightly changed reprint from his
Irish Elegies (1961).]

*4920. CONNOLLY, THOMAS E., ed. Scribbledehobble,
The Ur-Workbook for Finnegans Wake. Ev-
anston, Ill.: Northwestern University
Press, 1961.

4921. COOK, ALBERT. Prisms: Studies in Modern Literature. Bloomington, London: Indiana
University Press, 1967, pp. 48-50, et
passim.

4922. DALTON, JACK P. "- -," in A Wake Digest,
pp. 69-70, No. 4935. [See also his "The
FW Concordance: A Further Note." James
Joyce Quarterly, 6 (Spring 1960): 275,
and reply by Nathan Halper, 7 (Summer
1970): 375-376.]

4923. DALTON, JACK P., and CLIVE HART, eds. Twelve
and a Tilly: Essays on the Occasion of the
25th Anniversary of Finnegans Wake. Ev-
anston: Northwestern University Press;
London: Faber and Faber, 1966.
   Contents: Padraic Colum. "In Memory of
James Joyce," 9-10, No. 4919; Frank Budgen.
"Resurrection," 11-15, No. 5312; Frederick
J. Hoffman. "'The Seim Anew': Flux and Fam-
ily in Finnegans Wake," 16-25, No. 5316;
Vivian Mercier. "James Joyce and the Mac-
aronic Tradition," 26-35, No. 5362; Fritz
Senn. "Insects Appalling," 36-39, No. 5529;
Robert F. Gleckner. "Byron in Finnegans
Wake," 40-51, No. 5359; James S. Atherton.
"Sport and Games in Finnegans Wake," 52-
64, No. 5520; J. Mitchell Morse. "On Teach-
ing Finnegans Wake, 65-71, No. 4955; Nathan
Halper. "The Date of Earwicker's Dream,"
72-90, No. 5524; Richard M. Kain. "'Nothing Odd will do Long': Some Thoughts on
Finnegans Wake Twenty-five Years Later,"
91-98, No. 4946; A. Walton Litz. "Uses of
the Finnegans Wake Manuscript," 99-106,
No. 4948; David Hayman. "'Scribbledehobbles' and How they Grew: A Turning Point
in the Development of a Chapter," 107-118,
No. 4937; Jack P. Dalton. "Advertisement
for the Restoration," 119-137; Jack P.
Dalton. "Editorial Afterword," 141-142.

4924. DEUTSCH, BABETTE. This Modern Poetry. New York: Norton, 1935, pp. 134-138.

4925. _____ . Poetry in Our Time. New York: Holt, 1952, pp. 278-283; 2nd revised and enlarged edition, New York: Doubleday, 1963, pp. 287-319.

4926. DIXON, VLADIMIR (?) "A Letter to Mr. James Joyce," in Our Exagmination, pp. 193-194, No. 4906.

4927. DOBRÉE, BONAMY. Modern Prose Style. Oxford: Clarendon, 1934, pp. 244-249.

4928. ECO, UMBERTO. "My exagmination round his factification for incamination to reduplication with ridecolation of a portrait of the artist as Manzoni," in his Diario minimo. Milan: Mondadori, 1963, pp. 109-125. [Originally in Il verri (March 1962); translated by Adrienne Foulke as "The Betrothed by James Joyce." Chelsea, no. 18-19 (June 1966): 168-179.]

4929. FORSTER, LEONARD. "James Joyce, Dadaism, Surrealism and After," in The Poet's Tongues: Multilingualism in Literature. The de Carle Lectures at the University of Otago, 1968. London: Cambridge University Press in Association with University of Otago Press, 1970, pp. 74-96.

4930. GILBERT, STUART. "Prologomena to 'Work in Progress,'" in Our Exagmination, pp. 49-75, No. 4906.

4931. _____ . "Sketch of a Scenario of 'ALP'," in James Joyce Yearbook, pp. 10-19, No. 1596.

4932. HACKETT, FRANCIS. On Judging Books. New York: John Day, 1947, pp. 51-60. [Reprinted Freeport, New York: Books for Libraries, 1971, pp. 51-60, 251-254.]

4933. HART, CLIVE. A Concordance to Finnegans Wake. Austin: University of Texas Press, 1963.

4934. _____ . "Finnegans Wake in Perspective," in James Joyce Today, pp. 135-165, No. 1659.

4935. _____ , and FRITZ SENN, eds. A Wake Digest. Sydney: Sydney University Press, 1968; University Park, Pa.: Pennsylvania State University Press; London: Methuen, 1968.
        Contents: Clive Hart. "The Elephant in the Belly: Exegesis of Finnegans Wake," 3-12, No. 5648; Jack P. Dalton. "Music Lesson," 13-16, No. 5590; Philip L. Graham. "re'furloined notepaper," 17-20, No. 5416; Clive Hart. "The Earwickers of Sidlesham," 21-22, No. 5645; Fritz Senn. "Dublin Theatres," 23-26, No. 5735; Fritz Senn. "Every Klitty of a scoldermeid: Sexual-Political

Analogies," 27-38, No. 5736; James S. Atherton. "French Argot in Finnegans Wake," 41-42*; Jack P. Dalton. "Kiswahili Words in Finnegans Wake," 43-47, No. 5394; Adaline Glasheen. "Finnegans Wake and the Secret Languages of Ireland," 48-51, No. 5289; Philip L. Graham. "japlatin, with my yuonkle's owlseller," 52-53, No. 5623; Nathan Halper. "A Passage in Albanian," 54-55, No. 5418; M. J. C. Hodgart. "Kiswahili Words in Finnegans Wake," 56-58*; M. J. C. Hodgart. "Some Lithuanian Words in Finnegans Wake," 59-61, No. 5431; Fritz Senn. "Borrowed Brogues," 62-63, No. 5487; Jack P. Dalton. "A More Modern Instance," 67-68, No. 5031; Jack P. Dalton. "- - -," 69-70*; Adaline Glasheen. "Dilmun," 71-72, No. 5607; Adaline Glasheen. "Instances Perhaps of the Tetragrammaton in Finnegans Wake," 73-74, No. 5608; Clive Hart. "The Geometry Problem," "The Sheep-Tally," "The Crampton Bust," "A Haka," 75-79, No. 5649; Breon Mitchell. "Marginalia from Conversations with Joyce," 80-81*; Ruth Von Phul. "The Four Absolutes," 82, No. 5806. [All previously published in A Wake Newslitter, except items marked with *.]

4936. HAYMAN, DAVID, ed. A First-Draft Version of Finnegans Wake. Austin: University of Texas Press, 1963.

4937. _____ . "'Scribbledehobbles' and How They Grew: A Turning Point in the Development of a Chapter," in Twelve and a Tilly, pp. 107-118, No. 4923.

4938. HIGGINSON, FRED H. Anna Livia Plurabelle: The Making of a Chapter. Minneapolis: University of Minnesota Press, 1960. [Abstract of "Introduction" appeared as "Style in Finnegans Wake," in Style in Language. Edited by Thomas A. Sebeok. Cambridge, Mass.: MIT Press; New York, London: John Wiley, 1960.]

4939. _____ . "The Text of Finnegans Wake," in New Light on Joyce, pp. 120-130, No. 1656.

4940. HOWARTH, HERBERT. "The Waste Land and Joyce," in Notes on Some Figures Behind T. S. Eliot. Boston: Houghton Mifflin, 1964, pp. 242-246.

4941. HOWARTH, R. G. Literary Particles. London, Sydney: Angus and Robertson, 1946, pp. 42-55. [Reprinted Port Washington, New York, London: Kennikat Press, 1970, pp. 42-55.]

4942. JACQUET, CLAUDE. Joyce et Rabelais: Aspects de la création verbale dans Finnegans Wake. Études Anglaises; Cahiers et documents, no. 4. Paris: Didier, 1972. [Same as No. 937.]

4943. JENNINGS, PAUL. "Joyce a Beckett," in Oodles of Oddlies. London: Max Reinhardt, 1963,

FINNEGANS WAKE

pp. 15-18. [Reprinted from Observer; double parody of FW and Beckett.]

4944. JOLAS, EUGENE. "My Friend James Joyce," in James Joyce: Two Decades of Criticism, pp. 3-18, No. 1570.

4945. JOLAS, MARIA. "Joyce's Friend Jolas," in A James Joyce Miscellany, 1957, pp. 62-74, No. 1612.

4946. KAIN, RICHARD M. "'Nothing Odd Will do Long': Some Thoughts on 'Finnegans Wake,'" in Twelve and a Tilly, pp. 91-98, No. 4923.

4947. LITZ, A. WALTON. "The Making of Finnegans Wake," in A James Joyce Miscellany, Second Series, pp. 209-224, No. 1613.

4948. _____. "Uses of the 'Finnegans Wake' Manuscripts," in Twelve and a Tilly, pp. 99-106, No. 4923.

*4949. McALPINE, W. R., and MOTOKI TODA. "Fineganz Weiku," in Joisu Nyumon [An Introduction to James Joyce], pp. 108-129, No. 1511.

4950. MACHINO, SHIZUO. "A Study of Finnegans Wake," in A Study of Joyce, pp. 365-406, No. 1592.

4951. McMULLEN, ROY. "Since Finnegans Wake," in Art, Affluence, and Alienation: The Fine Arts Today. New York, London: Praeger, 1968, pp. 196-228.

4952. McSHANE, PHILIP. Plants and Pianos: Two Essays in Advanced Methodology. Dublin: Milltown Institute of Theology and Philosophy, 1971, passim.

4953. MANET, MARIANO. "El Tercer Mr. Joyce," in Notes sobre Literatura Estrangera. Barcelona: Publications de 'La Revista,' 1934, pp. 224-234.

4954. MASON, EUDO C. "Joyce's Finnegans Wake," in his Exzentrische Bahnen: Studien zum Dichterbewusstsein der Neuzeit. Gottingen: Vandenhoeck and Ruprecht, 1963, pp. 284-292, 341.

4955. MORSE, J. MITCHELL. "On Teaching Finnegans Wake," in Twelve and a Tilly, pp. 65-71, No. 4923. [Expanded as "Take for Example Finnegans Wake," in his The Irrelevant English Teacher. Philadelphia: Temple University Press, 1972, pp. 123-142.]

4956. REICHERT, KARL. "Reise ans Ende der Möglichen: James Joyce," in Romananfänge: Versuch zu einer Poetik des Romans. Edited by Norbert Miller. Berlin: Literarisches Colloquium, 1965, pp. 317-343.

4957. SAGE, ROBERT. "Before Ulysses--and After," in Our Exagmination, pp. 149-170, No. 4906.

4958. SCHMIDT, ARNO. "Der Triton mit dem Sonnenschirm: Überlegungen zu einer Lesbarmachung von Finnegans Wake," "Das Buch Jedermann: James Joyce zum 25. Todestage," "Kaleidoskopische Kollidier-Eskapaden," "Der Mimus von Mir, Dir & den Mädies," in his Der Triton mit dem Sonnenschirm: Grossbritannische Gemütsergetzungen. Karlsruhe: Stahlberg, 1969, pp. 194-253, 254-291, 292-320, 322-328. [First two given as radio programs; third reprinted from Konkret, 20 October 1961, pp. 9-10; fourth a review of Dublin Diary reprinted from Spiegel, 3 June 1964.]

4959. SERRANO PONCELA, SEGUNDO. "El experimento nihilista: James Joyce," in La literatura occidental. Caracas: Ediciones de la Biblioteca de la Univ. Central de Venezuela, 1971, pp. 658-661.

*4960. SETTANNI, ETTORE. James Joyce e la prima versione italiana del Finnegans Wake. Venice: Cavallino, 1955.

4961. SLINGSBY, G. V. L. "Writes a Common Reader," in Our Exagmination, pp. 189-191, No. 4906.

4962. SOLOMON, MARGARET C. Eternal Geomater. Carbondale and Edwardsville: Southern Illinois University Press; Amsterdam: Feffer and Simons, 1969.

4963. STOLL, ELMER EDGAR. From Shakespeare to Joyce. Garden City: Doubleday Doran, 1944, pp. 350-388; New York: Ungar, 1965, pp. 350-358.

4964. THOMPSON, JOHN HINSDALE. "Finnegans Wake," in Modern Poetry: American and British. Edited by Kimon Friar and John Brinnin. New York: Appleton-Century-Crofts, 1951, pp. 88-97.

4965. _____. Bio-biblio-graphiti of James Joyce gulled from the Pages of Finnegans Wake and Prepared with Meaner Intercessions by John H. Thompson. New York: YM-YWHA Poetry Center, 1950.

4966. TINDALL, WILLIAM YORK. A Reader's Guide to Finnegans Wake. New York: Farrar, Strauss and Giroux, 1969; London: Thames and Hudson.

4967. USSHER, ARLAND. "James Joyce: Doubting Thomist and Joking Jesuit," in his Three Great Irishmen: Shaw, Yeats, Joyce. New York: Devin-Adair, 1953, pp. 115-160; London: Gollancz. [Brief extract, "Joyce's Ulysses," "'Treasure Chest,'" NYTBR, 30 August 1953, p. 2; reprinted New York: Biblio and Tannen, 1968, pp. 115-160.]

4968. WEIDLÉ, WLADIMIR. The Dilemma of the Arts. Translated by Martin Jarret-Kerr. London: S.C.M. Press, 1948, pp. 60ff.

4969. WILDER, THORNTON. "Joyce and the Modern Novel," in A James Joyce Miscellany, 1957, pp. 11-19, No. 1612. [Translated in Configuration critique I, pp. 272-282, No. 1636.]

4970. WILLIAMS, WILLIAM CARLOS. "A Point for American Criticism," in Our Exagmination, pp. 173-185, No. 4906.

4971. WILSON, EDMUND. "Antrobuses and the Earwickers," "A Guide to Finnegans Wake," in his Classics and Commercials: A Literary Chronicle of the Forties. New York: Farrar, Strauss, 1950, pp. 81-86, 182-189.

Periodical Articles

*4972. ALDINGTON, RICHARD. "A Critical Attitude: All Art is Tending to the Condition of Journalism." The Referee, 24 November 1929.

4973. ATHERTON, J. S. "The Chapter Titles of Finnegans Wake." Notes and Queries, 199 (June 1954): 270-271.

4974. _____. "James Joyce and Finnegans Wake." Manchester Review, 9 (1961): 97-108.

4975. AUBERT, JACQUES. "Finnegans Wake: Pour en finir avec les traductions." James Joyce Quarterly, 4 (Spring 1967): 217-222.

*4976. B., W. C. New York Herald Tribune (Paris), 8 April 1929. [Review of transition.]

4977. [BACKLUND], PERCIVAL. "Finnegans Wake-- James Joyce i ala tider." Horisont (Vasa), 15 (1968): 45-50.

4978. BEGNAL, MICHAEL. "The Narrator of Finnegans Wake." Éire-Ireland, 4 (Autumn 1969): 38-49.

4979. BEHAR, JACK. "McLuhan's Finnegans Wake." Denver Quarterly, 3 (Spring 1968): 5-27. [McLuhan's version of reality like FW.]

*4980. BENNETT, ARNOLD. "Books and Persons." Evening News (Manchester), 12 June 1930.

*4981. _____. "Back to Riceyman Steps." Evening Standard (London), 12 June 1930.

*4982. _____. "Books and Persons." Evening Standard (London), 19 September 1929.

*4983. BENSTOCK, BERNARD. "Joyce's Finnegans Wake." Explicator, 15 (June 1957): item 59.

4984. _____. "A Portrait of the Artist in Finnegans Wake." Bucknell Review, 9 (March 1961): 259-271.

4985. _____. "Anna Livia and the City Builder." Notes and Queries, 206 (September 1961): 352-353.

4986. _____. "The Final Apostacy: James Joyce and Finnegans Wake." ELH: Journal of English Literary History, 28 (December 1961): 417-437.

4987. _____. "The Quiddity of Shem and the Whatness of Shaun." James Joyce Quarterly, 1 (Fall 1963): 26-33.

4988. _____. "L. Bloom as Dreamer in Finnegans Wake." Publications of the Modern Language Association, 82 (March 1967): 91-97.

4989. _____. "The Reel Finnegans Wake." New Orleans Review, 1 (Fall 1968): 60-64.

4990. BERNBAUM, ERNEST. "The Crucial Question Concerning Finnegans Wake." College English, 7 (December 1945): 151-154.

4991. BIERMAN, ROBERT. "White and Pink Elephants: Finnegans Wake and the Tradition of Unintelligibility." Modern Fiction Studies, 4 (Spring 1958): 62-70.

4992. _____. "The Dreamer and the Dream in Finnegans Wake." Renascence, 11 (Spring 1959): 197-200.

4993. BLISH, JAMES. "A Prayer for James Joyce." James Joyce Quarterly, 7 (Summer 1970): 379. [In the style of FW.]

4994. _____. "Announcement: A Wake Appendix." Wake Newslitter, 8 (December 1971): 91-93. [Proposed list of corrections.]

4995. _____. "The Long Night of a Virginia Author." Journal of Modern Literature, 2 (Third Issue, 1972): 393-409. [Compares Cabell's Nightmare has Triplets trilogy with FW.]

4996. BOGAN, LOUISE. "Finnegans Wake." Nation, 148 (May 1939): 533-535; 149 (August 1944): 214. [Appeared in her Selected Criticism: Prose, Poetry. New York: Noonday Press, 1955, pp. 132-148, 149-153.]

4997. BONHEIM, HELMUT. "Umana in Finnegans Wake." Umana, 20 (May-September 1971): 21-22.

*4998. 'Book Taster.' "On the Table." Post (Liverpool), 8 April 1932.

4999. BOORUM, TED. "Finnegans Wake." Poetry, 62 (August 1943): 250-251. [Poem.]

5000. BROPHY, LIAM. "The Vague, The Verbose, The Venomous." The Word (1957): 12-15.

FINNEGANS WAKE

5001. BROWN, T. J. "Finnegans Wake." British Museum Quarterly, 17 (1952): 4-5. [Surviving MS. Add. Mss. 47471-85.]

5002. BURGUM, EDWIN B. "The Interpretation of Joyce." Virginia Quarterly Review, 21 (Winter 1945): 134-144. [Appeared as "The Paradox of Scepticism in Finnegans Wake," in his The Novel and the World's Dilemma. New York: Oxford University Press, 1947, pp. 109-119; reprinted in Joyce, pp. 109-118, No. 1526.]

5003. BUTLER, TERENCE. "The Day of the Wake: A Joycean Anniversary." Irish Times, 2 February 1962, p. 7.

5004. BUTOR, MICHEL. "Finnegans Wake est certainement traduisible." Figaro littéraire, 20 January 1966, p. 9.

5005. _____. "La traduction, dimension fondamentale de notre temps." James Joyce Quarterly, 4 (Spring 1967): 215-216.

5006. _____. "Crossing the Joycean Threshhold," translated by Jerry A. Stewart. James Joyce Quarterly, 7 (Spring 1970): 160-176.

5007. BYRNE, PATRICK. "Joyce's Dream Book Took Seventeen Years to Write." Irish Digest, 81 (July 1964): 73-76. [From Sunday Independent.]

*5008. CALMER, EDGAR. Chicago Sunday Tribune (Paris), 17 November 1929. [Review of transition.]

5009. CAMPBELL, JOSEPH. "Finnegan the Wake." Chimera, 4, no. 3 (Spring 1946): 63-80. [Also in James Joyce: Two Decades of Criticism, pp. 368-389, No. 1570.]

5010. _____. "Clave Esquematica Para Finnegans Wake." Las Armas y las Letras, 2 (June 1949): 9-20. [Translation from "Introduction" to A Skeleton Key to Finnegans Wake, No. 5523.]

5011. _____. "Finnegans Wake." Explicator, 14 (May 1956): item 52.

5012. _____, and HENRY MORTON ROBINSON. "Skin of Whose Teeth? Strange Case of Mr. Wilder's New Play and Finnegans Wake." SatR, 25 (19 December 1942): 3-4; 26 December 1942 and 2 January, 9 January, 13 February 1943.

*5013. CAMPOS, AUGUSTO de. "Um lance de 'des' do Grande Sertao." Revista do livro, 4 (December 1959): 9-28. [Comparison of FW with Guimaraes Rosa's work.]

*5014. CARGEEGE, F. B. "The Mystery of James Joyce." Everyman, 5 (11 June 1931). [See also Michael Petch. "The Approach to James Joyce." Everyman, 5 (25 June 1931): 701-702.]

*5015. 'Casimir.' Soir (Brussels), 8 November 1931.

5016. CELATI, GIANNI. "Da 'Finnegans Wake': Elaborazioni sul Tema visita al Museo Willigton [sic.]." Il Cafè, 3/4 (1972): 26.

5017. CERNY, JAMES W. "Joyce's Mental Map." James Joyce Quarterly, 9 (Winter 1971): 218-224.

5018. CHAPMAN, GERALD. "The Modern Search for Tradition." University of Denver Magazine, 3 (December 1965): 20-25.

5019. CHASTAING, MAXINE. "Tentatives pour une traduction de Finnegans Wake." Romàn, no. 3 (June 1951): 269-271.

*5020. CHEON, HENRI. "Snobisme et littérature." Latinite (1931).

5021. CLARKIN, FRANKLIN. "New Prose from Dr. Joyce." New York Times Book Review, 24 May 1931, p. 2.

5022. COLLINS, BEN L. "Joyce's 'Haveth Childers Everywhere.'" Explicator, 10 (December 1951): item 21.

*5023. COLUM, MARY. New York Herald Tribune, 24 April 1927. [Review of transition (April 1929).]

5024. COLUM, PADRAIC. "River Episode from James Joyce's Uncompleted Work." Dial, 84 (April 1928): 318-322. [Appeared as "Preface" to Joyce's Anna Livia Plurabelle. New York: Crosby Gaige, 1928, pp. vii-ix; reprinted in Our Friend James Joyce, pp. 139-143, No. 298.]

*5025. _____. "Joyce: From a 'Work in Progress.'" New Republic, 64 (17 September 1930): 131-132. [Reprinted in The Critic as Artist: Essays on Books, 1920-1970. Edited by Gilbert A. Harrison. New York: Liveright, 1972, pp. 65-70.]

*5026. _____. "Notes on Finnegans Wake." Yale Review, 30 (March 1941): 640-645.

5027. COSTANZO, W. V. "The French version of Finnegans Wake: Translation, Adaptation, Recreation." James Joyce Quarterly, 9 (Winter 1971): 225-236.

5028. CUNNINGHAME, A. T. "On Hearing James Joyce." The Modern Scot, 2 (October 1931): 207-215.

*5029. CURLING, JONATHAN. "Obscurity in Modern Art." Spectator, 143 (24 August 1929): 241. [On transition, no. 13.]

*5030. CURRIE, GEORG. Brooklyn Eagle, 27 January 1929. [Review of Transition Stories.]

5031. DALTON, JACK P. "A More Modern Instance." Wake Newslitter, no. 9 (January 1963): 8-10. [Also in A Wake Digest, pp. 67-68, No. 4935.]

5032. _____. "Letter to the Editor." James Joyce Quarterly, 4 (Winter 1967): 156-157. [Errors in Scribbledehobble, No. 4920.]

5033. _____. "Some Notes on the Finnegans Wake Concordance." James Joyce Quarterly, 5 (Winter 1968): 171-175.

5034. _____. "A Letter from T. S. Eliot." James Joyce Quarterly, 6 (Fall 1968): 79-81.

5035. _____. "The Finnegans Wake Concordance: A Further Note." James Joyce Quarterly, 6 (Spring 1969): 275.

5036. _____. "Two Joyce Titles." Wake Newslitter, 10 (April 1973): 26.

*5037. DMITRIEVA, M., translator. [Letter of H. G. Wells to James Joyce, November 1928]. Voprosey Lit., no. 8 (1959): 162-163.

5038. DOLMATCH, THEODORE B. "Notes and Queries Concerning the Revision in Finnegans Wake." Modern Language Quarterly, 16 (June 1955): 142-148.

5039. DUFF, CHARLES C. "Magnificent Leg-Puller." Saturday Review of Literature, 33 (9 September 1950): 24.

5040. ECKLEY, GRACE. "1600." Wake Newslitter, 10 (October 1973): 81.

5041. ECO, UMBERTO. "Le moyen âge de James Joyce," translated by Louis Bonalumi. Tel quel, no. 11 (Fall 1962): 39-52; no. 12 (Winter 1963): 83-92.

*5042. EDEL, LEON. "New Writers." Canadian Forum, 10 (June 1930): 329-330.

5043. EDELHEIT, HENRY. "Reflections on 'Scribbledehobble': A Note on Joyce's Debt to Édouard Dujardin." Analyst, 24 (March 1965): 2-4.

5044. ELLENBOGEN, EILEEN. "The Pattern of Finnegans Wake." Changing World, no. 7 (February-March-April 1949): 87-91.

*5045. FADIMAN, CLIFTON P. Nation, 27 February 1929. [Review of Transition Stories. Edited by Eugene Jolas and Robert Sage.]

5046. FAGERBERG, SVEN. "Finnegan og de øde Land." Heretica, 3 (1950): 327-373. [Also in Poesi, 3, no. 1 (1950): 11-40.]

5047. FERREIRA, JÕAO PALMA. "Odespertar de Finnegan." Diário de Noticias (Lisbon), 6 January 1972, pp. 17, 19.

*5048. FRANK, ANDRÉ. La République, 8 May 1931.

*5049. FURNAS, J. C. "Penaninkumpoops." New Freeman, 1 (9 July 1930): 399-401.

5050. GARVIN, JOHN. "Bruinoboroff." Moderna Språk, 67, no. 3 (1973): 212-216.

5051. GIEDION-WELCKER, CAROLA. "Ein Sprachliches Experiment von James Joyce." Neue Schweizer Rundschau, 22, no. 9 (September 1929): 660-671. [Translated by Eugene Jolas in transition, no. 19-20 (June 1930): 174-183; appeared in In Memoriam James Joyce, pp. 37-50, No. 1038; appeared in her Schriften, 1926-1971: Statimen zu einer Zeitbild, pp. 39-48, No. 1566.]

5052. GILBERT, STUART. "Thesaurus Minusculus: A Short Commentary on a Paragraph of 'Work in Progress.'" transition, no. 16-17 (June 1929): 15-24.

*5053. _____. "The Growth of a Titan." Saturday Review of Literature, 7 (2 August 1930): 17-19.

5054. _____. "Understanding James Joyce." Golden Book Magazine, 14 (November 1931): 340.

5055. _____. "The Joycean Protagonist." Échanges, no. 5 (December 1931): 154-157.

5056. _____. "A Footnote to 'Work in Progress.'" Contempo, 3 (February 1934): 4-5. [Also in Experiment (Cambridge), no. 7 (Spring 1931): 30-33.]

5057. _____. "On comprendra Finnegans Wake dans cent ans!" Figaro littéraire, 20 January 1966, p. 8.

5058. GILLET, LOUIS. "Mr. James Joyce et son nouveau Roman 'Work in Progress.'" Revue des Deux Mondes, 84 (August 1931): 928-939. [Excerpts in Lu, no. 20 (6 November 1931); translated by Ronald Symond in transition, no. 21 (March 1932): 263-272; later appeared in Claybook for James Joyce, No. 1568; original article discussed by Frederic Lefevre. La République, 16 August 1931 and in "Literarische Chronik: Joyce in der Revue des Deux Mondes." Neue Zürcher Zeitung, 25 August 1931.]

5059. _____. "A Propos de Finnegans Wake." Babel, 1 (1940): 101-113. [Translated by D. D. Paige as "Joyce's Testament: Finnegans Wake." Quarterly Review of Literature (Chapel Hill), 1, no. 1 (Autumn 1944): 87-99.]

FINNEGANS WAKE

5060. _____ . "Finnegans Wake." Revue des deux Mondes, 60 (December 1940): 502-513.

5061. GILMAN, SANDER L. "Finnegans Wake in Germany." Wake Newslitter, 3 (October 1966): 116-117.

5062. GLASHEEN, ADALINE. "Joyce and Yeats." Wake Newslitter, 4 (February 1967): 30.

5063. _____ . "Molly and Finnegans Wake." Wake Newslitter, 4 (June 1967): 56-57.

5064. _____ . "Notes Towards A Supreme Understanding of the Use of 'Finnegans Wake' in Finnegans Wake." Wake Newslitter, 5 (February 1968): 4-15.

5065. _____ . "Joyce's Letters and Finnegans Wake." Wake Newslitter, 6 (February 1969): 25-26.

5066. _____ . "Rough Notes on Joyce and Wyndham Lewis." Wake Newslitter, 8 (October 1971): 67-75.

*5067. GOMEZ de la SERNA, RAMON. "El Escritor y la Pruebas." La Nacion (Santiago), 23 October 1930.

*5068. GOPALEEN, MYLES na (Flann O'Brien, Brian Nolan). "Cruiskeen Lawn." Irish Times, 2 February 1942.

*5069. _____ . "Cruiskeen Lawn." Irish Times, 1 June 1942.

*5070. _____ . "Cruiskeen Lawn." Irish Times, 17 February 1943.

*5071. _____ . "Cruiskeen Lawn." Irish Times, 18 March 1944.

*5072. _____ . "Cruiskeen Lawn." Irish Times, 9 May 1947.

*5073. _____ . "Cruiskeen Lawn." Irish Times, 7 July 1950.

*5074. _____ . "Cruiskeen Lawn." Irish Times, 16 February 1954.

*5075. _____ . "Cruiskeen Lawn." Irish Times, 13 July 1957.

*5076. _____ . "Cruiskeen Lawn." Irish Times, 6 December 1957.

*5077. _____ . "Cruiskeen Lawn." Irish Times, 28 December 1957.

*5078. _____ . "Cruiskeen Lawn." Irish Times, 14 February 1961.

5079. _____ . "Cruiskeen Lawn." Irish Times, 22 December 1964.

5080. GRIFFIN, GERALD. "James Joyce: An Explanation of His Methods." Everyman, 4, no. 81 (14 August 1930): 76.

*5081. GUILLEMIN, BERNARD. "Der Irrtum des James Joyce." Hamburger Fremdenblatt, 14 April 1928; Magdeburger Zeitung, 4 March 1928.

5082. HALPER, NATHAN. "Joyce and Eliot: A Tale of Shem and Shaun." Nation, 200 (31 May 1965): 590-595. [Appears in slightly different form in Wake Newslitter, 2 (June 1965): 3-10; (August 1965): 17-23; (December 1965): 22-26.]

5083. _____ . "James Joyce and His Peers." Wake Newslitter, 4 (October 1967): 96-97.

5084. _____ . "Joyce and 'Anna Livia.'" James Joyce Quarterly, 4 (Spring 1967): 223-228.

5085. _____ . "Differing with Dalton." James Joyce Quarterly, 7 (Summer 1970): 375-376. [Reply to Jack P. Dalton. ". . ." in A Wake Digest, pp. 69-70, No. 4935 and Dalton's "The Finnegans Wake Concordance: A Further Note." James Joyce Quarterly, 6 (Spring 1969): 275.]

5086. HANNEY, MARGARET. "Notes in Basic English on the 'ALP' Record." Psyche, 12, nos. 2 and 4 (1932): 86-95.

*5087. HANSEN, KURT HEINRICH. "Grosse Kunst mit kleinem Gelächter." Die Zeit, 16 (3 February 1961): 7.

*5088. HARLONG, R. [n.t.]. Gringoire (Paris), 9 May 1931.

5089. HART, CLIVE. "Notes on the Text of Finnegans Wake." Journal of English and Germanic Philology, 59 (April 1960): 229-239. [Addendum to Higginson article, No. 5101.]

5090. _____ . "Concordance: Errata." Wake Newslitter, 2 (February 1965): 11-12.

5091. _____ . "The Hound and the Type-Bed: Further Notes on the Text of Finnegans Wake." Wake Newslitter, 3 (August 1966): 77-84.

5092. _____ . "Concordance--Corrigend." Wake Newslitter, 6 (October 1969): 74-76.

5093. HASSAN, IHAB. "Joyce-Beckett: A Scenario in Eight Scenes and a Voice." Journal of Modern Literature, 1 (First Issue 1970): 7-18. [Also in New Light on Joyce, pp. 180-194, No. 1656.]

5094. HÄUSERMANN, H. W. "'Finnegans Wake': Hinweis auf ein neues Personenverzeichnis." Neue Zürcher Zeitung, 29 June 1963.

5095. HAYMAN, DAVID. "Dramatic Motion in Finnegans Wake." Texas Studies in English,
37 (1958): 155-176.

5096. _____ . "Letter to the Editor." James
Joyce Quarterly, 1 (Spring 1964): 55-56.
[Corrections to First Draft Version of
FW.]

5097. _____ . "A List of Corrections for the
Scribbledehobble." James Joyce Quarterly,
1 (Winter 1964): 23-39.

5098. _____ . "The Distribution of the Tristan
and Isolde Notes under 'Exiles' in the
Scribbledehobble." Wake Newslitter, 2
(October 1965): 3-14.

5099. HEATH, STEPHEN. "Ambiviolences: Notes pour
la lecture de Joyce." Tel quel, no. 50
(Summer 1972): 22-43; no. 51 (Autumn
1972): 64-76.

*5100. HENNECKE, HANS. "Fragment eines Fragmentes."
Frankfurter Allgemeine Zeitung (August
1959).

5101. HIGGINSON, FRED H. "Notes on the Text of
Finnegans Wake." Journal of English and
Germanic Philology, 55 (July 1956): 451-
456. [See also article by Clive Hart,
No. 5089.]

5102. _____ . "Two Letters from Dame Anna Earwicker." Critique, 1 (1957): 3-14.

5103. HODGART, MATTHEW. "The Earliest Sections of
Finnegans Wake." James Joyce Review, 1,
no. 1 (February 1957): 3-18; errata in
(June 1957): 25-26.

*5104. HOHOFF, CURT. "'Finnegans Wake,' James
Joyces Letzter Roman." Süddeutsche
Zeitung, 7/8 April 1951.

*5105. HOLTEY, WINIFRED. "The Assault on Time: A
Modern Enmity." Yorkshire Post, 3 August 1929.

5106. JENNINGS, PAUL. "Double Parody: Vowelmouthed
Garbledabook of Brutish Erkingman."
Punch, 246 (26 February 1964): 308-310.
[Room at the Top parodied in the style of
FW.]

5107. JOHNSTON, DENIS. "Clarify Begins At: The
Non-Information of Finnegans Wake."
Massachusetts Review, 5 (Winter 1964):
357-364.

*5108. JOLAS, EUGENE. "transition: An Epilogue."
American Mercury, 23 (June 1931): 185-192.

5109. _____ . "Marginalia to James Joyce's
'Work in Progress.'" transition, no. 22
(February 1933): 101-105.

5110. _____ . "Verbirrupta for James Joyce."
Contempo, 3, no. 13 (February 1934): 3.

*5111. _____ . "Frontierless Decade." transi-
tion, no. 27 (April-May 1938): 8.

5112. _____ . "Homage to the Mythmaker."
transition, no. 27 (May 1938): 169-175.

5113. JOLAS, MARIA. "James Joyce as a Revolutionary: Reply to Max Lerner." New Republic,
107 (9 November 1942): 613.

5114. JONES, C. A. "Finnegans Wake and Its De-
tractors." Graffiti, 1 (September-
December 1941): 5-11.

5115. JONES, T. H. "Once it was the Colour of
Saying: or, Are they the same all over?
A Note on Joyce's Basic Humanity." Wake
Newslitter, 1 (April 1964): 10-12.

*5116. KIELY, BENEDICT. "A Key to James Joyce."
Irish Bookman, 2 (December 1947): 9-19.

5117. KNUTH, LEO. "The Finnegans Wake Translation
Panel at Trieste." James Joyce Quarterly,
9 (Winter 1971): 266-269.

5118. KORG, JACOB. "Literary Esthetics of Dada."
Works, 1 (Spring 1968): 43-54.

*5119. KOSPOTH, B. J. "All James Joyce says has
been said many times in French, declares
M. Souday: Paris Critic scoffs at 'New
Vocabulary.'" Chicago Tribune (Paris),
5 May 1929, p. 2.

5120. LAVERGNE, PHILIPPE. "Avant-propos." Tel
quel, no. 30 (Summer 1967): 67-68.

5121. LAMB, MARGARET. "'I wish I had written Pride
and Prejudice'--James Joyce." Little Magazine, 4 (Winter 1970-71): 24-25. [In
parody of FW.]

*5122. LAWRENCE, RAYMOND. [n.t.]. Oregonian (Port-
land), 18 December 1927.

*5123. LeFEVRE, FREDERIC. "Snobisme et littérature."
La République, 4 May 1931.

*5124. _____ . "l'Erreur de James Joyce." La
République, 5 May 1931.

*5125. LEWIS, WYNDHAM. "Mustard and Cress." Sunday
Referee (London), 30 August 1931.

5126. LITZ, A. WALTON. "The Genesis of Finnegans
Wake." Notes and Queries, 198 (October
1953): 445-447.

5127. _____ . "The Evolution of Joyce's 'ALP.'"
Philological Quarterly, 36 (October 1957):
36-48.

FINNEGANS WAKE

5128. LOCKSPEISER, EDWARD. "Humphrey Searle and James Joyce." Listener, 54 (29 September 1955): 521.

*5129. MacDIARMID, HUGH. "A Plea for Synthetic Scots." Scots Observer, 1 September 1952.

*5130. MacENERY, MARCUS. "The Joyce Country." Irish Times, 13 September 1947.

5131. McHUGH, ROLAND. "Chronology of the Buffalo Notebooks." Wake Newslitter, 9 (June 1972): 19-31, 36-38.

*5132. MacKENZIE, COMPTON. [n.t.]. The Gramaphone (March 1930).

5133. McMICHAEL, CHARLES T., and TED R. SPIVEY. "'Chaos--Hurray!--is come again': Heroism in James Joyce and Conrad Aiken." Studies in the Literary Imagination, 3 (October 1970): 65-68. [Aiken's The Coming Forth by Day of Osiris Jones and FW.]

5134. MANNING, MARY. "Myth-carriage of Joyce-stice." Reporter, 26 (15 March 1962): 38-39.

*5135. MARYE, EDWARD. [n.t.]. Nouvelles littéraire, 4 April 1931.

5136. MASON, EUDO C. "Zu James Joyce's Finnegans Wake." Du (Zürich), 8, no. 12 (December 1948): 32, 135-136.

*5137. MEADE, NORAH. [n.t.]. New York Herald Tribune Books, 13 September 1931.

*5138. MERCANTON, JACQUES. "Finnegans Wake." Nouvelle Revue Française, 27 (1 May 1939): 858-864.

5139. MERLE, ROBERT. "Finnegans Wake est certainement intraduisible." Figaro littéraire, 20 January 1966, p. 9.

*5140. MICHAUD, REGIS. "Lettres Americaines: Les Nouveaux Ferments." Les nouvelles, 3 February 1929.

*5141. MODIC, JOHN. "The Eclectic Mr. Wilder." Ball State Teachers College Forum, 1 (Winter 1960-61): 55-61. ["Skin of our Teeth."]

5142. MONOD, SYLVÈRE. "'Brother Wearers of Motley.'" Essays and Studies, 26 (1973): 66-82.

5143. MONTGOMERY, NIALL. "The Pervigilium Phoenicis." New Mexico Quarterly, 23 (Winter 1953): 437-472.

5144. MORSE, J. MITCHELL. "Finnegans Wake, These Ten Years After." New York Herald Tribune Books, 1 May 1949, section 7, pp. 1-2.

5145. _____. "Cain, Abel, and Joyce." ELH: Journal of English Literary History, 22 (March 1955): 48-60.

*5146. NICKALLS, BARBARA. [n.t.]. Bookfinder Illustrated (May 1932): 3.

5147. NOON, WILLIAM T., S.J. "'Roll away the Reel World.'" America, 111 (31 October 1964): 517-520.

*5148. O., Y. (AE, George Russell). "Magazines." Irish Statesman, 16 March 1929. [About transition.]

5149. O'BRIEN, DARCY. "The Twins that Tick Homo Vulgaris: A Study of Shem and Shaun." Modern Fiction Studies, 12 (Summer 1966): 183-199.

5150. _____. "Joyce, Dogs, Eros, Metamorphosis, Revolution and the Unity of Creation." New Blackbriars, 53 (October 1972): 466-470.

*5151. O'CONNOR, FRANK. "Joyce--The Third Period." Irish Statesman, 12 April 1930, pp. 114-116.

5152. O'FAOLAIN, SEAN. "The Cruelty and Beauty of Words." Virginia Quarterly Review, 4 (April 1928): 208-225. [Same article appeared as "Style and the Limitations of Speech." Criterion, 8 (September 1928): 67-87; article plus O'Faolian's "Letter" and Review of ALP (next item) attacked by Eugene Jolas. "The New Vocabulary." transition, no. 15 (February 1929): 171-174, which also appeared as "Style and the Limitations of Speech." Irish Statesman, 26 January 1929, pp. 414, 416; O'Faolain reply in "Letter to the Editor." Irish Statesman, 2 March 1929, pp. 513-514; Jolas responded to O'Faolain with "The Revolution of Language and James Joyce," in Our Exagmination, No. 4906; O'Faolain in "Letter to the Editor." Criterion (October 1930): 147, acknowledges that he did not do "complete justice to Mr. Joyce's new prose."]

5153. _____. "Literature and Life: New Language." Irish Statesman, 10, no. 25 (25 August 1928): 492-493.

5154. _____. "Correspondence: ALP." Irish Statesman, 11 (5 January 1929): 354-355. [Same article appeared as "Almost Music." Hound and Horn, 2 (January-March 1929): 178-180 which is a reply to a review of ALP by Y. O. (AE, George Russell). Irish Statesman, 11 (29 December 1928): 339.]

*5155. OGDEN, C. K. "The Joyce Record." Psyche, 11 (July 1930): 95-96. [Reprinted as "Notes in Basic English on the ALP Record." Joycenotes, 2 (September 1969): 10-18.]

5156. _____ . "James Joyce's 'ALP' in Basic English." transition, no. 21 (March 1932): 259-262.

5157. PETCH, MICHAEL. "The Approach to James Joyce." Everyman, 5 (25 June 1931): 701-702. [Reply to earlier article by F. B. Cargeege, No. 5014; see also letters to editor, 16 July 1931, by Matt, Richardson, Cargeege, J. T. Price.]

*5158. PETERS, MARJORIE. "A New Tongue for Literary Snobs." New York World, 14 August 1927.

5159. PITNEY, R. H. "Pilgrim's Work not in Progress a fifth avenview with no Soapoliiologies to James Joyce." Argo (Princeton), 1, no. 1 (November 1930): 45-59.

5160. POLSKY, NED H. "Literary Background of Finnegans Wake." Chicago Review, 3 (Winter 1949): 1, 8.

5161. POOLE, ROGER C. "Structuralism and Phenomenology: A Literary Approach." Journal of the British Society for Phenomenology, 2, no. 2 (May 1971): 3-16.

5162. POWYS, JOHN COWPER. "Finnegans Wake," Modern Reading, no. 7 (1943): 75-88. [Reprinted in his Obstinate Cymric. Carmarthen: Druid Press, 1947, pp. 19-36; reprinted in Obstinate Cymric: Essays 1935-1947. London: Village Press, 1973, pp. 19-36; translated by Didier Coupaye and Michel Gresset in Nouvelle revue française, 16 (1 February 1968): 273-289.]

5163. PRESCOTT, JOSEPH. "Concerning the Genesis of Finnegans Wake." Publications of the Modern Language Association, 69 (December 1954): 1300-1302. [Translated by J. deM. in Sur, no. 260 (October-September 1959): 36-40.]

5164. _____ . "Two Manuscripts by Paul Léon Concerning James Joyce." Modern Fiction Studies, 2 (May 1956): 71-76.

*5165. 'Querist.' Irish Statesman, 16 April 1927. [Review of transition (April 1927).]

5166. RANKIN, H. D. "Joyce's Remove from Aristotle to Plato." Wake Newslitter, 2 (June 1965): 10-13.

5167. _____ . "After Looking into Finnegans Wake." The Age (Melbourne), 15 April 1967, p. 24. [Poem.]

5168. REED, HENRY. "Joyce's Progress." Orion, no. 4 (Autumn 1947): 131-146.

5169. REICHERT, KLAUS. "Finnegans Wake--Zum Problem einer übersetzung." Neue Rundschau, 83 (1972): 165-169. [Answers Richard

Gerber's review of the Hildescheimer and Wollschlager translation of ALP; see Gerber's rebuttal, pp. 170-172.]

*5170. REIFENBERG, BENNO. "7 Rue de l'Odeon." Frankfurter Zeitung, 30 March 1931.

*5171. REYES, ALFONSO. "El calambur en Joyce." Monterrey, no. 8 (March 1942). [Reprinted in his A lápiz, 1923-1946. Mexico City: Stylo, 1947, pp. 183-185; reprinted in his Obras Completos, vol. 8. Mexico City: Fondo de Cultura Económica, 1958, pp. 318-319.]

5172. RISSET, JACQUELINE. "Joyce traduit par Joyce." Tel quel, no. 55 (Autumn 1973): 47-58. [On the Italian translation of ALP.]

5173. RITCHIE, A. M. "Awake at the Wake, or How to Tell When Not Seeing What is Not is Seeing what Is." Wake Newslitter, 3 (April 1966): 39-42.

5174. ROBINSON, HENRY M. "The Curious Case of Thornton Wilder." Esquire, 47 (March 1957): 70-71, 124-126.

5175. ROSATI, SALVATORE. "Inghilterra." Almanacco Letterario Bompiani (Milan) (1940): 168-171.

*5176. ROWLAND, JOHN H. S. "Letters to the Editor." Everyman, 5, no. 127 (2 July 1931): 733.

*5177. ROY, F. C. [n.t.]. South London Press, 6 March 1931.

5178. RUSHTON, G. WYNNE. "The Case Against James Joyce." Everyman, 5 (9 July 1931): 765-766.

5179. RYBERG, WALTER. "How to Read Finnegans Wake." New Horizons, 3 (November-December 1940): 14-19, 31.

*5180. SAGE, ROBERT. [n.t.]. Chicago Tribune (Paris), 20 March 1927.

5181. _____ . "ETC." transition, no. 14 (Fall 1928): 171-176.

*5182. _____ . [n.t.]. Chicago Tribune (Paris), 17 May 1931.

5183. SALEMSON, HAROLD J. "James Joyce and the New Word." Modern Quarterly, 5 (Fall 1929): 294-312.

*5184. _____ . "Desarticulation." Anthologie du Groupe Moderne d'Art (Liege), February 1930.

5185. SAUTOY, PETER du. "The Published Text." Wake Newslitter, 4 (October 1967): 97-99.

FINNEGANS WAKE

*5186. SCHIFF, GERT. "James Joyces Finnegans Wake: Ein paar Umrisse des Werks." Frankfurter Allgemeine Zeitung, 28 February 1959. [Reprinted as "James Joyce: 'Finnegans Wake': Umrisse des Werks." Die Tat (Zürich), 12 September 1959.]

*5187. _____. "Das Schwierigste Werk der Welt Literatur." Die Zeit, 16 (June 1961): 7.

5188. SCHLAUCH, MARGARET. "Linguistic Aspects of 'Work in Progress.'" Washington Square College Review, 3 (February 1939): 9-12, 33.

*5189. SCHMIDT, ARNO. "Das Geheimnis von Finnegans Wake." Die Zeit, 9 December 1960, p. 7; "Seines Brüders Schumaher," 16 December 1960, p. 6; "Der Hölleenschlüssel," 16 December 1960, p. 7. [Replies by: Gert Schiff. "Das Schwierigste Werk der Welt-literatur." Die Zeit, 3 February 1961, p. 7; Kurt Heinrich Hansen. "Grosse Kunst mit kleinem Gelachter." Die Zeit, 10 February 1961, p. 7--all in the U.S. edition; in the Hamburg edition dates are one week earlier and pagination is different.]

5190. SENN, FRITZ. "James Joyce über die Schweizer Frauen Stimmrecht--ein Anweis in Finnegans Wake." Die Tat (Zürich), 31 January 1959, p. 15. [Reprinted in his James Joyce: Aufsätze von Fritz Senn, pp. 10-11, No. 1654.]

5191. _____. "A Test Case of Over-Reading." Wake Newslitter, 1 (April 1964): 1-8.

5192. _____. "James Joyce: Eigenheiten im Werk des grossen Iren." Zolliker Bote (Zürich), no. 24 (17 June 1966): 9-11 and Zürcher Woche, 17 June 1966, pp. 9-11. [Reprinted as second part of "In het struikgewas van Finnegans Wake," translated by B. Wijffels-Smulders. Levende Talen, no. 269 (June-July 1970): 456-461.]

5193. _____. "The Issue is Translation." James Joyce Quarterly, 4 (Spring 1967): 163-164.

5194. _____. "The Tellings of the Taling." James Joyce Quarterly, 4 (Spring 1967): 229-233.

5195. _____. "Reading in Progress: Words and Letters in Finnegans Wake." Leuvense Bijdragen (Louvain), 57 (1968): 2-18.

5196. _____. "A Reading Exercise in Finnegans Wake." Levende Talen, no. 269 (June-July 1970): 469-480.

5197. SEMMLER, CLEMENT. "Vladimir Dixon." Wake Newslitter, no. 18 (December 1963): 6-7.

*5198. SETTANNI, ETTORE. "I Fiumi Scorrono di James Joyce." Prospettive, 4, no. 11-12 (15 December 1940): 14-16.

5199. SHERWOOD, JOHN C. "Joyce and the Empire: Some Thoughts on Finnegans Wake." Studies in the Novel, 1 (Fall 1969): 357-363.

5200. SLOMCZYŃSKI, MACIEJ. "Klucze otchlani." Literatura na świecie, no. 5 (May 1973): 4-41.

*5201. SMALL, ALEX. Chicago Tribune (Paris), 10 April 1927. [About transition.]

*5202. SOSKIN, WILLIAM. [n.t.]. Evening Post (New York), 24 January 1929. [Review of Transition Stories.]

*5203. SOUPAULT, PHILIPPE. "A Propos de la traduction d'Anna Livia Plurabelle." Nouvelle revue française, 19 (May 1931): 633-636. [Reprinted in Souvenirs de James Joyce, No. 547; article accompanying the French translation of ALP by Samuel Beckett, A. Person, Ivan Goll, Eugene Jolas, Paul Léon, Adrienne Monnier, Soupault, and Joyce.]

5204. STONE, JAMES. "Lacunae: Part I (Poem)." James Joyce Quarterly, 9 (Winter 1971): 270-277; Part II. James Joyce Quarterly, 9 (Spring 1972): 390-396.

*5205. STONIER, G. W. [n.t.]. Sun (New York), 16 May 1930.

5206. _____. "Mr. James Joyce in Progress." New Statesman, 35 (28 June 1930): 372, 374.

5207. STRONG, L. A. G. "James Joyce and the New Fiction." American Mercury, 35, no. 140 (August 1935): 433-437. [Also appeared as "What is Joyce Doing with the Novel?" John O'London's Weekly, 34, no. 881 (29 February 1936): 821-822, 826.]

5208. _____. "Symbols, Words, and Finnegans Wake." Irish Writing, no. 1 (1946): 101-113.

*5209. STRZETELSKI, JERZY. "Slopiewnie James Joyce'a." Tworczosc (Warsaw), 15 (December 1959): 60-61. [Compares Tuwim's poem with FW.]

5210. _____. "Finnegans Wake w oczach krytyki." Literatura na świeci, no. 5 (May 1973): 54-84.

5211. STUART, MICHAEL. "Joyce after Ulysses." This Quarter, 2 (October-December 1929): 242-248.

5212. _____. "The Dubliner and his Dowdili (A Note on the Sublime)." transition, no. 18 (November 1929): 152-161.

5213. _____ . "James Joyce au Travail," translated by Yves de Longevialle. La revue
européenne, no. 3-4 (March-April 1930):
367-370.

5214. SUZUKI, YUKIO. [On Translating Finnegans
Wake]. Eigo seinen, 118, no. 4 (1972):
44.

5215. SVENDSEN, JOHN. "A Structural Analysis of
a Passage from Finnegans Wake." Language
and Literature, 1 (1971): 76-89.

5216. SYMOND, RONALD. "Third Mr. Joyce: Comments
on 'Work in Progress.'" London Mercury,
29 (February 1934): 318-321. [Reprinted
in Living Age, 346 (April 1934): 160-164.]

*5217. T., M. A. "Jottings." Dublin Evening Mail,
7 November 1961.

5218. THOMA, RICHARD. "Dream in Progress."
Contempo, 3, no. 13 (February 1934): 3.

5219. TITUS, EDWARD W. "Mr. Joyce Explains."
This Quarter, 4 (December 1931): 371-372.

5220. TORRE, GUILLERMO de. "Para una polemica
sobre la nueva novela." Mundo Nuevo
(Paris), no. 34 (April 1969): 81.

5221. TROY, WILLIAM. "Notes on Finnegans Wake."
Partisan Review, 6 (Summer 1939): 97-110.
[Appeared in James Joyce: Two Decades of
Criticism, pp. 302-318, No. 1570; trans-
lated in Configuration critique I, pp.
209-228, No. 1636; reprinted in his Se-
lected Essays. Edited by Stanley Edgar
Hyman. New Brunswick: Rutgers University
Press, 1967, pp. 94-109.]

5222. TYSDAHL, BJØRN. "Litt mer om Joyce og hans
kritikere." Edda, 68 (1968): 212-213.

5223. _____ . "Two Translations by Joyce."
James Joyce Quarterly, 4 (Spring 1967):
240-241.

5224. van LAERE, FRANCOIS. "Finnegans Wake, text-
uellement." L'Arc, 36 (1968): 88-93.

5225. _____ . "Les traducteurs français devant
Finnegans Wake." Revue des langues vivantes (Brussels), 34 (1968): 126-133.

5225a. _____ . "Finnegans Wake, ou le triomphe
des figures matricelles." Umana, 20
(May-September 1971): 22-25.

5226. VICKERY, JOHN B. "Finnegans Wake and Sexual
Metamorphosis." Contemporary Literature,
13 (Spring 1972): 213-242.

5227. VON PHUL, RUTH. "A Sketch of the Artist as
the Self-Parodist." James Joyce Quarterly,
3 (Fall 1965): 62.

5228. WAGNER, GEOFFREY. "Wyndham Lewis and James
Joyce: A Study in Controversy." South
Atlantic Quarterly, 56 (January 1957): 57-
66. [Appeared in his Wyndham Lewis. New
Haven: Yale University Press, 1957, pp.
168-188; reprinted Westport, Conn.: Greenwood Press, 1973.]

5229. WAIN, JOHN. [n.t.]. New Republic, 153 (7
August 1965): 20-22. [Review of John
Lennon's A Spainard in the Works and its
FW style.]

*5230. WEIGEL, JOHN. "Teaching the Modern Novel:
From Finnegans Wake to A Fable." College
English, 21 (December 1959): 172-173.

5231. WEST, REBECCA. "Letter from Europe." Bookman (New York), 70 (September 1929): 664-
668.

*5232. _____ . "James Joyce and His Followers."
New York Herald Tribune Books, 12 January 1930, pp. 1, 6.

*5233. Unsigned. "Die Deutsche Ausgabe von 'Finne-
gans Wake.'" Frankfurter Allgemeine
Zeitung, 16 June 1951.

5234. Unsigned. "In a Second Revolution a New Role
for Culture." Life, 26 December 1960,
p. 45.

*5235. Unsigned. "In the Latin Quarter." New York
Herald (Paris), 24 September 1929.

*5236. Unsigned. "Jimmys Hassegesang." Spiegel,
14 (14 December 1960): 81-83.

5237. Unsigned. "Joyce-übersetzung: Wsch! Ne Möwe."
Spiegel, 22 (15 January 1968): 104.

*5238. Unsigned. "La Nouvelle aventure de James
Joyce." Action Française, 25 June 1931.

*5239. Unsigned. "Les Lettres." Intranigeant
(Paris), 26 April 1931.

*5240. Unsigned. "M. James Joyce et son 'Ouvrage en
train.'" Le Mois, Synthèse de l'activité
mondiale, no. 26 (February-March 1933):
185-190.

*5241. Unsigned. "Magazines." Irish Statesman,
10 September 1927.

*5242. Unsigned. "O Jamesovi Joyceovi, Nejzajima-
vejsin a Nejsensaonejsim Avtorovi Sou-
casne." Narodni Politika Prahe (Prague),
15 August 1930.

*5243. Unsigned. "Pages in Waiting." Daily Tele-
graph (London), 13 May 1930.

*5244. Unsigned. [n.t.]. Ammilles (Saint-Etienne),
July 1931.

FINNEGANS WAKE

*5245. Unsigned. [n.t.]. Chicago Tribune (Paris), 2 April 1928. [Review of transition, no. 12.]

*5246. Unsigned. [n.t.]. Daily Express (London), 10 September 1930.

*5247. Unsigned. [n.t.]. Daily Sketch (London), 12 November 1929.

*5248. Unsigned. [n.t.]. Enquirer (Cincinnati), 5 May 1928.

*5249. Unsigned. [n.t.]. Evening News (Newark), 11 May 1929. [Review of Transition Stories.]

*5250. Unsigned. [n.t.]. Evening Sun (New York), 15 June 1927. [Review of transition, no. 2.]

*5251. Unsigned. [n.t.]. Journal (Minneapolis), 31 July 1927.

*5252. Unsigned. [n.t.]. Literary Review (Autumn 1929).

*5253. Unsigned. [n.t.]. New York Times, 24 February 1929. [Review of Transition Stories.]

*5254. Unsigned. [n.t.]. New York Times, 23 August 1929.

*5255. Unsigned. [n.t.]. Post (Liverpool), 30 October 1933.

*5256. Unsigned. [n.t.]. Quinzaine Critique (Paris), 25 September 1931. [Review of Soupault's translation of ALP in Nouvelle revue française (May 1931).]

*5257. Unsigned. [n.t.]. Soir (Paris), 5 November 1931.

LANGUAGE STUDIES

Books

5258. CHRISTIANI, DOUNIA BUNIS. "The Polyglot Poetry of Finnegans Wake," in James Joyce: His Place in World Literature, pp. 23-38, No. 1688.

5259. ECO, UMBERTO. "Dalla Summa al Finnegans Wake: le poetiche di Joyce," in his Opera aperta. Milan: Bompiani, 1962, pp. 215-361. [2nd edition appeared as Le poetiche di Joyce in 1966; translated by C. Roux de Bézieux and André Boucourechilliev as "De la Somme à Finnegans Wake: Les poétiques de James Joyce," in Oeuvre ouverte. Paris: Editions du Seuil, 1965, pp. 169-288.]

5260. _____. "Semantica dello metafora," in his Le forme del contenuto. Milan: Bompiani, 1971, pp. 93-125. [Translated by

Marida di Francesco as "Semantique de la metaphore." Tel quel, no. 55 (Autumn 1973): 25-46, omitting last five pages of original.]

5261. HODGART, M. J. C. "Artificial Languages," in A Wake Digest, pp. 56-58, No. 4935.

5262. JOLAS, EUGENE. "The Revolution of Language and James Joyce," in Our Exagmination, pp. 79-92, No. 4906. [Discussion of O'Faolain articles; see controversy summarized No. 5152.]

5263. KOCH, WALTER A. "Der Idiolekt des James Joyce," in Varia Semiotica. Studia Semiotica, series practica, no. 3. Hildesheim, New York: Georg Olms, 1971, pp. 396-416.

5264. LLONA, VICTOR. "I Don't Know What to call it but it's Mighty unlike Prose," in Our Exagmination, pp. 95-102, No. 4906. [Translated by Tomas G. Escajadillo and Marco A. Gutiérrez as "No sé cómo ila marlo pero es algo sumament distinto della prosa." Revista peruana de Cultura, no. 7-8 (June 1966): 213-220.]

5265. McALMON, ROBERT. "Mr. Joyce Directs an Irish Word Ballet," in Our Exagmination, pp. 105-116, No. 4906.

5266. PURDY, STROTHER B. "Mind your Genderous: Toward a Wake Grammar," in New Light on Joyce, pp. 46-78, No. 1656.

5267. WINTERS, YVOR. "The Extension and Reintegration of the Human Spirit through the Poetry Mainly French and American since Poe and Baudelaire," in The New American Caravan. Edited by Alfred Kreymborg, Lewis Mumford, and Paul Rosenfeld. New York: Macaulay, 1929, pp. 383-389.

Periodical Articles

*5268. 'AFFABLE HAWK' (Desmond MacCarthy). "Current Literature." New Statesman, 29 (14 May 1927): 151. [On Joyce and Gertrude Stein.]

5269. ATHERTON, J. S. "Finnegans Wake: The Gist of the Pantomime." Accent, 15 (Winter 1956): 14-26. [Translated as a revised and corrected version in Configuration critique de James Joyce, II, pp. 181-199, No. 1584.]

5270. BEYER, THOMAS P. "A Note on the Diction of Finnegans Wake." College English, 2 (December 1940): 275-277.

5271. BIERMAN, ROBERT. "Streameress Mastress to the Sea: A Note on Finnegans Wake." Modern Fiction Studies, 2 (May 1956): 79-80.

5272. BOGAN, LOUISE. "Proteus; Or Vico's Road." Nation, 148 (May 1939): 533-535. [Appeared in her Selected Criticism: Prose,

Poetry. New York: Noonday Press, 1955, pp. 142-148; reprinted in A Poet's Alphabet: Reflections on the Literary Art and Vocation. Edited by Robert Phelps and Ruth Limmer. New York: McGraw-Hill, 1970, pp. 262-266.]

5273. BORGES, JORG LUIS. "Joyce y los Neologismos." Sur, 62 (November 1939): 59-61.

5274. BRUNS, GERALD L. "Silent Orpheus: Annihilating Words and Literary Language." College English, 31 (May 1970): 821-827.

5275. BUTOR, MICHEL. "Esquisse d'un Seuil pour Finnegan." Nouvelle nouvelle revue française, 5e Année, no. 60 (December 1957): 1033-1053. [Translated by Juan Petit in Sobre literatura. Barcelona: Soix Barral, 1960; reprinted in his Répertoire. Paris: Les Éditions de Minuit, 1960, pp. 219-233; reprinted in his Essais sur les modernes. Paris: Gallimard, 1964, pp. 283-309; reprinted as "Introduction" to André du Bouchet's James Joyce: Finnegans Wake. Paris: Gallimard, 1962.]

*5276. CANBY, HENRY SEIDEL. "Gyring and Gibbling: Or Lewis Carroll in Paris." Saturday Review of Literature, 3, no. 40 (30 April 1927): 777, 782-783. [Later reprinted in his American Estimates. 1939, pp. 170-177.]

5277. COLUM, PADRAIC. "Notes on Finnegans Wake." Yale Review, 30 (March 1941): 640-645.

5278. COWDREY, MARY B. "The Linguistic Experiments of James Joyce." Horn Book Magazine, 6 (March 1933): 16-19.

5279. CRÉMIEUX, BENJAMIN. "Le Règne des Mots." Candide (Paris), 14 November 1929, p. 3. [Review of transition group's "Revolution of the Word."]

5280. FORD, FORD MADOX. "Finnegans Wake." Saturday Review of Literature, 20 (3 June 1939): 9. [Reply to Paul Rosenfeld's review, No. 2262; also in The Letters of Ford Madox Ford. Edited by Richard M. Ludwig. Princeton: Princeton University Press, 1965, pp. 320-323.]

*5281. GIEDION-WELCKER, CAROLA. "James Joyce und die Sprache." Die Weltwoche (Zürich), no. 225 (4 March 1938): 5. [Reprinted in her Schriften, 1926-1971: Statimen zu einer Zeitbild, pp. 49-51, No. 1566.]

5282. GILBERT, STUART. "Souvenirs de Voyage." Mercure de france, 309 (May 1950): 38-44.

5283. GLASHEEN, ADALINE. "Finnegans Wake and the Secret Languages of Ireland." Wake Newslitter, no. 10 (February 1963): 1-3. [Reprinted in A Wake Digest, pp. 48-51,

No. 4935; see also Vivian Mercier's addendum, no. 14 (June 1963): 7, 10.]

5284. _____. "AEsopian Language." Wake Newslitter, 4 (June 1967): 57.

*5285. HEARD, GERALD. "The Language of James Joyce." The Week-End, 14 June 1930, pp. 492-493.

5286. HEDBERG, JOHANNES. "'Smugging': An Investigation of a Joycean Word." Moderna Språk, 66 (1972): 19-25. [See also article by Alarik Rynell, No. 3387.]

*5287. HIGHET, GILBERT. "The Revolution of the Word." New Oxford Outlook, 1 (February 1934): 288-304.

5288. HILL, ARCHIBALD. "A Philologist Looks at Finnegans Wake." Virginia Quarterly Review, 15 (October 1939): 650-656.

5289. JOLAS, EUGENE. "The Revolution of the Word (A Symposium)." Modern Quarterly, 5 (Fall 1929): 273-292.

5290. _____. "transition's Revolution of the Word Dictionary." transition, no. 21 (March 1932): 323-324; no. 22 (February 1933): 122-123.

5291. LEAVIS, F. R. "Joyce and the Revolution of the Word." Scrutiny, 2, no. 2 (September 1933): 193-201. [Appeared in The Importance of Scrutiny. Edited by Eric Bentley. New York: Stewart, 1948, pp. 316-323, which was a reprint of the same article in For Continuity. Cambridge: Minority Press, 1933, pp. 207-219; former volume reprinted New York: New York University, 1964, pp. 316-323.]

5292. PETITJEAN, ARMAND. "Signification de Joyce." Études anglaises, 1 (September 1937): 405-417.

5293. _____. "El Tratamiento del Lenguaje en Joyce." Sur, no. 78 (March 1941): 42-59.

5294. PRESCOTT, JOSEPH. "James Joyce: A Study in Words." Publications of the Modern Language Association, 54 (March 1939): 304-315. [Also in his Exploring James Joyce, No. 1637; reprinted in Portrait: Notes, No. 3039a.]

5295. RANSOM, TIMOTHY. "The P-p-p-p-power of the Words, Words, Words: Finnegans Wake as Words Wake." James Joyce Quarterly, 9 (Winter 1971): 259-265.

5296. RODKER, JOHN. "Proteus, de James Joyce," translated by Ludmila Savitsky. La revue européenne, n.s. no. 1-2 (January-February 1928): 164-169.

FINNEGANS WAKE

5297. _____. "The Word Structure of 'Work in Progress.'" _transition_, no. 14 (Fall 1928): 229-232. [Appeared in _Our Examination_, pp. 141-146, No. 4906.]

5298. ROSENFELD, PAUL. "_Finnegans Wake._" _Saturday Review of Literature_, 20 (10 June 1939): 9, 20. [Response to Ford Madox Ford, No. 5280.]

5299. ROTHWELL, KENNETH. "Who Now Reads--?" _CEA Critic_, 14, no. 2 (February 1952): 4. [Excerpts from an article in the Dallas _Times-Herald_.]

5300. RUSSELL, FRANCIS. "Joyce and Alexandria." _Catacomb_, 2 (1951): 36-57. [Appeared in _Irish Writing_, no. 17 (December 1951): 33-53 and in _Three Studies in Twentieth Century Obscurity_. Aldington, Kent: Hand and Flower Press, 1954, pp. 7-44; reprinted New York: Haskell House, 1966, pp. 7-44; reprinted New York: Gordon Press, 1973, pp. 7-44.]

5301. SCHLAUCH, MARGARET. "The Language of James Joyce." _Science and Society: A Marxian Quarterly_, 3 (Fall 1939): 482-497. [Reprinted Folcroft, Pa.: Folcroft Library Editions, 1973.]

5302. SOLOMON, MARGARET. "The Phallic Letter of _Finnegans Wake._" _Language and Literature in Hawaii_, 1 (April 1968): 45-47. [An abstract of full article in _The Celtic Master_, pp. 37-43, No. 1583.]

*5303. STRAUMANN, HEINRICH. "Kernveränderungen in der englischen Literatursprache." _Neue Zürcher Zeitung_, 27 March 1954.

5304. STUART, MICHAEL. "Mr. Joyce's Word Creatures." _Colophon_, Part 7 (1931); also appeared in _Symposium_, 2 (October 1931): 459-469.

5305. TAPLIN, WALTER. "James Joyce Wrote English." _The Critic_, 1 (Spring 1947): 11-16.

5306. THOMPSON, WILLIAM IRWIN. "The Language of _Finnegans Wake._" _Sewanee Review_, 72 (Winter 1964): 78-90.

5307. WORTHINGTON, MABEL P. "Joyce's _Finnegans Wake._" _Explicator_, 14 (May 1956): item 52.

*5308. Unsigned. "James Joyce and the New Prose." _T.P.'s Weekly_, 12, no. 307 (14 September 1929): 573-574.

*5309. Unsigned. "Literature and Life: 'New Language.'" _Irish Statesman_, 25 August 1928.

STUDIES OF TECHNIQUE AND STRUCTURE

Books

5310. BEGNAL, MICHAEL H. "Who Speaks When I Dream? Who Dreams When I Speak?: A Narrational Approach to _Finnegans Wake_," in _Litters from Aloft_, pp. 74-90, No. 1516.

5311. BENSTOCK, BERNARD. "Here Comes Everybody: _Finnegans Wake_ as Epic," in _Nine Essays in Modern Literature_. Louisiana State University Studies, Humanities Series, no. 15. Edited by Donald E. Stanford. Baton Rouge: Louisiana State University Press, 1965, pp. 3-35.

5312. BUDGEN, FRANK. "Resurrection," in _Twelve and a Tilly_, pp. 11-15, No. 4923.

5313. EDWARDS, A. L. R. "_Finnegans Wake_," in _Personal Landscape_. Compiled by Robin Fedden. London: Editions Poetry Limited, 1945, pp. 27-36.

5314. GARZILLI, ENRICO. "Myth, Dream and Self: _Finnegans Wake_--James Joyce," in his _Circles without Centers: Paths to the Discovery and Creation of Self in Modern Literature_. Cambridge: Harvard University Press, 1972, pp. 65-74.

5315. HART, CLIVE. _Structure and Motif in Finnegans Wake_. London: Faber and Faber, 1962. [Translation of revised section, "Le motif 'Quinet' dans _Finnegans Wake_," appeared in _Configuration critique de James Joyce_, II, pp. 201-222, No. 1584.]

5316. HOFFMAN, FREDERICK J. "'The Seim Anew': Flux and Family in _Finnegans Wake_," in _Twelve and a Tilly_, pp. 16-25, No. 4923.

5317. PAUL, ELLIOTT. "Mr. Joyce's Treatment of Plot," in _Our Exagmination_, pp. 131-137, No. 4906.

5318. RAMNOUS, CLEMENCE. "The Finn Cycle: The Atmosphere and Symbols of a Legend," in _James Joyce Yearbook_, pp. 130-158, No. 1596.

5319. VON PHUL, RUTH. "Circling the Square: A Study of Structure," in _A James Joyce Miscellany_, Third Series, pp. 239-277, No. 1614.

Periodical Articles

5320. ASSENJO, F. G. "The General Problem of Sentence Structure: An Analysis Prompted by the Loss of Subject in _Finnegans Wake._" _Centennial Review_, 8 (Fall 1964): 398-408.

5321. AUBERT, J. A. "The Genealogy of Grammar." _Wake Newslitter_, 4 (April 1967): 39.

5322. BENSTOCK, BERNARD. "Ever Telling has a Tale: A Reading of the Narrative of _Finnegans Wake_." _Modern Fiction Studies_, 15 (Spring 1969): 3-25.

5323. BURINCK, J. R. "_Finnegans Wake_ is an Oral Book: It is Something to be Read Aloud." _Utopia_, 8 (June 1969): 27-28.

5324. FITZMORRIS, T. J. "Vico Adamant and Some Pillars of Salt." _Catholic World_, 156 (February 1943): 568-577.

5325. FLEMING, WILLIAM S. "Formulaic Rhythms in _Finnegans Wake_." _Style_, 9 (Winter 1972): 19-37.

5326. FROBERG, HERLUF. "Om Begreber og Vaerdier i Moderne Aesthetik." _Heretica_, 4 (1951): 190-209.

*5327. GIEDION-WELCKER, CAROLA. "Mythisches und Sprachliches in _Finnegans Wake_." _Neue Zürcher Zeitung_, 28 March 1954.

5328. GRAHAM, PHILIP L. "The Middlewhite Fair." _Wake Newslitter_, 6 (October 1969): 67-69.

5329. HALPER, NATHAN. "Joyce, Earwicker, and the Performing Arts." _Center_, 1 (1954): 7-11.

5330. HENSELER, DONNA L. "'Harpsdichord,' The Formal Principle of HCE, ALP, and the Cad." _James Joyce Quarterly_, 6 (Fall 1968): 53-68.

5331. HIGGINSON, FRED H. "Homer: Vico: Joyce." _Kansas Magazine_ (1956): 83-88.

5332. KUMAR, SHIV K. "Space-Time Polarity in _Finnegans Wake_." _Modern Philology_, 54 (May 1957): 230-233.

5333. LLOYD, P. C. "Developments of Motifs in James Joyce." _Mandrake_, 1, no. 6 (1949): 6-12.

5334. McHUGH, ROLAND. "A Structural Theory of _Finnegans Wake_." _Wake Newslitter_, 5 (December 1968): 83-87.

5335. McLUHAN, HERBERT M. "Radio & TV vs. the ABCED-Minded." _Explorations_, no. 5 (1956): 12-18.

5336. MAGALANER, MARVIN. "The Myth of Man: Joyce's _Finnegans Wake_." _University of Kansas City Review_, 16 (Summer 1950): 265-277. [Reprinted in _Myth and Literature_. Edited by John B. Vickery. Lincoln: University of Nebraska Press, 1966, pp. 201-212.]

*5337. MERCANTON, JACQUES. "L'esthetique de Joyce." _Études de lettres_ (Lausanne), 13 (October 1938): 20-[46?].

5338. MORSE, J. MITCHELL. "Jacob and Esau in _Finnegans Wake_." _Modern Philology_, 52 (November 1954): 123-130.

5339. PELORSON, GEORGES. "_Finnegans Wake_ ou les Livres de l'Homme." _Aux écoutes_, 23, no. 1096 (20 May 1939): 29. [Appeared in expanded form in _Revue de Paris_, 1 (September 1939): 227-235.]

5340. PETITJEAN, ARMAND. "James Joyce et l'Absorption du Monde par le Langage." _Cahiers du sud_, 11 (October 1934): 607-623.

5341. _____. "Joyce and Mythology: Mythology and Joyce," translated by Maria Jolas. _transition_, no. 23 (July 1935): 133-142.

5342. RANSOM, JOHN CROWE. "Aesthetic of _Finnegans Wake_." _Kenyon Review_, 1 (Autumn 1939): 424-428.

5343. ROSENFELD, PAUL. "James Joyce: Charlatan or Genius?" _American Mercury_, 47 (July 1939): 367-371. [Translated in _Babel_, 1 (September 1939): 135-137; a revision of his _SatR_ review, No. 2262.]

5344. SEMMLER, CLEMENT. "Some Notes on the Themes and Language of _Finnegans Wake_." _Southerly_, 15 (1954): 156-171. [Also in his _For the Uncanny Man_, pp. 93-108, No. 1653.]

5345. TALLENTIRE, D. R. "Mathematics and Style." _Times Literary Supplement_, 13 August 1971, p. 973.

5346. THEALL, DONALD. "Here Comes Everybody." _Explorations_ (April 1954): 66-77.

5347. THOMPSON, FRANCIS J. "A Portrait of the Artist Asleep." _Western Review_, 14 (Summer 1950): 245-253.

5348. TYLER, HAMILTON. "Finnegans Epic." _Circle_, no. 7-8 (1946): 14-26.

5349. VON PHUL, RUTH. "Who Sleeps at Finnegans Wake?" _James Joyce Review_, 1, no. 2 (February 1957): 27-38.

5350. WILLIAMS, WILLIAM CARLOS. "A Note on the Recent Work of James Joyce." _transition_, no. 8 (November 1927): 149-154. [Appeared in his _Selected Essays_. New York: Random House, 1954, pp. 75-79; reprinted in his _Imaginations_. Edited by Webster Schott. New York: New Directions, 1970, pp. 333-338.]

ALLUSIONS

Books

5351. ATHERTON, J. S. _Books at the Wake_. New York: Viking Press, 1960.

FINNEGANS WAKE

5352. _____. "French Argot in Finnegans Wake," in A Wake Digest, pp. 41-42, No. 4935.

5353. BOLDEREFF, FRANCES. Hermes to His Son Thoth: Being Joyce's use of Giordano Bruno in Finnegans Wake. Woodward, Pa.: Classic Non-Fiction Library, 1968.

5354. BONHEIM, HELMUT W. A Lexicon of the German in Finnegans Wake. Berkeley: University of California Press, 1967.

5355. BUDGEN, FRANK. "James Joyce's 'Work in Progress' and Old Norse Poetry," in Our Exagmination, pp. 37-46, No. 4906.

5356. CHRISTIANI, DOUNIA BUNIS. Scandanavian Elements of Finnegans Wake. Evanston, Ill.: Northwestern University Press, 1965.

5357. GLASHEEN, ADALINE. A Census of Finnegans Wake. Northwestern University Studies, Humanities Series, no. 32. Evanston, Ill.: Northwestern University Press, 1956.

5358. _____. A Second Census of Finnegans Wake: An Index of the Characters and Their Roles. Evanston, Ill.: Northwestern University Press, 1963.

5359. GLECKNER, ROBERT F. "Byron in Finnegans Wake," in Twelve and a Tilly, pp. 40-51, No. 4923.

5360. LITZ, A. WALTON. "Vico and Joyce," in Giambatista Vico. Edited by Giorgio Tagliacozzo and Hayden V. White. Baltimore: Johns Hopkins University Press, 1969, pp. 245-258.

5361. MERCIER, VIVIAN. "In the Wake of the Fianna: Some Additions and Corrections to Glasheen and a Footnote or Two to Atherton," in A James Joyce Miscellany, Third Series, pp. 226-238, No. 1614.

5362. _____. "James Joyce and the Macronic Tradition," in Twelve and a Tilly, pp. 26-35, No. 4923.

5363. O HEHIR, BRENDAN. A Gaelic Lexicon for Finnegans Wake and Glossary for Joyce's Other Works. Berkeley: University of California Press, 1967.

5364. SCOTT, L. H. "'Sprats ye, gus paudheen!: Notes from a Survey-in-Progress of Slavs and Slavicisms in Finnegans Wake," in Studies Presented to Professor Roman Jakobson by his Students. Edited by Charles E. Gribble. Cambridge, Mass.: Slavica Publishers, 1968, pp. 289-298.

5365. SULLIVAN, KEVIN. "The House by the Churchyard: James Joyce and Sheridan le Fanu," in Modern Irish Literature: Essays in Honor of William York Tindall. Library of Irish Studies, vol. 1. Edited by Raymond J. Porter and James D. Brophy. New York: Iona College Press and Twayne, 1972, pp. 315-334.

Periodical Articles

5366. ASHRAF, SYED MOHMMED. "A Note on Dr. Benstock's Article--'Persian in Finnegans Wake.'" Wake Newslitter, 7 (December 1970): 90-91. [See Benstock article, No. 5385.]

5367. ATHERTON, JAMES S. "Arrah-na-pogue and Finnegans Wake." Notes and Queries, 194 (October 1949): 430-432.

5368. _____. "Finnegans Wake and Poverty." Times Literary Supplement, 23 November 1951, p. 749.

5369. _____. "Lewis Carroll and Finnegans Wake." English Studies, 33 (February 1952): 1-15.

5370. _____. "Joyce and Cricket." Times Literary Supplement, 9 May 1952, p. 313. [Discussion by Gerald Brodribb. 16 May 1952, p. 329; W. P. Hone. 30 May 1952, p. 361; Eoin O'Mahony. 20 June 1952, p. 405; P. R. Butler. 27 June 1952, p. 421; D. D. Dunkley. 1 August 1952, p. 501.]

5371. _____. "Cardinal Newman in Finnegans Wake." Notes and Queries, 198 (March 1953): 120-121.

5372. _____. "Ghazi Power: Frank le Boer Power in Finnegans Wake." Notes and Queries, 198 (September 1953): 399-400.

5373. _____. "Islam and Koran in Finnegans Wake." Comparative Literature, 6 (Summer 1954): 240-255.

5374. _____. "A Royal Divorce in Finnegans Wake." James Joyce Review, 1, no. 3 (September 1957): 39-42.

5375. _____. "A Few More Books at the Wake." James Joyce Quarterly, 2 (Spring 1965): 142-149.

5376. _____. "To Give Down the Banks and Hark from the Tomb!" James Joyce Quarterly, 4 (Winter 1967): 75-83. [Huckleberry Finn.]

5377. _____. "Classical Commentary." Wake Newslitter, 4 (April 1967): 40-41.

5378. _____. "Scandinavian Elements." Wake Newslitter, 4 (April 1967): 41.

5379. _____. "The Maunder's Praise of his Strolling Mort." Joycenotes, 1 (June 1969): 18.

5380. _____ . "Lodge's The Survival of Man in
Finnegans Wake." Wake Newslitter, 8
(February 1971): 8-10. [See also his
"Still More Peacock in the Oxen." Wake
Newslitter, 8 (August 1971): 53 and Phil-
ip Herring. "More Peacock in the Oxen."
ibid., 51-53.]

5381. AUBERT, JACQUES. "Notes on the French Element in Finnegans Wake." James Joyce
Quarterly, 5 (Winter 1968): 110-124.

5382. BATES, RONALD. "Finnish in Finnegans Wake."
Wake Newslitter, 3 (February 1966): 3-4.

5383. BEGNAL, MICHAEL. "The Fables of Finnegans
Wake." James Joyce Quarterly, 6 (Summer
1969): 357-367.

5384. BENSTOCK, BERNARD. "Americana in Finnegans
Wake." Bucknell Review, 12 (March 1964):
64-81.

5385. _____ . "Persian in Finnegans Wake."
Philological Quarterly, 44 (January 1965):
100-109. [See No. 5366.]

5386. BROES, ARTHUR T. "The Bible in Finnegans
Wake." Wake Newslitter, 2 (December
1965): 3-11. [See also ibid., 3 (1966):
102-105.]

5387. _____ . "More People at the Wake." Wake
Newslitter, 3 (December 1966): 125-128.

5388. _____ . "More People at the Wake." Wake
Newslitter, 4 (February 1967): 25-30.

5389. _____ . "More Books at the Wake." James
Joyce Quarterly, 9 (Winter 1971): 189-217.

5390. BURGESS, ANTHONY. "Mark Twain and James
Joyce." Mark Twain Journal, 13 (Winter
1966-67): 1-2.

*5391. CARLSON, MARVIN. "Henrik Ibsen and Finnegans
Wake." Comparative Literature, 12 (Spring
1960): 133-141.

5392. CHRISTIANI, DOUNIA. "H. C. Earwicker the
Ostman." James Joyce Quarterly, 2 (Spring
1965): 150-157.

5393. COPE, JACKSON I. "From Egyptian Rubbish-
heaps to Finnegans Wake." James Joyce
Quarterly, 3 (Spring 1966): 166-170.

5394. DALTON, JACK P. "Re 'Kiswahili Words in
Finnegans Wake' by Philipp Wolff." Wake
Newslitter, no. 12 (April 1963): 6-12.
[See WN, no. 8 (December 1962): 2-4;
Dalton article reprinted in A Wake Digest,
pp. 43-47, No. 4935.]

5395. _____ . "Finnegans Wake at Large." Wake
Newslitter, no. 15 (August 1963): 1-2.
[S. J. Perelman.]

5396. _____ . "A Mother." Wake Newslitter, 1
(June 1964): 4-5.

5397. DAVIES, ANEIRIN. "A Note on Finnegans Wake."
Welsh Review, 7 (Summer 1948): 141-143.

5398. EPSTEIN, EDMUND L. "Another Book at the
Wake." James Joyce Quarterly, 5 (Spring
1968): 278. [Joseph Collins' The Doctor
Looks at Literature.]

5399. FAJ, ATTILA. "La filosofia vichiana in
Joyce." Forum Italicum, 2 (1968): 470-
482. [Presented as paper at Third International James Joyce Symposium: "Some
Important, Hitherto Unnoticed, Sources
of Finnegans Wake."]

5400. _____ . "Alcune fonti importanti, finora
ignorate, del Finnegans Wake." Revista di
letterature moderne e comparate, 24 (September 1971): 223-234. [Translated as
"Some Important, Hitherto Unnoticed
Sources for Finnegans Wake." Wake Newslitter, 10 (February 1973): 3-12; reprinted in Neuphilologische Mitteilungen, 75,
no. 4 (1974): 650-662. Stoics and Imre
Madách.]

5401. FORD, WILLIAM J. "Old Parr." Bulletin of
the History of Medicine, 24 (1950): 219-
226.

5402. FRYE, NORTHROP. "Quest and Cycle in Finne-
gans Wake." James Joyce Review, 1, no. 1
(February 1957): 39-47. [Reprinted in his
Fables of Identity. New York: Harcourt,
Brace and World, 1959, pp. 256-264; trans-
lated by Alain Delahaye in Change, no. 11
(May 1972): 111-119, No. 157.]

5403. GLASHEEN, ADALINE. "Finnegans Wake and the
Girls from Boston, Mass." Hudson Review,
7 (Spring 1954): 89-96.

5404. _____ . "Out of my Census." Analyst,
no. 17 (September 1960).

5405. _____ . "avtokinatown." Wake Newslitter,
no. 18 (December 1963): 4-5. [Chinoiser-
ie.]

5406. _____ . "Semper as Oxhousehumper." Wake
Newslitter, 1 (February 1964): 7-11.
[Hebrew.]

5407. _____ . "Some References to Thoth." Wake
Newslitter, 1 (December 1964): 6-8.

5408. _____ . "Dublin Firms." Wake Newslitter,
4 (August 1967): 78.

5409. _____ . "Census Revisions." Wake Newslitter, 6 (October 1969): 77-78.

5410. _____ . "The Authoress of Paradise Lost."
Wake Newslitter, 7 (December 1970): 83-88.
[Marie Corelli's Sorrows of Satan.]

FINNEGANS WAKE

5411. GLECKNER, ROBERT F. "In the Wake of The Census." Analyst, no. 20 (September 1961): 5-11.

5412. GOODWIN, DAVID. "Hebrew in The Wake." Wake Newslitter, 9 (October 1972): 68-75.

*5413. GOPALEEN, MYLES na (Flann O'Brien, Brian Nolan). "Cruiskeen Lawn." Irish Times, 20 December 1957.

*5414. _____ . "Cruiskeen Lawn." Irish Times, 7 July 1958.

*5415. _____ . "Cruiskeen Lawn." Irish Times, 2 August 1958.

5416. GRAHAM, PHILIP L. "re-furloined notepaper (419.29)." Wake Newslitter, no. 7 (November 1962): 1-4. [Supplemented by "More Groseness." WN, no. 9 (January 1963): 7-8; reprinted in A Wake Digest, pp. 17-20, No. 4935.]

5417. HALPER, NATHAN. "The Most Eyeful Hoyth of Finnegans Wake." New Republic, 124 (7 May 1951): 20-23. [Also appeared in Minerva, 71 (October 1951): 329-333.]

5418. _____ . "A Passage in Albanian." Wake Newslitter, no. 14 (June 1963): 5-6. [Reprinted in A Wake Digest, pp. 54-55, No. 4935.]

5419. _____ . "Notes on Late Historical Events." Wake Newslitter, 2 (October 1965): 15-16. [See also comments by Ruth Von Phul, ibid., December 1965, pp. 26-29.]

5420. _____ . "Another Anecdote in Ellmann." Wake Newslitter, 3 (June 1966): 56-57. [Ellmann's JJ, p. 720.]

5421. _____ . "A Plea for Intolerance." Wake Newslitter, 3 (June 1966): 68-76. [Contra Glasheen's Census; see reply by Ruth Von Phul, ibid. (August 1966): 85-87.]

5422. _____ . "Another Anecdote in Ellmann." Wake Newslitter, 5 (December 1968): 90-93. [Ellmann, JJ, p. 411n misses pun in FW 353.]

5423. _____ . "Joyce and James Branch Cabell." Wake Newslitter, 6 (August 1969): 51-60. [Also revised and enlarged as "Joyce/Cabell and Cabell/Joyce." Kalki, 4 (Winter 1969): 9-24.]

5424. HART, CLIVE. "Shem's Bodily Getup; A Note on Some Unused Theology." James Joyce Quarterly, 3 (Fall 1965): 66-68.

5425. _____ , and PHILIP B. SULLIVAN. "Australiana in Finnegans Wake." Wake Newslitter, no. 9 (January 1963): 1-5.

5426. HAYMAN, DAVID. "Tristan and Isolde in Finnegans Wake: A Study of the Sources and Evolution of a Theme." Comparative Literature Studies, 1 (Summer 1964): 93-112.

5427. _____ . "Pound at the Wake or the Uses of a Contemporary." James Joyce Quarterly, 2 (Spring 1965): 204-216.

5428. HENRICI, WALDTRAUD B. "Anspielungen auf Ibsens Dramen in Finnegans Wake." Orbis litterarum, 23 (1968): 127-160.

5429. HEWES, HENRY. "Two Masterpieces in Search of an Audience." Saturday Review of Literature, 38 (31 December 1955): 25.

5430. HODGART, M. J. C. "Shakespeare and Finnegans Wake." Cambridge Journal, 6 (September 1953): 735-752.

5431. _____ . "Some Lithuanian Words in Finnegans Wake." Wake Newslitter, no. 15 (August 1963): 6-7. [Reprinted in A Wake Digest, pp. 59-61, No. 4935.]

5432. _____ . "Word-Hoard." Wake Newslitter, 1 (February 1964): 1-5. (Albanian, Kiswahili); ibid., 9-10 (Basque).

5433. HOLLINGDALE, R. J. "A Note on Joyce and Bruno." Wake Newslitter, no. 11 (March 1963): 4-5.

5434. IOANNIDOU, IOANNA, and LEO KNUTH. "Greek in 'The Mookse and the Gripes.'" Wake Newslitter, 8 (December 1971): 83-88; ibid., 10 (February 1973): 12-16.

5435. JARRELL, MACKIE L. "Swiftiana in Finnegans Wake." ELH: Journal of English Literary History, 26 (June 1959): 271-294.

5436. JENKINS, WILLIAM D. "Algernon Charles Swinburne, Rex of Regums." Wake Newslitter, 6 (February 1969): 8-11.

5437. KARRFALT, DAVID H. "James II and the Earl of Lucan." Wake Newslitter, 8 (December 1971): 89.

5438. KELLEHER, JOHN V. "Notes on Finnegans Wake and Ulysses." Analyst, no. 10 (1956): 1-9.

5439. _____ . "Notes on Finnegans Wake." Analyst, no. 12 (April 1957): 9-15.

5440. _____ . "Identifying the Irish Printed Sources for Finnegans Wake." Irish University Review, 1 (Spring 1971): 161-177.

5441. KIRALIS, KARL. "Joyce and Blake: A Basic Source for Finnegans Wake." Modern Fiction Studies, 4 (Winter 1958-59): 329-334.

5442. KNUTH, LEO. "Dutch Elements in Finnegans Wake, pp. 75-78 Compared with Holograph Workbook VI.B.46." Wake Newslitter, 5 (April 1968): 19-28.

5443. _____. "Some Notes on Malay Elements in Finnegans Wake." Wake Newslitter, 5 (August 1968): 51-63.

5444. _____. "Dutch in Finnegans Wake Holograph Workbooks VI.B.22 and VI.B.26." James Joyce Quarterly, 7 (Spring 1970): 218-228.

5445. _____. "Correspondence." Wake Newslitter, 7 (August 1970): 63. [More Malay.]

5446. _____. "Beckett's 'Come in.'" Wake Newslitter, 7 (December 1970): 96. [Ellmann, JJ, p. 662.]

5447. _____. "Dutch in Finnegans Wake." Wake Newslitter, 8 (April 1971): 24-32; 8 (June 1971): 35-43; 8 (August 1971): 54-62.

5448. KOCH, RONALD J. "Giordano Bruno and Finnegans Wake: A New Look at Shaun's Objection to the 'Nolanus Theory.'" James Joyce Quarterly, 9 (Winter 1971): 237-249.

5449. KOPPER, EDWARD A., JR. "Some Additional Christian Allusions in the Wake." Analyst, no. 24 (March 1965): 5-22.

5450. _____. "Saint Patrick in Finnegans Wake." Wake Newslitter, 4 (October 1967): 109.

5451. _____. "Three More Legends in Finnegans Wake." Wake Newslitter, 4 (December 1967): 119-120.

5452. _____. "'An Encounter' in the Wake." Wake Newslitter, 6 (April 1969): 20-21.

5453. _____. "More Legends in Finnegans Wake." Wake Newslitter, 6 (June 1969): 39-43.

5454. LAIDLAW, R. P. "More Huck Finn in Finnegans Wake." Wake Newslitter, 5 (October 1968): 71-73.

5455. LEE, L. L. "Some Uses of Finnegans Wake in John Barth's The Sot-Weed Factor." James Joyce Quarterly, 5 (Winter 1968): 177-178.

5456. _____. "The Mormons at the Wake." James Joyce Quarterly, 6 (Fall 1968): 87-88.

5457. McCARTHY, KEVIN M. "Turkish References in Finnegans Wake." James Joyce Quarterly, 9 (Winter 1971): 250-258.

5458. MacCARVILL, EILEEN. "Les Années de Formation de James Joyce à Dublin." Archives des lettres modernes, no. 12 (1958): 1-31.

5459. McGREEVY, THOMAS. "Note on 'Work in Progress.'" transition, no. 14 (Fall 1928): 216-219. [Reprinted as "The Catholic Element in 'Work in Progress,'" in Our Exagmination, pp. 119-127, No. 4906; reprinted in A Bash in the Tunnel, pp. 213-219, No. 1644.]

5460. McHUGH, ROLAND. "The Languish of Tintangle." Wake Newslitter, 8 (October 1971): 76-77. [Cornish word-list.]

5461. MALINGS, RON. "Cricketeers at the Wake." James Joyce Quarterly, 7 (Summer 1970): 333-349.

5462. MARCUS, PHILIP L. "The Wake and Piers Plowman." Wake Newslitter, 3 (April 1966): 36-37.

5463. _____. "Conchubar Mac Nessa and Finnegans Wake." Wake Newslitter, 4 (April 1967): 36-37.

5464. _____. "Irish Warriors Once Again." Wake Newslitter, 4 (October 1967): 101-102.

5465. MISRA, B. P. "Joyce's Use of Indian Philosophy in Finnegans Wake." Indian Journal of English Studies (Calcutta), 1 (1960): 70-78.

5466. _____. "Sanskrit Translations." Wake Newslitter, 1 (December 1964): 8-10; 2 (February 1965): 9-11.

5467. MITCHELL, BREON. "The Newer Alchemy: Lord Rutherford and Finnegans Wake." Wake Newslitter, 3 (October 1966): 96-102.

5468. _____. "Swobbing Grouguen Eeriesh Myth Brockendootsch: Two German Novelists in Finnegans Wake." Wake Newslitter, 5 (October 1968): 70-71. [Alfred Döblin, 490.15; Hermann Broch, 272.24.]

5469. MONTGOMERY, NIALL. "Joyeux Quicum Ulysses-- Swissairis Dubellay Gadelice." Envoy, 5 (May 1951): 31-43. [Reprinted in A Bash in the Tunnel, pp. 61-72, No. 1644.]

5470. MORLANG, WERNER. "Those Lips." Wake Newslitter, 7 (December 1970): 95. [Shakespeare allusion at FW 628.]

5471. MORSE, J. MITCHELL. "Burrus, Caseous, and Nicholas of Cusa." Modern Language Notes, 75 (April 1960): 326-334.

5472. _____. "Charles Nodier and Finnegans Wake." Comparative Literature Studies, 5 (Summer 1968): 195-201.

5473. MURPHY, JIM. "More from the Book of Kells." Wake Newslitter, 6 (October 1969): 73.

FINNEGANS WAKE

5474. NAG, MARTIN. "Hamsum i Finnegans Wake." Edda, 54 (1967): 356-360. [See reply by Bjørn Tysdahl, No. 5509.]

5475. NAGAHARA, KAZUO. ["Joyce and Vico"]. Otaru shoka daigaku jinmon Kenkyu, no. 42 (March 1971): 41076. [In Japanese.]

5476. O HEHIR, BRENDAN. "Anna Livia Plurabelle's Gaelic Ancestry." James Joyce Quarterly, 2 (Spring 1965): 158-166.

5477. _____ . "A Gaelic Lexicon for Finnegans Wake: Supplement." Wake Newslitter, 5 (December 1968): 87-90.

5478. PEERY, WILLIAM. "Shakhisbeard at Finnegans Wake." Studies in English (Texas), 30 (1951): 243-257.

5479. RANKIN, H. D. [Additions and Corrections to Atherton and Glasheen]. Wake Newslitter, 2 (December 1965): 14-17.

5480. RITCHIE, A. M. "Notae in Programma Quoddam." Wake Newslitter, no. 12 (April 1963): 3-5. [Australiana]

5481. RODEWALD, CLARK. "A Note on the Names in Finnegans Wake." English Language Notes, 2 (June 1965): 292-293.

5482. ROSE, ELLEN C. "Hawthorne Allusions in 'Anna Livia Plurabelle.'" Wake Newslitter, no. 12 (April 1963): 1-3.

5483. SEDELOW, WALTER A. "Joyce's Finnegans Wake." Explicator, 13 (February 1955): item 27.

5484. SENN, FRITZ. "Early Russian History in Finnegans Wake." James Joyce Review, 2, nos. 1-2 (June 1958): 63-64.

5485. _____ . "Schweizerdeutsches in Finnegans Wake." Du (Zürich), May 1960, pp. 51-52. [Privately printed in Zürich, 1960; reprinted in his James Joyce: Aufsätze von Fritz Senn, pp. 12-15, No. 1654.]

5486. _____ . "Some Zürich Allusions in Finnegans Wake." Analyst, no. 19 (December 1960): 1-23.

5487. _____ . "Borrowed Brogues." Wake Newslitter, no. 3 (June 1962): 4-6. [Reprinted in A Wake Digest, pp. 62-63, No. 4935.]

5488. _____ . "rheadoromanscing." Wake Newslitter, no. 11 (March 1963): 1-2. [Rhaeto-Romanic words.]

5489. _____ . "Pat as Ah Be Seated." Wake Newslitter, 1 (June 1964): 5-7. [Hebrew, Phoenician, and Egyptian references.]

5490. _____ . "One White Elephant." Wake Newslitter, 1 (August 1964): 1-3. [Buddhist legend]

5491. _____ . "Ossianic Echoes." Wake Newslitter, 2 (April 1966): 25-36.

5492. _____ . "Old Celtic Romances." Wake Newslitter, 4 (February 1967): 8-11.

5493. _____ . "Old Celtic Romances." Wake Newslitter, 4 (April 1967): 8-10.

5494. _____ . "The Short and the Long of It." Joycenotes, 1 (June 1969): 20-21.

5495. _____ . "Buybibles." James Joyce Quarterly, 7 (Spring 1970): 257-258.

5496. _____ . "The Localization of Legend." Wake Newslitter, 8 (February 1971): 10-13.

5497. STAPLES, HUGH B. "Beckett in the Wake." James Joyce Quarterly, 8 (Summer 1971): 421-424.

5498. _____ . "Mirror in His House." Wake Newslitter, 8 (June 1971): 44-45. [References to O'Casey's autobiography.]

5499. SULLIVAN, PHILIP B. "Father Finn Again." Analyst, no. 20 (September 1961): 1-2.

5500. _____ . "Four Notes on the Census." Wake Newslitter, no. 11 (March 1963): 2.

5501. _____ . "Henry van Dyke would have left early." Wake Newslitter, no. 11 (March 1963): 3.

5502. _____ . "Tolstoy's War and Peace at the Wake." James Joyce Quarterly, 1 (Fall 1964): 64.

5503. _____ . "Notes." James Joyce Quarterly, 2 (Spring 1965): 232-236.

5504. _____ . "Dedalus Hyperboreus." Wake Newslitter, 6 (April 1969): 26-27. [Swedenborg's Dedalus Hyperboreus.]

5505. _____ . "The Decline of the West." Wake Newslitter, 7 (December 1970): 92-93.

5506. TANNER, GODFREY. "Classical Language References in Finnegans Wake: A Philological Commentary with Versions." Wake Newslitter, 3 (April 1966): 37-39; (June 1966): 58-60; (October 1966): 105-108.

5507. TEELE, ROY E. "Kungfusian Sinicisms and Budhy Jape-words in Finnegans Wake." South Central Bulletin, 26 (March 1966): 9.

5508. TYSDAHL, BJØRN. "A Norse 'Hundredlettered Name' in Finnegans Wake." Orbis litterarum, 19 (1964): 232-233.

5509. _____ . "Til vinning for perspektivet." Edda, 68 (1968): 70-73. [Reply to Martin Nag No. 5474; Nag's rebuttal, ibid., 213-

214; Tysdahl's reply, "Litt mer om Joyce og hans kritikere," 212-213.]

5510. _____. "Joyce's Use of Norwegian Writers." English Studies, 50 (June 1969): 261-273.

5511. _____, and CLIVE HART. "Norwegian Captions." Wake Newslitter, 1 (October 1964): 6-9; (December 1964): 11-13; 2 (1965): 7-9, 13-15.

5512. VON PHUL, RUTH. "Shaun in Brooklyn." Analyst, no. 16 (1959): 1-22; "Shaun in Brooklyn: Errata." ibid., no. 17 (1959): 73; "Shaun in Brooklyn: Corrigenda and Addenda." ibid., no. 20 (September 1961): 12-14.

5513. WAGNER, RICHARD. "Danish at the Wake." James Joyce Quarterly, 6 (Winter 1968): 171-173.

5514. WERCKMEISTER, O. K. "Das Book of Kells in Finnegans Wake." Neue Rundschau, 87 (1966): 44-63.

5515. WILSON, ROBERT A. "Joyce and Tao." James Joyce Review, 3, nos. 1-2 (February 1959): 8-15.

5516. WOLFF, PHILIPP. "Kiswahili Words in Finnegans Wake." Wake Newslitter, no. 8 (December 1962): 2-4.

5517. WORTHINGTON, MABEL P. "Another Classical Allusion in Finnegans Wake." Wake Newslitter, 4 (April 1967): 38.

5518. Unsigned. "Cletter Clutter." Times Literary Supplement, 11 February 1965, p. 107. [Response by Remo Ceserani, 18 March 1965.]

EXPLICATIONS

Books

5519. AIKEN, CONRAD. "I'm a Water-Witch Mostly Incurable," in A Seizure of Limericks. New York: Holt, Rinehart and Winston, 1964, p. 37.

5520. ATHERTON, JAMES S. "Sport and Games in Finnegans Wake," in Twelve and a Tilly, pp. 52-64, No. 4923.

5521. BOLDEREFF, FRANCES MOTT. Reading Finnegans Wake. New York: Barnes and Noble, 1959.

5522. BURKE, KENNETH. Philosophy of Literary Form. Baton Rouge: Louisiana State University Press, 1941, passim.

5523. CAMPBELL, JOSEPH, and HENRY MORTON ROBINSON. A Skeleton Key to Finnegans Wake. London: Faber and Faber; New York: Harcourt, Brace, 1944; paperback reprint. Viking-

Compass, 1961. [Incorporates "Unlocking the Door to Joyce." SatR, 26 (19 June 1943): 4-6; extract "Introducão a um assunto estranho," in Panaroma do Finnegans Wake. Edited by Augusto and Haroldo de Campos. São Paulo: Conselho Estadual de Cultura, Comissão de Literature, 1962, pp. 61-73.]

5524. HALPER, NATHAN. "The Date of Earwicker's Dream," in Twelve and a Tilly, pp. 72-90, No. 4923.

5525. HARVEY, DAVID DOW. Ford Madox Ford, 1873-1939: A Bibliography of Works and Criticism. Princeton: Princeton University Press, 1962, pp. 541-543, et passim.

5526. HILDESHEIMER, WOLFGANG. "Übersetzung und Interpretation einer Passage aus Finnegans Wake von James Joyce," in Interpretationen: James Joyce, Georg Büchner, Zewi Frankfurter Vorlesungen. Frankfurt am.M.: Suhrkamp, 1969, pp. 7-29.

5527. MITCHELL, BREON. "Marginalia from Conversations with Joyce," in A Wake Digest, pp. 80-81, No. 4935.

5528. ROBINSON, HENRY MORTON. "Hardest Crux Ever," in A James Joyce Miscellany, Second Series, pp. 195-208, No. 1613.

5529. SENN, FRITZ. "Insects Appalling," in Twelve and a Tilly, pp. 36-39, No. 4923.

5530. WILSON, EDMUND. "The Dream of H. C. Earwicker," in his The Wound and the Bow. New York: Oxford University Press, 1947, pp. 243-271. [Appeared in James Joyce: Two Decades of Criticism, pp. 319-342, No. 1570; reprinted in Modern British Fiction. Edited by Mark Schorer. New York: Oxford University Press, 1961, pp. 358-375.]

5531. WORTHINGTON, MABEL P. "The Moon and the Sidhe: Songs of Isabel," in New Light on Joyce, pp. 167-179, No. 1656.

Periodical Articles

5532. ALWAN, M. BAKIR. "Another Interpretation of the Thunderwords in Finnegans Wake." Wake Newslitter, 10 (April 1973): 20-21.

5533. ARMSTRONG, ALISON. "Shem the Penman as Glusg as the Wolf-man." Wake Newslitter, 10 (August 1973): 51-59.

5534. ATHERTON, JAMES S. "Joyce's Finnegans Wake." Explicator, 11 (May 1953): item 52.

5535. _____. "Spiritualism in Finnegans Wake." Notes and Queries, 199 (1954): 222.

5536. _____. "Hall Caine and the Isle of Man." Wake Newslitter, 2 (August 1965): 6-8.

FINNEGANS WAKE

5537. _____ . "Bell's Flocutionist." Wake Newslitter, 4 (April 1967): 39-40.

5538. _____ . "The Identity of the Sleeper." Wake Newslitter, 4 (October 1967): 83-85.

5539. _____ . "The Real Slim Jim at Last." Wake Newslitter, 4 (October 1967): 106.

5540. _____ . "Some American Notes, Mulberry Bend Park." Wake Newslitter, 4 (October 1967): 102-103. [Comments on Bird. WN, 3 (1966): 119-124 and Halper. WN, 4 (October 1967): 72-76.]

5541. _____ . "Periodicals in Finnegans Wake." Joycenotes, 1 (June 1969): 3-5.

5542. _____ . "Three Notes." Wake Newslitter, 7 (December 1970): 94. [FW 361.27, 157.02, 94.02.]

5543. _____ . "A Man of Four Watches: Macrobins in Finnegans Wake." Wake Newslitter, 9 (June 1972): 39-40.

5544. _____ . "Sus in Cribro (A Wake Newslitter, I.1.12; I.3.11) and Other Prophecies of Malachy." Wake Newslitter, 10 (December 1973): 111-113.

5545. AUBERT, J. "A Monument of Impropriety." Wake Newslitter, 1 (June 1964): 1-4; (August 1964): 4-5.

5546. BARBER, STEPHEN. "Nichthemerical Litter." Wake Newslitter, 2 (June 1965): 15-17. [On Senn. WN (April 1964).]

5547. BATES, RONALD. "The Feast is a Flyday." James Joyce Quarterly, 2 (Spring 1965): 174-187.

5548. BAUERLE, RUTH. "Dolando." Wake Newslitter, 10 (April 1973): 26.

5549. _____ . "Potato Preservative." Wake Newslitter, 10 (October 1973): 80.

5550. BEECHHOLD, HENRY F. "Finn MacCool and Finnegans Wake." James Joyce Review, 2, nos. 1-2 (June 1958): 3-12.

5551. _____ . "Joyce's Finnegans Wake." Explicator, 19 (January 1961): item 27.

5552. BEGNAL, MICHAEL H. "The Prankquean in Finnegans Wake." James Joyce Quarterly, 1 (Spring 1964): 14-18.

5553. _____ . "Shaunspeare in Finnegans Wake." Wake Newslitter, 2 (August 1965): 3-6.

5554. _____ . "Mourners at the Wake: The Family and Friends of HCE." Western Humanities Review, 24 (Autumn 1970): 383-393.

5555. _____ . "Some Further Notes on the Prankquean and Grainne O'Mailly." Wake Newslitter, 8 (February 1971): 14-15.

5556. _____ . "The Sommerfool in the Elephant's Belly, or Come Back to the Text Again, Peg, Honey!" Wake Newslitter, 8 (February 1971): 7. [Reply to Margaret Solomon. WN, 7 (October 1970): 67-72.]

5557. BENSTOCK, BERNARD. "Joyce's Finnegans Wake, Book II, Chapter II, Footnotes." Explicator, 20 (December 1961): item 37.

5558. _____ . "The Gastronome's Finnegans Wake." James Joyce Quarterly, 2 (Spring 1965): 188-194.

5559. _____ . "A Finnegans Wake Address Book." James Joyce Quarterly, 2 (Spring 1965): 195-203.

5560. _____ . "Mick and Nick in Finnegans Wake." Ball State University Forum, 6 (Autumn 1965): 25-28.

5561. _____ . "Echoes and Reverberations." Wake Newslitter, 2 (August 1965): 28-29.

5562. BIRD, STEPHEN B. "Some American Notes to Finnegans Wake." Wake Newslitter, 3 (December 1966): 119-124.

5563. BISHOP, JOHN P. "Finnegans Wake." Southern Review, 5 (Winter 1949): 439-453. [Appeared in his Collected Essays. Edited by Edmund Wilson. New York: Scribner, 1948, pp. 146-165; translated in Configuration critique I, pp. 229-260, No. 1636.]

5564. BLAKE, ARTHUR W. "Identifications from Brewer." Wake Newslitter, 4 (August 1967): 38-39.

5565. BLISH, JAMES. "Kram Revisited." Wake Newslitter, 4 (August 1967): 76-77.

5566. _____ . "Formal Music at the Wake." Wake Newslitter, 7 (April 1970): 19-27; 7 (June 1970): 34-43; 7 (August 1970): 51-58.

5567. BONHEIM, HELMUT. "The Father in Finnegans Wake." Studia neophilologica, 31, no. 2 (1959): 182-190.

5568. _____ . "'Tory' in Finnegans Wake." Notes and Queries, 206 (September 1961): 349-350.

5569. _____ . "God and the Gods in Finnegans Wake." Studia neophilologica, 34 (1962): 294-314.

5570. _____ . "Goldsmith's Spectacles." Wake Newslitter, 8 (August 1971): 62.

5571. BOSINELLI, ROSA MARIA, and FRITZ SENN. "We've found Rerembrandtsers." Wake Newslitter, 7 (August 1970): 62-63.

5572. BOUCHET, ANDRÉ du, ed. "Lire Finnegans Wake?" Nouvelle revue française (December 1957): 1054-1064.

5573. BOYLE, ROBERT. "Finnegans Wake, Page 185: An Explication." James Joyce Quarterly, 4 (Fall 1966): 3-16.

5574. BRINGHURST, ROBERT. "The Koran, the Wake, and Atherton." Wake Newslitter, 10 (December 1973): 92-93.

5575. BUDGEN, FRANK. "Joyce's Chapter on Going Forth by Day." Horizon, 4 (September 1941): 172-191. [Appeared in James Joyce: Two Decades of Criticism, pp. 343-367, No. 1570.]

5576. CARLSON, MARVIN. "Henrik Ibsen and Finnegans Wake." Comparative Literature, 12 (Winter 1960): 133-141.

5577. CHALENDAR, RENÉ. "La lettre dans Finnegans Wake." Univ. de Saint-Étienne, travaux de linguistique et littérature, 3 (1972): 57-66 (?).

5578. CHASE, RICHARD V. "Finnegans Wake: An Anthropological Study." American Scholar, 13 (Autumn 1944): 418-426. [Excerpts reprinted in Library of Literary Criticism, pp. 106-117, No. 250.]

5579. COHEN, DAVID. "Further Suggestions on the Museyroom." Wake Newslitter, 3 (February 1966): 14-15.

5580. COHEN, DAVID, and CLIVE HART. "Evovae." Wake Newslitter, 4 (April 1967): 42-43.

5581. COHN, ALAN M. "Rosenbach, Copinger, and Sylvia Beach in Finnegans Wake." Publications of the Modern Language Association, 78 (June 1962): 342-344.

5582. _____. "Some Anachronisms in and an Addition to Hodgart and Worthington." Wake Newslitter, 4 (July 1962): 3.

*5583. COLEMAN, ELLIOTT. "Heliotropical Noughttime: Light and Color in Finnegans Wake." Texas Quarterly, 4 (Winter 1961): 162-177.

5584. COOK, ALBERT. "The Portable and the Wonderful." Halcyon, 1, no. 2 (Spring 1948): 3-25. [Later appeared as the first chapter in his The Dark Voyage and the Golden Mean: A Philosophy of Comedy. Cambridge: Harvard University Press, 1949, pp. 155-160.]

5585. COWAN, THOMAS A. "Johnny Like Joyce was once a Drama Critic for a Newspaper."

Wake Newslitter, 7 (December 1970): 83-84. [FW, 386-388.]

5586. _____. "What I shall call a Research Project on the Four Evangelists." Wake Newslitter, 8 (April 1971): 19-24.

5587. _____. "St. Humphrey as Tesseract." Wake Newslitter, 10 (February 1973): 19-20.

5588. _____. "Jeff Earwicker." Wake Newslitter, 10 (October 1973): 69-75.

5589. DALTON, JACK P. "Re Article by Thornton Wilder." Wake Newslitter, no. 10 (February 1963): 4-6. [See WN, no. 6 (October 1962): 1-7 and Hudson Review, 16 (Spring 1963): 74-79.]

5590. _____. "Music Lesson." Wake Newslitter, no. 16 (September 1963): 1-5. [Also in A Wake Digest, pp. 13-16, No. 4935.]

5591. _____. "More Numbers." Wake Newslitter, 1 (February 1964): 5-7; addendum (June 1964): 10.

5592. _____. "Hardest Crux." James Joyce Quarterly, 1 (Spring 1964): 45-49.

5593. _____. "Habemus Dominationis." James Joyce Quarterly, 1 (Winter 1964): 10-14.

5594. _____. "Advertisement for the Restoration." Partially rewritten article, based on his "Hardest Crux." JJQ, 1 (Spring 1964): 45-49, and "Habemus Dominationis." JJQ, 1 (Winter 1964): 10-14, in Twelve and a Tilly, pp. 109-137, No. 4923.

5595. _____. "FW 549.11: 'Horrible.'" James Joyce Quarterly, 4 (Winter 1967): 154. [See reply by Edmund L. Epstein. JJQ, 4 (Summer 1967): 355-356, and Dalton's answer. "Letter to the Editor." JJQ, 5 (Winter 1968): 181.]

5596. _____. "Letter to the Editor." James Joyce Quarterly, 6 (Fall 1968): 99. [Various corrections.]

5597. _____. "Late Historical Events, Again." Wake Newslitter, 6 (December 1969): 91-92.

5598. ECKLEY, GRACE. "'Petween peas like ourselves': The Folklore of the Prankquean." James Joyce Quarterly, 9 (Winter 1971): 177-188.

5599. _____. "Eggoarchicism and the Bird Lore of Finnegans Wake." Literary Monographs, 5 (1973): 139-184, 208-212.

5600. EPSTEIN, EDMUND L. "Tom and Tim." James Joyce Quarterly, 6 (Winter 1968): 158-162.

FINNEGANS WAKE

5601. _____ . "Hostius Quadra." Wake News-litter, 6 (February 1969): 19-20.

5602. _____ . "Chance, Doubt, Coincidence and the Prankquean's Riddle." Wake Newslitter, 6 (February 1969): 3-7.

5603. FAYE, JEAN-PIERRE. "J. Joyce: Post-Scriptum--Shem trouvé." Tel quel, no. 30 (Summer 1967): 56-57.

5604. GILMAN, SANDER L. "Joyce and Sealsfield?" Wake Newslitter, 3 (February 1966): 5-6.

5605. GLASHEEN, ADALINE. "The Strange Cold Fowl in Finnegans Wake." Spectrum, 6 (Spring 1961): 38-64.

5606. _____ . Wake Newslitter, no. 14 (June 1963): 3-4.

5607. _____ . "Dilmun." Wake Newslitter, no. 15 (August 1963): 2-3. [Also in A Wake Digest, pp. 71-72, no. 4935; see also David Hayman. WN, no. 18 (December 1963): 6.]

5608. _____ . "Instances Perhaps of the Tetragrammaton in Finnegans Wake." Wake Newslitter, no. 16 (September 1963): 5-6. [Also in A Wake Digest, pp. 73-74, No. 4935.]

5609. _____ . "On First Looking into the 11th Britannica." Wake Newslitter, no. 18 (December 1963): 3-4.

5610. _____ . "Part of What the Thunder Said in Finnegans Wake." Analyst, no. 23 (November 1964): 1-29. [See reply by Ruth Von Phul. Analyst, no. 24 (March 1965): 23-28.]

5611. _____ . "The Opening Paragraphs." Wake Newslitter, 2 (1965): 3-8, no. 3, 21-25, no. 4, 24-27, no. 6, 1-22; 3 (1966): 6-14.

5612. _____ . "A Garner of Littles." Wake Newslitter, 3 (June 1966): 63-65.

5613. _____ . "Flesh and Blood Games." Wake Newslitter, 4 (October 1967): 99-100.

5614. _____ . "A Riddle Not Answered." Wake Newslitter, 4 (April 1967): 100-101.

5615. _____ . "Further Garner of Littles." Wake Newslitter, 4 (April 1967): 77-78.

5616. _____ . "Beaumont and Fletcher." Wake Newslitter, 10 (April 1973): 24.

5617. _____ . "G. A. A." Wake Newslitter, 10 (April 1973): 24-25.

5618. _____ . "Schoppin hour" [and] "Jon Jacobsen (424.27)." Wake Newslitter, 10 (April 1973): 25.

5619. _____ . "The Yeats Letters and Finnegans Wake." Wake Newslitter, 10 (October 1973): 76.

5620. _____ . "Laurens County," "Riverrun," "!" [and] "My Cubarola Glide (618.22)." Wake Newslitter, 10 (October 1973): 77-78, 80.

5621. _____ . "Fay Arthur," "Phoenix Park," "Jonah in Dolphin's Barn," "Watches." Wake Newslitter, 10 (December 1973): 95-97.

5622. GOODWIN, DAVID. "Nathandjoes (3.12)." Wake Newslitter, 10 (December 1973): 96.

5623. GRAHAM, PHILIP L. "japlatin, with my yuonkle's owlseller." Wake Newslitter, no. 5 (September 1962): 1-2; "Addenda." Wake Newslitter, no. 9 (January 1963): 6-7. [Reprinted in A Wake Digest, pp. 52-53, No. 4935.]

5624. _____ . "Bees at the Wake." Wake Newslitter, no. 5 (September 1962): 2-4.

5625. _____ . "Jam of the Cross." Wake Newslitter, 4 (April 1967): 45.

5626. _____ . "The Birds." Wake Newslitter, 10 (June 1973): 39.

5627. _____ , PHILIP B. SULLIVAN, G. F. RICHTER. "Mind Your Hats goan In! Notes on the Museyroom Episode of Finnegans Wake." Analyst, no. 21 (July 1962): 1-21; no. 22 (October 1962): 1-24.

5628. GYSEN, RENE. "Links en Rechts." Komma, 2 (1966): 57-63.

5629. HALPER, NATHAN. "James Joyce and the Russian General." Partisan Review, 18 (July-August 1951): 424-431.

5630. _____ . "Twelve O'Clock in Finnegans Wake." James Joyce Review, 1, no. 2 (June 1957): 40-41.

5631. _____ . "The Question of Leap-Year." James Joyce Quarterly, 3 (Spring 1966): 223.

5632. _____ . "On an Anecdote of Beckett's." Wake Newslitter, 3 (June 1966): 54-56. [See also Atherton, WN (October 1966).]

5633. _____ . "Thurkells." Wake Newslitter, 3 (June 1966): 57-58.

5634. _____ . "Variations on a Theme." Wake Newslitter, 4 (February 1967): 10-14.

5635. _____ . "Mulberry Bend Park." Wake Newslitter, 4 (August 1967): 72-76.

5636. _____. "Organs." Wake Newslitter, 4 (October 1967): 94-96.

5637. _____. "The Ram." Wake Newslitter, 4 (December 1967): 122.

5638. _____. "Mrs. Cornwallis-West." Wake Newslitter, 4 (December 1967): 124-126.

5639. _____. "A Few Phrases on Page 4." Wake Newslitter, 6 (February 1969): 22-23.

5640. _____. "Being a Sommerfool." Wake Newslitter, 8 (February 1971): 3-6. [See also Fritz Senn. WN, 7 (October 1970): 74-76.]

5641. _____. "Malachy Again." Wake Newslitter, 10 (June 1973): 44.

5642. HANSEN, KURT HEINRICH. "Der Ungerhorsam des Einzelgängers: Anklage und Identifikation in Finnegans Wake; Versuch einer Interpretation des J'schen Protestes." Eckart-Jahrbuch (1968): 117-135.

5643. HART, CLIVE. "Joyce's Finnegans Wake, page 285, lines 23-26." Explicator, 17 (June 1959): item 63.

5644. _____. "Explications—for the greeter glossary of code." Wake Newslitter, no. 1 (March 1962): 3-10; "Addenda." no. 2 (April 1962): 1-5; no. 4 (July 1962): 4-8; no. 5 (September 1962): 4-9.

5645. _____. "The Earwickers of Sidlesham." Wake Newslitter, no. 4 (July 1962): 1-2. [Also in A Wake Digest, pp. 21-22, No. 4935.]

5646. _____. "Nullnull, Medical Square." Wake Newslitter, no. 9 (January 1963): 5.

5647. _____. "Wake-Time." Wake Newslitter, no. 10 (February 1963): 4.

5648. _____. "The Elephant in the Belly: Exegesis of Finnegans Wake." Wake Newslitter, no. 13 (May 1963): 1-8. [Also in A Wake Digest, pp. 3-12, No. 4935.]

5649. _____. "The Geometry Problem." Wake Newslitter, no. 14 (June 1963): 2-3. [FW 283.30; also in A Wake Digest, pp. 75-79, No. 4935.]

5650. _____. "His Good Smetterling of Entymology." Wake Newslitter, 4 (February 1967): 14-24.

5651. _____. "More Entymology." Wake Newslitter, 4 (June 1967): 57.

5652. HAYMAN, DAVID. "From Finnegans Wake: A Sentence in Progress." Publications of the Modern Language Association, 73 (March 1958): 136-154. [Slightly revised version in Bibliography and Textual Criticism: English and American Literature, 1700 to the Present. Edited by O. M. Brack, Jr., and Warner Barnes. Chicago, London: University of Chicago Press, 1969, pp. 256-294.]

5653. HEATH, STEPHEN. "Trames de lecture (à propos de la dernière section de Finnegans Wake)." Tel quel, no. 54 (Summer 1973): 4-15.

5654. HODGART, M. J. C. "Work in Progress." Cambridge Journal, 6 (October 1952): 23-39.

5655. _____. [Three Notes]. Wake Newslitter, no. 18 (December 1963): 2-3.

5656. HORNIK, MARCEL P. "Page in Finnegans Wake Explained." Modern Language Notes, 75 (February 1960): 123-126.

5657. HUNTER, AIDA L. "If in Finnegans Wake." Wake Newslitter, 9 (June 1972): 45-46.

5658. JENKINS, WILLIAM D. "Tales of a Bayside Inn." Wake Newslitter, 3 (April 1966): 20-24.

5659. _____. "Kram of Llawnroc." Wake Newslitter, 4 (April 1967): 35.

5660. _____. "David and Jonathan." Wake Newslitter, 4 (April 1967): 35-36.

5661. _____. "Plums." Wake Newslitter, 4 (October 1967): 105.

5662. _____. "Nepman." Wake Newslitter, 4 (October 1967): 107.

5663. _____. "Zerothruster and the Twelve Morphios." Wake Newslitter, 4 (December 1967): 123-124.

5664. _____. "From a Hugglebeddy Fann." James Joyce Quarterly, 6 (Fall 1968): 89-91.

5665. _____. "From Solation to Solution." Wake Newslitter, 7 (February 1970): 3-11.

5666. _____. "Have a Glimpse of Proteus." Wake Newslitter, 10 (June 1973): 35-37.

5667. KAIN, RICHARD M. "Why is the Thunder a Hundred-Letter Word?" Wake Newslitter, 8 (February 1971): 15.

5668. KELLEHER, JOHN V. "Notes on Finnegans Wake." Analyst, 12 (April 1957): 9-15; 15 (1957): 9-16.

5669. KELLEY, WILLIAM M. "Oswhole'stalking." L'Arc, 36 (1968): 94-95. [From his A Wake in Progress.]

5670. KENNER, HUGH. "Frank Budgen." Wake Newslitter, 9 (February 1972): 10-11.

FINNEGANS WAKE

5671. KNUTH, A. M. L. "Joyce's Ouroboros: Kop en staart." Levende Talen, no. 269 (June–July 1970): 461–469.

5672. KNUTH, LEO. "The Key to 'Lps. The Keyes to.'" Wake Newslitter, 5 (April 1968): 28–29.

5673. _____. "Shem's Riddle of the Universe." Wake Newslitter, 9 (October 1972): 79–88.

5674. KOPPER, EDWARD A., JR. "The Two Saint Lawrences in Finnegans Wake." Wake Newslitter, no. 8 (December 1962): 6.

5675. _____. "Notes on Two Saints at the 'Wake.'" Notes and Queries, 10 (April 1963): 150.

5676. _____. "Joyce's Finnegans Wake." Explicator, 22 (January 1964): item 34.

5677. _____. "Notes on Grace O'Malley and the 'Wake.'" James Joyce Quarterly, 5 (Fall 1967): 68–70.

5678. _____. "A Note on St. Genesius in the 'Wake.'" Wake Newslitter, 4 (October 1967): 106–107.

5679. _____. "Some Elements of the Phoenix Park Murders in Finnegans Wake." Wake Newslitter, 4 (December 1967): 115–119.

5680. _____. "Hostius Quadra." Wake Newslitter, 6 (April 1969): 19–20.

5681. _____. "Egan O'Rahilly." Wake Newslitter, 5 (April 1968): 29.

5682. _____. "Saint Olaf in Finnegans Wake." Wake Newslitter, 6 (June 1969): 35–38.

5683. _____. "Lady Gregory and Finnegans Wake." Wake Newslitter, 10 (December 1973): 103–107.

5684. LEE, L. L. [FW 339.2-3]. James Joyce Quarterly, 3 (Spring 1966): 221.

5685. LEINWALL, GEORGE. "Carolan." Wake Newslitter, 4 (October 1967): 109.

5686. LeWINTER, OSWALD. "Aristotle's 'Fear' and Joyce's 'Terror.'" Wake Newslitter, 6 (October 1962): 7–9.

5687. LYONS, J. B. "Fin u cane Lives! Or Does He?" Wake Newslitter, 10 (June 1973): 42–43.

5688. McGARRITY, ANN K. "Chaplin." Wake Newslitter, 10 (October 1973): 75.

5689. McHUGH, ROLAND. "Direct References to Sigla." Wake Newslitter, 7 (August 1970): 61.

5690. _____. "283 A.D." Joycenotes, 1 (June 1969): 19.

5691. _____. "Two More Songs." Joycenotes, 1 (June 1969): 17.

5692. MARGERUM, EILEEN G. "First Music." Wake Newslitter, 10 (August 1973): 60–65.

5693. MATHEWS, F. X. "Festy King in Finnegans Wake." James Joyce Quarterly, 6 (Winter 1968): 154–157.

5694. MINK, L. O. "O's and Mae's." Wake Newslitter, 10 (April 1973): 25–26.

5695. _____. "Bowlbeggar Bill." Wake Newslitter, 10 (June 1973): 38–39.

5696. _____. "Schwalby Words" [and] "Dear Dirty Hazelwood Ridge." Wake Newslitter, 10 (December 1973): 110, 114–115.

5697. MITCHELL, BREON. "On the Verge of the Gutter, More French Slang in the Wake." Wake Newslitter, 6 (April 1969): 27–28.

5698. MORLEY, PATRICIA A. "Fish Symbolism in Chapter Seven of Finnegans Wake: The Hidden Defence of Shem the Penman." James Joyce Quarterly, 6 (Spring 1969): 267–270.

5699. MORSE, J. MITCHELL. "1132." James Joyce Quarterly, 3 (Summer 1966): 272–275.

5700. _____. "HCE's Chaste Ecstasy." Yale Review, 56 (Spring 1967): 397–405.

5701. _____. "The Coach with the Six Insides." Wake Newslitter, 8 (June 1971): 46–47.

5702. _____. "The Solence of That Stilling." Wake Newslitter, 10 (December 1973): 107–109.

5703. MOSELEY, VIRGINIA. "Ramasbatham." Wake Newslitter, 2 (June 1965): 10–15.

5704. MUELLER, LAVONNE M. "A Wind-Schlemihl in the Museyroom." Wake Newslitter, 2 (August 1965): 13–17.

5705. NEWELL, ELAIN. "More Song in Finnegans Wake." Wake Newslitter, 6 (February 1969): 23–25.

5706. NOON, WILLIAM T., S.J. "Distant Music in Finnegans Wake." Oral English, 1 (Winter 1972): 6–9.

5707. O'DWYER, RIANA. "Belinda's Dungheap and 'A Strate that was called Strete' (110.33)." Wake Newslitter, 8 (June 1971): 47.

5708. O'HANLON, DANIS. "In Explication of Commodius." Wake Newslitter, 9 (December 1972): 96–97.

5709. O HEHIR, BRENDAN. "The Humptyhilhead of Mulachy our Kingable Khan according to Dinny Finneen." Wake Newslitter, 1 (August 1964): 3-4.

5710. _____. "The Names of Shem and Shaun." Wake Newslitter, 1 (October 1964): 1-6; 3 (October 1966): 91-93.

5711. _____. "The Name of Humphrey." Wake Newslitter, 3 (October 1966): 93-96.

5712. _____. "The Cute Old Speckled Church." Wake Newslitter, 3 (December 1966): 124-125.

5713. _____. "O'Cannochar, O Conchobhair, Conchobhar." Wake Newslitter, 4 (August 1967): 67-72.

5714. O'ROURKE, MAMIE. "Mulberry Park Revisited." Wake Newslitter, 4 (October 1967): 103-105. [Comments on Nathan Halper. WN, 4 (1967).]

5715. PARIS, JEAN. "Finnegans Wake." Tel quel, no. 30 (Summer 1967): 58-66.

5716. PHILLIPS, GARY J. "Moonface the Murderer." Wake Newslitter, 8 (February 1971): 13.

5717. PHILLIPS, JOSEPH M. "Time, Pace." Wake Newslitter, 5 (October 1968): 68-70.

5718. _____. "Locating J. W. Dunne in Finnegans Wake." Modern Language Studies, 3 (Spring 1973): LI-LII. [Abstract: in extenso in Wake Newslitter, 11 (August 1974): 59-64.]

5719. PHILLIPS, LEWIS. "How to Teach Geometry and Theology Simultaneously." James Joyce Quarterly, 3 (Summer 1966): 295-297.

5720. POLSKY, NED. "Joyce's Finnegans Wake." Explicator, 9 (December 1950): item 24.

5721. RANKIN, H. D. "Nogger, Family and the Priapic Theme." Wake Newslitter, no. 15 (August 1963): 4-5; no. 16 (September 1963): 6-7.

5722. _____. "'Taylorised World' and Platonism." Wake Newslitter, 2 (December 1965): 11.

5723. _____. "Myopper." Wake Newslitter, 4 (April 1967): 43-44.

5724. RICHEY, CLARENCE W. "'The Riverrun': A Note upon a Joycean Quotation in Wright Morris' In Orbit." Notes on Contemporary Literature, 2 (January 1972): 14-15.

5725. _____. "On the Use of the Phopetia de Summis Pontificibus Ascribed Popularly to S. Malacy in the Fable of the Mookse and the Gripes." Wake Newslitter, 10 (April 1973): 27-28.

5726. ROSE, DANIS. "His Canonicititions Existence," "An Emendation," [and] "Ad Maturing Daily Glory Aims (282.6)." Wake Newslitter, 10 (June 1973): 43, 44, 45-47.

5727. _____. "A Note on Strawberry Beds Schoolhouse [265.6]," "About Kitty the Beads [530]," "Chuff and Glugg." Wake Newslitter, 10 (August 1973): 66.

5728. _____, and THOMAS A COWAN. "Commodius Vicus of Recirculation." Wake Newslitter, 10 (October 1973): 79-80.

5729. _____. "Who Wrote the Rann." Wake Newslitter, 10 (December 1973): 85.

5730. ROVIT, EARL H. "James Joyce's Use of Sidney Lanier." Notes and Queries, 7 (April 1960): 151.

5731. SANTISTÉBAN, RICARDO SILVA, translator. "La última página de Finnegans Wake." Creación y crítica, no. 2 (February 1971): 1-4. [FW 626-628.]

5732. SCARRY, JOHN. "Finnegans Wake III.i: A Portrait of John McCormack." Irish University Review, 3 (Autumn 1973): 155-162.

5733. SCHWIMMER, HELMUT. "Die Musik in Finnegans Wake." Melos, 35 (April 1968): 133-140.

5734. SEMMLER, CLEMENT. "Radio and James Joyce." BBC Quarterly, 9, no. 2 (1954): 92-96. [Also in his For the Uncanny Man, pp. 121-126, No. 1653.]

5735. SENN, FRITZ. "Dublin Theatres." Wake Newslitter, no. 2 (April 1962): 5-8. [Also in A Wake Digest, pp. 23-26, No. 4935.]

5736. _____. "Every Klitty of a scolderymeid: Sexual-Political Analogies." Wake Newslitter, no. 3 (June 1962): 1-7. [Also in A Wake Digest, pp. 27-38, No. 4935.]

5737. _____. "A Touch of Manichaeism." Wake Newslitter, 1 (June 1964): 9-10.

5738. _____. "First Words and No End." Wake Newslitter, 2 (June 1965): 17-20.

5739. _____. "Ailments of Jumeantry." Wake Newslitter, 3 (June 1966): 51-54.

5740. _____. "Tellforth's Glory." Wake Newslitter, 4 (April 1967): 42.

5741. _____. "The Lifewand." Wake Newslitter, 4 (April 1967): 44.

5742. _____. "Bitterness." Wake Newslitter, 4 (April 1967): 44.

FINNEGANS WAKE

5743. _____. "Pass the Fish." Wake Newslitter, 4 (April 1967): 44.

5744. _____. "Pass the Loaf." Wake Newslitter, 4 (April 1967): 44-45.

5745. _____. "A Gap." Wake Newslitter, 4
(April 1967): 45.

5746. _____. "Strange Worms." Wake Newslitter, 4 (April 1967): 45.

5747. _____. "Bygmesters." Wake Newslitter,
4 (April 1967): 45.

5748. _____. "Litterish Fragments." Wake
Newslitter, 4 (June 1967): 52-55.

5749. _____. "Indecent Behavior." Wake
Newslitter, 4 (June 1967): 55-56.

5750. _____. "Nepman." Wake Newslitter, 4
(June 1967): 56.

5751. _____. "Minxing Marriage." Wake Newslitter, 4 (June 1967): 56.

5752. _____. "Bang." Wake Newslitter, 4
(June 1967): 56.

5753. _____. "Loose Carollaries." Wake
Newslitter, 4 (August 1967): 78-79.

5754. _____. "Universal Word." Wake Newslitter, 4 (October 1967): 108-109.

5755. _____. "Charting Old Ireland." Wake
Newslitter, 6 (June 1969): 43-45.

5756. _____. "Some Conjectures About Homosexuality in Finnegans Wake." Wake Newslitter, 6 (October 1969): 70-72.

5757. _____. "Being a Sommerfool." Wake
Newslitter, 7 (October 1970): 74-76.
[Reply by Nathan Halper. WN, 8 (Febru-
ary 1971): 3-6.]

5758. _____. "Unknown Quantity." Wake Newslitter, 7 (October 1970).

5759. _____. "Quoint a quincidence." James
Joyce Quarterly, 7 (Spring 1970): 210-
217. [FW 299.8.]

5760. _____. "Cattermole Hill." Wake Newslitter, 8 (April 1971): 32.

5761. _____. "Terminals Four." Wake Newslitter, 8 (June 1971): 46.

5762. _____. "Bush Abob." Wake Newslitter,
8 (June 1971): 46.

5763. _____. "His Pillowscone Sharpened"
[and] "All Agog." Wake Newslitter, 10
(December 1973): 109-110, 110-111.

5764. SHELLY, BETTY W. "Tower of London." Wake
Newslitter, 7 (December 1970): 96. [FW
77. 18-20.]

5765. SHIBLEY, ALLEN M. "A Joycean Slip." New
York Times Magazine, 28 February 1954,
p. 6.

5766. SKRABANEK, PETR. "Cheka and OGPU." Wake
Newslitter, 8 (February 1971): 13-14.

5767. _____. "355.11 Slavansky Slavar, R.
Slavanskii Slovar (Slovanic Dictionary)."
Wake Newslitter, 9 (October 1972): 51-68.

5768. _____. "Imaginable Itinerary Through
the Particular Universal (260.R3)." Wake
Newslitter, 10 (February 1973): 22-23.

5769. _____. "Wassaily Booslaeugh (of Rieen-
geborg) (5.05)." Wake Newslitter, 10
(June 1973): 42.

5770. _____. "O quanta virtus est interseca-
tionibus circulorum." Wake Newslitter,
10 (December 1973): 86-87.

5771. _____. "More Hebrew." Wake Newslitter,
10 (December 1973): 88-91.

5772. SMIDT, KRISTIAN. "More Flutters." Wake
Newslitter, 8 (February 1971): 6. [See
Gary J. Phillips and Fritz Senn. WN
(December 1971): 90-91.]

5773. SMITH, G. RALPH. "Identity and Opposition."
Wake Newslitter, no. 18 (December 1963):
1-2. [FW 414.16ff.]

5774. SOLLERS, PHILIPPE. "Argument." Tel quel,
no. 54 (Summer 1973): 17-18.

5775. SOLOMON, MARGARET. "Sham Rocks: Shem's
Answer to the First Riddle of the Universe." Wake Newslitter, 7 (October
1970): 67-72. [See Michael Begnal. WN,
8 (February 1971): 7.]

5776. SPIELBERG, PETER. "Addenda: More Food for
the Gastonome's Finnegans Wake." James
Joyce Quarterly, 3 (Summer 1966): 297-
298. [See article by Benstock, No. 5558.]

5777. _____. "The Infant Tantalus." Zeitgeist, 2 (February 1967): 30. [Poem on
FW 260 n.2.]

5778. STAPLES, HUGH B. "Some Notes on the One
Hundred and Eleven Epithets of HCE."
Wake Newslitter, 1 (December 1964): 3-6;
2 (1965): 9-13; 2 (1965): 25-28.

5779. _____. "Some Notes on Book 1, Chapter
2." Wake Newslitter, 2 (December 1965):
12-13.

5780. _____ . "A Painful Case." Wake Newslitter, 3 (December 1966): 130-131. [FW,
490.3-5.]

5781. _____ . "Finucane Lives!" [and] "Notes
Toward a Gazetteer of Finnegans Wake."
Wake Newslitter, 10 (April 1973): 23-24,
28-30.

*5782. STARTSEV, A. "Eksperiment v sovremennoĭ
burzhuaznoĭ literature (Tretiĭ period
Dzhema Dzhoisa)." Literaturny Kritik,
no. 6 (1934): 57-59.

5783. SULLIVAN, PHILIP B. "Vortigern-A Dramatic
Suggestion." Wake Newslitter, no. 9
(January 1963): 5-6.

5784. _____ . "A New Light on Lipoleum."
Wake Newslitter, no. 18 (December 1963):
6. [See also WN, 7 (August 1970): 59-
60.]

5785. _____ . "A Matter of Spelling." James
Joyce Quarterly, 1 (Spring 1964): 50.

5786. _____ . "Fly and/or Sparks." James
Joyce Quarterly, 4 (Fall 1966): 35.

5787. _____ . "The Queen of Heaven." James
Joyce Quarterly, 4 (Fall 1966): 52.

5788. _____ . "Browne/Brown." James Joyce
Quarterly, 4 (Winter 1967): 160. [FW,
567.22-23.]

5789. _____ . "The White Sister." James Joyce
Quarterly, 7 (Winter 1969): 153. [FW,
184.]

5790. _____ . "Elanio Vitale." James Joyce
Quarterly, 7 (Winter 1969): 153. [FW,
221.22.]

5791. _____ . "Lipoleum Redefined." Wake
Newslitter, 7 (August 1970): 59-60. [FW,
008-010.]

5792. _____ . "Caesar the Victor." Wake Newslitter, 8 (June 1971): 45. [FW, 281.22.]

5793. _____ . "Seventy-Nine Graften Street."
Wake Newslitter, 8 (June 1971): 45.

5794. _____ . "J. J. & S." Wake Newslitter,
8 (June 1971): 45.

5795. _____ . "Sem the Pencil Man" [and] "Wil-
lingtoned." Wake Newslitter, 10 (April
1973): 26.

5796. _____ . "The Freeman's Cuticatura by
Fennella (291.F6)," "Sophy as Dublin
Drama," "Two More Books at the Wake,"
[and] "Donatus." Wake Newslitter, 10
(October 1973): 78.

5797. _____ . "Poet and Publisher," "Copen-
hague--Marengo," [and] "Room at the Inn."
Wake Newslitter, 10 (October 1973): 80,
81.

5798. SWINSON, WARD. "Macpherson in Finnegans
Wake." Wake Newslitter, 9 (December
1972): 89-95.

5799. _____ . "Riddle in Finnegans Wake."
Twentieth Century Literature, 19 (July
1973): 165-180.

5800. TANNER, GODFREY, translator. "The Latin
Passages." Wake Newslitter, 3 (February
1966): 4-5. [FW, 185.14ff. and 287.20ff.]

5801. TELLO, JAIME. "Un Experimento en Español."
Bolívar, 17 (1953): 345-363. [Also in
Revista nacional de Cultura, no. 148-149
(September-December 1961): 61-79.]

5802. THOMPSON, DIANE, and PAUL. "A Geometry
Problem in Finnegans Wake." Analyst,
no. 20 (September 1961): 2-4.

5803. THOMPSON, JOHN H. "Soft Morning, City: A
Paraphrase of the end of Finnegans Wake."
Analyst, no. 12 (1957): 1-8.

5804. VEALE, EILEEN. "Tansy Sauce." Wake Newslitter, 7 (December 1970): 96. [FW,
164.20.]

5805. VON PHUL, RUTH. "A Note on the Donkey in
Finnegans Wake." James Joyce Review, 1,
no. 1 (February 1957): 47-48.

5806. _____ . "The Four Absolutes." Wake
Newslitter, no. 18 (December 1963): 2.
[Also in A Wake Digest, p. 82, No. 4935.]

5807. _____ . "Late Historical Events." Wake
Newslitter, 1 (October 1964): 13-15.

5808. _____ . "Gorgios." Wake Newslitter, 2
(June 1965): 20-21.

5809. _____ . "Tantrist." Wake Newslitter, 2
(August 1965): 8-9.

5810. _____ . "Tristan." Wake Newslitter, 2
(August 1965): 9-10.

5811. _____ . "Thunderstruck: A Reply to Mrs.
Glasheen." Analyst, no. 24 (1965): 24-29.

5812. _____ . "Five Explications." Wake Newslitter, 3 (August 1966): 84-85.

5813. _____ . "Carmina Woodbiniana." Wake
Newslitter, 4 (February 1967): 24.

5814. _____ . "Addendum and (?) Corrigenda to
Arthur T. Broes' Entry on Anastasia.
AWN, iii.6." Wake Newslitter, 4 (Febru-
ary 1967): 25.

FINNEGANS WAKE

5815. _____ . "Nepmen." Wake Newslitter, 4 (October 1967): 107.

5816. _____ . "Haec Olim Meminisse Juvat." Wake Newslitter, 4 (October 1967): 107-108.

5817. _____ . Wake Newslitter, 5 (February 1968): 3.

5818. _____ . "Not a Leetle Beetle." James Joyce Quarterly, 6 (Spring 1969): 265-266. [FW, 417.3-4.]

5819. _____ . "Two Vicious Circles." Wake Newslitter, 7 (December 1970): 95. [FW, 18.24-28.]

5820. _____ . "A Portion of Glue and Gravy." Wake Newslitter, 7 (December 1970): 88-89.

5821. WATSON, DR. J. A. L. "August Weismann." Wake Newslitter, no. 12 (April 1963): 5-6.

5822. WEATHERS, WINSTON. "Finnegans Wake as Final Word." ETC, 26 (June 1969): 217-220.

5823. WELSSMAN, STEPHEN B. "Seudodanto [47.22]," "Throw the cobwebs from your eyes woman [214.13]." Wake Newslitter, 10 (December 1973): 94.

5824. _____ . "Phoebe." Wake Newslitter, 10 (December 1973): 96.

5825. WIGGIN, L. A. "The First Thunderword." James Joyce Review, 3, nos. 1-2 (February 1959): 56-59.

5826. _____ . "The Voice of the Frogs." Wake Newslitter, 6 (August 1969): 60-63.

5827. WILDER, THORNTON. "Giordano Bruno's Last Meal in Finnegans Wake." Hudson Review, 16 (Spring 1963): 74-79. [See reply by Jack P. Dalton. WN, no. 7 (November 1962): 7-9.]

5828. WOODFIN, HENRY. "The Loves of H. C. Earwicker." Chicago Review, 4 (Autumn 1949): 29-33.

5829. WORTHINGTON, MABEL P. "American Folksongs in Joyce's Finnegans Wake." American Literature, 28 (May 1956): 198-210.

5830. _____ . "Nursery Rhymes in Finnegans Wake." Journal of American Folklore, 70 (January-March 1957): 37-48.

5831. _____ . "The World as Christ Church, Dublin." Wake Newslitter, 2 (February 1965): 3-7.

5832. _____ . "Whip Jamboree." Wake Newslitter, 4 (April 1967): 37-38.

5833. _____ . "'Old Roger': Death and Rebirth." Wake Newslitter, 4 (December 1967): 121-122.

5834. _____ . "More Songs at the 'Wake.'" Joycenotes, 3 (December 1969): 4-9.

5835. _____ . "Not for Joe (170.03 and Ulysses 160.32)." Wake Newslitter, 10 (December 1973): 91.

5836. _____ . "Antony Romeo." Wake Newslitter, 10 (December 1973): 93.

5837. WRIGHT, HOPE M. "High Fa Luting." Wake Newslitter, 4 (April 1967): 3-8.

5838. ZETTERSTEN, ARNE. "Graphs and Symbols in Finnegans Wake." English Studies, 50 (1969): 516-524.

Uncategorized and Unverified Items

UNCATEGORIZED ITEMS

Books

5839. BALOTA, NICOLAE. "Resurectia lui Joyce," in _Labirint_. Bucharest: Editura Eminescu, 1970, pp. 39-44.

5840. ECO, UMBERTO. _James Joyce and the Aesthetics of Chaosmos_. University of Tulsa Monograph Series, vol. 15. Fall/Winter 1971-1972.

5841. HART, CLIVE. "Musical Qualities in Joyce's Late Prose," in _Proceedings of the Eighth Congress of the Australian Universities Language and Literature Association_. Canberra: [n.p., n.d.], pp. 32-33.

5842. ITO, HITOSHI. _Joyce_. Tokyo: Kenkyusha, 1969.

5843. MAGGIO PALAZZOLO, EGLE. _Joyce poeta_. Palermo: Pezzino, 1964.

Periodical Articles

5844. ALISTAR, D. J. "Joyce." _Ateneu_, 4, no. 6 (20 June 1967): 19.

*5845. BALOGH, L. "James Joyce: Kamarazene." _Alföld_ (Debrecen), 11, no. 3 (1960): 158-159.

5846. BEECHHOLD, HENRY F. "Joyce's Otherworld." _Éire-Ireland_, 8 (Spring 1972): 103-115.

5847. BERGSTEN, STEFAN. "Nyare Joyceforskning." _Samlaren_ (Uppsala), 90 (1969): 201-211.

*5848. BLOCKER, GÜNTER. "Literarische Weltfahrt." _Süddeutsche Zeitung_, 16 February 1957.

*5849. BLOCKER, GÜNTER. "Seine Welt heiss Dublin: Ein Wichtiges Buch zum Verständnis des grossen Iren James Joyce." _Der Zeit_, 12 August 1960.

5850. BROPHY, LIAM. "The Stagey Irishman." _Apostle_, 41 (February 1963): 9-13.

5851. CIXOUS, HELÉNE. "Joyce, la ruse de l'écriture." _Poetique_, no. 4 (1970): 419-432.

*5852. COLBERG, KLAUS. "Müncher Funktagebuch: Das zusätzliche Sonderprogramm." _Süddeutsche Zeitung_, 28 May 1957.

*5853. COLBERG, KLAUS. "Müncher Funktagebuch: Das rar gewordene Hörspiel." _Süddeutsche Zeitung_, 28 January 1958.

*5854. ELLMANN, RICHARD. "James Joyce's Luck with Chicago." _Chicago Sunday Tribune Magazine of Books_, 29 November 1959, p. 6.

*5855. FARWER, GOTTFRIED. "'Ahn, alter Künstler, steh mir bei...' Anmerkungen zu James Joyce." _aachener prisma_, 9, no. 1 (1960-61): 24-25.

5856. GARCIA GONZALEZ, ENRIQUE. "El enigma de James Joyce." _Revista mexicana de cultura_ (Supplement to _El nacional_), 24 January 1965, p. 4.

5857. GLESCH-BRUNNINGEN, HANS. "James Joyce y la medicina." _Semana_ (Guayaquil, Ecuador), no. 121 (20 April 1962): 1-2.

5858. GÜRSTER, EUGEN. "Kronzeuge eines Genies." _Die Welt der Literatur_, 1 (1964): 221.

*5859. HOLTHUSEN, HANS EGON. "Der Junge Joyce." _Süddeutsche Zeitung_, 18/19 October 1958.

*5860. KAUFMANN, RICHARD. "Gedanken wie Infusorien: die drei Gestalten des James Joyce." _Christ und Welt_, 14 (10 November 1961): 15.

5861. KENSIK, A. Cl. "James Joyce." _Neue Zürcher Zeitung_, 15 March 1964, pp. 5-5B. [In the Fernausgabe appears 14 March 1964, pp. 14-14B.]

5862. KURELLA, ALFRED. "Der frühling, die Schwalben und Franz Kafka." _Sonntag_, no. 31 (1963).

UNCATEGORIZED ITEMS

5863. KURELLA, ALFRED. "Die Demokratisierung des Helden." Sonntag, no. 2 (1965): 5.

*5864. LEVIN, HARRY. "James Joyce, mediador entre al mundo de la realidad y el mundo de los suenos." La Gaceta, 5 (June 1959): 1, 3.

5865. McHUGH, ROGER. "Joyce, gesprochen." Neue Zürcher Zeitung, 14 March 1964.

*5866. NEESON, EOIN. "The Devil of Dublin?" Sunday Review (Dublin), 8 February 1959.

5867. NIKULA, KARL H. "Om James Joyces engagemang." Horisont (Vasa), 2, no. 13 (1966): 20-21.

5868. PRACHT, ERWIN. "Prazisierung oder Preisgabe des Realismus-Begriffs." Sonntag, no. 11 (1964): 7.

*5869. SATTLER, ANDREAS. "'Ich interessiere mich nur für Stil': Eiseskälte und erloschene Augen bei James Joyce: Kein Versuch Einer Neudeutung." Die Zeit, 19 September 1958.

*5870. SCHMIDT, ARNO. "Der Kritiker erwidert." Frankfurter Allgemeine Zeitung, 6 December 1957.

*5871. SCHWABACH, ERIK-ERNST. "Zwei wichtige Biographien Liegen endlich vor." Zeitschrift für Bücherfreunde, n.F. 19 (1927): 61-62.

5872. ULBRICHT, WALTER. "Über die Entwicklung einer Volksverbundenen sozialistischen Nationalkultur." Supplement to Sonntage, no. 20 (1964).

5873. WEL. "Der Joyce-Turm in Irland." Volksrecht (Zürich), 1 April 1966.

*5874. Unsigned. "What of James Joyce." Irish Rosary (March 1941).

UNVERIFIED ITEMS

5875. BERTI, LUIGI. "Dell'elemento distrittivo in Joyce." Boccaporto Secondo (Firenze, Parenti) (1944): 260-264.

5876. BRION, MARCEL. "L'Actualité littéraire à l'etranger." Les Nouvelles littéraires (Paris), 15 October 1927.

5877. COLUM, PADRAIC. Gregonian (Portland), 18 December 1927.

5878. ELLMANN, RICHARD. "James Joyce: The Growth of Imagination." Tri-Quarterly, 2(?) (Fall 1959?): 3-8.

5879. GIEDION-WELCKER, CAROLA. "Dazu Besprechung." Mannheimer Tageblatt, no. 5 (1932).

5880. LeBRETON, GEORGES. "La methode de James Joyce." Mercure de France, 338 (1960): 123-132.

5881. LINATI, CAROLO. "Ricordi su Joyce." Prospettiva, 4, no. 2 (15 February 1940): 16. [Reprinted in his Scrittori anglo-americani d'oggi. 2nd edition. Milan: A. Corticelli, 1944.]

5882. MILLER-BUDNITSKAYA, R. [n.t.]. Literaturny kritik, no. 1 (1934).

5883. MIRSKY, D. S. [n.t.]. God shestnadtsaty, nos. 1 and 2 (1933).

5884. RUIZ DEUÑAS, J. "Joyce: Conciencia literaria del siglo." Excelsior magazine dominical (Mexico City), 1 February 1970, pp. 2-3.

5885. WILDER, THORNTON. [n.t.]. Herald (Boston), 31 March 1929.

Index

Index of authors, editors, translators, reviewers, and unsigned articles and reviews. Numbers refer to items, not to pages.

A

AE (See George Russell, Y. O.)
A., E. L., 3682
A., F., 1077
A., M., 1853
A., R., 1855
Abbas, M. A., 167
Abbott, H. Porter, 3111
Abbs, Peter, 1796
Abel, Lionel, 1353, 1417
Abernathy, F. W., 3286
Abin, César, 910
Acton, Harold, 818
Abrahami, Izzy, 155, 2633
Abrams, M. H., 184
Absono, D'ámaso (A. Donado), 1771
Adam, George, 3544
Adams, Franklin P., 819
Adams, J. Donald, 1330, 4905
Adams, Leonie, 2732
Adams, Michael, 290
Adams, Robert M., 61, 62, 645, 1501, 1540, 2852,
     3298, 3492, 3493, 3534, 4256
Adamson, Donald, 624
Adicks, Richard, 2891
Adler, Gerhard, 3603
"Affable Hawk" (See Desmond MacCarthy)
Aggeler, Geoffrey, 1418
Agrawal, I. N., 2824
Ahearn, Edward J., 3684
Aiken, Conrad, 4453, 5133, 5519
Aitken, D. J. F., 157, 3494
Ajame, Pierre, 555
al'Atiwi, Amin, 2642
Alberes, R. M., 168, 3535, 4184
Albert, Leonard, 2390, 3545, 4778
Alberts, Julian, 159
Aldebert, Monique, 2731
Aldington, Richard, 820, 2309, 3685, 4454, 4972
Aldridge, John W., 1507, 1603, 4298
Alexander, Herbert, 781
Alexander, Sidney, 4653
Algaux, Pierre, 711
Alien, Pierre, 724
Alistar, D. J., 5844
Allen, Charles, 8
Allen, Creighton, 2540

Allen, Walter, 169, 1354, 3686
Allott, Miriam, 1508
Allt, Peter, 291
Aloyse, Sister M., 3212, 3233
Alsop, Joseph W., Jr., 1078
Altichieri, Gilberto, 63
Altieri, Charles, 3288
Altschul, Carlos, 1689
Alvarez, A., 713
Alwan, M. Bakir., 5532
Ames, Van Meter, 664, 954
Amor, José Blanc, 3289
Amorós, Andrés, 170
Anceshi, Luciano, 3687
And Trieste, Ah Trieste, 100
Anderson, Chester G., 159, 292, 362, 595, 924, 1909,
     2438, 2706, 2795, 2833, 3195, 3213, 3222, 3223,
     3255, 3260, 3287, 3290, 3291, 3471, 4549
Anderson, George K., 3013
Anderson, John, 1509, 3536
Anderson, Marcia Lee, 1254
Anderson, Margaret, 1036, 1510, 1612, 4355, 4356
Anderson, Sherwood, 156, 1355, 1356
Ando Ichiro, 1079, 1592, 2781, 2849
Andrade, Raul, 3688
Andreach, Robert J., 649, 2367, 3214
Andreasen, N. J. C., 363
Angeli, Diego (?), 1937, 3213, 3292
Angelis, Guilio de, 260, 1659, 3565
Anghinetti, Paul W., 2368
Angioletti, G. B., 171, 3537
Angioletti, Paola, 435
Angus, Ian, 1055, 4508
Anibal, José, 4385
Anonymous, Finnegans Wake, 2652
Anonymous Announcer, "Voorang: Ulysses van James
     Joyce," 154
Antheil, George, 626, 2541, 2580
Antoni, Claudio, 364
Appel, Alfred, 106, 704
Apollonio, U., 149, 781
apRoberts, Robert P., 2972
Aquin, Hubert, 4257
Ara, Masato, 1511
"Aramis," 2058
Archibald, R. C., 2708
Arciniega, Rosa, 3689
Arendt, Hannah, 3555

Arias, Augusto, 4409
Armstrong, Alison, 5533
Arnieri, Gabrijeal, 4852
Arnett, Earl, 1080
Arnold, Allen D., 3428
Arnold, Armin, 1512, 1690
Arnold, I., 172
Arns, Karl, 1898, 3538, 4185
Aronne Amestoy, Lida, 4198
Aschauer, Joseph C., S.J., 261
Aschcroft, Edward, 3539
Ashmore, Basil, 2021
Ashraf, Syed Mohmmed, 5366
Aspell, Joseph, 3472
Assenjo, F. G., 5320
Aston, Paul, 4438
Astre, Georges-Albert, 955
Asturias, Miguel Angel, 2140
Atherton, James S., 1255, 1584, 1659, 1664, 2850,
    2866, 2973, 4682, 4840, 4841, 4923, 4935, 4973,
    4974, 5269, 5351, 5352, 5367, 5368, 5369, 5370,
    5371, 5372, 5373, 5374, 5375, 5376, 5377, 5378,
    5379, 5380, 5520, 5534, 5535, 5536, 5537, 5538,
    5539, 5540, 5541, 5542, 5543, 5544, 5632
Atkinson, Brooks, 262, 3495
Atlas, Nicholas, 4357
Aubert, Jacques, 150, 163, 164, 1513, 3293, 4975,
    5321, 5381, 5345
Aubert, Jean Paul, 2653
Auclair, George, 2634
Auden, W. H., 956
August, Eugene R., 3294
"Auseinandersetzung mit James Joyces Ulysses," 3690
Austin, Avel, 2459
Austin, William W., 645
Avery, George C., 3215
Aycock, Wendell M., 2868

B

B., B., 2270
B., M., 1976
B., S. S., 3691
B., W. C., 4976
Baake, Josef, 2460, 3540
Babel, Isaacs, 1142
Bacca, Juan David Garcia, 4455
Bach, Robyn, 3295
Backlund, Percival, 4977
Bacon, Wallace A., 2974
Baez, Joan, 2759
Baim, Joseph, 4201
Baird, Donald, 31
Baird, Edwin, 2133
Bajarlía, Juan Jacobo, 3541
Baker, E. A., 249
Baker, Denys Val, 1039
Baker, James R., 1614, 2796, 2851, 2852, 3138, 3260,
    3429, 3430
Baker, Joseph E., 3112
Baker, Terence, 2021
Baker, William, 1419
Bakos, Mikulas, 3610
Bălăiță, George, 3145
Baldwin, Peter, 4762
Balogh, L., 5845
Balota, Nicolae, 3296, 3542, 5839
Baltzell, E. D., 3692
Bambrough, J. R., 957

Bandler, Bernard, 3496
Barab, Seymour, 2762
Barantono, Adelchi, 1081
Barber, Samuel, 2542, 2543, 2544, 2545, 2546, 2709,
    2762
Barber, Stephen, 5546
Bard, Joseph, 1514
Barfoot, C. C., 64
Barkentin, Marjorie, 2634
Barker, George, 2218
Barnes, A. C., 3497
Barnes, Djuna, 596
Barnes, Warner, 5652
Barois, Jean, 609
Barr, Alan P., 747
Barr, Isabelle H., 3146
Barrett, William, 1515
Barroll, J. Leeds, 2975
Barrow, Craig Wallace, 2461
Barrows, Herbert, 3086
Barth, John, 4510
Barucca, Primo, 3693
Basalla, George, 4783
Bass, Richard K., 4410, 4872, 4873
Bass, Richard N., 4683
Bassi, Marcella, 1677
Bassoff, Bruce, 3694
Bate, Stanley, 2547
Bates, H. E., 3125, 3147
Bates, Ronald, 1516, 2398, 3473, 5382, 5547
Báti, László, 191
Battistessa, A. J., 2064
Bauerle, Ruth, 3498, 4411, 4758, 4779, 4842, 5548,
    5549
Bauman, Lise, 3695
Bax, Arnold, 2580
Beach, Joseph Warren, 1420, 3543
Beach, Sylvia, 107, 132, 156, 2695, 2710, 2758, 2763,
    3544, 3551, 3696, 3697, 3698, 3906, 3944, 3960,
    3961, 4058, 4182, 4654, 4667, 4906
Beachcroft, T. S., 2853
Beard, M. C., 2711
Beardslee, Bethany, 2742
Beardsley, Harry M., 4456
Beare, W., 4149
Beaslai, Piaras, 857, 958
Beatty, Jerome S., Jr., 446
Beaudry, Pierre, 150
Beaulire, Lester A., 308
Beaumont, Germaine, 263
Beausang, Michael, 159, 4550
Beauvoir, Simone de, 313
Beck, Emily Morison, 190
Beck, Warren, 2854
Beckett, Samuel, 1256, 1644, 4906, 4907, 5203
Becher, Johannes, 1142
Beckley, Paul V., 1999
Beckmann, G., 1691
Beckson, Karl, 785, 2825, 2892, 3474, 3798
Beckwith, Ethel, 2278
Beddow, Bruce, 4177, 4457
Bedford, Patrick, 2728
Bedford, Sybille, 821
Beebe, Maurice, 29, 30, 65, 157, 158, 161, 959, 1516,
    1613, 1636, 2439, 2855, 3213, 3216, 3223, 3431,
    3699
Beechhold, Henry F., 2515, 5550, 5551, 5846
Begnal, Michael H., 1516, 2516, 3700, 4908, 4978,
    5310, 5383, 5552, 5553, 5554, 5555, 5556, 5775

Butler, Anthony, 1088
Butler, Francelia, 2890
Butler, P. R., 5370
Butler, Terence, 5003
Butor, Michel, 149, 265, 1702, 1703, 4910, 5004,
5005, 5006, 5275
Butt, Mary, 1190
Byrd, Don, 3746
Byrne, Barry, 1333, 2319, 2345
Byrne, John Francis, 296, 1644
Byrne, Sister Mary E., 2369
Byrne, Patrick F., 4588, 5007

C

C., A., 2322
C., J., 1704, 1899
C., R. H. (pseud of A. R. Orage), 2049, 3747
Cabanis, José, 266
Cabibbe, Giorgio, 4460
Cage, John, 2559
Cahill, Susan, 177
Cahill, Tom, 177
Cahoon, Herbert, 1, 17, 18, 19, 1613, 1614, 2354,
2887, 3198, 3200
Calder-Marshall, Arthur, 1537
Calderwood, James L., 4443
Callaghan, Morley, 825, 2304
Callahan, Edward F., Jr., 2391
Calmer, Edgar, 598, 2172, 5008
Calvert, J., 2200
Cambon, Glauco, 1358, 1429, 1538, 1677, 1705
Camerino, Aldo, 3559
Cameron, K. N., 1706, 2896
Cami, Ben, 3207
Camino, Aurelio Corazón del, 1632
Campbell, John W., 3221
Campbell, Joseph, 160, 1551, 1570, 2718, 3475, 3749,
4915, 5009, 5010, 5011, 5012, 5523
Campbell, Kenneth, 3750
Campbell, Sandy, 381
Campos, Augusto de, 1539, 4915, 4916, 4917, 5013,
5523
Campos, Haroldo de, 1539, 4915, 4918, 5523
Canby, Henry Seidel, 1030, 2073, 5276
"Candida," 2653
Canis, Domini, see Shane Leslie
Canning, John, 245
C[ano], J[osé] L[uis], 2141
Cantwell, Robert, 1430, 1707, 1708, 2130
Carballo, Emmanuel, 1359
Carbonaro, A., 1606
Card, James Van Dyck, 2464, 4894, 4895, 4896
Card, William, 3751
Carducci, Edgardo, 2580
Carens, James F., 320, 1656, 3560
Cargeege, F. B., 2225, 5014, 5157
Cargill, Oscar, 1360
Carleton, V. B., 313
Carlini, Franco, 161, 754
Carlson, Marvin, 5391, 5576
Carothers, Robert L., 3476
Carpeaux, Otto Maria, 178, 1361
Carpenter, Edmund, 528
Carpenter, Richard, 3059
Carrier, Warren, 2897
Carroll, Lewis, 4915
Carroll, Paul, 1203
Carroy, Jean-Roger, 150

Carruthers, John (John Young Thompson Grieg), 4437
Carter, Boyd, 702
Carter, Eileen, 702
"Casimir," 5015
Casotti, Francesco, 1431
Cass, Andrew, see John Garvin
Cassidy, Thomas E., 2357
Cassola, Carlo, 1261
Cassou, Jean, 2108
Castagna, Barbara, 3306
Castigliano, Luigi, 1089
Castresana, Luis de, 3778
Castris, A. Leone d, 755
Castronovo, David, 4692
Casty, Alan, 3037
Catherton, L., 1262
Cattabiani, Anna Rosso, 1616
Caulfield, Edward, 3798
Cazamian, Louis, 1709
Cecchi, Emilio, 2088, 3752
Cela, Camila Jose, 3753
Celati, Gianni, 68, 4286, 5016
Cerf, Bennett, 3759
Cerny, James W., 5017
Ceresani, Remo, 5518
Chabay, Leslie, 2755
Chace, William M., 1540
Chadourne, Marc, 2113
Chalendar, René, 5577
Chalon, Jean, 383, 1090
Chambers, R. L., 795
Chamson, André, 156, 3755
Chapman, Gerald, 5018
Chapple, J. A. V., 179
Charlton, Linda, 3755
Charques, R. D., 3561
Chase, Richard V., 250, 5578
Chastaing, Maxine, 5019
Chatman, Seymour, 2898
Chattopadhyaya (or Chatterjee), Sisir, 180, 181,
1541, 4785
Chávez, Oscar, 4493
Chayes, Irene Hendry, 1507, 1570, 2244, 2833, 3213,
3223, 3260, 3273
Cheon, Henri, 5020
Chevevière, Jacques, 1883
Chesterton, G. K., 1031, 2074, 3757
Chic, Antonio, 2031
Chilton, Eleanor Carroll, 2204, 2217
Chisholm, Francis P., 384
Chocron, Isaac, 385
Christ, Ronald, 299
Christen, Arnold, 1308
Christiani, Dounia Bunis, 1688, 2520, 5258, 5356,
5392
Church, Margaret, 967, 1542, 2899, 4732, 4879
C[hurch], S[amuel] H[arden], 2126
"Churchman," 4145
Chruchill, R. C., 182
Churchill, Thomas, 903
Cicogna, O., 3758
Cierpial, Leo Joseph, 2465
Cingria, Charles-Albert, 267
Cinigho, Ada V., 3026
Cismaru, Alfred, 1432
Citkowitz, Israel, 2560, 2762
Cixous, Helène, see Helène Cixous Berger
Clarke, Austin, 67, 386, 710, 2695, 3759
Clark, Earl John, 3502

Clarke, Edward Murray, 1614
Clarke, John, 1461
Clarke, Laurence, 2719
Clarkin, Franklin, 5021
Clemens, Thomas Craine, 2466
Clement-Janin, 3760
Clery, Arthur, 1848
Clissmann, Anne, 1433
Cluny, Claude-Michel, 4211
Clutton-Brock, A., 1910, 1962
Cody, Morril, 599
Cohen, David, 5579, 5580
Cohen, Hazel E., 3300, 3307
Cohn, Alan M., 2, 3, 33, 34, 35, 36, 37, 38, 39, 40,
    41, 42, 43, 44, 45, 46, 48, 70, 109, 387, 1584,
    2536, 2654, 2800, 3308, 4827, 4843, 4856, 5581,
    5582
Cohn, Ruby, 1362, 4462, 4854
Coginard, Jerome, 1091
Colberg, Klaus, 5852, 5853
Cole, David W., 4815
Coleman, Elliott, 152, 673, 1263, 4463, 5583
Collingwood, Frank, 3222
Collins, Ben L., 1710, 2441, 2862, 2981, 3107, 5022
Collins, John T., 388
Collins, Joseph, 2066, 3562, 5398
Collins, Norman, 1363
Collins, Robert G., 159, 2370, 3309, 3761
Collis, J. S., 1092, 2292
Collobert, Danielle, 150
Colum, Mary, 297, 298, 328, 389, 446, 659, 926,
    2072, 2158, 2327, 3688, 3762, 5023
Colum, Padraic, 298, 299, 390, 391, 392, 393, 394,
    395, 852, 923, 1264, 1265, 1309, 1312, 1612,
    1966, 2124, 2151, 2222, 2266, 2580, 2634, 2644,
    2721, 2727, 2782, 2858, 3486, 3503, 4786, 4919,
    4923, 5024, 5025, 5026, 5277, 5877
Comisso, Giovanni, 396
Common, Jack, 3763
Conklin, Groff, 1909
Conley, Joh, 4651
Connell, Charles, 183
Connelly, Steve, 397
Connolly, Cyril, 156, 250, 300, 1544, 1711
Connolly, Francis, 3060
Connolly, Thomas E., 4, 968, 2852, 2866, 2946, 3087,
    3201, 3223, 3436, 3437, 4920
Conroy, Jack, 2305
Consiglio, Alberto, 3764, 3765, 4552
Contat, Michel, 1802
Cook, Albert, 4921, 5584
Cooke, Deryck, 2537
Cooke, Greville, 2226
Cooke, John, 4524
Cooke, M. G., 2900
Cope, Jackson I., 969, 1093, 2901, 4287, 4413, 5393
Copland, R. A., 4880
Corbeillier, Philippe, 4759
Corcoran, A. T., 301
Cordell, R. A., 2634
Core, George, 1410
Corelli, Marie, 5410
Corkery, Tom, 398
Corn, Mary, 1712
Corran, H. S., 1094
Corrington, J. W., 2432, 2852, 2866, 2947, 3088
Corsini, Gianfranco, 2634
Cort, David, 2173
Cos Cob Song Volume, 2561
Costa, Richard H., 1364, 4464

Costanzo, W. V., 5027
Coupaye, Didier, 5162
Cournos, John, 1938
Couroy, André, 308
Courtenay, Jennifer, 1713, 2227
Coveney, Peter, 1545
Cowan, S. A., 3062, 3063
Cowan, Thomas A., 5585, 5586, 5587, 5588
Cowdrey, Mary B., 5278
Cowie, Alfred T., 134
Cowley, Malcolm, 156, 750, 826, 860, 904, 1032,
    3224, 3766
Cowley, Robert, 750
Cox, C. B., 198
Cox, Roger L., 3153
Cox, Sidney, 3038
Coxhead, Elizabeth, 302
Coyle, Kathleen, 399
Craig, Maurice, 17
Crane, Hart, 3310
Crane, Melville H., 1380
Crastre, Victor, 268
Creighton, Joanne Vanish, 2433
Crémieux, Benjamin, 5279
Crews, Frederick C., 1532
Crise, Stelio, 105, 161, 303, 400, 401, 402, 403
Critchley, Julian, 163
Croessmann, H. K., 44, 1613, 4258
Croisille, Nicole, 2713
Cronin, Anthony, 404, 1540, 3767, 3768, 3769, 4540
Cronin, John, 405, 611, 3103
Crosby, Caresse, 595, 827
Crosby, Harry, 595, 1095, 1102
Crosman, Robert, 4881
Cross, Amanda, 1033
Cross, Gustav, 3770
Cross, Richard K., 1546, 2371
Crothers, George D., 4016
Crowley, Aleister, 1096
Crowley, Christine, 406
Csillaghy, Andrea, 161, 756
Cunard, Nancy, 828, 829
Cunningham, Everett V., 4465
Cunningham, Frank R., 3114, 3504
Cunningham, J., 3798
Cunningham, Louis A., 1097
Cunninghame, A. T., 5028
Curling, Jonathan, 5029
Curran, C. P., 153, 304, 305, 407, 970, 1331, 2695
Curran, Stuart, 3311
Currie, George, 5030
Curtayne, Alice, 408, 409
Curtius, Ernst Robert, 1551, 4259
Curtnesse, D. M., 3771
Cusack, Cyril, 2666, 2722, 2746
Cwiakala, Jodwiga, 1098, 4288

D

D., A., 1310
D., F., 2320
D., H. E., 3772
Dadufalza, Concepcion D., 2982
Daglish, Robert, 1434
D'Agostino, Nemi, 1547, 1551
Dahl, Liisa, 4186, 4212, 4213, 4214
Dahlberg, Edward, 830
Daiches, David, 71, 184, 410, 1365, 1548, 1549, 1649,
    2862, 3438, 3563

Duncan, Edward, 975, 4414
Duncan, Iris June Autry, 2468
Duncan, Joseph E., 4291
Dundes, Alan, 3785, 4734
Dunkley, D. D., 5370
Dunn, J. Tyler, 2737
Dunseath, Thomas K., 4568
Duplaix, Georges, 1875, 3786
Durant, Ariel, 187
Durant, Will, 187
Durinck, J. R., 162, 414, 5323
Durzak, Manfred, 1367, 4469
DuSautoy, Peter, 5185
Dütsch, Adolf, 2042
Duthie, G. S., 1618
Duvan, K. D., 686
Duwell, Bernhard, 3787
Duytschaever, Joris, 1101, 1556, 3788
Dwyer, Richard A., 417
Dyrkøb, Jan Ulrik, 3315
Dyson, A. E., 198
Dyson, Anne Jane, 51

E

E., 1974
E., P., 2203
Earnshaw, H. G., 188
Easson, Angus, 3067
East, Sara Toll, 4392
Eastman, Max, 581, 1102
Eastman, Richard M., 189
Eaton, Edward E., 2405
Eaton, W. P., 1963
Eberly, Ralph S., 2372
Eckley, Grace, 2521, 5039, 5598, 5599
Eco, Umberto, 149, 831, 1717, 2828, 3316, 4928,
    5041, 5259, 5260, 5840
Edel, Leon, 190, 418, 666, 1103, 1368, 1436, 1568,
    1597, 1612, 1718, 2328, 4217, 5042
Edelheit, Henry, 5043
Edgar, Pelham, 4188
Edge, Charles, 1675
Edgerton, William B., 269
Edwards, A. L. R., 5313
Edwards, Calvin R., 4415
Edwards, Owen D., 708
Edwards, Philip, 4292
Eggleshaw, J. H., 2292
Eglinton, John, see W. K. Magee
Egri, Péter, 161, 191, 688, 689, 748, 1104, 1557,
    2358, 2770, 2771, 2908, 3317, 3318, 4218, 4219,
    4438, 4738
Ehrenburg, Ilya, 1142, 1437
Ehrenstein, Albert, 3789
"Eichinger," 1973
Eisenstein, S. M., 150, 156, 3790
Elektorowicz, Leszek, 3791
Eliot, T. S., 112, 156, 329, 696, 697, 804, 1105,
    1507, 1558, 1570, 1636, 1720, 2048, 3792, 4293
Elizondo, Salvador, 3793
Ellenbogen, Eileen, 4554, 4855, 5044
Ellegard, Alvar, 1721
Elliott, John R., 4805
Ellis, Charles R., 3227
Ellis, Havelock, 3567

Ellmann, Richard, 149, 155, 161, 192, 250, 308, 309,
    310, 329, 420, 421, 422, 423, 424, 425, 426, 759,
    805, 1106, 1535, 1540, 1551, 2769, 2776, 2777,
    2855, 2881, 2885, 3138, 3157, 3213, 3223, 3228,
    3260, 3273, 3568, 3794, 3795, 3796, 3797, 3798,
    4058, 4294, 4592, 4627, 5420, 5422, 5446, 5854,
    5878
Emery, Laurence K., 3799
Emeth, Omer (Elimio Vaisse), 3800
Emié, Louis, 2107
Empson, William, 1614, 1722, 4416, 4417
Engel, Fritz, 1986, 3507
Engel, Monroe, 2861
Engstrom, Alfred G., 4439
Enkemann, Jürgen, 1574
Enroth, C. A., 3130
Epstein, David, 2742
Epstein, Edmund L., 5, 73, 976, 1723, 2442, 3027,
    3229, 3801, 3802, 4295, 4555, 5398, 5595, 5600,
    5601, 5602
Erdman, Jean, 2636, 2720
Ernst, Morris, 3690, 4343, 4344, 4364
Ervine, St. John, 1988
Erzgraber, Willi, 3230
Escalera, Manuel de al, 3580
Esch, Arno, 3569, 4260
Escajadillo, Thomas G., 5264
Evans, B. Ifor, 193, 2273
Evans, Fallon, 3231, 3233
Evans, William A., 160, 4695
Eversole, Finley, 3674
Every, George, 194, 1369
Ewen, Frederic, 2637
Exner, Julian, 2007

F

F., 1987
F., L., 2094
F., S., 2286
Faas, Egbert, 4220
Fabian, David R., 2949
Fabricant, Noah D., 311
Fackler, Herbert V., 3439
Fadiman, Clifton, 2123, 2261, 2663, 3570, 5045
Fagerberg, Sven, 5046
Fahey, William, 2950
Faibani, Enzo, 427
Fáj, Atilla, 1724, 5399, 5400
Fallon, Padraic, 2802
Fallon, William G., 852
Falqui, Enrico, 977, 1438
Fanger, Donald, 978
Fargue, Leon-Paul, 1439, 4023
Farkas, Paul D., 3440
Farley, Earl, 2882
Farmer, Paul, 3013
Farrell, James T., 710, 1035, 1059, 1570, 2128, 3196,
    3232, 3319, 3487
Farrow, Anthony, 2373
Farwer, Gottfried, 5855
Fauchereau, Serge, 1131
Faulkner, William, 904
Faverty, Frederick E., 3803
Fay, Gerard, 2667
Faye, Jean-Pierre, 5603
Fechter, Paul, 3804

Fritz, Helen M., 983
Froberg, Herluf, 5326
Frye, Northrop, 150, 2913, 3658, 5402
Fuentes, Carlos, 1728, 4472
Füger, Wilhelm, 201, 2957, 3236, 3325, 3478
Fuhrmann, Mandred, 4264
Fukynaga, Kazutoshi, 1562, 1592
Fulford, Robert, 906, 1111
Fuller, Edmund, 929
Fuller, James A., 2985
Fuller, Roy, 1268
Furbank, P. N., 760, 778
Furnas, J. C., 5049
Furst, Lilian, 690

G

G., E., 436
G., I., 437
G., J. W., 1961
G., Y., 1882
Gabler, Hans Walter, 3236, 3237
Gabrieli, Vittorio, 1547
Gafney, Wilbur, 3798
Gallacher, Tom, 2638
Gallagher, Michael P., 700
Galli, Lina, 761
Galligan, Edward L., 1269
Galloway, David D., 4558
Gandon, Yves, 1563
Gangewere, Robert J., 4201
Gannett, Lewis, 2249, 4366
Gararry, Paul, 1946
García González, Enrique, 5856
Garcia Ponce, Juan, 702
Garcia Sabell, D., 1564
Gardair, Jean-Michel, 149, 762, 781
Gardiner, H. C., 1383
Garfeldt-Klever de Leal, Irene, 4200
Garnett, David, 3819
Garnett, Edward, 308, 3213, 3260
Garrett, Peter K., 1565, 2376, 2862
Garrison, Joseph M., Jr., 2986
Garvin, John (Andrew Cass), 153, 382, 438, 1644, 4628, 4696, 5050
Garzilli, Enrico F., 2377, 5314
Gaudebout, Pierre, 150
Gaugeard, Jean, 1112
Gaunt, Roger, 658
Gaunt, William, 583
Gaupp, F., 2104
Gaya Nuño, Juan Antonio, 3820
Geckle, George L., 3326, 4611
Genêt, see Janet Flanner
Genieva, E. Iu., 3511
Genissieux, L. E., 984
Genzmer, Harald, 2571
George, Manfred, 2095
George, W. L., 1443
Gerard, Albert, 3445
Gerassimowa, W., 1142
Gerber, Albert B., 4345
Gerber, Richard, 5169
Germanetto, 1142
Gerö, 1956
Gerold-Tuchoisky, Mary, 4099
Gerould, Daniel C., 3914
Gerstenberg, Joachim, 3821
Gertsfelde, V., 1113

Gessner, Robert, 1142
Getlein, Frank, 1037
Gettman, Royal A., 3090
Gheerbrant, Bernard, 114
Gheorghiu, Mihnea, 275
Ghiselin, Brewster, 2852, 2855, 2862, 2885, 2914
Gibbon, Monk, 622, 710, 1060, 1644, 3578, 3648
Gibbons, T. H. 2915
Gibbs-Smith, C. H., 1040
Gibson, George H., 4559
Gibson, Morgan, 1729
Gide, André, 156, 1445, 1568
Gidley, M., 1444
Giedion-Welcker, Carola, 315, 321, 439, 440, 441, 442, 443, 864, 1038, 1114, 1311, 1329, 1566, 1655, 2695, 3579, 3822, 3823, 4367, 5051, 5281, 5327, 5879
Gifford, Don, 2863
Gilbert, Allan, 4788
Gilbert, Bernard, 3824
Gilbert, Jean, 6
Gilbert, Martin, 316
Gilbert, Stuart, 7, 202, 309, 317, 984, 1039, 1115, 1312, 1523, 1551, 1570, 1591, 1596, 2229, 3580, 3581, 4187, 4225, 4739, 4763, 4769, 4906, 4930, 4931, 5052, 5053, 5054, 5055, 5056, 5057, 5282
Gill, Richard, 4299
Gillam, Doreen M. E., 3327, 3479
Gillespie, Robert, 2638
Gillet, Eric, 1567
Gillet, Guillaume, 865
Gillet, Louis, 444, 1568, 1596, 3328, 3825, 5058, 5059, 5060
Gillie, Christopher, 3238
Gillon, Adam, 1270
Gilman, Sander L., 5061, 5604
Ginden, James, 3582
Giorgianni, Enio, 1569
Giovanelli, Felix, 476
Giovanni, Norman Thomas de, 1258
Giroux, Roger, 156, 4416
Guidiei, Giovanni, 1551
Givens, Seon, 1570
Gladkow, Fjodor, 1142
Glasgow, Ellen, 3826
Glasheen, Adaline, 930, 1613, 2866, 3068, 4413, 4856, 4935, 5062, 5063, 5064, 5065, 5066, 5283, 5284, 5357, 5358, 5403, 5404, 5405, 5406, 5407, 5408, 5409, 5410, 5421, 5479, 5605, 5606, 5607, 5608, 5609, 5610, 5611, 5612, 5613, 5614, 5615, 5616, 5617, 5618, 5619, 5620, 5621
Glassco, John, 834
Gleckner, Robert F., 1571, 1614, 4923, 5359, 5411
Gleeson, W. F., 2952
Glendinning, Alex, 2316
Glesch-Brunningen, Hans, 5857
Glicksberg, Charles I., 1572
Glikin, Gloria, 4226
Globocnik, Amalija, 881
Godin, Genri, 3329
Godwin, Murray, 3827, 4418
Gogarty, Oliver St. John, 318, 319, 320, 328, 389, 393, 394, 445, 446, 835, 836, 837, 838, 866, 2267, 2695, 4629, 4724
Going, William T., 2987
Gold, Ed, 152, 3828
Goldberg, Gerald J., 2444
Goldberg, M. A., 3239
Goldberg, S. L., 1116, 1540, 1573, 1574, 1584, 2852, 2862, 3273, 3446, 3829

H

I

J

Jarret-Kerr, Martin, 4968
Jarrett, Jack, 2581, 2582, 2583
Jauss, Hans Robert, 4442
Jay, Maurice Le Verne, 2526
Jedlicka, Gottehard, 1457
Jedynak, Stanley Louis, 2435, 2920
Jenkins, Ralph, 158, 4789
Jenkins, William D., 158, 640, 3878, 5436, 5658,
    5659, 5660, 5661, 5662, 5663, 5664, 5665, 5666
Jennings, Paul, 4943, 5106
Jense, Gregory, 2011
Jeremic, Ljibisa, 4231
Jewett, Sarah Orne, 3380
Joerden, Erika, 24
John, Augustus, 473, 2580
Johnson, Robert G., 3250
Johnston, Denis, 153, 993, 1154, 1644, 2646, 4658,
    5107
Joho, Wolfgang, 270, 280
Jolas, Eugene, 555, 648, 871, 1312, 1315, 1570,
    1596, 2169, 3555, 3879, 3880, 4259, 4906, 4944,
    5045, 5051, 5108, 5109, 5110, 5111, 5112, 5152,
    5203, 5262, 5289, 5290
Jolas, Maria, 156, 451, 547, 555, 603, 614, 631,
    680, 1029, 1044, 1155, 1596, 1612, 1613, 2695,
    3555, 4945, 5113, 5341
Jones, Alun, 3881
Jones, C. A., 5114
Jones, David E., 3449
Jones, E. S., 3706
Jones, H. M., 1356
Jones, T. H., 5115
Jones, W. Powell, 1156, 3260, 3602
Jordan, John, 615, 846, 1644
Jordan-Smith, Paul, see Smith, Paul Jordan
Josephson, Matthew, 750, 2078, 2732, 3882, 4483
Jost, François, 293, 1362, 4444
Joyce, Eva, 2695
Joyce, Helen, 475, 2667
Joyce, Stanislaus, 60, 328, 329, 330, 331, 446, 476,
    477, 478, 763, 764, 765, 781, 1523, 1551, 1644,
    2678, 2695, 2765, 2881, 2921, 3138
Joyce, Stephen, 919
Juchhoff, Rudolf, 9
Jude the Obscure, 632
Jung, Carl Gustav, 3603
Just, Gottfried, 1458

K

Kaestlin, John, 2812
Kagen, Sergius, 2584, 2585
Kahane, Jack, 847
Kahn-Ackerman, Susanne, 1033
Kahn, Ludwig W., 3236, 3450
Kain, Richard M., 46, 48, 49, 50, 137, 159, 160,
    281, 332, 1157, 1274, 1459, 1516, 1597, 1613,
    1614, 1659, 1751, 1752, 2772, 2813, 2852, 2866,
    3119, 3203, 3255, 3260, 3272, 3344, 3345, 3604,
    3605, 3606, 3657, 3883, 3884, 3885, 3886, 3942,
    4284, 4544, 4612, 4634, 4740, 4770, 4790, 4791,
    4792, 4793, 4876, 4923, 4946, 5667
Kaiser, Gerhard R., 3607
Kanters, Robert, 79, 737, 1158
Kaplan, Frederick, 4598
Kaplan, Harold J., 3608
Kaplan, Marian, 4818
Kaplan, Robert B., 1460
Karl, Frederick R., 210

Karling, Karin, 3887
Karpowitz, Stephen, 3451
Karrfalt, David H., 5437
Kastor, Robert N., 603, 2668, 2675
Kataoka, Jintaro, 211
Katz, Leslie, 156
Kauder, Hugo, 2586
Kaufmann, Richard, 5860
Kauver, Elaine M., 3120
Kavanagh, Patrick, 153, 1275, 1276, 1277, 1644,
    3888
Kawaguchi, Kyoichi, 3889, 3890
Kaye, Julian B., 157, 1598, 1612, 1613, 2852, 2968,
    3166, 3222, 3255, 3260, 3346, 4545
Kazin, Alfred, 1335, 2298
Keener, Ulysses Grant, 2476
Kell, Richard, 3347
Kelleher, John V., 1997, 3167, 3260, 3418, 5438,
    5439, 5440, 5668
Kelleher, V. M. K., 3452
Keller, Dean H., 3517
Kelley, William Melvin, 149, 5669
Kellogg, Charles E., 1159
Kellogg, Robert, 1648
Kelly, Blanche Mary, 1045
Kelly, Edward H., 3348
Kelly, H. A., 4232
Kelly, John, 163
Kelly, P., 1160
Kelly, Richard, 3349
Kelly, Robert G., 1599, 1659, 2380, 3350
Kelly, Seamus ("Quidnunc"), 163, 164, 282, 710,
    4667
Kelly, Sean, 1278
Kelvin, Norman, 2988
Kempf, Roger, 149, 872
Kennedy, Sister Eileen, 2922, 3891
Kennedy, Richard S., 1416
Kennedy, Sighle, 1378
Kennelly, Brendan, 3168
Kenner, Hugh, 80, 212, 333, 671, 717, 1161, 1461,
    1540, 1570, 1600, 1636, 2855, 2862, 3032, 3213,
    3223, 3251, 3260, 3273, 3351, 3352, 3518, 3557,
    4306, 4420, 4443, 4485, 4486, 4487, 4511, 4599,
    4659, 5670
Kenner, William H., 2413
Kenny, Sean, 2645
Kensik, A. C., 1162, 5861
Keogh, J. G., 4771
Kerel, François, 841
Kermode, Frank, 3609
Kerr, Alfred, 1612, 4371
Kerrigan, Anthony, 1279, 1865
Kershner, Richard B., 2381
Kesser, Armin, 1046
Kesting, Marianne, 1462
Kestner, Joseph A., 994
Kettle, Arnold, 213, 4546
Kettle, Thomas, 1847
Khan, Frank, 166
Khezlop, G., 2331
Kiashvili, N., 310
Kieckhefer, Patricia, 3070
Kiely, Benedict, 334, 1047, 1644, 5116
Kilburn, Patrick E., 2477
Kilchenmann, Ruth J., 2869
Kileen, A., 3892
Kileen, J. F., 4488
Kilgallin, Anthony R., 1463

L

Laurence, William, 2656
LaValley, Albert J., 2872
Lavergne, Philippe, 725, 5120
Lawrence, D. H., 696, 4146
Lawrence, Raymond, 5122
Lawson, David, 3797
Lawson, Jack, 1282
Lazarett, Pierre, 481
Leal, Antonio Castro, 1603
Leary, Daniel, 3059
Leary, Wilson, 2129
Leavis, F. R., 4372, 5291
LeBreton, Georges, 5880
LeComte, Marcel, 3908
Ledgard, Rudolfo, 4493
Lee, Jae-Ho, 4613
Lee, Robin, 4310
Lee, L. L., 5455, 5456, 5684
LeFevre, Frederic, 909, 5058, 5123, 5124
LeFleming, Christopher, 2590
Léger, David, 1580
Legris, Renée, 4257
Lehmann, John, 1165
Lehmann, Trevor, 1614, 4794
Leinwall, George, 152, 698, 1080, 4662, 5685
Leitch, Vincent B., 4772
Lelay, Yves, 3603
Lemarchand, Jacques, 3520
Lemon, Lee T., 3273, 3356
Lennartz, Franz, 218
Lennon, John, 5229
Lennon, Michael J., 482, 483, 4848
Lennon, Peter, 874
Lennox, Maud, 907
Lenz, Siegfried, 692
Léon, Lucie Noël, 340, 704, 911, 2669, 2695
Léon, Paul, 875, 911, 1596, 1613, 4158, 5203
Leonard, Hugh, 2641, 2642, 3357
Lerdahl, Fred, 2742
LeRoy, Anne, 2835
LeRoy, Gaylord C., 228, 2904, 3679
Lescure, Pierred, 1758
Leslie, Shane ("Domini Canis"), 2077, 2080, 3690, 4373
Lester, John A., 2924
Lester, Leigh, 3909
Lestra, André, 1759
"Les Treize," 910
Leventhal, A. J., 1760, 4567
Levenston, E. A., 4726
Levin, Harry, 250, 484, 767, 938, 1049, 1055, 1166, 1507, 1540, 1551, 1603, 1604, 1636, 1649, 1761, 1762, 2245, 2325, 2355, 2855, 3204, 3213, 3223, 3255, 3260, 3273, 3910, 3915, 5864
Levin, Lawrence, 4821
Levin, Richard, 1570, 2925
Levitt, Morton P., 1656, 1763, 3571, 3615, 4568
Lewers, Constance E., 3911
Lewicki, Zbigniew, 155, 3912, 3913, 3914
LeWinter, Oswald, 5686
Lewis, Janet Elizabeth O'Brien, 2482
Lewis, Sinclair, 616, 1380
Lewis, Wyndham, 718, 1049, 2324, 3577, 3616, 3617, 3618, 3880, 3915, 3975, 4195, 5125
Lewisohn, Ludwig, 1381
Leyris, Pierre, 156
Lidderdale, Jane, 335, 485, 3916
Liddy, James, 1167, 1282, 1283, 1284, 1317
Lief, Leonard, 1678
Liepman, Heinz, 486

Liljegren, Stan Bodvar, 3619
Lilly, Katherine A., 3254
Lillyman, W. J., 4234
Lima, Robert, 1259
Limmer, Ruth, 5272
Linati, Carlo, 283, 5881
Lincecum, J. B., 4235
Lind, Ilse, Dusior, 3419
Lind, L. Robert, 2293
Lindberger, Örjan, 738
Lindenberg, A., 3555
Lindner, G., 3917
Lindsay, Jack, 250, 739, 939, 1465
Lindsay, Norman, 4374
Link, Frederick M., 3455
Link, Victor, 2483, 4421, 4860
Linn, Robert, 2591
Lippman, Bertram, 3227, 3918
Liss, Archie K., 1765, 2417
List, Robert Nelson, 2418
Little, George A., 3358, 3359
Little, Sherry B., 2419
Littlejohn, David, 1466
Littmann, Mark E., 4422
Litz, A. Walton, 29, 30, 157, 158, 1605, 1606, 1613, 1636, 2420, 2866, 2885, 3028, 3919, 3920, 3921, 3942, 4311, 4923, 4947, 4948, 5126, 5127, 5360
Livermore, Ana, 4494
Llona, Victor, 4906, 5264
Lloyd, P. G., 1764, 5333
Lockspeiser, Edward, 5128
Loda, Motoki, 4691
Lodge, David, 219, 638
Loehrich, Rolf Rudolf, 3620
Loeppert, Elsbeth, 3922
Loftus, Richard, 3423
Logan, Dorothy, 3171
Lombardo, Agostino, 2766
Longaker, Mark, 220
Longhead, W. C., 325
Loomis, C. C., Jr., 2862, 2885, 3138, 3172
López, Naravaez, Froylán, 1168
Lorch, Thomas M., 4495
Lord, George De F., 4312
Loreis, Hector-Jan, 1467
Lorenzini, Amleto, 1603, 3923
Lotringer, Sylvere, 487
Lottman, Herbert R., 603
Lovett, Robert M., 208, 3621
Low, Donald A., 685
Low, Stephen, 3924
Lowenfels, Walter, 1169, 2169
Luce, Robert B., 391
Lüdeke, Henry, 653
Ludwig, Jack, 2852, 2873, 3135
Ludwig, Richard M., 661, 2262, 3575, 5280
Lukács, Georg, 3622
Lundell, Roger H., 3066
Lundkvist, Artur, 1607, 1608
Lundström, Bengt, 1766
Lutter, Tibor, 1609
Luzi, Mario, 3623
Lynd, Robert, 1170, 2251, 2290
Lynd, Sylvia, 876, 1252, 2310
Lyngstad, Sverre, 2383
Lyner, A., 1171
Lynskey, Winifred, 10, 3071
Lyon, Thomas E., 4496
Lyons, F. S. L., 488

Mariategui, José Carlos, 3366
Marichalar, Antonio, 1336, 1771, 3937
Marie, Aristide, 3625
Marienstros, Richard, 1257
Marin Morales, José A., 719
Mariño-Palacio, Andris, 3626, 3938
Marion, Denis, 1176
Marriott, R. B., 115
Markovic, Vida E., 3257
Markow-Totevy, Georges, 665, 667, 1568, 1612, 1617
Marks, J., 1772
Marks, Lester, 4773
Markson, David, 4571
Marmon, C., 3939
Marschall, Hiltrud, 2620
Marshall, Beatrice, 725, 726, 4375
Marshall, E. G., 2745
Marshall, William H., 1003
Martin, Augustine, 1469
Martin, E. W., 194
Martin, Graham, 222
Martin, Jean Paul, 1741
Martin, Kingsley, 497
Martín-Santos, Luis,
Martindale, C. C., 1941, 4314
Martino, Donald, 2593
Martinson, Moa, 3627
Maruya, Saiichi, 1592, 3258
Marye, Edward, 5135
Masaryk, Thomas G., 223
Mason, Ellsworth, 151, 476, 496, 2485, 2765, 2767, 2774, 2775, 2776, 3260, 3457, 3940, 3941, 4315, 4572, 4849
Mason, Eudo C., 224, 4954, 5136
Mason, Michael, 3628, 3942
Masuda, Yoshio, 1511, 3197, 3259
Mathews, F. X., 3075, 5693
Mathews, Jackson, 156, 3943, 3944
Matlack, David, 3945
Matlaw, Myron, 1678
Matson, L., 2634
Matthews, Herbert L., 2231
Mattioui, Stelio, 878
Maudlin, A. A., 4145
Maugeri, Aldo, 4728
Maule, Harry E., 1380
Maura, Sister, 1287
Mauriac, François, 904
Maurois, André, 1470
Maxwell, J. C., 4704
Mayhew, G., 4424
Mayo, W. K., 3946
Mayoux, Jean-Jacques, 849, 1319, 1385, 1618, 1619
Mazzi, Libero, 3947
Meade, Norah, 2201, 5137
Meagher, James Anthony, 879, 3948, 3949
Medioli, Joann, 3545, 4797
Meenan, James, 338
Meeting of the Joyce Society, 2747, 2748
Meeuwesse, Karel, 4501
Megret, Frederic, 3950
Mehren, Günther, 2044
Meister, Guido G., 1632
Melchiori, Giorgio, 1526, 3629
Mellard, James M., 2997
Meller, Horst, 644, 1471
DeMenasce, Jean, 1177
Mencken, H. L., 699
Mendilow, A. A., 4262
Menendez, Aldo, 3951

Mengelberg, Rudolf, 2594
Menicanti, Daria, 1632
Menton, Seymour, 1472
Mercanton, Jacques, 880, 1620, 2247, 3952, 5138, 5337
Mercer, Caroline G., 3367
Merchant, W. M., 2778
Mercier, 84, 95, 498, 1178, 1386, 1473, 1474, 1570, 1584, 1614, 2350, 4236, 4265, 4446, 4665, 4923, 5283, 5361, 5362
Meredith, Burgess, 2634
Merkling, Frank, 3953
Merle, Robert, 5139
Merrill, Jean, 2635
Mertner, Edgar, 225
Merton, Thomas, 86, 4861
Meskin, Carol, 3545, 4602, 4837
Metzger, Deena P., 3524
Metzner, John, 56
Meyer, R. W., 1668
Meyers, Stanley, 2749
Meylan, Jean-Pierre, 226
Miasnikov, A. S., 252
Micha, René, 149, 499
M[ichalski], H[ieronim], 500
Michaud, Regis, 5140
Michel, André, 156
Michelson, Peter, 4350
Mignot, Yvan, 150
Mikelson, Anne, 4705
Mikhalskaya, N. P., 3954
Miles, Hamish, 2195, 2213
Miles, Josephine, 4293
Milgate, W., 4889
Millar, Gavin, 2682
Miller, Henry, 741
Miller, J. Hillis, 3600
Miller, James E., 3093
Miller, Mildred, 2726
Miller, Milton, 1773
Miller, Nolan, 87
Miller, Norbert, 3646, 4956
Miller-Budnitskaia, R., 1774, 3955, 5882
Millet, Fred B., 227, 229
Millstein, Gilbert, 116
Milne, Ewart, 1288, 4626
Milner, Ian, 4425
Mink, Louis O., 4856, 5694, 5695, 5696
Minkoff, George Robert, 11
Miomandre, Francis de, 2110, 3956
Mirkovic, Radoslava, 4316
Mirkovic, Vladimir, 881
Miroiu, Michai, 800, 4237, 4238
Mirskii, Dmitrii Petrovich, 742, 1035, 5883
Misiorny, Michal, 2047
Misra, B. P., 941, 1004, 5465, 5466
"Miss Modern," 4146
Mitchell, Breon, 3957, 3958, 4239, 4935, 5467, 5468, 5527, 5697
Mitchell, Carol, 2715
Mitchell, Caroline, 4666
Mitchell, Charles, 3601
Mitchell, Evelyn, 2755
Mitchison, Naomi, 2187
Mizener, Arthur, 12, 662, 2998, 3076
Miyata, Kyoko, 3368
Mjöberg, Jöran, 1775
Mochizuki, Mitsuko, 1776, 4751
Modic, John, 5141

N

Nickson, Richard, 310
Nicolson, Harold, 294, 850, 851, 1183, 2257, 4147
Nicolson, Mary, 335, 485
Nicolson, Nigel, 851
Niebyl, Karl H., 1182
Niemeyer, Carl, 2852, 3124
Nightingale, Benedict, 2017, 2029
Nikula, Karl H., 5867
Nims, John Frederick, 1184, 3233, 3263
Nishiwaki, Junzaburo, 1592, 1626
Noakes, David, 1423
Noël, Lucie, see Lucie Noël Léon
Nöhbauer, Hans, 3970
Nojima, Hidekatsu, 1627
Nolan, Brian, see Myles na Gopaleen
Noma, Hiroshi, 1592, 3264
Noon, William T., S.J., 159, 232, 267, 284, 308,
    341, 322, 505, 943, 1185, 1659, 1688, 1781,
    1782, 2393, 2852, 3077, 3138, 3260, 3265, 3373,
    3635, 3971, 4821, 5147, 5706
Nordio, Mario, 506, 885
Norman, Charles, 719, 1392
Norris, Margot Christa, 2531
"Northerner," 2301
Novak, Jane, 4899
Nowell, Elizabeth, 1393
Nowell-Smith, Simon, 309
Nowlan, David, 2036
Noyes, Alfred, 1052, 3636, 3972
Nunez, Estuardo, 1479
Nyholm, J., 117

O

O., K., 1655
O., Y., see George Russell, AE
Oakes, E., 507
Obler, Paul C., 4809
Obradovic, Adelheid B., 2492
O'Brien, Conor Cruise, 886
O'Brien, Darcy, 161, 1628, 1629, 1656, 1703, 2421,
    3657, 3993, 4596, 4604, 4605, 5149, 5150
O'Brien, Edna, 1053, 1644
O'Brien, Flann, see Myles na Gopaleen
O'Brien, Justin, 156, 674
O'Brien, Kate, 2335
O'Brien, Maurice N., 1293
O'Callaghan, J., 3974
O'Casey, Sean, 710, 5498
O'Conluain, Proinsias, 509
O'Connell, Daniel, 4574
O'Connor, Frank (Michael O'Donovan), 233, 342, 621,
    710, 904, 1784, 2695, 2750, 2751, 2855, 2862,
    2878, 2879, 2885, 3138, 3178, 3213, 3460, 3975,
    5151
O'Connor, Michael, 2659
O'Connor, Ulick, 234, 343, 508, 670, 852, 1202, 1644,
    2659
O'Connor, William Van, 410, 3438, 3461
Oda, Motoi, 1785
Odajimi, Yuji, 1511, 2785
O'Dea, Richard J., 3462
O'Doherty, Brian, 912
O'Donnell, Donat, 322
O'Donnell, Thomas Daniel, 2397
O'Duffy, Eimar, 2085
O'Dwyer, Riana, 5707
O'Faolain, Sean, 802, 944, 1186, 2168, 2169, 2685,
    3266, 4393, 5152, 5153, 5154, 5262

Offenburg, Kurt, 2105
O'Flaherty, Gerard, 91, 4670
Ogawa, Yoshihiko, 4822
Ogden, C. K., 2209, 5155, 5156
O'Grady, Desmond, 510
O'Hanlon, R. Davis, 4722, 5708
O hAodha, Michael, 2686
Ohaski, Kenzaburo, 1394, 1511, 4863
O'Hegarty, P. S., 13, 1940, 2079
O'Hehir, Brendan P., 3138, 3179, 4708, 5363, 5476,
    5477, 5709, 5710, 5711, 5712, 5713
O Hehir, Diana F., 2384
O heithirt, Brendan, 1187
Ohmann, Richard, 2999, 3002
Ó hUrmoltaigh, Seán, 1786
Oketani, Hideaki, 1630
Olden, G. A., 2687, 2688, 3976
Oldmeadow, E., 2205, 2220
Olfson, Lewy, 3267
Oliass, Heinz Gunther, 1903
Olinto, Antonio, 720, 1787
"Oliver," 4145
Oljeschs, Jurij, 1142
Olmstead, Nelson, 2689
Olmstead, Sterling P., 3047
Olson, Richard D., 118
O'Mahony, Eoin, 511, 1644, 5370
O'Malley, Glenn, 1026
O'Neill, Bridget, 3374
O'Neill, Michael J., 323, 344, 1613, 2779, 2881,
    3109
O'Neill, Samuel J., 4240
"Onlooker," 913
Ono, Kyoichi, 1511, 3268
Ono, Yasuko, 345, 1054, 1511
Opasi, E., 512
Opfermann, H. C., 3977
Oppel, Horst, 235, 3230
Orage, Alfred R., 1921, 3637, 3638
O'Rahilly, Father A., 2644
O'Reilly, James P., 1480
O'Riordan, Conal, 1190
Orlov, Yu. K., 1011
Ormsby, Frank, 3103
Ornstein, William, 3978
O'Rourke, Mamie, 5714
Orr, C. W., 2580, 2601
Ortembach, Enrique, 2031
Orwell, George, 1055, 4508
Orwell, Sonia, 1055, 4508
Osborne, Marianne, 2446
Oscott, Hanni, 4575
Ostroff, Anthony, 2929
O'Sullivan, Terry, 163, 164
Ota, Saburo, 1056, 1057, 1395, 1592
Otten, J. F., 3979
O'Tuama, Sean, 2752

P

P., B. C., 1191
Paci, Francesca Roma, 1631
Pack, Claus, 711
Paez, Urdaneta, Iraset, 4241
Pagé, Pierre, 4257
Paige, D. D., 721, 769, 5059
Painter, George D., 744, 791
Paley, Morton D., 1614, 4449

Pratt, Kenneth, 3233, 3269
Praz, Mario, 159, 238, 348, 1385, 1794, 3270, 3629, 3998, 3999
Prescott, Joseph, 151, 375, 1200, 1320, 1486, 1613, 1614, 1636, 1637, 1795, 2493, 2757, 2768, 2839, 3207, 3222, 3223, 3260, 3273, 4000, 4001, 4271, 4272, 4322, 4323, 4371, 4512, 4576, 4607, 4617, 4710, 4711, 4823, 5163, 5164, 5294
Preston, Harold P., 4379
Preston, Hayter, 4002
Price, J. T., 5157
Price, Rosemary, 3545, 4867
Priestly, J. B., 239, 4380
Pritchard, William H., 2931, 4513
Pritchett, V. S., 787, 792, 1201, 2769, 2932, 4003, 4004
Proffer, Carl R., 1398
Proust, Marcel, 982
Puccini, Dario, 2786
Punnini, Mario, 4005
Puner, Helen Walker, 946
Purcell, Sally A. J., 1543
Purdon, C. B., 285
Purdy, Andrew, 4577
Purdy, Strother B., 1656, 4514, 5266
Purnal, Roland, 240
Purser, John T., 2979, 3058
Pusack, James P., 4279
Putman, Samuel, 584
Pütz, Manfred, 32
Pyle, Hilary, 752

Q

Quarantoti-Gambini, R. A., 520, 521
Quasha, George, 2880, 3438
Queneau, Raymond, 854, 891
"Querist," 5165
Quidnunc, see Seamus Kelly
Quinn, John, 1925
Quinn, Owen, 1487

R

R., D., 294
R., H., 1897
R., L., 2232
R., S., 2083
Raabe, Paul, 1632
Rabinovitz, Rubin, 241
Raddatz, Fritz J., 4099
Radek, Karl, 1035, 1059, 1142
Rader, Ralph W., 1638
Radford, F. L., 4798
Raimond, Michel, 4199
Raimondi, Guiseppe, 855
Raine, Kathleen, 984
Raleigh, John Henry, 522, 4006, 4007
Ramnoux, Clémence, 1596, 5318
Ranald, Margaret L., 3465
Randolph, John, 2637
Rank, Otto, 1022
Rankin, H. D., 1013, 4833, 5166, 5167, 5479, 5721, 5722, 5723
Ransom, John Crowe, 3961, 5342
Ransom, Timothy, 5295
Rasbridge, W. J., 4838
Rascoe, Burton, 2268, 4451

Rathkey, W. A., 1297
Rauter, Herbert, 3138, 3644
Ray, Gordon N., 192
Ray, Man, 585
Raymont, Henry, 310
Read, Forrest, 724, 725, 726, 1198, 1635, 1793, 1873, 3213, 4378, 4511
Read, Gardner, 2605
Read, Herbert, 1202, 1203, 1555, 1796, 1934, 3603, 3645, 4008
Readdy, Coral Ann, 4242
Ready, W. B., 265
Reavey, George, 634
Rebecchi-Piperata, Carlina, 349
Rebora, Piero, 1639
Reck, Rima Drell, 1488, 4009
Recondo, Pablo, 149
Reddick, Bryan, 3381
Reddin, Kenneth, 153
Redfern, J., 1989
Redford, Grant H., 157, 3222, 3223, 3260, 3383
Reding, Josef, 770
Redman, Ben R., 4381
Reece, Shelley C., 2448
Reed, Alfred, 2606
Reed, Henry, 1797, 2692, 5168
Rees, G. E., 1798, 4010, 4145
Rees, Leslie, 892
Rees, Richard, 743
Reeves, Paschal, 1416, 4515
Rehm, George, 2053, 2057
Reichert, Klaus, 308, 310, 351, 2045, 2881, 3527, 3646, 4956, 5169
Reid, B. L., 587
Reid, Marjorie, 4011
Reid, Stephen, 3094
Reifenberg, Benno, 2197, 5170
Reilly, James P., 3233, 3426, 3466
Rembar, Charles, 4352
Renard, Marie-Jo, 150, 4290
Renda, Agostino, 4012
"Reno," 2002
Renzi, Dorothy, 2719
Rergner, George 1879
Rest, Jaimé, 1204, 3207
Reutter, Hermann, 2607
Reverdy, Pierre, 156
Revol, E. L., 635, 3647
Reyes, Alfonso, 5171
Reyes, Pedro A., 3383
Reynolds, Horace, 2207, 2243, 2339
Reynolds, Mary L., 523, 4516
Reynolds, Michael S., 2956
Rhind, Neil, 3384
Rice, Howard C., 140
Richards, Howard, 2608, 2609
Richardson, Dorothy, 156, 2317, 4013, 4185
Richardson, Robert O., 4900
Richey, Clarence W., 5724
Richter, G. F., 5627
Rickword, Edgell, 939
Riddell, John, 4014
Rideout, W. B., 1356
Ridgeway, Ann, 4517
Rieman, Fritz, 4200
Riesner, Dieter, 224
Rigolot, François, 150
Riley, Sister Mary Geraldine, 3385
Rimanelli, Giose, 150

S

Sahl, Hans, 4035
Saillet, Maurice, 156, 3944
Sainer, Arthur, 2030
St. John-Stevas, Norman, 4353
St. Lawrence, Henry, 1338
Sale, Richard B., 1491
Sale, William M., 3141
Salemson, Harold J., 2208, 5183, 5184
Salerno, George, 1015
Saliņš, Gunars, 1401
Sallenave, Daniele, 4244
Salus, Peter H., 4824
Samilowitz, Hazel, 4036
Sampson, George, 182
Sánchez, Luis Alberto, 1646
Sandgren, Gustav, 4037
Sandulescu, C. G., 1801, 2840
Sanesi, Roberto, 3264
San Juan, Epifanio, 2883, 2957, 3014, 3034, 3095, 3104
Santiago, Luciano, 4038
Santini, Lea Ritter, 1551
Santoyo, J. C., 3808
Sarraute, Nathalie, 1402
Sardi, Francesco Saba, 4906
Sartre, Jean-Paul, 1802
Sarukhonian, A. P., 243
Sasayama, Takashi, 1511, 3489
Sasse, Carl, 1492
Sattler, Andreas, 5869
Saul, George Brandon, 1493, 2884
Savage, Derek S., 1526, 1647
Savage, Henry, 1300
Savio, Antonio Fonda, 893
Savio, Letizia Fonda, 893
Savitsky, Ludmilla, 550, 5296
Saxer, Johann, 2788
Scarfe, Francis, 1403
Scarry, John M., 536, 2424, 3110, 3181, 3182, 3183, 5732
Schaarschmidt, G., 4245
Scharaf, Lester, 2161
Schardt, Alois, 3233, 3427
Scharper, Philip, 322
Schauder, Karlheinz, 1321
Schaurek, Eileen Joyce, 902, 2695
Schawlow, R., 2348
Schd., H., 2097
Schechner, Mark, 2495, 4039, 4040, 4674
Scheffrin, Gladys, 1803
Scherbacher, Wolfgang, 2366
Scheuerle, William H., 3184, 4714
Schickele, Peter, 2759
Schiefele, Hans, 2496, 4200
Schiff, Gert, 537, 5186, 5187, 5189
Schirokauer, Arno, 694
Schlauch, Margaret, 5188, 5301
Schlesak, Dieter, 1322
Schlien, Helmut, 1323
Schlumberger, Jean, 156
Schmidt, Arno, 329, 330, 2142, 4958, 5189, 5870
Schmidt, Hugo, 3185
Schneidau, Herbert N., 727
Schneider, Daniel, 4327
Schneider, Duana, 4518
Schneider, Ulrich, 2497, 4404, 4868
Schneiders, Heinz-Ludwig, 4041
Schoeck, R. J., 4042

Scholes, Robert E., 16, 308, 1494, 1584, 1614, 1648, 1804, 2363, 2780, 2816, 2829, 2841, 2842, 2866, 2885, 2935, 2936, 3052, 3079, 3186, 3203, 3213, 3272, 3388, 3389, 3942, 4043
Schonberg, Harold C., 1805
Schoolfield, G. C., 4519
Schoonbroodt, Jean, 149, 2498, 4044, 4275
Schorer, Mark, 421, 1548, 1603, 1649, 3044, 3390, 4097, 4265, 4293, 5530
Schott, Webster, 5350
Schow, Howard W., 2451
Schrenk, M., 1324
Schulte, Edvige, 1650
Schumach, Murray, 2540
Schunemann-Killian, Peter, 538
Schutte, William M., 2499, 3273, 3657, 4276, 4405, 4579, 4799
Schwab, Raymond, 1211
Schwabach, Erik-Ernst, 5871
Schwartz, Alan U., 4344
Schwartz, Delmore, 2340
Schwartz, Edward, 3391
Schwartz, Harry W., 53
Schwartz, Kessel, 244
Schwartz, Lewis M., 4608
Schwartz, Nathan, 2719
Schwegel, Douglas M., 4753
Schweikart, Hans, 2642
Schwerin, Christoph, 1971, 4125
Schwerte, Hans, 1743
Schwieghauser, Charles A., 4422
Schwimmer, Helmut, 5733
Scott, Alexander, 1285
Scott, Evelyn, 1495
Scott, George R., 1806, 4382
Scott, L. H., 5364
Scott, Nathan A., Jr., 1651
Scott, Robert Ian, 286, 3392
Scott, Virgil, 3041, 3053
Scott-James, Rolfe, 1652
Scotti, Giacomo, 539
Scotto, Robert M., 2452, 3393
Scribe, Oliver, 2155, 4045
Searle, Humphrey, 2611
Sebeok, Thomas A., 4938
Sedelow, Walter A., 5483
Seelmann-Eggebert, Ulrich, 2046
Segur, Nicholas, 4520
Seiber, Mátyás, 2612, 2613, 2760, 4046
Seidman, Robert J., 2863
Selby, John, 2253
Seldes, Gilbert, 2076, 2125
Selig, Karl L., 773
Sell, Frederick C., 1807
Selver, Paul, 2051, 4047
Semmler, Clement, 1212, 1653, 2696, 5197, 5344, 5734
Semple, I., 1896
Sen, Mihir Kumar, 2817
Sencourt, Robert, 624
Sender, Ramon J., 1213
Senn, Fritz, 93, 123, 155, 162, 308, 310, 351, 352, 353, 540, 541, 542, 913, 918, 1060, 1214, 1325, 1516, 1654, 1655, 1656, 1808, 1809, 1810, 1811, 1812, 2866, 2881, 2958, 2969, 3187, 3188, 3273, 3394, 3395, 3482, 3657, 4048, 4049, 4050, 4051, 4052, 4053, 4054, 4055, 4056, 4057, 4151, 4638, 4715, 4716, 4717, 4736, 4741, 4754, 4810, 4811,

T

T., M. A., 5217
Th.,-P., M., 1655
Tadie, Marie, 330
Tagliaboue, John, 1304
Tagliaiozzo, Giorgio, 5360
Takada, Kunio, 557
Takamura, Katsuji, 1413, 1592
Takano, Fumi, 1511, 4801
Talarico, E., 783
Talbot, Francis, 2135, 4387
Tallentire, D. R., 5345
Tambimuttu, M. J., 4499
Taniguchi, Satoji, 2818, 3529
Tannenbaum, Samuel, 3528
Tanner, Godfrey, 5506, 5800
Tanselle, G. Thomas, 22, 126
Taplin, Walter, 126, 2701, 2702, 5305
Taranierko, Zbigniew, 156, 1822, 4332
Tarbox, Raymond, 3404
Tarnaud, Claude, 1603
Tate, Allen, 156, 1400, 2885, 3131, 3191
Tatsumiya, Sakae, 1592, 1672
Tau, Max, 1823, 4085
Taube, Myron, 3018
Taubman, Howard, 2650
Taylor, Estella R., 1071
Teele, Roy E., 5507
Tegenbosch, Lambert, 915
Tellegen, A. O. H., 155, 4086
Tello Quijano, Jaime (Jaime Tello), 4620, 5801
Temple, Michael, 4087
Temple, Ruth Z., 250
Tery, Simone, 916, 1673
Thatcher, David S., 625
Thayer, Scofield, 1824
Theall, Donald F., 1, 96, 2387, 5346
Theile, Harald, 4088
Thiebaut, Marcel, 1878, 4089
Thieme, Karl, 1222
Thoma, Richard, 5218
Thomas, Donald, 4388
Thomas, Vlad Ivan, 2507
Thompson, Alan R., 4090
Thompson, Diane, 5802
Thompson, Francis J., 5347
Thompson, George, 4756
Thompson, John H., 4964, 4965, 5803
Thompson, Lawrence, 1674
Thompson, Marjorie,
Thompson, Morton, 2277
Thompson, Paul, 5802
Thompson, Ralph, 2254
Thompson, William Irwin, 5306
Thomson, Allan, 2428
Thomson, M. T., 1018
Thomson, Virgil, 728
Thorn, Erie P., 1825
Thornburn, David, 2970
Thornton, Helen, 3013
Thornton, Weldon, 23, 1675, 2508, 3657, 4091, 4406, 4407, 4731, 4737, 4745, 4757
Thorpe, Michael, 97
Thrall, William F., 4204
Thrane, James R., 1614, 3314, 3405
Thurston, Jarvis, 2888
Tierney, Michael, 359
Tillyard, E. M. W., 3664

Timpe, Eugene P., 3665
Tindall, William York, 159, 250, 360, 951, 1019, 1497, 1584, 1676, 1677, 1678, 1861, 2664, 2693, 2793, 2819, 2852, 3138, 3213, 3222, 3260, 4530, 4531, 4587, 4902, 4966
Titus, Edward, 1225, 2202, 4092, 5219
Tobin, Patricia, 3210
Toda, Motoki, 1511
Todorov, Tzvetan, 4093
Toliver, Harold E., 4443
Toller, Ernst, 1142
Tolomeo, Diane, 4903
Tomas, Cabot, José, 745
Tomasi, Barbara R., 4094, 4588, 4589
Tomkinson, Neil, 1343
Tompkins, Phillip K., 4095, 4772
Toor, David, 4720
Torchiana, Donald T., 1026, 2937, 3019, 3023, 3029
Torre, Guillermo de, 251, 794, 5220
Torrents, J. Montserrat, 1631
Toth, Alexander S., Jr., 2389
Toynbee, Philip, 1570, 1649, 4096, 4097
Tracy, Robert, 4590
Traschen, Isadore, 3116
Traversi, Derek, 294
Treach, Leon, 1881
Treacher, Graham, 2627, 2628, 2629
Treece, Henry, 1072
Trench, W. F., 811
Tretjakow, Sergei, 1142
Triesch, Gisela, 1533
Triesch, Manfred, 1533
Triggs, Harold, 2629
Trilling, Jacques, 1826
Trilling, Lionel, 1498, 1499, 1540, 2852, 3144
Troy, William, 1500, 1570, 1636, 2127, 2308, 2343, 4098, 5221
Tsuchiya, Toru, 1511, 4767
Tuchoisky, Karl, 4099
Tucker, Martin, 250
de Tuoni, Dario, 361, 558
Turaj, Frank, 3005
Turner, G. W.,
Turner, Susan Jane, 2365, 3666
Tyler, Hamilton, 5348
Tysdahl, Bjørn J., 952, 3530, 5222, 5223, 5474, 5508, 5509, 5510, 5511

U

U., 1971
Uchida, Michiko, 1511, 3667, 4746
Ulbricht, Walter, 5872
Ullmann, Thilo, 1522
Ulrich, Carolyn F., 8
"Ulysses," 4163
Undurrago, Antonio de, 4493
Ungvari, T., 1020
Unsigned articles:
    "A Commentary," 4393
    "A Critical Commentary," 3284
    "A Fellow Dubliner," 1233
    "A Fragment and Four Furrow," 102
    Aberdeen Journal (30 June 1922), 4173
    Adelphi (April 1927), 683
    Ammilles (July 1931), 5244
    "An Irishman's Diary," 4680
    "Another Appeal," 4392

V

W

Y

Yamakawa, Gakuji, 1511, 4281, 4851
Yañez, J. Agustín, 1359
Yamella, Philip R., 573
Yankwich, Leon R., 4251
Yaron, Mark S., 2456
Yeats, J. B., 1026, 1612
Yeats, William Butler, 300, 813, 814, 815, 816,
   3678, 4149
Young, B. A., 4123
Young, Calvin Eugene, 2457
Young, Frederic J., 1230
Young, Philip, 3088a

Z

Zabel, Morton D., 1636, 1686, 1857, 2146, 2153,
   2821
Zaniello, Thomas, 2430, 2846
Zants, Emily, 2847

Zarek, Otto, 1231, 2092, 4124
Zaraleta, C. E., 2822
Zayalefa, C. E., 2673
Zbierzchowska, Hanna, 155, 1510
Zemelman, Steven A., 2382
Zeraffa, Michel, 594
Zettersten, Arne, 5838
Zhantieva, B., 3679
Zhantieva, D. G., 257, 258
Zhdanov, A., 1059
Ziedonis, Arvide, 1338a
Zimmer, Carl E., 2295
Zimmer, Dieter E., 574, 1232, 2881
Zimmerman, Hans-Joachim, 644, 4028, 4071
Zingrone, Frank D., 2458
Ziolkowski, Theodore, 259, 2848
Zipf, George K., 1842
Zochert, Donald, 3502a
Zolla, Elemire, 1843, 3680
Zorn, Walther, 288
Zurowski, M., 4298
Zweig, Stefan, 817, 2099, 4125
Zyla, Wolodymyr T., 1688, 2867, 3133

Other Reference Works in Literature
Published by G. K. Hall & Co.

Maxwell Anderson and S. N. Behrman:
A Reference Guide
William Robert Klink
6 x 9. xii, 104 pp.   ISBN 0-8161-7824-0 $12.00

Sherwood Anderson: A Reference Guide
Ray Lewis White
6 x 9. xii, 430 pp.   ISBN 0-8161-7818-6 $25.00

Louis Auchincloss and His Critics:
A Bibliographical Record
Jackson R. Bryer   Preface by Louis Auchincloss
6 x 9. xiii, 273 pp.   ISBN 0-8161-7965-4 $18.00

W. H. Auden: A Reference Guide
Martin E. Gingerich
6 x 9. xii, 146 pp. .   ISBN 0-8161-7889-5 $15.00

John Berryman: A Reference Guide
Gary Q. Arpin
5⅜ x 8. xii, 158 pp.   ISBN 0-8161-7804-6 $17.00

Index to Black Poetry
Dorothy H. Chapman
Foreword by Samuel W. Allen
7 x 10. xxii, 542 pp.   ISBN 0-8161-1143-X $25.00

Van Wyck Brooks: A Reference Guide
James R. Vitelli
6 x 9. xvi, 122 pp.   ISBN 0-8161-7978-6 $12.00

Jack London: A Reference Guide
Joan R. Sherman
6 x 9. xxviii, 323 pp.   ISBN 0-8161-7849-6 $22.00

Flannery O'Connor and Caroline Gordon:
A Reference Guide
Robert E. Golden and Mary C. Sullivan
6 x 9. vi, 342 pp.   ISBN 0-8161-7845-3 $22.00

John Osborne: A Reference Guide
Cameron Northouse and Thomas P. Walsh
5⅜ x 8. x, 158 pp.   ISBN 0-8161-1152-9 $9.50

Theodore Roethke's Career:
An Annotated Bibliography
Keith Moul
6 x 9. xxii, 254 pp.   ISBN 0-8161-7892-5 $20.00

William Styron: A Descriptive Bibliography
James L. W. West III
Preface by William Styron
6 x 9. xxxviii, 250 pp.   ISBN 0-8161-7968-9 $30.00

Eudora Welty: A Reference Guide
Victor H. Thompson
6 x 9. xviii, 175 pp.   ISBN 0-8161-7801-1 $18.00

Thomas Wolfe: A Reference Guide
John S. Phillipson
6 x 9. xiv, 218 pp.   ISBN 0-8161-7878-X $18.00

Prices subject to change without notice